State Names, Seals, Flags, and Symbols

State Names, Seals, Flags, and Symbols

A HISTORICAL GUIDE

Third Edition, Revised and Expanded

Benjamin F. Shearer
and Barbara S. Shearer

Illustrations by Jerrie Yehling Smith

GREENWOOD PRESS
Westport, Connecticut • London

Library of Congress Cataloging-in-Publication Data

Shearer, Benjamin F.
    State names, seals, flags, and symbols : A historical guide / Benjamin F. Shearer and
  Barbara S. Shearer.—3rd ed., rev. and expanded.
      p. cm.
    Includes bibliographical references and index.
    ISBN 0–313–31534–5 (alk. paper)
      1. Names, Geographical—United States—States. 2. Seals (Numismatics)—United
States—States. 3. Flags—United States—States. 4. Mottoes—United States—States. 5. State
flowers—United States. 6. State birds—United States. 7. State songs—United States. 8.
U.S. states—Miscellanea. 9. United States—History, Local—Bibliography. I. Shearer,
Barbara Smith. II. Title.
E155 .S44 2002
929.9'2'0973—dc21   2001023525

British Library Cataloguing in Publication Data is available.

Library of Congress Catalog Card Number: 2001023525
ISBN: 0–313–31534–5

First published in 2002

Greenwood Press, 88 Post Road West, Westport, CT 06881
An imprint of Greenwood Publishing Group, Inc.
www.greenwood.com

Printed in the United States of America

The paper used in this book complies with the
Permanent Paper Standard issued by the National
Information Standards Organization (Z39.48–1984).

10 9 8 7 6 5 4 3 2

Copyright Acknowledgments

For the Huey sisters

Lois Huey Smith
Marjorie Huey Carrick
Elizabeth Huey Damron

Contents

Introduction   xiii

1   State and Territory Names and Nicknames   1

2   State and Territory Mottoes   17

3   State and Territory Seals   27

4   State and Territory Flags   53

5   State and Territory Capitols   77

6   State and Territory Flowers   97

7   State and Territory Trees   109

8   State and Territory Birds   125

9   State and Territory Songs   147

10 State and Territory Legal Holidays and Observances   155

11 State and Territory License Plates   195

12 State and Territory Postage Stamps   215

13 Miscellaneous Official State and Territory Designations   225

14 State and Territory Fairs and Festivals   249

15 State and Territory Universities   319

16 State and Territory Governors   373

17 State Professional Sports Teams   443

    Selected Bibliography of State and Territory Histories   453

    Index   471

Introduction

This third revised and expanded edition of *State Names, Seals, Flags, and Symbols* incorporates the numerous changes and additions that have occurred since the publication of the second edition in 1994. There have been, for example, 118 additions and changes in miscellaneous state and territory designations alone since the second edition went to press. The four new chapters on postage stamps, fairs and festivals, legal holidays and special observances, and license plates that were added to the second edition remain in this edition and have been updated or completely revised. In addition, three new chapters have been added to this edition covering state and territory universities, governors, and professional sports teams.

State publications and state codes have again provided much of the documentation for state symbols and other official designations. State websites were also valuable sources of information. United States government publications provided several sources of descriptive material. John P. Harrington's scholarship on the origin of state names, found in the *Annual Report of the Smithsonian Institution, 1954*, remains an excellent source of historical information. *The Yearbook of Agriculture, 1949* provided descriptive information on state trees. *Bulletins of the United States Museum*, numbers 50, 107, 113, 121, 162, 174, 176, 179, 191, 195, 211, and 237, provided behavioral and descriptive information on state birds.

State and Territory Names and Nicknames

The names of the states taken all together honor the important players in the early exploration and history of the nation. Georgia, the Virginias, the Carolinas, New Jersey, New Hampshire, and Maryland, among others, were named by the English. Maine, Vermont, and Louisiana were named by the French. The Spanish left their names to Florida, Colorado, California, Nevada, and Texas. The Dutch were responsible for naming Rhode Island. The United States honored the first president when it created the state of Washington and the Native Americans displaced by the country's westward expansion when it named Indiana. In fact, the majority of state names are derived from Indian names. From the Choctaw in Alabama, to the Aleuts in Alaska, to the Massachusetts on the East Coast, Indian tribes left their mark on the naming of the states.

Nicknames for the states have come out of particular incidents and events or in an effort to promote state industries, businesses, and tourism. The nicknames listed below are those that have stood the test of time and illustrate some historical or economic fact. Not included here are the many slogans devised by the states to promote a particular industry or image.

ALABAMA

The Alabama River was named after the Indian tribe that was settled in central Ala-

bama when early European explorers first arrived there. The state received its name from the river. The name Alabama first occurs in chronicles of DeSoto's 1540 expedition, spelled variously Alibamu, Limamu, and Alibamo. Numerous other variant spellings were set down by English, French, and Spanish explorers.[1]

The origin of the name Alabama is probably in two Choctaw words. "Alba" in Choctaw means vegetation, herbs, plants, or weeds. "Amo" means a gatherer, picker, or shearer. It was not unusual that a tribe would accept a descriptive name from a contiguous tribe. The description "vegetation gatherers" was appropriate for the Alabama Indians, who cleared land for agricultural purposes.[2]

While the state of Alabama has no officially adopted nickname, Alabamians proudly display the nickname "The Heart of Dixie" on their license plates. Alabama is also known as the Yellowhammer State. The state bird is the yellowhammer, chosen because of the color of the uniforms of a company of Alabama confederate soldiers. The NASA-Marshall Space Flight Center in Huntsville has provided Alabama with another nickname—The Pioneer Space Capital of the World.

ALASKA

Alaska is taken directly from the Aleut "aláxsxaq," meaning "the object toward which the action of the sea is directed," or the mainland.[3] Alaska was known as Russian America until its purchase by the United States in 1867. The Russians had used the term Alaska to refer only to the Alaskan peninsula. The name was appropriated by the United States to refer first to the Territory of Alaska and then to the state.[4]

The American purchase of Alaska, negotiated by Secretary of State William Seward, gave Alaska two of its first American nicknames—Seward's Folly and Seward's Ice Box. While obviously meant to be derisive, Seward's purchase of Alaska for $7,200,000 has proved a fine investment. Alaska has also been spoken of more fondly as the Land of Midnight Sun and America's Last Frontier.

ARIZONA

The name Arizona is derived from two words in the Papago Indian dialect of the Pima language—"Aleh-zon," which means "little spring." Spaniards used the term as early as 1736. The springs, now located in Mexican territory, are near a large silver find made in 1735 in the Arizona Creek. Arizona was chosen as the territorial name, in part owing to Charles D. Poston. Poston was a mining speculator who claimed to have first suggested the name Arizona in a petition to Congress to make Arizona a territory.[5]

Arizona is known as the Copper State because of its large copper production and as the Apache State because of the large number of Apache Indians who once lived there. Arizona's most familiar nickname today is the Grand Canyon State.

ARKANSAS

The pronunciation of the word Arkansas is actually prescribed by an 1881 state statute. Although Arkansas is actually another form of Kansas, the Arkansas legislature declared

that the correct pronunciation of the three-syllable word should have the final "s" silent, all "a's" with the Italian sound, and the accent on the first and third syllables. This pronunciation follows from the fact that Arkansas was first written in French, as Frenchmen tried to record the sounds they heard from native American Indians.[6] The Kansas Indians are a tribe of the Sioux. Fr. Marquette first used the word Arkansas in a 1673 map.[7]

Arkansas has many nicknames, including the Bowie State and the Toothpick State, which refer to Bowie knives and to the handles for them. The Hot Water State is a nickname that refers to the hot springs in the state.[8] In 1947, The Land of Opportunity became the officially designated nickname of Arkansas.[9] As time passed, however, "Arkansas Is a Natural" was the slogan used to promote recreation and tourism. Then in 1995, the legislature designated The Natural State as the official nickname of the state.[10]

CALIFORNIA

California was an island filled with gold in an early sixteenth-century novel, *Las Sergas de Esplandian*, by Garcia Ordoñez de Montalvo. Although the eleventh-century *Song of Roland* mentions a capital city called Califerne, it is most probable that Spanish explorers Ortuno Ximenez and Hernando Cortés were familiar with the contemporary Spanish novel and drew their inspiration for naming California, which they thought to be an island, from Montalvo's book. By 1541, California had become an established place name and location on the maps.[11]

Although several slogans have been used by the state of California over the years to promote business and tourism, the only official nickname, designated by the California legislature in 1968, is The Golden State.[12] This nickname was chosen not only in reference to the discovery of gold in 1848, but also to the fields of yellow poppies that bloom in California in the spring.[13]

COLORADO

The Pike's Peak Region, land attained originally from the Louisiana Purchase, Mexican cession, and Texas, became the Colorado Territory soon after gold was discovered near Denver. A number of names were suggested for the territory, including Osage, Idaho, Jefferson, and Colona; however, the name Colorado, Spanish for red, referring to the color of the Colorado River whose headwaters lie within the boundaries of the state, was chosen over the others. Local native Indians from a number of tribes had referred to the river's color in naming it even before the Spanish arrived.[14]

Colorado is known as the Centennial State because it attained statehood in 1876, the one-hundred-year anniversary of the signing of the Declaration of Independence. It is also known as the Highest State and the Switzerland of America for its elevation and mountainous terrain. Many slogans have also been used over the years to promote skiing and tourism in Colorado.

CONNECTICUT

The name Connecticut was clearly established in the early seventeenth century as applied to the Connecticut River.[15] The native Indian word "Quinnehtukqut" was translated into the current English spelling and means "beside the long tidal river."[16]

In 1959, the Connecticut legislature officially adopted the nickname The Constitution State[17] because Connecticut was the first of all the states to have a written constitution. Connecticut is also known unofficially as the Nutmeg State, not because the state produces the spice in large quantities, but because its early citizens were so skilled and industrious that they could make and sell wooden nutmegs.[18]

DELAWARE

The state of Delaware and the Delaware Indians are both named after the Delaware River. The Delaware River was named by the English after Sir Thomas West, Lord de la Warr, who was the Virginia Company's first governor.[19]

Delaware was the first state to ratify the United States Constitution, thus earning it the nickname the First State. Delaware is also known as the Diamond State, a sobriquet originated by Thomas Jefferson, who referred to Delaware as like a diamond—small but of great value.[20]

FLORIDA

Florida was named for the day on which it was discovered by Spanish explorer Ponce de Leon. On Easter Sunday in 1513, de Leon named the new land La Florida in honor of Pascua Florida, the Spanish Feast of the Flowers at Eastertime.[21]

Florida has a number of nicknames owing to its geographical location and the importance of tourism. Florida is commonly known as the Sunshine State. It is also called the Alligator State, the Everglades State, and the Southernmost State for obvious reasons. The Orange State is still another nickname that acknowledges the importance of the citrus industry to Florida's economy.

GEORGIA

Georgia was founded in 1733 by James Oglethorpe, who had been granted a charter by King George II in 1732 to found a colony named after the king. Oglethorpe carried out the terms of the charter by naming the last of the thirteen British colonies in America Georgia.[22]

The state of Georgia has no officially designated nickname, although it recognizes the use of several unofficial nicknames. Georgia is known as the Peach State and the Goober State for the importance of peaches and peanuts in the state's agricultural economy. Two nicknames refer to the determination and will of Georgia's citizens to lead the South in industrial and economic development—the Empire State of the South and the Yankee-land of the South. Georgia is also known as the Cracker State and the Buzzard State. Crackers, originally a derogatory term meaning braggarts, was the term used to describe immigrants into Georgia who came from the mountains of Virginia and North Carolina. The Buzzard State refers to the fact that buzzards were once protected by law in Georgia.[23]

HAWAII

Captain James Cook named the islands he discovered in 1778 the Sandwich Islands in honor of his patron, the Earl of Sandwich. By 1819, however, King Kamehameha I had united the formerly independent islands under his rule in the Kingdom of Hawaii. In 1893, Hawaii became a republic and a territory in 1898 when the islands were annexed by the United States. Statehood came in 1959.

The name Hawaii itself is said to have come from the traditional discoverer of the islands, Hawaii Loa. Another explanation is that Hawaii means a small or new homeland. "Hawa" means a traditional homeland, and "ii" means both small and raging. The latter meaning may refer to Hawaii's volcanoes.[24]

The state of Hawaii recognized the Aloha State as its official popular name in a 1959 legislative act.[25] Hawaii is also known unofficially as the Pineapple State for its extensive pineapple industry, the Paradise of the Pacific for its natural beauty, and the Youngest State because it is the last state to join the Union.

IDAHO

Contrary to long-held common belief, Idaho is not a Shoshone word meaning "gem of the mountains." In fact, the name Idaho was invented by George M. Willing, who unsuccessfully sought to become a delegate from what would become the territory of Colorado. The more traditional name of Colorado was maintained when Colorado became a territory, partly because the name Idaho was discovered to have been a coined term. Nevertheless, the name Idaho took hold in settlements such as Idaho Springs and gold discoveries on the Salmon and Clearwater rivers known as the Idaho mines. Even a Columbia River steamship was christened *The Idaho*. In 1863, Congress designated the Idaho Territory with the erroneous understanding that Idaho meant "gem of the mountains," while Montana, another name proposed for the territory, was said to mean nothing.[26] In spite of the misunderstanding concerning the origin of the name Idaho, the state of Idaho continues to be known as the Gem State and the Gem of the Mountains.

ILLINOIS

When La Salle traveled up the Illinois River in 1679, he named it after the native Americans he found living along its banks. Illinois is a French spelling for the Illinois and Peoria Indian word "ilini," the plural of which is "iliniwok," meaning a man or a warrior and also possibly a member of the Illinois tribe.[27]

The Illinois legislature officially adopted "Land of Lincoln" as its slogan in 1955, referring to Illinois as the state where Abraham Lincoln began his political career.[28] Illinois is also known unofficially as the Prairie State, a fitting sobriquet for a state that sets aside the third full week of September each year as Illinois Prairie Week "to demonstrate the value of preserving and reestablishing native Illinois prairies."[29] The Corn State is another fitting nickname for Illinois, owing to the importance of that crop to the state's agricultural economy.

INDIANA

The United States Congress created the name Indiana, meaning "Land of the Indians," when it created the Indiana Territory out of the Northwest Territory in 1800.[30]

"Crossroads of America" was designated by the Indiana legislature as the state's official motto or slogan.[31] Indiana is popularly known, however, as the Hoosier State. The origin of the term Hoosier is unclear. It may be a corruption of the terse pioneer question "Who's here?" Another explanation has it that the men who worked for an Indiana contractor, Sam Hoosier, became known as Hoosiers. Still another explanation is that the term Hoosier is a corruption of "husher," a term applied to early riverboat workers who could hush anyone with brute force.[32]

IOWA

The Iowa District was the name of the territory of Wisconsin west of the Mississippi. The district became first a territory and then, in 1846, a state. The Iowa River was named for the Iowa Indians who inhabited the area, and the name of the state was derived from the river. The tribal name " 'Ayuxwa" means "one who puts to sleep." The French spelled Iowa as Ayoua and the English, as Ioway.[33]

Iowa's most enduring but unofficial nickname, the Hawkeye State, was first suggested in an 1838 newspaper article by James G. Edwards as a tribute to Chief Black Hawk. Black Hawk had come back to Iowa to die after his release from prison, where he had served a sentence for fighting the encroachment of white settlers on Indian land.[34]

KANSAS

Kansas is the French spelling of the Kansas, Omaha, Kaw, Osage, and Dakota Sioux Indian word "KaNze." In the language of the Kansas, the word Kansas means the "south wind." The tribal name was applied to the Kansas River and also to the territory occupied by the tribe.[35]

Kansas has several nicknames that describe its history, resources, and weather. Kansas was known at one time as "Bleeding Kansas," an apt appellation for pre–Civil War Kansas and the carnage that occurred there at the time. In a sense, Kansas was a precursor of things to come as the United States was about to embark on civil war. Kansas is also called the Squatter State for the squatters who settled the new territory. The Cyclone State is a nickname that calls to mind the worst of Kansas weather; the Sunflower State calls to mind the wild sunflowers of the plains, the official flower of the state. The Wheat State is a nickname from Kansas' most famous crop; and Midway, USA is a nickname based on the state's geographic location. Finally, Kansas is called the Jayhawk State for the unruly irregulars and pillagers who first occupied the Kansas borders. Kansas soldiers came to be known as a result as Jayhawkers.[36]

KENTUCKY

The name Kentucky, the Wyandot word for "plain," referring to the central plains of the state, was first recorded in 1753. Kentucky, which had been a province of Virginia, became a territory in 1790, a state in 1792.[37]

Kentucky is commonly nicknamed the Bluegrass State, in spite of the fact that it is officially a commonwealth. Bluegrass is actually green, but its bluish-purple buds, when seen from afar, give a field of bluegrass a bluish tint.[38] Kentucky is also nicknamed for two crops that have figured in its economic history—the Hemp State and the Tobacco State. Finally, Kentucky has been called the Dark and Bloody Ground, a nickname passed down by Daniel Boone from an Indian chief to describe the battles Indians and whites fought in Kentucky.[39]

LOUISIANA

In 1682, explorer Sieur de La Salle was the first European to descend the Mississippi River all the way to its delta. He named the area he discovered La Louisianne after Louis XIV of France. The state of Louisiana was carved out of the New Orleans Territory, which was only a portion of the Louisiana Purchase.[40]

Nicknames for Louisiana are plentiful and descriptive. Louisiana is known as the Bayou State for its numerous bayous and the Fisherman's Paradise for the variety of excellent fishing available in the state. The Child of the Mississippi is a nickname that describes the state's geological origin. The Sugar State is a tribute to Louisiana's sugar industry, and the Pelican State is a tribute to the state bird, the brown pelican, which is native to Louisiana.[41]

MAINE

The origin of the name Maine is uncertain. French colonists may have named the area after the French province of Mayne. "Main" was also a common term among early explorers to describe a mainland.[42]

The state of Maine recognizes the nickname the Pine Tree State. The white pine is the state tree and Maine possesses 17 million acres of forest.[43] Maine is also known as the Lumber State for its lumber industry and as

the Border State for its geographical position below Canada. The Old Dirigo State refers to the state's motto "Dirigo," which means "I lead" or "I direct."[44]

MARYLAND

When Lord Baltimore received the charter for the colony from Charles I of England, it contained the proviso that the colony be named Maryland in honor of Charles I's wife, Queen Henrietta Maria, who was popularly known as Queen Mary.[45]

Maryland is known as the Free State and the Old Line State. The first of these nicknames originated in 1923. Hamilton Owens, editor of the *Baltimore Star*, coined the term after Maryland refused to pass an enforcement act for Prohibition. He continued to use the nickname in his editorials. The second nickname, by some accounts, was created by George Washington in praise of Maryland's regular line troops who served well in many Revolutionary War skirmishes.[46]

MASSACHUSETTS

Massachusetts was named after the Massachusetts Indian tribe, which populated the Massachusetts Bay region before Columbus first arrived in the New World. Massachusetts means "large hill place." The tribe was named after Great Blue Hill, which lies south of Milton.[47]

Massachusetts Bay lends the state two common nicknames—the Bay State and the Old Bay State. Massachusetts' early settlers were responsible for two more nicknames—the Pilgrim State and the Puritan State. The Old Colony State is a nickname that refers to the original Plymouth Colony. Finally, the Puritan practice of serving baked beans for Sunday meals gives Massachusetts the nickname the Baked Bean State.[48]

MICHIGAN

The name Michigan first appeared in written form in 1672 in connection with a clearing on the west side of the lower peninsula. In Chippewa, the word "majigan" means "clearing." European explorers named Lake Michigan after the clearing. The attribution of Michigan's name to the Chippewa word "micigami," meaning "large water," is not accurate.[49]

Michigan has long been known as the Wolverine State for the large numbers of wolverines that once roamed the peninsula. The Great Lakes that surround Michigan lend it the nicknames the Lake State and the Lady of the Lake. Michigan's extensive auto industry, centered in Detroit, also gives Michigan another nickname, the Auto State.[50]

MINNESOTA

The state of Minnesota received its name from the Minnesota River in southern Minnesota. The Dakota word "mnishota" means "cloudy" or "milky water."[51]

Minnesota is known as the North Star State; its motto is translated from the French as the "Star of the North." Although having many more lakes than the nickname suggests, Minnesota is also called the Land of 10,000 Lakes. Minnesota is nicknamed the Gopher State for the many gophers that roamed its prairies and also the Bread and Butter State for its extensive production of wheat and dairy products.[52]

MISSISSIPPI

The state of Mississippi is named after the Mississippi River, although the river itself has had a number of names throughout history. Indians on the Gulf Coast called the river Malabouchia. Spaniards called it Rio del Espiritu Santo and Rio Grande del Flor-

ida during the sixteenth and seventeenth centuries. The French called it the Colbert River after La Salle explored it and then, after the founding of the colony at Fort Maurepas in 1699, the St. Louis River. Mississippi, the name given the river by Northwest Indians visited by La Salle and Marquette, is the name that finally won out. La Salle's map of 1695 actually uses the name Mississippi. Mississippi, contrary to common opinion, means "large river" in Chippewa, not "the father of waters."[53]

Mississippi is nicknamed the Magnolia State for the state flower and tree and the abundance of magnolias in the state. The state coat-of-arms, which depicts an American eagle, lends the nicknames the Eagle State and the Border-Eagle State to Mississippi. The numerous bayous in Mississippi, like Louisiana, lend the nickname the Bayou State to Mississippi. Finally, Mississippi is known as the Mud-cat State for the catfish that are abundant throughout the state's streams and swamps.[54]

MISSOURI

The Missouri Territory was named for the Missouri River, which, in turn, was named for the Missouri Indians. The earliest use of the word in writing occurs on the Marquette map of 1673. The Missouri, a small tribe, lived along the Missouri River with the Illinois to the east and the Little Osage to the west. The name means "canoe haver."[55]

The state of Missouri is commonly known as the Show Me State, a nickname attributed to Representative Willard Vandiver of Missouri. It connotes a certain self-deprecating stubbornness and devotion to simple common sense. Another politician, Thomas Hart Benton, gave Missouri the nickname the Bullion State for his advocacy of hard money, that is, gold and silver. Missouri is also called the Cave State for its numerous caves and caverns open to the public, the Lead

State for its lead production, and the Ozark State for the Ozark Mountains in southern Missouri.[56]

MONTANA

Montana's name is derived from the Latin word *montaanus* meaning "mountainous." Montana Territory was created in 1864 out of Idaho Territory.[57]

Montana is popularly known as the Big Sky Country, an allusion to its immense area of mountains and valleys. The Stub Toe State, another nickname, refers to the state's mountainous terrain. The Bonanza State and the Treasure State refer to the importance of mining in Montana. "Naturally Inviting Montana" is a slogan used to promote Montana tourism.[58]

NEBRASKA

The state of Nebraska is actually named after the Platte River, a French name meaning "broad river." The Omaha Indians called the river Nibôápka, or "broad river." When John Frémont was in Nebraska in 1842, he first used the word Nebraska in reference to the Platte River, and this name was applied to the territory created in 1854.[59]

Nebraska has had two official nicknames. In 1895, the legislature designated Nebraska as the Tree Planters' State because it is "preeminently a tree planting state."[60] In 1945, the legislature changed Nebraska's official nickname to the Cornhusker State in recognition of Nebraska football.[61] Nebraska is also unofficially nicknamed the Antelope State for the herds of antelope that once roamed its territory and the Bug-eating State for its numerous bull bats, which eat insects.[62]

NEVADA

Seventeenth- and eighteenth-century Spanish sailors traveling between the Philippines and Mexico saw mountain ranges in California from out at sea. They named these mountains Sierra Nevada or "snowy range." When a new territory was designated out of Utah, it was decided to name it Sierra Nevada, but the territory was named simply Nevada in 1859.[63]

Nevada is nicknamed the Sage State and the Sagebrush State for the wild sage that grows there prolifically. It is also known as the Silver State and the Mining State for its silver mines. Because Nevada was admitted to the Union in 1864 while the Civil War was raging, it has the additional nickname of the Battle Born State.[64]

NEW HAMPSHIRE

Captain John Mason of the Royal Navy received a grant in 1629 for the part of the land that became the state of New Hampshire. He named the area New Hampshire after the central English county of Hampshire, where he had spent a number of years of his youth.[65]

New Hampshire is nicknamed the Granite State for its extensive granite formations and quarries and the White Mountain State for the range of that name in northern New Hampshire. New Hampshire's mountains also lend it the nickname of the Switzerland of America. The mountains, which spawn five of New England's rivers, lend New Hampshire still another name, The Mother of Rivers.[66]

NEW JERSEY

New Jersey was named after the island of Jersey in the English Channel by Sir John Berkeley and Sir George Carteret. Berkeley and Carteret obtained a royal charter for this colony. Carteret was born on the island of Jersey and had been its lieutenant governor.[67]

New Jersey is known as the Garden State

for its truck farms which provide produce to nearby cities and as the Clam State for the clams taken in off its coast. The Camden and Amboy State is an old nickname that recalls the influence of the Camden and Amboy Railroad in New Jersey. Two other nicknames are derived from an even earlier period: the Jersey Blue State recalls the blue uniforms of the New Jersey soldiers in the Revolutionary War,[68] and the Pathway of the Revolution recalls the many battles fought on New Jersey soil in the American Revolution.[69]

NEW MEXICO

The upper region of the Rio Grande was called "Nuevo Mexico" as early as 1561 by Fray Jacinto de San Francisco in the hope that this area would hold the riches of Mexico. Mexico, which is the Aztec spelling, means "place of Mexìtli," one of the Aztec gods. When New Mexico came under American control, the Spanish name was anglicized.[70]

New Mexico is nicknamed the Cactus State for the numerous cacti that grow there and the Spanish State in honor of its history as a Spanish-speaking state.[71] While New Mexico has an official slogan for business, commerce, and industry—"Everybody Is Somebody in New Mexico"—the sobriquet the Land of Enchantment adorns automobile license plates and is used frequently in the state publications that promote tourism.[72]

NEW YORK

When the British took over New Amsterdam from the Dutch in 1664, the city's new name was proclaimed to be New York in honor of the brother of England's Charles II, the Duke of York and Albany. The Dutch colony was called New Netherlands, but New York became the name of both the city and the state.[73]

New York is commonly nicknamed the Empire State for its wealth and variety of resources. It is also known as the Excelsior State because the state motto is *Excelsior*. New York is also called the Knickerbocker State in reference to the breeches worn by early Dutch settlers.[74]

NORTH CAROLINA

North Carolina and South Carolina were one colony until they were divided in 1729. Carolina was originally named in honor of France's Charles IX and then in honor of England's Charles I and Charles II, both of whom made grants of Carolina. Carolina is the feminine form of the Latin word *Caroliinus*, an adjective derived from the name *Carolus*, or Charles.[75]

North Carolina is known as the Old North State in reference to its separation from South Carolina in 1729. It has also been called the Turpentine State for its large production of turpentine. Possibly the most familiar nickname of North Carolina, however, is the Tarheel State. Originally a derisive term, "tarheels" is said to have been a name given to North Carolina Civil War soldiers by soldiers from Mississippi when the Carolina soldiers were routed from a position on a hill. They had forgotten to "tar their heels" and could not maintain their position.[76] Today the term has lost its derogatory inference.

NORTH DAKOTA

The Dakotas were divided into North and South Dakota by an omnibus bill passed in 1889.[77] Dakota is a Sioux word meaning "friends" or "allies." When Dakota Territory was created in 1861, it was named for the Dakota tribe which inhabited the region.[78]

The International Peace Garden on North Dakota's border with Manitoba, Canada, caused the legislature to officially designate North Dakota as the Peace Garden State in 1957. During the 1960s and 1970s, the Roughrider State was used as a nickname for tourism promotion. The Sioux State is a nickname that recognizes the Dakota tribe, also called the Sioux. The Flickertail State is a nickname referring to the flickertail squirrel which inhabits North Dakota. North Dakota is also sometimes called the Land of the Dakotas.[79]

OHIO

The state of Ohio is named after the Ohio River. The French explorer La Salle noted as early as 1680 that the Iroquois called the river "Ohio," meaning "large" or "beautiful river."[80]

Ohio is commonly called the Buckeye State for the buckeye trees that grow abundantly in the state and for an incident that occurred in 1788 when a very tall Colonel Sproat led a procession to a fort and the onlooking Indians, impressed by his stature, referred to him as "Big Buckeye." Ohio is also sometimes referred to as the Mother of Modern Presidents, having spawned seven American presidents.[81]

OKLAHOMA

The word Oklahoma first appears in the 1866 Choctaw-Chickasaw Treaty. Allen Wright, a native American missionary who spoke Choctaw, made up the word by combining two Choctaw words: " 'ukla" or person and "humá" or red. Oklahoma therefore means "red person."[82]

Oklahoma is known as the Sooner State and as the Boomer's Paradise. Both of these nicknames derive from the opening of the Oklahoma Territory for settlement in 1889. Boomers were those who came in hordes to settle the new land and sooners were those who illegally entered the territory to stake claims before the designated date and time.[83]

OREGON

The origin of the name Oregon is unclear. There are at least three possibilities, each quite different. Oregon may come from the French Canadian word "ouragan" meaning "storm" or "hurricane." The Columbia River was probably at one time called "the river of storms" by Canadian fur traders. Another possibility is that the name Oregon comes from the Spanish word "orejon" or "big-ear." This term was applied to a number of tribes of the region. Still another possibility is that the name of Oregon comes from the Spanish word "orégano" or wild sage, which was corrupted to Oregon. Sage grows abundantly in eastern Oregon.[84]

Oregon is known as the Beaver State because the beaver has been declared the state animal and is depicted on the state flag and as the Web-foot State in reference to its abundant rainfall. The Hard-case State is a nickname that was given to Oregon because of the difficulties encountered by early settlers.[85]

PENNSYLVANIA

When William Penn was granted a charter in 1680 by England's Charles II, the king gave the name Pennsylvania to the land. *Sylvania* is Latin for woods or woodland and, thus, Pennsylvania means "Penn's woods."[86]

Pennsylvania is sometimes called the Quaker State in reference to William Penn's religious affiliation and the Quakers who settled the state.[87] More commonly, Pennsylvania is nicknamed the Keystone State. Although the origin of this nickname has been lost, it was used and accepted by the turn of the eighteenth century. The term probably refers to Pennsylvania's geographical location in the original thirteen colonies that straddled the Atlantic Ocean.[88]

RHODE ISLAND

When Dutch explorer Adrian Block came upon an island with red clay shores, he named it in his native tongue "Roodt Eylandt," meaning "red island." Under English rule, the name was anglicized in the then current spelling.[89]

Rhode Island's status as the smallest state lends it the nicknames Little Rhody and the Smallest State. Roger Williams, who founded Providence Plantation in 1636, is honored by the sobriquet the Land of Roger Williams. Rhode Island, whose full name is actually The State of Rhode Island and Providence Plantations, is also known as the Plantation State. Finally, Rhode Island uses the nickname the Ocean State to promote tourism.[90]

SOUTH CAROLINA

The Carolinas were originally named in honor of Charles IX of France and then in honor of Charles I and Charles II of England. The Carolinas were divided into north and south in 1729.[91]

South Carolina's rice production lends it the nicknames the Rice State and the Swamp State. Its shape, that of a wedge, gives it the nickname of the Keystone of the South Atlantic Seaboard. The Iodine State is a nickname that refers to the iodine content of South Carolina plants, and the Palmetto State refers to South Carolina's state tree, the palmetto.[92]

SOUTH DAKOTA

The Dakota Territory was named for the Dakota tribe that inhabited the region. The territory was divided into north and south in 1889. Dakota is a Sioux word meaning "friends" or "allies."[93]

South Dakota had long used the nickname the Sunshine State to promote tourism and it recognized also the nickname the Coyote State in tribute to its large coyote population.[94] Unofficially, South Dakota has also been known as the Blizzard State for its severe winter weather and the Artesian State for its many artesian wells.[95] In 1992, however, South Dakota's official nickname was declared to be The Mount Rushmore State.[96]

TENNESSEE

The original form of the name Tennessee was the Cherokee name "Tanasi." The Cherokee called two villages on the Little Tennessee River "Tanasi." The river was named after the villages and the region after the river. The meaning of the Cherokee name is unknown.[97]

Tennessee is widely known as the Volunteer State, a nickname resulting from the valor displayed by Tennessee volunteer soldiers fighting under Andrew Jackson in the Battle of New Orleans. Tennessee is also called the Big Bend State in reference to the Tennessee River and the Mother of Southwestern Statesmen for the three United States presidents it has spawned. At one time, Tennessee was called the Hog and the Hominy State for its pork and corn product production, but this nickname is no longer used.[98]

TEXAS

Texas, or "teysha" in the language of the Caddo, means "hello friend." The Spanish used this term to refer to friendly tribes throughout Louisiana, Oklahoma, and Texas. The tribes of the Caddo confederacy, who lived in Louisiana and eastern Texas, came to be called "the kingdom of the Texas." The name of Texas was firmly established in 1690 when the Spanish named their first mission St. Francis of the Texas.[99]

Texas is popularly called the Lone Star State. The lone star on the state flag connotes the history of Texas as an independent republic fighting alone against great odds for its freedom. Texas is also called the Beef State for its cattle production and the Banner State for its leading position in many pursuits.[100]

UTAH

The White Mountain Apache referred to the Navajo as "Yuttahih" or "one that is higher up." European settlers and explorers understood the Apache term to refer to the Utes, who dwelled farther up the mountains than the Navajo. The land of the Utes came to be called Utah.[101]

Utah's state emblem, the beehive, gives it the nickname of the Beehive State. The beehive is a symbol of industry. Utah's Mormon heritage provides Utah with two nicknames: the Mormon State and the Land of the Saints (the Mormon church is officially called The Church of Jesus Christ of the Latter-Day Saints). Finally, Utah's Great Salt Lake gives it the additional nickname of the Salt Lake State.[102]

VERMONT

The French explorer Champlain, who saw Vermont's Green Mountains only from a distance, designated them as "Verd Mont" or "green mountain" in a 1647 map. The English name Vermont is therefore directly derived from Champlain's naming of the Green Mountains.[103] Vermont's mountains lend it the nickname of the Green Mountain State.[104]

VIRGINIA

Virginia was named in 1584 in honor of Queen Elizabeth of England, who was pop-

ularly called the "Virgin Queen." The name Virginia is the feminine form of the Latin word *virginius*.[105]

Virginia has long been nicknamed the Old Dominion or the Ancient Dominion. Charles II of England quartered the arms of Virginia on his shield in 1663 thus adding Virginia to his dominions of France, Ireland, and Scotland. Virginia is often called the Cavalier State for its early settlers who were loyal to England and the Mother of States because it was the first to be colonized. The predominance of the Virginia aristocracy in early United States politics and diplomacy lends Virginia the additional nicknames of the Mother of Presidents and the Mother of Statesmen.[106]

WASHINGTON

Washington Territory was carved out of Oregon Territory in 1853. It was named in honor of George Washington.[107]

The state of Washington is best known as the Evergreen State for its many large fir and pine trees. The Chinook State, a nickname referring to Washington's salmon industry and the Chinook Indians, is no longer in common use.[108]

WEST VIRGINIA

West Virginia was not separated from Virginia until 1861. West Virginia, as part of Virginia, was named after Queen Elizabeth of England, who was called the "Virgin Queen."[109]

West Virginia's scenic Allegheny Mountains lend it the nicknames the Switzerland of America and the Mountain State. Its shape gives it the additional name of the Panhandle State.[110]

WISCONSIN

The state of Wisconsin is named after the Wisconsin River. In Chippewa, Wisconsin means "grassy place." When Hennepin first recorded the name in 1695, it referred either to the river itself or to a place on the river.[111]

Wisconsin is popularly, but unofficially, called the Badger State after the early lead miners who lived underground and were called badgers. The badger is also the state animal of Wisconsin. Wisconsin is also known as the Copper State for its copper mines in the north.[112]

WYOMING

The name Wyoming comes from two Delaware words "mecheweamiing" meaning "at the big flats." A popular interpretation translates the Delaware words as "large plains." Legh Richmond Freeman, publisher of *The Frontier Index* in Kearney, Nebraska, claimed to have been the first to suggest the name Wyoming for the southwest half of the Dakota Territory.[113]

Wyoming has three nicknames currently in use. The Equality State recognizes Wyoming as the first state to extend women the right to vote; "Equality" is also the state motto. Wyoming is also called Big Wyoming and the Cowboy State.[114]

DISTRICT OF COLUMBIA

The District of Columbia was carved out of Maryland and Virginia and created on January 24, 1791. Columbia is feminine, as used for a country, derived from a neo-Latin adjective "columbius," or pertaining to Columbus. The practice of calling the district "Washington" honors the nation's first president.

AMERICAN SAMOA

What is now American Samoa is thought to have been settled around 600 B.C. by Polynesians coming from Fiji, the New Hebrides, and Indonesia. Samoan people were,

therefore, quite established when Dutch explorer Jacob Roggeveen ended Samoa's isolation from the Western world in 1722. American Samoa, named for its inhabitants and its association with the United States since 1900, consists of seven islands 2,300 miles south-southwest of Honolulu. It is the only United States territory below the equator.[115]

COMMONWEALTH OF THE NORTHERN MARIANA ISLANDS

Ferdinand Magellan was the first Western explorer to sail through the Mariana Islands in 1521. He named the archipelago the "Island of the Latin Sails" because of the shape of the islanders' canoe sails. But when the islanders robbed his ship, he decided to call the place the "Islands of the Thieves." The islands were not renamed until 1668, when Spain established its first colony on Guam. They were named for the widow of King Philip IV of Spain, Queen Mariana of Austria. Germany bought the Northern Marianas from Spain in 1899 and fifteen years later, Japan seized the islands. After World War II, the U.S. Naval Administration governed until 1962 under a United Nations act making the Northern Marianas a trust territory of the United States. In 1976, a commonwealth was established and in 1986, the trusteeship was ended and the people of the Commonwealth of the Northern Mariana Islands (CNMI) became full U.S. citizens. The Commonwealth calls itself "Micronesia's Sun Belt."[116]

GUAM

Guam, or Guahan, is the southernmost island of the Mariana Archipelago. It was discovered and settled by Chamorros, who were probably of Indo-Malayan and Filipino descent, sometime before 1500 B.C. Magellan arrived there in 1521, but it was Miguel

Lopez de Legaspi who claimed the Marianas for Spain. Jesuit missionaries arrived in Agana in 1668. The mission was funded by Queen Mariana of Spain, and the Mariana Islands were christened in her name. Agana became the capital of Guam and the Northern Mariana Islands.

The United States took possession of Guam from Spain in 1898. Except for the Japanese occupation from late 1941 to July 1944, the United States has administered the island. Citizenship rights were granted to Guamanians by the 1950 Organic Act of Guam. The unincorporated territory of Guam is America's westernmost frontier, which is why it is known both as "Where America's Day Begins" and "America's Paradise in the Pacific."[117]

PUERTO RICO

In 1493, during his second voyage, Christopher Columbus discovered an island called Boringuen, which was inhabited by several Indian tribes. He named the island San Juan in honor of St. John the Baptist. The city was called Puerto Rico, meaning "rich port." Later, the names were switched. Puerto Rico has been an American territory since 1898. Puerto Ricans became U.S. citizens in 1917, and in 1952, the island became a semi-autonomous commonwealth voluntarily associated with the United States.[118]

U.S. VIRGIN ISLANDS

The U.S. Virgin Islands lie 1,500 miles south-southeast of New York in the Lesser Antilles. St. Croix, St. Thomas, and St. John are the three principal islands. Columbus found the islands on his second voyage to the New World, naming them "The Virgins," referring to the beauty of the 11,000 seafaring virgins of St. Ursula. According to legend, St. Ursula agreed to marry a pagan prince at her father's request only after 11,000 of the most beautiful virgins of the two kingdoms were gathered to be her companions for three years. Ursula trained her companions into a fighting force and set off up the Rhine to Basel and from there to Rome on foot. But all were martyred near Cologne in 238 A.D.

The Danish took control of all three islands in 1733. They were purchased on March 31, 1917, by the United States for $25,000,000 from Denmark. Today, the Virgin Islands are an unincorporated territory of the United States and everyone born in the Islands is a U.S. citizen. The Virgin Islands call themselves the "American Paradise."[119]

NOTES

1. *Alabama State Emblems* (Montgomery: Alabama State Department of Archives and History, n.d.), p. 2; "The Name Alabama," *Arrow Points* 10 (January 1925): 19–20.

2. *Alabama State Emblems*, pp. 3–4.

3. J. Ellis Ransom, "Derivation of the Word 'Alaska,'" *American Anthropologist* 42 (July–September 1940): 551.

4. John P. Harrington, "Our State Names," *Smithsonian Institution Annual Report* (1954): 376.

5. *Welcome to Arizona* (Phoenix: Arizona Office of Tourism, n.d.); Harrington, "Our State Names," p. 376; Adlai Feather, "Origin of the Name Arizona," *New Mexico Historical Review* 39 (April 1964): 90–100.

6. Ark. Stat. Ann. § 5–102.

7. Harrington, "Our State Names," p. 376.

8. *A Brief History of Arkansas* (n.p., n.d.).

9. Ark. Stat. Ann. § 5–110.

10. *A Brief History of Arkansas*; Ark. Code Ann. § 1–4–106.

11. *California's Legislature, 1984*, pp. 212–13.

12. Cal. Govt. Code § 420.75 (West).

13. *California's Legislature, 1984*, p. 203.

14. *Colorado State Capitol* (Denver: Colorado Department of Education, n.d.); Harrington, "Our State Names," p. 377.

15. Harrington, "Our State Names," p. 377.

16. *State of Connecticut Register and Manual, 1983*, p. 909.

17. Conn. Gen. Stat. Ann. § 3–110a (West).

18. George Shankle, *State Names, Flags, Seals, Songs, Birds, and Flowers, and Other Symbols*, rev. ed. (Westport: Greenwood Press, 1970, c 1938), pp. 105–6.

19. Harrington, "Our State Names," pp. 377–78.

20. *Delaware; Small Wonder* (Dover: Delaware State Travel Service, n.d.).

21. Harrington, "Our State Names," p. 378; *A Short History of Florida* (Tallahassee: Florida Department of State, n.d.), p. 1.

22. *Georgia's Capitol* (Atlanta: Max Cleland, n.d.).

23. Ibid.; Shankle, *State Names*, pp. 109–10.

24. *Hawaii, The Aloha State* (Honolulu: State of Hawaii, Hawaii Visitors Bureau, Chamber of Commerce of Hawaii, n.d.).

25. Haw. Rev. Stat. § 5–7.

26. *Idaho Blue Book, 1981–1982*, pp. 14–15.

27. Harrington, "Our State Names," p. 379.

28. Ill. Ann. Stat. ch. 1, § 3007 (Smith-Hurd).

29. Ibid., ch. 1, § 3131.

30. *Here Is Your Indiana Government*, 18th ed. (Indianapolis: Indiana State Chamber of Commerce, 1977), p. 135.

31. 1937 Indiana Acts, 1389.

32. *Here Is Your Indiana Government*, p. 135.

33. Benjamin F. Shambaugh, "The Naming of Iowa," *The Palimpsest* 38 (March 1957): 97–98; Harrington, "Our State Names," p. 379.

34. Shambaugh, "The Naming of Iowa," p. 98.

35. Harrington, "Our State Names," pp. 379–80.

36. Shankle, *State Names*, pp. 115–16; www.kansascommerce.com; *Kansas Directory 1982*, pp. 134–35.

37. Harrington, "Our State Names," p. 380.

38. *Oh! Kentucky* (Frankfort: Department of Travel Development, n.d.).

39. Frederick W. Lawrence, "The Origin of American State Names," *National Geographic* 38 (July 1920): 129.

40. *Louisiana Facts* (Baton Rouge: Louisiana Department of State, n.d.); Harrington, "Our State Names," p. 380.

41. Shankle, *State Names*, p. 119.

42. *Quick Facts About Maine* (Augusta: John L. Martin, n.d.).

43. Ibid.

44. Shankle, *State Names*, pp. 119–20.

45. Harrington, "Our State Names," p. 380.

46. Gregory A. Stiverson and Edward C. Papenfuse, *Maryland and Its Government in Brief* (Annapolis: Archives Division, Hall of Records Commission, Department of General Services, n.d.), p. 14.

47. Harrington, "Our State Names," p. 381.

48. Shankle, *State Names*, p. 123; information provided by the Citizen Information Service, State of Massachusetts.

49. Harrington, "Our State Names," p. 381.

50. Shankle, *State Names*, p. 124.

51. *Minnesota Facts* (St. Paul: Minnesota Historical Society, Education Division, December 1983); Harrington, "Our State Names," p. 381.

52. Shankle, *State Names*, pp. 125–26.

53. *Souvenir of Mississippi* (Jackson: Dick Molpus, n.d.), p. 19; Harrington, "Our State Names," p. 382.

54. Shankle, *State Names*, p. 127.

55. Harrington, "Our State Names," p. 382.

56. Shankle, *State Names*, pp. 128–29.

57. *Montana Highway Map, 1985–86* (Helena: Montana Promotion Division, 1985).

58. Ibid.; Shankle, *State Names*, p. 130.

59. Harrington, "Our State Names," p. 383.

60. 1895 Neb. Laws, 441.

61. *Nebraska Blue Book, 1982–1983*, p. 12.

62. Shankle, *State Names*, p. 130.

63. Harrington, "Our State Names," p. 383.

64. Shankle, *State Names*, pp. 131–32.

65. Harrington, "Our State Names," p. 383.

66. Shankle, *State Names*, pp. 132–33.

67. Harrington, "Our State Names," p. 383.

68. Shankle, *State Names*, pp. 133–34.

69. *Your Miniguide to New Jersey* (Trenton: New Jersey Department of Commerce and Economic Development, Division of Travel and Tourism, 1985).

70. Harrington, "Our State Names," pp. 383–84.

71. Shankle, *State Names*, p. 135.

72. *New Mexico USA: Where to Go, What to Do* (Santa Fe: Marketing Services Division, New Mexico Economic Development and Tourism Department, 1986); N. M. Stat. Ann. § 12-3-9.

73. Harrington, "Our State Names," p. 384.

74. Shankle, *State Names*, p. 136.

75. Harrington, "Our State Names," p. 384.

76. Shankle, *State Names*, pp. 137–38.

77. *Facts About North Dakota* (Bismark: North Dakota Economic Development Commission, 1983), p. 32.

78. Harrington, "Our State Names," p. 384.

79. N.D. Cent § 39–04–12; discovernd.com/about/symbols.html; *Emblems of North Dakota* (Bismark: Ben Meier, n.d.), n.p.; Shankle, *State Names*, pp. 138–39.

80. Harrington, "Our State Names," pp. 384–85.

81. Shankle, *State Names*, pp. 139–40.

82. Harrington, "Our State Names," p. 385.

83. Shankle, *State Names*, pp. 140–41.

84. Harrington, "Our State Names," p. 385.

85. Shankle, *State Names*, pp. 141–42.

86. Harrington, "Our State Names," p. 385.

87. Shankle, *State Names*, p. 143.

88. *1976–77 Pennsylvania Manual*, p. 846.

89. Harrington, "Our State Names," pp. 385–86.

90. *State of Rhode Island Official Emblems* (Providence: Office of the Secretary of State, n.d.); Shankle, *State Names*, p. 144.

91. Harrington, "Our State Names," p. 384.

92. Shankle, *State Names*, pp. 144–45.

93. Harrington, "Our State Names," p. 384.

94. *Great Seal of South Dakota* (Pierre: Alice Kundert, n.d.); *South Dakota Signs and Symbols*, n.p., n.d.

95. Shankle, *State Names*, pp. 146–47.

96. S.D. Codified Laws § 1–6–16.5.

97. Harrington, "Our State Names," p. 386.

98. *Tennessee Blue Book, 1985–1986*, p. 341.

99. Harrington, "Our State Names," p. 386.

100. Shankle, *State Names*, pp. 148–49.

101. Harrington, "Our State Names," p. 386.

102. Shankle, *State Names*, p. 150.

103. Harrington, "Our State Names," pp. 386–87.

104. Shankle, *State Names*, pp. 150–51.

105. Harrington, "Our State Names," p. 387.

106. Shankle, *State Names*, pp. 151–52.

107. Harrington, "Our State Names," p. 387.

108. *Our State Seal, Flag, Flower, etc.* (Olympia: Washington State Superintendent of Public Instruction, n.d.).

109. Harrington, "Our State Names," p. 387.

110. Shankle, *State Names*, p. 154.

111. Harrington, "Our State Names," p. 387.

112. Shankle, *State Names*, pp. 154–55.

113. *Wyoming; Some Historical Facts* (Cheyenne: Wyoming State Archives, Museums and Historical Department, n.d.), p. 2.

114. Ibid., p. 1.

115. *American Samoa: Where Polynesia Began . . . and the South Pacific Begins* (n.p., n.d.); pamphlet provided by the office of Eni Faleomavaega, member of congress for American Samoa.

116. *The Northern Marianas: Saipan, Tinian, Rota* (Saipan: Marianas Visitors Bureau, n.d.); *History and Geographic Tourist Map of Saipan* (Saipan: Economic Service Counsel, Inc., in cooperation with the Marianas Visitors Bureau, 1992).

117. *Guam and Micronesia* (Agana: Guam Visitors Bureau, 1989), p. 5; *Guam USA Fact Sheet* (Agana: Guam Visitors Bureau, n.d.).

118. *Puerto Rico: The Shining Star of the Caribbean* (San Francisco: Travel and Sports, Inc., 1992), p. 4.

119. *United States Virgin Islands Visitor's Guide* (n.p.: United States Virgin Islands, Division of Tourism, 1993), pp. 5, 8–9.

2

State and Territory Mottoes

The use of mottoes accompanied the development of heraldry, which began to take hold in the twelfth century. A motto might be considered a terse statement, sometimes humorous, sometimes serious, that describes a certain spirit of the bearer. State mottoes, whether in English, Latin, French, or Spanish, or a native American language, express simply the character and beliefs of the citizenry.

Many state mottoes express a fundamental belief in God. Arizona's motto, *Ditat Deus*, means "God enriches." Florida's motto, taken from United States coinage, states simply "In God We Trust." Colorado's motto states that there is "Nothing without Providence" and Ohio's, that "With God, All Things Are Possible." South Dakota combines two common themes: "Under God the People Rule." Arkansas' motto boldly states that "The People Rule." Some statements of democratic belief are more pugnacious than religious: Alabama, "We Dare Maintain Our Rights," Massachusetts, "By the Sword We Seek Peace, but Peace Only Under Liberty," and New Hampshire, more direct, "Live Free or Die." Still other mottoes are designed as slogans rather than philosophical statements. Alaska promotes itself with the motto "North to the Future." Indiana calls itself "The Crossroads of America." Tennessee touts "Agriculture and Commerce," and Utah's motto is one word— "Industry."

ALABAMA

Motto: Audemus Jura Nostra Defendere[1]

Translation: "We Dare Maintain Our Rights"

Origin: This motto was selected by Marie Bankhead Owen, director of the State Department of Archives and History, when she requested B. J. Tieman to design a coat of arms in 1923. The motto was translated into Latin by University of Alabama Professor W. B. Saffold. The positive statement made by this motto replaced what was considered a negative statement imposed by outsiders during Reconstruction through the motto "Here We Rest."[2]

ALASKA

Motto: "North to the Future"[3]

Origin: In 1963, the Alaska Centennial Commission announced a competition to determine a distinctive centennial motto and emblem for Alaska.[4] During the competition, which carried a $300 prize, 761 entries were received. In December 1963, the commission announced that "North to the Future," the entry submitted by Juneau newsman Richard Peter, had won.[5] The legislature adopted this motto officially in 1967.

ARIZONA

Motto: Ditat Deus[6]

Translation: "God Enriches"

Origin: The motto remains unchanged since its introduction by Richard Cunningham McCormick in 1864. It is an expression, probably biblical in origin, of deep religious sentiment.

ARKANSAS

Motto: Regnat Populus[7]

Translation: "The People Rule"

Origin: A 1907 act changed the motto to its current language from "Regnant Populi," the motto selected in 1864. While the direct origin of this motto is somewhat obscure, it clearly voices the democratic tradition of the state and the nation.

CALIFORNIA

Motto: Eureka[8]

Translation: "I Have Found It"

Origin: The great seal of California, first designed in 1849, included this Greek motto to signify either the admission of the state into the Union or a miner's success.[9] Clearly, this ancient expression refers to the discovery of gold in California.

COLORADO

Motto: Nil Sine Numine[10]

Translation: "Nothing without Providence"

Origin: This motto is credited to William Gilpin, first territorial governor of Colorado. It may actually be an adaptation of a line from Virgil's *Aeneid*.[11]

CONNECTICUT

Motto: Qui Transtulit Sustinet[12]

Translation: "He Who Transplanted Still Sustains"

Origin: This motto, dating back to the early colonial history of Connecticut, was part of the colonial seal that depicted a vineyard. The words are adapted from the Book of Psalms 79:3.

DELAWARE

Motto: "Liberty and Independence"[13]

Origin: This motto was added to the state's great seal in 1847 as an expression of the ideals of American government.[14]

FLORIDA

Motto: "In God We Trust"[15]

Origin: The state seal, adopted in 1868, is declared to be the size of a silver dollar. This motto is evidently taken from the motto used on the silver dollar.

GEORGIA

Mottoes: "Agriculture and Commerce, 1776"; "Wisdom, Justice, Moderation"[16]

Origins: These mottoes appear on the great seal of the state—one on the obverse, the other on the reverse. Agriculture and commerce, of course, describe the mainstay of Georgia's economic well-being. In 1914, the date of 1799 was changed to 1776, the date of national independence rather than the date of Georgia's admission to the Union. Wisdom, justice, and moderation refer to the virtues that should guide legislative, judicial, and executive branches of government.

HAWAII

Motto: Ua Mau ke Ea o ka Aina i ka Pono[17]

Translation: "The Life of the Land Is Perpetuated in Righteousness"

Origin: Before becoming the state of Hawaii's official motto, these words were part of the coat of arms of the Kingdom of Hawaii and the seals of the Republic of Hawaii and the Territory. King Kamehameha III issued this motto upon the restoration of the Hawaiian flag to the kingdom by the British in 1843.[18]

IDAHO

Motto: Esto Perpetua[19]

Translation: "It Is Forever"

Origin: This motto is attributed to Venetian theologian and mathematician Pietro Sarpi (1552–1623) who, in 1623, applied it to the Republic of Venice.[20] This motto was chosen by the Grange in 1867 and by the state of Idaho in 1891.

ILLINOIS

Motto: "State Sovereignty, National Union"

Origin: These words were inscribed on the original state seal adopted in 1818. The seal that came into use in 1868, contrary to an amendment disallowing it, reversed the motto and placed "National Union" above "State Sovereignty." Nevertheless, the official motto places "State Sovereignty" first.[21]

INDIANA

Motto: "The Crossroads of America"[22]

Origin: The 1937 law designates "The Crossroads of America" as Indiana's official state motto or slogan. When this motto was chosen, the theoretical center of the United States was in Indiana; furthermore, a number of north-south and east-west routes intersect in Indiana.

IOWA

Motto: "Our Liberties We Prize, and Our Rights We Will Maintain"[23]

Origin: This motto, expressing the sentiment of Iowans as they entered the Union in 1846, was placed on the state seal by the first General Assembly in 1847.

KANSAS

Motto: Ad Astra per Aspera[24]

Translation: "To the Stars Through Difficulties"

Origin: John J. Ingalls was responsible for including this motto in the design of the great seal in 1861. He was at the time secretary of the Senate. Ingalls claimed the phrase was "as old as Josephus," quite common in heraldry, and the most melodious of various phrases that express similar sentiments. He had first noticed it in the office of the gentleman under whom he had read law.[25]

KENTUCKY

Motto: "United We Stand, Divided We Fall"[26]

Origin: This familiar motto paraphrases a line from John Dickinson's "Liberty Song of 1768," which says "By uniting we stand; by dividing we fall." George Pope Morris, who wrote the poem "The Flag of Our Union," probably got the phrase from the original song.[27]

LOUISIANA

Motto: "Union, Justice and Confidence"

Origin: An exact explanation for the choice of this motto has been lost in time. Clearly, however, it represents the sentiments present at Louisiana's joining the Union. Until 1864, the motto had been "Justice, Union, and Confidence."[28]

MAINE

Motto: Dirigo[29]

Translation: "I Direct" or "I Guide"

Origin: In the design of the seal, the star above the motto is intended to symbolize the state. The motto continues a navigational metaphor to the effect that the state should be a guiding light to its citizens just as the citizens should direct their efforts to the well-being of the state.[30]

MARYLAND

Mottoes: Fatti Maschii Parole Femine; Scuto Bonae Voluntatis Tuae Coronasti Nos[31]

Translation: "Manly Deeds, Womanly Words"; "With Favor Wilt Thou Compass Us as with a Shield"

Origins: The first motto is the motto of the Calvert family, whose history is closely tied to the state. The second motto is derived directly from the twelfth verse of the Fifth Psalm.[32]

MASSACHUSETTS

Motto: Ense Petit Placidam Sub Libertate Quietem[33]

Translation: "By the Sword We Seek Peace, but Peace Only under Liberty"

Origin: This motto was first used on the seal commissioned in 1775, after which time royal authority, and therefore royal seals, lost legitimacy. The motto is attributed to Algernon Sydney, who penned it in 1659.[34]

MICHIGAN

Motto: Si Quaeris Peninsulam Amoenam Circumspice[35]

Translation: "If You Seek a Pleasant Peninsula, Look About You"

Origin: This motto was placed on the 1835 great seal, which was designed by Lewis Cass. Cass, by one story, paraphrased the

inscription on the north door of St. Paul's Cathedral in London, so that the lower peninsula took the place of the monument by which Christopher Wren wished to be remembered.[36]

MINNESOTA

Motto: L'Etoile du Nord[37]

Translation: "Star of the North"

Origin: This motto was substituted for the Latin motto on the territorial seal when Governor Sibley designed a new state seal. The seal was approved in 1861. This motto lies behind Minnesota's having become known as the North Star State.[38]

MISSISSIPPI

Motto: Virtute et Armis[39]

Translation: "By Valor and Arms"

Origin: James Rhea Preston, the superintendent of education, suggested this motto when the coat of arms was under consideration in 1894.[40]

MISSOURI

Motto: Salus Populi Suprema Lex Esto[41]

Translation: "The Welfare of the People Shall Be the Supreme Law"

Origin: This motto has always been found on the state seal, which was adopted in 1822. Its source is Cicero's *De Legibus*.[42]

MONTANA

Motto: Oro y Plata[43]

Translation: "Gold and Silver"

Origin: This motto first appeared on the territorial seal adopted in 1865. It had been suggested by a special committee charged with designing the seal. Curiously, it was decided that the motto should be Spanish, but no one knew enough Spanish to formulate the motto correctly in the committee report. The error was corrected before the seal was struck.[44]

NEBRASKA

Motto: "Equality Before the Law"[45]

Origin: This motto was adopted in 1867 along with the state seal. It speaks to the cornerstone of the American system of justice. In 1963, the legislature also adopted a state symbol, a sooner, and a slogan: "Welcome to Nebraskaland, where the West begins."[46]

NEVADA

Motto: "All for Our Country"[47]

Origin: This motto was adopted in 1866 along with the state seal. It is clearly an expression of patriotism.

NEW HAMPSHIRE

Motto: "Live Free or Die"[48]

Origin: These words were written as a toast for a veterans' reunion on July 31, 1809, by General John Stark. The motto was adopted by the legislature in 1945.[49]

NEW JERSEY

Motto: "Liberty and Prosperity"[50]

Origin: The state had used this patriotic, hopeful motto informally for at least a century before it was officially adopted in 1928 along with a new design of the state seal.[51]

NEW MEXICO

Motto: *Crescit Eundo*[52]

Translation: "It Grows as It Goes"

Origin: This motto, which has its origins in classical Latin literature, has been in use since 1851, when the territorial seal was first designed. It is a statement of belief in growth and progress. True to New Mexico's belief in growth and progress, the legislature adopted a slogan in 1975; the official state slogan for business, commerce, and industry in New Mexico is "Everybody Is Somebody in New Mexico."[53]

NEW YORK

Motto: Exselsior[54]

Translation: "Higher"

Origin: This ancient motto signifying progress has been New York's motto since 1778, when its original coat of arms was adopted.

NORTH CAROLINA

Motto: Esse Quam Videri[55]

Translation: "To Be Rather than to Seem"

Origin: This motto, adopted with the great seal in 1893, can be found in Cicero. It is an expression of the character of the citizens of North Carolina.

NORTH DAKOTA

Motto: "Liberty and Union Now and Forever, One and Inseparable"[56]

Origin: This motto is a quotation from Daniel Webster's *Reply to Hayne*. When the state seal was adopted in 1889, the law changed the wording of the motto used on the territorial seal to its present form.

OHIO

Motto: "With God, All Things Are Possible"[57]

Origin: Ohio's motto, adopted in 1959, is taken from the Bible, Matthew 19:26.

OKLAHOMA

Motto: Labor Omnia Vincit[58]

Translation: "Labor Conquers All Things"

Origin: The classical quotation from Virgil speaks to the virtue of hard work in the settlement and growth of Oklahoma. It was adopted in 1906 as part of the state's seal.

OREGON

Motto: Alis Volat Propriis[59]

Translation: "She Flies with Her Own Wings"

Origin: This motto was first found on the 1849 state seal in spite of the fact that a legislative committee had recommended the motto "The Union" in 1857 and the legislature adopted that motto in 1859. "The Union" remained Oregon's motto until 1987, when the legislature chose to change it back.[60]

PENNSYLVANIA

Motto: "Virtue, Liberty, and Independence"[61]

Origin: This motto was included in the state coat of arms designed in 1778 by Caleb Lownes of Philadelphia. In 1875, it was approved.

RHODE ISLAND

Motto: "Hope"[62]

Origin: The simple motto was added to the seal after the colony received a more liberal charter in 1644. The anchor, the symbol of hope, had been the colonial seal since the beginning.

SOUTH CAROLINA

Mottoes: Animis Opibusque Parati; Dum Spiro Spero

Translations: "Prepared in Mind and Resources"; "While I Breathe I Hope"

Origins: These mottoes and the state seal on which they appear symbolize the June 28, 1776, battle between what is now Fort Moultrie and the British fleet. These mottoes declaring South Carolina's determination, strength, and hope were chosen in 1776 after the colony had declared itself independent.[63]

SOUTH DAKOTA

Motto: "Under God the People Rule"[64]

Origin: This motto was adopted in the 1885 and 1889 South Dakota constitutions at the suggestion of Dr. Joseph Ward, the founder of Yankton College.[65]

TENNESSEE

Motto: "Agriculture and Commerce"

Origin: Tennessee adopted this motto officially in 1987, although it had been used on the state seal since 1801.[66] The legislature also adopted "Tennessee—America at Its Best" as the state slogan in 1965.[67]

TEXAS

Motto: "Friendship"[68]

Origin: This motto was adopted in 1930 in recognition that the name of the state is derived from the Indian word *tejas*, which means friendship.

UTAH

Motto: "Industry"[69]

Origin: This motto, adopted in 1896, is an appropriate motto for a state which uses the beehive as a symbol.

VERMONT

Motto: "Freedom and Unity"[70]

Origin: This motto, on the seal designed by Ira Allen in 1778 and adopted in 1779, expresses the desire that states remain free, but united.

VIRGINIA

Motto: Sic Semper Tyrannis[71]

Translation: "Thus Ever to Tyrants"

Origin: This motto, dating back to the revolutionary times of 1776, evokes the sentiment for independence among the colonists.

WASHINGTON

Motto: Alki

Translation: "Bye and Bye"

Origin: This Indian word appeared on the territorial seal designed by Lt. J. K. Duncan. When settlers landed at Alki Point in Seattle, they named their settlement New York-Alki. They had hoped Seattle would become the New York of the West Coast.[72]

WEST VIRGINIA

Motto: Montani Semper Liberi[73]

Translation: "Mountaineers Are Always Free"

Origin: This motto was adopted with the state seal in 1863. The seal was based on suggestions and designs by Joseph H. Diss Debar.

WISCONSIN

Motto: "Forward"[74]

Origin: This motto, part of the coat of arms, became Wisconsin's motto when the seal and coat of arms were revised in 1851. The seal was designed by Edward Ryan and John H. Lathrop. The motto "Forward" was a compromise between the two men when Ryan objected to Lathrop's Latin motto.[75]

WYOMING

Motto: "Equal Rights"[76]

Origin: This motto, which had been used on the seal, was officially adopted in 1955. It was chosen in recognition of the fact that Wyoming women had attained political rights in 1869, long before they could vote in national elections.

DISTRICT OF COLUMBIA

Motto: Justitia Omnibus

Translation: "Justice for All"

Origin: The first act passed by the District's first legislative assembly on August 3, 1871, created the corporate seal of the District of Columbia, which included this motto.[77]

AMERICAN SAMOA

Motto: Samoa—Muamua le Atua[78]

Translation: "Samoa—Let God Be First"

Origin: This motto, adopted officially in 1975, speaks to the religious fervor of the Chamorros, who populate American Samoa.

COMMONWEALTH OF THE NORTHERN MARIANA ISLANDS

The Commonwealth has not adopted an official motto.

GUAM

Guam has not adopted an official motto.

PUERTO RICO

Motto: Joannes Est Nomen Ejus[79]

Translation: "John Is His Name"

Origin: Christopher Columbus named the island of Puerto Rico San Juan in honor of St. John the Baptist. The coat of arms given by King Ferdinand to Puerto Rico in 1511 prescribed this motto.

U.S. VIRGIN ISLANDS

Motto: "United in Pride and Hope"[80]

Origin: This motto appears on the official seal of the Islands.

NOTES

1. Ala. Code § 1-2-1.
2. *Alabama State Emblems* (Montgomery: Alabama State Department of Archives and History, n.d.), pp. 9–11.
3. Alaska Stat. § 44.09.045.
4. *Centennial Press* 1 (September 1963): 1.
5. *Centennial Press* 1 (December 1963): 1.
6. Ariz. Rev. Stat. Ann. art. 22, § 20.
7. Ark. Stat. Ann. § 5–103.
8. Cal. Govt. Code § 420.5 (West).
9. *California's Legislature, 1984*, p. 207.
10. Colo. Rev. Stat. § 24–80–901.
11. George E. Shankle, *State Names, Flags, Seals, Birds, Flowers, and Other Symbols*, rev. ed. (Westport, Conn.: Greenwood Press, 1970, c 1938), pp. 158–59.
12. Conn. Gen. Stat. Ann. § 3–105.
13. Del. Code Ann. tit. 29, § 301.
14. *Official Insignia of Delaware* (Dover: Delaware State Development Department, n.d.).
15. Fla. Stat. Ann. § 15.03 (West).
16. Ga. Code Ann. § 50–3–30.
17. Haw. Rev. Stat. § 5–9.
18. 1959 Haw. Sess. Laws 365.
19. Idaho Code § 59–1005.
20. Shankle, *State Names*, p. 160.
21. *Illinois Blue Book, 1983–1984*, pp. 439–40.
22. 1937 Indiana Acts, 1389.
23. Iowa Code Ann. § 1A.1 (West).
24. Kan. Stat. Ann. § 75–201.
25. *Kansas Historical Collections* 8 (1903–04): 299.
26. Ky. Rev. Stat. Ann. § 2.020 (Baldwin).
27. *Louisville Times*, 19 November 1940 (copy supplied by Kentucky Department for Libraries and Archives).
28. La. Rev. Stat. Ann. § 49–153 (West); information provided by Richard H. Holloway, Archives, State of Louisiana, Division of Archivist, Records Management, and History.
29. Me. Rev. Stat. tit. 1, § 205.
30. *Resolves of the Legislature of the State of Maine* . . . (Portland: Francis Douglas, State Printer, 1820), p. 22.
31. Md. Ann. Code § 13–102.
32. Shankle, *State Names*, p. 162.
33. Mass. Laws Ann. ch. 2, § 1.
34. "The History of the Seal of the Commonwealth" (copied material supplied by the Massachusetts Secretary of State, Citizen Information Service).
35. Mich. Comp. Laws Ann. § 2.21; § 2.22.
36. *Michigan History Magazine* 13 (1929): 663–64; *The Great Seal of Michigan* (Lansing: Richard H. Austin, n.d.).
37. Minn. Stat. Ann. § 1.135 (West).
38. *Minnesota Legislative Manual, 1985*, p. 11.
39. *Souvenir of Mississippi* (Jackson: Dick Molpus, n.d.), p. 19.
40. *Mississippi Official and Statistical Register, 1980–1984*, p. 27.
41. Mo. Ann. Stat. § 10.060 (Vernon).
42. Shankle, *State Names*, p. 163.
43. Mont. Code Ann. § 1–1–501.
44. Rex C. Myers, *Symbols of Montana* (Helena: Montana Historical Society, 1976), p. 4.
45. Neb. Rev. Stat. § 84–501.
46. Ibid., § 90–105.
47. Nev. Rev. Stat. § 235.010.
48. N.H. Rev. Stat. Ann. § 3:8.
49. *Manual for the General Court, 1981*.
50. N.J. Stat. Ann. § 52:2–1 (West).

51. 1928 N.J. Laws 801.

52. N.M. Stat. Ann. § 12–3–1.

53. Ibid., § 12–3–9.

54. N.Y. State Law § 70 (McKinney).

55. N.C. Gen. Stat. § 144–2.

56. N.D. Cent. Code art. XI, § 2.

57. Ohio Rev. Code Ann. § 5.06 (Page).

58. Okla. Stat. Ann. art. 6, § 35 (West).

59. Or. Rev. Stat. Ann. § 186.040.

60. "Motto (Oregon's)" (information supplied by the Office of the Secretary of State of Oregon).

61. *Pennsylvania Symbols* (Harrisburg: House of Representatives, n.d.).

62. R.I. Gen. Laws § 42–4–2.

63. *South Carolina State Symbols and Emblems* (Columbia: House of Representatives, n.d.)

64. S.D. Codified Laws Ann. § 1–6–2.

65. *History of the South Dakota State Flag* (Pierre: Bureau of Administration, Division of Central Services, The State Flag Account, n.d.).

66. Tenn. Code Ann. § 4–1–315.

67. Tenn. Code Ann. § 4–1–304.

68. Texas Rev. Civ. Stat. Ann. art. 6143a (Vernon).

69. Utah Code Ann. § 63–13–11.

70. Vt. Stat. Ann. tit. 1, § 491.

71. Va. Code § 7.1–26.

72. *Our State Seal, Flag, Flower, etc.* (Olympia: Washington State Superintendent of Public Instruction, n.d.).

73. W. Va. Code art. 2, § 7.

74. Wis. Stat. Ann. § 1.07 (West).

75. *State of Wisconsin, 1983–1984 Blue Book*, p. 947.

76. Wyo. Stat. Ann. § 8–3–107.

77. *Symbols of the District of Columbia* (Washington, D.C.: Government of the District of Columbia, Office of the Secretariat, Office of Visual Information Management, n.d.).

78. A.S. Code tit. 1, § 1102.

79. P.R. Laws Ann. tit. 1, § 34, § 37.

80. V.I. Code Ann. tit. 1, § 108.

3

State and Territory Seals

Not merely decorative symbols of statehood, the seals of state have been used to designate official acts of state through the ages, and their use is strictly prescribed by law.

State seals are like snapshots of each state's history. Oklahoma's seal, for example, contains the symbols of the Cherokee, Chickasaw, Creek, Choctaw, and Seminole nations and forty-five small stars around a central star, representing the forty-five existing states before Oklahoma became the forty-sixth in 1907. The seal of Kansas, on which appear thirty-four stars for the thirty-fourth state, depicts a steamboat and a river to symbolize commerce, a settler's cabin and a mare plowing to represent agriculture and prosperity, a train of wagons heading west and a herd of buffalo retreating being chased by two Indians on horseback.

The symbols employed in the seals represent recurring themes—agriculture, commerce, mining, shipping, liberty, and union. These symbols celebrate the economic development of the state, the natural resources on which the state was built, and the freedom of a united people to pursue their lives in peace and harmony.

ALABAMA

In 1939, the Alabama legislature returned to the design of the great seal that had been used before 1868. At the same time, the legislature provided for an official coat of arms.

The seal, which celebrates the historical importance of Alabama's river systems, is set out by law to be

> circular, and the diameter thereof two and a quarter inches; near the edge of the circle shall be the word "Alabama," and opposite this word, at the same distance from the edge, shall be the words, "great seal." In the center of the seal there shall be a representation of a map of the state with its principal rivers.[1]

The coat of arms signifies the history of Alabama under five flags, its status as a maritime state, and the courage of its citizens. The law describes the coat of arms as

> a shield upon which is carried the flags of four of the five nations which have at various times held sovereignty over a part or the whole of what is now the state of Alabama: Spain, France, Great Britain and the Confederacy. The union binding these flags shall be the shield of the United States. The shield upon which the flags and shield of the United States are placed shall be supported on either side by an eagle. The crest of the coat of arms shall be a ship representing the "Badine" which brought the French colonists who established the first permanent white set-

tlements in the state. Beneath the shield there shall be a scroll containing the sentence in Latin: "Audemus jura nostra defendere," the English interpretation of which is "We Dare Maintain Our Rights." The word "Alabama" shall appear beneath the state motto.[2]

ALASKA

Alaska's state seal is 2⅛ inches in diameter and consists of "two concentric circles between which appear the words 'The Seal of the State of Alaska.' "[3] The design inside the inner circle represents northern lights, icebergs, railroads, and people native to the state as well as symbols for mining, agriculture, fisheries, and fur seal rookeries. This seal, with the substitution of the word "Territory" for "State," had been used as the territorial seal since 1913.[4] It officially became the state seal in 1960.

ARIZONA

The great seal of Arizona is set in the state's constitution, which was adopted in 1911.

> The seal of the State shall be of the following design: In the background shall be a range of mountains, with the sun rising behind the peaks thereof, and at the right side of the range of mountains there shall be a storage reservoir and a dam, below which in the middle distance are irrigated fields and orchards reaching into the foreground, at the right of which are cattle grazing. To the left in the middle distance on a mountain side is a quartz mill in front of which and in the foreground is a miner standing with pick and shovel. Above this device shall be the motto: "Ditat Deus." In a circular band surrounding the whole device shall be inscribed: "Great Seal of the State of

Arizona," with the year of admission of the State into the Union.[5]

The seal uses the symbols of Arizona's first primary enterprises: reclamation, farming, cattle raising, and mining.

ARKANSAS

The seal of Arkansas was adopted in 1864. Except for an editorial change affecting the motto made in 1907, the seal has remained the same.

> An eagle at the bottom, holding a scroll in its beak, inscribed "Regnat Populus," a bundle of arrows in one claw and an olive branch in the other; a shield covering the breast of the eagle, engraved with a steamboat at top, a bee-hive and plow in the middle, and sheaf of wheat at the bottom; the Goddess of Liberty at the top, holding a wreath in her right hand, a pole in the left hand, surmounted by a liberty cap, and surrounded by a circle of stars, outside of which is a circle of rays; the figure of an angel on the left, inscribed "Mercy," and a sword on the right hand, inscribed "Justice," surrounded with the words "Seal of the State of Arkansas."[6]

The Arkansas seal celebrates the importance of the steamboat in its development and the industry of its citizens in a peaceful, bountiful land.

CALIFORNIA

The great seal of California was adopted by the 1849 constitutional convention. The code provides a pictorial description.[7] The seal as it now appears is the fourth design, a standardized representation adopted in 1937.

In the circular design is a seated figure of the goddess Minerva, at her feet a grizzly bear, in the background ships upon a mountain-rimmed bay, in the mid-distance a goldminer at work and, near the top centre, the motto EU-REKA (I have found it!) beneath a semi-circle of 31 stars, the number of States in the Union after the admission of California (September 9, 1850).[8]

COLORADO

The Colorado legislature adopted the state seal in 1877. The seal recalls the beauty of the Rocky Mountains and the significance of mining in the state's development.

The seal of the state shall be two and one-half inches in diameter, with the following device inscribed thereon: An heraldic shield bearing in chief, or upon the upper portion of the same, upon a red ground three snow-capped mountains; above surrounding clouds; upon the lower part thereof upon a golden ground a miner's badge, as prescribed by the rules of heraldry; as a crest above the shield, the eye of God, being golden rays proceeding from the lines of a triangle; below the crest and above the shield, as a scroll, the Roman fasces bearing upon a band of red, white, and blue the words "Union and Constitution"; below the whole the motto, "Nil Sine Numine"; the whole to be surrounded by the words, "State of Colorado," and the figures "1876."[9]

CONNECTICUT

The seal of the state of Connecticut has a history that goes back to colonial times. The seal has undergone several modifications, but essential elements have remained as the 1931 description indicates.

The great seal of the state shall conform to the following description: It shall be a perfect ellipse with its major axis two and one-half inches in length and its minor axis two inches in length, the major axis being vertical. Within such ellipse shall appear another ellipse with its major axis one and fifteen-sixteenths inches in length and its minor axis one and one-half inches in length. The inner ellipse is separated from the outer ellipse only by a line two points one-thirty-sixth of an inch in width and with the space between the two ellipses, being seven-thirty-seconds of an inch, forming a border. In said space shall appear, letter spaced and in letters one-eighth of an inch in height and of twelve point century Roman, the words "SIGILLUM REIPUBLICAE CONNECTICUTENSIS," beginning and ending one and one-sixteenth inches apart in the lower space along such border. In the center of the inner ellipse shall be three grape vines, two above and one below, each with four leaves and three clusters of grapes intertwined around a support nine-sixteenths of an inch high, and the base of the supports of the two upper vines one inch from the base of the inner ellipse and eleven-sixteenths of an inch apart. The base of the lower support shall be nine-sixteenths of an inch from the base of the inner ellipse and halfway between said bases shall appear the motto "QUI TRANSTULIT SUSTINET," in number three, six point card Roman letters, or engraver's Roman letters, on a ribbon gracefully formed, with the ends of the ribbon turned upward and inward and cleft.[10]

The description of the official arms was revised slightly in 1990 from the original description of 1931.

The following-described arms shall be the official arms of the state: A shield of rococo design of white field, having in the center three grape vines, supported and bearing fruit. The vine located in the center of the shield and the vine located on the right side of the shield shall ascend in a counterclockwise manner. The vine located on the left side of the shield shall ascend in a clockwise manner. The bordure to the shield shall consist of two bands bordered by fine lines adorned with clusters of white oak leaves (Quercus alba) bearing acorns. Below the shield shall be a white streamer, cleft at each end, bordered with two fine lines, and upon the streamer shall be in block letters the motto, "QUI TRANSTULIT SUSTINET." A drawing of said arms, made in conformity herewith and filed in the office of the secretary, shall be the official drawing of the arms of the state.[11]

DELAWARE

The great seal of Delaware is essentially the same design as the seal of 1777.

It is emblazoned as follows: Party per fess, or and argent, the first charged with a garb (wheat sheaf) in bend dexter and an ear of maize (Indian Corn) in bend sinister, both proper; the second charged with an ox statant, ruminating, proper; fess, wavy azure, supporters on the dexter a husbandman with a hilling hoe, on the sinister a rifleman armed and accoutred at ease. Crest, on a wreath azure and argent, a ship under full sail, proper, with the words "Great Seal of the State of Delaware" and the words "Liberty and Independence" engraved thereon.[12]

The seal symbolizes the importance of shipping and farming in Delaware's history as well as Delaware's role in carving out American independence.

FLORIDA

The state seal was first designed in 1868 and remains substantially the same except for the substitution of the sabal palmetto for the cocoa tree in 1970.

The great seal of the state shall be of the size of the American silver dollar, having in the center thereof a view of the sun's rays over a highland in the distance, a sabal palmetto palm tree, a steamboat on water, and an Indian female scattering flowers in the foreground, encircled by the words "Great Seal of the State of Florida: In God We Trust."[13]

The seal signifies Florida's tropical climate and the importance of native Americans in its history and the steamboat in its modern development. In 1985, the seal was officially revised to correct previous errors and to bring it into conformity with the change made in 1970.

GEORGIA

The great seal of Georgia was adopted by the state constitution of 1798. It remains the same today except for changing the date 1799 to 1776.

The device on one side is a view of the seashore, with a ship bearing the flag of the United States riding at anchor near a wharf, receiving on board hogsheads of tobacco and bales of cotton, emblematic of the exports of this state; at a small distance a boat, landing from the interior of the state, with hogsheads, etc., on board, representing the state's internal traffic; in the back part of the same side a man in the act of plowing; and at a small distance a flock of sheep in different postures, shaded by a flourishing tree. The motto inscribed thereon is "Agriculture and Commerce, 1776."

The device on the other side is three pillars supporting an arch, with the word "Constitution" engraved within the same, emblematic of the Constitution, supported by the three departments of government, namely the legislative, judicial, and executive. The first pillar has engraved upon a scroll "Wisdom," the second, "Justice," the third, "Moderation"; between the second and third pillars a man stands with a drawn sword, representing the aid of the military in the defense of the Constitution, and the motto is "State of Georgia, 1776."[14]

HAWAII

Except for the legend "Republic of Hawaii" and the size of the seal, Hawaii's state seal is the same as that of the Republic of Hawaii.

The great seal of the State shall be circular in shape, two and three-quarters inches in diameter, and of the design being described, with the tinctures added as a basis for the coat of arms as follows:

Arms. An heraldic shield which is quarterly; first and fourth, stripes of the Hawaiian flag; second and third, on a yellow field, a white ball pierced on a black staff; overall, a green escutcheon with a five-pointed yellow star in the center.

Supporters. On the right side, Kamehameha I, standing in the attitude as represented by the bronze statue in front of Aliiolani Hale, Honolulu; cloak and helmet yellow; figure in natural colors. To the left, goddess of lib-

erty, wearing a Phrygian cap and laurel wreath, and holding in right hand the Hawaiian flag, partly unfurled.

Crest. A rising sun irradiated in gold, surrounded by a legend "State of Hawaii, 1959," on a scroll, black lettering.

Motto. "Ua mau ke ea o ka aina i ka pono" on the scroll at bottom, gold lettering.

Further accessories. Below the shield, the bird phoenix wings outstretched; arising from flames, body black, wings half yellow, half dark red; also eight taro leaves, having on either side banana foliage and sprays of maidenhair fern, trailed upwards.[15]

IDAHO

The Idaho state seal, designed by Emma Edwards Green, was adopted in 1891.[16] The designer described the seal in these words:

The question of Woman Suffrage was being agitated somewhat, and as leading men and politicians agreed that Idaho would eventually give women the right to vote, and as mining was the chief industry, and the mining man the largest financial factor of the state at that time, I made the figure of the man the most prominent in the design, while that of the woman, signifying justice, as noted by the scales, liberty, as denoted by the liberty cap on the end of the spear, and equality with man as denoted by her position at his side, also signifies freedom. The pick and shovel held by the miner, and the ledge of rock beside which he stands, as well as the pieces of ore scattered about his feet, all indicate the chief occupation of the State. The stamp mill in the distance, which you can see by using a magnifying glass, is also typical of the mining interest of Idaho. The shield between the man and the woman is emblematic of the protection they unite in giving the state. The large fir or pine tree in the foreground in the shield refers to Idaho's immense timber interests. The husbandman plowing on the left side of the shield, together with the sheaf of grain beneath the shield, are emblematic of Idaho's agricultural resources, while the cornucopias, or horns of plenty, refer to the horticultural. Idaho has a game law, which protects the elk and moose. The elk's head, therefore, rises above the shield. The state flower, the wild Syringa or Mock Orange, grows at the woman's feet, while the ripened wheat grows as high as her shoulder. The star signifies a new light in the galaxy of states. . . . The river depicted in the shield is our mighty Snake or Shoshone River, a stream of great majesty.[17]

ILLINOIS

The Illinois state seal, designed by Secretary of State Sharon Tyndale, dates back to 1867 and was first used in 1868. This seal, actually the third since statehood, is considerably altered from the earlier seals.[18]

The secretary of state is hereby authorized and required to renew the great seal of state, and to procure it as nearly as practicable of the size, form and intent of the seal now in use, and conforming with the original design, as follows: "American eagle on a boulder in prairie—the sun rising in distant horizon," and scroll in eagle's beak, on which shall be inscribed the words: "State Sovereignty," "National Union," to correspond with the original seal of state, in every particular.[19]

INDIANA

Until 1963, Indiana had no officially authorized state seal although pioneer scenes were used on territorial seals as early as 1801.[20] The 1963 law sets out this description:

The official seal for the state of Indiana shall be described as follows:

A perfect circle, two and five eighths (2⅝) inches in diameter, inclosed by a plain line. Another circle within the first, two and three eighths (2⅜) inches in diameter inclosed by a beaded line, leaving a margin of one quarter (¼) of an inch. In the top half of this margin are the words "Seal of the State of Indiana."

At the bottom center, 1816, flanked on either side by a diamond, with two (2) dots and a leaf of the tulip tree (liriodendron tulupifera), at both ends of the diamond. The inner circle has two (2) trees in the left background, three (3) hills in the center background with nearly a full sun setting behind and between the first and second hill from the left.

There are fourteen (14) rays from the sun, starting with two (2) short ones on the left, the third being longer and then alternating, short and long. There are two (2) sycamore trees on the right, the larger one being nearer the center and having a notch cut nearly half way through, from the left side, a short distance above the ground. The woodsman is wearing a hat and holding his ax nearly perpendicular on his right. The ax blade is turned away from him and is even with his hat.

The buffalo is in the foreground, facing to the left of front. His tail is up, front feet on the ground with back feet in the air—as he jumps over a log.

The ground has shoots of blue grass, in the area of the buffalo and woodsman.[21]

IOWA

In 1847, the first General Assembly of Iowa adopted the following act designating a state seal:

The secretary of state be, and he is, hereby authorized to procure a seal which shall be the great seal of the state of Iowa, two inches in diameter, upon which shall be engraved the following device, surrounded by the words, "The Great Seal of the State of Iowa"—a sheaf and field of standing wheat, with a sickle and other farming utensils, on the left side near the bottom; a lead furnace and pile of pig lead on the right side; the citizen soldier, with a plow in his rear, supporting the American flag and liberty cap with his right hand, and his gun with his left, in the center and near the bottom; the Mississippi river in the rear of the whole, with the steamer Iowa under way; an eagle near the upper edge, holding in his beak a scroll, with the following inscription upon it: Our liberties we prize, and our rights we will maintain.[22]

KANSAS

The 1861 resolution creating the great seal of Kansas describes the seal as follows:

The east is represented by a rising sun, in the right-hand corner of the seal; to the left of it, commerce is represented by a river and a steamboat; in the foreground, agriculture is represented as the basis of the future prosperity of the state, by a settler's cabin and a man plowing with a pair of horses; beyond this is a train of ox-wagons, going west; in the background is seen a herd of buffalo, retreating, pursued by two Indians, on horseback; around the top is the motto, "Ad astra per aspera," and beneath a cluster of thirty-four stars. The circle is surrounded by the words, "Great seal of the state of Kansas. January 29, 1861."[23]

KENTUCKY

Kentucky's seal has remained essentially unchanged since 1792. It combines friendship with a slogan of revolutionary fervor.

The seal of the Commonwealth shall have upon it the device, two (2) friends embracing each other, with the words "Commonwealth of Kentucky" over their heads and around them the words, "United We Stand, Divided We Fall."[24]

LOUISIANA

The code of Louisiana empowers the governor of the state to devise a public seal to authenticate official governmental acts.[25] In 1902, Governor William Wright Heard prescribed this description of the seal:

A Pelican, with its head turned to the left, in a nest with three young; the Pelican, following the tradition in act of tearing its breast to feed its young; around the edge of the seal to be inscribed "State of Louisiana." Over the head of the Pelican to be inscribed "Union, Justice," and under the Pelican to be inscribed "Confidence."[26]

The motto and the pelican have been employed in Louisiana seals since at least 1804.

MAINE

In 1820, when Maine became a state, a law was passed describing the state seal. The current law provides a bit more detail and retains all the features of the original seal.

The seal of the State shall be a shield; argent, charged with a pine tree (Americana, quinis ex uno folliculo setis) with a moose deer (cervus alces), at the foot of it, recumbent; supporters: on dexter side, a husbandman, resting on a scythe; on sinister side, a seaman, resting on an anchor.

In the foreground, representing sea and land, and under the shield, shall be the name of the State in large Roman capitals, to wit: MAINE.

The whole shall be surrounded by a crest, the North Star. The motto, in small Roman capitals, shall be in a label interposed between the shield and crest, viz.:—DIRIGO.[27]

MARYLAND

The Maryland seal, readopted in 1876, is the seal sent from England shortly after the colony was settled. The reverse of the seal is the official state seal. The obverse is used only for decorative purposes.[28]

Description of Great Seal:

(a) Obverse. On the obverse of the Great Seal of Maryland is an equestrian figure of the Lord Proprietary, arrayed in complete armour and bearing a drawn sword in his hand. The caparisons of the horse are adorned with the family coat of arms. On the ground below is represented a sparse growth of grass on sand soil, with a few small blue and yellow flowers. On the circle, surrounding the obverse of the seal, is the Latin inscription "Caecilius Abso-lutus Dominus Terrae Mariae et Avaloniae Baro de Baltemore" meaning "Cecil Absolute Lord of Maryland and Avalon Baron of Baltimore" (Avalon refers to Lord Baltimore's first settlement in the new world, in Newfoundland).

(b) Reverse. On the reverse of the Great Seal of Maryland is Lord Baltimore's hereditary coat of arms. The 1st and 4th quarters represent the arms of the Calvert family described in heraldic language as a paly of 6 pieces, or (gold) and sable (black) a bend counterchanged. The 1st and 4th quarters are the left-hand top quarter and the right-hand bottom quarter. The 2nd and 3rd quarters show the arms of the Crossland family, which Cecil inherited from his grandmother, Alicia, wife of Leonard Calvert, the father of George, 1st Lord Baltimore. This coat of arms is in quarters also, argent (silver) and gules (red) a cross bottony (boutonne, with a button or a three-leaf clover at the end of each radius of the cross) counterchanged. Above the shield is placed an Earl's coronet (indicating that though only a baron in England, Calvert was an earl or court palatine in Maryland). Above that, a helmet set full faced and over that the Calvert crest, (2 pennons, the dexter or the right one or (gold), the other sable (black) staffs gules (red) issuing from the ducal coronet). The supporters of the shield are a plowman and a fisherman with their hands on the shield, designated respectively by a spade held in the right hand of the plowman and a fish held in the left hand of the fisherman (the fish is heraldic and cannot, therefore, be identified as to any species). The plowman wears a high-crowned, broad-brimmed beaver hat; the fisherman wears a knitted cap (somewhat resembling a stocking cap). The motto in Italian on a ribbon at the feet of the plowman and fisherman is the motto of the Calvert family "Fatti maschii parole femine" loosely translated as "Manly deeds, womanly words." Behind and surrounding both shield and supporters is an ermine-lined mantle and on the circle around this part of the seal are the words "Scuto bonae voluntatis tuae coronasti nos" (5th Psalm, 12th verse: "With favor wilt thou compass us as with a shield") and the date 1632. The date refers to the year the charter was granted.[29]

MASSACHUSETTS

The seal and coat of arms of Massachusetts were adopted in 1885; some revisions were made in 1898 and 1971. The current law holds that the seal

> shall be circular in form, bearing upon its face a representation of the arms of the commonwealth encircled with the inscription within a beaded border, "Sigillum Reipublicae Massachusettensis." The colors of the arms shall not be an essential part of said seal, and an impression from a seal engraved according to said design, on any commission, paper, or document shall be valid without such colors or the representation thereof by heraldic lines or marks.[30]

The coat of arms is described as consisting of

> a blue shield with an Indian thereon, dressed in a shirt, leggings, and moccasins, holding in his right hand a bow, and in his left hand an arrow, point downward, all of gold; and, in the up-

per right-hand corner of the field a silver star of five points. The crest shall be, on a wreath of gold and blue, a right arm, bent at the elbow, clothed and ruffled, and grasping a broadsword, all of gold. The motto "Ense petit placidam sub libertate quietem" shall appear in gold on a blue ribbon.[31]

MICHIGAN

The great seal of Michigan, adopted in 1911, is the 1835 seal designed by Lewis Cass. The law now reads that

> the great seal shall be comprised of the coat of arms of the state around which shall appear the words "great seal of the state of Michigan, A.D. MDCCCXXXV."[32]

The coat of arms, simply the seal without the legend, was also adopted in 1911. It is described as follows:

> The coat-of-arms shall be blazoned as follows:
> Chief, Azure, motto argent Tuebor;
> Charge, Azure, sun-rayed rising sinister proper, lake wavey proper, peninsula dexter grassy proper, man dexter on peninsula, rustic, habited, dexter arm-raised, dexter turned, sinister arm with gun stock resting, all proper;
> Crest, On a wreath azure and or, an American eagle rising to the dexter, tips of wings partly lowered to base, all proper, dexter talon holding an olive branch with 13 fruit, sinister talon holding a sheaf of 3 arrows, all proper. Over his head a sky azure environed with a scroll gules with the motto "E Pluribus Unum" argent;
> Supporters:
> Dexter, An elk rampant, proper;

Sinister, A moose rampant, proper;

Mottoes, On the scroll unending superior narrow argent, in sable, the motto, "Si quaeris peninsulam, amoenam."

On the scroll unending inferior, broader argent in sable the motto "circumspice."

Observations:

Scroll support and conventional leaf design between shield and scroll superior or;

Escutcheon supporters rest on the scroll supports and leaf design.[33]

MINNESOTA

Even though Minnesota became a state in 1858, the territorial seal remained in use until 1861 when the Minnesota legislature approved Governor Sibley's design for a state seal.[34] The design was revised in 1983 to read as follows:

(a) The seal is composed of two concentric borders. The outside forms the border of the seal and the inside forms the border for the illustrations within the seal. The area between the two borders contains lettering.

(b) The seal is two inches in diameter. The outside border has a radius of one inch and resembles the serrated edge of a coin. The width of the border is 1/16 of an inch.

(c) The inside border has a radius of three-fourths of an inch and is composed of a series of closely spaced dots measuring $\frac{1}{32}$ of an inch in diameter.

(d) Within the area between the borders "The Great Seal of the State of Minnesota" is printed in capital letters. Under that is the date "1858" with two dagger symbols separating the date and the letters. The lettering is 14 point century bold.

(e) In the area within the inside border is the portrayal of an 1858 Minnesota scene made up of various illustrations that serve to depict a settler plowing the ground near the falls of St. Anthony while he watches an Indian on horseback riding in the distance.

(f) For the purposes of description, when the area within the inside border is divided into quadrants, the following illustrations should be clearly visible in the area described.

(1) In the upper parts of quadrants one and two, the inscription, "L'Etoile du Nord" is found on the likeness of a scroll whose length is equal to twice the length of the inscription, but whose ends are twice folded underneath and serve to enhance the inscription. The lettering is seven point century bold.

(2) In quadrant two is found a likeness of a rising sun whose ambient rays form a background for a male Indian in loincloth and plume riding on horseback at a gallop. The Indian is sitting erect and is holding a spear in his left hand at an upward 60-degree angle to himself and is looking toward the settler in quadrant four.

(3) In quadrant one, three pine trees form a background for a picturesque resemblance of St. Anthony Falls in 1858.

(4) In quadrants three and four, cultivated ground is found across the lower half of the seal, which provides a background for the scenes in quadrants three and four.

(5) In quadrant three, a tree stump is found with an ax embedded in the stump and a period muzzle loader resting on it. A powder flask is hanging towards the end of the barrel.

(6) In quadrant four, a white barefoot male pioneer wearing clothing and a hat of that period is plowing the earth, using an animal-drawn implement from that period. The animal is not visible. The torso of the man continues into quadrant two, and he has his legs spread apart to simulate movement. He is looking at the Indian.

Additional effects; size. Every effort shall be made to reproduce the seal with justification to the 12 o'clock position and with attention to the authenticity of the illustrations used to create the scene within the seal. The description of the scene in this section does not preclude the graphic inclusion of the effects of movement, sunlight, or falling water when the seal is reproduced. Nor does this section prohibit the enlargement, proportioned reduction, or embossment of the seal for its use in unofficial acts.

Historical symbolism of seal. The sun, visible on the western horizon, signifies summer in the northern hemisphere. The horizon's visibility signifies the flat plains covering much of Minnesota. The Indian on horseback is riding due south and represents the great Indian heritage of Minnesota. The Indian's horse and spear and the Pioneer's ax, rifle, and plow represent tools that were used for hunting and labor. The stump symbolizes the importance of the lumber industry in Minnesota's history. The Mississippi River and St. Anthony Falls are depicted to note the importance of these resources in transportation and industry. The cultivated ground and the plow symbolize the importance of agriculture in Minnesota. Beyond the falls three pine trees represent the state tree and three great pine

regions of Minnesota; the St. Croix, Mississippi, and Lake Superior.[35]

MISSISSIPPI

The great seal of the state of Mississippi adopted by the legislature is the same seal that has been in use since statehood was attained in 1817.[36] The 1817 law reads:

> The seal of this state, the inscription of which shall be "the great seal of the state of Mississippi" around the margin, and in the center an eagle, with the olive branch and quiver of arrows in his claws.[37]

MISSOURI

The Missouri state seal, designed by a select committee of legislators, was adopted by the legislature and signed into law in 1822.

> The device for an armorial achievement for the state of Missouri is as follows: Arms, parted per pale, on the dexter side; gules, the white or grizzly bear of Missouri, passant guardant, proper on a chief engrailed; azure, a crescent argent; on the sinister side, argent, the arms of the United States, the whole within a band inscribed with the words "UNITED WE STAND, DIVIDED WE FALL." For the crest, over a helmet full-faced, grated with six bars; or a cloud proper, from which ascends a star argent, and above it a constellation of twenty-three smaller stars, argent, on an azure field, surrounded by a cloud proper. Supporters on each side, a white or grizzly bear of Missouri, rampant, guardant proper, standing on a scroll, inscribed with the motto, "Salus populi su-

prema lex esto," and under the scroll numerical letters MDCCCXX. And the great seal of the state shall be so engraved as to present by its impression the device of the armorial achievement aforesaid, surrounded by a scroll inscribed with the words, "THE GREAT SEAL OF THE STATE OF MISSOURI," in Roman capitals, which seal shall be in a circular form and not more than two and a half inches in diameter.[38]

MONTANA

The Montana territorial seal, slightly altered since 1865, became the state seal by legislative act in 1893.[39]

The great seal of the state is as follows: a central group representing a plow and a miner's pick and shovel; upon the right, a representation of the Great Falls of the Missouri River; upon the left, mountain scenery; and underneath, the words "Oro y Plata." The seal must be 2½ inches in diameter and surrounded by these words, "The Great Seal of the State of Montana."[40]

NEBRASKA

The great seal of the state of Nebraska was laid by an 1867 law, which reads in part:

The eastern part of the circle to be represented by a steamboat ascending the Missouri river; the mechanic arts to be represented by a smith with hammer and anvil; in the foreground, agriculture to be represented by a settler's cabin, sheaves of wheat and stalks of growing corn; in the background a train of cars heading towards the Rocky Mountains, and on the extreme west, the Rocky Mountains to be plainly in view; around the top of this circle to be in capital letters, the motto, "EQUALITY BEFORE THE LAW," and the circle to be surrounded with the words, "Great Seal of the State of Nebraska, March 1st, 1867."[41]

NEVADA

The state seal was officially adopted in 1866. The current law states that

1. There shall be a seal of the State of Nevada called The Great Seal of the State of Nevada, the design of which shall be as follows: In the foreground, there shall be two large mountains, at the base of which, on the right, there shall be located a quartz mill, and on the left a tunnel, penetrating the silver leads of the mountain, with a miner running out a carload of ore, and a team loaded with ore for the mill. Immediately in the foreground, there shall be emblems indicative of the agricultural resources of the state, as follows: A plow, a sheaf and sickle. In the middle ground, there shall be a railroad train passing a mountain gorge and a telegraph line extending along the line of the railroad. In the extreme background, there shall be a range of snow-clad mountains, with the rising sun in the east. Thirty-six stars and the motto of our state, "All for Our Country," shall encircle the whole group. In an outer circle, the words "The Great Seal of the State of Nevada" shall be engraved with "Nevada" at the base of the seal and separated from the other words by two groups of three stars each.

2. The size of the seal shall not be more than 2¾ inches in diameter.[42]

NEW HAMPSHIRE

The current seal was adopted in 1931, when a committee was formed to recommend improvements in the seal of 1784. The statute describing the seal is reprinted with permission of Butterworth Legal Publishers.

The seal of the state shall be two inches in diameter, circular, with the following detail and no other: A field crossed by a straight horizon line of the sea, above the center of the field; concentric with the field the rising sun, exposed above the horizon about one third of its diameter; the field encompassed with laurel; across the field for the full width within the laurel a broadside view of the frigate Raleigh, on the stocks; the ship's bow dexter and higher than the stern; the three lower masts shown in place, together with the fore, main and mizzen tops, shrouds and mainstays; an ensign staff at the stern flies the United States flag authorized by act of Congress June 14, 1777; a jury staff on the mainmast and another on the foremast each flies a pennant; flags and pennants are streaming to the dexter side; the hull is shown without a rudder; below the ship the field is divided into land and water by a double diagonal line whose highest point is sinister; no detail is shown anywhere on the water, nor any on the land between the water and the stocks except a granite boulder on the dexter side; encircling the field is the inscription, SEAL OF THE STATE OF NEW HAMPSHIRE, the words separated by round periods, except between the parts of New Hampshire; at the lowest point of the inscription is the date 1776, flanked on either side by a five-pointed star, which group separates the beginning and end of the inscription.[43]

In 1945, the legislature also adopted a state emblem. The law, slightly amended in 1957, is reprinted with permission of Butterworth Legal Publishers.

The state emblem shall be of the following design: With an elliptical panel, the longest dimension of which shall be vertical, there shall appear an appropriate replica of the Old Man of the Mountains; surrounding the inner panel, and enclosed within another ellipse, there shall be at the bottom of the design the words of any state motto which may be adopted by the general court; and at the top of the design, between the inner and outer elliptical panels, the words, New Hampshire, appropriately separated from the motto, if adopted, by one star on each side. Said emblem may be placed on all printed or related material issued by the state and its subdivisions relative to the development of recreational, industrial, and agricultural resources of the state.[44]

NEW JERSEY

The great seal was authorized in 1776 and its design amended in 1928. The law describes the seal accordingly:

The great seal of this state shall be engraved on silver, which shall be round, of two and a half inches in diameter and three-eighths of an inch thick; the arms shall be three ploughs in an escutcheon, azure; supporters, Liberty and Ceres. The Goddess Liberty to carry in her dexter hand a pole, proper, surmounted by a cap gules, with band azure at the bottom, displaying on the band six stars, argent; tresses falling on shoulders, proper; head bearing over

all a chaplet of laurel leaves, vert; overdress, tenne; underskirt, argent; feet
sandaled, standing on a scroll. Ceres:
Same as Liberty, save overdress, gules;
holding in left hand a cornucopia, or,
bearing apples, plums and grapes surrounded by leaves, all proper; head
bearing over all a chaplet of wheat
spears, vert. Shield surmounted by sovereign's helmet, six bars, or; wreath
and mantling, argent and azure. Crest:
A horse's head, proper. Underneath the
shield and supporting the goddesses, a
scroll azure, bordered with tenne, in
three waves or folds; on the upper
folds the words "Liberty and Prosperity"; on the under fold in Arabic numerals, the figures "1776." These
words to be engraved round the arms,
viz., "The Great Seal of the State of
New Jersey."[45]

NEW MEXICO

The great seal of New Mexico is essentially
the one that was designed for the Territory
of New Mexico in 1851 and adopted in
1887. After becoming a state in 1912, the
state legislature adopted the old territorial
seal, appropriately changed for New Mexico's new status, as the state seal.[46]

The coat of arms of the state shall be
the Mexican eagle grasping a serpent
in its beak, the cactus in its talons,
shielded by the American eagle with
outspread wings, and grasping arrows
in its talons; the date 1912 under the
eagles and, on a scroll, the motto:
"Crescit Eundo." The great seal of the
state shall be a disc bearing the coat of
arms and having around the edge the
words "Great Seal of the State of New
Mexico."[47]

NEW YORK

The great seal of New York was officially
designated in 1882. The 1882 law seeks to
describe the seal first adopted in 1778.

The secretary of state shall cause to be
engraved upon metal two and one-half
inches in diameter the device of arms
of this state, accurately conformed to
the description thereof given in this article, surrounded with the legend, "The
great seal of the state of New York."[48]

NORTH CAROLINA

North Carolina's seal was adopted first in
1893 and has undergone some modifications
since then. The current law is as follows:

The Governor shall procure for the
State a seal, which shall be called the
great seal of the State of North Carolina, and shall be two and one-quarter
inches in diameter, and its design shall
be a representation of the figures of
Liberty and Plenty, looking toward
each other, but not more than half-
fronting each other and otherwise dis-
posed as follows: Liberty, the first
figure, standing her pole with cap on it
in her left hand and a scroll with the
word "Constitution" inscribed thereon
in her right hand. Plenty, the second
figure, sitting down, her right arm half
extended towards Liberty, three heads
of grain in her right hand, and in her
left, the small end of her horn, the
mouth of which is resting at her feet,
and the contents of the horn rolling
out.
    The background on the seal shall
contain a depiction of mountains running from left to right to the middle of
the seal and an ocean running from

right to left to the middle of the seal. A side view of a three-masted ship shall be located on the ocean and to the right of Plenty. The date "May 20, 1775" shall appear within the seal and across the top of the seal and the words "esse quam videri" shall appear at the bottom around the perimeter. The words "THE GREAT SEAL of the STATE of NORTH CAROLINA" shall appear around the perimeter. No other words, figures or other embellishments shall appear on the seal.[49]

NORTH DAKOTA

This North Dakota seal is described in the 1889 state constitution. It is essentially the same as the territorial seal approved in 1863.

The following described seal is hereby declared to be and hereby constituted the great seal of the state of North Dakota, to wit: a tree in the open field, the trunk of which is surrounded by three bundles of wheat; on the right a plow, anvil and sledge; on the left, a bow crossed with three arrows, and an Indian on horseback pursuing a buffalo toward the setting sun; the foliage of the tree arched by a half circle of forty-two stars, surrounded by the motto "Liberty and Union Now and Forever, One and Inseparable"; the words "Great Seal" at the top; the words "State of North Dakota" at the bottom; "October 1st" on the left and "1889" on the right. The seal to be two and one-half inches in diameter.[50]

OHIO

The current seal of Ohio was revised in 1967, but the revision is based on the first seal, adopted in 1803.

The great seal of the state shall be two and one-half inches in diameter and shall consist of the coat of arms of the state within a circle having a diameter of one and three-fourths inches, surrounded by the words "THE GREAT SEAL OF THE STATE OF OHIO" in news gothic capitals.[51]

The coat of arms used in the seal was also revised in 1967 and then again in 1996.

The coat of arms of the state shall consist of the following device: a circular shield; in the right foreground of the shield a full sheaf of wheat bound and standing erect; in the left foreground, a cluster of seventeen arrows bound in the center and resembling in form the sheaf of wheat; in the background, a representation of Mount Logan, Ross county, as viewed from Adena state memorial; over the mount, a rising sun three-quarters exposed and radiating thirteen rays to represent the thirteen original colonies shining over the first state in the northwest territory, the exterior extremities of which form a semicircle; and uniting the background and foreground, a representation of the Scioto river and cultivated fields. . . .

When the coat of arms of the state is reproduced in color, the colors used shall be substantially the same as the natural color of the terrain and objects shown.

Any official seal acquired on or after March 1, 2003, shall contain the official coat of arms of the state as described in section 5.04 of the Revised Code and surrounded by the appropriate words. Prior to that date, any official seal authorized by statute is valid for all purposes.[52]

OKLAHOMA

The design of Oklahoma's seal is laid out thusly in the 1906 state constitution:

> In the center shall be a five pointed star, with one ray directed upward. The center of the star shall contain the central device of the seal of the Territory of Oklahoma, including the words, "Labor Omnia Vincit." The upper left hand ray shall contain the symbol of the ancient seal of the Cherokee Nation, namely: A seven pointed star partially surrounded by a wreath of oak leaves. The ray directed upward shall contain the symbol of the ancient seal of the Chickasaw Nation, namely: An Indian warrior standing upright with bow and shield. The lower left hand ray shall contain the symbol of the ancient seal of the Creek Nation, namely: A sheaf of wheat and a plow. The upper right hand ray shall contain the symbol of the ancient seal of the Choctaw Nation, namely: A tomahawk, bow, and three crossed arrows. The lower right hand ray shall contain the symbol of the ancient seal of the Seminole Nation, namely: A village with houses and a factory beside a lake upon which an Indian is paddling a canoe. Surrounding the central star and grouped between its rays shall be forty-five small stars, divided into five clusters of nine stars each, representing the forty-five states of the Union, to which the forty-sixth is now added. In a circular band surrounding the whole device shall be inscribed, "GREAT SEAL OF THE STATE OF OKLAHOMA 1907."[53]

OREGON

The seal of the state of Oregon was designed by a legislative committee in 1857 and officially adopted in 1903. The statute describing the seal is reprinted with permission of Butterworth Legal Publishers.

> The description of the seal of the State of Oregon shall be an escutcheon, supported by 33 stars, and divided by an ordinary, with the inscription, "The Union." In chief—mountains, an elk with branching antlers, a wagon, the Pacific Ocean, on which there are a British man-of-war departing and an American steamer arriving. The second—quartering with a sheaf, plow and a pickax. Crest—the American eagle. Legend—State of Oregon, 1859.[54]

PENNSYLVANIA

A seal for the Commonwealth was designed in 1776 and approved in 1791. In 1809, a new die was cut. The seal currently in use was adopted in 1893.[55] The three symbols used in the seal were originally used in county seals. The ship was the crest of Philadelphia County; the plough, the crest of Chester County; and the sheaf of wheat, the crest of Sussex County, which is now in Delaware.[56]

> The shield shall be parted PER FESS, or, charged with a plough, PROPER, in chief; on a sea WAVY; PROPER, a ship under full sail, surmounted with a sky, Azure; and in BASE, on a field VERT, three GARBS, OR. On the SINISTER a stock of maize, and DEXTER an olive branch. And on the wreath of its colours a bald eagle—PROPER, PERCHED, wings extended, for the CREST. MOTTO: VIRTUE, LIBERTY, and INDEPENDENCE. Round the margin of the seal, COMMONWEALTH OF PENNSYLVANIA. The reverse, Liberty, trampling on a Lyon, Gules, the emblem of Tyranny.

MOTTO—"BOTH CAN'T SUR-VIVE."[57]

RHODE ISLAND

The state seal was adopted in 1875. The anchor was adopted in the 1647 seal by the assembly. The law states that

> There shall continue to be one (1) seal for the public use of the state; the form of an anchor shall be engraven thereon; the motto thereof shall be the word Hope; and in a circle around the same shall be engraven the words, Seal of the State of Rhode Island and Providence Plantations, 1636.[58]

The arms, found on the flag, are officially described as follows:

The arms of the state are a golden anchor on a blue field, and the motto thereof is the word Hope.[59]

SOUTH CAROLINA

The seal of South Carolina was commissioned in 1776 and first used in 1777. The design for the arms was made by William Henry Drayton and that for the reverse, by Arthur Middleton. The seal is a circle four inches in diameter and is described as follows:

> *Arms*: A Palmetto tree growing on the seashore erect (symbolical of the fort on Sullivan's Island, built on Palmetto logs); at its base, a torn up oak tree, its branches lopped off, prostrate, typifying the British Fleet, constructed of oak timbers and defeated by the fort; both proper. Just below the branches of the Palmetto, two shields, pendant; one of them on the dexter side is inscribed MARCH 26, (the date of ratification of the Constitution of

S.C.)—the other on the sinister side JULY 4, (the date of Declaration of Independence): Twelve spears proper, are bound crosswise to the stem of the Palmetto, their points raised, (representing the 12 states first acceding to the Union); the band uniting them together bearing the inscription QUIS SEPARABIT (Who shall separate?) under the prostrate oak, is inscribed MELIOREM LAPSA LOCAVIT (having fallen it has set up a better); below which appears in large figures, 1776 (the year the Constitution of S.C. was passed, the year of the Battle at Sullivan's Island and of the Declaration of Independence, and the year in which the Seal was ordered made). At the summit of Exergue, are the words SOUTH CAROLINA; and at the bottom of the same ANIMIS OPIBUSQUE PARATI (prepared in mind and resources).

> *Reverse*: A woman walking on the seashore, over swords and daggers (typifying Hope overcoming dangers, which the sun, just rising, was about to disclose); she holds in her dexter hand, a laurel branch, (symbolical of the honors gained at Sullivan's Island), and in her sinister hand, the folds of her robe; she looks toward the sun, just rising above the sea, (indicating that the battle was fought on a fine day, and also bespeaking good fortune); all proper. On the upper part is the sky azure. At the summit of Exergue, are the words DUM SPIRO SPERO (While I breathe I hope) and within the field below the figure, is inscribed the word SPES (Hope).[60]

SOUTH DAKOTA

The design of the state seal was set out in the constitutions of 1885 and 1889. In 1961, the legislature adopted the same design, but specified the colors to be used.

The design of the colored seal of the state of South Dakota shall be as follows: An inner circle, whose diameter shall be five-sevenths of the diameter of the outer circle of any seal produced in conformity herewith; within which inner circle shall appear; in the left foreground on the left bank of a river, a rust-colored smelting furnace from which grey smoke spirals upward and adjacent to which on the left are a rust-colored hoist house and mill, and to the left a grey dump; these three structures being set in a yellow field and above and back of a light green grove on the left bank of the river. In the left background is a series of three ranges of hills, the nearer range being a darker green than the said grove, the intermediate range of a blue-green and the higher range of blue-black coloration.

In the right foreground is a farmer with black hat, red shirt, navy-blue trousers and black boots, holding a black and silver breaking plow, drawn by a matched team of brown horses with a black harness. In the right background and above the horses in a pasture of grey-green, a herd of rust-colored cattle graze in front of a field of yellow-brown corn, part in shock and part in cut rows to the rear and above which are blue and purple hills forming a low background and receding into the distance. Between the right and left foregrounds and backgrounds is a light-blue river merging in the distance into a sky-blue and cloudless sky. Moving upstream on the river is a white steamboat with a single black funnel from which grey smoke spirals upward. Green shrubbery appears on the near bank of the river, in the left foreground and on the right bank of the river near the pasture is a yellow field. The farmer is turning black-brown furrows which reach across the circle and in his foreground is a field of brown-green-yellow.

Near the upper edge of the inner circle at the top on a golden quarter circle which is one-fifth in width the distance between the innermost and the outermost circles that compose the seal, shall appear in black, the state motto: "Under God the People Rule." This innermost circle is circumscribed by a golden band one-fourth as wide as the above-described quarter circle, which inner border, shall be circumscribed by a deep blue circle four and one-half times as wide as the above quarter circle, on which in golden letters one-third its width, in height, shall appear at the top the words, "State of South Dakota." In the lower half of the deep blue circle shall appear in words of equal height "Great" and "Seal" between which shall be the numerals "1889." Between the above-stated names and on either side shall appear a golden star one-half in size the width of the deep blue circle. Circumscribing this deep blue circle shall be a band of gold of the same width as of the inner golden band.

Outside of this outer golden band shall be a serrated or saw-toothed edge of small triangles whose base shall be of the same width as the above quarter circle.[61]

TENNESSEE

Tennessee has no officially designated seal. The seal in use now, however, is essentially the same as that recommended in 1801 by a special committee:

the said seal shall be a circle, two inches and a quarter in diameter, that the circumference of the circle contain the words THE GREAT SEAL OF TENNESSEE, that in the lower part of said circumference be inserted Feb. 6th 1796, the date of the constitution of this State; that in the inside of the upper part of said circle, be set in numerical letters XVI, the number of the state in chronological order; that under the base of the upper semicircle, there be the word AGRICULTURE; that above said base, there be the figure of a plough, sheaf of wheat and cotton plant; that in the lower part of the lower semicircle, there be the word COMMERCE, and said lower semicircle shall also contain the figure of a boat and boatman.

This seal was used until 1829, when a second seal began to come into use. The new seal was used until 1865. The so-called Brownlow Seal was used in 1865, after which time, two new seals came into use. The seal now used is the larger of the two new seals. It differs from the 1801 seal in that the boat is of different design and is pointed in the opposite direction, and the month and day have been dropped from the date.[62]

TEXAS

The seal of Texas is that adopted by the Republic of Texas in 1839. When Texas became a state in 1845, the word "Republic" was changed to "State." The seal is described as follows:

> There shall be a Seal of the State which shall be kept by the Secretary of State, and used by him officially under the direction of the Governor. The Seal of the State shall be a star of five points

encircled by olive and live oak branches, and the words "The State of Texas."

In 1993, the reverse of the seal and the state arms were prescribed by law:

> The reverse of the state seal contains a shield, displaying a depiction of the Alamo, the cannon of the Battle of Gonzales, and Vince's Bridge. The shield is encircled by live oak and olive branches, and the unfurled flags of the Kingdom of France, the Kingdom of Spain, the United Mexican States, the Republic of Texas, the Confederate States of America, and the United States of America. Above the shield is emblazoned the motto, "REMEMBER THE ALAMO," and beneath it are the words, "TEXAS ONE AND INDIVISIBLE," with a white five-pointed star hanging over the shield, centered between the flags.
>
> The state arms are a white star of five points, on an azure ground, encircled by olive and live oak branches. [63]

UTAH

The state seal of Utah, designed by Harry Edwards, was adopted in 1896. The symbols of the seal include the American eagle (protection in peace and war), the beehive (industry), and sego lilies (peace). The date 1847 represents the year the Mormons came to the Salt Lake Valley, and 1896 is the year in which Utah was granted statehood.[64]

> The Great Seal of the state of Utah shall be 2-½ inches in diameter, and of the following device: the center a shield and perched thereon an American eagle with outstretching wings; the top of the shield pierced by six arrows crosswise; under the arrows the motto "In-

dustry"; beneath the motto a beehive, on either side growing sego lilies; below the beehive the figures "1847"; and on each side of the shield an American flag; encircling all, near the outer edge of the seal, beginning at the lower left-hand portion, the words "The Great Seal of the State of Utah," with the figures "1896" at the base. [65]

VERMONT

In 1821, the original 1779 seal went into disuse. Until 1937, when the design of the first seal was adopted again, Vermont used a number of different seals. The current law reads as follows:

The state seal shall be the great seal of the state, a faithful reproduction, cut larger and deeper, of the original seal, designed by Ira Allen, cut by Reuben Dean of Windsor and accepted by resolution of the general assembly, dated February 20, 1779. The seal shall be kept by the secretary of civil and military affairs. [66]

The description of the coat of arms was set out in law in 1862:

The coat of arms, crest, motto and badge of the state shall be and are described as follows:

(1) Coat of arms. Green, a landscape occupying half of the shield; on the right and left, in the background, high mountains, blue; the sky, yellow. From near the base and reaching nearly to the top of the shield, arises a pine tree of natural color and between three erect sheaves, yellow, placed diagonally on the right side and a red cow standing on the left side of the field.

(2) Motto and badge. On a scroll beneath the shield, the motto: Vermont; Freedom and Unity. The Vermonter's badge: two pine branches of natural color, crossed between the shield and scroll.

(3) Crest. A buck's head, of natural color, placed on a scroll, blue and yellow. [67]

VIRGINIA

The seal of Virginia is described in a 1930 law:

The great seal of the Commonwealth of Virginia shall consist of two metallic discs, 2¼ inches in diameter, with an ornamental border one fourth of an inch wide, with such words and figures engraved thereon as will, when used, produce impressions to be described as follows: On the obverse, Virtus, the genius of the Commonwealth, dressed as an Amazon, resting on a spear in her right hand, point downward, touching the earth; and holding in her left hand, a sheathed sword, or parazonium, pointing upward; her head erect and face upturned; her left foot on the form of Tyranny represented by the prostrate body of a man, with his head to her left, his fallen crown nearby, a broken chain in his left hand, and a scourge in his right. Above the group and within the border conforming therewith, shall be the word "Virginia," and, in the space below, on a curved line, shall be the motto, "Sic Semper Tyrannis." On the reverse, shall be placed a group consisting of Libertas, holding a wand and pileus in her right hand; on her right, Aeternitas, with a globe and phoenix in her right hand; on the left of Libertas, Ceres, with a cornucopia in her left hand, and an ear of wheat in her right;

over this device, in a curved line, the word "Perseverando."[68]

The law also provides for a lesser seal:

The lesser seal. The lesser seal of the Commonwealth shall be 1⁹⁄₁₆ inches in diameter, and have engraved thereon the device and inscriptions contained in the obverse of the great seal.[69]

WASHINGTON

The seal of the state of Washington was prescribed in the 1889 state constitution and added to the body of law in 1967.

The seal of the state of Washington shall be, a seal encircled with the words: "The Seal of the State of Washington," with the vignette of General George Washington as the central figure, and beneath the vignette the figures "1889."[70]

WEST VIRGINIA

The state constitution of West Virginia designates the seal designed by Joseph H. Diss Debar and chosen by a legislative committee in 1863 as the official state seal.

The present seal of the State, with its motto, "Montani Semper Liberi," shall be the great seal of the State of West Virginia, and shall be kept by the secretary of state, to be used by him officially, as directed by law.[71]

The report of the committee, which was then adopted by a joint resolution in 1863, described the seal:

The disc of the Great Seal is to be two and one-half inches in diameter; the obverse to bear the legend "The State

of West Virginia," the constitutional designation of our Republic, which with the motto, "Montani Semper Liberi—Mountaineers always free"—is to be inserted in the circumference. In the center a rock with ivy, emblematic of stability and continuance, and on the face of the rock the inscription, "June 20, 1863," the date of our foundation, as if graven with a pen of iron in the rock forever. On the right of the rock a farmer clothed in the traditional hunting garb, peculiar to this region, his right arm resting on the plow handles, and his left supporting a woodman's axe, indicating that while our territory is partly cultivated, it is still in the process of being cleared of the original forest. At his right hand a sheaf of wheat and a cornstalk on the left hand of the rock, a miner, indicated by a pick-axe on his shoulder, with barrels and lumps of mineral at his feet. On his left anvil, partly seen, on which rests a sledge hammer, typical of the mechanic arts, the whole indicating the principal pursuits and resources of the state. In front of the rock and the hunter, as if just laid down by the latter and ready to be resumed at a moment's notice, two hunters' rifles, crossed and surmounted at the place of contact by the Phrygian cap, or cap of liberty, indicating that our freedom and liberty were won and will be maintained by the force of arms.

The reverse of the Great Seal is to be encircled by a wreath composed of laurel and oak leaves, emblematical of valor and strength, with fruits and cereals, productions of the State. For device, a landscape. In the distance, on the left of the disc, a wooded mountain, and on the right a cultivated slope with the log farmhouse peculiar to this region. On the side of the mountain, a representation of the viaduct on the line of the Baltimore & Ohio Railroad in Preston County, one of the great engineering triumphs of the age, with a train of cars about to pass over it. Near the center a factory, in front of which a river with boats, on the bank and to the right of it nearer the foreground, a derrick and a shed, appertaining to the production of salt and petroleum. In the foreground a meadow with cattle and sheep feeding and reposing, the whole indicating the leading characteristics, productions and pursuits of the State at this time. Above the mountain, etc., the sun merging from the clouds, indicating that former obstacles to our prosperity are now disappearing. In the rays of the sun the motto "Libertas et Fidelitate" Freedom and Loyalty—indicating that our liberty and independence are the result of faithfullness to the Declaration and the National Constitution.

The committee further recommend that the above device and motto, for the obverse of the Great Seal be also adopted as the Coat-of-Arms of the State.[72]

WISCONSIN

When Wisconsin became a state in 1848, a new seal was designed to replace the revised territorial seal of 1839. The state seal was itself revised in 1851 and finally prescribed by law in 1881.[73] The law sets out the following description:

The great seal of the state consists of a metallic disc, 2⅜ inches in diameter, containing, within an ornamental border, the following devices and legend: The coat of arms of the state . . . above the arms, in a line parallel with the border, the words, "Great Seal of the

State of Wisconsin"; in the exergue, in a curved line, 13 stars.[74]

The coat of arms is prescribed as follows:

The coat of arms of the state of Wisconsin is declared to be as follows:

Arms. Or, quartered, the quarters bearing respectively a plow, a crossed shovel and pick, an arm and held hammer, and an anchor, all proper; the base of shield resting upon a horn of plenty and pyramid of pig lead, all proper; overall, on fesse point, the arms and motto of the United States, namely: Arms, palewise of 13 pieces argent and gules; a chief azure; motto (on garter surrounding inescutcheon), "E pluribus unum."

Crest. A badger, passant, proper.

Supporters. Dexter, a sailor holding a coil of rope, proper; sinister, a yeoman resting on a pick, proper.

Motto. Over crest, "Forward."[75]

WYOMING

Wyoming's seal was adopted in 1893 and revised in 1921. The current law is as follows:

There shall be a great seal of the state of Wyoming, which shall be of the following design, viz: A circle one and one-half (1-½) inches in diameter, on the outer edge or rim of which shall be engraved the words "Great Seal of the State of Wyoming." The design shall conform substantially to the following description: A pedestal, showing on the front thereof an eagle resting upon a shield, the shield to have engraved thereon a star and the figures, "44," being the number of Wyoming in the order of admission to statehood. Standing upon the pedestal shall be a draped figure of a woman, modeled after the statue of the "Victory of the Louvre," from whose wrists shall hang links of a broken chain, and holding in her right hand a staff from the top of which shall float a banner with the words "Equal Rights" thereon, all suggesting the political position of woman in this state. On either side of the pedestal and standing at the base thereof, shall be male figures typifying the livestock and mining industries of Wyoming. Behind the pedestal, and in the background, shall be two (2) pillars, each supporting a lighted lamp, signifying the light of knowledge. Around each pillar shall be a scroll with the following words thereon: On the right of the central figure the words "Livestock" and "Grain," and on the left the words "Mines" and "Oil." At the base of the pedestal, and in front, shall appear the figures "1869–1890," the former date signifying the organization of the territory of Wyoming and the latter date of its admission to statehood.[76]

DISTRICT OF COLUMBIA

The District's seal was the subject of the first act of the District's first legislative assembly in 1871. The design of the corporate seal became law on August 3, 1871.

The Corporate Seal of the District of Columbia is a circular design that includes two central figures. One figure depicts George Washington on a pedestal. His right hand rests upon a staff and his left hand rests upon a fasces—an axe within a bundle of rods, which classically symbolizes power. Protruding from behind the fasces are the handles of a plow. Standing on the ground to the right of Washington is the figure of a woman. Blindfolded, she symbol-

izes justice. Her right hand, extended, holds a wreath, and, in her left hand, is a tablet bearing the word "CONSTITU-TION" in three lines.

Positioned beneath the presented wreath is an eagle with a shield across its breast. In its left talon are arrows and its right talon holds an olive branch. The eagle's beak clutches a ribbon. To the eagle's immediate left are two hogshead casks of tobacco, a sheaf of wheat and two sacks of agricultural products.

In the background, on the left, the Potomac River is depicted flowing between the Virginia and District of Columbia shores. Crossing the river on a trestle is a smoking, bulbous stack locomotive, emblazed by a radiating sun and trailed by several rail cars. In the background on the right, stands the United States Capitol with rolling hills in the distance.

Centered at the very bottom of the seal is a wreath embracing the year 1871. Flowing on a ribbon from both sides of the wreath are the words "JUSTITIA" (on the left) and "OMNIBUS" (on the right), which together mean "JUSTICE FOR ALL." Arched across the top of the seal are the words "DISTRICT OF COLUMBIA."

The official seal had been used also as the insignia of the District on numerous publications until May 15, 1979, when a mayor's memorandum discussing printing standards declared that it should be replaced "by a logo representing the D.C. flag." This logo, called the "Stars and Bars," employs the three stars over two bars as depicted in the flag.[77]

AMERICAN SAMOA

The territorial seal of American Samoa depicts a fly switch, which represents wisdom, and a staff, which represents authority, crossed above a kava bowl. The kava bowl represents service to the chief and is used in the traditional, formal Kava Ceremony. These symbols lie on a tapa cloth background that represents the artistry of traditional Samoan dress. Around the circumference at the top of the seal are the words "Seal of American Samoa" and the date "17 April 1900," the date on which the United States took possession. The motto *Samoa—Muamua le Atua* appears at the bottom. It means "Samoa—Let God Be First."[78]

COMMONWEALTH OF THE NORTHERN MARIANA ISLANDS

The seal of the Commonwealth employs the latte stone, a symbol of strength and tradition, with the star representing the Commonwealth as the newest star in the Pacific, represented by the field of blue. It was adopted in 1986.

> The official seal of the Commonwealth shall consist of a circular field of blue having in its center a white star superimposed on a gray latte stone, surrounded by the traditional Carolinian mwaar consisting of the following flowers: langilang, flores mayo (seyur) angagha, and teibwo, on the outer border, and the words encircling the imwaar, "Commonwealth of the Northern Mariana Islands" and "Official Seal."[79]

GUAM

The seal of Guam is described in its code of laws:

> The Great Seal of the Territory of Guam shall consist of the Coat of Arms of Guam surrounded by the following words, letters and punctuation, encircling the outer border of the Coat of Arms in such a manner as to be read when the Coat of Arms is in a proper position: "Great Seal of the Territory of Guam, United States of America". The Great Seal shall be approximately two and five-sixteenths (2⁵⁄₁₆) inches long.[80]

The coat of arms is also described in the code of laws:

> The official Coat of Arms of Guam shall consist of an upright, two-pointed oval scene which portrays an ancient flying proa (canoe) approaching the beach near the mouth of the Agana River, with a lone coconut palm tree in the foreground. The colors of the Coat of Arms shall be as follows: yellow, which represents the sand; brown, the tree trunk and canoe; green, the palm fronds; white, the canoe sail; grey, the distant flat-topped mountains; light blue, the sky; dark blue, the water; red, the letters GUAM emblazoned across the Coat of Arms; red, the border around the outer edge and surrounding the oval.[81]

PUERTO RICO

Puerto Rico's official seal is based on the coat of arms adopted in 1952 and amended in 1976, which is illustrated with the seals that King Ferdinand of Spain gave to Puerto Rico by royal order of November 8, 1511. The order described the coat of arms as " 'a green shield bearing in the center a silver lamb resting upon a red book, and bearing a flag with cross and banner, the streamer of the lance showing the device of SANCT JOAN and having for border castles and lions and flags and crosses of Jerusalem, and for a device an F. and a Y. with its crowns and yokes and arrows, and a motto around it reading as follows: Joannes est nomen ejus.' "

Puerto Rico was originally called St. John. Thus the green background, the color used by early Christians for St. John the Baptist, and the red book representing the Apocalypse of John the Apostle. The lamb represents Jesus Christ. Castles and lions symbolize Spain, the Jerusalem flags and crosses St. John the Baptist, and the "F" and "Y," King Ferdinand and Queen Isabella (Ysabella). That the cluster of arrows is made of seven arrows calls up the mystery of the number seven in the Apocalypse. The motto translates as "John is his name."[82]

The official coat of arms is prescribed by law:

The coat of arms of the Commonwealth of Puerto Rico shall be "a green shield" bearing a silver lamb resting upon a red book and bearing a flag with cross and banner, as shown in the device of Saint John, and having for border castles, lions, flags and crosses of Jerusalem, and having for a device an F and Y with its crown and yoke and arrows, and a motto around it as follows: *Joannes est nomen ejus.*[83]

U.S. VIRGIN ISLANDS

The great seal of the government of the Virgin Islands of the United States as described below came into use on January 1, 1991. The statute is reprinted with permission from Butterworth Legal Publishers.

In the foreground, a yellow breast (Coereba Flaveola), the official bird of the Virgin Islands, perched on a branch of the yellow cedar (Tecoma Stans), the official flower of the Virgin Islands, on the left end of which are three flowers, three seed pods and, on the right, three leaves of the plant; in the background, surrounding the bird and

plant, are three islands representing the three major islands of the United States Virgin Islands, one with a sugarmill located on it, representing St. Croix, another with the Annenberg Ruins, representing St. John, and the third with the Capitol Building, behind which are the flags of the United States of America and the Danneborg, representing St. Thomas; a sailboat is also located in the harbor of the island representing St. Thomas; a scroll bearing the words, "United in Pride and Hope," is located on the lower edge of the design directly below the island representing St. Croix. Encircling the above-described design the words "Government of" are inscribed in the upper portion of the circle, and the words "The United States Virgin Islands" are inscribed in the lower portion of the circle.[84]

NOTES

1. Ala. Code § 1–2–4.
2. Ibid., § 1–2–1.
3. Alaska Stat. § 44.09.010.
4. *Alaska Blue Book, 1977*, p. i.
5. Ariz. Rev. State. Ann. art. 22, § 20.
6. Ark. Code Ann. (1987) § 1–4–108.
7. Cal. Govt. Code tit. 1, § 400 (West).
8. *State Emblems* (Sacramento (?): n.d.).
9. Colo. Rev. Stat. § 24–80–901.
10. Conn. Gen. Stat. Ann. § 3–106 (West).
11. Ibid., § 3–105 (West).
12. Del. Code Ann. tit. 29, § 301.
13. Fla. Stat. Ann. § 15.03 (West).
14. Ga. Code Ann. § 50–3–30.
15. Haw. Rev. Stat. § 5–5.
16. Idaho Code § 59–1005.
17. Idaho Code § 59–1005A.
18. *Illinois Blue Book, 1983–1984*, pp. 439–40.
19. 1867 Ill. Laws 36.
20. *Indiana Emblems* (Indianapolis: Indiana Historical Bureau, 1982), p. 5.

21. Ind. Code Ann. § 1–2–4 (West).

22. Iowa Code Ann. § 1A.1 (West).

23. Kan. Stat. Ann. § 75–201.

24. Ky. Rev. Stat. § 2.020.

25. La. Rev. Stat. Ann. § 49–151 (West).

26. *Louisiana Facts* (Baton Rouge: Department of State, n.d.).

27. Me. Rev. Stat. tit. 1, § 201.

28. *Maryland Manual, 1981–1982*, p. 9.

29. Md. Ann. Code § 13–302.

30. Mass. Laws Ann. ch. 2, § 2.

31. Ibid., ch. 2, § 1.

32. Mich. Comp. Laws Ann. § 2.41.

33. Ibid., § 2.22.

34. *Minnesota Legislative Manual, 1985*, p. 11.

35. Minn. Stat. Ann. § 1.135 (West).

36. Miss. Code Ann. § 7–1–9.

37. *Souvenir of Mississippi* (Jackson: Dick Molpus, n.d.), p. 16.

38. Mo. Stat. Ann. § 10.060 (Vernon).

39. Rex C. Myers, *Symbols of Montana* (Helena: Montana Historical Society, 1976), p. 10.

40. Mont. Code Ann. § 1–1–501.

41. 1867 Neb. Stats. 863.

42. Nev. Rev. Stat. § 235.010.

43. N.H. Rev. Stat. Ann. § 3:9.

44. Ibid., § 3:1.

45. N.J. Stat. Ann. § 52:2–1 (West).

46. "The Great Seal of the State of New Mexico" (information provided by the New Mexico State Library).

47. N.M. Stat. Ann. § 12–3–1.

48. N.Y. Stat. Law § 73 (McKinney).

49. N.C. Gen. Stat. § 147–26.

50. N.D. Cent. Code art. XI, § 2.

51. Ohio Rev. Code Ann. § 5.10 (Page).

52. Ibid., § 5.04, § 5.101 (Page).

53. Okla. Stat. Ann. art. 6, § 35 (West).

54. Or. Rev. Stat. § 186.020.

55. *Pennsylvania Symbols* (Harrisburg: House of Representatives, n.d.).

56. *Pennsylvania Manual, 1976–1977*, pp. 846–47.

57. *Commonwealth of Pennsylvania Official Documents, 1893*, vol. 4, pp. 215–16.

58. R. I. Gen. Laws § 42–4–2.

59. Ibid., § 42–4–1.

60. *South Carolina State Symbols and Emblems* (Columbia: House of Representatives, n.d.).

61. S.D. Codified Laws Ann. § 1–6–2.

62. *Tennessee Blue Book, 1985–1986*, pp. 337–38.

63. Tex. Govt. Code art. 4, § 19 (Vernon); Tex. Rev. Civil Stats. Ann. tit. 106, art. 6139f.

64. *Symbols of the Great State of Utah* (Salt Lake City (?): n.d.).

65. Utah Code Ann. § 67–1a–8.

66. Vt. Stat. Ann. tit. 1, § 493.

67. Ibid., tit. 1, § 491.

68. Va. Code § 7.1–26.

69. Ibid., § 7.1–27.

70. Wash. Rev. Code Ann. § 1.20.080.

71. W. Va. Code art. 2, § 7.

72. *The Great Seal of West Virginia* (Charleston: A. James Manchin, n.d.).

73. *State of Wisconsin 1983–1984 Blue Book*, p. 947.

74. Wis. Stat. Ann. § 14.45 (West).

75. Ibid., § 1.07 (West).

76. Wyo. Stat. Ann. § 8–3–101.

77. *Description of the Corporate Seal of the District of Columbia* (n.p., n.d.); *The Corporate Seal of the District of Columbia and the Stars and Bars* (n.p., n.d.); information provided by W. C. Bradley III, Visual Information Specialist, Government of the District of Columbia, Office of the Secretary.

78. *American Samoa* (n.p., n.d.); pamphlet provided by the office of Eni Faleomavaega, member of Congress for American Samoa.

79. *Amendments to the Constitution of the Northern Mariana Islands* (Saipan: Marianas Printing Service, Inc., 1986), amendment 43.

80. Guam Code Ann. tit. 1, § 410.

81. Ibid., § 406.

82. *The Coat of Arms of Puerto Rico* (n.p., n.d.); information supplied by Commonwealth of Puerto Rico, Department of State.

83. P.R. Laws Ann. tit. 1, § 34, § 37.

84. V.I. Code Ann. tit. 1, § 108.

4

State and Territory Flags

Flags, like seals, are symbols that legitimize the sovereignty of each state, linked by vote of the people into the union of the United States.

The flags of the states, often displaying the coats of arms, are also tableaux of each state's history. Hawaii's flag proudly symbolizes its founding by displaying Great Britain's Union Jack. New Mexico retains the yellow and red colors of Spain in its flag together with the Zia symbol, an ancient Indian symbol of friendship. The crossed peace pipe and olive branch of Oklahoma's flag and the Indian figure and steamboat of Florida's flag vividly recall the history of these states.

ALABAMA

The state flag of Alabama was officially designated in 1895. The law declares that the flag, reminiscent of the Confederate battle flag, "shall be a crimson cross of St. Andrew on a field of white. The bars forming the cross shall be not less than six inches broad, and must extend diagonally across the flag from side to side."[1]

The governor's flag is the state flag with the addition of the coat of arms or great seal in the upper portion above the cross, and in the lower portion, the military crest of the state.[2]

ALASKA

In 1927, a contest was held among Alaska's school children for the design of a territorial flag. Benny Benson, then thirteen years old, submitted the winning design. In 1959, the territorial flag was declared to be the state flag.[3]

The design of the official flag is eight gold stars in a field of blue, so selected for its simplicity, its originality and its symbolism. The blue, one of the national colors, typifies the evening sky, the blue of the sea and of mountain lakes, and of wild flowers that grow in Alaskan soil, the gold being significant of the wealth that lies hidden in Alaska's hills and streams.

The stars, seven of which form the constellation Ursa Major, the Great Bear, the most conspicuous constellation in the northern sky, contains the stars which form the "Dipper," including the "Pointers" which point toward the eighth star in the flag, Polaris, the North Star, the ever constant star for the mariner, the explorer, hunter, trapper, prospector, woodsman, and the surveyor. For Alaska the northernmost star in the galaxy of stars and which at some future time will take its place as the forty-ninth star in the national emblem.[4]

The code goes on to describe the color of the stars as that of natural yellow gold and the shade of blue as that used in the United

States flag. Standard proportions and size are also delineated.

ARIZONA

Arizona's flag was adopted in 1917. It symbolizes the importance of the state's copper industry.

> The lower half of the flag a blue field and the upper half divided into thirteen equal segments or rays which shall start at the center on the lower line and continue to the edges of the flag, colored alternately light yellow and red, consisting of six yellow and seven red rays. In the center of the flag, superimposed, there shall be a copper-colored five pointed star, so placed that the upper points shall be one foot from the top of the flag and the lower points one foot from the bottom of the flag. The red and blue shall be the same shade as the colors in the flag of the United States. The flag shall have a four-foot hoist and a six-foot fly, with a two-foot star and the same proportions shall be observed for flags of other sizes.[5]

ARKANSAS

In 1913, at the urging of the Pine Bluff Chapter of the Daughters of the American Revolution, the Arkansas legislature adopted a state flag designed by Willie K. Hocker, a member of that chapter. In 1923, an additional star was added to the flag.[6] The current law states that

> (a) The official state flag shall be a rectangle of red on which is placed a large white diamond, bordered by a wide band of blue on which are twenty-five (25) white stars. Across the diamond shall be the word "ARKANSAS" and four (4) blue stars, with one (1) star above and three (3) stars below the word "ARKANSAS." The star above the word "ARKANSAS" shall be below the upper corner of the diamond. The three (3) stars below the word "ARKANSAS" shall be placed so that one (1) star shall be above the lower corner of the diamond and two (2) stars shall be placed symmetrically, parallel above and to the right and left of the star in the lower corner of the diamond.
>
> (b) The three (3) stars so placed are designed to represent the three (3) nations, France, Spain, and the United States, which have successively exercised dominion over Arkansas. These stars also indicated that Arkansas was the third state carved out of the Louisiana Purchase. Of these three (3) stars, the twin stars parallel with each other signify that Arkansas and Michigan are twin states, having been admitted to the Union together on June 15, 1836. The twenty-five (25) white stars on the band of blue show that Arkansas was the twenty-fifth state admitted to the Union. The blue star above the word "ARKANSAS" is to commemorate the Confederate States of America. The diamond signifies that this state is the only diamond-bearing state in the Union.[7]

The code also sets out a salute to the flag: "I salute the Arkansas Flag with its diamond and stars. We pledge our loyalty to thee."[8]

CALIFORNIA

The California Bear Flag was designed by an unknown person sometime between 1875 and 1899. In 1846, however, a bear flag had been chosen as the emblem of the republic. It was adopted by legislative action in 1911.

A new color rendering was approved in 1953.

> The Bear Flag is the State Flag of California. As viewed with the hoist end of the flag to the left of the observer there appears in the upper left-hand corner of a white field a five-pointed red star with one point vertically upward and in the middle of the white field a brown grizzly bear walking toward the left with all four paws on a green grass plot, with head and eye turned slightly toward the observer; a red stripe forms the length of the flag at the bottom, and between the grass plot and the red stripe appear the words CALIFORNIA REPUBLIC.[9]

The code goes on to specify exact colors and dimensions. The white background symbolizes purity, the red star and bar, courage. The star itself represents sovereignty and the grizzly bear, strength.

COLORADO

The 1911 law, amended slightly in 1929 and 1964, adopting the state flag, describes it as follows:

> The flag shall consist of three alternate stripes to be of equal width and at right angles to the staff, the two outer stripes to be blue of the same color as in the blue field of the national flag and the middle stripe to be white, the proportion of the flag being a width of two-thirds of its length. At a distance from the staff end of the flag of one-fifth of the total length of the flag there shall be a circular red C, of the same color as the red in the national flag of the United States. The diameter of the letter shall be two-thirds of the width of the flag. The inner line of the opening of the letter C shall be three-fourths of the width of its body or bar and the outer line of the opening shall be double the length of the inner line thereof. Completely filling the open space inside the letter C shall be a golden disk; attached to the flag shall be a cord of gold and silver intertwined, with tassels one of gold and one of silver.[10]

CONNECTICUT

The design of the state flag of Connecticut first approved by the General Assembly in 1897 was modified slightly by a 1990 amendment.

> The following-described flag is the official flag of the state. The dimensions of the flag shall be five feet and six inches in length, four feet and four inches in width. The flag shall be azure blue, charged with an argent white shield of rococo design, having in the center three grape vines, supported and bearing fruit in natural colors. The bordure to the shield shall be in two colors, gold on the interior and silver on the exterior, adorned with natural-colored clusters, of white oak leaves (Quercus alba) bearing acorns. Below the shield shall be a white streamer, cleft at each end, bordered by a band of gold within fine brown lines, and upon the streamer in dark blue block letters shall be the motto "QUI TRANSTULIT SUSTINET"; the whole design being the arms of the state.[11]

DELAWARE

The state flag of Delaware was adopted in 1913.

> The design of the official state flag shall be as follows: A background of colo-

nial blue surrounding a diamond of buff in which diamond is placed the correct coat of arms of the State in the colors prescribed by law and in accordance with § 301 of this title, with the words, "December 7, 1787," to be inscribed underneath the diamond.[12]

The code goes on to describe the exact colors of each element of the flag. A governor's flag is also provided by law.[13]

FLORIDA

The Florida state flag makes prominent use of the 1868 seal, which was changed in 1970, when the sabal palmetto replaced the cocoa tree as the state tree.

> The state flag shall conform with standard commercial sizes, and be of the following proportions and description: The seal of the state, in diameter one-half the hoist, shall occupy the center of a white ground. Red bars, in width one-fifth the hoist, shall extend from each corner toward the center, to the outer rim of the seal.[14]

GEORGIA

The current Georgia state flag was adopted in January 2001. It replaces the flags of 1799, 1861, 1879, 1905, and 1956.

> The flag of the State of Georgia shall be a blue field, centered upon which shall be placed a representation of that side of the great seal of the state described at subsection (c) of Code Section 50-3-30, centered in a circle of 13 equally spaced white mullets or five-pointed stars, and beneath the same shall be an escroll or ribbon, gold, two-thirds the length of the field, bearing the words "Georgia's History" and

charged below said words with a representation of five flags horizontally presented as follows: the first, to the left, being that version of the flag of the United States of America consisting of a field of 13 red and white stripes and, centered in a canton of blue, a circle of 13 equally spaced white mullets or five-pointed stars, as adopted by the Continental Congress in 1777 and commonly known as the "Stars and Stripes" or the "1777 Flag"; to the right thereof a flag consisting of a field of blue, centered upon which shall be placed a representation of the coat of arms of the state as the same appeared on the great seal of the state adopted in 1799, and which flag is commonly known as the "Pre-1879 Georgia State Flag"; to the right thereof a flag consisting of a vertical band of blue occupying the leftmost one-third of the entire flag, on which shall be placed a representation of that side of the great seal of the state approved in 1914 which contained the coat of arms of the state, and the remainder of which flag shall consist of a scarlet field horizontally bisected by a white band such that said band shall be equal in width to the remainder of the scarlet field both above and below, which flag is commonly known as the "Pre-1956 Georgia State Flag"; to the right thereof the flag of the State of Georgia as approved at Ga. L. 1956, p. 38, Section 1; and to the right thereof that version of the flag of the United States of America consisting of a field of 13 red and white stripes and a canton of blue bearing 50 white mullets or five-pointed stars, such that such flag shall represent the flag of the United States of America as the same appeared on July 4, 1960. And under the horizontal representation of the five flags, the phrase "In God We Trust" shall be written in the blue section and in the same gold color as the State Seal. Every force of the organized militia shall carry this flag when on parade or review.[15]

The pledge of allegiance to the Georgia flag is set in the state code: "I pledge allegiance to the Georgia flag and to the principles for which it stands: Wisdom, Justice, and Moderation."[16]

HAWAII

The Hawaiian state flag is the same flag that was used for the Kingdom of Hawaii, the Republic of Hawaii, and the Territory of Hawaii. Its alternating white, red, and blue stripes represent the eight islands. The field resembles the Union Jack of Great Britain, from which the flag was originally designed.

The official description of the flag is as follows:

(1) The Hawaiian flag shall consist of eight horizontal stripes, alternately white, red, blue, etc., beginning at the top, having a jack cantoned in the dexter chief angle next to the point of suspension;

(2) The jack shall consist of a blue shield charged with a compound saltire (crossing) of alternate tincture white and blue, the white having precedence; a narrow edge of white borders each red side of the saltire;

(3) A red cross bordered with white is charged (placed) over all;

(4) The proportion shall be as follows:

    (A) The fly (length) is twice the hoist (width);

    (B) The jack is half the hoist (width) in breadth and 7–16 the fly in length;

    (C) The arms of the red cross with border shall be equal in width to one of the horizontal stripes; the white border shall be one-third the width of the red cross;

    (D) The arms of the compound saltire (crossing) are equal in width to the red cross, the tinctures white, red, and the border being in the proportion of 3, 2, 1, respectively.[17]

IDAHO

The state flag was adopted in 1907. For twenty years, the state flag in actual use did not meet the specifications of the 1907 law. In 1927, this situation was corrected.

A state flag for the state of Idaho is hereby adopted, the same to be as follows:

A silk flag, blue field, five (5) feet six (6) inches fly, and four (4) feet four (4) inches on pike, bordered with gilt fringe two and one half (2½) inches in width, with state seal of Idaho twenty-one (21) inches in diameter, in colors, in the center of a blue field. The words "State of Idaho" are embroidered in with block letters, two (2) inches in height on a red band three (3) inches in width by twenty-nine (29) inches in length, the band being in gold and placed about eight and one half (8½) inches from the lower border of fringe and parallel with the same.[18]

ILLINOIS

The first Illinois state flag, which incorporated the great seal on the banner, was adopted in 1915. In 1969, the legislature amended the 1915 act to include the name of the state on the flag and to standardize production of the flag. The amended act reads as follows:

> The reproduction of the emblem only on the "great seal of the State of Illinois" is authorized and permitted when reproduced in black or in the national colors upon a white sheet or background and bearing underneath the emblem in blue letters the word "Illinois" and being an actual reproduction of the great seal except for the outer ring thereof for use as a State banner or insignia under the conditions and subject to the restrictions provided by the laws of the United States and the State of Illinois as to the United States or State flag or ensign.[19]

INDIANA

The Indiana state flag, designed by Paul Hadley of Mooresville, Indiana, was adopted in 1917. In 1979, an amendment standardized the size of the flag, but the 1917 law otherwise remains in force.

> A state flag is hereby adopted, and the same shall be of the following design and dimensions, to-wit: Its dimensions shall be three (3) feet fly by two (2) feet hoist; or five (5) feet fly by three (3) feet hoist; or any size proportionate to either of those dimensions. The field of the flag shall be blue with nineteen (19) stars and a flaming torch in gold or buff. Thirteen (13) stars shall be arranged in an outer circle, representing the original thirteen (13) states; five (5) stars shall be arranged in a half circle below the torch and inside the outer circle of stars, representing the states admitted prior to Indiana; and the nineteenth star, appreciably larger than the others and representing Indiana shall be placed above the flame of the torch. The outer circle of stars shall be so arranged that one (1) star shall appear directly in the middle at the top of the circle, and the word "Indiana" shall be placed in a half circle over and above the star representing Indiana and midway between it and the star in the center above it. Rays shall be shown radiating from the torch to the three (3) stars on each side of the star in the upper center of the circle.[20]

IOWA

The Iowa state banner was designed by Mrs. Dixie Cornell Gebhardt and sponsored by the Iowa Society of the Daughters of the American Revolution. It was approved in 1921.[21]

> The banner designed by the Iowa society of the Daughters of the American Revolution and presented to the state, which banner consists of three vertical stripes of blue, white, and red, the blue stripe being nearest the staff and the white stripe being in the center, and upon the central white stripe being depicted a spreading eagle bearing in its beak blue streamers on which is inscribed, in white letters, the state motto, "Our liberties we prize and our rights we will maintain" and with the word "Iowa" in red letters below such streamers, as such design now appears on the banner in the office of the governor of the state of Iowa, is hereby adopted as a distinctive state banner, for use on all occasions where a distinctive state symbol in the way of a banner may be fittingly displayed.[22]

KANSAS

The Kansas state flag was approved in 1927. In 1961, the name of the state was added to it. The laws describe the flag in this manner:

The official state flag of the state of Kansas shall be a rectangle of dark-blue silk or bunting, three (3) feet on the staff by five (5) feet fly.

The great seal of the state of Kansas, without its surrounding band of lettering, shall be located equidistant from the staff and the fly side of the flag, with the lower edge of the seal located eleven (11) inches above the base side of the flag. The great seal shall be surmounted by a crest and the word KANSAS shall be located underneath the seal. The seal shall be seventeen (17) inches in diameter. The crest shall be on a wreath or an azure, a sunflower slipped proper, which divested of its heraldic language is a sunflower as torn from its stalk in its natural colors on a bar of twisted gold and blue. The crest shall be six (6) inches in diameter; the wreath shall be nine (9) inches in length. The top of the crest shall be located two (2) inches beneath the top side of the flag. The letters KANSAS shall be imprinted in gold block letters below the seal, the said letters to be properly proportioned, and five (5) inches in height, imprinted with a stroke one (1) inch wide; and the first letter K shall commence with the same distance from the staff side of the flag as the end of the last letter S is from the fly side of the flag. The bottom edge of the letters shall be two (2) inches above the base side of the flag. Larger or smaller flags will be of the same proportional dimensions.

The colors in the seal shall be as follows: Stars, silver; hills, purple; sun, deep yellow; glory, light yellow; sky, yellow and orange from hills half way to motto, upper half azure; grass, green; river, light blue; boat, white; house, dark brown; ground, brown; wagons, white; near horse, white; off horse, bay; buffalo, dark, almost black; motto, white; scroll, light brown.[23]

Kansas also has a state banner, which was approved in 1925. The law holds that the official state banner

shall be of solid blue and shall be of the same tint as the color of the field of the United States flag, whose width shall be three-fourths of its length, with a sunflower in the center having a diameter of two-thirds of the space.[24]

KENTUCKY

The 1918 act creating Kentucky's state flag was amended in 1962 to read as follows:

The official state flag of the Commonwealth of Kentucky shall be of navy blue silk, nylon, wool or cotton bunting, or some other suitable material, with the seal of the Commonwealth encircled by a wreath, the lower half of which shall be goldenrod in bloom and the upper half the words "Commonwealth of Kentucky," embroidered, printed, painted or stamped on the center thereof. The dimensions of the flag may vary, but the length shall be one and nine-tenths ($1\frac{9}{10}$) times the width and the diameter of the seal and encirclement shall be approximately two-thirds ($\frac{2}{3}$) the width of the flag.[25]

LOUISIANA

Louisiana's flag was adopted officially in 1912 by the legislature.

The official flag of Louisiana shall be that flag now in general use, consisting of a solid blue field with the coat-of-arms of the state, the pelican feeding its young, in white in the center, with a ribbon beneath, also in white, containing in blue the motto of the state, "Union, Justice and Confidence."[26]

In 1981, the legislature adopted a state pledge of allegiance.

I pledge allegiance to the flag of the state of Louisiana and to the motto for which it stands: A state, under God, united in purpose and ideals, confident that justice shall prevail for all of those abiding here.[27]

MAINE

The Maine legislature adopted the state flag in 1909. This flag uses the coat of arms in a field of blue.

The flag to be known as the official flag of the State shall be of blue, of the same color as the blue field in the flag of the United States, and of the following dimensions and designs; to wit, the length or height of the staff to be 9 feet, including brass spearhead and ferrule; the fly of said flag to be 5 feet 6 inches, and to be 4 feet 4 inches on the staff; in the center of the flag there shall be embroidered in silk on both sides of the flag the coat of arms of the State, in proportionate size; the edges to be trimmed with knotted fringe of yellow silk, 2½ inches wide; a cord, with tassels, to be attached to the staff at the spearhead, to be 8 feet 6 inches long and composed of white and blue silk strands.[28]

Maine law also prescribes a merchant and marine flag.

The flag to be known as the merchant and marine flag of the State shall be of

white, at the top of which in blue letters shall be the motto "Dirigo"; beneath the motto shall be the representation of a pine tree in green color, the trunk of which shall be entwined with the representation of an anchor in blue color; beneath the tree and anchor shall be the name "Maine" in blue color.[29]

MARYLAND

Maryland's flag was officially adopted in 1904, although the flag was first flown in 1888 at Gettysburg Battlefield. The flag described below employs the arms of the Calvert and Crossland families.[30]

(a) *In general*. The State flag is quartered.

(b) *First and fourth quarters*. The 1st and 4th quarters are paly of 6 pieces, or sable, a bend dexter counterchanged and the 2nd and 3rd, quarterly, are argent and gules, a cross bottony countersigned. Thus, the 1st and 4th quarters consist of 6 vertical bars alternately gold and black with a diagonal band on which the colors are reversed.

(c) *Second and third quarters*. The 2nd and 3rd quarters are a quartered field of red and white, charged with a Greek cross, its arms terminating in trefoils, with the coloring transported, red being on the white ground and white on the red, and all being as represented upon the escutcheon of the State seal.[31]

MASSACHUSETTS

The Massachusetts flag, like many other state flags, includes a representation of the coat of arms. Unlike most other states, the law also prescribes a naval and maritime flag.

> The flag of the commonwealth shall consist of a white rectangular field, bearing on either side a representation of the arms of the commonwealth, except that the star shall be white. The naval and maritime flag of the commonwealth shall consist of a white rectangular field bearing on either side a representation of a green pine tree.[32]

In 1971, the governor's flag was prescribed by law.

> The flag of the governor shall conform to the design of the flag of the commonwealth, except that the field of the flag of the governor shall be triangular in shape.[33]

MICHIGAN

The 1911 law adopting the state flag states simply that "the state flag shall be blue charged with the arms of the state."[34] A pledge of allegiance, written by Harold G. Coburn, was adopted in 1972.

> I pledge allegiance to the flag of Michigan, and to the state for which it stands, 2 beautiful peninsulas united by a bridge of steel, where equal opportunity and justice to all is our ideal.[35]

A governor's flag is also provided in the 1911 law: "The governor's flag shall be white charged with the arms of the state."[36]

MINNESOTA

In 1957, the legislature approved the design for a new flag. The 1893 flag had been a double flag. The new law, revised only for editorial purposes in 1984, simplifies the design of the first flag.[37]

> The design of the flag shall conform substantially to the following description: The staff is surmounted by a bronze eagle with outspread wings; the flag is rectangular in shape and is on a medium blue background with a narrow gold border and a golden fringe. A circular emblem is contained in the center of the blue field. The circular emblem is on a general white background with a yellow border. The word MINNESOTA is inscribed in red lettering on the lower part of the white field. The white emblem background surrounding a center design contains 19 five pointed stars arranged symmetrically in four groups of four stars each and one group of three stars. The latter group is in the upper part of the center circular white emblem. The group of stars at the top in the white emblem consists of three stars of which the uppermost star is the largest and represents the north star. A center design is contained on the white emblem and is made up of the scenes from the great seal of the state of Minnesota, surrounded by a border of intertwining Cypripedium reginae, the state flower, on a blue field of the same color as the general flag background. The flower border design contains the figures 1819, 1858, 1893.
>
> The coloring is the same on both sides of the flag, but the lettering and the figures appear reversed on one side.[38]

MISSISSIPPI

The Mississippi flag was created by a special committee appointed by the legislature in 1894. The original law described a flag with width two-thirds length; with a union square, in width two-thirds of the width of the flag; the ground of the union to be red and a broak blue saltier thereon, bordered with white and emblazoned with thirteen (13) mullets or five-pointed stars, corresponding with the number of original states of the Union; the field to be divided into three bars of equal width, the upper one blue, the center one white, and the lower one, extending the whole length of the flag, red—the national colors.[39]

The official pledge of the State of Mississippi reads as follows:

I salute the flag of Mississippi and the sovereign state for which it stands with pride in her history and achievements and with confidence in her future under the guidance of Almighty God.[40]

MISSOURI

The Missouri flag, designed by Marie Elizabeth Watkins Oliver and Mary Kochtitzky, was approved by the legislature in 1913.[41]

The official flag of the state of Missouri is rectangular in shape and its vertical width is to the horizontal length as seven is to twelve. It has one red, one white and one blue horizontal stripe of equal width; the red is at the top and the blue at the bottom. In the center of the flag there is a band of blue in the form of a circle enclosing the coat of arms in the colors as established by law on a white ground. The width of the blue band is one-fourteenth of the vertical width of the flag and the diameter of the circle is one-third of the horizontal length of the flag. In the

blue band there are set at equal distances from each other twenty-four five pointed stars.[42]

MONTANA

The Montana flag had been the banner of the First Montana Infantry before it was adopted as the state flag in 1905. In 1981, the name of the state was added to the flag.

The state flag of Montana shall be a flag having a blue field with a representation of the great seal of the state in the center and with golden fringe along the upper and lower borders of the flag; the same being the flag borne by the 1st Montana Infantry, U.S.V., in the Spanish-American War, with the exception of the device, "1st Montana Infantry, U.S.V."; and above the great seal of the state shall be the word "MONTANA" in Roman letters of gold color equal in height to one-tenth of the total vertical measurement of the blue field.[43]

NEBRASKA

A state banner was adopted in 1925 according to a bill introduced by J. Lloyd McMaster. In 1963, the banner was designated the official state flag.[44]

The banner of the State of Nebraska shall consist of a reproduction of the Great Seal of the State, charged on the center in gold and silver on a field of national blue. The banner shall be the official state flag of the State of Nebraska and may be displayed on such occasions, at such times, and under such conditions as the flag of the United States of America.[45]

NEVADA

The Nevada state flag has been modified several times since 1866, when a flag was first adopted. The current law prescribes the following:

The official flag of the State of Nevada is hereby created. The body of the flag must be of solid cobalt blue. On the field in the upper left quarter thereof must be two sprays of sagebrush with the stems crossed at the bottom to form a half wreath. Within the sprays must be a five-pointed silver star with one point up. The word "Nevada" must also be inscribed below the star and above the sprays, in a semicircular pattern with the letters spaced apart in equal increments, in the same style of letters as the words "Battle Born." Above the wreath, and touching the tips thereof, must be a scroll bearing the words "Battle Born." The scroll and the word "Nevada" must be golden-yellow. The lettering on the scroll must be black-colored sans serif gothic capital letters.[46]

NEW HAMPSHIRE

New Hampshire's state flag was not adopted until 1909. The original flag was modified in 1931, when changes were made in the state seal. The statute is reprinted with permission of Butterworth Legal Publishers.

The state flag shall be of the following color and design: The body or field shall be blue and shall bear upon its center in suitable proportion and colors a representation of the state seal. The seal shall be surrounded by a wreath of laurel leaves with nine stars interspersed. When used for military

purposes the flag shall conform to the regulations of the United States.[47]

NEW JERSEY

The design of the state flag was adopted in 1896. The law states simply that

The state flag shall be of buff color, having in the center thereof the arms of the state emblazoned thereon.[48]

In 1965, the official state colors for use in the flag were designated:

The official colors of the State of New Jersey for use on the State Flag and for other purposes shall be buff and Jersey blue.

For the purposes of this act the specifications, references, and designations for the official colors of the state are as follows:

Jersey Blue (Cable No. 70087, Royal Blue. The Color Association of the United States, Inc.)
    Buff (Cable No. 65015, U.S. Army Buff. The Color Association of the United States, Inc.)[49]

NEW MEXICO

The current New Mexico state flag, adopted in 1925, replaced a flag adopted in 1915. The Daughters of the American Revolution had supported the movement for a distinctive new flag, and the design of Dr. Harry Mera was finally chosen.[50] The law reads as follows:

That a flag be and the same is hereby adopted to be used on all occasions when the state is officially and publicly represented, with the privilege of use by all citizens upon such occasions as they may deem fitting and appropriate. Said flag shall be the ancient Zia sun symbol of red in the center of a field of yellow. The colors shall be the red and yellow of old Spain. The proportion of the flag shall be a width of two-thirds its length. The sun symbol shall be one-third of the length of the flag. Said symbol shall have four groups of rays set at right angles; each group shall consist of four rays, the two inner rays of the group shall be one-fifth longer than the outer rays of the group. The diameter of the circle in the center of the symbol shall be one-third of the width of the symbol. Said flag shall conform in color and design described herein.[51]

In 1953, the legislature adopted both an English and a Spanish salute to the state flag. The official salute to the state flag is:

I salute the flag of the state of New Mexico, the Zia symbol of perfect friendship among united cultures.[52]

The official Spanish language salute to the state flag is:

Saludo la bandera del estado de Nuevo Méjico, el símbolo zía de amistad perfecta, entre culturas unidas.[53]

NEW YORK

In 1882, the legislature adopted the arms of the state that had first been designated in 1778. The flag was adopted in 1901 and modified in 1909. The current law reads as follows:

The device of arms of this state, as adopted March sixteenth, seventeen hundred and seventy-eight, is hereby declared to be correctly described as follows:

Charge. Azure, in a landscape, the sun in fess, rising in splendor or, behind a range of three mountains, the middle one the highest; in base a ship and sloop under sail, passing and about to meet on a river, bordered below by a grassy shore fringed with shrubs, all proper.

Crest. On a wreath azure and or, an American eagle proper, rising to the dexter from a two-thirds of a globe terrestrial, showing the north Atlantic ocean with outlines of its shores.

Supporters. On a quasi compartment formed by the extension of the scroll.

Dexter. The figure of Liberty proper, her hair disheveled and decorated with pearls, vested azure, sandaled gules, about the waist a cincture or, fringed gules, a mantle of the last depending from the shoulders behind to the feet, in the dexter hand a staff ensigned with a Phrygian cap or, the sinister arm embowed, the hand supporting the shield at the dexter chief point, a royal crown by her sinister foot dejected.

Sinister. The figure of Justice proper, her hair disheveled and decorated with pearls, vested or, about the waist a cincture azure, fringed gules, sandaled and manteled as Liberty, bound about the eyes with a fillet proper, in the dexter hand a straight sword hilted or, erect, resting on the sinister chief point of the shield, the sinister arm embowed, holding before her scales proper.

Motto. On a scroll below the shield argent, in sable, Excelsior.

State Flag. The state flag is hereby declared to be blue, charged with the arms of the state in the colors as described in the blazon of this section.[54]

NORTH CAROLINA

The flag of North Carolina was adopted in 1885.

The flag of North Carolina shall consist of a blue union, containing in the center thereof a white star with the letter "N" in gilt on the left and the letter "C" in gilt on the right of said star, the circle containing the same to be one third the width of said union. The fly of the flag shall consist of two equally proportioned bars, the upper bar to be red, the lower bar to be white; the length of the bars horizontally shall be equal to the perpendicular length of the union, and the total length of the flag shall be one third more than its width. Above the star in the center of the union there shall be a gilt scroll in semicircular form, containing in black letters this inscription: "May 20th, 1775," and below the star there shall be a similar scroll containing in black letters the inscription: "April 12th, 1776."[55]

NORTH DAKOTA

The North Dakota state flag was first adopted in 1911. An amendment was made to the original act in 1959. The current law reads as follows:

The flag of North Dakota shall consist of a field of blue silk or material which will withstand the elements four feet four inches [132.08 centimeters] on the pike and five feet six inches [167.64 centimeters] on the fly, with a border of knotted yellow fringe two and one-half inches [6.35 centimeters] wide. On each side of said flag in the center thereof, shall be embroidered or stamped an eagle with outspread wings

and with opened beak. The eagle shall be three feet four inches [101.6 centimeters] from tip to tip of wing, and one foot ten inches [55.88 centimeters] from top of head to bottom of olive branch hereinafter described. The left foot of the eagle shall grasp a sheaf of arrows, the right foot shall grasp an olive branch showing three red berries. On the breast of the eagle shall be displayed a shield, the lower part showing seven red and six white stripes placed alternately. Through the open beak of the eagle shall pass a scroll bearing the words "E Pluribus Unum." Beneath the eagle there shall be a scroll on which shall be borne the words "North Dakota." Over the scroll carried through the eagle's beak shall be shown thirteen five-pointed stars, the whole device being surmounted by a sunburst. The flag shall conform in all respects as to color, form, size, and device with the regimental flag carried by the First North Dakota Infantry in the Spanish American War and Philippine Insurrection, except in the words shown on the scroll below the eagle.[56]

OHIO

The flag of Ohio was first adopted in 1902. An amendment in 1953 was made so that the current law reads as follows:

The flag of the state shall be pennant shaped. It shall have three red and two white horizontal stripes. The union of the flag shall be seventeen five-pointed stars, white in a blue triangular field, the base of which shall be the staff end or vertical edge of the flag, and the apex of which shall be the center of the middle red stripe. The stars shall be grouped around a red disc superimposed upon a white circular "O." The proportional dimensions of the flag and of its various parts shall be according to the official design on file in the office of the secretary of state. One state flag of uniform dimensions shall be furnished to each company of the organized militia.[57]

In 1963, descriptions of other official flags were passed by the legislature.

The flag of the governor of this state will be of scarlet wool bunting, six feet eight inches hoist by ten feet six inches fly. In each of the four corners will be a white five-pointed star with one point upward. The centers of these stars will be twelve inches from the long edges and seventeen inches from the short edges of the flag. In the center of the flag will be a reproduction of the great seal of Ohio in proper colors, three feet in diameter, surrounded by thirteen white stars equally spaced with their centers on an imaginary circle four feet three inches in diameter. All stars shall be of such size that their points would lie on the circumference of an imaginary circle ten inches in diameter.

The official colors of the governor of Ohio will be of scarlet silk, four feet four inches on the pike by five feet six inches fly, of the same design as the flag of the governor of Ohio, with the seal and stars proportionately reduced in size and embroidered. The colors will be trimmed on three edges with a knotted fringe of yellow silk two and one half inches wide. Attached below the head of the pike will be a silk cord of scarlet and white eight feet six inches in length with a tassel at each end.

The naval flag of the governor of Ohio will be of scarlet wool bunting, three feet hoist by four feet fly. The design will be the same as the flag of the governor of Ohio with the seal and the stars proportionately reduced in size.

The automobile flag of the governor of Ohio will be of scarlet silk, or wool bunting, one foot six inches on the staff by two feet six inches on the fly. The design will be the same as the flag of the governor of Ohio with the seal and stars proportionately reduced in size. The flag will be trimmed on three edges with a knotted fringe of silk or wool one and one half inches wide.[58]

OKLAHOMA

The Oklahoma flag was adopted in 1925 and amended in 1941 to add the name of the state to the flag. The law reads as follows:

The banner, or flag, of the design prescribed by Senate Concurrent Resolution No. 25, Third Legislature of the State of Oklahoma shall be, and it hereby is superseded and replaced by one of the following design, to-wit:
A sky blue field with a circular rawhide shield of an American Indian Warrior, decorated with six (6) painted crosses on the face thereof, the lower half of the shield to be fringed with seven (7) pendant eagle feathers and superimposed upon the face of the shield a calumet or peace pipe, crossed at right angles by an olive branch, as illustrated by the design accompanying this resolution, and underneath said shield or design in white letters shall be placed the word "Oklahoma," and the same is hereby adopted as the official flag and banner of the State of Oklahoma.[59]

The same section describing the flag also sets out the official salute to the flag: "I salute the flag of the state of Oklahoma: Its symbols of peace unite all people." The salute was adopted in 1982.[60]

In 1957, the legislature approved a governor's flag:

> The flag of the Governor of the State of Oklahoma shall be forest green, bearing on each side the following: the Great Seal of the State of Oklahoma, centered, surrounded by five equidistant white stars with one of the stars placed directly above the Great Seal; and the flag to be edged with golden fringe.[61]

OREGON

The Oregon state flag was adopted in 1925, and the official colors were designated in 1959. The statute is reprinted with permission of Butterworth Legal Publishers.

> (1) A state flag is adopted to be used on all occasions when the state is officially and publicly represented, with the privilege of use by all citizens upon such occasions as may be fitting and appropriate. It shall bear on one side on a navy blue field the state escutcheon in gold, supported by 33 gold stars and bearing above the escutcheon the words "State of Oregon" in gold and below the escutcheon the figures "1859" in gold, and on the other side on a navy blue field a representation of the beaver in gold.
>
> (2) The official colors of the State of Oregon are navy blue and gold.[62]

PENNSYLVANIA

Pennsylvania's state flag was approved in 1907.

The flag to be known as the official flag of the commonwealth of Pennsylvania shall be of blue, same color as the blue field in the flag of the United States, and of the following dimensions and design; to wit, The length, or height of the staff to be nine feet, including brass spearhead and ferrule; the fly of the said flag to be six feet two inches, and to be four feet six inches on the staff; in the center of the flag there shall be embroidered in silk the same on both sides of the flag the coat of arms of the commonwealth of Pennsylvania, in proportionate size; the edges to be trimmed with knotted fringe of yellow silk, two and one-half inches wide; a cord, with tassels, to be attached to the staff, at the spearhead, to be eight feet six inches long, and composed of white and blue silk strands.[63]

RHODE ISLAND

The original act designating the state flag was passed in 1897. Although amended, the flag remains essentially unchanged.

> The flag of the state shall be white, five (5) feet and six (6) inches fly and four (4) feet and ten (10) inches deep on the pike, bearing on each side in the centre a gold anchor, twenty-two (22) inches high, and underneath it a blue ribbon twenty-four (24) inches long and five (5) inches wide, or in these proportions, with the motto "Hope" in golden letters thereon, the whole surrounded by thirteen (13) golden stars in a circle. The flag to be edged with yellow fringe. The pike shall be surmounted by a spearhead and the length of the pike shall be nine (9) feet, not including the spearhead, provided, however, that on the 29th day of August, 1978 the flag of the Rhode Island

first regiment shall be flown as the official state flag for that day.[64]

The law also allows for a flag and pennant of the governor.

The flag and pennant of the governor shall be white bearing on each side the following: A gold anchor on a shield with a blue field and gold border; above the shield a gold scroll bearing the words in blue letters "State of Rhode Island"; below the shield a gold scroll bearing in blue letters the word "Hope"; the shield and scrolls to be surrounded by four (4) blue stars; both the flag and pennant to be edged with yellow fringe.[65]

SOUTH CAROLINA

The first state flag was designed by Colonel William Moultrie at the request of the Revolutionary Council of Safety in 1775. It was in truth a flag for the troops. Moultrie chose the blue of the soldiers' uniforms as the color of the field. A crescent in the upper right of the flag reproduced the silver emblem worn by the soldiers on the front of their caps. A palmetto tree was added in the center of the flag after Moultrie's defense of a palmetto-log fort on Sullivan's Island in 1776. In 1861, with South Carolina's secession, this same flag was chosen as the state's national flag. It became the state flag again when South Carolina rejoined the union.[66]

A 1966 act designated the pledge of allegiance to the state flag.

The pledge to the flag of South Carolina shall be as follows: "I salute the flag of South Carolina and pledge to the Palmetto State love, loyalty and faith."[67]

SOUTH DAKOTA

South Dakota has two official state flags. The first flag, adopted in 1909, depicted the sun on the obverse and the seal on the reverse. Because of the expense of manufacturing a flag with two emblems, however, a new flag with a single emblem was designed and approved in 1963.[68] The description of the new flag is as follows:

The state flag or banner shall consist of a field of sky-blue one and two-thirds as long as it is wide. Centered on such field shall be the great seal of South Dakota made in conformity with the terms of the Constitution, which shall be four-ninths the width of the said flag in diameter; such seal shall be on a white background with the seal outlined in dark blue thereon, or, in the alternative shall be on a sky-blue background with the seal outlined in dark blue thereon; surrounding the seal in gold shall be a serrated sun whose extreme width shall be five-ninths the width of the said flag. The words "South Dakota" symmetrically arranged to conform to the circle of the sun and seal shall appear in gold letters one-eighteenth the width of the said field above said sun and seal and the words "The Sunshine State" in like-sized gold letters and in like arrangement shall appear below the said sun and seal. Flags designed of such material as may be provident for outdoor use need have no fringe but flags for indoor and display usage shall have a golden fringe one-eighteenth the width of said flag on the three sides other than the hoist.

All state flags made in conformity with state law prior to March 11, 1963 shall remain official state flags but the creation of a state flag from and after said date, other than in conformity with § 1-6-4, is prohibited.

In 1987, an official pledge to the state flag was adopted: "I pledge loyalty and support to the flag and state of South Dakota, land of sunshine, land of infinite variety."[69]

TENNESSEE

The Tennessee state flag was designed by LeRoy Reeves and adopted in 1905.[70]

The flag or banner of the state of Tennessee shall be of the following design, colors, and proportions, to wit, an oblong flag or banner in length one and two thirds (1⅔) times its width, the principal field of same to be of color red, but said flag or banner ending at its free or outer end in a perpendicular bar of blue, of uniform width, running from side to side, that is to say, from top to bottom of said flag or banner, and separated from the red field by a narrow margin or stripe of white of uniform width; the width of the white stripe to be one fifth (⅕) that of the blue bar; and the total width of the bar and stripe together to be equal to one eighth (⅛) of the width of the flag. In the center of the red field shall be a smaller circular field of blue, separated from the surrounding red field by a circular margin or stripe of white of uniform width and of the same width as the straight margin or stripe first mentioned. The breadth or diameter of the circular blue field, exclusive of the white margin, shall be equal to one half (½) of the width of the flag. Inside the circular blue field shall be three (3) five-pointed stars of white distributed at equal intervals around a point, the center of the blue field, and of such size and arrangement that one (1) point of each star shall approach as closely as practicable without actually touching one (1) point of each of the other two (2) around the center point of the field; and the two (2) outer points of each star shall approach as nearly as practicable without actually touching the periphery of the blue field. The arrangement of the three (3) stars shall be such that the centers of no two (2) stars shall be in a line parallel to either the side or end of the flag, but intermediate between same; and the highest star shall be the one nearest the upper confined corner of the flag.[71]

TEXAS

The flag of the Republic of Texas became the official state flag when it was adopted in the 1876 state constitution.

(a) The state flag is the 1839 national flag of the Republic of Texas.

(b) The state flag consists of a rectangle with a width to length ratio of two to three containing:

　(1) a blue vertical stripe one-third the entire length of the flag wide, and two equal horizontal stripes, the upper stripe white, the lower red, each two-thirds the entire length of the flag long; and

　(2) a white, regular five-pointed star in the center of the blue stripe, oriented so that one point faces upward, and of such a size that the diameter of a circle passing through the five points of the star is equal to three-fourths of the width of the blue stripe.

(c) The red, white, and blue of the state flag stand, respectively, for bravery, purity, and loyalty.

(d) The red and blue colors of the state flag are the same colors used in the United States flag and are defined as numbers 80108 (red) and 80075 (dark blue) of *The Standard Color Reference of America*, 10th edition.

(e) When displayed permanently mounted on a staff, as for indoor or parade use, the state flag may be decorated with gold fringe and its staff with gold cords and tassels.

The salute to the Texas flag is:

Honor the Texas Flag; I pledge allegiance to thee, Texas, one and indivisible.[72]

UTAH

The Utah state flag was adopted in 1896 and revised in 1933. It was designated the governor's flag in 1911.[73]

The state flag of Utah shall be a flag of blue field, fringed, with gold borders, with the following device worked in natural colors on the center of the blue field:
   The center a shield; above the shield and thereon an American eagle with outstretched wings; the top of the shield pierced with six arrows arranged crosswise; upon the shield under the arrows the word "Industry," and below the word "Industry" on the center of the shield, a beehive; on each side of the beehive, growing sego lilies; below the beehive and near the bottom of the shield, the word "Utah," and below the word "Utah" and on the bottom of the shield, the figures "1847"; with the appearance of being back of the shield there shall be two American flags on flagstaffs placed crosswise with the flags so draped that they will project beyond each side of the shield, the heads of the flagstaffs appearing in front of the eagle's wings and the bottom of each staff appearing over the face of the draped flag below the shield; below the shield and flags and

upon the blue field, the figures "1896"; around the entire design, a narrow circle in gold.[74]

VERMONT

The current state flag of Vermont was adopted in 1923. It replaced the state flags adopted in 1803 and 1837. The 1923 law states simply that "the flag of the state shall be blue with the coat of arms of the state thereon."[75]

VIRGINIA

The flag of the Commonwealth of Virginia was adopted by legislative act in 1930.

The flag of the Commonwealth shall hereafter be made of bunting or merino. It shall be a deep blue field, with a circular white centre of the same material. Upon this circle shall be painted or embroidered, to show on both sides alike, the coat of arms of the State . . . for the obverse of the great seal of the Commonwealth; and there shall be a white silk fringe on the outer edge, furthest from the flagstaff. This shall be known and respected as the flag of Virginia.[76]

WASHINGTON

The state flag of Washington was adopted in 1923 and amended slightly in 1925. The law declares

That the official flag of the state of Washington shall be of dark green silk or bunting and shall bear in its center a reproduction of the seal of the state of Washington embroidered, printed, painted or stamped thereon. The edges of the flag may, or may not, be fringed. If a fringe is used the same shall be of gold or yellow color of the same shade as the seal. The dimensions of the flag may vary.[77]

WEST VIRGINIA

The current state flag of West Virginia was adopted in 1929, after numerous other flags had come into use and become infeasible. The flag is described as follows:

The proportions of the flag of the state of West Virginia shall be the same as those of the United States ensign; the field shall be pure white, upon the center of which shall be emblazoned in proper colors, the coat-of-arms of the state of West Virginia, upon which appears the date of the admission of the state into the Union, also with the motto "Montani Semper Liberi" (Mountaineers Always Freemen) above the coat-of-arms of the state of West Virginia there shall be a ribbon lettered, state of West Virginia, and arranged appropriately around the lower part of the coat-of-arms of the state of West Virginia a wreath of rhododendron maximum in proper colors. The field of pure white shall be bordered by a strip of blue on four sides. The flag of the state of West Virginia when used for parade purposes shall be trimmed with gold colored fringe on three sides and when used on ceremonial occasions with the United States ensign, shall be trimmed and mounted in similar fashion to the United States flag as regards fringe cord, tassels and mounting.[78]

WISCONSIN

In 1979, the legislature revised the state flag, which had been adopted in 1913. The 1979 law became effective in 1981 and sets out these requirements:

(1) The Wisconsin state flag consists of the following features:
   (a) Relative dimensions of 2 to 3, hoist to fly.
   (b) A background of royal blue cloth.
   (c) The state coat of arms, as described under s. 1.07, in material of appropriate colors, applied on each side in the center of the field, of such size that, if placed in a circle whose diameter is equal to 50% of the hoist, those portions farthest from the center of the field would meet, but not cross, the boundary of the circle.
   (d) The word "WISCONSIN" in white, capital, condensed Gothic letters, one-eighth of the hoist in height, centered above the coat of arms, midway between the uppermost part of the coat of arms and the top edge of the flag.
   (e) The year "1848" in white, condensed Gothic numbers, one-eighth of the hoist in height, centered below the coat of arms, midway between the lowermost part of the coat of arms and the bottom edge of the flag.
   (f) Optional trim on the edges consisting of yellow knotted fringe.
(2) The department of administration shall ensure that all official state flags that are manufactured on or after May 1, 1981 conform to the requirements of this section. State flags manufactured before May 1, 1981 may continue to be used as state flags.[79]

WYOMING

The state flag of Wyoming, designed by Mrs. A. C. Keyes of Casper, was adopted in 1917. The colors of the flag carry important symbolism: the red border symbolizes the Indian and the blood of the pioneers; the white signifies purity; the blue symbolizes fidelity and justice.[80] The current law reads as follows:

A state flag is adopted to be used on all occasions when the state is officially and publicly represented. All citizens have the privilege of use of the flag upon any occasion they deem appropriate. The width of the flag shall be seven-tenths ($7/10$) of its length; the outside border shall be in red, the width of which shall be one-twentieth ($1/20$) of the length of the flag; next to the border shall be a stripe of white on the four (4) sides of the field, which shall be in width one-fortieth ($1/40$) of the length of the flag. The remainder of the flag shall be a blue field, in the center of which shall be a white silhouetted buffalo, the length of which shall be one-half ($1/2$) of the length of the blue field; the other measurements of the buffalo shall be in proportion to its length. On the ribs of the buffalo shall be the great seal of the state of Wyoming in blue. The seal shall be in diameter one-fifth ($1/5$) the length of the flag. Attached to the flag shall be a cord of gold with gold tassels. The same colors shall be used in the flag, red, white and blue, as are used in the flag of the United States of America.

Wyoming also has an official state territorial flag:

(a) The state territorial flag shall be a flag with a field of blue, the name "WYOMING" printed across the top of the flag and the phrase, "CEANT ARMA TOGAE" printed across the bottom of the flag. In the center of the flag shall be a shield with a border of gold divided into three (3) parts:

(i) The top half of the shield shall have the numbers "1869" across the top and depict mountains and a train;

(ii) The lower left part of the shield shall depict a staff, shovel, plow and pick; and

(iii) The lower right part of the shield shall depict an arm and hand holding a sword.[81]

DISTRICT OF COLUMBIA

The flag of the District of Columbia was created by an October 15, 1938, act of the District Commission. Its design was adapted from George Washington's family crest. The insignia, which is illustrated, employs the same design with shorter stripes.

This flag shall consist of a rectangular white background with two horizontal bars in red, and with three red stars in the upper white space of the flag. The proportions of this design are prescribed in terms of the hoist, or vertical height of the flag as follows: The upper white portion is $3/10$ of the hoist; the two horizontal red bars are each $2/10$ of the hoist; the white space between bars is $1/10$ of the hoist; and the base, or lowest white space, is $2/10$ of the hoist. The three red five-pointed stars have a diameter of $2/10$ of the hoist and are spaced equidistant in the fly or horizontal dimension of the flag. So long as the proportions herein prescribed are observed, the dimensions of the flag both in hoist and fly may vary in accordance with the size of the flag desired.[82]

AMERICAN SAMOA

The flag of American Samoa was adopted in 1960 when internal self-government was introduced. It employs the red, white, and blue of the American flag as well as the United States symbol of the bald eagle and the Samoan symbols of a fly whisk and a ceremonial dancing knife. A white triangle going from the fly to the hoist is defined by a red stripe. Toward the hoist within the white triangle an eagle holds and safeguards the symbols of Samoan culture. The remainder of the flag is blue.[83]

COMMONWEALTH OF THE NORTHERN MARIANA ISLANDS

The design of the flag of the Islands appears in an amendment to the constitution that made them a commonwealth in 1986.

> The official flag of the Commonwealth shall consist, on both sides of a rectangular field of blue, a white star in the center, superimposed on a gray latte stone, surrounded by the traditional Carolinian mwaar. The dimensions of the flag, the mwaar, the star and latte stone shall be provided by law. The field of blue represents the Pacific Ocean; the star represents the Commonwealth as the newest star in the western Pacific; the latte stone represents Chamorro culture; and the mwaar is a headband with flowers used for official ceremonies.[84]

GUAM

> The official territorial flag of Guam consists, on both sides, of a rectangular field of marine blue seventy-eight inches long and forty inches wide, trimmed on all sides with a border of deep red two inches in width and having in its center the Guam Coat of Arms, such Coat of Arms to be twenty-four (24) inches high and sixteen (16) inches wide. The territorial flag may be

reproduced for unofficial purposes in smaller or larger sizes, but in such cases, the dimensions shall be in proportion to those stated herein.

> The official territorial flag of Guam for holiday uses shall be the same design as stated herein, but shall be fifty percent (50%) larger with identical proportions as the flag described above. The holiday flag shall be displayed on official buildings and flag staffs belonging to the government of Guam on all territorial and national Holidays.[85]

PUERTO RICO

The design of the current Puerto Rican flag became effective on July 25, 1952, although the flag that had been used before commonwealth status remained the flag of the commonwealth.

> The flag of the Commonwealth of Puerto Rico shall be the one traditionally known heretofore as the Puerto Rican Flag, and which is rectangular in form, with five alternate horizontal stripes, three red and two white, and having next to the staff a blue equilateral triangle with a five-point white star. On the vertical side this triangle stretches along the entire width of the flag.[86]

> The official salute to the flag of Puerto Rico is as follows: "I swear before the Flag of the Commonwealth of Puerto Rico to honor the fatherland it symbolizes, the people it represents, and the ideals it embodies of liberty, justice and dignity."[87]

U.S. VIRGIN ISLANDS

The design of the U.S. Virgin Islands flag was approved in 1950 and the statute describing it is reprinted with permission of Butterworth Legal Publishers.

Upon a field argent (white) between the block letters V and I azure (blue) an American Eagle (yellow) displayed and bearing upon his breast the shield of the United States of America and having in his dexter talon a sprig of laurel vert (green) and in his sinister talon a bundle of three arrows azure (blue). The blue of the letters V.I. and the three arrows shall be azure blue. The blue of the chief of the shield is the blue of the arms and flag of the United States of America.[88]

NOTES

1. Ala. Code § 1–2–5.
2. Ibid., § 31–2–54.
3. *Alaska Blue Book, 1979*, p. 123.
4. Alaska Stat. § 44.09.020.
5. Ariz. Rev. Stat. Ann. § 41–851.
6. *Arkansas Almanac, 1972* (Little Rock: Arkansas Almanac, Inc., 1972), p. 31.
7. Ark. Code Ann. (1987) § 1–4–101.
8. Ibid., § 1–4–102.
9. Cal. Govt. Code § 420 (West).
10. Colo. Rev. Stat. § 24–80–904.
11. Conn. Gen. Stat. Ann. § 3–107 (West).
12. Del. Code Ann. tit. 29, § 306.
13. Ibid., tit. 29 § 307.
14. Fla. Stat. Ann. § 15.012 (West).
15. Georgia General Assembly, House Bill 16 (Committee Substitute), 2001–02 (www2.state.ga.us/Legis/2001_02/fulltext/hb16.htm).
16. Georgia Code Ann. § 50–3–2.
17. *Hawaii, The Aloha State* (Honolulu: State of Hawaii, Hawaii Visitors Bureau, Chamber of Commerce of Hawaii, n.d.; Haw. Rev. Stat. § 5–19.
18. Idaho Code § 46–801.
19. Ill. Comp. Stat. Ann. ch. 1, § 3001 (Smith-Hurd).
20. Ind. Code Ann. § 1–2–2–1 (West).
21. *1985–86 Iowa Official Register*, vol. 61, p. 236.
22. Iowa Code Ann. § 31.1 (West).
23. Kan. Stat. Ann. § 73–702.
24. Ibid., § 73–704.
25. Ky. Rev. Stat. Ann. § 2.030.
26. La. Rev. Stat. Ann. § 9–153 (West).
27. Ibid., § 49–167 (West).
28. Me. Rev. Stat. tit. 1, § 206.
29. Ibid., tit. 1, § 207.
30. *Maryland Manual, 1981–82*, p. 10.
31. Md. Ann. Code § 13–202.
32. Mass. Laws Ann. ch. 2, § 3 (West).
33. Ibid., ch. 2, § 4 (West).
34. Mich. Comp. Laws Ann. § 2–23.
35. Ibid., § 2.29.
36. Ibid., § 2.24.
37. *Official Minnesota Symbols* (St. Paul: Minnesota Historical Society, Education Division, December 1983).
38. Minn. Stat. Ann. § 1.141 (West).
39. 1894 Miss. Laws 154.
40. Miss. Code Ann. § 37–13–7.
41. *State of Missouri Official Manual, 1975–1976*, p. 1438.
42. Mo. Ann. Stat. § 10.020 (Vernon).
43. Mont. Code Ann. § 1–1–502.
44. *Nebraska Blue Book, 1982–83*, p. 12.
45. Neb. Rev. Stat. § 90–102.
46. Nev. Rev. Stat. § 235.020.
47. N.H. Rev. Stat. Ann. § 3:2.
48. N.J. Stat. Ann. § 52:3–1 (West).
49. Ibid., § 52:2A-1 (West).
50. Information provided by the New Mexico State Library.
51. N.M. Stat. Ann. § 12–3–2.
52. Ibid., § 12–3–3.
53. Ibid., § 12–3–7.
54. N.Y. State Law § 70 (McKinney).
55. N.C. Gen. Stat. § 144–1.
56. N.D. Cent. Code § 54–02–02.
57. Ohio Rev. Code Ann. § 5.01 (Page).
58. Ibid., § 5.011 (Baldwin).
59. Okla. Stat. Ann. tit. 25, § 91 (West).
60. Ibid., tit. 25, § 92 (West).
61. Ibid., tit. 25, § 93.1 (West).
62. Or. Rev. Stat. Ann. § 186.010.
63. Pa. Stat. Ann. tit. 44, § 45 (Purdon).

64. R.I. Gen. Laws § 42–4–3.

65. Ibid., § 42–7–4.

66. *South Carolina State Symbols and Emblems* (Columbia: House of Representatives, n.d.).

67. S.C. Code § 1–1–670.

68. *History of the South Dakota State Flag* (Pierre: Bureau of Administration, Division of Central Services, The State Flag Account, n.d.).

69. S.D. Codified Laws Ann. § 1–6–4, § 1–6–5, § 1–6–4–1.

70. *Tennessee Blue Book, 1985–1986,* pp. 338–39.

71. Tenn. Code Ann. § 4–1–301.

72. Tex. Rev. Civ. Stat. Ann. tit. 106, art. 6139a.

73. *Symbols of the Great State of Utah* (n.p., n.d.).

74. Utah Code Ann. § 63–13–5.

75. Vt. Stat. Ann. tit. 1, § 495.

76. Va. Code § 7.1–32.

77. Wash. Rev. Code Ann. § 1.20.010.

78. 1929 W. Va. Acts 495.

79. Wis. Stat. Ann. § 1.08 (West).

80. *Wyoming: Some Historical Facts* (Cheyenne: Wyoming State Archives, Museums and Historical Department, n.d.), p. i.

81. Wyo. Stat. Ann. § 8–3–102, § 8–3–114.

82. Text provided by W. C. Bradley III, Visual Information Specialist, Government of the District of Columbia, Office of the Secretary.

83. Information provided by the office of Eni Faleomavaega, member of Congress for American Samoa.

84. *Amendments to the Constitution of the Northern Mariana Islands* (Saipan: Marianas Printing Service, Inc., 1986), amendment 43.

85. Guam Code Ann. tit. 1, § 407.

86. P.R. Laws Ann. tit. 1, § 31.

87. *Regulations to Establish the Official Salute to the Flag of the Commonwealth of Puerto Rico* (San Juan: Commonwealth of Puerto Rico, Department of State, n.d.).

88. V.I. Code Ann. tit. 1, § 101.

5

State and Territory Capitols

The history of American state and territory capitols is replete with political intrigue, architectural blunderings, frequent destruction by fire, and occasional destruction by war. This history is also, however, a record of the deep and abiding patriotism of the citizens of each state and territory and their respect for and pride in the functions of their governments.

Many of today's capitols were constructed at the end of the nineteenth or beginning of the twentieth century. The architecture of these buildings is clearly informed by the style of the United States Capitol—neoclassical, domed capitols that call to mind ancient democracies. Some states, however, chose contemporary architecture to express their belief in progress. Notable among all the capitols in this regard are the "skyscraper" style capitols of Nebraska and Louisiana, built in the second and third decades of this century. The capitols of Hawaii and New Mexico, completed in the 1960s, are contemporary designs that express the individual history and heritage of those states. But whatever their design, state and territory capitols stand as monuments to the people, to their hard work, and to their belief in the progress of democracy.

session. Since becoming a state in 1817, the legislature had met in Huntsville, Cahaba, and Tuscaloosa before choosing Montgomery as a permanent capital. Because the legislative act designating Montgomery stipulated that the state should bear no expense in purchasing land or building a capitol, the city floated a $75,000 bond issue, which paid for the site known as Goat Hill and the erection of a Greek revival capitol designed by Stephen D. Dutton. Completed in 1847, it was destroyed in December 1849. The legislature appropriated $60,000 in 1850 and employed Barachias Holt to design a new building to be erected on the foundation of the destroyed capitol. The new capitol, also in the Greek revival style embellished with Corinthian columns and a towering, white dome, was completed in 1851. In 1885, an east wing was erected at a cost of $25,000. A south wing was added in 1905–1906 for $150,000 and a north wing, in 1911 for $100,000. The wings, constructed of brick with a stucco finish, maintain the box-like, Greek style and are adorned with Ionic columns. Frank Lockwood was the architect for all of the additions. The Legislature has met in the State House, formerly the State Highway Department Building, since renovations on the capitol began in 1985.[1]

ALABAMA

Montgomery was chosen as the capital city of Alabama during the 1845–1846 legislative

ALASKA

The six-story Alaska State Capitol in Juneau, begun in 1929, was completed in 1931 as the Federal and Territorial Building. When Alaska became a state in 1958, the state was given possession of the building. In fact, the people of Juneau had donated half of the property to the federal government, as Congress had not appropriated enough money to pay for the building site. Construction and site costs approximated $1 million.

The capitol was designed by James A. Wetmore, who was the federal government's supervising architect. It is made of reinforced concrete with a brick facing. Indiana limestone was used for the lower facade and Tokeen marble, native to Alaska, was used for the four Doric columns of the portico as well as the interior trim.[2]

ARIZONA

The Arizona Capitol, designed by James Riely Gordon, is located in Phoenix. The Victorian four-story structure is made primarily from Arizona materials, as mandated by the legislature. The exterior is made of granite, tuff stone, and malapai. Oak woodwork adorns the interior. The building was completed in 1900 at a cost of $135,744. Today the capitol houses the Arizona State Capitol Museum. Government offices have been moved to nearby or adjacent buildings, which became the capital city in 1889, succeeding Prescott (1863–67), Tucson (1867–77), and again Prescott.[3]

ARKANSAS

The Arkansas State Capitol in Little Rock was begun in 1899 when the existing building became inadequate with the growth of the government. It was completed after numerous delays in 1916. Final construction costs totalled about $2.5 million, considerably more than the $1 million originally appropriated. The Grecian design of the building, including the dome, which is copied from St. Paul's via the Mississippi Capitol, is essentially that of George R. Mann. Cass Gilbert became the architect toward the end of the project, but he made few changes in the exterior design. The exterior is constructed of Batesville marble and some Indiana Bedford limestone. The interior is finished in Alabama marble.[4]

CALIFORNIA

In 1854, after meeting in San Jose, Vallejo, Sacramento, Vallejo again, and Benicia, the California legislature moved the state capital to Sacramento. Construction of the permanent capitol building, designed by M. F. Butler, began in September 1860, and the cornerstone was laid in May 1861. Although some offices were occupied as early as 1869, the building was not fully completed until 1874. Remodeling work was undertaken from 1906 to 1908 and again in 1928. The capitol was completely restored between 1976 and 1981 at a cost of $68 million.

The "Old Capitol," as it is known today, is a four-story building topped by a copper-clad dome. A cupola extending from the dome is supported by twelve columns. Its roof is covered with gold plate and supports a copper ball, 30 inches in diameter, which is plated with gold coins. The building itself, Roman Corinthian in design, is 219 feet 11 ½ inches in height, 320 feet in length, and 164 feet wide. The dome rises on a two-story drum. A colonnade of twenty-four Corinthian columns supports the roof, from which a clerestory rises. The first story was constructed from granite out of nearby quarries, and stuccoed brick construction was used for the top three stories.

In 1949 construction of an annex was begun. Completed in January 1952, at a cost of $7.6 million (about three times the cost of the Old Capitol), the annex is 103 feet high, 210 feet long, and 269 feet wide. This six-story building, designed by the State Division of Architecture, is joined to the Old

Capitol and, although it is contemporary in style, blends with the lines of the older building.[5]

COLORADO

When Colorado entered the Union in 1876, Denver had been its capital city for nine years. Although a ten-acre site had been donated and accepted for erection of a capitol in 1874, excavation did not begin until 1886. The government continued to operate out of rented quarters until 1894, when offices in the permanent capitol were first used. The building was not completed, however, until twenty-two years after work first began at a cost of almost $3 million.

Colorado's capitol was designed by architect E. E. Myers to resemble the U.S. Capitol. The building measures 383 feet in length and 315 feet in width; its floor plan is in the form of a Greek cross. Gunnison granite was used for the five-foot-thick exterior walls, sandstone from Fort Collins for the foundations, marble from Marble, Colorado, for the floors and stairs, and rose onyx unique to Beulah, Colorado, for wainscoting. The dome rises 272 feet above the ground. Copper was first used to cover the dome, but, because of the public outcry that copper was not native to Colorado, sheets of gold leaf donated by Colorado miners were applied to the dome. A second coating of gold was applied to the dome in 1950.[6]

CONNECTICUT

The Capitol of Connecticut is located in Hartford, overlooking Bushnell Memorial Park on a site contributed by the city. Funds were appropriated for the building in 1871 and it was completed in 1879 at a cost of $2,532,524. Built by James G. Batterson and designed by Richard M. Upjohn, this Victorian Gothic capitol is constructed of New England marble and granite and is topped by a gold-leaf dome. In 1972, the capitol was declared a national historical landmark.[7]

DELAWARE

In 1787, the Levy Court of Kent County, in which the capital city of Dover is located, decided that the 1722 courthouse had grown too small for county and state offices. Using bricks from the old building as the foundation for the new, the building was finally opened in April 1792 with the proceeds of a state lottery to overcome financial difficulties. The cost was £2107:7:5. In 1795, the General Assembly appropriated £404:4:4 to complete the brick, colonial-style state house, including a copper roof.

In 1836, when it was necessary to expand the facility, $3,000 was spent on a two-story plus basement addition that measured 40 by 50 feet. Finally, in April 1873, the legislature purchased the statehouse for its exclusive use at a cost of $15,000. After some remodeling, the capitol was ready for use in 1875. Another addition, built during 1895–1897, added 40 feet to the 1836 addition, and a south wing was added in 1910 at a cost of $62,500. In 1925–1926, a three-story annex was erected to the east side of the original building.[8]

FLORIDA

Tallahassee was chosen to be Florida's capital city in 1824. Two years later, a 40 by 26 foot, two-story masonry building was constructed as the capitol. Although this was to be the wing of a larger building, by 1839, no further addition had been made. Instead, the original structure was razed and a new brick capitol was finally completed in 1845. In 1902, a copper dome was added along with four bay wings. Further enlargements were made in 1923, 1936, and 1947.

By 1972 it was clear that the old capitol

did not provide enough space to carry on government operations. A capitol complex was authorized by the legislature that included new legislative chambers and offices as well as a 307-foot, twenty-two-story executive office building. The new concrete and steel capitol, completed in 1977 and dedicated in 1978, cost $43,070,741. It was designed jointly by Edward Durell Stone of New York and Reynolds, Smith and Hills of Jacksonville.[9]

GEORGIA

The people of Georgia voted in 1877 to make the city of Atlanta the state's capital. When Georgia became a state in 1788, Augusta was the capital, and the capital city was subsequently moved to Louisville, Milledgeville, Macon, back to Milledgeville, and, finally, to Atlanta in 1868. In 1883, the legislature appropriated $1 million for the construction of a capitol, to be supervised by a board of five commissioners.

The firm of Edbrooke and Burnham in Chicago was awarded the contract for its Classic Renaissance design. Georgia marble was used for the interior finish and Indiana limestone for the exterior. Construction began in 1884 and was completed within the amount appropriated in 1889. Its largest dimensions are 347 feet, 9 inches in length and 272 feet, 4 inches in width. A rotunda extends from the second floor to a height of 237 feet, 4 inches. The gilded dome is 75 feet in diameter. The cupola is adorned by a 15-foot statue that represents freedom. The main entrance to the capitol is a four-story portico supported by six Corinthian columns.

Renovation work, which included applying native Georgia gold to the dome, was authorized in 1957. In 1981, it was necessary to apply more gold to the dome. The capitol was dedicated as a national historic landmark in 1977.[10]

HAWAII

The Hawaiian State Capitol in Honolulu is certainly one of the most unique of any of the state capitols. The concrete and steel building rises from an 80,000-square-foot reflecting pool to symbolize the creation of the islands out of the water. The legislative chambers are shaped like the volcanoes that gave birth to the islands. The forty columns that surround the capitol are shaped like royal palms.

The architectural firms of Belt, Lemmon and Lo of Honolulu and John Carl Warnecke and Associates of San Francisco planned and designed the 558,000-square-foot structure. Ground was broken late in 1965 and the capitol was dedicated in 1969. Construction costs came to $21,745,900. Total costs, including construction, equipment, furnishings, design, and fine arts totalled $24,576,900.[11]

IDAHO

The Capitol Building in Boise was designed by the local firm of Tourtellette and Hummell in the same style as the U.S. Capitol. Construction began in 1905. By 1911, the central part of the building was completed, and, by 1920, the east and west wings were ready for use by the legislature. Construction costs totalled nearly $2.3 million.

Idaho sandstone, quarried by convicts, was used for exterior facing. Marble from Vermont, Alaska, Georgia, and Italy was used in the interior. The dome, which rises 208 feet, is topped by a solid copper eagle dipped in bronze, itself standing 5 feet, 7 inches tall. Eight massive columns ring the rotunda and support the dome. The columns are scagliola—a mixture of granite, marble dust, glue, and gypsum that is dyed to look like marble. Artisans from Italy were brought to Boise to do the scagliola veneer.[12]

ILLINOIS

Illinois became a state in 1818. Its capital at that time was Kaskaskia. In 1820, the capital was moved to Vandalia and then, in 1839, with the help of Abraham Lincoln, to its permanent location, Springfield. The building used today is the sixth capitol and the second built in Springfield. Its construction was authorized in 1867, the cornerstone was laid in 1868, and it was completed in 1888 at a cost of $4.5 million. Situated on nine acres of land, the building was designed by John C. Cochrane of Chicago in the form of a Latin cross combining classical Greek and Roman styles. Its height from ground to dome is 361 feet. From north to south the capitol measures, at its extreme, 379 feet and from east to west, 268 feet. The walls supporting the dome are made from granular magnesian limestone. The interior walls are constructed of Niagara limestone. The corridors and walls of the rotunda employ decorative mosaics of marble. Bedford blue limestone and Missouri red granite were used to face the interior stone walls.[13]

INDIANA

In 1824 the Indiana capital was moved to Indianapolis from Corydon, which had been the capital even before Indiana became a state in 1816. The first statehouse, a Greek revival building occupied in 1835, had been outgrown by 1877. Construction of the new Modern Renaissance capitol, designed by local architect Edwin May, began in 1878 and was completed in 1888 at a cost of approximately $2 million. The four-story capitol, constructed of Indiana limestone, contains over twelve acres of floor space. It is distinguished by the dome, 72 feet in diameter, which reaches a height of 234 feet. The inner dome, rising 108 feet above the main floor, is a 48-foot-wide work of stained glass, which was installed in 1887.[14]

IOWA

When the first General Assembly met in Iowa City after Iowa became a state in 1846, it began the search for a new capital. In 1857, the governor finally declared Des Moines to be the capital city. The government occupied temporary quarters in Des Moines until the new capitol was completed in 1884.

A capitol commission was formed in 1870 to construct a capitol for $1.5 million. The commission named John C. Cochrane and A. H. Piquenard architects, and the cornerstone for the traditional, modified Renaissance building was laid in 1871. The cornerstone had to be laid again in 1873 owing to the deterioration of the stone used. The capitol was finally completed eleven years later at a cost of $2,873,294. A fire in 1904, which occurred during repair and modernization work, resulted in additional expenditures for renovation that brought the total cost of the capitol to $3,296,256.

The steel and stone dome, covered with gold leaf that was replaced in 1964–1965, is surmounted by a lookout lantern and terminates in a filial that reaches 275 feet. The capitol was constructed of Iowa stone for the foundation, Iowa granite, Missouri limestone, and Anamosa from Iowa, Ohio, Minnesota, and Illinois. Interior wood came entirely from Iowa hardwood forests, and twenty-nine different foreign and domestic marbles were used for interior facing. Extensive interior and exterior renovations of the building, including regilding the dome with 150 ounces of gold leaf, are scheduled to be completed in 2000 at a cost of $59.5 million.[15]

KANSAS

In 1861, the citizens of the new state of Kansas voted to make Topeka their capital city.

The next year, the state accepted a donation of twenty acres on which to build a capitol building. In 1866 the cornerstone of the east wing was laid, but it had to be replaced in 1867. By 1870 the building was opened for use by the legislature. In 1879 work started on a west wing with a $60,000 appropriation and a tax increase. The Kansas House of Representatives met in the still unfinished west wing in 1881. Finally, the legislature authorized erection of the central portion, which was completed in 1903. Total costs came to approximately $3.2 million. McDonald Brothers of Louisville were the designing architects.

The classical capitol is 399 feet north to south, 386 feet east to west, and 304 feet to the top of the dome, on which is situated a statue of the goddess Ceres. The central part of the building is five stories high. Each wing is four stories. The interior is decorated with a number of rich marbles, and the rotunda contains eight murals designed by David H. Overmyer. The second floor contains a series of murals by John Stewart Curry.[16]

KENTUCKY

In 1904 the legislature of Kentucky passed a bill providing for the construction of a capitol in Frankfort, thus ending a long debate as to where the permanent capital should be located. Collection of $1 million of debt left from the Civil and Spanish-American wars owed Kentucky by the United States War Department provided the funding. F. M. Andrews and Company had been retained as architects and work commenced in 1905, with the cornerstone having been laid in 1906. The building was dedicated in 1910.

Kentucky's capitol combines French Renaissance and neoclassical designs in a building that measures 402 feet, 10 inches east to west, 180 feet north to south, and 212 feet from the top of the lantern to the terrace floor, on a thirty-four-acre site. The base of the exterior is Vermont granite, and the facework on the three-story building is Bedford limestone. The exterior walls are adorned with seventy Ionic columns of limestone. The rotunda, 57 feet in diameter, the dome, and the lantern were copied from the Hôtel des Invalides of Napoléon's tomb in Paris. The State Reception Room is a copy of Marie Antoinette's drawing room in the Grand Trianon Palace. Total construction and furnishing costs totaled $1,820,000.[17]

LOUISIANA

When Huey Long became governor of Louisiana in 1928, one of his top priorities was to centralize the state's government under one roof. The 100-year-old neo-Gothic capitol in downtown Baton Rouge had grown inadequate. In 1930, the legislature granted Long's wish and appropriated $5 million for a new capitol building. Work commenced in December 1930 and was completed only fourteen months later.

The New Orleans architectural firm of Weiss, Dreyfous, and Seiferth designed a statehouse that replaced the traditional dome and rotunda with a thirty-four-story, 450-foot tower, and a public hall in accordance with the governor's wishes. The capitol became, at the time, the tallest building in the South, and it remains a fine example of the Art Moderne school of American architecture. The 10 percent savings in building costs were used to embellish the capitol with art deco ornamentation.

The capitol is surrounded by twenty-seven acres of formal gardens, which were once occupied by Louisiana State University. In 1935, Huey Long was assassinated in the very building he had envisioned to be a monument to the people of Louisiana. His grave is located at the center of the formal gardens.[18]

MAINE

Augusta was selected as Maine's capital in 1827, seven years after Maine became a state. Charles Bulfinch was chosen to design the building for a thirty-four-acre plot that had been chosen. The cornerstone of the Greek and Renaissance influenced capitol was laid in 1829 and was completed in time for the legislative session beginning in January 1832. The completed capitol, made of Hallowell granite, cost $139,000, including furnishings and grounds.

The interior was remodeled in 1852 and again in 1860. A three-story wing was added at the rear in 1890–1891. Major remodeling work was accomplished in 1909 and 1910. The length of the structure was doubled to 300 feet, but the original front was maintained. However, a dome that reaches to 185 feet, surmounted by a statue of Wisdom made of copper covered with gold, replaced the original cupola.[19]

MARYLAND

The Maryland State House in Annapolis, begun in 1772 and first occupied in 1779, is the oldest state capitol still used for legislative purposes. The roof was refashioned in 1785 and the dome, designed by Joseph Clark, in 1789. The interior height of the cypress-beamed dome is 113 feet, the largest wooden dome in the country. Annexes were added in 1858 and 1886, but they were replaced between 1902 and 1904. This brick colonial building, trimmed in stone, was built originally for £7,500. Most of the rooms of the original building have been restored to their eighteenth-century luster, a task that has occupied most of the years of this century.[20]

MASSACHUSETTS

The site of the statehouse of Massachusetts in Boston was formerly John Hancock's cow pasture. The building was designed by Charles Bulfinch and completed in 1798 after three years of construction. Bulfinch designed the brick capitol after months of studying Greek and Roman temples. The large wooden dome, now covered with 23 karat gold, was originally covered with copper from Paul Revere. Except for two marble wings on each side added in this century and a yellow brick north annex, the original building still looks much as it did in 1798.[21]

MICHIGAN

In 1847, ten years after becoming a state, Michigan moved its capital from Detroit to Ingham township. A new capital city, temporarily named Michigan, was fashioned out of the woods. After only a few months, the city's name was changed to Lansing.

Having quickly outgrown a temporary statehouse, a permanent brick building was erected in 1854 and added to in 1863 and 1865. These buildings were also outgrown within a few years. In 1871, the legislature set a limit of $1.2 million for the construction of a new capitol. Elijah E. Myers, a self-taught architect from Springfield, Illinois, was named the winner of the architectural contest to build the capitol in 1872. The cornerstone was laid in 1873, and the academic-classical structure was completed in 1879.

The capitol building covers more than an acre of land. It is 420 feet long, 274 feet wide, and 267 feet high. It is made of Ohio sandstone, Illinois limestone, Massachusetts granite, and Vermont marble. It has a cruciform floor plan, a high dome in the center, and a two-story portico at the head of the outside stairway above the central entrance. The exterior facade of the top floors is decorated with Corinthian, Tuscan, and Ionic columns.[22]

MINNESOTA

Ground was broken for the Minnesota Capitol in St. Paul in 1896. The legislature had recognized by 1893 that its Romanesque capitol building had become too small to conduct the state's business. Cass Gilbert won the architectural competition with a familiar domed design in the classical Renaissance style. The capitol was ready for occupancy in 1905 at a cost of $4.5 million, including grounds and furnishings.

The basement of the Michigan Capitol is constructed of St. Cloud granite and the rest of the building of Georgia marble. It measures 434 feet from east to west and 229 feet from north to south. The white dome reaches a height of 223 feet.[23]

MISSISSIPPI

In 1822, Mississippi moved its capital to Jackson from Natchez. Eleven years later, a new capitol, Greek revival in style, was planned. What is now referred to as the "Old Capitol" was completed in 1839 and remained in use as the capitol building until the current capitol was completed in 1903.

The "New Capitol," designed by Theodore C. Link of St. Louis, was constructed at a cost of $1,093,641 from 1901–1903. The exterior of this beaux arts classic masterpiece is Bedford limestone and the base course, Georgia granite. Blue Vermont marble, Italian white marble, Belgian black marble, jet black New York marble, and columns of scagliola adorn the interior. The dome rises to a height of 180 feet. An 8-foot eagle of copper coated in gold leaf stands atop the dome.[24]

MISSOURI

Having moved its capital from St. Louis and temporarily to St. Charles, the legislature of Missouri chose Jefferson City to be the cap-
ital and appropriated $18,373 in 1825 to construct a permanent capitol there. In 1837, this building was destroyed by fire. A new capital was constructed in 1848 and enlarged in 1888. In 1911 this structure was also destroyed by fire. A $3.5 million bond issue was floated to construct a new capitol. The design contest was won by Tracy and Swartwout and construction began in 1913. Ready for occupancy in 1918, it cost $4,215,000, including furnishings and grounds. The Renaissance-classical capitol, constructed of Burlington limestone, is five stories high, 437 feet east to west, 300 feet wide at the center, and 200 feet wide in the wings. It houses 500,000 square feet of floor space. The dome stretches to a height of 238 feet. Above the dome is a bronze statue of Ceres. Extensive renovation and restoration activities have been completed recently.[25]

MONTANA

Six years after becoming a state in 1889, the Montana legislature authorized $1 million to be spent on a permanent capitol in Helena. Owing to depression and scandal, the original plan was abandoned, and, in 1897, the legislature authorized a less grandiose capitol that would cost, when completed in 1902, only $485,000.

Charles Emlen Bell and John Hackett Kent of Council Bluffs, Iowa, were selected as architects. The cornerstone of the Greek Ionic neoclassical capitol was laid in 1899. Sandstone quarried in Columbus, Montana, was used for the exterior. The rotunda decoration suggests that of a nineteenth-century opera house. The copper-clad dome above the rotunda was refaced in 1933–1934. East and west wings were added to the original building in 1909–1912. The wings, which maintain the style of the first building, were designed by Frank M. Andrews in association with John G. Link and Charles S. Haire. The facing of the wings is Jefferson County granite, chosen over sandstone for its durability. Some alterations were made in the central and end blocks of the original building during reconstruction in 1963–1965.[26]

NEBRASKA

The Nebraska Capitol, constructed in Lincoln between 1922 and 1932, is unlike any other state capitol building. Rather than imitating the architecture of the U.S. Capitol or harkening back to classical style, this statehouse is thoroughly modern in inspiration, and it received the Building Stone Institute's Award for architectural excellence in 1982. The Indiana limestone building was designed by Bertram Goodhue who, in turn, chose August Vincent Tack to execute the murals, Hildreth Meiere to design the mosaic and tile decoration, and Lee Lawrie to do the sculpture. The base of the capitol is 437 feet square and two stories high. A 400-foot tower, adorned with a bronze statue of "The Sower," rises from the base. The capitol, including grounds and furnishings, was completed at a cost exceeding $10 million.[27]

NEVADA

Early in 1869, the Nevada legislature designated a ten-acre site in Carson City, where it had been using temporary facilities, on which to construct a new capitol for no more than $100,000. The design submitted by Joseph Gosling, which called for a "two-story building in the form of a Grecian Cross, compounded of the Corinthian, Ionic and Doric," was chosen. The plans called for the building to be 148 feet long and 98 feet wide and the cupola to be 30 feet in diameter and 120 feet high.

The cornerstone was laid in 1870, and the capitol was completed on time in 1871. Sandstone from the state prison quarry was used for the facade, and Alaskan marble was used for inlay to the interior arches, floors,

and wainscoting. The completed building cost $169,830. An annex was added in 1905, and north and south wings were added in 1913.[28]

NEW HAMPSHIRE

The New Hampshire statehouse in Concord is the oldest state capitol in the country in which the legislature uses its original chambers. The cornerstone for the original building, designed with simple classical lines by Stuart Park, was laid in 1816. The capitol was ready for use in 1819. The two-story New Hampshire granite structure which measures 126 feet wide and 57 feet deep, was completed for $82,000.

In 1864 a project to double the size of the original building was begun using the design of Gridley J. F. Bryant. At this time, a portico was added with Doric and Corinthian columns. A new dome replaced the original, but the gilded eagle that had first been perched on the capitol dome in 1818 was placed on the new dome. In 1909, under the auspices of Peabody and Stearns, the capitol building was again enlarged. The legislature, however, retained its same quarters. The Senate chamber was refurbished in 1974 and the Representatives Hall in 1976.[29]

NEW JERSEY

The New Jersey statehouse in Trenton is the second oldest in continuous use of all the statehouses in the United States. Traces of the original two-story colonial structure, built in 1792 by Jonathan Doanne, can still be seen. In the mid-1800s, John Notman was employed to do a major restructuring of the capitol, at which time the building attained a Greek revival flavor with the addition of columned porticoes and a rotunda.

When fire destroyed much of the capitol in 1885, repairs and renovation were begun at once under the supervision of architect

Lewis Broom. When completed in 1889, the capitol had taken on the French academic classic style popular at the time. Additions were made to the refurbished building in 1891, 1898, 1900, 1903, 1906, 1911–1912, and 1917. Major renovations were planned for 1986–1988 to improve the functional aspects of the building and to return it aesthetically to its original design.[30]

NEW MEXICO

Santa Fe, New Mexico's capital city, boasts the oldest capitol building—El Palacio, built in 1610—and one of the newest—the Round House or Bull Pen, completed in 1966. The exterior of the new capitol is modified New Mexico territorial design. The interior is circular and contains four levels. The adobe-colored building with a total area of 232,206 square feet was designed by W. C. Kruger and Associates. Construction costs totaled $4,676,860.

The capitol was designed to include the shape of the Zia, an Indian sun symbol. The Zia, a sign of friendship, is composed of four rays around an inner circle. The entrances to the circular building continue this symbolism. Native marble adorns the interior. The rotunda is 24 feet in diameter and 60 feet high.[31]

NEW YORK

By 1865 the New York legislature had moved to erect a new capitol building in Albany, since Philip Hooker's Greek revival capitol, which had first been occupied in 1809, had clearly become inadequate. Late in 1867, the design of an Italian Renaissance capitol by Arthur D. Gilman and Thomas Fuller was accepted, and ground was broken very shortly thereafter. The 1868 legislature set the spending limit at $4 million, but, by 1874, the commissioners overseeing construction knew that at least $10 million

would be needed. The cornerstone was laid in 1871, with architect Fuller still in command. Fuller was dismissed in 1876 and replaced by a board of advisors that included Frederick Law Olmstead and architects Leopold Eidlitz and H. H. Richardson. Plans were redrawn by Eidlitz and Richardson that called for completion of the capitol in 1879 and an additional expenditure of only $4.5 million. Finishing touches were still under way, however, in 1898. As a result of changes in architects and the collaboration of two architects whose styles were quite different, the capitol represents an admixture of Gilman's Italian Renaissance, Richardson's romanesque, Eidlitz's Victorian Gothic, and a bit of Moorish-Saracenic finished with French Renaissance. By 1879, the building was ready for occupancy. The granite building was partially destroyed by fire in 1911. Reconstruction costs amounted to $2 million. From 1978 to 1980, renovation work restored some parts of the building to their original splendor. In 1979, the capitol was designated a national historic landmark.[32]

NORTH CAROLINA

Raleigh was chosen as North Carolina's permanent capital city in 1792, and, by 1796, a two-story brick statehouse had been completed. Between 1820 and 1824, additions were made to this simple building, which was completely destroyed by fire in 1831. The general assembly that met during the 1832–1833 session appropriated $50,000 to construct a new capitol, which was to be a larger version of the old statehouse. Architect William Nichols was hired to prepare plans for a building in the shape of a cross with a central, domed rotunda. Nichols was replaced in August 1833 by the New York firm of Ithiel Town and Alexander Jackson Davis. The firm is responsible for giving the capitol its present appearance, although David Paton, who replaced Town and Davis early in 1835, made several changes to the interior.

The cornerstone for the Greek revival capitol was laid in 1833, and soon after construction began another $75,000 had to be appropriated. By the time the building was completed in 1840, its total cost with furnishings came to $532,682. The capitol measures 160 feet by 140 feet. The exterior walls are North Carolina gneiss and the interior walls, stone and brick. The Doric exterior columns are modeled after the Parthenon. The new capitol has been extensively renovated.[33]

NORTH DAKOTA

The "Skyscraper Capitol of the Plains" in Bismarck was completed in 1934 at a cost of $2 million, after the original capitol had been destroyed by fire in 1930. The nineteen-story Indiana limestone building in modern American style was designed by Holabird and Root of Chicago, Joseph Bell De Remer of Grand Forks, and William F. Kurke of Fargo. A four-story judicial wing and state office building was added to the original capitol in the 1970s. The annex, finished in limestone to match the capitol, provides another 100,000 square feet of space. Between 1971 and 1981, over $10 million was spent on various renovation projects.[34]

OHIO

The Ohio legislature voted in 1817, fourteen years after Ohio became a state, to locate the capital in Columbus, which at the time possessed no name. The capital was first located in Chillicothe, moved to Zanesville in 1809, and moved back to Chillicothe in 1812. The desire of the legislature was to fashion a capital city in the center of the state. In December 1816, the legislature moved into the new capital city, Columbus.

The first statehouse, which was destroyed by fire in 1852, had become inadequate by 1838, when the legislature approved a new capitol. The building commission decided on a composite plan, designed from plans received in a competition. The plan decided on was a Greek revival capitol with Doric columns made of native stone. Henry Walter of Cincinnati was named architect, and construction began in 1839. In 1840, construction stopped as the legislature repealed the authorization, and work was not resumed until 1846. In 1848, William R. West was named architect and work was proceeding rapidly. In 1854, when N. B. Kelly became the architect, all the stonework but the cupola had been finished. By 1856, with the appointment of Thomas U. Walter and Richard Upjohn as consulting architects, the legislative chambers had been completed. In 1858, Isaiah Rogers was appointed the architect to complete the interior designs. Finally, the 184 foot by 304 foot capitol was completed in 1861 at a cost of $1,359,121. From 1899 to 1901, an annex was added at a cost of $450,000.[35]

OKLAHOMA

The capitol of Oklahoma, located in Oklahoma City, is unique among state capitol buildings if only for the oil wells that surround the grounds. The structure itself, designed by the firm of Layton-Smith in modern classic style based on Greek and Roman architecture, was begun in 1914 and completed in 1917. The Indiana limestone capitol with a pink and black granite base is six stories high, 480 feet east to west, and 380 feet north to south. There are in fact only five main floors excluding the basement, as the dome and legislative chambers are two stories in height. The exterior facade is ornamented with smooth columns that have Corinthian capitals. The capitol cost approximately $1.5 million. In 1966, a seal was inlaid in the rotunda area at a cost of $4,000.[36]

OREGON

The Oregon statehouse in Salem is the third capitol building in that city; the previous two were destroyed by fire like so many earlier capitols of other states. The first capitol was erected in 1854 at a cost of $40,000. In 1872 another capitol was begun, modeled somewhat after the U.S. Capitol, at a cost of about $325,000. It was destroyed in 1935. Construction began on the present capitol in 1935 and was completed in 1938.

The four-story, modern Greek capitol, designed by Francis Keally of New York, is constructed of white Vermont marble and bronze. It cost approximately $2.5 million. An 8½-ton bronze statue enameled with gold leaf stands atop the capitol tower. The "Golden Pioneer" looks to the west in tribute to Oregon's early settlers. In 1977, wings were added to the capitol, which added 144,000 square feet of usable area to the 131,750 feet in the original building at a cost of $12,025,303.[37]

PENNSYLVANIA

In 1810, the General Assembly passed an act making Harrisburg Pennsylvania's capital city after 1812. Philadelphia was the capital from 1683 to 1799, and Lancaster was the capital from 1799 until the move to Harrisburg. Construction of a capitol was authorized in 1816, and it was occupied in 1821. An addition was authorized in 1864. The main building was destroyed by fire in 1897.

The present capitol was authorized in 1897, supplemented by a 1901 act, and was dedicated by Theodore Roosevelt in 1906. Designed by Joseph M. Houston in the classic style adapted from the Italian Renaissance, the five-story capitol is constructed of Vermont granite. It measures 520 feet in

length and 254 feet in width. The dome reaches a height of 272 feet and is surmounted by a figure symbolic of the Commonwealth. The interior is finished in marble, bronze, mahogany, and tiling. Exclusive of furnishings, the building cost $10,073,174.[38]

RHODE ISLAND

In 1895, groundbreaking ceremonies were held in Providence for a new statehouse. Charles Follen McKim designed a capitol in the Greek Renaissance tradition with exterior walls of white Georgia marble. It is 333 feet long and 180 feet wide at the center. The dome, one of four unsupported marble domes in the world, is surmounted by an 11-foot-high, gold-leafed statue of the "Independent Man." Some offices of the capitol were occupied as early as 1900, but the building and grounds were totally completed in 1904 at a cost including furnishings of $3,018,416.[39]

SOUTH CAROLINA

The building of South Carolina's capitol spanned over fifty years owing to war and scandal. In 1851, the legislature began the process of erecting the new capitol. In 1854, the first architect was dismissed and the new architect, Major John R. Niernsee, determined that the workmanship and materials were defective. A new site was chosen and work began, but not according to schedule. Still not completed in 1865, work was suspended when Sherman's army destroyed Columbia. Although the building was not heavily damaged, work did not recommence until 1885. John Niernsee died in the same year. He was succeeded by J. Crawford Neilson and, in 1888, Frank Niernsee replaced Neilson. The younger Niernsee worked primarily on the interior, but work was suspended in 1891. In 1900, Frank P. Milburn was appointed architect. He built the dome and the north and south porticoes. In 1904, Charles C. Wilson became the architect, and the building was finally completed. In the end, the granite capitol was a freely interpreted Roman Corinthian structure that cost $3,540,000.[40]

SOUTH DAKOTA

Pierre had been the temporary capital city since South Dakota became a state in 1889. Not until 1904 did an election determine that Pierre would be the permanent capital. Construction began in 1907 on the capitol building. It was completed in 1910 at a cost of $1 million. C. E. Bell of Minneapolis designed the building, patterning it after Montana's capitol. The exterior is limestone. The rotunda is decorated with marble, scagliola pillars, and mosaic floors. The inner dome rises 96 feet and is made of leaded stained glass. The outer dome rises 159 feet. Its now blackened roof is fashioned from 40,000 pounds of copper. An annex was added to the original building in 1932.[41]

TENNESSEE

Forty-seven years after joining the Union, a bitter debate was ended when Nashville was designated the permanent capital city in 1843. An area known as Campbell's Hill was purchased by the city in the same year for $30,000 and was given to the state for the capitol site. William Strickland, a strong adherent of the Greek revival style, was chosen as architect. The cornerstone for the Tennessee marble structure was laid in 1845. State convicts and slaves performed much of the labor. Although the building was not entirely completed then, it was first occupied by the General Assembly in 1853. By 1857, building costs had amounted to $711,367.

The capitol is designed after an Ionic temple. Eight fluted Ionic columns adorn the

north and south porticoes and six adorn the east and west porticoes. The tower rises 206 feet, 7 inches from the parallelogram-shaped structure, which measures 112 feet by 239 feet. Exterior restoration was performed beginning in 1956 and interior restoration and repair, in 1958. In 1969 and 1970, more restoration work was undertaken in the assembly chambers and in various offices and meeting rooms.[42]

TEXAS

Austin was chosen as the permanent capital of the Republic of Texas in 1839. It remained the capital city after Texas joined the Union in 1845. The present capitol was begun in 1882 to replace an 1852 structure that burned down in 1881. A temporary building, constructed in 1881, was used until the completion of the new capitol in 1888. The temporary structure burned down in 1889. The classical Renaissance capitol, shaped as a Greek cross, was designed by E. E. Myers of Detroit. The exterior walls are Texas pink granite; the interior and dome walls, Texas limestone. The building measures 585 feet, 10 inches in length and 299 feet, 10 inches in width. It is 309 feet, 8 inches from the basement floor to the top of the sixteen-foot statue of the goddess Liberty that stands atop the dome. The capitol provides 273,799 square feet of usable space. The builders of the capitol accepted 3 million acres of land in the Texas Panhandle as payment for constructing the capitol.[43]

UTAH

Utah became a state in 1896, and, although Salt Lake City had long been a capital city, it was not until 1911 that the legislature authorized the construction of a permanent capitol. The Renaissance revival design of Richard K. A. Kletting was chosen for the Utah granite and Georgia marble building.

Groundbreaking took place in 1913, and the capitol was completed at a cost of $2,739,528 in 1915.

The capitol is 404 feet in length and 240 feet in width. The ceiling of the copper dome is 165 feet above the floor of the rotunda. The dome itself rises above a pediment and a colonnade of twenty-four Corinthian columns.[44]

VERMONT

Vermont entered the Union in 1791. Its legislature designated Montpelier as the permanent capital city in 1805. The first capitol, in use from 1808 to 1836, was torn down and replaced by a new structure designed by Ammi B. Young after the Greek temple of Theseus. This capitol was destroyed by fire in 1857. The present statehouse, occupied since 1859, was modeled after the building that had burned down except for the dome and larger wings.

The exterior is constructed of Barre granite. The building is accented by a six-columned Doric portico and a 57-foot-high wooden dome. The dome is sheathed in copper and is covered with gold leaf. A statue of Ceres surmounts the dome. The original statue of the goddess of agriculture was replaced in 1938. Construction cost approximately $220,000.[45]

VIRGINIA

The Virginia General Assembly, the oldest law-making body in the Western Hemisphere, held its first session at Jamestown in 1619. The capitol was moved to Williamsburg in 1699 and then to Richmond in 1779. In 1785, Thomas Jefferson was asked to consult an architect for the design of a capitol. Jefferson chose an architect who shared his interest in classical buildings. Charles Louis Clerisseau, with Jefferson's assistance, modeled a capitol after a Roman temple in France known as "La Maison Carrée." The cornerstone was laid in 1785, and the General Assembly first met in the new capitol in 1788. The two-story brick structure is rectangular with a portico secured by Ionic columns. Between 1904 and 1906, wings were added to each side of the original building. Extensive renovation and remodeling, begun in 1962, was completed in 1963.[46]

WASHINGTON

When Olympia became the territorial capital of Washington in 1855, a wooden capitol was built there. When Washington entered the Union in 1889, a more suitable capitol was desired. In 1893, the design submitted by Ernest Flagg was chosen, and work began in 1894 only to be delayed while the foundation and basement were being constructed. In 1901, what is now known as the "Old Capitol" was purchased by the state and utilized as the statehouse until 1928.

By 1909, the government had decided that the Old Capitol had become inadequate. Ernest Flagg visited Olympia in 1911 and proposed a group concept for the capitol. Architects Walter R. Wilder and Harry K. White of New York were chosen to carry out Flagg's idea. In 1919, work began on an enlarged foundation for Flagg's original building. Construction began in 1922 and continued until completion in 1928.

The Wilkeson sandstone legislative building cost $6,798,596. It is 413 feet long and 179.2 feet wide. The total height is twenty-two stories. The dome, crowned by the "Lantern of Liberty," which rises 287 feet, is the fifth largest in the world. Doric columns adorn the colonnade around the building. Corinthian columns decorate the main north entrance and south portico.[47]

WEST VIRGINIA

Wheeling was the location of West Virginia's first capital. In 1870, the capital was moved to Charleston and, in 1875, back to Wheeling. In 1877, the capital was moved again to Charleston by vote of the people. A capitol was built in 1885 in downtown Charleston, but it was destroyed by fire in 1921 as was the temporary capitol six years later. The capitol now in use was built in stages—the west wing in 1924–1925, the east wing in 1926–1927, the center in 1930–1932—and was dedicated in 1932. Total construction costs came to $10 million.

The capitol was designed by Cass Gilbert, who also designed the U.S. Supreme Court. This Renaissance building provides over fourteen acres of floor space. Porticoes at the north and south entrances are supported by limestone pillars, each of which weighs 86 tons. The exterior of the capitol is buff Indiana limestone, and an assortment of marbles was used to finish the interior. The dome reaches 293 feet, 5 feet higher than the dome of the U.S. Capitol.[48]

WISCONSIN

The state capitol in Madison is Wisconsin's fifth capitol building, the third in Madison. The first Madison capitol was in use from 1838 to 1863. The second building was destroyed by fire in 1904. The current capitol was designed by George B. Post and Sons of New York. Construction began in 1906 and was completed in 1917 at a cost of $7.5 million.

The capitol is situated between Monona and Mendota lakes in a 13.4-acre park. The Roman Renaissance marble and granite structure itself occupies 2.42 acres and rises to a height of 285.9 feet, from the ground to the top of Daniel Chester French's gilded bronze statue "Wisconsin." This capitol boasts the only granite-domed capitol in the nation. The interior is finished in forty-three varieties of stone, glass mosaics, and murals.[49]

WYOMING

Wyoming became a state in 1890. Cheyenne had been the territorial capital, and, in 1886, the first of three separate contracts for a capitol was let, with David W. Gibbs and Company as architect. The cornerstone for the pseudo-Corinthian building, reminiscent of the U.S. Capitol, was laid in 1887, and, by 1888, it was ready for use. The first wings were finished in 1890. New east and west wings were approved in 1915 and completed in 1917. The cost of the original building and its additions totaled $389,569. The sandstone capitol was renovated between 1974 and 1980 at a cost of almost $7 million. The 24-karat gold-leafed dome, 145 feet high, has been leafed four times, most recently in 1980.[50]

DISTRICT OF COLUMBIA

The stately District Building at 1350 Pennsylvania Avenue had been the home to District government for a number of years. However, in November 1992, offices other than those used for Council business were moved and consolidated in a modern concrete, steel, and glass office building at 441 4th Street at Judiciary Square. The building is called One Judiciary Square.[51]

AMERICAN SAMOA

Government House overlooks Pago Pago Bay on the Mountain of Chiefs. Built in 1903 at a cost of $18,651, it has been the home of civilian and naval governors since its construction. The two-story white mansion designed by the U.S. Navy has been enlarged and remodelled over the years, but without losing its original charm as an excellent example of an old South Pacific home.[52]

The Fono or legislature building is a new building that features traditional Samoan architecture. It incorporates both a long oval-shaped residence and a round meeting house.[53]

COMMONWEALTH OF THE NORTHERN MARIANA ISLANDS

Government offices are located on Capitol Hill in Saipan. Capitol Hill is actually a complex of offices and houses that was constructed by the U.S. Naval Technical Training Unit between 1954 and 1956. In fact, these mostly precast concrete buildings were off-limits headquarters for a Central Intelligence Agency program to train Nationalist Chinese for guerrilla warfare against China during the 1950s. Thus the Commonwealth's capitol holds a singular distinction. In 1962, the CIA vacated the complex and the government of the trust territory moved in, to be replaced eventually by the Commonwealth government.[54]

GUAM

The Adelup Complex in Agana is now the site of the governor's office. It had served originally as a school for military children during the naval administration. The school itself had been a rather undistinguished and decaying rectangular structure. The government set out to renovate the school in Spanish style, and in 1985 the governor's office moved to this prime beach location. The renovated complex is replete with Spanish arches, but traditional Chamorro architecture at the front of the complex can be seen in the two porticos supported by latte stones, the pillars on which ancient homes were built, which serve as a symbol of strength.

Government House itself, the official residence of the governor, likewise combines Chamorro and Spanish architecture. It sits on Kasamate Hill in Agana Heights, commanding a beautiful view of Agana and Agana Bay. Originally constructed in 1952 and completed in 1954, Government House was reconstructed after sustaining damages by Typhoon Pamela in 1976.[55]

PUERTO RICO

The Puerto Rican capitol building in San Juan was authorized in 1907, but not constructed until 1925. It was designed by architect Rafael Carmoega of Puerto Rico. The rotunda was finished at a later date under the architect's supervision. Sixteen columns of rose marble, grouped in fours, form support for the third floor. Four arches reach to the vaulted ceilings. Venetian mosaics, designed from the work of Puerto Rican artists, occupy the vaulting between the arches. The mosaics depict Puerto Rico's conquest, colonization, and discovery as well as the autonomy movement and the abolition of slavery. In the dome's interior are eight figures in mosaic representing freedom, justice, health, the arts, agriculture, education, science, and industry. These figures are surrounded by mythological motifs in a background of rolled gold. The coat of arms, made of leaded glass, is at the center of the dome. Marble friezes occupy the second floor. The north frieze depicts an Indian council, a sixteenth-century Spanish council, and mayors. The west frieze represents the twentieth century. The east frieze depicts Puerto Rican history from 1582 to 1867 and the south frieze, the history for 1671 to 1898, when U.S. forces arrived on the island.[56]

U.S. VIRGIN ISLANDS

There are two government houses in the U.S. Virgin Islands. Government House on St. Croix actually consists of two separate buildings. The older central wing was constructed in 1747 and purchased by the government in 1771 for the governor's residence. The western end of the building was built in the late 1700s and purchased in 1828 for government offices. They were joined together in the 1830s.

Today the capital city of the U.S. Virgin Islands is Charlotte Amalie on St. Thomas. Government House, which is both the home and the office of the governor, was built by the Colonial Council of St. Thomas and St. John, the body that governed under the Danish. It was completed in 1867 at a cost of $33,500 and housed the Vice Governor of the Danish West Indies, who was president of the Colonial Council. Under U.S. administration, Government House became the governor's residence.

Government House is a neoclassical building with Georgian overtones. Danish ballast brick was used in construction. It is stuccoed over in the interior and painted white on the exterior. A two-story cast-iron veranda is its most prominent feature. Native mahogany can be found inside as well as murals painted by Pepino Mangravatti in the 1930s under the Works Progress Administration.

The Legislative Building, home of the Virgin Islands Senate, was planned originally as a marine barracks for the Danish. Although conceived in 1827, construction did not begin until 1829 and was not completed until 1879.[57]

NOTES

1. *Alabama Capitol Complex* (Montgomery: Bureau of Publicity and Information, n.d.); *Alabama Emblems* (Montgomery: Alabama State Department of Archives and History, n.d.), pp. 1–2; "Visitor's Guide to the Alabama Legislature," www. legislature. state. al. us / misc / visitorsguide / visitorsguide.

2. *Alaska Blue Book, 1979*, p. 82.

3. Information provided by Anne Wallace, Museum Educator, Arizona State Capitol Museum, Phoenix, Arizona; "Arizona State Capitol Welcome to the Complex Tour," www.Azleg. state.az.us/museum/museum.

4. Clara B. Eno, "Old and New Capitols of Arkansas," *The Arkansas Historical Quarterly* 4 (Autumn 1945): 246–48; John A. Treon, "Politics and Concrete: The Building of the Arkansas State Capitol, 1899–1917," *The Arkansas Historical Quarterly* 31 (Summer 1972): 127, 132.

5. *California's Legislature, 1984*, pp. 135–48.

6. *Colorado State Capitol* (Denver: Colorado Department of Education, n.d.).

7. *State of Connecticut Register and Manual, 1983*, p. 905.

8. *Official Insignia of Delaware* (Dover: Delaware State Development Department, n.d.).

9. *Florida's Capitol* (Tallahassee: Department of State, 1983); *The State of Florida's Heritage and Emblems* (Tallahassee: Department of State, n.d.); information provided by the Florida Legislative Library.

10. *Georgia's Capitol* (Atlanta: Max Cleland, n.d.).

11. *Hawaii State Capitol Fact Sheet* (Honolulu: State Archives, February 1975), pp. 1–2.

12. *Idaho Blue Book, 1981–1982*, p. 214.

13. *Illinois Blue Book, 1983–1984*, pp. 28–32.

14. *The State House, 1888 to Present* (Indianapolis: Indiana Department of Commerce, n.d.); *A Guide to the Indiana State Capitol . . .* (Indianapolis: Indiana Sesquicentennial Commission, 1967).

15. *1985–86 Iowa Official Register*, vol. 61, pp. 228–31; "Iowa Department of General Services: Capitol Restoration," www.state.ia.us/ government/dgs/Services/restoration.

16. *Kansas Directory, 1982*, pp. 104–13.

17. *Kentucky's Capitol* (Frankfort: Kentucky Department of Public Information, n.d.); *75th Birthday Celebration, State Capitol Building, 1910–1985; Commemorative Program, October 26, 1985*, p. 10.

18. *Louisiana Facts* (Baton Rouge: Louisiana Department of State, n.d.); *The Louisiana State Capitol* (n.p., n.d.).

19. *Maine, the Pine State* (n.p., n.d.).

20. *The Maryland State House, Annapolis* (Annapolis: Maryland Commission on Artistic Property of the State Archives and Hall of Records, Commission for the Maryland Heritage Committee, September 1984).

21. "Additions and Corrections to *Massachusetts*"; material provided by the Massachusetts Citizen Information Service.

22. *Michigan History Salutes . . . The Historic State Capitol Built in 1879* (Lansing: Michigan Department of State, 1980), pp. 3–15.

23. *Minnesota Legislative Manual, 1985*, pp. 2–3.

24. *Souvenir of Mississippi* (Jackson: Dick Molpus, n.d.), pp. 8–16.

25. *Official Manual, State of Missouri, 1975–76*, pp. 1428–30.

26. *The Montana Capitol: A Self-Guiding Tour* (Helena: Montana Historical Society, n.d.), pp. 1–10.

27. *Nebraska Blue Book, 1982–83*, pp. 8–9.

28. *The History of the Capitol Building* (Carson City: Department of Economic Development, n.d.); information supplied by the Nevada State Library.

29. *New Hampshire's State House: A Visitor's Guide* (n.p., n.d.).

30. *New Jersey's Historic State Capitol* (n.p., n.d.); records of the State Capitol Building Commission, 1945–1946 (supplied by John T. Jacobsen, Assistant to the Secretary of State).

31. Information from clippings files provided by Michael Miller, Southwest Librarian, New Mexico State Library, Santa Fe, New Mexico.

32. C. R. Roseberry, *Capitol Story* (Albany: New York State Office of General Services, 1982), pp. 24–25, 45, 126.

33. Information from *North Carolina Manual* provided by Thad Eure, Secretary of State, North Carolina.

34. Lloyd B. Omdahl, *Governing North Dakota, 1981–83* (Grand Forks: Bureau of Governmental Affairs, University of North Dakota, 1981), pp. 72–73; *Facts About North Dakota* (Bismark: North Dakota Economic Development Commission, revised July 1983), p. i; "History of the State Capitol and Grounds Renovations" (n.p., n.d.), one page.

35. *Ohio's Capitals and the Story of Ohio's Emblems* (Columbus: n.p., n.d.), pp. 5–12.

36. *Directory of Oklahoma, 1981*, pp. 36–38.

37. *Oregon Blue Book, 1977–1978*, pp. 141–42.

38. *1976–77 Pennsylvania Manual*, 103 ed., pp. 848–53.

39. *The State of Rhode Island and Providence Plantations 1983–1984 Manual*, pp. 1–5.

40. *South Carolina State Symbols and Emblems* (Columbia: House of Representatives, n.d.).

41. Jan Clark, *South Dakota State Capitol* (Pierre: South Dakota Department of State Development and G. F. Thomsen and Associates, n.d.); *South Dakota History and Heritage* (n.p., n.d.).

42. *Tennessee Blue Book, 1985–86*, pp. 308–12.

43. *Texas Capitol Guide* (Austin: State Department of Highways and Public Transportation, Travel and Information Division, 1983).

44. *Utah: A Guide to Capitol Hill* (n.p., n.d.).

45. *Vermont Legislative Directory and State Manual, 1979–1980*, pp. 4–5.

46. *The Virginia State Capitol, Richmond, Virginia* (Richmond: Division of Engineering and Buildings, 1974).

47. Shanna Stevenson, *A Guide to Washington's Capitol—Walking Tour* (Olympia: Prepared for Office of the Secretary of State, December 1984), pp. 1–4, 11.

48. *State Capitol* (Charleston: Ken Hechler, n.d.).

49. *Wisconsin State Capitol* (Madison: Department of Administration, n.d.); information provided by Kim Varnell, Capitol Tour Guide, Department of Administration, Madison, Wisconsin.

50. *Wyoming Facts* (Cheyenne: Wyoming Travel Commission, n.d.).

51. Information received from the Mayor's Office of Public Information.

52. *Facts about American Samoa* (n.p., n.d.); pamphlet provided by office of Eni Faleomavaega, member of Congress for American Samoa.

53. *American Samoa* (n.p., n.d.); pamphlet provided by office of Eni Faleomavaega, member of Congress for American Samoa.

54. Information provided by Pete Torres, Federal Relations and Programs, Office of the Resident Representative to the United States, Commonwealth of the Northern Mariana Islands.

55. *Guam and Micronesia* (Agana: Guam Visitors Bureau, 1989), p. 14; personal interview with Terence G. Villaverde, Special Assistant to the Governor, Washington Office of the Governor of Guam.

56. *Capitol of Puerto Rico* (n.p., n.d.); information supplied by Commonwealth of Puerto Rico, Department of State.

57. *Echoes from "Our Journey through History"* (n.p.: United States Virgin Islands Diamond Jubilee Committee, 1992); *Government House, Charlotte Amalie, St. Thomas, U.S. Virgin Islands* (Charlotte Amalie: Government Information Office, n.d.).

6

State and Territory Flowers

Reasons for selecting a particular state flower are as varied as their colors and varieties. Some flowers have historical significance—the golden poppy caught the attention of early explorers in California who nicknamed the state the Land of Fire upon observing its golden blooms spread across the countryside. The mountain laurel, state flower of Connecticut, was first discovered by the Swedish explorer, Peter Kalm, who sent it to Linnaeus in 1750 for identification. Kansas designated the wild sunflower as a symbolic emblem of early Kansas settlement.

School children and agriculturalists in Delaware lobbied for the peach blossom because the peach was often associated with the state. Florida, of course, named the orange blossom as its state flower in recognition of the orange industry. The apple blossom, named as the state flower of Michigan, pays tribute to their apple industry. Proud of its pine forests, Maine designated the pine cone and tassel as its floral emblem.

A commercial peony grower in Indiana convinced fellow state representatives to name the peony the state flower, in spite of strong opposition. It seems likely, however, that naturalists will try again to see that a flower native to the state will be named the state flower.

Many states seemed to have chosen flowers on the basis of their beauty, such as New York's selection of the rose, Minnesota's pink and white lady slipper, and New Hampshire's purple lilac. Hawaii not only chose a state flower, the hibiscus, but also designated an official flower for each of its eight islands.

Two states selected the apple blossom, Arkansas and Michigan. Nebraska and Kentucky favored the goldenrod, and Louisiana and Mississippi named the magnolia. The mountain laurel was chosen by Connecticut and Pennsylvania. Several states have named varieties of the violet and rose as their state flowers.

ALABAMA

The camellia was named the official state flower of Alabama by the legislature in 1959,[1] repealing the 1927 act designating the goldenrod as the state flower. Unofficially, the red camellia variety with red and white colors similar to those in the state flag is considered the Alabama state flower.[2]

ALASKA

The wild, native forget-me-not, *Myosotis alpestris Schmidt Boraginaceae*, became the state flower and floral emblem of Alaska in 1949 by act of the legislature.[3] Forget-me-nots are sturdy blue perennial flowers, which grow throughout the Arctic region.[4]

ARIZONA

The flower of the saguaro, *Carnagiea gigantea*, was officially designated the state flower of Arizona by legislative act in 1931.[5] The saguaro is a member of the cactus family, which includes around 40 genera and 1,000 species mostly native to North America.[6]

ARKANSAS

The apple blossom, *Pyrus malus*, was declared the state floral emblem of Arkansas by act of the legislature in 1901.[7]

CALIFORNIA

The golden poppy, *Eschscholtzia californica*, was named the official state flower of California by the legislature in 1903. A 1973 amendment designated April 6 of each year as California Poppy Day.[8] Also called the *Copa de Oro*, or "cup of gold," because of the brilliantly colored golden bloom, they grew so widely that early explorers nicknamed California the Land of Fire. Indians used poppy oil on their hair and boiled and consumed the edible portions. As perennials, they bloom several times a year if treated to an occasional trimming.[9]

COLORADO

The white and lavender columbine, *Columbine aquilegia caerulea*, was declared by the legislature to be the state flower of Colorado in 1899.[10] Further provisions of Colorado state law protect the columbine from needless destruction and waste, forbid tearing up the plant by the roots from any public lands, and limit the number of stems, buds, or blossoms that may be picked from public lands to twenty-five.[11] Violation of these provisions is a misdemeanor and is punishable upon conviction by a fine of not less than $5 nor more than $50.[12]

CONNECTICUT

The mountain laurel, *Kalmia latifolia*, was designated by legislative act in 1907 to be the state flower of Connecticut.[13] The Swedish explorer Peter Kalm sent the fragrant white and pink blossomed flower to Linnaeus in 1750 for identification. Linnaeus named it the *Kalmia latifolia*, the first part to honor Kalm and the second to indicate that it had wide leaves. The mountain laurel blooms most brilliantly every two or three years making different sections of the Connecticut countryside host to a beautiful display of blooms depending upon the cycle of a particular growth of plants. Other names for this brightly colored flower are calico bush and spoonwood.[14]

DELAWARE

The peach blossom was adopted as the floral emblem of Delaware by legislative act in 1895. It was also named the official state flower in 1955.[15] Agriculturalists and school children, fearing that the popular goldenrod would be named the state flower, flooded the state legislators with petitions requesting that the peach blossom be adopted as the official state flower. It was felt that the orchards with over 800,000 peach trees were responsible for the Delaware nickname, the Peach State, and had a significant economic impact on the state. As a consequence, the peach blossom was given its due recognition and named the state flower.[16]

FLORIDA

In 1909, the state legislature of Florida adopted the orange blossom as the state flower. A fragrant reminder of Florida's multibillion dollar orange industry, the white blossoms bloom throughout central and southern Florida.[17] Florida has also designated the Coreopsis, which is planted extensively along its highways, as the official state wildflower.[18]

GEORGIA

The Cherokee rose was adopted as the floral emblem of Georgia by legislative act in 1916.[19] Although the Georgia Federation of Women's Clubs supported the adoption of the Cherokee rose, *Rosa sinica*, as the official state flower, they were probably under the mistaken notion that the flower was native to the South. Instead, it is believed that the white, thorny shrub hails from China and was first introduced in England before it arrived in the new world in the latter half of the eighteenth century. The common name of the plant emanates from the Cherokee Indians, who were fond of the plant and were responsible for its widespread propagation. This beautiful plant blooms in the early spring and often in the fall. It is a popular hedge in the South.[20]

In 1979, the Georgia legislature also designated a state wild flower, the azalea.[21]

HAWAII

The *Pua Aloala*, the hibiscus, was designated the flower emblem of Hawaii in 1923.[22] The hibiscus grows abundantly in all color shades throughout the Hawaiian Islands. In addition to a state flower, the Hawaii legislature has designated an official flower for each island:

Hawaii Island	Red *Lehua (Ohia)*
Maui	*Lokelani* (pink cottage rose)
Molokai	White *Kukui* blossom
Kahoolawe	*Hinahina* (beach heliotrope)
Lanai	*Kaumaoa* (yellow and orange air plant)
Oahu	*Ilima*
Kauai	*Mokihana* (green berry)
Niihau	White *Pupu* shell[23]

IDAHO

The syringa, *Philadelphus lewisii*, was designated the official state flower of Idaho by that state's legislature in 1931.[24] The four-petaled syringa blossoms, white and fragrant, cluster at the ends of short branches.[25]

ILLINOIS

The native violet was declared the state flower of Illinois by legislative act in 1908.[26] School children voted in 1907 from among three floral candidates, the violet, wild rose, and goldenrod. The violet won by nearly 4,000 votes.

INDIANA

The flower of the peony, *Paeonia*, was designated by legislative act in 1957 as the official state flower of Indiana.[27] The 1957 act repealed a 1931 act that had named the zinnia the state flower. The 1931 act also repealed a 1923 act that had designated the flower of the tulip tree as the state flower, for in 1931 the tulip tree had been designated the official state tree. From 1919 until 1923, the carnation had been Indiana's state flower.[28]

Since the adoption of the first state flower in 1913, there seems to have been much shuffling of floral emblems and discussions concerning the merits of each candidate. In 1957, a House committee changed a Senate-committee-proposed entry, the dogwood blossom, to the peony.

It has been conjectured that a commercial peony grower, also a state representative, had some influence in this decision. Though the peony is not indigenous to Indiana and, for this reason, has been criticized as inappropriately named as the state flower, it nonetheless continues to be the official state flower. If history repeats itself, however, it will not be long before naturalist agitators try again to change the state floral emblem to one that is native to Indiana.

Blooming in late May or early June, the peony sports its apparel in a variety of shades of pink and red, as well as white.[29]

IOWA

The wild rose was designated the official state flower of Iowa by that state's General Assembly in 1897. Specifically, the *Rosa pratincola*, the wild prairie rose, is considered to be the unofficial selection since there are several species and none was singled out for the designation. The wild rose blooms from June throughout the summer. It has large pinkish flowers with yellow centers.[30]

KANSAS

The *Helianthus*, or wild native sunflower, was designated the state flower and floral emblem of Kansas in 1903. The laws speak to the symbolism of the sunflower as connoting "frontier days, winding trails, pathless prairies" as well as "the majesty of a golden future."[31]

The law's author, Senator George P. Morehouse, very eloquently expressed his love for the flower as well as the people of the state when he addressed the National Guard at Fort Riley after passage of the law. To quote his heartfelt speech:

This flower has to every Kansan a historic symbolism . . . it is not a blossom lingering a few brief hours, but lasts for a season. It gracefully nods to the caresses of the earliest morning zephyrs. Its bright face greets the rising orb

of day and faithfully follows him in his onward course through the blazing noontime, till the pink-tinted afterglow of sunset decorates the western sky and marks the quiet hour of eventide.

It is hard to imagine that the sunflower will ever be dethroned as the state flower.[32]

KENTUCKY

The goldenrod became the official state flower of Kentucky in 1926 by legislative act.[33] Most of the 125 species of goldenrod have yellow flowers, though a few species sport white flowers instead. This perennial herb is also called the yellow-top or flower-of-gold.[34]

LOUISIANA

The magnolia was designated the state flower of Louisiana by act of the legislature in 1900. The magnolia family, which includes about ten genera and seventy-five species, is most commonly found throughout eastern North America. The flower from the magnolia tree or shrub is large and extremely fragrant.[35] Louisiana also designated the Louisiana iris, *Giganticaerulea*, as the official state wildflower in 1990.[36]

MAINE

The pine cone and tassel, *Pinus strobus Linnaeus*, was named the floral emblem of the state of Maine by legislative act in 1895.[37] It is obvious from the state seal, the nickname of the state, and the state tree that Maine is proud of its 17 million acres of forestland. It is no surprise that the pine cone and tassel was designated the official state flower of the Pine Tree State.

MARYLAND

The black-eyed susan, *Rudbeckia hirta*, was proclaimed to be the floral emblem of Maryland by legislative act in 1918.[38] Also called the yellow daisy, this herb is a member of the thistle family, with orange or orange-yellow petals and a purplish brown center.[39]

MASSACHUSETTS

The mayflower, *Epigea repens*, was named the flower or floral emblem of the Commonwealth of Massachusetts by legislative act in 1918. A provision was added in 1925 to protect the mayflower, making it unlawful to dig up or injure a mayflower plant, other than to pick the flower, if growing on public lands. A fine of not more than $50 may be levied upon conviction, unless a person violates this law while in disguise or in the secrecy of night, in which case the punishment is increased to a fine of not more than $100.[40]

Large patches of the mayflower, or ground laurel, may be found growing as far north as Newfoundland and as far south as Florida. The pink or white flowers grow in fragrant clusters at the ends of branches.[41]

MICHIGAN

The apple blossom became the state flower of Michigan by joint resolution of the legislature in 1897. The law cites the apple blossom, in particular the *Pyrus coronaria*, which is native to Michigan, as adding to the beauty of the landscape, while Michigan apples have gained a reputation throughout the world. In 1998, Michigan also designated a state wildflower, the dwarf lake iris (*Iris lacustrus*).[42]

MINNESOTA

The pink and white lady slipper, *Cypripedium reginae*, was adopted by the legislature of Minnesota as the official state flower in 1902.[43] The pink and white lady slipper, an orchid, blooms in June and July, thriving in tamarack and spruce marshes. It has been protected by law since 1925.[44]

MISSISSIPPI

The flower of the evergreen magnolia, *Magnolia grandiflora*, was designated the state flower of Mississippi by legislative act in 1952. In 1900 the children of the state had selected the magnolia as the state flower, but their selection was not officially acted on until 52 years later.[45]

MISSOURI

The blossom of the red haw or wild haw, *Crataegus*, was declared the floral emblem of Missouri by the state legislature in 1923. Further, the legislature declared in the same act that the state department of agriculture shall encourage its cultivation because of the beauty of its flower, fruit, and foliage.[46]

The hawthorn's many species are found throughout Missouri and the Ozarks. The most common species are the margaretta, the turkey apple, and the cockspur thorn. A member of the rose family, the shrubby tree ranges from 3 to 30 feet in height with thorns 3 inches long on some trees. Its white blossoms spring forth in April and May.[47]

MONTANA

The bitterroot, *Lewisia rediviva*, was designated the floral emblem of Montana by legislative act in 1895.[48]

First chosen as the Montana Women's Christian Temperance Union's state flower in 1891, the bitterroot was selected as the official state flower after the Montana Floral Emblem Association held a statewide vote in 1894 and recommended it to the legislature. Of the over 5,800 ballots cast, the bitterroot received 3,621 votes far outdistancing the next runner-up, the evening primrose, which received a mere 787 votes. Early Indians boiled the root of the plant and combined it with meat or berries, making it a nutritious dietary staple.[49]

NEBRASKA

The late goldenrod, *Solidago serotina*, was declared the floral emblem of Nebraska by the legislature in 1895.[50] A member of the thistle family, it is a perennial herb that grows best in moist soil from Canada south to Georgia, Texas and Utah.[51]

NEVADA

The sagebrush, *Artemisia tridentata* or *A. trifida*, was designated the state flower of Nevada by legislative act in 1967. It had been the unofficial state floral emblem since 1917.[52] An odorous silvery-gray member of the thistle family, the sagebrush thrives in the rocky soil or dry plains of the western United States and Canada.[53]

NEW HAMPSHIRE

The purple lilac, *Syringa vulgaris*, was named the state flower of New Hampshire by the legislature in 1919. After months of arguments and committee debates, including an exasperated move by a legislative committee to ask two college botany professors to choose between the Senate preferred purple aster and the House preferred apple blossom, the purple lilac was finally selected. (The two college professors could not agree either, but finally the committee was able to break its deadlock.)[54] In 1991, New Hampshire also designated an official state wildflower, the pink lady's slipper, *Cypripedium acaule*.[55]

NEW JERSEY

The common meadow violet, *Viola sororia*, was designated the state flower of New Jersey by a legislative act in 1971 that became effective during 1972.[56]

NEW MEXICO

The yucca flower was adopted as the official flower of New Mexico by legislative act in 1927.[57] The yucca flower was selected after a vote by school children and subsequent recommendation by the First Federation of Woman's Clubs. Blooming in early summer, the yucca flowers appear at the ends of long stalks. The base of the yucca consists of sharply pointed leaves making the plant both dastardly and delicate as the lower leaves contrast with the gentle ivory colored flowers. Amole, a soap substitute, can be made from its ground roots, a practice still found in some New Mexican Indian villages.[58]

NEW YORK

The rose, in any color or color combination common to it, was designated the official flower of the state of New York by the legislature in 1955.[59]

NORTH CAROLINA

The dogwood was adopted as the official flower of North Carolina by that state's legislature in 1941.[60]

NORTH DAKOTA

The wild prairie rose, *Rosa blanda* or *R. arkansana*, was named the floral emblem of North Dakota by legislative act in 1907.[61] An erect shrub, its stems are usually free of prickles, though sometimes they have a few slender thorns. The pink flowers bloom in June or July.[62]

OHIO

The scarlet carnation was adopted by the Ohio General Assembly in 1904 as that state's official flower in memory of William McKinley. The carnation was considered a good luck piece by McKinley because, during an early campaign for a seat in the U.S. House of Representatives, his opponent gave McKinley a red carnation for his buttonhole. After winning the election, he continued to wear a red carnation during later campaigns.[63] In 1987, Ohio adopted the large white trillium, *Trillium grandiflorum*, as the official state wildflower.[64]

OKLAHOMA

The mistletoe, *Phoradendron serotinum*, was designated the floral emblem of Oklahoma by legislative act in 1893; and in 1910, the Indian Blanket (*Gaillardia pulthella*) was designated the state wildflower.[65] Mistletoe has the dubious distinction of being a tree parasite. There are over 100 American species in the mistletoe family.[66]

OREGON

The Oregon grape, *Berberis aquifolium*, was designated the official flower of Oregon by legislative act in 1899.[67] The Oregon grape, also known as the Rocky Mountain grape or the holly-leaf barberry, is a low trailing shrub. Its spherical berry, about 3 inches in diameter, is blue or purple.[68]

PENNSYLVANIA

The mountain laurel, *Kalmia latifolia*, was adopted as the state flower of Pennsylvania by that state's legislature in 1933.[69] Blooming in June, the laurel's soft pink color is so popular that Tioga County celebrates an annual laurel festival where hundreds attend to soak up its beauty.[70]

RHODE ISLAND

The violet, *Viola palmata*, was designated the state flower of Rhode Island by legislative act in 1968.[71] Also called the early blue violet and Johnny-jump-up, this violet-purple member of the abundant violet family is found from Massachusetts to Minnesota and south to Florida.[72]

SOUTH CAROLINA

In 1924 the General Assembly adopted the yellow jessamine as the official state flower of South Carolina. Reasons given for its selection include its fragrance and resilience. Growing throughout the state, the golden flower's reawakening in the spring has been considered a sign of its constancy and loyalty to the state of South Carolina.[73]

SOUTH DAKOTA

The American pasque flower, *Pulsatilla hirsutissima*, with the motto "I Lead" was made the floral emblem of South Dakota by legislative act in 1903.[74] Also known as the May Day flower, the wild crocus, the Aprilfools, the rock lily, the badger, and the wind flower, its lavender blooms appear in early spring.[75] It grows best in the arid prairie soil of South Dakota and other midwestern states north to British Columbia.[76]

TENNESSEE

Tennessee has two state flowers, a wild flower and a cultivated flower. The passion flower, *Passiflora incarnata*, officially became the state wildflower in 1973 by act of the General Assembly.[77] In 1919 a resolution was passed providing that a vote by the state's school children would determine the state flower, and the passion flower was chosen. In 1933, however, the General Assembly passed another resolution adopting the iris as the state flower without rescinding the earlier resolution. This curious situation was finally rectified by the 1973 act that made the passion flower the state wildflower and the iris the state cultivated flower.[78]

The passion flower, also called the maypop, the wild apricot, and the Indian name *ocoee* grows in the southern United States and South America. Early South American Christian missionaries gave the flower its name upon seeing such crucifixion symbols as the crown of thorns and three crosses within the flower.[79]

TEXAS

The bluebonnet, *Lupinus subcarnosis*, was adopted as the state flower of Texas by legislative act in 1901.[80] A member of the pea family, the bluebonnet is one of the over 100 species in this mostly herbaceous family.[81]

UTAH

The sego lily, *Calochortus nuttalli*, was declared to be the state flower of Utah by the legislature in 1911.[82] This slender stemmed member of the lily family has white, lilac, or yellow flowers which bloom in midsummer. It is native from South Dakota to Nebraska and California.[83]

VERMONT

The red clover, *Trifolium pratense*, was designated the state flower of Vermont by legislative act in 1894.[84] The red clover, not native to Vermont, was brought to the United States from Europe.[85] A perennial member of the pea family, it grows wild in fields and meadows. It is also called cowgrass, sugar plum, and honeysuckle clover.[86]

VIRGINIA

The American dogwood, *Cornus florida*, was declared the floral emblem of Virginia by legislative act in 1918.[87] The flowering dogwood is known also as boxwood, white cornel, Indian arrowwood, and nature's mistake. The dogwood is a small tree or large shrub, with greenish yellow flowers and scarlet fruit. Found from Maine to Florida and from Minnesota to Texas, it spruces up the landscape in the fall with its red leaves.[88]

WASHINGTON

The Pink Rhododendron, *Rhododendron macrophyllum* was designated the state flower of Washington by that state's legislature in 1949.[89]

WEST VIRGINIA

The *Rhododendron maximum*, or big laurel, was named the state flower of West Virginia by the legislature in 1903, following a vote by school children.[90] Found from Nova Scotia to Alabama, along streams and in low-lying wooded areas, the big laurel often forms dense thickets. It is also called deer-laurel, cow-plant, rose bay, and spoon-hutch. A tall branching shrub, sometimes a tree, its flowers are rose colored or white, lightly spotted in yellow or orange.[91]

WISCONSIN

The wood violet, *Viola papilionacea*, was officially adopted as the state flower of Wisconsin by legislative act in 1949.[92] The violet won in an election over the wild rose, the trailing arbutus, and the white water lily. After the Arbor Day vote in 1909, the school children's choice was unofficial until voted into law in 1949.[93]

WYOMING

The Indian paintbrush, *Castilleja linariae-folia*, was made the state flower of Wyoming by legislative act in 1917.[94] Other names for this scarlet-leaved member of the figwort family include prairie fire, bloody warrior, and nose-bleed. Parasitic on plant roots, it can be found in meadows and damp thickets from Maine to Wyoming and Texas.[95]

DISTRICT OF COLUMBIA

The District of Columbia commissioners designated the American Beauty rose as the District's official flower on April 17, 1925.[96]

AMERICAN SAMOA

In 1973, the Paogo (Ula-fala) was designated the official flower of American Samoa.[97]

COMMONWEALTH OF THE NORTHERN MARIANA ISLANDS

The Commonwealth designated the Flores Mayo or plumeria (*Plumeria acuminata*) as its official flower in 1986.[98]

GUAM

The official territorial flower of Guam, a local flower called the puti tai nobio, was adopted in 1968. This flower, known also as the bougainvillea, blooms throughout the year on the island.[99]

PUERTO RICO

Puerto Rico has not designated an official flower.

U.S. VIRGIN ISLANDS

In 1950, the *Tecoma stans* was named the official flower of the Virgin Islands. This trumpet-shaped flower is also called the yellow elder or yellow cedar.[100]

NOTES

1. Ala. Code §1–2–11.
2. *Alabama Official and Statistical Register* (Montgomery: Alabama Department of Archives and History, 1979), pp. 24–25.
3. Alaska Stat. §44.09.050.
4. *Alaska Blue Book 1979*, p. 173.
5. Ariz. Rev. Stat. Ann. §41–855.
6. Nathaniel Lord Britton and Addison Brown, *An Illustrated Flora of the Northern United States, Canada and the British Possessions*, 2d ed., rev. and enl. (New York: Scribners, 1913), vol. 2, p. 568.
7. Ark. Stat. Ann. §5–109.
8. Cal. Govt. Code §421 (West).
9. *California's Legislature 1984*, pp. 202–3.
10. Colo. Rev. Stat. §24–80–905.
11. Ibid., §24–80–906, §24–80–907.
12. Ibid., §24–80–908.
13. Conn. Gen. Stat. Ann. §3–108 (West).
14. *State of Connecticut Register and Manual, 1983*, p. 900.
15. Del. Code Ann. tit. 29, §308.
16. *Delaware State Manual, 1975–1976*, p. 14.
17. 1909 Fla. Laws 688; *The State of Florida's Heritage and Emblems* (Tallahassee: Florida Department of State, 1986).
18. Fla. Stat. Ann. §15.0345 (West).
19. Ga. Code Ann. §50–3–53.
20. *The State of Georgia and Its Capitol* (Atlanta: State Museum of Science and Industry, Department of Archives and History, 1979), p. 16.
21. Ga. Code Ann. §50–3–54.
22. Haw. Rev. Stat. §5–9.
23. *Hawaii, The Aloha State* (Honolulu: State of Hawaii, Hawaii Visitors Bureau, Chamber of Commerce of Hawaii, n.d.).
24. Idaho Code §67–4502.
25. *Idaho Blue Book*, 1981–82, p. 209.
26. Ill. Ann. Stat. ch. 1, §3009 (Smith-Hurd).

27. Ind. Code Ann. §1–2–7–1 (West).

28. George Shankle, *State Names, Flags, Seals, Songs, Birds, Flowers, and Other Symbols*, rev. ed. (Westport, Conn.: Greenwood Press, 1970, c 1938), pp. 336–37.

29. Information provided by Indiana State Library, Indianapolis, Indiana.

30. *1985–86 Iowa Official Register*, vol. 61, p. 237.

31. Kan. Stat. Ann. §73–1801.

32. *Kansas Directory, 1984*, p. 128.

33. Ky. Rev. Stat. Ann. §2.090.

34. Britton and Brown, *An Illustrated Flora*, vol. 3, p. 380.

35. La. Rev. Stat. Ann. §49–154 (West); Britton and Brown, *An Illustrated Flora*, vol. 2, pp. 80–83.

36. La. Rev. Stat. Ann. §49–154.1 (West).

37. Me. Rev. Stat. tit. 1, §211.

38. Md. Ann. Code §13–305.

39. Britton and Brown, *An Illustrated Flora*, vol. 3, p. 470.

40. Mass. Laws Ann. ch. 2, §7.

41. Britton and Brown, *An Illustrated Flora*, vol. 2, p. 692.

42. Mich. Comp. Laws Ann. §2.11; §2.81.

43. Minn. Stat. Ann. §1.142 (West).

44. Information provided by the Minnesota Historical Society, St. Paul, Minnesota.

45. 1952 Miss. Laws 465.

46. Mo. Ann. Stat. §10.030 (Vernon).

47. *Official Manual, State of Missouri, 1975–1976*, p. 1439.

48. Mont. Code Ann. §1–1–503.

49. Rex C. Myers, *Symbols of Montana* (Helena: Montana Historical Society, 1976), p. 12.

50. 1895 Neb. Laws 441.

51. Britton and Brown, *An Illustrated Flora*, vol. 3, p. 394.

52. Nev. Rev. Stat. §235.050.

53. Britton and Brown, *An Illustrated Flora*, vol. 3, p. 530.

54. N.H. Rev. Stat. Ann. §3:5; *Manual for the General Court, 1981*.

55. N.H. Rev. Stat. Ann. §3:17.

56. N.J. Stat. Ann. §52:9 A-2 (West).

57. N.M. Stat. Ann. §12–3–4.

58. *New Mexico Blue Book 1977–1978*, p. 86.

59. N.Y. State Law §75 (McKinney).

60. N.C. Gen. Stat. §145–1.

61. N.D. Cent. Code §54–02–03.

62. Britton and Brown, *An Illustrated Flora*, vol. 2, p. 283.

63. Ohio Rev. Code Ann. §5.02 (Page); Ohio Almanac (Lorain: Lorain Journal Company, 1977), p. 60.

64. Ohio Rev. Code Ann. §5.021 (Baldwin).

65. Okla. Stat. Ann. tit. 25, §92, §92–1 (West).

66. Britton and Brown, *An Illustrated Flora*, vol. 1, p. 639.

67. Or. Rev. Stat. Ann. §186.

68. Britton and Brown, *An Illustrated Flora*, vol. 2, p. 128.

69. Pa. Stat. Ann. tit. 71, §1006 (Purdon).

70. *Pennsylvania Symbols* (Harrisburg: House of Representatives, n.d.).

71. R.I. Gen. Laws §42–4–9.

72. Britton and Brown, *An Illustrated Flora*, vol. 2, p. 547.

73. *South Carolina State Symbols and Emblems* (Columbia: House of Representatives, n.d.).

74. S.D. Codified Laws Ann. §1–6–10.

75. *South Dakota Legislative Manual, 1981*, p. 145.

76. Britton and Brown, *An Illustrated Flora*, vol. 2, p. 102.

77. Tenn. Code Ann. §4–1–306.

78. Ibid., §4–1–307.

79. *Tennessee Blue Book, 1985–1986*, p. 342.

80. Tex. Rev. Civ. Stat. Ann. art. 6143b (Vernon).

81. Britton and Brown, *An Illustrated Flora*, vol. 2, p. 347.

82. Utah Code Ann. §63–13–6.

83. Britton and Brown, *An Illustrated Flora*, vol. 1, p. 508.

84. Vt. Stat. Ann. tit. 1, §498.

85. *Vermont Legislative Directory and State Manual, 1979–80*, p. 15.

86. Britton and Brown, *An Illustrated Flora*, vol. 2, p. 355.

87. Va. Code §7.1–38.

88. Britton and Brown, *An Illustrated Flora*, vol. 2, p. 664.

89. Wash. Rev. Code Ann. §1.20.030.

90. *West Virginia Blue Book, 1980*, p. 925.

91. Britton and Brown, *An Illustrated Flora,* vol. 2, p. 681.

92. Wis. Stat. Ann. §1.10 (West).

93. *State of Wisconsin, 1983–1984 Blue Book,* p. 948.

94. Wyo. Stat. Ann. §8–3–104.

95. Britton and Brown, *An Illustrated Flora,* vol. 3, p. 214.

96. *Symbols of the District of Columbia* (Washington, D.C.: Government of the District of Columbia, Office of the Secretariat, Office of Visual Information Management, n.d.).

97. A.S. Code tit. 1, §1103.

98. C.M.C. tit. 1, §232.

99. Guam Code Ann. tit. 1, §1022.

100. V.I. Code Ann. tit. 1, §102.

7

State and Territory Trees

In 1919, Texas became the first state to select a state tree, the pecan. All of the other states have since chosen state trees, and one state, New Jersey, has named a state tree and a state memorial tree.

Out of the thirty-five trees designated by the states, the white oak and the sugar maple tie for first place. Each was named the state tree for four states. Connecticut, Maryland, Illinois, and Iowa named the white oak their state tree. Iowa, in fact, designated all species of the oak. New York, Vermont, West Virginia, and Wisconsin selected the sugar maple. Tying for second place in popularity are the southern pine, designated by Alabama, Arkansas, and North Carolina, and the dogwood, named by Missouri, Virginia, and New Jersey. New Jersey named the dogwood its state memorial tree.

Two states chose the American elm (Massachusetts and North Dakota), the white pine (Maine and Michigan), the cottonwood (Kansas and Nebraska), the palmetto (Florida and South Carolina), the blue spruce (Colorado and Utah), and the tulip poplar (Indiana and Tennessee).

Probably the most frequently cited reason for the selection of a particular state tree is the part that tree played in the early history of a state. The palmetto was used to build colonial forts off the coast of South Carolina. The live oak was used to construct homes by early Georgia settlers. In Tennessee, the tulip poplar was used to construct homesteads and barns. The white oak was chosen by Connecticut in remembrance of a famous tree, the Charter Oak, and its role in the American fight for independence. Kansas recognized the cottonwood planted by pioneers.

New Hampshire's white birch, Maine's white pine, and Oregon's Douglas fir, are but a few examples of trees that are strongly identified with a particular state and, therefore, have been made state emblems. Delaware is proud of the many ornamental uses of its state tree, the American holly.

ALABAMA

The southern longleaf pine was designated the official tree of Alabama in 1949.[1]

Scientific name: *Pinus palustris* Mill.

Synonyms: Longleaf yellow pine, pitch pine, hard pine, heart pine, turpentine pine, rosemary pine, brown pine, fat pine, longstraw pine, longleaf pitch pine.

Native to: South Atlantic and Gulf coastal plains.

Physical description: The southern longleaf pine is a large tree with coarsely scaly, orange-brown bark and slender dark green needles, three in a cluster and from 10 to 15 inches long. The large cones are from 5 to 10 inches long and are dull brown and prickly.

The bill does not specify which species was intended, even though twelve exist in Alabama. However, the person who introduced the bill, Hugh Kaul of Birmingham, has stated that he meant the longleaf pine.[2]

ALASKA

The Sitka spruce, *Picea sitchensis*, became the official tree of Alaska by legislative act in 1962.[3]

Scientific name: *Picea sitchensis* (Bong.) Carr.

Synonyms: Yellow spruce, tideland spruce, western spruce, silver spruce, coast spruce, Menzies' spruce.

Native to: Pacific coast region north to Canada and Alaska.

Physical description: The bark on this large to very large tree is reddish brown and thin with loosely attached scales. The flat, dark green needles are from ⅝ to 1 inch long, and the light orange-brown cones are from 2 to 3½ inches long with long stiff scales.

ARIZONA

The paloverde, genus *cercidium*, was adopted as the state tree of Arizona in 1954.[4]

Scientific name: *Cercidium torreyanum* (Wats.) Sargent.

Synonym: Green barked Acacia.

Native to: Southern California and Arizona; south into Mexico.

Physical description: The bark of this short, stout tree is yellow to yellow green. Leaves are oblong in shape and paired with two or three leaflets on each side. Soon after the leaves mature in March or April, they fall, making the tree bare of leaves the rest of the year. The brilliant yellow-gold flowers bloom in early spring, and the pod-shaped fruit ripens in July.

ARKANSAS

The pine tree was designated the state tree of Arkansas in 1939.[5] See the Alabama entry for a description.

CALIFORNIA

Two species of the California redwood, *Sequoia sempervirens* and *Sequoia gigantea*, were named the official state trees of California in 1937.[6]

Scientific names: *Sequoia sempervirens* (D. Don) Endl. and *Sequoiadendron giganteum (Lindl.) Buchholz.*

Synonyms: Coast redwood and redwood for the first variety; giant sequoia, bigtree, Sierra redwood, and mammoth tree for the second.

Native to: The coast redwood is native to the Pacific coast of California and southwestern Oregon. The giant sequoia is native to the Sierra Nevada in California.

Physical description: The coast redwood is the world's largest species. Its reddish-brown bark is thick, deeply furrowed, and fibrous. The leaves are scalelike and needlelike, flat, slightly curved, and unequal in length ranging from ¼ to ¾ of an inch. They are dark green, spreading in two rows. The reddish-brown cones are from ¾ to 1 inch long and mature in the first year.

The giant sequoia's bark is reddish brown, thick, deeply furrowed, and fibrous. The tree is swollen at the base. The cones range from 1¾ to 2¾ inches in length, are reddish brown, and mature the second year. The leaves are from ⅛ to ¼ inch long and may grow from leading shoots ½ inch long. The blue-green, sharply pointed leaves grow all around the twig and overlap.

The tallest known *sequoia sempervirens* is 364 feet high. Protected by the state, which matched monies raised by the Save-the-Redwoods League, they are allowed to grow uncut in designated groves.[7]

Located in thirty-two groves on the western slopes of the Sierra Nevada mountains, the *sequoia gigantea* was voted the United States tree by school children across the United States. The largest of these trees, nicknamed "General Sherman" is 36½ feet in diameter, and it is estimated that it could supply enough lumber to build forty houses.[8] It is estimated that this tree is from 3,000 to 4,000 years old.[9]

COLORADO

The unofficial state tree of Colorado is the blue spruce, as designated in 1939.[10]

Scientific name: *Picea pungens* Engelm.

Synonyms: Colorado blue spruce, balsam, Colorado spruce, prickly spruce, white spruce, silver spruce, Parry's spruce.

Native to: Rocky Mountain region.

Physical description: The four-angled needles of the blue spruce are from ¾ to 1⅛ inches long and are dull blue green. This large tree has gray or brown bark that is furrowed into scaly ridges. Cones are from 2½ to 4 inches long and are light brown with long, thin, irregularly toothed scales.

CONNECTICUT

The white oak, *Quercus alba*, was designated the state tree of Connecticut in 1947.[11]

Scientific name: *Quercus alba* Linn.

Synonym: Stave oak.

Native to: Eastern half of United States and adjacent Canada.

Physical description: The white oak is a large tree with light gray bark, fissured into scaly ridges. The smooth leaves are oblong, from 4 to 9 inches long, and are deeply or shallowly 5 to 9 lobed. They are bright green above, pale or whitish beneath, and turn a deep red in the fall. The acorns are from ¾ to 1 inch long, with shallow cups.

The Charter Oak, a famous oak of the colonial period, was the inspiration for the oak tree's being named the state tree of Connecticut. In 1687 the Charter Oak was a hiding place for a charter earlier given to the General Court of Connecticut by King Charles II that was rescinded twenty-five years later by King James II. The colonists were not eager to return the charter to James's emissary, and, while they were seated at a table holding the charter, the candles went out. When they were re-lit, the charter was gone.[12]

DELAWARE

The American holly, *Ilex opaca Aiton*, was adopted as the state tree of Delaware in 1939.[13]

Scientific name: *Ilex opaca* Ait.

Synonyms: Holly, white holly, evergreen holly, boxwood.

Native to: Atlantic and Gulf coasts; Mississippi valley region.

Physical description: A medium-sized to large tree, the American holly's bark is light gray, thin, and smoothish, with wart-like projections. The evergreen elliptical leaves are from 2 to 4 inches long and are coarsely spring toothed, stiff, and leathery. They are green above and yellowish green beneath. The small male and female flowers, which are on different trees, are greenish white. Spherical in shape, the red berrylike fruit is from ¼ to ⅜ of an inch in diameter.

Holly boughs with their colorful red berries make attractive and lucrative Christmas decorations. It is for this reason that the holly tree is considered one of Delaware's most treasured trees.[14]

FLORIDA

The sabal palmetto palm, known also as the cabbage palm, was designated the state tree of Florida in 1953. This act declares further that such designation should not be construed to limit the use of this tree in any way for commercial purposes.[15]

Scientific name: *Sabal palmetto* (Walt.) Lodd.

Synonyms: Cabbage palmetto, palmetto, tree palmetto, Bank's palmetto.

Native to: South Atlantic to Gulf coasts from North Carolina to Florida.

Physical description: The trunk of this medium-sized palm tree is stout and unbranched, grayish brown, roughened or ridged, with a cluster of large leaves at the top. The 4- to 7-foot-long evergreen leaves are coarse, fan-shaped, thick, and leathery, much folded and divided into narrow segments with threadlike fibers hanging between. Leafstalks are from 5 to 8 feet long. Fruits are numerous in a much-branched cluster about 7 feet long and are black, ⅜ to ½ inch in diameter, and one seeded.

GEORGIA

The live oak was adopted as the official tree emblematic of the state of Georgia in 1937.[16]

Scientific name: *Quercus virginiana* Mill.

Synonyms: Chêne Vert.

Native to: South Atlantic and Gulf coast regions, lower California, southern Mexico, Central America, and Cuba.

Physical description: The live oak is a medium-sized widespreading tree. Its bark is dark brown, furrowed, and slightly scaly. The leaves are evergreen, shiny dark green above and whitish hairy beneath. They are elliptical or oblong, 2 to 5 inches long, and usually rounded at the apex; their edges are usually smooth and rolled under. There are from one to five acorns on stalks ½ to 3 inches long. The narrow acorns are from ¾ to 1 inch long and have deep cups.

The Edmund Burke Chapter of the Daughters of the American Revolution first introduced the native oak as a candidate for state tree. Many of the earlier settlers lived along the coast or on islands where the oak was plentiful. A few of the better known Georgians who seemed appreciative of the tree's beauty were James Oglethorpe, John Wesley, and Sidney Lanier.[17]

HAWAII

The *kukui* tree, *Aleurites moluccana*, which is also known as the candlenut tree, was designated the official tree of Hawaii in 1959.[18]

Scientific name: *Aleurites moluccana* (L.) Willd.

Physical description: The sharply pointed or regularly shaped leaves are greyish green due to a grey fur adorning the surface of the leaf, which is especially pronounced beneath. The five-petalled flowers are small, forming delicate white clusters. The nuts are edible if roasted. The fruits were also once used for torch oil.[19]

IDAHO

The white pine, *Pinus monticola*, was declared the state tree of Idaho in 1935.[20]

Scientific name: *Pinus monticola* Dougl.

Synonyms: Western white pine, Idaho white pine, finger-cone pine, mountain pine, little sugar pine, mountain Weymouth pine.

Native to: Northern Rocky Mountain and Pacific coast regions, including southern British Columbia.

Physical description: The bark on this large tree is gray, thin, and smoothish, becoming fissured into rectangular, scaly plates. The blue-green needles are stout, from 2 to 4 inches long, and are five in a cluster. The cones are long stalked, from 5 to 12 inches long, and yellow brown with thin, rounded scales.

ILLINOIS

Following a vote of school children the Illinois legislature, in 1908, declared the native oak to be the official state tree. Since at least two oaks are native to Illinois, however, another selection was held among school children, this time between the northern red oak and the white oak. The white oak won, and, in 1973, the legislature officially designated the white oak as the official tree of Illinois.[21] See the Connecticut entry for a description.

INDIANA

The tulip tree, *Liriodendron tulipifera*, was designated the official state tree of Indiana in 1931.[22]

Scientific name: *Liriodendron tulipifera* L.

Synonyms: Yellow poplar, blue poplar, hickory poplar, basswood, cucumber tree, tulipwood, whitewood, white poplar, poplar, old-wife's-shirt-tree.

Native to: Eastern third of the United States and southern Ontario.

Physical description: The tallest eastern hardwood, the tulip tree's bark is brown, becoming thick and deeply furrowed. The unusually shaped leaves are squarish with a broad, slightly notched or nearly straight apex and two or three lobes on each side. They are from 3 to 6 inches long and are shiny dark green above and pale green beneath. The flowers are large and tulip shaped, from 1½ to 2 inches in diameter, and usually green except in the spring when they are orange. The fruit is conelike, from 2½ to 3 inches long and ½ inch thick.

IOWA

The oak, *Quercus spp.*, was officially designated as the state tree of Iowa in 1961.[23] See the Connecticut and New Jersey entries for descriptions.

KANSAS

The cottonwood was designated the official tree of Kansas in 1937.[24]

Scientific name: *Populus deltoides* Bartr.

Synonyms: Eastern poplar, Carolina poplar, eastern cottonwood, necklace poplar, big cottonwood, Vermont poplar, whitewood, cotton tree, yellow cottonwood.

Native to: Eastern half of the United States and adjacent Canada.

Physical description: A large tree, the cottonwood's bark is at first yellowish green and smooth, becoming gray and deeply furrowed. The leaves are triangular, from 3 to 6 inches long, and wide, long pointed, and coarsely toothed with curved teeth. The smooth leaves are light green and shiny.

The cottonwood has been termed the pioneer tree of Kansas because many homesteaders planted cottonwood. The cottonwood flourished giving the settlers the courage to continue and to lay claim to the land.[25]

KENTUCKY

The coffee tree was the state tree from 1976 until 1994, when the tulip poplar was named the state tree. See description under Indiana.[26]

LOUISIANA

The bald cypress, *Taxodium distichum*, commonly called the cypress tree, was designated the official state tree of Louisiana in 1963.[27]

Scientific name: *Taxodium distichum* (L.) Rich.

Synonyms: Southern cypress, red cypress, yellow cypress, white cypress, black cypress, gulf cypress, swamp cypress, deciduous cypress, tidewater red cypress.

Native to: Swamps and riverbanks of the South Atlantic and Gulf coastal plains and the Mississippi valley.

Physical description: The bald cypress is a large tree with a swollen base and "knees." The bark is reddish brown or gray with long fibrous or scaly ridges. The leaves are light yellow green, whitish beneath, and are crowded featherlike in two rows on slender horizontal twigs. They are flat, from ⅜ to ¾ of an inch long, and are shed in the fall. The cones are from ¾ to 1 inch in diameter with hard scales.

MAINE

The white pine was named the official tree of Maine in 1959.[28]

Scientific name: *Pinus strobus* Linn.

Synonyms: Eastern white pine, northern white pine, soft pine, Weymouth pine, spruce pine.

Native to: Northeastern United States, adjacent Canada, and the Appalachian Mountain region.

Physical description: The largest northeastern conifer, the white pine's bark is gray or purplish and is deeply fissured into broad ridges. Its slender needles are blue green, from 2½ to 5 inches long, and grow five in a cluster. The cones are long stalked, narrow, from 4 to 8 inches long, and yellow brown with thin, rounded scales.

MARYLAND

The white oak, *Quercus alba*, was declared the arboreal emblem of Maryland in 1941.[29] See the Connecticut entry for a description.

MASSACHUSETTS

The American elm, *Ulmus americana*, was named the state tree of Massachusetts in 1941.[30]

Scientific name: *Ulmus americana* Linn.

Synonyms: White elm, soft elm, water elm, gray elm, swamp elm, rock elm, Orme Maigre.

Native to: Eastern half of the United States and adjacent Canada.

Physical description: The American elm is a large, spreading tree with gray bark that is deeply furrowed with broad, forking, scaly ridges. Twigs are soft and hairy, becoming smooth, not corky winged. Fruits are elliptical and flat, from ⅜ to ½ inch long. Leaves are in two rows, elliptical, from 3 to 6 inches long, and coarsely and doubly toothed with unequal teeth. The two sides of the leaf are unequal. They are dark green and smooth or slightly rough above, and pale and usually soft and hairy beneath.

MICHIGAN

The white pine, *Pinus strobus*, was adopted as the official state tree of Michigan in 1955.[31] See the Maine entry for a description.

MINNESOTA

The red pine or Norway pine, *Pinus resinosa*, was designated the official state tree of Minnesota in 1953.[32]

Scientific name: *Pinus resinosa* Ait.

Synonyms: Canadian red pine, hard pine.

Native to: Northeastern United States and adjacent Canada.

Physical description: A medium-sized to large tree, the red pine has reddish-brown bark with broad, flat, scaly plates. Needles are two in a cluster, dark green and slender, from 5 to 6 inches long. Cones are 2 inches long and light brown without prickles.

MISSISSIPPI

The magnolia or evergreen magnolia, *Magnolia grandiflora*, was designated the state tree of Mississippi in 1938.[33]

Scientific name: *Magnolia grandiflora* Linn.

Synonyms: Big laurel, bull bay, great laurel magnolia, bat-tree, laurel-leaved magnolia, large-flowered magnolia, laurel bay.

Native to: South Atlantic and Gulf coastal plains.

Physical description: A medium-sized to large tree, the magnolia has gray to light brown bark, broken into small, thin scales. Leaves are evergreen, oblong or elliptical, from 5 to 8 inches long, short pointed, and leathery with smooth edges. They are shiny bright green and smooth above, rusty and hairy beneath. The flowers are cup shaped, from 6 to 8 inches across, white and fragrant during spring and summer. The fruit is conelike, from 3 to 4 inches long, from 1½ to 2½ inches thick, rusty and hairy.

MISSOURI

The flowering dogwood, *Cornus florida*, was declared the arboreal emblem of Missouri in 1955.[34]

Scientific name: *Cornus florida* Linn.

Synonyms: Dogwood, boxwood, false box-dogwood, New England boxwood, flowering cornel, cornel.

Native to: Eastern half of the United States and southern Ontario.

Physical description: A small tree, the flowering dogwood's bark is dark reddish brown, broken into small square or rounded blocks. The leaves are paired, elliptical or oval, from 3 to 6 inches long, and short pointed; their edges appear to be smooth but are minutely toothed. They are bright green and nearly smooth above, whitish and slightly hairy beneath; and they turn bright scarlet above in the fall. The greenish-yellow flowers grow in a dense head with four showy, white, petal-like bracts from 2¼ to 4 inches in diameter, and bloom in the early spring. The egg-shaped fruits are ⅜ inch long, bright scarlet, shiny, fleshy, and 1 or 2 seeded.

MONTANA

The ponderosa pine was designated the official state tree of Montana in 1949.[35]

Scientific name: *Pinus ponderosa* Laws.

Synonyms: Western yellow pine, western soft pine, yellow pine, bull pine, foothills yellow pine, red pine, big pine, long-leaved pine, pitch pine, heavy-wooded pine, heavy pine, Sierra brownbark pine, Montana black pine.

Native to: Rocky Mountains and Pacific coast regions, including adjacent Canada; southward to western Texas and Mexico.

Physical description: The ponderosa pine is a large tree with brown or blackish bark, furrowed into ridges. On older trunks, the bark is yellow brown and irregularly fissured into large, flat, scaly plates. The needles are three, or two and three, in a cluster, stout, from 4 to 7 inches long, and dark green. The cones are from 3 to 6 inches long and short stalked with prickly scales, and they are light reddish brown.

NEBRASKA

The cottonwood was declared the state tree of Nebraska in 1972.[36] See the Kansas entry for a description.

NEVADA

The single-leaf piñon, *Pinus monophylla*, was designated the official state tree of Nevada in 1953. In 1987, the bristlecone pine, *Pinus longaeva*, was also named the official state tree. The first state tree is described below and illustrated.[37]

Scientific name: *Pinus monophylla* Torr. and Frém.

Synonyms: Nut pine, pinyon, gray pine, Nevada nut pine, singleleaf pinyon pine.

Native to: Great Basin region to California.

Physical description: The single-leaf piñon is a small tree with dark brown bark, furrowed into scaly ridges. The needles are one per sheath, stout, from 1 to 2 inches long, and gray green. The egg-shaped cones are light brown with stout, blunt scales and are from 2 to 2½ inches long. The large, edible seeds, ¾ inch long, are commonly known as pinyon nuts.

NEW HAMPSHIRE

The white birch, *Betula papyrifera*, was named the state tree of New Hampshire in 1947.[38]

Scientific name: *Betula papyrifera* Marsh.

Synonyms: Canoe birch, silver birch, paper birch, large white birch.

Native to: Northeastern United States; across Canada to Alaska; northern Rocky Mountain region.

Physical description: A medium-sized to large tree, the white birch has smooth, thin, white bark, separating into papery strips. Leaves are oval, from 2 to 4 inches long, long pointed and wedge shaped or rounded at the base. They are coarsely and usually doubly toothed, mostly with five to nine main veins on each side, dull dark green and smooth above, and light yellow green and smooth or slightly hairy beneath. The cones are narrow, from 1½ to 2 inches long and ⅜ inch wide, and hang from slender stalks.

The New Hampshire Federation of Garden Clubs recommended that the white birch be designated the state tree for the obvious reason that it is natively so abundant throughout the state. This graceful and beautiful tree had the practical historical use learned by every school child—its bark was used by Indians to construct their canoes.[39]

NEW JERSEY

The northern red oak was designated the official state tree of New Jersey in 1950.[40]

Scientific name: Quercus rubra Linn.

Synonyms: Red oak, black oak, Spanish oak.

Native to: Eastern half of the United States except the southern border; adjacent Canada.

Physical description: The northern red oak is a large tree with dark brown bark, fissured into broad, flat ridges. The leaves are from 5 to 9 inches long, oblong, and seven to eleven lobed less than halfway to the middle; the lobes have a few irregular bristle-pointed teeth. The smooth leaves are a dull dark green above and pale yellow green beneath, and they turn red in the fall. Acorns have either a shallow or deep cup and are from 5/8 to 1 1/8 inch long.

The dogwood was designated the state memorial tree in 1951 by Assembly Concurrent Resolution No. 12.[41] See the Missouri entry for a description of the dogwood.

NEW MEXICO

The nut pine or piñon, *Pinus edulis*, was adopted as the official state tree of New Mexico in 1948.[42]

Scientific name: Pinus edulis Engelm.

Synonyms: Nut pine, pinyon pine, Colorado pinyon pine, New Mexico piñon.

Native to: Southern Rocky Mountain region and adjacent Mexico.

Physical description: A small tree, the nut pine has reddish-brown bark, furrowed into scaly ridges. The needles are two (sometimes three) in a cluster, stout, from 3/4 to 1 1/2 inches long, and dark green. The egg-shaped cones are from 1 1/2 to 2 inches long and light brown with stout, blunt scales and large, edible seeds 1/2 inch long and known as pinyon nuts.

As long ago as the 1500s, when the Spanish first came to New Mexico, they noticed that the piñon nut was a popular food item. People still watch for the periodic over-abundant years when there are enough piñons for everyone who is willing to spend some effort to gather them. A close runner-up, the aspen, lost to the piñon after the New Mexico Federation of Women's Clubs selected the piñon for nomination to the state legislature.[43]

NEW YORK

The sugar maple, *Acer saccharum*, was designated the official tree of New York in 1956.[44]

Scientific name: Acer saccharum Marsh.

Synonyms: Hard maple, rock maple, sugar maple, black maple.

Native to: Eastern half of the United States and adjacent Canada.

Physical description: The sugar maple is a large tree with gray bark, furrowed into irregular ridges or scales. The leaves are paired, heart shaped, with three or five lobes, long pointed and sparingly, coarsely toothed. From 3 to 5 1/2 inches in diameter, they are dark green above and light green and usually smooth beneath, turning yellow, orange, or scarlet in the fall. The fruits, 1 to 1 1/4 inches long, mature in the fall.

NORTH CAROLINA

The pine tree was adopted as the official state tree of North Carolina in 1963.[45] See the Alabama entry for a description.

NORTH DAKOTA

The American elm, *Ulmus americana*, was designated the official tree of North Dakota in 1947.[46] See the Massachusetts entry for a description.

OHIO

The buckeye tree, *Aesculus glabra*, was adopted as the official tree of Ohio in 1953.[47]

Scientific name: Aesculus glabra Willd.

Synonyms: Ohio buckeye, fetid buckeye, stinking buckeye, American horse chestnut.

Native to: Midwestern United States, chiefly Ohio and Mississippi valley regions.

Physical description: The buckeye is a small to medium-sized tree with gray bark, much furrowed and broken into scaly plates. The leaves are paired together with leafstalks from 4 to 6 inches long. Leaflets are five per leafstalk, from 3 to 5 inches long, long pointed, narrowed at the base, and finely toothed. (The shrubby variety of the buckeye tree has from five to seven leaflets.) The showy flowers grow in branched clusters, from 4 to 6 inches long, and are pale greenish yellow with petals nearly as long as the flower, or from ¾ to 1¼ inches long. The one or two poisonous seeds are from 1 to 1½ inches wide and are encased in a prickly fruiting capsule from 1¼ to 2 inches in diameter.

The buckeye got its name because the Indians thought the seed of the tree looked like the "eye of a buck"; in the Indian, the *hetuck*.[48]

OKLAHOMA

The redbud tree, *Cercis canadensis*, was adopted as the official tree of Oklahoma in 1937.[49]

Scientific name: Cercis canadensis Linn.

Synonyms: Judas tree, red Judas tree, saladtree, Canadian Judas tree.

Native to: North central and eastern United States.

Physical description: A small tree, the redbud branches at 10 to 15 feet from the ground and forms a narrow and erect or a spreading, flattened, or rounded head. An ornamental tree, it flowers in late February to April in a profusion of small, light pink to purple blossoms.

OREGON

The Douglas fir, *Pseudotsuga menziessi*, was declared the official state tree of Oregon in 1939.[50]

Scientific name: Pseudotsuga menziessi (Mirb.) Franco.

Synonyms: Douglas spruce, red fir, yellow fir, Oregon pine, red pine, Puget Sound pine, spruce, fir, Douglas tree, corkbarked Douglas spruce.

Native to: Pacific coast and Rocky Mountain region, including Canada and Mexico.

Physical description: The Douglas fir is a very large tree, next to the giant sequoia and the redwood in size. The bark is reddish brown, thick, and deeply furrowed into broad ridges. The dark yellow-green or blue-green needles are short stalked, flat, and from ¾ to 1¼ inches long. The cones are from 2 to 4 inches long and light brown with thin, rounded scales and long, three-toothed bracts.

The Douglas fir was chosen as the state tree because Oregon is the major supplier of this indispensable lumber tree. Because its wood is relatively lightweight when compared with its strength, it is considered one of the foremost trees in the world for its lumber.[51]

PENNSYLVANIA

The hemlock tree, *Tsuga canadensis*, was adopted as the state tree of Pennsylvania in 1931.[52]

Scientific name: *Tsuga canadensis* (Linn.) Carr.

Synonyms: Eastern hemlock, Canadian hemlock, hemlock spruce, spruce pine, New England hemlock, spruce.

Native to: Northeastern United States, adjacent Canada, and the Appalachian Mountain region to northern Alabama and Georgia.

Physical description: The hemlock tree is a medium-sized to large tree with brown or purplish bark, deeply furrowed into broad, scaly ridges. The needles are short stalked, flat, soft, blunt pointed, and from ⅜ to ⅝ inch long. They are shiny dark green above and lighter beneath, appearing in two rows. The cones are brownish and from ⅝ to ¾ inch long.

RHODE ISLAND

The red maple, *Acer rubrum*, was designated the state tree of Rhode Island in 1964.[53]

Scientific name: *Acer rubrum* Linn.

Synonyms: Soft maple, water maple, scarlet maple, white maple, swamp maple, shoepeg maple, erable.

Native to: Eastern half of the United States and adjacent Canada; west to the Dakotas, Texas, and Nebraska.

Physical description: A large tree with a large trunk, the red maple's bark is gray, thin, smooth, and broken into long, thin scales. The twigs are reddish, and the leaves are dark green and shiny above, whitish and slightly hairy beneath, turning scarlet or yellow in the fall. The leaves are paired, heart shaped, from 2½ to 4 inches long, and three to five lobed. The lobes are short pointed and are irregularly and sharply toothed. The fruits, ¾ inch long, mature in the spring.

SOUTH CAROLINA

The palmetto tree, *Inodes palmetto*, was adopted as the official tree of South Carolina in 1939.[54] See the Florida entry for a description.

Palmetto logs, used in the construction of the fort on Sullivan's Island, helped withstand the British attack during the American Revolution. For this reason, the palmetto has been memorialized as the state tree and appears on both the flag and the seal.[55]

SOUTH DAKOTA

The Black Hills spruce, *Picea glauca densata*, was named the state tree of South Dakota in 1947.[56]

Scientific name: *Picea glauca* (Moench) Voss.

Synonyms: White spruce, single spruce, bog spruce, skunk spruce, cat spruce, spruce, pine, double spruce.

Native to: Northeastern United States, Black Hills, Canada, Alaska.

Physical description: The Black Hills spruce is a medium-sized tree with thin and scaly gray or brown bark. The blue-green needles are four-angled, from ½ to ¾ inch long, and of disagreeable odor when crushed. The cones are slender, from 1½ to 2 inches long, pale brown, and shiny with scales that are thin, flexible, and rounded with smooth margins.

TENNESSEE

The tulip poplar, *Liriodendron tulipifera*, was designated the official state tree of Tennessee in 1947.[57] See the Indiana entry for a description.

The tulip poplar is plentiful throughout the state of Tennessee. Early settlers found it particularly useful for dwelling and barn construction.[58]

TEXAS

The pecan tree was designated the state tree of Texas in 1919. An amendment in 1927 made it the duty of the State Board of Control 69 the State Parks Board "to give due consideration to the pecan tree when planning beautification of state parks or other public property belonging to the state."[59]

Scientific name: *Carya illinoensis* (Wangenh.) K. Koch.

Synonyms: Pecan nut, pecanier, pecan (hickory).

Native to: Mississippi valley region, Texas, and Mexico.

Physical description: A large tree, the pecan tree has deeply and irregularly furrowed and cracked light brown or gray bark. The compound leaves are from 12 to 20 inches long. The leaflets number from eleven to seventeen and are short stalked, lance shaped, and slightly sickle-shaped. They

are from 2 to 7 inches long, long pointed, finely toothed, smooth, and slightly hairy. The nuts are slightly four winged, oblong, and pointed, and they have thin husks. From 1 to 2 inches long, they are sweet and edible.

UTAH

The blue spruce was designated the Utah state tree in 1933.[60] See the Colorado entry for a description.

VERMONT

The sugar maple was named the state tree of Vermont in 1949.[61] See the New York entry for a description.

VIRGINIA

The flowering dogwood was designated the state tree of Virginia in 1956.[62] See the Missouri entry for a description.

WASHINGTON

The western hemlock, *Tsuga heterophylla*, was designated the official tree of the state of Washington in 1947.[63]

Scientific name: *Tsuga heterophylla* (Raf.) Sargent.

Synonyms: West coast hemlock, Pacific hemlock, hemlock spruce, California hemlock spruce, western hemlock fir, Prince Albert's fir, Alaska pine.

Native to: Pacific coast and northern Rocky Mountain regions north to Canada and Alaska.

Physical description: The western hemlock is a large tree with reddish-brown bark, deeply furrowed into broad, flat ridges. The needles are short stalked, flat, from ¼ to ¾ inch long, and shiny dark green above and lighter beneath. The brownish cones are from ¾ to 1 inch long.

WEST VIRGINIA

The sugar maple, *Acer saccharum* Marsh., was designated the state tree of West Virginia in 1949.[64] See the New York entry for a description.

Because it is used in furniture building and is enjoyed for its maple syrup, the state's school children and civic clubs voted to recommend the sugar maple as West Virginia's state tree.[65]

WISCONSIN

The sugar maple, *Acer saccharum*, was designated the official state tree of Wisconsin in 1949.[66] See the New York entry for a description.

Wisconsin's school children recommended the sugar maple by popular vote in 1948. Though others tried to overrule the 1948 vote by lobbying for the white pine, the legislature followed the recommendation of the Youth Centennial Committee vote.[67]

WYOMING

The cottonwood tree, *Populus sargentii*, was designated the state tree of Wyoming in 1947 and 1961.[68]

Scientific name: *Populus deltoides* var. *occidentalis* Ryb.; *P. sargentii* Dode is the name given in the state law.

Synonyms: Plains cottonwood, plains poplar.

Native to: Great plains and eastern border of Rocky Mountains north into Canada.

Physical description: The plains cottonwood is a large tree with gray, deeply furrowed bark. The leaves are smooth, light green, shiny, and broadly oval. They are often

wider than long, from 3 to 4 inches long and wide, long pointed, and coarsely toothed with curved teeth. The leafstalks are flat.

DISTRICT OF COLUMBIA

The commissioners declared the scarlet oak to be the official tree of the District on November 8, 1960. This particular oak tree is known for its brilliant color in fall and it can be seen throughout the area around the nation's capital.[69]

AMERICAN SAMOA

American Samoa has designated the Paogo or Pandanus tree as the territorial tree. Samoan chiefs wear necklaces made from the seeds of this tree and its leaves are used to weave mats, baskets, and other items.[70]

COMMONWEALTH OF THE NORTHERN MARIANA ISLANDS

The Commonwealth designated the Trongkon Atbot or flame tree, *Delonix regia*, as its official tree in 1986.[71] Also known as the flamboyant, this tree, as its name suggests, is a beautiful ornamental that may reach almost twenty feet and sports a flat crown adorned by clusters of flowers each with five petals. Four of the petals of each flower are scarlet, one is white, and each flower is about four inches wide.

GUAM

Guam declared the ifit, *Intsia bijuga*, its official tree in 1969. This tree, a member of the ironwood family, was used frequently to build homes on the island and thus symbolizes the strength of the family.[72]

PUERTO RICO

Puerto Rico has not designated an official tree.

U.S. VIRGIN ISLANDS

The U.S. Virgin Islands has not designated an official tree.

NOTES

1. Ala. Code §1–2–12.
2. *Alabama State Emblems* (Montgomery: Alabama State Department of Archives and History, n.d.).
3. Alaska Stat. §44.09.070.
4. Ariz. Rev. Stat. Ann. §41–856.
5. *State Trees and Arbor Days* (Washington, D.C.: Government Printing Office, 1981), p. 4; 1939 Ark. Acts, 1092.
6. Cal. Govt. Code §422 (West).
7. *State Emblems* (Sacramento: Secretary of State, n.d.).
8. Ibid.
9. *California's Legislature, 1984*, p. 204.
10. *State Trees and Arbor Days*, p. 5.
11. Conn. Gen. Stat. Ann. §3–110 (West).
12. *State of Connecticut Register and Manual, 1983*, p. 907.
13. Del. Code Ann. tit. 29, §305.
14. *Discover Wonderful Delaware!* (Dover: Delaware State Development Department, n.d.).
15. Fla. Stat. Ann. §15.031 (West).
16. Ga. Code Ann. §50–3–55.
17. *The State of Georgia and Its Capitol* (Atlanta: State Museum of Science and Industry, Department of Archives and History, 1979), p. 15.
18. Haw. Rev. Stat. §5–8.
19. Loraine E. Kuck and Richard C. Tongg, *Hawaiian Flowers and Flowering Trees: A Guide to Tropical and Semitropical Flora* (Rutland, Vt.: Charles E. Tuttle, 1960), p. 12.
20. Idaho Code §67–450.
21. Ill. Comp. Stat. Ann. ch. 5, §460/40 (Smith-Hurd); *Illinois Blue Book, 1983–1984*, p. 436.
22. Ind. Code Ann. §1–2–7–1 (West).

23. *State Trees and Arbor Days*, p. 8.
24. Kan. Stat. Ann. §73–1001.
25. *Kansas Directory* (Topeka: Secretary of State, 1981), p. 129.
26. Ky. Rev. Stat. Ann. §2.095.
27. La. Rev. Stat. Ann. §49–160 (West).
28. Me. Rev. Stat. tit. 1, §208.
29. Md. Ann. Code art. 41, §76.
30. Mass. Laws Ann. ch. 2, §8 (West).
31. Mich. Comp. Laws Ann. §2.31.
32. Minn. Stat. Ann. §1.143 (West).
33. Miss. Code Ann. §3–3–9.
34. Mo. Ann. Stat. §10.040 (Vernon).
35. *State Trees and Arbor Days*, p. 11.
36. Neb. Rev. Stat. §90–113.
37. Nev. Rev. Stat. §235.040.
38. N.H. Rev. Stat. Ann. §3:6.
39. *Manual for the General Court, 1981.*
40. *State Trees and Arbor Days*, p. 12.
41. Edward J. Mullin, ed., *Manual of the Legislature of New Jersey* (Princeton, N.J.: Century Graphics, 1984), p. 11.
42. N.M. Stat. Ann. §12–3–4.
43. *New Mexico Blue Book, 1977–1978*, p. 86.
44. N.Y. State Law §76 (McKinney).
45. N.C. Gen. Stat. §145–3.
46. N.D. Cent. Code §54–02–05.
47. Ohio Rev. Code Ann. §5.05 (Page).
48. *Ohio Almanac* (Lorain, Ohio: Lorain Journal Co., 1977), p. 61.
49. Okla. Stat. Ann. tit. 25, §97 (West).
50. Or. Rev. Stat. §186.
51. *Oregon Blue Book, 1977–1978*, p. 139.
52. Pa. Stat. Ann. tit. 71, §1004 (Purdon).
53. R.I. Gen. Laws st42–4–8.
54. S.C. Code §1–1–660.
55. *1978 South Carolina Legislative Manual*, 59th ed., n.p.
56. S.D. Codified Laws Ann. §1–6–11.
57. Tenn. Code Ann. §4–1–305.
58. *Tennessee Blue Book, 1983–1984*, p. 372.
59. Tex. Rev. Civ. Stat. Ann. art. 6143 (Vernon).
60. Utah Code Ann. §63–13–7.
61. Vt. Stat. Ann. tit. 1, §499.
62. *State Trees and Arbor Days*, p. 16.
63. Wash. Rev. Code Ann. §1.20.020.
64. *State Trees and Arbor Days*, p. 17.

65. *West Virginia Blue Book 1980*, p. 925.

66. Wis. Stat. Ann. §1.10 (West).

67. *Wisconsin Blue Book, 1983–84*, p. 948.

68. Wyo. Stat. Ann. §8–3–106; *State Trees and Arbor Days*, p. 18.

69. *Symbols of the District of Columbia* (Washington, D.C.: Government of the District of Columbia, Office of the Secretariat, Office of Visual Information Management, n.d.).

70. *American Samoa* (n.p., n.d.); pamphlet supplied by the office of Eni Faleomavaega, member of Congress from American Samoa.

71. C.M.C. tit. 1, §231.

72. Guam Code Ann. tit. 1, §1024.

8

State and Territory Birds

Beginning in 1926, when Kentucky officially named the handsome red bird or cardinal as its state bird, campaigns were launched nationwide until each state had selected at least one favorite bird as its avian symbol. Audubon societies and women's clubs from 1926 through the early 1930s were largely responsible for fueling public interest and holding popular votes, many of them among school children. Since then, of course, several states have established or changed state birds.

The cardinal is not only the first to have been proclaimed a state bird, but it also holds the distinction of having been designated by seven states: Illinois, Indiana, Kentucky, North Carolina, Ohio, Virginia, and West Virginia. The western meadow lark holds second place, having been honored by Kansas, Montana, Nebraska, North Dakota, Oregon, and Wyoming. The mockingbird, another favorite, has been named the state bird of Arkansas, Florida, Mississippi, Tennessee, and Texas.

Though the robin is probably the most remembered in idiom and fable, it has surprisingly been selected by only three states: Connecticut, Michigan, and Wisconsin. Maine and Massachusetts concurred that the chickadee was a fine emblem for their states, while Iowa and New Jersey agreed on the Eastern goldfinch.

Both Missouri and New York selected the bluebird in 1927, but New York waited for more than forty years to make it official. Again, over thirty years elapsed between the decisions of Idaho and Nevada to designate the mountain bluebird. Finally, two states, Alabama and South Carolina, chose the wild turkey as the state game bird. Altogether, thirty-two birds have been named as state birds, state game birds, or state waterfowl; four states, Alabama, Georgia, Mississippi, and South Carolina, have designated two birds.

In some cases, it is clear that a state selected a bird for patriotic or economic reasons, but, typically, a bird was selected by sheer popularity based on a number of aesthetic factors. Delaware and Alabama named birds symbolic of Revolutionary and Civil War companies who were nicknamed after the blue hen chicken and the yellowhammer. Utah honored the sea gull for saving farmers' crops in 1848 from pests. On the other hand, the rich blue colors of the mountain bluebird or the bold black and white patterns of Minnesota's loon are reason enough to designate a state symbol.

The names of the birds listed below are a mixture of correct, colloquial, and common names used in the state laws. In some cases, even names once correct have changed. Alabama's yellowhammer is the northern flicker. The California valley quail is properly called the California quail. The robin is the American robin. Georgia's bobwhite quail is actually the northern bobwhite.

Hawaii's nene is properly called the Hawaiian goose. The cardinal is the northern cardinal. The eastern goldfinch of New Jersey and Iowa and the willow goldfinch of Washington is the American goldfinch. The chickadee of Maine and Massachusetts is the black-capped chickadee. Minnesota's loon is the common loon. New Mexico's chapparal bird is the greater roadrunner and Utah's sea gull is the California gull.

ALABAMA

The bird commonly called the yellowhammer, *Colaptes auratus*, was designated the state bird in 1927.[1] Other common names for the yellowhammer include the yellow-shafted woodpecker and the flicker.

The Ladies' Memorial Association was responsible for encouraging the legislature to adopt this emblem because the gray and yellow plumage resembled the colors of the Confederate Army uniforms.[2] An incident during the Civil War involving a company from Huntsville, Alabama, resulted in the nickname "yellowhammers" being assigned to all Alabama troops. When the Huntsville company rode into camp at Hopkinsville, Kentucky, newly clad in Confederate uniforms trimmed in bright yellow cloth, they were met with the greeting "Yellerhammer, yellerhammer, flicker, flicker!" When the yellowhammer was adopted as the official state bird in 1927, the old soldiers were pleased, noting that the black breast spots were like bullet holes and the red patch on the neck like a bandana.[3]

Size: Total length: 10 to 11 inches; tail length: 4 inches.

Range: North America except treeless Arctic districts; south to Nicaragua and Cuba; mostly found from Florida and Texas to Kansas, Illinois, Indiana, and North Carolina.

Physical description: The back is grayish brown sharply barred in black; the head and hindneck are plain gray with a red crescent-shaped patch at nape; the shafts of the tail feathers (except the middle pair) are bright pure cadmium yellow as are the underwing feathers and the undersurface of the tail. There is a conspicuous black crescent-shaped patch on the chest; the underparts are pale cinnamon or dull buff-pink fading into pale yellow or white and spotted in black. Males have a broad black stripe across the lower side of the head.

Behavior: While on short flights, flickers glide and dip in rhythmic undulations, but at other times they exhibit a strong and steady flight pattern. As they feed on ants, beetles, grasshoppers, grubs, and other harmful insects, they hop from one choice spot to another within a self-prescribed small perimeter. Flickers consume more ants than any other bird, which in turn keeps enemies of ants, such as the destructive aphid, in check as well. Eggs are white and oval in shape and usually average six to eight per set. If the eggs are destroyed, the persistent flicker will lay another set, sometimes laying as many as forty eggs per season.

Alabama also designated an official state game bird, the wild turkey, in 1980.[4]

The wild turkey, *Meleagris gallopavo*, is the largest of the gallinaceous birds; the males measure from 41 to 49 inches in length, and the females are noticeably smaller.

Size: Body weight: 16 to 40 pounds; tail length: 12½ to 15 inches.

Range: Eastern and south central United States; mountains of Mexico; southern Ontario.

Physical description: The bluish head and red upper neck area is nude, warted, and corrugated in the adult male. The female's head and neck are smoother and are covered with short, dusky, downy feathers. The general color is dusky, glossed with brilliant metallic coppery, golden, and greenish hues. Many of the feathers are margined terminally in velvety black. There is a black pectoral tuft or "beard," greenish at the base and wine-tinted brown gloss distally. The female is duller in color with a smaller beard.

Behavior: Perhaps the most distinctive behavioral trait of the wild turkey is his courtship dance in which he gobbles, struts, spreads his fan-shaped tail, and generally makes a spectacle of himself in order to attract the female. During this season, the male's chest becomes a mass of gooey tissue consisting of oil and fat. From this he may draw nutritional sustenance after his frenzied dances. Wild turkeys feed primarily on fruit, berries, and seeds, and they consume large amounts of insects such as grasshoppers and crickets. Though they travel mostly on foot in flocks, they are able to fly to avoid danger and to cross rivers.

ALASKA

The Alaska willow ptarmigan (*Lagopus lagopus alascensis* Swarth) became the official state bird in 1955.[5]

Size: Wing length: 7 ½ inches; tail length: 4 inches.

Range: Alaska; Arctic and subarctic regions of North America, Europe, and Asia.

Physical description: Also known as the willow grouse, the male and female have quite different plumages. The male has a hazel to chestnut forehead, crown, and nape; the back feathers are darker with white tips; the upper tail feathers are hazel; the wings are white; the tail feathers are generally brownish gray tipped with white; the sides of the head, throat, and upper breast are hazel becoming darker on the lower breast, barred with gray or black; the scarlet comb over the eyes swells when the bird is sexually aroused; and the underparts are mostly white. In winter, the male plumage is pure white except for the gray or black median pair of tail feathers. The female is mostly tawny olive above; each feather is barred with black and tipped with pale olive buff; the wings are white; the tail feathers are dark brownish gray tipped with white; the sides of the head, chin, and upper throat are cinnamon buff; the lower throat, abdomen, sides, and flanks are yellow buff to yellow tawny and heavily barred with wavy bands of clove brown; the comb is pale vermilion.

Behavior: Typically, a set of willow ptarmigan eggs are laid one day at a time over a period of from seven to ten days. The eggs are oval and shiny, and upon first being laid are a vivid bright red. As they dry, they turn blackish brown flecked with red to brown spots. During the winter, the bird adapts so completely to its environment that it grows hairlike feathers on its feet allowing it to glide effortlessly across snow as though clad in snowshoes.

ARIZONA

The Arizona legislature adopted the cactus wren, known also as Coues' cactus wren or *Heleodytes brunneicapillus couesi* (Sharpe), as the state bird in 1931.[6]

Size: Total length: 7 to 7½ inches; tail length: 3 inches.

Range: Desert region of southwestern United States and northern Mexico.

Physical description: The top of the head and hindneck are plain deep brown; the back region is pale, grayish brown conspicuously variegated with white; the tail feathers are brownish gray to black and barred with dusky to white; the sides of the head are mostly white except for a brown postocular stripe occupying the upper portion of the auricular region. The underparts are white deepening into cinnamon buff; the whole surface is heavily spotted with black.

Behavior: The wren's disposition is good; the bird rarely becomes embroiled in battle and is insatiably curious. The interested human bystander is often entertained as the playful little bird energetically inspects cracks, crevices, containers, and trash. The cactus wren builds flask-shaped nests from 3 to 9 feet above the ground on thorny shrubs, trees, or cactus. Cactus wrens feed mostly on beetles, ants, wasps, grasshoppers, and other pests. They also consume a significant amount of fruit.

ARKANSAS

The mockingbird was adopted by the Arkansas legislature as the official state bird in 1929.[7] When it was first introduced to the legislature by the State Federation of Women's Clubs, the legislators thought the issue was a joke. However, they were forthwith presented with rousing speeches enumerating the bird's worth to the farmer. The vote was unanimous, and the issue was settled in favor of the mockingbird.[8]

Size: Total length: 8½ to 9 inches; tail length: 4 to 4½ inches.

Range: Eastern United States and southern Canada; along the Gulf coast to Texas; Bahama Islands.

Physical description: The mockingbird, *Mimus polyglottos*, is mostly plain gray or brownish gray from the top of the head over most of the back region; the lateral tail feathers are white; the wings and tail are dull blackish slate; the middle and greater wing coverts are tipped with dull or grayish white; the primary coverts are white with a subterminal dusky spot or streak; the auricular region is gray; the area beneath the eye and along the side of the head is dull white transversely flecked with gray or dusky; the chin and throat are dull white margined along each side by a distinct dusky streak; the chest is pale smoke gray turning to white on the center of the breast and abdomen; the feathers under the tail are pale buff or buffy white. When the mockingbird is in flight, the broad white spots above can easily be seen against the slate black of the upper wings.

Behavior: Mockingbirds are sturdy creatures which build nests that often last several seasons. From the time when the nest is completed to the time when the fledglings take flight is usually from three to four weeks. Eggs range from bright blue to bluish green or greenish blue spotted with hazel or cinnamon. Both sexes not only build the nests, but also care for the young. Mockingbirds are lively and bellicose, fighting among themselves as well as tormenting cats and dogs. A masterful imitator, the mockingbird is considered one of the most versatile and beautiful songsters, sometimes changing tunes as many as thirty times within a ten-minute period. The diet of the mockingbird consists equally of insects and wild fruit.

CALIFORNIA

The California valley quail, *Lophortyx californica*, was designated the official bird and avifaunal emblem of California by the state's legislature in 1931,[9] winning in a vote involving twenty-four other birds nominated by the California Audubon Society.[10]

Size: Tail length: 3 to 3½ inches; wing length: 4 inches.

Range: Semiarid interior of California as well as the coastal belt south of San Francisco; east to Nevada. (The valley quail has been successfully introduced to other areas.)

Physical description: The adult male is mostly brownish olive on the back and rump; the wings are mostly dark olive brown; the tail feathers are between slate gray and deep mouse gray; the area under the eye, chin, and throat is jet black, the throat bordered by a broad white band extending from each eye to the center throat region in a v-shape; the forehead is pale olive buff with a white line of demarcation across the crown followed by a broader black line. There is a crest on the crown of the head consisting of six forward-drooping, terminally expanded black feathers; a bright design is created by brownish gray feathers of the hindneck speckled with white; the breast is solid deep neutral gray; and the abdomen is warm buff or white with a central bright hazel patch margined in black. The female is the same as the male above but is darker and more brownish; the crest on the crown is smaller and is brownish gray in color; the forehead is a pale buffy brown. There is a light buffy brown speckled pattern on the nape and lower sides of the neck; the chin and throat are grayish white; and the breast is grayish brown.

Behavior: The California valley quail makes little effort to build a safe, sturdy nest for her young. Instead, eggs are found in nests near houses or roads, even in other birds' nests. Traveling in flocks, they feed primarily on seeds, grass, and fruit, consuming minute amounts of flies and insects. Preyed upon by man and animal alike, they make especially easy targets for snakes, raccoons, owls, jays, cats, and dogs. When startled, however, they can make an amazingly quick retreat.

COLORADO

The lark bunting, *Calamospiza melancorys stejneger*, was adopted as the Colorado state bird in 1931.[11] A first statewide vote yielded the name of the meadowlark as the most popular bird in the state. A second vote, spearheaded by the *Denver Post*, the Colorado Mountain Club, and the Colorado Federation of Women's Clubs, determined that the mountain bluebird should receive the title. Finally, the Colorado Audubon Society convinced state legislators that since the bluebird and meadowlark were already state birds of other states, the lark bunting was a more appropriate choice.[12]

Size: Total length: 6 inches; tail length: 2½ inches.

Range: Great plains; migrating south through Texas to the Gulf coast and Mexico.

Physical description: In summer, the adult male is black with a grayish cast on his back; the middle and greater wing coverts are mostly white, forming a conspicuous patch; the tertials are edged with white; and the tail coverts (especially the lower) are margined with white. The adult female is grayish above and brown streaked with dusky; the wing is white patched as in the male but smaller, more interrupted, and tinged with buffy; the underparts are white, streaked with dusky. In winter, the female is less grayish brown with paler markings tinged with buff; the adult male in the winter is similar to the adult female, but the feathers of the underparts and the chin are black beneath the surface.

Behavior: A highly sociable bird, the lark bunting is happiest when safely tucked away in a large flock. During courtship, lark buntings perform a dazzling air show commencing with soaring ascents, then drifting back to earth, all the while whistling a lively tune. From this behavior comes the common expression "happy as a lark." The lark's cheerful life can be tragically cut short by such natural enemies as hawks when his song attracts the attention of those for whom it was not intended. Because larks feed on harmful grasshoppers and waste grain, they are held in high regard by farmers.

CONNECTICUT

The American robin, *Turdus migratorius*, became the state bird of Connecticut by action of the state legislature in 1943.[13]

Size: Total length: 8½ to 9 inches; tail length: 4 inches.

Range: Eastern and northern North America; westward to the Rocky Mountains; northwestward to Alaska; winters southward to Florida and along the Gulf coast to Texas.

Physical description: The largest thrush in North America, the male is mostly deep mouse gray or brownish slate gray on the back; the head is black with white spots from the eye to the bill and on both the upper and lower eyelids; the chin is white; the feathers of the neck are black in the center, margined with brownish slate gray or mouse gray; the tail is a dull slate black or sooty black with a large and conspicuous white spot; the chest, flanks, breast, and upper abdomen are a plain, deep cinnamon red color; and the lower abdomen is white. The female is much duller in color with gray of upper parts lighter and chest browner than in the male.

Behavior: Named by the English colonists because of the similarity between this and their robin redbreast, the colonists did not notice the close resemblance to their blackbird or the *Turdus*, a thrush. A bird suggestive of the type-A personality, the robin is jittery and easily upset. However, he sails through the air without faltering, chest out and back straight. It is no wonder that we often think of the robin arising early to catch the first worm. A strong singer, he is up at dawn regaling the neighborhood with lengthy, energetic, and cheerful songs. The pale blue eggs (hence the color "Robin's egg blue") are usually laid in sets of three or four. The male cares for the young almost exclusively while the female prepares for a new brood. Sometimes three separate sets of eggs are laid in a year. Robins subsist mostly on beetles and caterpillars supplemented by an intake of spiders, earthworms, and snails. Since the robin also enjoys fruit, both cultivated and wild, he poses a potential threat to orchards. Fortunately, when the preferred insect or wild fruit is available, the robin leaves the fruit crops alone.

DELAWARE

The blue hen chicken was adopted as Delaware's state bird in 1939.[14] During the Revolutionary War, a company of soldiers from Kent County in Delaware entertained themselves between battles by staging cockfights between blue hen chickens. The cockfights became so famous that, when the soldiers fought fiercely in battle, they became known as the Blue Hen's Chickens. This nickname was again adopted during the Civil War by a company from the same county.[15]

Physical description: The throat is nude and wattled; there is a median fleshy "comb" on the forehead; the middle tail feathers are strongly hooked; and the feathers of the rump are elongated and linear, or pointed.

FLORIDA

In 1927, the mockingbird was officially designated the state bird of Florida.[16] The Audubon Society of St. Petersburg was responsible for a statewide vote for a state bird. The mockingbird won by a large margin over such other possibilities as the hummingbird, pelican, and buzzard. One can only imagine the chagrin of the Audubon Society when an entire school voted for the buzzard because the students had been studying the bird as part of an airplane building project.[17] See the Arkansas entry for a description.

GEORGIA

The brown thrasher was designated the state bird of Georgia by the legislature in 1970,[18] even though the governor had officially proclaimed the brown thrasher to be the state bird in 1935.[19]

Size: Total length: 10 inches; tail length: 5 inches.

Range: Eastern United States and southeastern Canada; breeding southward to Florida, Alabama, Mississippi, and Texas and westward to the Rocky Mountains; wintering from North Carolina to Florida and Texas.

Physical description: The plumage above is plain, dull, cinnamon red or tawny red, becoming duller above the eye; the wings are tipped with white or pale buff producing two distinct bands across the wing; the outermost tail feathers are tipped with buff; the auricular region is a light rusty brown, narrowly streaked with dull whitish or pale buffy; the underparts are a pale buff, approaching buffy white on the chin, throat, and abdomen; the chest and sides are streaked with brown or dusky; the throat is margined along each side by a series of blackish streaks forming a distinct stripe along the lower side of the head; the iris is bright lemon or sulphur yellow; and the tail feathers are long.

Behavior: The brown thrasher, *Toxostoma rufum*, is a fickle creature, often changing partners with each new brood during a single mating season. However, both sexes are fiercely protective of their young, launching attacks on any and all creatures, including humans, who dare disturb their nests. Eggs are pale blue, sometimes white, tinged with green, and are evenly spotted in reddish or dull brown. A well-balanced meal consists of the favored beetle, acorns, and wild berries.

Georgia also designated an official state game bird, the bobwhite quail, in 1970.[20] When the thrasher was officially designated the state bird of Georgia, it seemed a proper time to make the bobwhite quail the official state game bird. Known as the "Quail Capital of the World," Georgia was proud to give this designation to a bird so plentiful in Georgia and beloved by sportsmen everywhere.[21]

Size: Wing length: 4½ inches; tail length: 2 to 2½ inches.

Range: Resident of open uplands from Maine through southern New England; westward through Minnesota, North Dakota, and Wyoming; south through northern Florida, the Gulf coast region, northern Texas, and eastern Colorado; southern Ontario.

Physical description: The bobwhite quail, *Colinus virginianus*, is mostly dark amber brown to chestnut above, heavily blotched with fuscous-black and narrowly tipped with pale, warm buff; the lateral feathers of the upper back and the feathers of the lower back and rump are paler, narrowly barred with dusky and crossed by numerous pale warm buffy bands; the tail feathers are gray; the chin, upper throat, and forehead are white with a broad white stripe extending from above the eye to the back of the neck (in the female, the stripe, chin, and throat are pale orange-yellow, and the forehead and crown are between tawny and russet). There is a fairly broad blackish band across the lower throat (auburn in the female), followed by a broader one of cinnamon; the upper abdomen is white washed with pale warm buff; the feathers are crossed by four or five narrow black bars.

Behavior: The bobwhite quail, also commonly referred to as the partridge, feeds on grain left in the field after harvest, as well as locusts, grasshoppers, and potato beetles, making it a popular friend of farmers. The bobwhite quail's plumage makes it possible for the bird to conceal himself quite effectively from hunters and other threats. When it becomes too dangerous to remain stationary, the bobwhite launches himself into sudden flight giving the impression that he is a strong flyer. However, this is not the case, as quail have been known to collapse into the water in failed attempts to cross wide rivers.

HAWAII

The *nene, Nesochen sandwicensis* or *Bernicata sandwicensis*, was designated the state bird in 1957.[22]

Physical description: The *nene*, or Hawaiian goose, is a land goose, only recently saved from extinction by being bred in England and returned to Hawaii by Herbert Shipman and Peter Scott with U.S. financial support. The Hawaiian goose has a long, creme-colored neck, streaked vertically in black, with the light coloring extending upward into the malar region. The back of the neck and head are black. There is a black ring around the neck separating the creme color from the variegated pattern of the grayish brown back.[23]

IDAHO

The mountain bluebird, *Sialia arctica*, was designated and declared to be the state bird of Idaho in 1931.[24] The Idaho State Federation Conservation chairman initially indicated that the western tanager was the best choice for state bird. However, the state's school children felt differently, and the mountain bluebird received the most votes.[25]

Size: Total length: 6½ inches; tail length: 2½ to 3 inches.

Range: Mountain districts of western North America; winters southward to southern California and northern Mexico.

Physical description: A thrush, the male and female plumage differ as follows: The male is a plain, rich turquoise blue, sky blue, or porcelain blue; the head, throat, chest, and sides are paler in color than the upper parts; the abdomen and lower parts are white; the tail and wing feathers are black with longer undertail feathers a pale turquoise or sky blue tipped with white. The female head and back are plain mouse or smoke gray, sometimes tinged with greenish blue; the chin, throat, breast, and sides are a pale brownish gray passing into dull white on the abdomen; the longer undertail feathers are dusky sometimes tinged with blue; the rump, upper tail feathers, tail, and wings are mostly turquoise blue or light sky blue, sometimes nile blue. The adult male in winter turns a duller blue; the adult female's color deepens, especially the buffy grayish underparts.

Behavior: The *Sialia arctica* is now called the *Sialia currucoides* because, unlike previously thought, it is not native to the Arctic region. (Instead, it only summers there.) Mountain bluebirds feed mostly on ants and beetles with a small dietary component of grapes and berries. Flocks of bluebirds may be identified by their strange way of pausing between their deep swooping movements. They build nests in holes in trees, along river banks, in houses, and even in other birds' nesting holes. Bluebird fledglings sometimes fall prey to flickers who have been known to keep parents from feeding their young by blocking the entrance to the nests.

ILLINOIS

The cardinal, *Cardinalis cardinalis*, was designated the state bird of Illinois by the legislature in 1929,[26] after a vote of Illinois school children. The cardinal received 39,226 votes; the next runner-up was the bluebird which received 30,306 votes.[27]

Size: Total length: 7½ to 8 inches; tail length: 4 inches.

Range: Eastern United States, west to the Great Plains, southern Arizona, and northwestern Mexico, and south through Georgia to the Gulf states.

Physical description: A finch, the cardinal is conspicuously crested and thick-billed with the tail longer than the rather short and rounded wing. Adult males are entirely bright red, except for the black patchy band from the eye to the throat on both sides of the bill. The female has a dull grayish patch on the face and throat, is brownish above and dull tawny or pale buffy below; the crest, wings, and tail are a dull reddish color, and the underwing feathers are pinkish red.

Behavior: The cardinal builds its nest in shrubs and bushes, seemingly oblivious to its proximity to people. Eggs are whitish with brown spots incubating over a twelve- to thirteen-day period. Both parents attend to the young with frequent feedings of insects. As the young mature, they become primarily grain and fruit eaters, though insect pests still make up a third of their diet. Cardinals are beautiful birds, popular not only for their striking plumage, but also for their pleasant songs, which are loud, flutelike whistles. The trills last approximately three seconds.

INDIANA

The red bird or cardinal, *Richmondena Cardinalis cardinalis*, was designated the state bird of Indiana by act of legislature in 1933.[28] See the Illinois entry for a description.

IOWA

In 1933, the eastern goldfinch, *Spinus tristis tristis*, was designated the state bird of Iowa by the forty-fifth General Assembly.[29]

Size: Total length: 4½ inches; tail length: 1½ to 2 inches.

Range: United States and southern Canada east of the Rocky Mountains; wintering southward to the Gulf coast.

Physical description: The adult male in the summer is generally pure lemon yellow or canary yellow; the forehead, crown, wings, and tail are black; and white stripes appear near the base of the wings and along the ends of the tail feathers. The adult female and the adult male in the winter are olive brownish or grayish above; the wings and tail are blackish or dusky marked with white; the upper tail feathers are pale grayish or grayish white; and the underparts are dull grayish white tinged with yellow.

Behavior: The eastern goldfinch is a flock bird, often seen in undulating flight, cheerfully singing with his friends. The birds usually sing in choral fashion, whistling their high-pitched tunes which last from two to three seconds. Breeding very late in the season (from July to September), the male and female are constant companions as they build their nests and raise their young. Egg sets average five in number, and the coloration is plain bluish white. Seeds are the mainstay of their diet, supplemented in the winter months by a delicacy, plant lice eggs.

KANSAS

The western meadowlark, *Sturnella neglecta* (Audubon), was designated by the legislature in 1937 as the official state bird of Kansas, as preferred by a vote of school children in the state.[30]

Size: Total length: 8 to 9 inches; tail length: 2½ to 3 inches.

Range: Western United States, southwestern Canada, northwestern Mexico; east to the prairie areas of the Mississippi valley, in Minnesota, Iowa, Missouri, and Texas.

Physical description: The head and back of the neck are a pale dull buffy or white with broad lateral crown stripes of pale grayish brown; the lower sides of the head are largely yellow, topped by a dull grayish white area streaked with gray; mostly buffy or grayish brown above streaked with black; the outermost tail feathers are mostly white; the throat, breast, and abdomen are a deep yellow sometimes with an orangish hue. The yellow area is relieved by a black horseshoe-shaped patch on the chest.

Behavior: An oriole, the western meadowlark feeds mostly on insects with perhaps one third of its diet consisting of grain. Its loud, distinctive song is considered one of its most appealing qualities; the bird

sometimes hammers out as many as 200 notes per minute. The young leave their nests early, unable to fly but still under the protection of their parents until they are able to care for themselves. Fledglings are easy prey for weasels, skunks, snakes, owls, and hawks.

KENTUCKY

The native red bird commonly known as the Kentucky cardinal (*Cardinalis cardinalis*) was designated the official state bird by the legislature in 1926.[31] See the Illinois entry for a description.

LOUISIANA

The brown pelican, as it appears on the seal of the state, was designated as the official state bird of Louisiana by the legislature in 1966.[32] This amended a 1958 act naming the pelican, with no further designation, as the official state bird.

Physical description: Mostly grayish brown streaked with brown, the pelican feathers are white tipped, and he has a long brown neck (white in the winter), a white head and white stripe that extends under the bill in a straplike fashion, a yellow forehead that turns to white at the crown followed by a rust-colored tuft at the back of the head, a long bill, and a throat pouch.

Behavior: The *Pelecanus occidentalis occidentalis*, or brown pelican, usually lays three dull white eggs after a solemn courtship culminating on the water's surface. As is the case with many newly hatched birds, the young pelican is fed regurgitated food of a parent. However, it has the unique experience as it grows older of selecting meals smorgasbord-style from the parent's pouch, until it is old enough to capture its own meal from the sea. A hunting expedition is carried out when the pelican dives head first into the water at a downwind angle, making a somersault beneath the surface and emerging against the wind. This remarkable spectacle usually results in catching a supply of fresh fish that is stashed in the pouch for digestion later.

MAINE

The chickadee, *Penthestes atricapillus*, was adopted as official state bird of Maine in 1927.[33]

Size: Total length: 4½ to 5 inches; tail length: 2 to 2½ inches.

Range: Northern United States and Canada.

Physical description: The entire top and back of the head is black; most of the upper back is plain olive gray, passing into buffy gray on the rump and upper tail feathers; the wings and tail are a dusky or blackish slate color; the chin and throat are black; the sides of the head and most of the underparts are white, the sides tinged with buffy. In autumn and winter, this long-tailed small bird is much more deeply colored, contrasting even more strongly with the white abdomen and white wing edgings.

Behavior: The black-capped chickadee is a member of the titmouse family. Beloved by early colonial settlers, the chickadee is friendly and somewhat tame. It has been known to perch fearlessly on fingers and to feed from the hand. One of its songs is calling its own name—"chicka" followed by "dee dee dee."

MARYLAND

The Baltimore oriole, *Icterus galbula*, was designated the official state bird of Maryland

by the General Assembly in 1947. The assembly has also made special provision for its protection.[34] The first Lord Baltimore chose orange and black as the colors for his coat of arms because of his fondness for the bird, which he saw often on his estate, that was later named the Baltimore Oriole.[35]

Size: Total length: 6½ to 7 inches; tail length: 2½ to 3 inches.

Range: Eastern United States, west to the Rocky Mountains; winters in Mexico and Central America to Colombia and Venezuela.

Physical description: The male's head, back, and upper chest area are black; the rump, upper tail feathers, and underparts range from cadmium yellow to intense orange; the upper wings are black, broadly tipped with white. The female's head and back are saffron olive, with distinct central spots of black or dusky; the rump and tail feathers are olive saffron; the wings are dusky, narrowly tipped with white or gray; the underparts are saffron yellow or dull orange-yellow, duller on the abdomen and tinged with olive on the sides and flanks.

Behavior: The Baltimore oriole is a talented weaver, building a nest from grapevine bark, plant fibers, and milkweed silk. The nest hangs pouchlike from 30 feet above the ground. Fledglings are strangely quiet until a few days prior to leaving the nest, when they then cry for days in a high-pitched monotonous whine. The oriole feeds heavily on caterpillars and other insects and exhibits a taste for green peas and berries.

MASSACHUSETTS

The chickadee, *Penthestes atricapillus*, was designated the state bird of the Commonwealth of Massachusetts by legislative act in

1941.[36] See the Maine entry for a description. In 1991, the wild turkey (*Meleagris gallopavo*) was designated as the Commonwealth's game bird in honor of the first Thanksgiving dinner.[37]

MICHIGAN

A 1931 House concurrent resolution made the robin the official state bird of Michigan.[38] See the Connecticut entry for a description.

MINNESOTA

The loon, *Gavia immer*, was adopted as the official bird of Minnesota by the legislature in 1961.[39]

Size: Total length: 3 feet; wing span: 5 feet.

Physical description: The head is black with black and white stripes around the head in a vertical zebra pattern; the lower neck is coal black; the upper chest and underparts are white. Above there appears a black-and-white checkerboard pattern and, along the sides, the same colors give an an appearance of polka dots. The winter plumage is grayish brown above, with a brownish head and white underparts.

Behavior: The loon mates for life and returns to the same lake in the spring of every year. After laying two or three eggs, one usually infertile, the loon incubates the eggs for nearly a month. Within two days, the young loons are led into the water by their mother where they exhibit great skill in swimming and diving. They remain in the water, relatively safe from attack, until they are able to fly. Fish eaters, loons capture their prey with great alacrity and strength. Trout are often the objects of their underwater escapades; the loons quickly swallow them before resurfacing. Half running and half flying, the loon puts forth a considerable effort in taking flight, sometimes gliding along the surface for quite a distance before ascending.

MISSISSIPPI

The mockingbird was designated the state bird of Mississippi by the legislature in 1944.[40] See the Arkansas entry for a description.

The state of Mississippi also designated the wood duck, *Aix sponsa*, as the official state waterfowl in 1974.[41]

Range: United States and southern Canada.

Physical description: The crown of the head is metallic green streaked laterally with two white stripes; two white stripes also appear under the chin area; the breast is russet; metallic green, bronze, blue, and purple appear above and buffy to white below; the back, breast, and side regions are separated by white stripes. In July or August, the adult male begins to molt and takes on brownish shades above and yellowish tones below. The female is similar but duller, mostly brownish gray above, brown on the sides, and white below. There is a white ring around the eye.

Behavior: Also called the summer duck because it breeds and summers regularly throughout the South and a tree duck because it nests in tree trunks or branch cavities, the wood duck lays from ten to fifteen eggs per season. After incubating for nearly a month, the whitish eggs hatch and, from then on, the fledglings know little peace until their mother has managed to acclimate them to the water. Sometimes carrying them on her back or in her bill, the mother coaxes and protects her brood as they learn to manage for themselves. The wood duck feeds primarily on vegetable matter such as nuts, weeds, and seeds retrieved by scavenging under leaves and feeding on aquatic plants. The rest of his diet consists of miscellaneous insects, dragonflies, beetles, and locusts, as well as a few small fish, minnows, and frogs. A good swimmer and flyer, the wood duck is usually hunted as he goes from his sheltered roosting spot to his feeding spot along marshy streams.

MISSOURI

The bluebird, *Sialia sialis*, native to Missouri, became that state's official bird by legislative act in 1927.[42]

Size: Total length: 6 inches; tail length: 2½ inches.

Range: United States and southern Canada east of the Rockies; breeds south to Texas, along the Gulf coast and Florida.

Physical description: Above, the male is bright blue, the average hue being between ultramarine and deep blue; the shafts of the wing and tail feathers are black; the sides of the head are light or gray blue; the underparts are mostly a dull cinnamon red or cinnamon chestnut except the abdomen and under the tail feathers, which are white. The female is bluish gray above, tinged with grayish brown; the rump and tail feathers are bright blue; the wings are blue, edged with whitish gray; the underparts are mostly dull cinnamon; the chin, abdomen, and under tail feathers are white.

Behavior: Known as the eastern bluebird, this tiny bird was nicknamed the blue robin by early settlers because it reminded them of the English robin redbreast. Though an amorous and flirtatious suitor, the male loses no time in selecting another companion upon the loss of his mate. The courtship is marked by alluring songs from the male, who attentively pays friendly visits to the female. On such visits he may even feed her by placing food in her mouth. Once egg incubation begins, the singing stops until it is time to begin again with a new nesting (and often a new mate). The majority of the bluebird's diet is insect matter, such as harmful beetles, grasshoppers, crickets, and katydids.

MONTANA

The western meadowlark, *Sturnella neglecta* (Audubon), was declared to be the official state bird of Montana by the legislature in 1931, following a referendum vote of Montana school children.[43]

In 1805 the famous explorer, Meriwether Lewis, entered into his journal the observance of a lark he found similar to the eastern lark. This is believed to be the first recorded mention of what is now known as the western meadowlark. The most notable difference between the two larks is their song.[44]

See the Kansas entry for a description.

NEBRASKA

The western meadowlark was designated the state bird of Nebraska by the legislature in 1929.[45] See the Kansas entry for a description.

NEVADA

The mountain bluebird, *Sialia currucoides*, was designated the official state bird of Nevada by the legislature in 1967.[46] See the Idaho entry for a description.

NEW HAMPSHIRE

The New Hampshire legislature designated the purple finch, *Carpodacus purpureus*, the official state bird in 1957,[47] the year in which a Dartmouth College forester, Robert

S. Monahan, along with the Audubon Society of New Hampshire, the New Hampshire Federation of Garden Clubs, and the State Federation of Women's Clubs recommended the designation of the purple finch. Thereupon, Republican Doris M. Spollett, who had previously tried with no success to name the New Hampshire hen as the state bird, began again to campaign for her personal favorite. She lost when, within three months of its introduction, the bill making the purple finch the state bird was signed into law.[48]

Size: Total length: 5½ inches; tail length: 2 inches; wing length: 3 inches.

Range: Eastern North America; winters south to Gulf coast area.

Physical description: The male's top of head and back of the neck are deep wine purple (more crimson in the summer). There is a dusky brownish red spot near the ear and along the side of the head; the rest of the head is pinkish wine purple; the back is reddish brown or wine purplish with dark streaks; the wings and tail are dusky with light brownish red or light brown edgings; the abdomen and under tail feathers are white. The female is olive or olive grayish above streaked with dusky and white; the wings and tail are dusky with light olive or olive grayish edgings; the upper sides of the head are mostly white streaked with olive; the underparts are white, broadly streaked with olive.

Behavior: The purple finch feeds on seeds in the winter and spring, insects in the late spring, and fruit in the summer. Finches are considered generally beneficial by orchard growers, since they prune rather than destroy fruit trees. They also eat such harmful insects as plant lice, cankerworms, and caterpillars. Courtship consists of a wild dance and song by the male, sometimes followed by an equally eccen-

tric response by the female who first ignores the male and then pecks at him before they fly off together to build a nest. The four or five eggs commonly produced by the happy couple are bluish green or pale blue, with black or brown spots mostly located at the large end of each egg.

NEW JERSEY

The eastern goldfinch was designated the state bird of New Jersey by the legislature in 1935.[49] See the Iowa entry for a description.

NEW MEXICO

The chaparral bird, commonly known as the roadrunner, was adopted as the official bird of New Mexico by the legislature in 1949.[50]

Size: Total length: 20 to 21 inches; tail length: 11½ inches.

Range: Southwestern United States; east to Gulf coast of Texas; northern and central Mexico.

Physical description: The roadrunner is a large, long-tailed, long-billed cuckoo. The feathers of the forehead and front of the crown are black, each with a broad lateral spot of russet or light tawny brown; the occipital bushy crest is glossy black or blue-black broken by edgings of tawny brown or pale buffy; above is mostly black broadly edged with light tawny brown passing into dull buffy white on the edges creating a conspicuous streaked effect; the lower back and wing coverts are glossy bronze or bronze greenish and edged with black; the tail feathers are mostly bronzy olive glossed with purplish and margined with dull white; the sides of the head are dull whitish and tawny brown, barred and spotted with black; the chin and throat are mostly dull white; the rest of the underparts are plain grayish white, the neck and chest streaked with black.

Behavior: Many observers have described the roadrunner in unflattering terms such as odd looking and uniquely entertaining. Perhaps because of the barren habitat in which the roadrunner resides, it has had to adapt for survival by exhibiting stealth, speed, ferocity, and strength. This combination of traits and its outward appearance of awkwardness explains why it has attracted such bemused attention. When hungry, the roadrunner runs quickly in pursuit of lizards, scorpions, snakes, tarantulas, mice, insects, and small birds.

NEW YORK

The bluebird, *Sialia sialis*, became the official bird of the state of New York by legislative act in 1970.[51] The robin had been selected initially as the state bird, but, after a vote in 1927 and 1928, the bluebird was determined to be more popular.[52] It was not until 1970, however, that this designation was made official. See the Missouri entry for a description.

NORTH CAROLINA

The cardinal was declared to be the official state bird of North Carolina by the legislature in 1943.[53] See the Illinois entry for a description.

NORTH DAKOTA

The meadowlark, *Sturnella neglecta*, was named the official bird of North Dakota by the legislature in 1947.[54] See the Kansas entry for a description.

OHIO

The cardinal, *Cardinalis cardinalis*, was named the official bird of Ohio by the legislature in 1933.[55] See the Illinois entry for a description.

OKLAHOMA

The scissor-tailed flycatcher, *Muscivora forticata*, was designated the state bird of Oklahoma by joint resolution of the legislature in 1951.[56] The joint resolution notes that the flycatcher's nesting range is centered in Oklahoma, and, because its diet consists of harmful and useless insects, the flycatcher is of great economic value. Furthermore, the scissor-tailed flycatcher has been endorsed as the official state bird by numerous ornithologists, biologists, and wildlife societies.[57]

Size: Total length: 11 to 13 inches; tail length: 6 to 9 inches.

Range: Texas to Kansas, less commonly in Missouri, Arkansas, and Louisiana; migrates to Mexico and Central America.

Physical description: The male's head is clear pale gray with a small concealed orange-red patch on the center of the crown; the back is light gray strongly suffused with a pink wine color; the upper tail feathers are black or dusky, margined with gray; the six middle tail feathers are black; the three outermost tail feathers on each side are white, strongly tinged with salmon pink, terminally black; the tail is deeply forked, especially in the male, the lateral tail feathers more than twice as long as the middle pair and longer than the wing; the cheek, chin, and throat are white, shading into gray on the breast; the sides and flanks are a salmon color to an almost saturn red; there is a large concealed patch of bright orange-red on either side of the breast. The female is similar to the male but duller in color; the breast patches are more restricted and orangish; and the concealed crown spot is often missing.

Behavior: Fondest of open terrain, the fly-catcher perches on telephone wires and posts. Its diet is composed mainly of noxious insects such as beetles, wasps, and bees. Favorites are grasshoppers and crickets. Interestingly enough, flycatchers do not seem to care much for flies. An extremely energetic bird when provoked or frightened, it is nonetheless a sloppy nest builder who carelessly leaves strings and twine hanging from the nest. The eggs are a creamy white color spotted with brown and gray.

OREGON

The western meadowlark, *Sturnella neglecta*, was declared the official bird of Oregon by gubernatorial proclamation in 1927, following a vote of the state's school children sponsored by the Oregon Audubon Society.[58] See the Kansas entry for a description.

PENNSYLVANIA

Pennsylvania is the only state that has designated only an official state game bird, the ruffed grouse, *Bonasa umbellus*, which was adopted by the legislature in 1931.[59]

Size: Total length: 15 to 19 inches; tail length: 5 to 6 inches.

Range: Wooded portions of North America.

Physical description: A medium-sized wood grouse, the upperparts are brown and rusty or gray variegated with black; the underparts are buff or whitish, broken by broad bars of brownish; the lower half of the tarsus is nude and scalelike; the tail at approximately 5 inches is nearly as long as the wing and has from eighteen to twenty tail feathers; the tail is gray or rusty with numerous zigzag narrow bars of blackish and a broad subter-minal band of black or dark brown; the feathers on the crown are distinctly elongated, forming when erected a conspicuous crest. The male in the summer has a bright orange or red naked space above the eye.

Behavior: The courtship behavior of the ruffed grouse has been the source of much interest throughout the years. The drumming noise made by either the wild flapping of the wings against the sides or by the sheer force of the wings against the air is ear splitting, though no one can seem to agree on the exact noise-making mechanism. The ruffed grouse is primarily a fruit and vegetable eater; insects account for approximately ten percent of his diet. Grouse are remarkably tame by nature and, when allowed, they have become pets. The birds who reside in areas where grouse are hunted are much more wary of humans and take the appropriate evasive actions. A popular game bird, the grouse is called a pheasant in the South and a partridge in the northern states. Its enemies include raccoons, weasels, skunks, and opossum. In addition, disease and parasites take a heavy toll on the grouse population.

RHODE ISLAND

The breed of fowl known commonly as the Rhode Island Red was designated the official state bird of Rhode Island by the legislature in 1954.[60]

Physical description: The Rhode Island Red is a well-known American breed of domesticated fowl. It weighs from 6½ to 8½ pounds, has yellow skin beneath brownish red feathers, and a single rose-colored comb extending from the base of its beak to the upper back of its head. The hen lays brown eggs.

SOUTH CAROLINA

The Carolina wren, a member of the family *Troglodytidae*, was designated the official state bird of South Carolina in 1948 by the state legislature.[61] In 1939, however, the legislature had adopted the mockingbird as the state bird, in spite of the fact that the Carolina wren had been recognized unofficially as the state bird prior to that time. The 1948 act designating the Carolina wren as the official state bird repealed the 1939 act.[62]

Size: Total length: 5 inches; tail length: 2 inches.

Range: Eastern United States.

Physical description: The upperparts of the Carolina wren, *Thryothorus ludovicianus*, are plain rusty brown; the wings and tail are a duller brown than the back, narrowly barred with dusky. There is a sharply defined and conspicuous stripe of white or buffy white on each side from the bill and above the eye to the back of the neck, bordered above in black; beneath the white stripe is a broad area of rufous brown covering the upper half of the auricular region; the underparts are a plain dull buffy white to buff color on the chest, sides, and flanks; the under tail feathers are buffy whitish broadly barred with black. In autumn and winter, the colors are decidedly brighter, and the superciliary stripe is buffy.

Behavior: A sweet and vigorous songster, the wren whistles a variety of loud, cheerful songs. A set of wren eggs usually numbers five, and the eggs are creamy or pinkish white with reddish brown spots encircling the larger end of the egg. The wren is a pest eater; its diet comprises mostly beetles, caterpillars, grasshoppers, crickets, and cockroaches. It is no surprise, then, that the wren is an especially quick and energetic bird able to capture its tiny prey, as well as to escape the perceived danger posed by nosy humans. However, the wren is also a curious creature and will often bravely and swiftly investigate the source of suspicious noises before considering its own safety.

In 1976, the legislature made the South Carolina wild turkey, *Meleagris gallopavo*, the official state wild game bird.[63] See the Alabama entry for a description of the wild turkey.

SOUTH DAKOTA

The ring-necked pheasant, *Phasianus colchicus*, was adopted as the state bird of South Dakota by act of the state legislature in 1943.[64]

Size: Total length: 20 to 27 inches; the tail is proportionally long ranging from 10 inches in the female to 18 inches in the male.

Range: Native to eastern China; now well established in the northern half of the United States, southern Canada, Hawaii, and Europe.

Physical description: The male's head, crown, and neck are of varying shades of glossy green from Roman green to bottle green and dark zinc green; the nape of the neck is tinged with a glossy dark violet-blue that also predominates along the sides of the neck; erectile tufts of iridescent blue-green blackish feathers are located on each side toward the back of the crown. There is a white collar around the neck; the exposed interscapulers are a bright buff yellow with a white triangular space at the base; much of the upperparts are light neutral gray or brown tinged with pale olive buff and broadly edged with russet or black; the lower back region is yellow-green to deep lichen green; the breast is a dark coppery hazel, broadly glossed with magenta purple; the bare skin on the side of the head is bright red; the tail is brown or dark olive buff with black transverse markings. The female is brownish and buffy, variegated with black; the interscapulars are a bright hazel to tawny russet, the central area terminating in a brownish gray or black distally pointed "V"; the scapulars and upper wing feathers are brown to tawny olive, edged and tipped with pale buffy; the back and upper tail feathers are brownish black, broadly edged with pale pinkish buff; the tail feathers are a light pinkish hazel transversely blotched with black; the chin, upper breast, and abdomen are white to buffy.

Behavior: The ring-necked, or Chinese, pheasant was introduced in 1881 in Oregon by Judge O. N. Denny, the American consul general of Shanghai. The muted earth tones of the female's plumage serve as effective camouflage, making it possible for potential intruders to come within a few feet and yet never notice her in her nest. The female has no scent, making her even more secure from attack. The ten to twelve eggs in a set are usually brownish olive. Upon hatching, the newborn chicks follow their mother who helps them scavenge for food and protects them from predators. Though pheasant eat a good many harmful insects, they also attack farm and garden crops such as corn, tomatoes, and beans causing severe damage. Able to escape from danger by a rapid vertical movement if trapped by buildings or trees, the pheasant makes a noisy exit by madly fluttering its wings and croaking loudly in alarm. Very sensitive to earth tremors, caused by explosions or earthquakes, they make their alarm known by crowing loudly.

TENNESSEE

After a popular vote in April 1933, the mockingbird, *Mimus polyglottos*, was selected over the robin, cardinal, bobwhite, and bluebird, among others. In 1933 the General Assembly adopted Senate Joint Resolution 51 naming the mockingbird the official state bird of Tennessee.[65] See the Arkansas entry for a description.

TEXAS

The mockingbird, *Mimus polyglottos*, was adopted as the state bird of Texas by legislative act in 1927, following the recommendation of the Texas Federation of Women's Clubs.[66] See the Arkansas entry for a description.

UTAH

The sea gull, *Larus californicus*, was selected as the state bird of Utah by an act of the legislature in 1955.[67]

Size: Tail length: 6 inches; wing length: 14½ to 16 inches.

Range: Western North America, inland to Nevada, Utah, Kansas, Texas, and Colorado near large lake areas.

Physical description: The head, neck, upper tail feathers, tail, and all underparts are entirely white; the back, scapulars, and wings are between pale and light neutral gray, the wings tipped with white; the eye ring and rictus are vermillion-red; the subterminal third of the bill is red, immediately preceded by a black spot; the legs and feet are a pale grayish green.

Behavior: A faithful friend of the farmer, the California gull eats crickets, grasshoppers, and even mice. This gratitude of the farmer was the primary rationale behind the designation of the gull as the state bird. In 1848 the gulls were credited with saving farmers' crops by consuming the insects endangering them.[68] Aeronautic wizards, gulls are gymnasts of the sky, making the seemingly impossible appear effortless. They can appear motionless in midair by catching wind currents with perfect timing and precision while positioning their bodies at just the right angle. They are quiet birds, considered quite beneficial by agriculturalists, and are usually gentle creatures, exhibiting neither antagonism to nor fondness for man.

VERMONT

The hermit thrush, *Hylocichla guttata faxoni*, became the state bird of Vermont by an act of the legislature in 1941.[69]

Size: Total length: 6½ inches; tail length: 2½ to 3 inches.

Range: Eastern North America; southern migration to Gulf states.

Physical description: The upper parts are a cinnamon brown; the sides and flanks are buffy brown; there is a conspicuous orbital ring of dull white; the ear region is a grayish brown streaked with dull whitish; the underparts are a dull white tinged with a pale cream buff; the throat is streaked along each side in a sooty color; the chest has large triangular spots of dusky grayish brown, broader and more rounded on the lower chest; the tail is a dull cinnamon brown. Spring and summer plumage is brighter.

Behavior: A hardy bird, the hermit thrush arrives in early spring and departs in late fall for its migration southward. Traveling at night, thrushes sometimes become so tired and cold that they lose all natural shyness and feed from the human hand.

Hermit thrushes have been observed performing a curious activity known as "anting." The bird catches ants and places them in its feathers beneath the wings. It is thought that either the formic acid in the ants is effective in combating parasitic attacks or the ants are being horded for later consumption during migration. Talented singers, hermit thrushes sometimes sing in unison to form a harmonious chorus. Other times, they are capable of completely fooling the listener into thinking they are farther away or closer than they actually are by calling upon their extraordinary powers of ventriloquism. Protective of their young, thrushes fight so vigorously against predators that they can often fend off attacks.

VIRGINIA

The cardinal was designated the official state bird of Virginia by legislative act in 1950.[70] See the Illinois entry for a description.

WASHINGTON

The willow goldfinch, *Astragalinus tristis salicamans*, was designated the official bird of the state of Washington in 1951 by an act of the legislature.[71]

Size: Total length: 4½ inches; tail length: 1½ to 2 inches.

Range: Pacific coast region.

Physical description: The willow goldfinch is very similar to the eastern goldfinch (see the New Jersey entry), but the wings and tail are shorter and the coloration is darker. The adult male summer plumage of the back is tinged with pale olive green, and the winter adults and the young are decidedly darker or browner than the corresponding eastern goldfinch, with broader markings on the wings.

Behavior: Called the willow goldfinch because of its gravitation to damp areas conducive to the growth of willows, this small bird is a cheery singer and a graceful flyer. Very similar to the eastern goldfinch, this goldfinch begins to nest earlier than its counterparts, usually in April or May. The willow goldfinch is primarily a seed eater, munching mostly on seeds from harmful or neutral plants and occasionally supplementing his diet with harmful insects.

WEST VIRGINIA

The cardinal, *Richmondena cardinalis*, was designated the official bird of West Virginia by legislative act in 1949.[72] See the Illinois entry for a description.

WISCONSIN

The robin, *Turdus migratorius*, was designated the official state bird of Wisconsin by an act of the legislature in 1949.[73] When the school children of Wisconsin voted in 1926–1927 to select a state bird, the robin received twice as many votes as any other bird, but it was not until 1949 that the robin officially became the state bird.[74] See the Connecticut entry for a description.

WYOMING

The meadowlark, genus *Sturnella*, became the state bird of Wyoming by legislative act in 1927.[75] See the Kansas entry for a description.

DISTRICT OF COLUMBIA

Although the wood thrush was first proposed as the District's official bird in 1927,

it was not officially designated until January 31, 1967, by the commissioners.[76]

Size: Total length: 8½ inches.

Range: Eastern United States and southeastern Canada; wintering in Central America and Mexico.

Physical description: The plumage of *Hylocichia mustelina* is reddish-cinnamon above becoming olive-brown to tail; auricular region with white, yellowish-brown to tan streaks; underparts are white with large black spots; white ring surrounds eyes.

AMERICAN SAMOA

American Samoa has not designated an official bird.

COMMONWEALTH OF THE NORTHERN MARIANA ISLANDS

The Mariana fruit dove or Paluman tottut was adopted as the official Commonwealth bird in 1989.[77] See entry under Guam for description.

GUAM

The totot (*Ptilinopus*) was named the official territorial bird of Guam in 1969.[78]

Size: Total length: 9 inches.

Range: Mariana Islands.

Physical description: The totot, *Ptilinopus roseicapilla*, is also called the Mariana fruit dove and the love bird. Upper parts are very bright green with gray head, breast, upper back, and tail band; red cap; underparts with purple bar below breast, yellow belly, orange flanks, and pink-orange coverts beneath the tail.

Behavior: Rarely seen, preferring lofty perches and quiet, avoiding populated areas.

PUERTO RICO

Puerto Rico has not designated an official bird.

U.S. VIRGIN ISLANDS

In 1970, the United States Virgin Islands adopted the yellow breast (*Coereba flaveola*) as its official bird.[79]

Size: Total length: 5 inches.

Range: West Indies, Central and South America.

Physical description: Coereba flaveola, commonly called the bananaquit, is black above with white stripes over the eyes and white spots at the base of the wing tips; breast is bright yellow and throat and underparts are white; tail black with white spots; decurved short bill.

Behavior: The bananaquit is a very active honeycreeper that feeds on nectar, fruit, and small insects.

NOTES

1. Ala. Code §1–2–7.
2. Katherine B. Tippetts, "Selecting State Birds," *Nature* 19, no. 4 (1932): 231.
3. *Alabama State Emblems* (Montgomery: Alabama State Department of Archives and History, n.d.), pp. 17–18.
4. Ala. Code §1–2–17.
5. Alaska Stat. §44.09.060.
6. Ariz. Rev. Stat. Ann. §41–854.
7. 1929 Ark. Acts 1536.
8. *Nature* 19, no. 4 (1932): 231.
9. Cal. Govt. Code §423 (West).
10. *Nature* 19, no. 4 (1932): 231.
11. Colo. Rev. Stat. §24–80–910.
12. *Nature* 19, no. 4 (1932): 231, 234.
13. Conn. Gen. Stat. Ann. §3–109 (West).
14. Del. Code Ann. tit. 29, §304.
15. *Discover Wonderful Delaware: Official Insignia of Delaware* (Dover: Delaware State Development Department, n.d.).
16. 1907 Fla. Laws 1612.
17. *Nature* 19, no. 4 (1932): 234.
18. Ga. Code Ann. §50–3–50.
19. *Georgia's Official State Symbols* (Atlanta: Office of the Secretary of State, n.d.).
20. Ga. Code Ann. §50–3–51.
21. *The State of Georgia and Its Capitol* (Atlanta: State Museum of Science and Industry, Department of Archives and History, n.d.), p. 18.
22. Haw. Rev. Stat. §5–9.
23. *Grzimek's Animal Life* (New York: Van Nostrand Reinhold, 1975), vol. 7, pp. 284, 299.
24. Idaho Code §67–4501.
25. *Nature* 19, no. 4 (1932): 234.
26. Ill. Comp. Stat. Ann. ch. 5, §460/10 (Smith-Hurd).
27. *Illinois Blue Book, 1983–84*, p. 436.
28. Ind. Code Ann. §1–2–8–1 (West).
29. *1985–1986 Iowa Official Register*, p. 241.
30. Kan. Stat. Ann. §73–901.
31. Ky. Rev. Stat. Ann. §2.080.
32. La. Rev. Stat. Ann. §49–159 (West).
33. Me. Rev. Stat. tit. 1, §209.
34. Md. Ann. Code §13–302.
35. *Nature* 19, no. 4 (1932): 235.
36. Mass. Laws Ann. ch. 2, §9 (West).
37. Ibid., ch. 2, §36.
38. Information supplied by the Michigan Department of State.
39. Minn. Stat. Ann. §1.145 (West).
40. Miss. Code Ann. §3–3–11.
41. Ibid., §3–3–25.
42. Mo. Ann. Stat. §10.010 (Vernon).
43. Mont. Rev. Codes Ann. §1–1–504.
44. Rex C. Myers, *Symbols of Montana* (Helena: Montana Historical Society, 1976), p. 16.
45. Neb. Rev. Stat. §90–107.
46. Nev. Rev. Stat. §235.060.
47. N.H. Rev. Stat. Ann. §3:10.
48. *Manual for the General Court, 1981*.
49. N.J. Stat. Ann. §52:9A–1 (West).
50. N.M. Stat. Ann. §12–3–4.
51. N.Y. State Law §78 (McKinney).
52. *Nature* 19, no. 4 (1932): 235.

53. N.C. Gen. Stat. §145–2.

54. N.D. Cent. Code §54–02–06.

55. Ohio Rev. Code Ann. §5.03 (Page).

56. Okla. Stat. Ann. tit. 25, §98.

57. 1951 Okla. Sess. Laws 356.

58. Or. Rev. Stat. Ann. §186; *Oregon State Blue Book, 1977–78,* p. 139.

59. Pa. Stat. Ann. tit. 71, §1005 (Purdon).

60. R.I. Gen. Laws §42–4–5.

61. S.C. Code §1–1–630.

62. *1978 South Carolina Legislative Manual,* 59th ed.

63. S.C. Code §1–1–635.

64. S.D. Codified Laws Ann. §1–6–9.

65. *Tennessee Blue Book, 1983–84,* p. 373.

66. Tex. Rev. Civ. Stat. Ann. art. 6143c (Vernon).

67. Utah Code Ann. §63–13–9.

68. *Nature* 19, no. 4 (1932): 235.

69. Vt. Stat. Ann. tit. 1, §497.

70. Va. Code §7.1–39.

71. Wash. Rev. Code Ann. §1.20.040.

72. Information supplied by the West Virginia Department of Culture and History.

73. Wis. Stat. Ann. §1.10 (West).

74. *Wisconsin Blue Book, 1983–84,* p. 948.

75. Wyo. Stat. Ann. §8–3–105.

76. *Symbols of the District of Columbia* (Washington, D.C.: Government of the District of Columbia, Office of the Secretariat, Office of Visual Information Management, n.d.).

77. C.M.C. tit. 1, §233.

78. Guam Code Ann. tit. 1, §1023.

79. V.I. Code Ann. tit. 1, §105.

9

State and Territory Songs

State songs may celebrate a state's natural beauty and resources, its history and progress, or the hard work of its citizens. Some are quite familiar: "You Are My Sunshine" (Louisiana), "Home on the Range" (Kansas), and "Yankee Doodle" (Connecticut). Although others may be less familiar, forty-eight states have designated songs that express the unique character of the state. Among the states, only New Jersey and New York have never proclaimed state songs. On the other hand, Tennessee has five official songs and West Virginia has three. Furthermore, Georgia also has a state waltz; Kansas and North Dakota, a state march; Massachusetts, a state folk song; New Mexico, a Spanish language song; and Texas, a state flower song.

ALABAMA

The poem "Alabama" was adopted as the state song of Alabama in 1931. The poem was written by Julia S. Tutwiler and gifted to the state. Edna Gockel Gussen put the poem to music.[1] By the time the legislature officially adopted the song, it had already been in use for ten years as the state song. In 1917 the Alabama Federation of Music Clubs endorsed the song and gave it an award at its annual convention.[2]

ALASKA

"Alaska's Flag," composed by Elinor Dusenbury with words by Marie Drake, was adopted as the state song of Alaska in 1955.[3] The poem entitled "Alaska's Flag" first appeared in the October 1935 *School Bulletin*, published by the state's Department of Education. Marie Drake was an employee of that department for twenty-eight years, having become assistant commissioner of education in 1934 and remaining in that post until her retirement in 1945.[4]

ARIZONA

The Arizona state song or anthem, adopted by the Fourth State Legislature, is entitled "Arizona March Song." The words were written by Margaret Rowe Clifford; the music, by Maurice Blumenthal.[5]

ARKANSAS

In 1987, the Arkansas legislature clarified the state song situation by declaring two state songs, one state historical song, and one state anthem. The songs "Arkansas (You Run Deep in Me)," by Wayland Holyfield, and "Oh, Arkansas," words by Gary Klaff, music by Terry Rose, were both declared to be official state songs. "The Arkansas Traveler," which was composed and approved by the State Song Commission in 1949, was declared to be the official state historical song. The song "Arkansas" by Eva Ware Barnett, first named the state song in 1917, was now declared the official state anthem. However, this 1987 law further instructs the secretary of state to furnish copies of the song "Arkansas" by Eva Ware Barnett when filling requests for the state song.[6]

CALIFORNIA

"I Love You, California," words by F. B. Silverwood and music by A. F. Frankenstein, was first introduced to the public in 1913 by Mary Garden. In 1915, it became the official song of the San Francisco and San Diego Expositions. In 1951 "I Love You, California" was adopted as the official state song by the legislature.[7]

COLORADO

The song "Where the Columbines Grow," words and music by A. J. Flynn, was declared the official state song of Colorado by the legislature in 1915.[8]

CONNECTICUT

"Yankee Doodle" was adopted as the state song of Connecticut in 1978. The composer is unknown.[9]

DELAWARE

In 1925 "Our Delaware" was adopted as Delaware's state song. The words were written by George B. Hynson, and the music by Will M. S. Brown.[10]

FLORIDA

Stephen Foster's well-known song "Old Folks at Home," also known as "The Swanee River," was adopted as Florida's state song in 1935. The song was originally published in 1851.[11]

GEORGIA

"Georgia on My Mind" was designated the official state song of Georgia in 1979. The lyrics were written by Stuart Gorrell, and the music was composed by Hoagy Carmichael.[12] The 1979 act repealed a 1922 resolution designating "Georgia," words by Lottie Bell Wylie and music by Robert Loveman, as the official state song.[13]

Georgia also adopted an official state waltz, "Our Georgia," in 1951. Composed by James B. Burch to depict the glory of the state, this waltz was first played at the Georgia Democratic Convention in 1950.[14]

HAWAII

The song "Hawaii Ponoi" was adopted as the state song of Hawaii in 1967.[15]

IDAHO

In 1931 the Idaho legislature adopted "Here We Have Idaho" as the state song. The music, composed by Sallie Hume Douglas, had been copyrighted under the title "Garden of Paradise" in 1915. In 1930, the state obtained use of the melody forever from the composer. In 1917, McKinley Helm wrote the chorus, and, later, Albert J. Tompkins wrote additional verses to the song. Although other verses to the song had been written for use as an alma mater, the law cites the verses written by Helm and Tompkins as the official text for the state song.[16]

ILLINOIS

The song "Illinois," words by C. H. Chamberlain and music by Archibald Johnston, was established as the Illinois state song in 1925.[17]

INDIANA

In 1913 the song "On the Banks of the Wabash, Far Away" became the state song of

Indiana. Paul Dresser wrote both the words and the music.[18]

IOWA

In 1911 the Iowa legislature adopted "The Song of Iowa" as the official state song. Although inspired to write the song while in a Confederate prison in Richmond, Virginia, S. H. M. Byers did not do so until 1897. Byers chose the melody of "O Tannenbaum," the same melody used for "My Maryland," for the song. He thus put "loyal words" to the confederate song "My Maryland," which he had heard in prison.[19]

Although it is not officially designated, the "Iowa Corn Song" is recognized by popular approval as another Iowa song. This marching tune was written by George Hamilton and popularized as early as 1912.[20]

KANSAS

The Kansas legislature designated "Home on the Range," words by Dr. Brewster Higley and music by Dan Kelly, as the official state song in 1947.[21] This was originally titled "My Western Home" when it was penned by Dr. Higley, a pioneer physician in Kansas, in 1871 or 1872.[22]

Kansas has also designated two state marches. "The Kansas March" by Duff E. Middleton was named an official march in 1935 and then in 1992, "Here's Kansas" by Bill Post also became an official march of Kansas.[23]

KENTUCKY

"My Old Kentucky Home" by Stephen Collins Foster was designated the official state song of Kentucky in 1928. Kentucky also designated an official bluegrass song, "Blue Moon of Kentucky" by Bill Monroe, in 1994.[24]

LOUISIANA

Louisiana has two officially designated songs. The first song, "Give Me Louisiana," was written and composed by Doralice Fontane and arranged by John W. Schaum. In 1977 the legislature also designated "You Are My Sunshine" as an official state song. The words and music are by Jimmy H. Davis and Charles Mitchell.

In 1990, Louisiana also designated "The Gifts of Earth," music and lyrics by Frances LeBeau, as its official state environmental song.[25]

MAINE

"State of Maine Song" is the title of the state's official song. The music and lyrics were written by Roger Vinton Snow.[26]

MARYLAND

"Maryland! My Maryland!" was designated the official state song in 1939. The song, a poem written in 1861 by James Ryder Randall, is sung to the tune of "Lauriger Horatius."[27] Randall, a Marylander who lived in the Confederacy during the Civil War, wrote the poem after Union troops went through Baltimore in 1861.[28]

MASSACHUSETTS

In 1981 Massachusetts designated both an official commonwealth song and a folk song. The official commonwealth song is "All Hail to Massachusetts," words and music by Arthur J. Marsh. "Massachusetts," words and music by Arlo Guthrie, is the official commonwealth folk song.

In 1989, the Commonwealth also adopted an official patriotic song, "Massachusetts (Because of You Our Land Is Free)." Bernard Davidson wrote the music and lyrics. Then in 1997, "The Great State of Massachusetts," words by George A. Wells and music by J. Earl Bley, was named the state's glee club song. And in 1998, "Say Hello to Someone from Massachusetts" by Jenny Gomulka became the state polka song.[29]

MICHIGAN

"My Michigan," words by Giles Kavanagh and music by H. O'Reilly Clint, was designated an official state song of Michigan in 1937. In 1936 Governor Fitzgerald had designated this song as the official state song, but senate amendments changed a house resolution from designating "My Michigan" as the official song, to designating it as an official state song.[30]

MINNESOTA

"Hail! Minnesota," written in 1904–1905, was adopted as the state song of Minnesota in 1945. The music and the first verse were written by Truman E. Rickard. Arthur E. Upson wrote the words to the second verse. The song had first been used as the song of the University of Minnesota. Thus, the law adopting the song included a change from the original phrase "Hail to thee our college dear" to "Hail to thee our state so dear."[31]

MISSISSIPPI

The Board of Realtors of Jackson, Mississippi, set up an advisory committee to select an appropriate state song. The committee recommended the song "Go, Mississippi," words and music by Houston Davis, to the legislature for adoption. In 1962, the legislature acted positively on this recommendation.[32]

MISSOURI

"Missouri Waltz," arrangement by Frederick Knight Logan, melody by John Valentine

Eppel, and lyrics by J. R. Shannon, was designated the Missouri state song in 1949. The song was first published in 1914.[33]

MONTANA

In 1945 the Montana legislature declared the song "Montana," words by Charles C. Cohan and music by Joseph E. Howard, to be the official state song. The legislature had also designated an official state ballad, "Montana Melody," written by Carleen and LeGrande Harvey.[34]

NEBRASKA

"Beautiful Nebraska," words and music by Jim Fras, was adopted as Nebraska's official state song in 1967. The song was copyrighted in 1965.[35]

NEVADA

"Home Means Nevada" was adopted as the official state song of Nevada in 1933. It was written by Mrs. Bertha Raffetto of Reno.[36]

NEW HAMPSHIRE

New Hampshire recognizes nine state songs: "Old New Hampshire," words by Dr. John F. Holmes and music by Maurice Hoffman; "New Hampshire, My New Hampshire," words by Julius Richelson and music by Walter P. Smith; "New Hampshire Hills," words by Paul Scott Mowrer and music by Tom Powers; "Autumn in New Hampshire" by Leo Autumn; "New Hampshire's Granite State" by Anne B. Currier; "Oh, New Hampshire (You're My Home)" by Brownie McIntosh; "The Old Man of the Mountain" by Paul Belanger; "The New Hampshire State March" by Rene Richards; and "New Hampshire Naturally" by Rick Shaw and Ron Shaw.[37]

NEW JERSEY

The state of New Jersey does not have a state song. Attempts to make such a designation in 1940, 1954, and 1970 failed. Even an attempt in 1980 to designate "Born to Run" as the state's unofficial rock song failed for lack of legislative action.[38]

NEW MEXICO

In 1917 New Mexico adopted "O, Fair New Mexico," words and music by Elizabeth Garrett, as its official state song. In 1971 the legislature declared "Asi Es Nuevo Mejico," written by Amadeo Lucero, to be the Spanish language state song. Thus New Mexico has both an English language and a Spanish language official song.[39]

New Mexico also designated "Land of Enchantment—New Mexico," lyrics and music by Martin Murphy, Chick Raines, and Don Cook, as its official state ballad in 1989.[40]

NEW YORK

New York has no state songs. All bills to adopt a state song have thus far failed to pass the legislature.[41]

NORTH CAROLINA

The song "The Old North State" was declared the official state song of North Carolina in 1927. Another song, "A Toast" to North Carolina, was declared the official toast in 1957.[42]

NORTH DAKOTA

North Dakota has an official state song and a state march. The state song, "North Dakota Hymn," was written by James W. Foley and composed by Doctor C. S. Putnam. It was declared the state song in 1947.[43] In 1989 the legislature adopted "Flickertail March" by James D. Ployhar as the state march. The state march is to be played at appropriate state functions.[44]

OHIO

"Beautiful Ohio" was designated the official state song of Ohio in 1969. It was written by Ballard MacDonald and composed by Mary Earl.[45] Special lyrics were written by Wilbert B. White. Curiously, this 1918 waltz refers not to the state of Ohio, but to the Ohio River.[46]

OKLAHOMA

"Oklahoma," composed and written by Richard Rogers and Oscar Hammerstein, was declared the Oklahoma state song in 1953. The 1953 act repealed a 1935 act designating "Oklahoma (A Toast)" by Harriet Parker Camden as the state song. In 1996, "Oklahoma, My Native Land" by Martha Kemm Barrett was designated the state children's song.[47]

OREGON

"Oregon, My Oregon," words by J. A. Buchanan and music by Henry B. Murtagh, was adopted as the Oregon state song in 1927.[48]

PENNSYLVANIA

In 1990, Pennsylvania adopted the song "Pennsylvania," music and lyrics by Eddie Khoury and Ronnie Bonner, as its official state song.[49]

RHODE ISLAND

"Rhode Island," music and words by T. Clarke Brown, was declared to be the state song of Rhode Island in 1946. However, in

1996, a new state song, "Rhode Island's It for Me," words by Charlie Hall, music by Maria Day, and arrangement by Kathryn Chester, was named and the old state song became the new state march.[50]

SOUTH CAROLINA

The song "Carolina," words by Henry Timrod and music by Anne Custis Burgess, was declared to be the state song of South Carolina in 1911, when the legislature acted on the memorial of the South Carolina Daughters of the American Revolution. There is, however, another state song. "South Carolina on My Mind" was designated as an official state song in 1984 to promote the image of South Carolina beyond its borders "by further developing tourism and industry through the attraction of vacationers, prospective investors, and new residents."[51]

SOUTH DAKOTA

"Hail! South Dakota," music and words by Deecort Hammitt, was adopted as the official state song of South Dakota in 1943.[52]

TENNESSEE

Tennessee has five official state songs. In designating new official songs, the legislature has not repealed formerly designated songs. The first official song, "My Homeland, Tennessee" by Nell Grayson Taylor and Roy Lamont Smith was adopted in 1925. In 1935 "When It's Iris Time in Tennessee" by Willa Mae Waid became Tennessee's second official song. "My Tennessee" by Francis Hannah Tranum was adopted as the third song in 1955, and "The Tennessee Waltz" by Redd Stewart and Pee Wee King, was designated the fourth in 1965. The fifth official state song, "Rocky Top," by Boudleaux and Felice Bryant, was adopted in 1982.[53]

TEXAS

In 1928 the Texas legislature adopted "Texas, Our Texas" by William J. Marsh and Gladys Yoakum Wright as the official state song. This song was chosen following contests in each senatorial district and a final contest in Dallas, after which a legislative committee chose it twice.[54]

In 1933 the legislature designated a state flower song: "Bluebonnets," words by Julia D. Booth and music by Lora C. Crockett.[55]

UTAH

"Utah We Love Thee" was designated Utah's state song in 1937. It was written by Evan Stephens.[56]

VERMONT

In 1937 a committee was empowered to select an official state song. "Hail, Vermont!" was selected from over 100 songs in 1938, and the governor was informed of the selection. The song was written by Josephine Hovey Perry.[57]

VIRGINIA

"Carry Me Back to Old Virginia" by James B. Bland was declared by the General Assembly to be the official Commonwealth of Virginia song in 1940 and in 1997 it became known as the song emeritus.[58]

WASHINGTON

"Washington My Home" by Helen Davis was designated the official state song of Washington in 1959. In 1987, Washington also designated an official state folk song, "Roll On Columbia, Roll On," which was composed by Woody Guthrie.[59]

WEST VIRGINIA

West Virginia has adopted three state songs. "This Is My West Virginia" was written and composed by Mrs. Iris Bell of Charleston. "West Virginia My Home Sweet Home," words and music by Colonel Julian G. Hearne, Jr., was designated the official state song in 1947. The third song, "The West Virginia Hills," was written in 1879 by the Reverend David King as a poem for his wife, Ellen King. Mrs. King's name may be found on the music, as this was the request of the poet. H. E. Engle put the poem to music in 1885, and it was designated an official state song in 1961.[60]

WISCONSIN

"On, Wisconsin" was designated the state song of Wisconsin in 1959.[61] The song was composed in 1909 by William T. Purdy as a football fight song. While the song was recognized unofficially as the state song, several lyrics had come into existence in the fifty years before it was officially designated the state song. The 1959 law therefore actually prescribes the words to be used.[62]

WYOMING

In 1955 the march song "Wyoming," words by Charles E. Winter and music by George E. Knapp, was designated Wyoming's official state song.[63]

DISTRICT OF COLUMBIA

"The Star Spangled Banner" is the District of Columbia's official song.[64]

AMERICAN SAMOA

In 1973, "Amerika Samoa" was designated the official song of the territory.[65]

COMMONWEALTH OF THE NORTHERN MARIANA ISLANDS

The Commonwealth has not declared an official song.

GUAM

Guam has both an official territorial hymn and an official territorial march. "Guam Hymn," composed by Dr. Ramon M. Sablan, is the official hymn and "Guam March," composed by Jose Martinez Torres, is the official march.[66]

PUERTO RICO

"La Borinqueña" was made the Commonwealth's anthem in 1952. In 1977, the music and lyrics of this *danza* by Don Manuel Fernandez Juncos were adopted as the anthem.[67]

U.S. VIRGIN ISLANDS

"Virgin Islands March," composed by Alton A. Adams, Sr., is the official Virgin Islands anthem. It was adopted in 1982.[68]

NOTES

1. Ala. Code §1–2–16; *Alabama State Emblems* (Montgomery: Alabama State Department of Archives and History, n.d.), pp. 20–21.
2. 1931 Ala. Acts 190.
3. Alaska Stat. §44.09.040.
4. *Alaska Blue Book 1979*, p. 123.
5. *Welcome to Arizona* (Phoenix: Arizona Office of Tourism, n.d.).
6. Ark. Code Ann. (1987) §1–4–116.
7. *California's Legislature, 1984*, p. 203.
8. Colo. Rev. Stat. §24–80–909.
9. Conn. Gen. Stat. Ann. §3–110c (West).
10. *Official Insignia of Delaware* (Dover: Delaware State Development Department, n.d.).
11. 1935 Fla. Laws 1540.
12. Ga. Code Ann. §50–3–60.

13. *The State of Georgia and Its Capitol* (Atlanta: State Museum of Science and Industry, Department of Archives and History, 1979), p. 11.

14. 1951 Ga. Laws 842.

15. Haw. Rev. Stat. §5–10.

16. "Idaho State Song," Idaho Historical Society Reference Series no. 125 (Boise: Idaho Historical Society, December 1984), p. 1.

17. Ill. Ann. Stat. ch. 1, §3008 (Smith-Hurd).

18. Ind. Code Ann. §1–2–6–1 (West).

19. *1985–86 Iowa Official Register*, vol. 61, p. 238.

20. Ibid., p. 239.

21. Kan. Stat. Ann. §73–1301.

22. *Kansas Directory, 1982*, p. 128.

23. Kan. Stat. Ann. §73–801, §73–802.

24. Ky. Rev. Stat. Ann. §2.100.

25. *Louisiana Facts* (Baton Rouge: Louisiana Department of State, n.d.); La. Rev. Stat. Ann. §49–155.2 (West).

26. Me. Rev. Stat. tit. 1, §210.

27. Md. Ann. Code §13–307.

28. *Maryland Manual, 1981–1982*, p. 10.

29. Mass. Laws Ann. ch. 2, §19, §20, §31, §43, §44.

30. *Journal of the Michigan House of Representatives, 1937*, pp. 171, 1183.

31. *Minnesota Legislative Manual, 1958*, pp. 16–17; *Official Minnesota Symbols* (St. Paul: Minnesota Historical Society, December 1983), p. 1.

32. *Souvenir of Mississippi* (Jackson: Dick Molpus, n.d.), p. 28.

33. Mo. Ann. Stat. §10.050 (Vernon).

34. Mont. Code Ann. §1–1–511; Rex C. Myers, *Symbols of Montana* (Helena: Montana Historical Society, 1976), p. 14.

35. Neb. Rev. Stat. §90–111.

36. Nev. Rev. Stat. §235.030.

37. N.H. Rev. Stat. Ann. §3:7.

38. *Manual of the Legislature of New Jersey, 1984*, pp. 11–12.

39. N.M. Stat. Ann. §12–3–5, §12–3–6.

40. Ibid., §12–3–10.

41. Information supplied by Maureen Bigness, Director of Information Services, Department of State, Albany, New York.

42. N.C. Gen Stat. §149–1, §149–2.

43. N.D. Cent. Code §54–02–04.

44. Ibid., §54–02–09.

45. Ohio Rev. Code Ann. §5.09 (Page).

46. *Ohio Almanac* (Lorain: Lorain Journal Co., 1977), pp. 46, 60.

47. Okla. Stat. Ann. tit. 25, §94.1, §94.3, §94.5 (West).

48. *Journals of the Oregon Senate and House of the 34th Legislative Assembly, Regular Session, 1927*, p. 35.

49. Pa. Stat. Ann. tit. 1, §1010.4 (Purdon).

50. R.I. Gen. Laws §42–4–4, §42–4–4.1.

51. S.C. Code §1–1–685; *South Carolina State Symbols and Emblems* (Columbia: House of Representatives, n.d.).

52. *South Dakota Signs and Symbols* (n.p., n.d.).

53. Tenn. Code Ann. §4–1–302.

54. Tex. Rev. Civ. Stat. Ann. art. 6143b (Vernon).

55. Ibid., art. 6143bb (Vernon).

56. Utah Code Ann. §63–13–8.

57. 1937 Vt. Acts 350; *Vermont Legislative Directory and State Manual, 1979–80*, p. 19.

58. Va. Code §7.1–37.

59. Wash. Rev. Code Ann. §1.20.070, §1.20.073.

60. *West Virginia Blue Book, 1980*, p. 924.

61. Wis. Stat. Ann. §1.10 (West).

62. *State of Wisconsin 1983–84 Blue Book*, p. 948.

63. Wyo. Stat. Ann. §8–3–108.

64. www.ci.washington.dc.us/facts

65. A.S. Code tit. 1, §1105.

66. G.C.A. tit. 1, §416.

67. P.R. Laws Ann. tit. 1, §38, §39.

68. V.I. Code Ann. tit. 1, §104.

10

State and Territory Legal Holidays and Observances

Legal holidays are prescribed by law to commemorate important historical events, religious holidays, or people who have made significant contributions to society. Many of the states and territories recognize federal holidays, but they also add to the list of legal holidays their own special celebrations. Robert E. Lee's Birthday, for example, is a holiday in many southern states. Hawaii celebrates King Kamehameha I Day; Illinois celebrates Casimir Pulaski's Birthday; and Guam celebrates Lady Camarin Day.

Observances are not necessarily legal holidays, but days, weeks, or months recognized in the laws of many of the states and territories as worthy of special honor and remembrance. Some state codes may designate a legal holiday also as a special day of observance. Massachusetts sets out some 135 observances in its laws. They include such things as Homeless Unity Day, Armenian Martyrs' Day, Visiting Nurse Association Week, Rose Fitzgerald Kennedy Day, and Commodore John Barry Day. Taken all together, the observances provide an outline of historical, cultural, and social events in the states and territories.

ALABAMA

Legal Holidays

1. Sunday
2. New Year's Day (January 1)
3. Robert E. Lee's Birthday (third Monday in January)
4. Martin Luther King, Jr.'s Birthday (third Monday in January)
5. George Washington's Birthday (third Monday in February)
6. Thomas Jefferson's Birthday (third Monday in February)
7. Confederate Memorial Day (fourth Monday in April)
8. National Memorial Day (last Monday in May)
9. Jefferson Davis's Birthday (first Monday in June)
10. Independence Day (July 4)
11. Labor Day (first Monday in September)
12. Columbus Day (second Monday in October)
13. Fraternal Day (second Monday in October)
14. Veterans' Day (November 11)
15. Christmas Day (December 25)
16. Any day proclaimed by the governor as Thanksgiving

Notes: In Mobile and Baldwin counties, Mardi Gras is a legal holiday. Holidays falling on a Sunday are observed the next day. Holidays falling on a Saturday are observed on the preceding day.[1]

ALASKA

Legal Holidays

1. Sunday
2. New Year's Day (January 1)
3. Martin Luther King, Jr.'s Birthday (third Monday in January)
4. Presidents' Day (third Monday in February)
5. Seward's Day (last Monday in March)
6. Memorial Day (last Monday in May)
7. Independence Day (July 4)
8. Labor Day (first Monday in September)
9. Alaska Day (October 18)
10. Veterans' Day (November 11)
11. Thanksgiving Day (fourth Thursday in November)
12. Christmas Day (December 25)
13. Any day publicly proclaimed by the governor or the president of the United States as a legal holiday[2]

Notes: When a holiday (other than a Sunday itself) falls on a Sunday, both that Sunday and the following Monday are legal holidays. When a holiday falls on a Saturday, both that Saturday and the preceding Friday are both legal holidays.[3]

Observances

Ernest Gruening Day (February 6)[4]

Elizabeth Peratrovich Day (February 16)[5]

Bob Bartlett Day (April 20)

Preservation of the Family Month (May)

Family Day (May 1)

Dutch Harbor Remembrance Day (June 3)

Alaska Flag Day (July 9)[6]

Wickersham Day (August 24)[7]

William A. Egan Day (October 8)[8]

Anthony J. Dimond Day (November 30)

Pearl Harbor Remembrance Day (December 7)[9]

ARIZONA

Legal Holidays

1. Sunday of each week
2. New Year's Day (January 1)
3. Martin Luther King, Jr./Civil Rights Day (third Monday in January)
4. Lincoln/Washington Presidents' Day (third Monday in February)
5. Mother's Day (second Sunday in May)
6. Memorial Day (last Monday in May)
7. Father's Day (third Sunday in June)
8. Independence Day (July 4)
9. American Family Day (first Sunday in August)
10. Labor Day (first Monday in September)
11. Constitution Commemoration Day (September 17)
12. Columbus Day (second Monday in October)
13. Veterans' Day (November 11)
14. Thanksgiving Day (fourth Thursday in November)
15. Christmas Day (December 25)

Notes: Except for holidays numbered 1, 5, 7, 9, and 11, when a holiday falls on a Sunday, it is observed on the following Monday. If New Year's Day, Independence Day, Veterans' Day, or Christmas Day falls on a Saturday, it is observed on the preceding Friday. If Constitution Day falls on a day other than Sunday, it is observed on the Sunday preceding September 17.[10]

Observances

Prisoners of War Remembrance Day (April 9)

Arbor Day (Last Friday in April)

Korean War Veterans' Day (July 27)[11]

ARKANSAS

Legal Holidays

1. New Year's Day (January 1)
2. Martin Luther King, Jr.'s Birthday and Robert E. Lee's Birthday (third Monday in January)
3. George Washington's Birthday (third Monday in February)
4. Memorial Day (last Monday in May)
5. Independence Day (July 4)
6. Labor Day (first Monday in September)
7. Veterans' Day (November 11)
8. Thanksgiving Day (fourth Thursday in November)
9. Christmas Eve (December 24)
10. Christmas Day (December 25)

Notes: State employees are granted holidays for their birthdays. Holidays falling on Sunday are observed on the next Monday and holidays falling on Saturday are observed on the preceding Friday.[12]

Observances

General Douglas MacArthur Day (January 26)

Abraham Lincoln's Birthday (February 12)

Arkansas Teachers' Day (first Tuesday in March)

Arbor Day (third Monday in March)

Patriots' Day (April 19)

Arkansas Bird Day (April 26)

Good Friday (Friday preceding Easter)

Jefferson Davis's Birthday (June 3)

Columbus Day (October 12)[13]

In addition, the state of Arkansas has designated six other special observances:

Arkansas Agriculture Recognition Day (first Friday in March)

Prisoners of War Remembrance Day (April 9)[14]

Confederate Flag Day (Saturday preceding Easter Sunday)[15]

National Garden Week (first full week in June)

POW/MIA Recognition Day (third Friday in September)

White Cane Safety Day (October 15)[16]

CALIFORNIA

Legal Holidays

1. Every Sunday
2. New Year's Day (January 1)
3. Dr. Martin Luther King, Jr., Day (third Monday in January)
4. Lincoln Day (February 12)
5. Presidents' Day (third Monday in February)
6. Cesar Chavez Day (March 31)
7. Memorial Day (last Monday in May)
8. Independence Day (July 4)
9. Labor Day (first Monday in September)
10. Admission Day (September 9)
11. Columbus Day (second Monday in October)
12. Veterans' Day (November 11)

13. Christmas Day (December 25)

14. Good Friday from noon to 3:00 P.M. (Friday preceding Easter)

15. Days proclaimed by the governor or the president of the United States for public fast, thanksgiving, or holiday[17]

Notes: If the holidays of January 1, February 12, July 4, September 9, November 11, or December 25 fall on Sunday, the following Monday is a holiday. If Veterans' Day (November 11) falls on a Saturday, the preceding Friday is a holiday.[18]

Observances

A Day of Remembrance: Japanese American Evacuation (February 19)[19]

Arbor Day (March 7)[20]

John Muir Day (April 21)[21]

Native American Day (fourth Friday in September)[22]

Cabrillo Day (September 28)[23]

Stepparents' Day (first Sunday in October)[24]

Pearl Harbor Day (December 7)[25]

COLORADO

Legal Holidays

1. New Year's Day (January 1)

2. Dr. Martin Luther King, Jr.'s Birthday (third Monday in January)

3. Washington-Lincoln Day (third Monday in February)

4. Memorial Day (last Monday in May)

5. Independence Day (July 4)

6. Labor Day (first Monday in September)

7. Columbus Day (second Monday in October)

8. Veterans' Day (November 11)

9. Thanksgiving Day (fourth Thursday in November)

10. Christmas Day (December 25)

11. Any days proclaimed by the governor or the President of the United States for thanksgiving, prayer, or fasting

12. Saturdays from noon until midnight during the months of June, July, and August in cities with a population of 25,000 or more

Note: When holidays fall on Sundays, the following day is considered to be the holiday.[26]

Observances

Susan B. Anthony Day (February 15)

Arbor Day (third Friday in April)

Good Roads Day (second Friday in May)

Colorado Day (first Monday of August)

Leif Erikson Day (October 9)[27]

CONNECTICUT

Legal Holidays

1. New Year's Day (January 1)

2. Martin Luther King Day (first Monday after January 15)

3. Lincoln Day (February 12)

4. Washington's Birthday (third Monday in February)

5. Memorial Day (last Monday in May)

6. Independence Day (July 4)

7. Labor Day (first Monday in September)

8. Columbus Day (second Monday in October)

9. Veterans' Day (November 11)

10. Christmas Day (December 25)

11. Any day proclaimed or recommended by the governor or the President of the

United States for thanksgiving, fasting, or religious observance

Notes: When holidays fall on a Sunday, the following Monday is a legal holiday; when holidays fall on a Saturday, the preceding Friday is a legal holiday. In the public schools, Presidents' Day may be observed on the third Monday in February in lieu of observing Washington's Birthday and Lincoln Day.[28]

Observances

Martin Luther King Day (first Monday on or after January 15)

Youth to Work Day (second Sunday in February)

Retired Teachers Day (third Wednesday in February)

Iwo Jima Day (February 23)

St. Patrick's Day (March 17)

Greek-American Day (March 25)

Pan American Day (April 14)

Green Up Day (last Saturday in April)

Friends Day (fourth Sunday in April)

Workers' Memorial Day (April 28)

Loyalty Day (May 1)

Senior Citizens Day (first Sunday in May)

Polish-American Day (May 3)

Austrian-American Day (May 15)

Christa Corrigan McAuliffe Day (May 24)

Arbor Day (last Friday in May)

Flag Day (June 14)

Destroyer Escort Day (third Saturday in June)

Disability Awareness Day (July 26)

Korean Armistice Day (July 27)

Volunteer Fire Fighter and Volunteer Emergency Medical Services Personnel Day (first Saturday in August)

End of World War II Day (August 14)

Ukrainian-American Day (August 24)

Women's Independence Day (August 26)

Prudence Crandall Day (September 3)

911 Day (September 11)

School Safety Patrol Day (second Monday in September)

Nathan Hale Day (last Friday in September)

Indian Day (last Friday in September)

Puerto Rico Day (fourth Sunday in September)

German-American Day (October 6)

Leif Erikson Day (a day within the first nine days of October)

Fire Prevention Day (on or about October 9)

Republic of China on Taiwan-American Day (October 10)

National Children's Day (second Sunday in October)

Columbus Day (second Monday in October)

Hungarian Freedom Fighters Day (October 23)

Veterans' Day (November 11)

Romanian-American Day (December 1)

Lithuanian Day (a date certain in each year)

Powered Flight Day (a date certain in each year)[29]

DELAWARE

Legal Holidays

1. New Year's Day (January 1)
2. Martin Luther King, Jr. Day (third Monday in January)
3. Presidents' Day (third Monday in February)
4. Good Friday (Friday preceding Easter)
5. Memorial Day (last Monday in May)

6. Independence Day (July 4)

7. Labor Day (first Monday in September)

8. Columbus Day (second Monday in October)

9. Veterans' Day (November 11)

10. Thanksgiving Day (fourth Thursday in November)

11. Friday after Thanksgiving

12. Christmas Day (December 25)

13. Saturdays

14. Day of the biennial election

Notes: Return Day (the second day after the general election) is a legal holiday after noon in Sussex County. If a legal holiday falls on Sunday, the following Monday is a legal holiday. If a legal holiday falls on Saturday, the preceding Friday is a legal holiday.[30]

Observances

Arbor Day (last Friday in April)

Native American Day (first Saturday in September after Labor Day)

Delaware Day (December 7)[31]

FLORIDA

Legal Holidays

1. Sundays

2. New Year's Day (January 1)

3. Martin Luther King, Jr.'s Birthday (January 15)

4. Robert E. Lee's Birthday (January 19)

5. Lincoln's Birthday (February 12)

6. Washington's Birthday (third Monday in February)

7. Good Friday (Friday preceding Easter)

8. Pascua Florida Day (April 2)

9. Confederate Memorial Day (April 26)

10. Memorial Day (last Monday in May)

11. Jefferson Davis's Birthday (June 3)

12. Flag Day (June 14)

13. Independence Day (July 4)

14. Labor Day (first Monday in September)

15. Columbus Day and Farmers' Day (second Monday in October)

16. Veterans' Day (November 11)

17. General Election Day

18. Thanksgiving Day (fourth Thursday in November)

19. Christmas Day (December 25)

20. Days of mourning proclaimed by the President of the United States and the governor

Notes: In counties where carnival organizations exist to celebrate Mardi Gras, Shrove Tuesday is a legal holiday. Chief judges are authorized to designate Rosh Hashanah and Yom Kippur as legal holidays for courts in their judicial circuit. In Hillsborough County, Gasparilla Day and Parade Day of the Hillsborough County Fairs and Plant City Strawberry Festival are legal holidays. Desoto Day, the last Friday of Desoto Week, is a legal holiday in Manatee County. The days following holidays that fall on Sunday are public holidays.[32]

Observances

Arbor Day (third Friday in January)

Save the Florida Panther Day (third Saturday in March)

Pascua Florida Week (March 27 to April 2)

Florida State Day known as Pascua Florida Day (April 2)

Children's Day (second Tuesday in April)

Pan-American Day (April 14)

Patriots' Day (April 19)

Law Week (week starting with Monday preceding May 1)

Law Day (May 1)

Teacher's Day (third Friday in May)

Law Enforcement Appreciation Month (May)

Law Enforcement Memorial Day (May 15)

Juneteenth Day (June 19)

Grandmother's Day (second Sunday in October)

I Am an American Day (third Sunday in October)

Retired Teachers' Day (Sunday beginning the third week of November)[33]

GEORGIA

Legal Holidays

1. New Year's Day (January 1)
2. Martin Luther King, Jr., Day (third Monday in January)
3. Washington's Birthday (third Monday in February)
4. Memorial Day (last Monday in May)
5. Independence Day (July 4)
6. Labor Day (first Monday in September)
7. Columbus Day (second Monday in October)
8. Veterans' Day (November 11)
9. Thanksgiving Day (fourth Thursday in November)
10. Christmas Day (December 25)

Notes: In addition, any days proclaimed by the governor for fasting, prayer, or religious observance are also legal holidays. The governor is obligated by statute to close state offices for twelve days per year and must choose January 19, April 26, or June 3 as one of those legal holidays.[34]

Observances

Sundays (only official religious holidays)

American History Month (February)

Georgia History Month (February)

Home Education Week (first week in February)

Firefighter Appreciation Day (first Tuesday in February)

Girls and Women in Sports Day (first Thursday in February)

Law Enforcement Officer Appreciation Day (second Monday in February)

Wildflower Week (fourth week in March)

Former Prisoners of War Recognition Day (April 9)

Peace Officer Memorial Day (May 15)

Police Week (week in which May 15 falls)

Children's Day (first Sunday in October)

Bird Day (second Thursday in October)[35]

Clean Water Week (third week in October)

Bill of Rights Day (December 15)

HAWAII

Legal Holidays

1. New Year's Day (January 1)
2. Dr. Martin Luther King, Jr., Day (third Monday in January)
3. Presidents' Day (third Monday in February)
4. Prince Jonah Kuhio Kalanianaole Day (March 26)
5. Good Friday (Friday preceding Easter)
6. Memorial Day (last Monday in May)
7. King Kamehameha I Day (June 11)
8. Independence Day (July 4)
9. Admission Day (third Friday in August)
10. Labor Day (first Monday in September)

11. Veterans' Day (November 11)

12. Thanksgiving Day (fourth Thursday in November)

13. Christmas Day (December 25)

14. Election days other than primaries and special elections in counties where elections are occurring

15. Any days designated as a holiday by the governor or the President of the United States

Notes: When a holiday falls on a Sunday, the following Monday is observed as a holiday. When a holiday falls on a Saturday, the preceding Friday is observed as a holiday.[36]

Observances

Baha'i New Year's Day (March 21)

Buddha Day (April 8)

Father Damien De Veuster Day (April 15)

Ocean Day (first Wednesday in June)

Children and Youth Month (October)

Children and Youth Day (first Sunday in October)

Discoverers' Day (second Monday in October)

Respect for Our Elders Day (third Sunday in October)

Arbor Day (first Friday in November)

Bodhi Day (December 8)[37]

IDAHO

Legal Holidays

1. Sundays

2. New Year's Day (January 1)

3. Martin Luther King, Jr.-Idaho Human Rights Day (third Monday in January)

4. Washington's Birthday (third Monday in February)

5. Decoration Day (last Monday in May)

6. Independence Day (July 4)

7. Labor Day (first Monday in September)

8. Columbus Day (second Monday in October)

9. Veterans' Day (November 11)

10. Thanksgiving Day (fourth Thursday in November)

11. Christmas Day (December 25)

12. Any day designated by the governor or the President of the United States as a holiday or day of fasting or thanksgiving

Notes: When a holiday other than a Sunday itself falls on a Sunday, the following Monday is a holiday. When a holiday falls on a Saturday, the preceding Friday is a holiday.[38]

Observances

Constitutional Commemorative Day (September 17)[39]

ILLINOIS

Legal Holidays

1. New Year's Day (January 1)

2. Martin Luther King, Jr.'s Birthday (third Monday in January)

3. Abraham Lincoln's Birthday (February 12)

4. Presidents' Day (third Monday in February)

5. Casimir Pulaski's Birthday (first Monday in March)

6. Good Friday (Friday preceding Easter)

7. Memorial Day (May 30)

8. Independence Day (July 4)

9. Labor Day (first Monday in September)

10. Columbus Day (second Monday in October)

11. Veterans' Day (November 11)

12. Thanksgiving Day (fourth Thursday in November)

13. Christmas Day (December 25)

14. Election days (when House of Representatives elections occur)

15. Any days proclaimed as legal holidays by the governor

Note: Saturdays from noon to midnight are half-holidays.[40]

Observances

American History Month (February)

Viet Nam War Veterans Day (March 29)

Arbor and Bird Day (last Friday in April)

Chaplain's Day (first Sunday in May)

Mothers' Day (second Sunday in May)

Citizenship Day (third Sunday in May)

Senior Citizens' Day (third Sunday in May)

Retired Teachers' Week (fourth week of May)

Flag Day (June 14)

Fathers' Day (third Sunday in June)

Korean War Armistice Day (July 27)

Gold Star Mothers' Day (second Sunday in August)

Prairie Week (third full week of September)

POW/MIA Recognition Day (third Friday in September)

Grandmothers' Day (second Sunday in October)

Coal Miners Memorial Day (November 13)[41]

Pearl Harbor Remembrance Day (December 7)

INDIANA

Legal Holidays

1. Sundays

2. New Year's Day (January 1)

3. Martin Luther King, Jr.'s Birthday (third Monday in January)

4. Abraham Lincoln's Birthday (February 12)

5. George Washington's Birthday (third Monday in February)

6. Good Friday (Friday preceding Easter)

7. Memorial Day (last Monday in May)

8. Independence Day (July 4)

9. Labor Day (first Monday in September)

10. Columbus Day (second Monday in October)

11. Election Day (any general, municipal, or primary election)

12. Veterans' Day (November 11)

13. Thanksgiving Day (fourth Thursday in November)

14. Christmas Day (December 25)

Notes: When a holiday other than a Sunday itself falls on a Sunday, the following Monday is the legal holiday. When a holiday falls on a Saturday, the preceding Friday is the legal holiday.[42]

Observances

George Rogers Clark Day (February 25)

Casimir Pulaski Day (first Monday in March)

Flag Day (June 14)

Northwest Ordinance Day (July 13)

Indiana Day (December 11)[43]

IOWA

Legal Holidays

1. New Year's Day (January 1)
2. Dr. Martin Luther King, Jr.'s Birthday (third Monday in January)
3. Lincoln's Birthday (February 12)
4. Washington's Birthday (third Monday in February)
5. Memorial Day (last Monday in May)
6. Independence Day (July 4)
7. Labor Day (first Monday in September)
8. Veterans' Day (November 11)
9. Thanksgiving Day (fourth Thursday in November)
10. Christmas Day (December 25)[44]

Observances

Dr. Martin Luther King, Jr., Day (third Monday in January)

Iowa State Flag Day (March 29)

Arbor Week (last week in April)

Arbor Day (last Friday in April)

Mother's Day (second Sunday in May)

Father's Day (third Sunday in June)

Independence Sunday (Sunday preceding July 4 or July 4 if on a Sunday)

Herbert Hoover Day (August 10)

Columbus Day (October 12)

Youth Honor Day (October 31)

Veterans' Day (November 11)

Note: Veterans' Day is to be observed as a legal holiday.[45]

KANSAS

Legal Holidays

1. New Year's Day (January 1)
2. Lincoln's Birthday (February 12)
3. Washington's Birthday (third Monday in February)
4. Memorial Day (last Monday in May)
5. Independence Day (July 4)
6. Labor Day (first Monday in September)
7. Columbus Day (second Monday in October)
8. Veterans' Day (November 11)
9. Thanksgiving Day (fourth Thursday in November)
10. Christmas Day (December 25)[46]

Observances

Arbor Day (last Friday in March)

Mother's Day (second Sunday in May)

Flag Day (June 14)

American Indian Day (fourth Saturday in September)

General Pulaski's Memorial Day (October 11)

Family Day (Sunday after Thanksgiving)

Pearl Harbor Remembrance Day (December 7)[47]

KENTUCKY

Legal Holidays

1. New Year's Day (January 1)
2. Martin Luther King, Jr.'s Birthday (third Monday in January)
3. Robert E. Lee Day (January 19)
4. Franklin D. Roosevelt Day (January 30)
5. Lincoln's Birthday (February 12)
6. Washington's Birthday (third Monday in February)
7. Memorial Day (last Monday in May)
8. Confederate Memorial Day and Jefferson Davis' Birthday (June 3)

9. Independence Day (July 4)

10. Labor Day (first Monday in September)

11. Columbus Day (second Monday in October)

12. Veterans' Day (November 11)

13. Christmas Day (December 25)

14. Any days proclaimed as holidays or days of thanksgiving by the governor or the President of the United States

Note: If a holiday falls on a Sunday, the following Monday is observed as a holiday.[48]

Observances

Environmental Education Month (March)

Commonwealth Cleanup Week (fourth week in March)

Barrier Awareness Day (May 7)

Mother's Day (second Sunday in May)

Retired Teachers' Week (fourth week of May)

Garden Week (first week of June)

Flag Day (June 14)

Disability Day (August 2)

Grandmother's Day (second Sunday in October)

General Pulaski's Birthday (October 11)

Native American Indian Month (November)

Kentucky Harvest Day (November 15)[49]

LOUISIANA

Legal Holidays

1. Sundays

2. New Year's Day (January 1)

3. Battle of New Orleans (January 8)

4. Dr. Martin Luther King, Jr.'s Birthday (third Monday in January)

5. Robert E. Lee Day (January 19)

6. Washington's Birthday (third Monday in February)

7. Good Friday (Friday before Easter)

8. National Memorial Day (last Monday in May)

9. Confederate Memorial Day (June 3)

10. Independence Day (July 4)

11. Huey P. Long Day (August 30)

12. Labor Day (first Monday in September)

13. Columbus Day (second Monday in October)

14. All Saints' Day (November 1)

15. Veterans' Day (November 11)

16. Thanksgiving Day (fourth Thursday in November)

17. Christmas Day (December 25)

18. Any days proclaimed by the governor

Notes: When January 1, July 4, or December 25 falls on a Sunday, the next day is a holiday; when they fall on a Saturday, the preceding Friday is a holiday, if declared by ordinance.

Governing authorities of the parishes may declare Saturdays to be holidays, but if that is not accomplished, Saturdays from noon until midnight are half-holidays. The provision for Saturday half-holidays does not apply to the Parish of Orleans or Baton Rouge. In certain parishes and municipalities, Mardi Gras is a holiday if declared so by local authorities. When the governor declares the Friday following Thanksgiving Day a holiday, that holiday is designated as Acadian Day.[50]

Observances

Arbor Day (third Friday in January)

Doctors' Day (March 30)

Garden Week (first week in June)

My Nationality American Day (December 17)[51]

MAINE

Legal Holidays

1. Sundays
2. New Year's Day (January 1)
3. Martin Luther King, Jr., Day (third Monday in January)
4. Washington's Birthday (third Monday in February)
5. Patriot's Day (third Monday in April)
6. Memorial Day (last Monday in May)
7. Independence Day (July 4)
8. Labor Day (first Monday in September)
9. Columbus Day (second Monday in October)
10. Veterans' Day (November 11)
11. Christmas Day (December 25)

Notes: If the federal government designates May 30 as Memorial Day, it will be celebrated on May 30. When holidays fall on a Sunday, the following Monday is a holiday.[52]

Observances

American History Month (February)

Maine Cultural Heritage Week (week containing March 15)

Statehood Day (March 15)

Edmund S. Muskie Day (March 28)

Former Prisoner of War Recognition Day (April 9)

Arbor Week (third full week in May)

Maine Merchant Marine Day (May 22)

Maine Clean Water Week (first full week in June)

Garden Week (first full week in June)

Samantha Smith Day (first Monday in June)

Seamen's Memorial Day (second Sunday in June)

Saint Jean-Baptiste Day (June 24)

R. B. Hall Day (last Saturday in June)

Old Home Week (week beginning second Sunday in August)

Alcohol Awareness Week (first full week in September)

Landowner Recognition Day (third Saturday in September)

Children's Day (last Friday in September)

Deaf Culture Week (last full week in September)

Poetry Day (October 15)

Maine Business Women's Week (third full week in October)

Margaret Chase Smith Day (December 14)

Chester Greenwood Day (December 21)[53]

MARYLAND

Legal Holidays

1. New Year's Day (January 1)
2. Dr. Martin Luther King, Jr.'s Birthday (January 15)
3. Lincoln's Birthday (February 12)
4. Washington's Birthday (third Monday in February)
5. Maryland Day (March 25)
6. Good Friday (Friday preceding Easter)
7. Memorial Day (last Monday in May)
8. Independence Day (July 4)
9. Labor Day (first Monday in September)
10. Defenders' Day (September 12)
11. Columbus Day (second Monday in October)

12. Veterans' Day (November 11)
13. Thanksgiving Day (fourth Thursday in November)
14. Christmas Day (December 25)
15. General statewide election days
16. Any days designated by the President of the United States or governor for businesses to be closed

Note: Holidays falling on a Sunday are observed on the following Monday.[54]

Observances

John Hanson's Birthday (April 13)
Law Day USA (May 1)
Poetry Day (October 15)[55]

MASSACHUSETTS

Legal Holidays

1. New Year's Day (January 1)
2. Martin Luther King, Jr.'s Birthday (third Monday in January)
3. Presidents' Day (third Monday in February)
4. Patriots' Day (third Monday in April)
5. Memorial Day (last Monday in May)
6. Independence Day (July 4)
7. Labor Day (first Monday in September)
8. Columbus Day (second Monday in October)
9. Veterans' Day (November 11)
10. Thanksgiving Day (fourth Thursday in November)
11. Christmas Day (December 25)

Note: If January 1, July 4, November 11, or December 25 falls on a Sunday, the following Monday is a holiday.[56]

Observances

New Orleans Day (January 8)
Albert Schweitzer's Reverence for Life Day (January 14)
Martin Luther King, Jr. Day (January 15)
Jaycee Week (third week in January)
Jaycee Day (Wednesday of the third week in January)
Child Nutrition Week (last week in January)
American History Month (February)
Tadeusz Kosciuszko Day (first Sunday in February)
USO Appreciation Day (February 4)
Boy Scout Week (first full week of February)
Lincoln Day (February 12)
Spanish War Memorial Day and Maine Memorial Day (February 15)
Lithuanian Independence Day (February 16)
Iwo Jima Day (February 19)
Washington's Day (third Monday in February)
Homeless Unity Day (February 20)
Homeless Awareness Week (last week in February)
Kalevala Day (February 28)
Boston Massacre Anniversary (March 5)
Lucy Stone Day (March 8)
Slovak Independence Day (March 14)
Peter Francisco Day (March 15)
Robert Goddard Day (March 16)
Evacuation Day (March 17)
Employ the Older Worker Week (third week in March)
Practical Nursing Education Week (last full week in March)
Greek Independence Day (March 25)
Italian American War Veterans of the United States, Inc. Day (March 27)
Vietnam Veterans Day (March 29)

Parliamentary Law Month (April)

School Library Media Month (April)

Student Government Day (first Friday in April)

Veterans of World War I Hospital Day (first Sunday in April)

Bataan-Corregidor Day (April 9)

Former Prisoner of War Recognition Day (April 9)

Aunt's and Uncle's Day (second Sunday in April)

Patriots' Day (April 19)

Secretaries Week (last full week in April)

Licensed Practical Nurse Week (last full week in April)

Secretaries Day (Wednesday in the last full week in April)

Armenian Martyrs' Day (April 24)

Arbor and Bird Day (last Friday in April)

School Principals' Recognition Day (April 27)

Exercise Tiger Day (April 28)

Workers' Memorial day (fourth Friday in April)

Earth Week (one week in April, unspecified)

Senior Citizens Month (May)

Keep Massachusetts Beautiful Month (May)

Law Enforcement Memorial Month (May)

Loyalty Day (May 1)

Polish Constitution Day (May 3)

Horace Mann Day (May 4)

Massachusetts Whale Awareness Day (first Thursday in May)

Mother's Day (second Sunday in May)

Massachusetts Emergency Responders Memorial Day (second Sunday in May)

Emergency Management Week (week following the second Sunday in May)

Police Officers' Week (week in which May 15 occurs)

Police Memorial Day (May 15)

Visiting Nurse Association Week (third week in May)

National Family Week (third week in May)

American Indian Heritage Week (third week in May)

Massachusetts National Guard Week (week preceding third Saturday in May)

Joshua James Day (third Sunday in May)

Anniversary of the Death of General Marquis de Lafayette (May 20)

Massosoit Day (Wednesday of the third week in May)

Maritime Day (May 22)

Anniversary of the Enlistment of Deborah Samson (May 23)

Special Needs Awareness Day (May 23)

Massachusetts Art Week (last week in May)

Memorial Day (last Monday in May)

Presidents' Day (May 29)

Teachers' Day (first Sunday in June)

Retired Members of the Armed Forces Day (first Monday in June)

Public Employees Appreciation Day (first Wednesday in June)

Rabies Prevention Week (second week in June)

Children's Day (second Sunday in June)

Fire Fighters Memorial Sunday (second Sunday in June)

State Walking Sunday (second Sunday in June)

Flag Day (June 14)

Anniversary of the Battle of Bunker Hill (June 17)

Father's Day (third Sunday in June)

Destroyer Escort Day (third Saturday in June)

Saint Jean de Baptiste Day (fourth Sunday in June)

John Carver Day (fourth Sunday in June)

Battleship Massachusetts Memorial Day (last Saturday in June)

Reflex Sympathetic Dystrophy Awareness Month (July)

Independence Day (July 4)

Lead Poisoning Prevention Week (third Sunday in July)

Rose Fitzgerald Kennedy Day (July 22)

Korean War Veterans Day (July 27)

Public Employees Week (first week in August)

Jamaican Independence Day (first Monday in August)

Youth in Government Day (first Friday in August)

Purple Heart Day (August 7)

Social Security Day (August 14)

Liberty Tree Day (August 14)

Caribbean Week (last week in August)

Susan B. Anthony Day (August 26)

Sight-saving Month (September)

Literacy Awareness Month (September)

Labor Week (first week in September)

Endangered Species Day (second Saturday in September)

Grandparents' Day (Sunday after the first Monday in September)

Alzheimer's Awareness Week (week after the Sunday after the first Monday)

Commodore John Barry Day (September 13)

Constitution Day (September 17)

Cystic Fibrosis Week (third full week in September)

POW/MIA Day (third Friday in September)

National Hunting and Fishing Day (fourth Saturday in September)

Pro-Life Month (October)

Lupus Awareness Month (October)

Head Injury Awareness Month (October)

Polish-American Heritage Month (October)

Employee Involvement and Employee Ownership Week (first week in October)

Eddie Eagle Gun Safety Week (first week in October)

Employ Handicapped Persons Week (first full week in October)

Senior Citizens' Day (first Sunday in October)

Independent Living Center Day (first Sunday in October)

Social Justice for Ireland Day (first Saturday in October)

Town Meeting Day (October 8)

Leif Ericson Day (October 8)

Columbus Day (second Monday in October)

Home Composting Recognition Week (second week in October)

Anniversary of the Death of Brigadier General Casimir Pulaski (October 11)

White Cane Safety Day (October 15)

United Nations Day (October 24)

State Constitution Day (October 25)

Statue of Liberty Awareness Day (October 26)

Robert Frost Day (fourth Saturday in October)

Youth Honor Day (October 31)

American Education Week (an unspecified week in October or November)

Massachusetts Hospice Week (second week in November)

Geographic Education Awareness Week (second week in November)

United States Marine Corps Day (November 10)

Veterans' Day (November 11)

Armistice Day (November 11)

Silver-Haired Legislature Days (third Wednesday, Thursday, and Friday in November)

John F. Kennedy Day (last Sunday in November)

American Education Week (an unspecified week in October or November)

Disabled American Veterans' Hospital Day (first Sunday in December)

Pearl Harbor Day (December 7)

Civil Rights Week (December 8–15)

Human Rights Day (December 10)

Army and Navy Union Day (second Saturday in December)

Samuel Slater Day (December 20)

Clara Barton Week (week commencing on December 25)

Traffic Safety Week (unspecified)

Veteran Firemen's Muster Day (unspecified)[57]

11. Christmas Day (December 25)

12. Saturdays from noon until midnight

Note: When January 1, February 12, July 4, November 11, or December 25 falls on a Sunday, the following Monday is a holiday.[58]

Observances

Rosa L. Parks Day (first Monday after February 4)

Grandparents' and Grandchildren's Day (March 18)

John Fitzgerald Kennedy Day (May 29)

Flag Month (June 14 to July 14)

American Family Day (last Sunday in August)

Michigan Indian Day (fourth Friday in September)

Casimir Pulaski Day (October 11)

Arbor Day (unspecified, to be designated by governor)[59]

MICHIGAN

Legal Holidays

1. New Year's Day (January 1)
2. Martin Luther King, Jr. Day (third Monday in January)
3. Lincoln's Birthday (February 12)
4. Washington's Birthday (third Monday in February)
5. Memorial Day (last Monday in May)
6. Independence Day (July 4)
7. Labor Day (first Monday in September)
8. Columbus Day (second Monday in October)
9. Veterans' Day (November 11)
10. Thanksgiving Day (fourth Thursday in November)

MINNESOTA

Legal Holidays

1. New Year's Day (January 1)
2. Martin Luther King's Birthday (third Monday in January)
3. Washington's and Lincoln's Birthday (third Monday in February)
4. Memorial Day (last Monday in May)
5. Independence Day (July 4)
6. Labor Day (first Monday in September)
7. Christopher Columbus Day (second Monday in October)
8. Veterans' Day (November 11)
9. Thanksgiving Day (fourth Thursday in November)
10. Christmas Day (December 25)

Note: When New Year's Day, Independence Day, Veterans' Day, or Christmas Day falls on a Sunday, the following day is a holiday. When they fall on a Saturday, the preceding day is a holiday.[60]

Observances

American Family Day (first Sunday in August)[61]

MISSISSIPPI

Legal Holidays

1. New Year's Day (January 1)
2. Robert E. Lee's and Dr. Martin Luther King, Jr.'s Birthday (third Monday in January)
3. Washington's Birthday (third Monday in February)
4. Confederate Memorial Day (last Monday in April)
5. National Memorial Day and Jefferson Davis' Birthday (last Monday in May)
6. Independence Day (July 4)
7. Labor Day (first Monday in September)
8. Veterans' Day (November 11)
9. Thanksgiving Day (fourth Thursday in November)
10. Christmas Day (December 25)

Note: When a holiday falls on a Sunday, the following Monday is a legal holiday.[62]

Observances

Hernando de Soto Week (first week of May)

Hernando de Soto Day (May 8)

Elvis Aaron Presley Day (August 16)

Retired Teachers Day (Sunday preceding Thanksgiving Day)[63]

MISSOURI

Legal Holidays

1. New Year's Day (January 1)
2. Martin Luther King Day (third Monday in January)
3. Lincoln Day (February 12)
4. Washington's Birthday (third Monday in February)
5. Truman Day (May 8)
6. Memorial Day (last Monday in May)
7. Independence Day (July 4)
8. Labor Day (first Monday in September)
9. Columbus Day (second Monday in October)
10. Veterans' Day (November 11)
11. Christmas Day (December 25)

Note: When holidays fall on a Sunday, the following Monday is considered the holiday.[64]

Observances

Arbor Day (first Friday in April)

Prisoner of War Remembrance Day (April 9)

Jefferson Day (April 13)

Law Day (May 1)

Truman Day (May 8)

Peace Officers Memorial Day (May 15)

Flag Day (June 14)

Korean War Veterans Day (July 27)

Missouri Day (third Wednesday of October)

Pearl Harbor Remembrance Day (December 7)[65]

MONTANA

Legal Holidays

1. Sundays
2. New Year's Day (January 1)

3. Martin Luther King, Jr. Day (third Monday in January)

4. Lincoln's and Washington's Birthdays (third Monday in February)

5. Memorial Day (last Monday in May)

6. Independence Day (July 4)

7. Labor Day (first Monday in September)

8. Columbus Day (second Monday in October)

9. Veterans' Day (November 11)

10. Thanksgiving Day (fourth Thursday in November)

11. Christmas Day (December 25)

12. State general election day

Note: When holidays other than Sundays fall on a Sunday, the following Monday is a holiday.[66]

Observances

Right to Keep and Bear Arms Week (week beginning first Monday in March)

Arbor Day (last Friday in April)

Montana's Hunting Heritage Week (week beginning the third Monday in September)[67]

NEBRASKA

Legal Holidays

1. New Year's Day (January 1)

2. Birthday of Martin Luther King, Jr. (third Monday in January)

3. Presidents' Day (third Monday in February)

4. Arbor Day (last Friday in April)

5. Memorial Day (last Monday in May)

6. Independence Day (July 4)

7. Labor Day (first Monday in September)

8. Columbus Day (second Monday in October)

9. Veterans' Day (November 11)

10. Thanksgiving Day (fourth Thursday in November)

11. Day after Thanksgiving

12. Christmas Day (December 25)

Notes: The following Monday is a holiday when any holiday listed above falls on a Sunday. Except for Veterans' Day, the federal holiday takes precedence over the state-designated day.[68]

Observances

George W. Norris Day (January 5)

Martin Luther King, Jr. Day (January 15)

State Day (March 1. If falling on a weekend, the governor may proclaim either the preceding Friday or the following Monday as State Day.)

Workers Memorial Day (April 28)

Pioneers' Memorial Day (second Sunday in June)

Howard's Day (September 2)

American Indian Day (fourth Monday in September)

Pulaski's Memorial Day (October 11)

White Cane Safety Day (October 15)

Veterans' Day (November 11)

Thanksgiving Day (fourth Thursday in November)[69]

NEVADA

Legal Holidays

1. New Year's Day (January 1)

2. Martin Luther King, Jr.'s Birthday (third Monday in January)

3. Washington's Birthday (third Monday in February)

4. Memorial Day (last Monday in May)

5. Independence Day (July 4)

6. Labor Day (first Monday in September)

7. Nevada Day (October 31)

8. Veterans' Day (November 11)

9. Thanksgiving Day (fourth Thursday in November)

10. Family Day (Friday after Thanksgiving)

11. Christmas Day (December 25)

12. Any day other than the fourth Monday in October, observed as Veterans' Day, appointed by the President of the United States as a legal holiday or a day of public fast or thanksgiving

Notes: If New Year's Day, Independence Day, Nevada Day, Veterans' Day, or Christmas Day falls on a Sunday, the next Monday must be observed as a legal holiday. If any of those holidays falls on a Saturday, the preceding Friday must be observed as a legal holiday.[70]

Observances

Tartan Day (April 6)

Arbor Day (last Friday in April)

Law Day USA (May 1)

Mother's Day (second Sunday in May)

Osteoporosis Prevention and Awareness Week (week beginning with Mother's Day)

Nevada Mineral Industry Week (first week in June)

Nevada All-Indian Stampede Days (third week in July)

Constitution Day (September 17)

Constitution Week (third week in September)

Nevada Indian Day (fourth Friday in September)

Columbus Day (second Monday in October)[71]

NEW HAMPSHIRE

Legal Holidays

1. New Year's Day (January 1)

2. Civil Rights Day (third Monday of January)

3. Washington's Birthday (third Monday of February)

4. Memorial Day (May 30)

5. Independence Day (July 4)

6. Labor Day (first Monday of September)

7. Columbus Day (second Monday of October)

8. Day on which biennial election is held

9. Veterans' Day (November 11)

10. Thanksgiving Day (whenever appointed)

11. Christmas Day (December 25)

Observances

State Constitution Day (January 5)

American History Month (February)

Teacher Appreciation Day (first Tuesday in May)

Law Enforcement Memorial Week (calendar week of May 15)

Lafayette Day (May 20)

Federal Constitution Day (September 17)

New Hampshire Pearl Harbor Day (December 7)[72]

NEW JERSEY

Legal Holidays

1. Saturdays (after noon)

2. Sundays

3. New Year's Day (January 1)
4. Martin Luther King's Birthday (third Monday in January)
5. Lincoln's Birthday (February 12)
6. Washington's Birthday (third Monday in February)
7. Good Friday (Friday before Easter)
8. Memorial Day (last Monday in May)
9. Independence Day (July 4)
10. Labor Day (first Monday in September)
11. Columbus Day (second Monday in October)
12. Veterans' Day (November 11)
13. Thanksgiving Day (fourth Thursday in November)
14. Christmas Day (December 25)
15. General Election Days
16. Any days declared as holidays, bank holidays, or days of fasting and prayer or other religious observance by the governor or the President of the United States

Notes: When holidays fall on Sundays, the following Mondays are public holidays. When holidays fall on Saturdays, the preceding Fridays are public holidays.[73]

Observances

Volunteer Fireman's Day (second Sunday in January)

Volunteer First Aid and Rescue Squad Day (third Sunday in January)

Crispus Attucks Day (March 5)

Women's History Week (second week in March)

New Jersey Day (April 17)

Law Day (May 1)

Mother's Day (second Sunday in May)

Grandparent's Day (last Sunday in May)

American Flag Week (June 7–14)

Lidice Memorial Day (June 10)

Father's Day (third Sunday in June)

New Jersey P.O.W.-M.I.A. Recognition Day (July 20)

New Jersey Retired Teachers Day (first Sunday in November)

Kristallnacht Memorial Night (November 9–10)[74]

NEW MEXICO

Legal Holidays

1. New Year's Day (January 1)
2. Martin Luther King, Jr.'s Birthday (third Monday in January)
3. Presidents' Day (third Monday in February)
4. Memorial Day (last Monday in May)
5. Independence Day (July 4)
6. Labor Day (first Monday in September)
7. Columbus Day (second Monday in October)
8. Veterans' Day (November 11)
9. Thanksgiving Day (fourth Thursday in November)
10. Christmas Day (December 25)

Note: When a holiday falls on a Sunday, the next Monday is a legal holiday.[75]

Observances

American History Month (February)

American Indian Day (first Tuesday of February)

Guadalupe-Hidalgo Treaty Day (February 2)

Arbor Day (second Friday in March)

Bataan Day (April 9)

Onate Day (a day in the month of July)

Ernie Pyle Day (August 3)[76]

NEW YORK

Legal Holidays

1. New Year's Day (January 1)
2. Dr. Martin Luther King, Jr. Day (third Monday in January)
3. Lincoln's Birthday (February 12)
4. Washington's Birthday (third Monday in February)
5. Memorial Day (last Monday in May)
6. Flag Day (second Sunday in June)
7. Independence Day (July 4)
8. Labor Day (first Monday in September)
9. Columbus Day (second Monday in October)
10. Veterans' Day (November 11)
11. Thanksgiving Day (fourth Thursday in November)
12. Christmas Day (December 25)
13. Days following all holidays except Flag Day, if they fall on Sunday
14. General Election Days
15. Any days declared by the governor or the President of the United States as days of general fasting or prayer, thanksgiving, or religious observances
16. Saturdays, from noon until midnight[77]

Observances

Haym Salomon Day (January 6)

Lithuanian Independence Day (February 16)

Pulaski Day (March 4)

Workers' Memorial Day (April 28)

Korean War Veterans' Day (June 25)

John Barry Day (September 13)

Uncle Sam Day in the State of New York (September 13)

Friedrich Wilhelm von Steuben Memorial Day (September 17)

War of 1812 Day (last Saturday in September)

Raoul Wallenberg Day (October 5)

New Netherland Day in the State of New York (October 11)

Theodore Roosevelt Day (October 27)

New York State History Month (November)

Pearl Harbor Day (December 7)[78]

NORTH CAROLINA

Legal Holidays

1. New Year's Day (January 1)
2. Martin Luther King, Jr.'s Birthday (third Monday in January)
3. Robert E. Lee's Birthday (January 19)
4. Washington's Birthday (third Monday in February)
5. Greek Independence Day (March 25)
6. Anniversary of Signing of Halifax Resolves (April 12)
7. Good Friday (Friday before Easter)
8. Anniversary of Mecklenburg Declaration of Independence (May 20)
9. Memorial Day (last Monday in May)
10. Confederate Memorial Day (May 10)
11. Independence Day (July 4)
12. Labor Day (first Monday in September)
13. Columbus Day (second Monday in October)
14. Yom Kippur
15. Veterans' Day (November 11)
16. Election Days (Tuesday after the first Monday in November when elections are held)

17. Thanksgiving Day (fourth Thursday in November)
18. Christmas Day (December 25)

Note: When a holiday falls on a Sunday, the following Monday is a public holiday.[79]

Observances

Arbor Week (week in March containing March 15)

Prisoner of War Day (April 9)

American Family Day (first Sunday in August)

Indian Solidarity Week (last full week in September)

National Employ the Physically Handicapped Week (first full week in October)

Pearl Harbor Remembrance Day (December 7)

Indian Day (unspecified day named by governor)[80]

NORTH DAKOTA

Legal Holidays

1. Sundays
2. New Year's Day (January 1)
3. Martin Luther King Day (third Monday in January)
4. George Washington's Birthday (third Monday in February)
5. Good Friday (Friday before Easter)
6. Memorial Day (last Monday in May)
7. Independence Day (July 4)
8. Labor Day (first Monday in September)
9. Veterans' Day (November 11)
10. Thanksgiving Day (fourth Thursday in November)
11. Christmas Day (December 25)

12. Any days declared public holidays by the President of the United States or the governor

Note: If New Year's, Independence, Veterans', or Christmas day falls on a Sunday, the following day is a holiday. If any of these days falls on a Saturday, the preceding Friday is a holiday.[81]

Observances

Temperance Day (third Friday in January)

Four Chaplains Sunday (first Sunday in February)

Bird Day (April 26)

Workers' Memorial Day (April 28)

Arbor Day (first Friday in May)

Mother's Day (second Sunday in May)

Gold Star Mothers' Day (last Sunday in September)[82]

OHIO

Legal Holidays

1. New Year's Day (January 1)
2. Martin Luther King Day (third Monday in January)
3. Washington-Lincoln Day (third Monday in February)
4. Memorial Day (last Monday in May)
5. Independence Day (July 4)
6. Labor Day (first Monday in September)
7. Columbus Day (second Monday in October)
8. Veterans' Day (November 11)
9. Thanksgiving Day (fourth Thursday in November)
10. Christmas Day (December 25)

11. Days appointed and recommended by the President of the United States or the governor

12. Saturdays from noon until midnight

13. Election Days from noon to 5:30 P.M.

Note: If a legal holiday falls on a Sunday, the next day is a legal holiday.[83]

Observances

Ohio Braille Literacy Week (first week in January)

Ohio Township Day (February 1)

Ohio Statehood Day (March 1)

School Energy Conservation Day in Ohio (third Friday in March)

World War I Day (April 6)

Child Care Worker Appreciation Week (week beginning on Sunday that includes April 19)

Workers' Memorial Day (April 28)

Arbor Day (last Friday in April)

Prostate Cancer Awareness Month (June)

Destroyer Escort Day in Ohio (third Saturday in June)

Ohio National Guard Day (July 25)

Korean War Veterans' Day (July 27)

Gold Star Mothers Day (last Sunday in September)

Ohio Hepatitis C Awareness Month (October)

Ohio Breast Cancer Awareness Month (October)

General Pulaski Memorial Day (October 11)

Native American Indian Day (fourth Saturday in November)

Ohio Aviation and Aerospace History Education Week (week beginning on Sunday including December 17)[84]

OKLAHOMA

Legal Holidays

1. Each Saturday

2. Each Sunday

3. New Year's Day (January 1)

4. Martin Luther King, Jr.'s Birthday (third Monday in January)

5. Presidents' Day (third Monday in February)

6. Memorial Day (last Monday in May)

7. Independence Day (July 4)

8. Labor Day (first Monday in September)

9. Veterans' Day (November 11)

10. Thanksgiving Day (fourth Thursday in November)

11. Day after Thanksgiving Day

12. Christmas Day (December 25)

13. Monday before Christmas, if Christmas is on Tuesday

14. Friday after Christmas, if Christmas is on Thursday

Note: If holidays other than Saturdays fall on Saturdays, the preceding Fridays are holidays; if holidays other than Sundays fall on Sundays, the succeeding Mondays are holidays.[85]

Observances

Arbor Day (Friday after second Monday in February)

Youth Day (third Sunday in March)

Vietnam Veterans Day (third Thursday in March)

Prisoners of War Remembrance Day (April 9)

Jefferson Day (April 13)

Oklahoma City Bombing Remembrance Day (April 19)

Oklahoma Day (April 22)

Bird Day (May 1)

Senior Citizens Week (beginning with first Sunday in May)

Senior Citizens Day (Wednesday of Senior Citizens Week)

Mother's Day (second Sunday in May)

Jim Thorpe Day (May 22)

Purple Heart Week (last week in May)

Shut-In Day (first Sunday in June)

Flag Week (June 8–14)

Juneteenth National Freedom Day (third Saturday in June)

Indian Day (first Saturday after first full moon in September)

Grandparents' Week (beginning with second Sunday in September)

Cherokee Strip Day (September 16)

Oklahoma Historical Day (October 10)

Will Rogers Day (November 4)

Oklahoma Week (November 11–16)

Oklahoma Statehood Day (November 16)

Oklahoma Heritage Week (week in which November 16 falls)

Oklahoma Native American Day (third Monday in November)

Oklahoma Pearl Harbor Remembrance Day (December 7)

Bill of Rights Day (December 15)

Bill of Responsibilities Day (December 16)

Citizenship Recognition Day (fixed by governor)

Holiday for each Indian tribe in state, chosen by tribes[86]

OREGON

Legal Holidays

1. Sundays
2. New Year's Day (January 1)

3. Martin Luther King, Jr.'s Birthday (third Monday in January)
4. Presidents' Day (third Monday in February)
5. Memorial Day (last Monday in May)
6. Independence Day (July 4)
7. Labor Day (first Monday in September)
8. Veterans' Day (November 11)
9. Thanksgiving Day (fourth Thursday in November)
10. Christmas Day (December 25)
11. Days appointed by the governor or the President of the United States as holidays

Notes: When holidays other than Sundays fall on Sundays, the next Mondays are legal holidays. When holidays fall on Saturdays, the preceding Fridays are holidays.[87]

Observances

Arbor Week (first full week of April)

Garden Week (first full week of June)[88]

PENNSYLVANIA

Legal Holidays

1. New Year's Day (January 1)
2. Dr. Martin Luther King, Jr. Day (third Monday in January)
3. Presidents' Day (third Monday in February)
4. Good Friday (Friday before Easter)
5. Memorial Day (last Monday in May)
6. Flag Day (June 14)
7. Independence Day (July 4)
8. Labor Day (first Monday in September)
9. Columbus Day (second Monday in October)

10. Election Day (first Tuesday after the first Monday in November)
11. Veterans' Day (November 11)
12. Thanksgiving Day (fourth Thursday in November)
13. Christmas Day (December 25)
14. Saturdays, from noon to midnight
15. Days appointed by the governor or the President of the United States as days of fasting, prayer, or thanksgiving

Note: When New Year's Day, July 4, or Christmas Day falls on a Sunday, the next Monday may be a holiday.[89]

Observances

Pennsylvanians with Disabilities Day (January 30)

Lithuanian Independence Day (February 16)

Charter Day (March 14)

Bird Day (March 21)

Local Government Day (April 15)

Earth Day (April 22)

Rothrock Memorial Conservation Week (last Friday in April)

Arbor Day (last Friday in April)

American Loyalty Day (May 1)

Commonwealth Day of Prayer and Celebration of Religious Freedom (first Thursday in May)

Police Officers Memorial Day (May 15)

See Pennsylvania's Covered Bridges Week (from the first Saturday after the first Sunday in May to and including the third Sunday of May)

Hubert H. Humphrey, Jr. Day (May 27)

Rachel Carson Day (May 27)

Pennsylvania German Day (June 28)

Commodore John Barry Day (September 13)

National Anthem Day (September 14)

Pennsylvania POW/MIA Recognition Day (third Friday in September)

Shut-In Day (third Sunday in October)

William Penn's Birthday (October 24)[90]

RHODE ISLAND

Legal Holidays

1. Sundays
2. New Year's Day (January 1)
3. Dr. Martin Luther King, Jr.'s Birthday (third Monday in January)
4. Washington's Birthday (third Monday in February)
5. Rhode Island Independence Day (May 4)
6. Memorial Day (last Monday in May)
7. Independence Day (July 4)
8. Victory Day (second Monday in August)
9. Labor Day (first Monday in September)
10. Columbus Day (second Monday in October)
11. Veterans' Day (November 11)
12. Christmas Day (December 25)
13. General election days
14. Any days that the governor, general assembly, President, or Congress appoints as holidays for any purpose

Note: When holidays fall on Sundays, the following Mondays are holidays.[91]

Observances

George Washington Carver Recognition Day (January 5)

Viet Nam Veterans' Day (January 27)

American History Month (February)

Founders Day of the Italian American War Veterans of the United States, Inc. (February 15)

Lithuanian Independence Day (February 16)

Retired Teachers' Day (first Wednesday of March)

National Women's History Week (week containing March 8)

Rhode Island School Bus Safety Week (second week of March)

Social Workers' Day (second Wednesday of March)

Peter Francisco Day (March 15)

Dauphine Day (April 21)

Motorcycle Safety Awareness Week (fourth week in April)

Workers' Memorial Day (fourth Friday in April)

Arbor Day (last Friday in April)

V.F.W. Loyalty Day (May 1)

Rhode Island Speech-Language-Hearing Awareness Week (first week of May)

Nurses' Day (first Monday in May)

Friendship Day (second Friday in May)

National Police Week (week containing May 15)

National Police Awareness Day (May 15)

Itam-Vets Daisy Day (first Saturday in June)

Gaspee Days (second Saturday and following Sunday in June)

Destroyer Escort Day (third Saturday in June)

Saint Jean-Baptiste Day (June 24)

Cape Verdian Recognition Week (July 2–9)

Old Home Week (week beginning with the first Sunday in July, or any subsequent week during July, August, or September)

Puerto Rican Recognition Week (July 23–29)

Korean War Veterans Memorial Day (July 27)

POW/MIA's Day (third Friday in September)

American Indian Heritage Day (September 24)

General Casimir Pulaski Day (October 11)

Narragansett Indian Day (last Saturday before second Sunday in August)

White Cane Safety Day (October 15)

Disabled American Veterans Day (December 7)

Veteran Firemen's Muster Day (date not specified)[92]

SOUTH CAROLINA

Legal Holidays

1. New Year's Day (January 1)
2. Martin Luther King, Jr.'s Birthday (January 15)
3. Robert E. Lee's Birthday (January 19)
4. Washington's Birthday (third Monday in February)
5. Confederate Memorial Day (May 10)
6. National Memorial Day (last Monday in May)
7. Jefferson Davis's Birthday (June 3)
8. Independence Day (July 4)
9. Labor Day (first Monday in September)
10. Veterans' Day (November 11)
11. Thanksgiving Day and the following day (fourth Thursday in November and the following day)
12. Christmas Day and the following day (December 25 and December 26)
13. General election days

Notes: Christmas Eve may be declared a holiday by the governor. When holidays fall on

Sundays, the next Mondays are holidays. When they fall on Saturdays, the preceding Fridays are holidays.[93]

Observances

Martin Luther King Day (January 15)

American History Month (February)

South Carolina Day (March 18)

Golf Week (last week in April)

Loyalty Day (May 1)

Mother's Day (second Sunday in May)

Garden Week (week beginning the first Sunday in June)

Carolina Day (June 28)

Family Week (last week in August)

General Pulaski Memorial Day (October 11)

Frances Willard Day (fourth Friday in October)

Arbor Day (first Friday in December)[94]

SOUTH DAKOTA

Legal Holidays

1. Sundays
2. New Year's Day (January 1)
3. Martin Luther King, Jr. Day (third Monday in January)
4. Washington's and Lincoln's Birthdays (third Monday in February)
5. Memorial Day (last Monday in May)
6. Independence Day (July 4)
7. Labor Day (first Monday in September)
8. Native Americans' Day (second Monday in October)
9. Veterans' Day (November 11)
10. Thanksgiving Day (fourth Thursday in November)
11. Christmas Day (December 25)

12. Any day declared by the governor or the President of the United States as a holiday

Notes: When January 1, July 4, November 11, or December 25 falls on a Sunday, the following Monday is a legal holiday. When they fall on a Saturday, the preceding Friday is a legal holiday.

Observances

Arbor Day (last Friday in April)

Little Big Horn Recognition Day (June 25)

Bill of Rights Day (December 15)

Wounded Knee Day (December 29)[95]

TENNESSEE

Legal Holidays

1. Saturdays from noon until midnight
2. New Year's Day (January 1)
3. Martin Luther King, Jr. Day (third Monday in January)
4. Washington Day (third Monday in February)
5. Good Friday (Friday before Easter)
6. Memorial Day (last Monday in May)
7. Independence Day (July 4)
8. Labor Day (first Monday in September)
9. Columbus Day (second Monday in October)
10. Veterans' Day (November 11)
11. Thanksgiving Day (fourth Thursday in November)
12. Christmas Day (December 25)
13. Any days declared holidays by the governor or the President of the United States
14. Election Days

Notes: The following Monday is substituted for holidays that fall on Sunday. The preceding Friday is substituted for holidays falling on Saturday.[96]

Observances

Robert E. Lee Day (January 19)

Franklin D. Roosevelt Day (January 30)

Abraham Lincoln Day (February 12)

Andrew Jackson Day (March 15)

Mother's Day (second Sunday in May)

Statehood Day (June 1)

Confederate Memorial Day (June 3)

Scottish, Scots-Irish Heritage Day (June 24)

Nathan Bedford Forrest Day (July 13)

Family Day (last Sunday in August)

American Indian Day (fourth Monday in September)

Tennessee P.O.W.–M.I.A. Recognition Week (September 18–24)

Veterans' Day (November 11)

Free Sport Fishing Day (date not specified)[97]

TEXAS

Legal Holidays

1. New Year's Day (January 1)
2. Confederate Heroes Day (January 19)
3. Martin Luther King, Jr. Day (third Monday in January)
4. Presidents' Day (third Monday in February)
5. Texas Independence Day (March 2)
6. San Jacinto Day (April 21)
7. Memorial Day (last Monday in May)
8. Emancipation Day in Texas (June 19)
9. Independence Day (July 4)

10. Lyndon B. Johnson's Birthday (August 27)
11. Labor Day (first Monday in September)
12. Election Days
13. Veterans' Day (November 11)
14. Thanksgiving Day (fourth Thursday in November)
15. Friday after Thanksgiving Day
16. December 24
17. Christmas Day (December 25)
18. December 26[98]

Observances

Sam Rayburn Day (January 6)

Texas Week (entire week in which March 2 is contained)

Former Prisoners of War Recognition Day (April 9)

Texas Conservation and Beautification Week (April 19–26)

International Trade Awareness Week (May 22–26)

Columbus Day (second Monday in October)

Father of Texas Day (November 3)[99]

UTAH

Legal Holidays

1. Sundays
2. New Year's Day (January 1)
3. Martin Luther King, Jr.'s Birthday (third Monday in January)
4. Presidents' Day (third Monday in February)
5. Memorial Day (last Monday in May)
6. Independence Day (July 4)
7. Pioneer Day (July 24)
8. Labor Day (first Monday in September)

9. Columbus Day (second Monday in October)

10. Veterans' Day (November 11)

11. Thanksgiving Day (fourth Thursday in November)

12. Christmas Day (December 25)

13. Days of thanksgiving or fasting designated by the governor or the President of the United States

Notes: When a holiday other than a Sunday falls on a Sunday, the following Monday is the holiday. When a holiday falls on a Saturday, the preceding Friday is the holiday.[100]

VERMONT

Legal Holidays

1. New Year's Day (January 1)

2. Martin Luther King, Jr.'s Birthday (third Monday in January)

3. Lincoln's Birthday (February 12)

4. Washington's Birthday (third Monday in February)

5. Town Meeting Day (first Tuesday in March)

6. Memorial Day (May 30)

7. Independence Day (July 4)

8. Bennington Battle Day (August 16)

9. Labor Day (first Monday in September)

10. Columbus Day (second Monday in October)

11. Veterans' Day (November 11)

12. Thanksgiving Day (fourth Thursday in November)

13. Christmas Day (December 25)

Notes: When holidays fall on Sundays, they are observed on the following Mondays. When they fall on Saturdays, they are observed on the preceding Fridays.[101]

Observances

American History Month (February)

Arbor Day (first Friday in May)

POW/MIA Recognition Day (third Friday in September)[102]

VIRGINIA

Legal Holidays

1. New Year's Day (January 1)

2. Lee-Jackson-King Day (third Monday in January)

3. George Washington Day (third Monday in February)

4. Memorial Day (last Monday in May)

5. Independence Day (July 4)

6. Labor Day (first Monday in September)

7. Columbus Day and Yorktown Victory Day (second Monday in October)

8. Veterans' Day (November 11)

9. Thanksgiving Day (fourth Thursday in November)

10. Friday following Thanksgiving Day

11. Christmas Day (December 25)

12. Any day appointed as a legal holiday by the governor or the President of the United States

Notes: When a holiday falls on a Sunday, the following Monday is a legal holiday. When a holiday falls on a Saturday, the preceding Friday is a legal holiday.[103]

Observances

Religious Freedom Week (second full week of January)

Virginia and American History Month (January 19–February 22)

Motherhood and Apple Pie Day (January 26)

Arbor Day (second Friday in March)

Bone Marrow Donor Programs Recognition Day (April 8)

Landscape Architecture Week in Virginia (second full week in April)

Dogwood Day (third Saturday in April)

Month for Children (May)

Commonwealth Day of Prayer (first Thursday in May)

Mother's Day (second Sunday in May)

First Lady's Day in Virginia (June 2)

Citizenship Day (September 17)

Constitution Week (September 17–23)

Virginia Championship Applebutter Making Contest (third week in September)

Native American Indian Week (last full week in September)

Yorkstown Day (October 19)

Early Childhood and Day-Care Providers and Professionals Recognition Day (October 22)

Virginia Drug Free Day (Saturday of last week in October)

American Indian Month (November)

Vietnam War Memorial Dedication and Veterans' Recognition Day (second Saturday in November)

Day of Appreciation for American Indians (Wednesday preceding Thanksgiving)

Pearl Harbor Remembrance Day (December 7)

Bill of Rights Day (December 15)[104]

WASHINGTON

Legal Holidays

1. Sundays
2. New Year's Day (January 1)
3. Martin Luther King, Jr.'s Birthday (third Monday in January)
4. Presidents' Day (third Monday in February)
5. Memorial Day (last Monday in May)
6. Independence Day (July 4)
7. Labor Day (first Monday in September)
8. Veterans' Day (November 11)
9. Thanksgiving Day (fourth Thursday in November)
10. Friday following Thanksgiving Day
11. Christmas Day (December 25)

Notes: When a holiday other than a Sunday itself falls on a Sunday, the following Monday is the legal holiday. When a holiday falls on a Saturday, the preceding Friday is the legal holiday.[105]

Observances

Washington Army and Air National Guard Day (January 26)

Former Prisoner of War Recognition Day (April 9)

Purple Heart Recipient Recognition Day (August 7)

Columbus Day (October 12)[106]

WEST VIRGINIA

Legal Holidays

1. New Year's Day (January 1)
2. Martin Luther King, Jr.'s Birthday (third Monday in January)
3. Lincoln's Birthday (February 12)
4. Washington's Birthday (third Monday in February)
5. Memorial Day (last Monday in May)
6. West Virginia Day (June 20)
7. Independence Day (July 4)
8. Labor Day (first Monday in September)

9. Columbus Day (second Monday in October)

10. Veterans' Day (November 11)

11. Thanksgiving Day (fourth Thursday in November)

12. Christmas Day (December 25)

13. Election Days

14. Any days appointed as days of thanksgiving or business holidays by the President of the United States or the governor

Note: When a holiday falls on a Sunday, the following Monday is observed as the legal holiday.[107]

Observances

Native American Indian Heritage Week (week beginning the Sunday before Thanksgiving)[108]

WISCONSIN

Legal Holidays

1. New Year's Day (January 1)

2. Martin Luther King, Jr.'s Birthday (January 15)

3. Presidents' Day (third Monday in February)

4. Memorial Day (last Monday in May)

5. Independence Day (July 4)

6. Labor Day (first Monday in September)

7. Veterans' Day (November 11)

8. Thanksgiving Day (fourth Thursday in November)

9. Christmas Day (December 25)

10. September Primary and November General Election Days

Notes: Good Fridays, from 11:00 A.M. to 3:00 P.M., are to be used for worship. When a holiday falls on a Sunday, the legal holiday is the following Monday.[109]

Observances

American History Month (February)

Mother's Day (second Sunday in May)

Citizenship Day (third Sunday in May)

Indian Rights Day (July 4—if it falls on Sunday, the day may be observed on July 3 or July 5)

Labor Day (first Monday in September)

Wonderful Wisconsin Week (third week in September)

Gold Star Mother's Day (last Sunday in September)

Wisconsin Family Month (November)

Wisconsin Family Week (first seven days of November)

Family Sunday (first Sunday of November)

Hire a Veteran Week (second week in November)

Arbor and Bird Day (unspecified date)[110]

WYOMING

Legal Holidays

1. New Year's Day (January 1)

2. Martin Luther King, Jr., Wyoming Equality Day (third Monday in January)

3. Washington's and Lincoln's Birthdays (third Monday in February)

4. Memorial Day (last Monday in May)

5. Independence Day (July 4)

6. Labor Day (first Monday in September)

7. Veterans' Day (November 11)

8. Thanksgiving Day (fourth Thursday in November)

9. Christmas Day (December 25)

10. Any days appointed by the President of the United States and declared by the governor for rejoicing, mourning, or national emergency

Note: When January 1, July 4, November 11, or December 25 falls on a Sunday, the following Monday is a legal holiday.[111]

Observances

Arbor Day (last Monday in April)

Native American Day (third Friday in September)

Nellie Tayloe Ross's Birthday (November 29)

Pearl Harbor Remembrance Day (December 7)

Wyoming Day (December 10)[112]

DISTRICT OF COLUMBIA

Legal Holidays

1. New Year's Day (January 1)
2. Martin Luther King, Jr.'s Birthday (third Monday in January)
3. Washington's Birthday (third Monday in February)
4. Memorial Day (last Monday in May)
5. Independence Day (July 4)
6. Labor Day (first Monday in September)
7. Columbus Day (second Monday in October)
8. Veterans' Day (November 11)
9. Thanksgiving Day (fourth Thursday in November)
10. Christmas Day (December 25)
11. Presidential Inauguration Day every four years

Notes: When a holiday other than Inauguration Day falls on a Sunday, the next day is a holiday. When a holiday other than Inauguration Day falls on a Saturday, the preceding day is a holiday.[113]

AMERICAN SAMOA

Legal Holidays

1. New Year's Day (January 1)
2. Washington's Birthday (February 22)
3. Good Friday (Friday before Easter)
4. American Samoa Flag Day (April 17)
5. Memorial Day (May 30)
6. Independence Day (July 4)
7. Labor Day (first Monday in September)
8. Veterans' Day (November 11)
9. Thanksgiving Day (fourth Thursday in November)
10. Christmas Day (December 25)[114]

COMMONWEALTH OF THE NORTHERN MARIANA ISLANDS

Legal Holidays

1. New Year's Day (January 1)
2. Commonwealth Day (January 9)
3. Presidents' Day (third Monday in February)
4. Covenant Day (March 25)
5. Good Friday (Friday before Easter)
6. Memorial Day (last Monday in May)
7. Independence Day (July 4)
8. Labor Day (first Monday in September)
9. Columbus Day (second Monday in October)
10. Citizenship Day (November 4)
11. Veterans' Day (November 11)

12. Thanksgiving Day (fourth Thursday in November)
13. Constitution Day (December 9)
14. Christmas Day (December 25)

Observances

Ash Wednesday (varies)
Assumption of Mary (August 1)
All Saints Day (November 1)[115]

GUAM

Legal Holidays

1. Sundays
2. New Year's Day (January 1)
3. Martin Luther King, Jr.'s Birthday (January 18)
4. Presidents' Day (third Monday in February)
5. Guam Discovery Day (first Monday in March)
6. Good Friday (Friday before Easter)
7. Memorial Day (last Monday in May)
8. Independence Day (July 4)
9. Liberation Day (July 21)
10. Labor Day (first Monday in September)
11. Columbus Day (second Monday in October)
12. Veterans' Day (November 11)
13. Thanksgiving Day (fourth Thursday in November)
14. Lady Camarin Day (December 8)
15. Christmas Day (December 25)
16. Election Days
17. Any day proclaimed by the governor or the President of the United States as a holiday or day of fasting or thanksgiving

Notes: If any holiday other than a Sunday falls on a Sunday, the next Monday is a holiday. If any holiday falls on a Saturday, the preceding Friday is a holiday.[116]

Observances

Gubernatorial Inauguration Day (first Monday in January every fourth year)
Chamorro Week (beginning first Monday in March and ending eight days later)
Farmers Appreciation Days (last Saturday in March and the immediately following Sunday)
Guam Youth Month (April)
White Cane Days (second Saturday and Sunday in April)
Earth Week (third week in April)
Children and Youth Sunday (fourth Sunday in April)
Family Sunday (Sunday following Children and Youth Sunday)
Guam Youth Week (a week in April)
Senior Citizens Month (May)
Teacher Appreciation Day (first Saturday in May)
Atbot de Fuego (Flame Tree) and Arbor Day Week (first week in June)
Gold Star Mothers' Day (second Sunday in August)[117]

PUERTO RICO

Legal Holidays

1. Sundays
2. New Year's Day (January 1)
3. Three Kings' Day (January 6)
4. Eugenio Maria de Hostos' Birthday (second Monday in January)
5. Martin Luther King's Birthday (third Monday in January)

6. Washington's Birthday (third Monday in February)
7. Abolition of Slavery (March 22)
8. Good Friday (Friday preceding Easter)
9. Antonio R. Barcelo Day (second Sunday in April)
10. José de Diego Day (third Monday in April)
11. Memorial Day (last Monday in May)
12. Independence Day (July 4)
13. Luis Muñoz Rivera Day (third Monday in July)
14. Day of the Constitution (July 25)
15. Dr. José Celso Barbosa's Birthday (July 27)
16. Labor Day (first Monday in September)
17. Santiago Iglesias Pantin Day (first Monday in September)
18. Columbus Day (October 12)
19. Discovery Day (October 12)
20. Veterans' Day (November 11)
21. Christmas Day (December 25)
22. Election Days
23. Any day appointed by the governor or the President of the United States or the Legislative Assembly for fasting or thanksgiving or as a holiday[118]

Note: When holidays fall on Sundays, the next day is the holiday.

Observances

Eugenio María de Hostos Week (second week in January)

Educational Week Pro Tourism in Puerto Rico (first week after last Sunday in January)

Birth Date of Armando Sanchez Martinez (January 28)

Luis Muñoz-Marín Week (week including February 18)

Day in Commemoration of the Birthday of Don Luis Muñoz-Marín (February 18)

Police Day (February 21)

Rotary Week (third week in February)

Roman Baldorioty de Castro Day (February 28)

Advent of American Citizenship in Puerto Rico Day (March 2)

International Women's Day (March 8)

Puerto Rican Boxer's Day (March 23)

Cancer Prevention and Control Month (April)

Ramon Emeterio Betances Commemorative Day (April 8)

Renowned Puerto Rican Statesmen's Day (April 18)

José de Diego Week (third week in April)

Rafael Martinez Nadal's Birthday (April 22)

Ernesto Ramos Antonini Day (April 24)

Puerto Rico Land Week (last week in April)

Land Day (Sunday of last week in April)

Arbor Day (Monday of last week in April)

School Janitors' Day (last Friday in April)

Day in Honor of the Aged (April 30)

Day of Homage to Old Age (a day in April)

Natural Resources and Environmental Quality and Health Educational Term (May 1–June 5)

Teachers Week (first week beginning with first Monday in May)

Teachers Day (Friday of first week beginning with first Monday in May)

International Red Cross Day (May 8)

Mother's Day (second Sunday in May)

Week of the Puerto Rican Danza (week including May 16)

Juan Morel Campos's Birthday and Day of the Puerto Rican Composer (May 16)

Accountant Week (third week in May)

Puerto Rican Solidarity Week (first week in June)

Gastronomical Week (first week in June)

Recreational Leaders Week (third week in June)

Puerto Rico Youth Organizations Week (week ending in fourth Sunday in June)

Youth Day (fourth Sunday in June)

Members of Municipal Assembly Week (first week in July)

Puerto Rican Domino Players Week (first week in July)

Puerto Rican Press Day (first Friday in July)

Gilberto Concepción de Gracia Memorial Day (July 9)

Transportation Week (second week in July)

Luis Muñoz-Rivera Week (third week in July)

Day of the Flag, Anthem, and Coat of Arms (July 24)

José Celso Barbosa Week (week including July 27)

Press Week (week including July 31)

National Journalist Day (July 31)

Day of the Child (second Sunday in August)

Roberto Clemente Day (August 18)

Small and Medium-Sized Retail Merchants Week (third week in August)

Bible Day (September 1)

Lola Rodriguez de Tio's Birthday (September 14)

Grito de Lares Day (September 23)

National Guard Week (a week in September proclaimed by governor)

General Casimir Pulaski Day (October 11)

White Cane Day (October 15)

Natural Resources Rangers Corps Week (third week in October)

Quality of Life Week (last week in October)

Ramon Power y Giralt Day (October 27)

Day of Peace (November 1)

Pedrin Zorrilla Memorial Day (November 9)

Women Devoted to the Religious Vocation Commemorative Week (November 13–19)

Historical Archivist's Day (Friday of Historical Archives Week)

Historical Archives Week (third week in November)

Day of the Composer (November 22)

Day of No More Violence Against Women (November 25)

Day of the Blind (December 13)

Librarian's Day (Friday of Library Week)

School Lunchroom Employee's Day (Friday of School Lunchroom Week)

Native Industries Week (a week to be proclaimed by governor)[119]

U.S. VIRGIN ISLANDS

Legal Holidays

1. Sundays
2. New Year's Day (January 1)
3. Three Kings' Day (January 6)
4. Martin Luther King, Jr.'s Birthday (third Monday in January)
5. Presidents' Day (third Monday in February)
6. Transfer Day (March 31)
7. Holy Thursday (Thursday before Easter)
8. Good Friday (Friday before Easter)
9. Easter Monday (Monday following Easter)
10. Memorial Day (last Monday in May)
11. Organic Act Day (last Monday in May)
12. Danish West Indies Emancipation Day (July 3)

13. Independence Day (July 4)
14. Supplication Day (fourth Monday in July)
15. Labor Day (first Monday in September)
16. Columbus Day and Puerto Rico Friendship Day (second Monday in October)
17. Local Thanksgiving Day (third Monday in October)
18. D. Hamilton Jackson day (November 1)
19. Veterans' Day (November 11)
20. Thanksgiving Day (fourth Thursday in November)
21. Christmas Day (December 25)
22. Christmas Second Day (December 26)
23. Any days the President of the United States or governor proclaims as holidays

Note: When holidays other than Sundays fall on Sundays, the following Monday is a legal holiday.[120]

Observances

Midwives Week (second week in February)

Cyril Emmanuel King Day (April 7)

Earth Day (April 22)

Secretaries Week (last week in April)

Timothy Theodore Dunean Day (April 25)

Teachers' Day (first Friday in May)

Peace Officers Memorial Day (May 15)

Peace Officers Memorial Week (week in which May 15 occurs)

African Liberation Day (May 25)

Virgin Islands African Heritage Week (third week in May)

French Heritage Week (week in June ending on Father's Day)

Ferry Boat Transportation Day (July 2)

Nicole Robin Day (August 4)

Melvin H. Evans Day (August 7)

Eastern Caribbean–Virgin Islands Friendship Week (August 4 and the following ten days)

Caribbean Friendship Week (fourth Friday in August and the following ten days)

Virgin Islands Citizenship Day (a day in August or September)

Support Our Public Schools Month (September)

West Indies Solidarity Day (first Monday in September)

Rothschild Francis Day (October 5)

Virgin Islands Taxi Week (last week in October)

Human Relations Week (second week in December)

George Scott Day (Monday of Fire Prevention Week)[121]

NOTES

1. Ala. Code §1–3–8.
2. Alaska Stat. §44.12.010.
3. Ibid., §44.12.020, §44.12.025.
4. Alaska Stat. §44.12.050.
5. Ibid., §44.12.065.
6. Ibid., §44.12.055, §44.12.075, §44.12.072, §44.12.085, §44.12.070.
7. Ibid., §44.12.030.
8. Ibid., §44.12.060.
9. Ibid., §44.12.040, §44.12.080.
10. Ariz. Rev. Stat. Ann. §1–301.
11. Ibid., §1–304, §1–306, §1–307.
12. Ark. Code Ann. §1–5–101.
13. Ibid., §1–5–106.
14. Ibid., §1–5–111, §1–5–109.
15. Ibid., §1–5–107.
16. Ibid., §1–5–110, §1–5–112, §1–5–108.
17. Cal. Govt. Code §6700 (West).
18. Ibid., §6701 (West).
19. Ibid., §6711 (West).
20. Ibid., §6710 (West).
21. Ibid., §6714 (West).
22. Ibid., §6712 (West).
23. Ibid., §6708 (West).
24. Ibid., §6713 (West).

25. Ibid., §6716 (West).

26. Colo. Rev. Stat. §24–11–101, §24–11–103.

27. Ibid., §24–11–108, §24–11–104, §24–11–106, §24–11–111, §24–11–109.

28. Conn. Gen. Stat. Ann. §1–4 (West).

29. Ibid., §10–29a (West).

30. Del. Code Ann. tit. 1, §501.

31. Ibid., tit. 1, §601, §603, §602.

32. Fla. Stat. Ann. §683.01, §683.13, §683.19, §683.08, §683.12, §683.09 (West).

33. Ibid., §683.04, §683.18, §683.06, §683.17, §683.05, §683.14, §683.15, §683.22, §683.11, §683.115, §683.21, §683.21, §683.10, §683.145, §683.16 (West).

34. Ga. Code Ann. §1–4–1.

35. Ibid., §1–4–2, §1–4–3, §1–4–14, §1–4–12, §1–4–10, §1–4–6, §1–4–4, §1–4–9, §1–4–7, §1–4–8, §1–4–5, §1–4–11, §1–4–13.

36. Haw. Rev. Stat. §8–1, §8–2.

37. Ibid., §8–4–5, §8–4, §8–8, §8–12, §8–11, §8–1.5, §8–9, §8–7, §8–10.

38. Idaho Code §73–108.

39. Ibid., §73–108B.

40. Ill. Stat. Ann. ch. 17, §2201 (Smith-Hurd).

41. Ill. Comp. Stat. ch. 5, §490/5, §490/95, §490/10, §490/20, §490/70, §490/25, §490/85, §490/80, §490/45, §490/40, §490/100, §490/50, §490/75, §490/105, §490/55, §490/30, §490/70.

42. Ind. Code Ann. §1–1–9–1 (Burns).

43. Ibid., §1–1–13–1, §1–1–12.5–1, §1–1–11–1, §1–1–14–1, §1–1–10–1 (Burns).

44. Iowa Code Ann. §1C.1.

45. Ibid., §1C.9, §1C.11, §1C.10, §1C.3, §1C.4, §1C.8, §1C.5, §1C.7, §1C.6.

46. K.S.A. §35–107.

47. Ibid., §35–204, §35–202, §73–705, §35–205, §35–203, §35–201, §35–206.

48. Ky. Rev. Stat. Ann. §2.110 (Baldwin).

49. Ibid., §2.255, §2.135, §2.130, §2.245, §2,250, §2.120, §2.135, §2.132, §2.140, §2.230, §2.145.

50. La. Rev. Stat. Ann. §1–55 (West).

51. Ibid., §1–57, §1–56, §49–170.1, §1–58 (West).

52. Me. Rev. Stat. Ann. tit. 30–A, §1051.

53. Ibid., tit. 1, §113, §118, §116, §130, §131, §111–A, §127, §121, §127, §128, §126, §123, §120, §119; tit. 30–A, §2902; tit. 1, §125, §133, §134, §132, §112, §124, §129, §117.

54. Md. Ann. Code (1957) art. 1, §27.

55. Md. State Govt. Code Ann. §13–401, §13–402, §13–403.

56. Mass. Gen. Laws Ann. ch. 7, §7, cl. 18th.

57. Ibid., ch. 6, §12F, §12T, §15S, §15Y, §15X, §15C, §12BB, §12RR, §15H, §13, §14A, §12GG, §12AA, §12T, §12QQ, §15CCC, §15T, §12D, §12II, §15DDDD, §12S, §12K, §15AAAA, §15GG, §15UU, §15RR, §15J, §15MM, §15QQ, §15AAA, §12M, §12T, §15Z, §12PP, §12T, §12J, §15AA, §15LL, §15AA, §15II, §15, §12UU, §1200, §15KKK, §14C, §15B, §15O, §12O, §15TTT, §12R, §12T, §15ZZ, §12T, §15N, §15RRR, §15SSS, §15JJJ, §12JJ, §15KK, §12I, §15BB, §15XX, §12H, §12I, §12Y, §12FF, §15D, §15BBBB, §12Q, §15VV, §12X, §15CC, §15TT, §15EEE, §12U, §15JJ, §15NN, §14, §12C, §12T, §12TT, §15OO, §15HH, §15M, §15OOO, §15DD, §12SS, §15XXX, §12MM, §12CC, §12Z, §15WW, §12T, §12LL, §15I, §15QQQ, §15E, 12W, §15NNN, §12KK, §15EE, §12EE, §15GGG, §12E, §15A, §15K, §15BBB, §15W, §15FF, §15LLL, §15VVV, §15WWW, §15HHH, §15ZZZ, §15F, §12T, §15III, §15U, §15PP, §15YY, §15UUU, §12V, §12B, §15V, §12N, §14B, §15CCCC, §12HH, §15G, §12G, §15SS, §15MMM, §15Q, §12A, §15R, §15DDD, §15L, §12G, §12T, §12DD, §12P, §12NN, §12T, §15PPP, §15YYY, §15P, §12L.

58. Mich. Comp. Laws. Ann. §435.101, §435.102.

59. Ibid., §435.11, §435.121, §435.181, §2.91, §435.191, §435.161, §435.141, §435.171.

60. Minn. Stat. Ann. §645.44 (West).

61. Ibid., §517.21 (West).

62. Miss. Code Ann. §3–3–7.

63. Ibid., §3–3–8, §3–3–7, §3–3–35.

64. Mo. Stat. Ann. §9.010 (Vernon).

65. Ibid., §9.100, §9.070, §9.030, §9.050, §9.035, §9.060, §9.120, §9.080, §9.040 §9.110. (Vernon).

66. Mont. Code Ann. §1–1–216.

67. Ibid., §1–1–224, §1–1–225, §1–1–226.

68. Neb. Rev. Stat. §62–301.

69. Ibid., §84.104.04, §83.104.02, §84.107, §84.104.09, §82–112, §83–454, §84.104.07, §84–108, §20–130, §84.104.01, §84.104.

70. Nev. Rev. Stat. Ann. §236.015.

71. Ibid., §236.055, §236.018, §236.030, §236.020, §236.050, §236.065, §236.040, §236.035, §236.040, §236.025.

72. N.H. Rev. Stat. Ann. tit. 25, §288.1; tit. 1, §4:13–c, §4:13–d, §4:13–g, §4:13–e, §4:13–b, §4:13–c, §4:13–f.

73. N.J. Stat. Ann. §36: 1–1, 1–1.2 (West).

74. Ibid., §36: 1–8, 1–9, 2–1, 2–4, 2–3, 2–6, 1–5, 1–7, 2–2, 1–11, 1–6, 2–7, 2–9; §1–13 (West).

75. N.M. Stat. Ann. §12–5–2, §12–5–3.

76. Ibid., §12–5–6, §12–5–9, §12–5–10, §12–5–1, §12–5–7, §12–5–5, §12–5–4.

77. N.Y. Gen. Constr. Law §24 (McKinney).

78. N.Y. Exec. Law §161–a (McKinney); N.Y. Cons. Laws Ann. §57.02.

79. N.C. Gen. Stat. §103–4.

80. Ibid., §103–6, §103–9, §103–7, §103–8, §143–283.3, 103–10, §147–18.

81. N.D. Cent. Code §1–03–01, §1–03–02, §1–03.02.1.

82. Ibid., §15–38–05, §1–03–12, §1–03–08, §1–03–10, §1–03–07, §1–03–06, §1–03–11.

83. Ohio Rev. Code Ann. §1.14, §5.30, §5.20 (Page).

84. Ibid., §5.226, §5.2214, §5.224, §5.2212, §5.221, §5.2211, §5.225, §5.22, §5.2217, §5.227, §5.2216, §5.228, §5.229, §5.2215, §5.2213, §5.222, §5.223, §5.2210 (Page).

85. Okla. Stat. Ann. tit. 25, §82.1 (West).

86. Ibid., tit. 70, §24–107; tit. 25, §82.2, §90.11, §90.4, §90.9, §82.2, §90.3, §90.8, §83, §88, §90.7, §82.4, §82.2, §90.12; tit. 70, §24–109; tit. 25, §90.10, §90.1, §90.6, §89 (West).

87. Or. Rev. Stat. §187.010, §187.020.

88. Ibid., §336.01, §187.200.

89. Pa. Stat. Ann. tit. 44, §11 (Purdon).

90. Ibid., tit. 44, §40, §40.1, §28, §34, §40.7, §33, §19.3, §19.2, §40.8, §40.4, §30, §35, §39, §40.2, §38, §26, §27, §40.3, §36, §22 (Purdon).

91. R.I. Gen. Laws §25–1–1.

92. Ibid., §25–2–39, §25–2–20, §25–2–16, §25–2–11, §25–2–28, §25–2–26, §25–2–25, §25–2–19, §25–2–34, §25–2–33, §25–2–17, §25–2–22, §25–2–31, §25–2–30, §25–2–9, §25–2–36, §25–2–24, §25–2–27, §25–2–12, §25–2–10, §25–2–32, §25–2–38, §25–2–29, §25–2–23, §25–2–5, §25–2–21, §25–2–40, §25–2–35, §25–2–37, §25–2–15, §25–2–4, §25–2–14, §25–2–8, §25–2–7.

93. S.C. Code §53–5–10, §53–5–20, §53–5–30.

94. Ibid., §53–3–80, §1–1–615, §53–3–60, §53–3–130, §53–3–70, §53–3–40, §53–3–110, §53–3–140, §53–3–90, §53–3–30, §53–3–20, §53–3–10.

95. S.D. Codified Laws §1–5–1, §1–5–10, §1–5–8, §1–5–11, §1–5–9.

96. Tenn. Code Ann. §15–1–101.

97. Ibid., §15–2–101, §15–2–105, §15–2–102, §15–2–103, §15–2–108, §15–2–105, §15–2–106, §15–2–10, §70–2–109.

98. Tex. Govt. Code Ann. tit. 6, §662.003 (Vernon).

99. Ibid., tit. 6, §662.041; Tex. Civ. Code Ann. tit. 106, §6144a; Tex. Govt. Code Ann. tit. 6, §662.042; Tex. Civ. Code Ann. tit. 106, §6144d; Tex. Govt. Code Ann. tit. 6, §662.043, §662.044, §662.045.

100. Utah Code Ann. §63–13–2.

101. Vt. Stat. Ann. tit. 1, §371.

102. Ibid., tit. 1, §373, §372, §374(102).

103. Va. Code §2.1–21.

104. Ibid., §57–2.01, §2.1–28, §2.1–21.2, §2.1–25, §2.1–27.7, §2.1–27.11, §2.1–26, §2.1–27.9, §2.1–24.2, §2.1–24, §2.1–27, §2.1–27.4, §2.1–21.1, §2.1–27.1, §2.1–27.6, §2.1–27.3, §2.1–27.1, §2.1–27.8, §2.1–27.4, §2.1–27.1, §2.1–27.2, §2.1–27.10.

105. Wash. Rev. Code Ann. §1.16.050.

106. Ibid., §1.16.050.

107. W. Va. Code Ann. §2–2–1.

108. Ibid., §2–2–1a.

109. Wis. Stat. Ann. §895.20 (West).

110. Ibid., §14.16; §895.23, §895.22 (West).

111. Wyo. Stat. §8–4–101.

112. Ibid., §8–4–102, §8–4–105, §8–4–104, §8–4–106, §8–4–103.

113. D.C. Code §1.613.2.

114. A.S. Code tit. 1, §951.

115. C.N.M.I. Public Law 5–21.

116. Guam Code Ann. tit. 1, §1000, §1001.

117. Ibid, tit. 1, §1017, §1025, §1016, §1014, §1027, §1020, §1028, §1029, §1014, §1032, §1015, §1021, §1019.

118. P.R. Laws Ann., tit. 1., §71, §74–84.

119. Ibid., tit. 1, §150x, §102, §150n, §150x, §150o, §132, §150aa, §134, §143, §142, §150cc, §150h, §131a, §150j, §150x, §144, §130, §127, §105, §120, §150e, §135, §104, §150k, §150c, §113, §150v, §139, §147, §138, §149, §150w, §150z, §150n, §140, §116, §146, §148, §141, §150j–l, §150y, §150x, §150b, §150x, §117, §116, §501, §137, §150t, §100, §133, §150s, §119, §150a, §150bb, §150q, §136, §150, §150f, §150i, §142a, §150u, §150p, §122, §150m, §150g, §124.

120. V.I. Code Ann. tit. 1, §171.

121. Ibid., tit. 1, §190, §188, §193, §182, §196, §172, §184, §192, §185, §192, §185, §194, §183, §186, §181, §176, §191, §171c, §187, §189, §179, §180.

11

State and Territory License Plates

License plates today are commonplace symbols of a mobile society that are often taken for granted as we go about our daily business. The practice of states' registering vehicles and thereby giving a registration number to a vehicle began about a century ago in 1901, when New York became the first state to require motor vehicle registration. At first, vehicle owners had to make their own plates because the municipality or state with which they registered did not provide them. Everything from leather to porcelainized iron was used to display registration numbers. But the quick spread of the popularity of motorized cars across the nation led to the need for systematic registration at the state level. Not only did vehicles and their owners need to be identified, but governments recognized at once the taxation opportunities automobiles gave them.

The first state-issued plates were quite simple and came in a variety of shapes, sizes, and colors. Not until 1956 was a nationwide standard for license plates adopted. This brought us the familiar six-inch by twelve-inch plate of today, which will fit on any automobile. But variety remains in the colors and designs of the plates. State flags, seals, nicknames, and symbols adorn many license plates. A buffalo roams the North Dakota plate and a bighorn sheep the Nevada plate. Mount Rainier majestically dominates the state of Washington plate and Mount Rushmore appears on South Dakota's plate. The Wright brothers' first airplane still flies on the North Carolina plate. There are canoes on lakes (Minnesota), bisons' skulls (Montana), and Idaho continues to remind us of its "famous potatoes."

The illustrations presented in this book are of standard-issue passenger-car plates. Vanity plates and specialized plates are available now in most states. In addition, the states have numerous special plates, often in colors different from the passenger-car plates, for different kinds of vehicles—trailers, trucks, motorcycles, tractors, and so on. There has never before been such a variety of license plates available to the citizens of all the states and territories.

ALABAMA

The state of Alabama began issuing license plates in 1912. From 1905 until 1912, license plate issues were controlled locally rather than at the state level. The first Alabama plate was white on blue. A host of color combinations have been used throughout the years. In 1955, the slogan "Heart of Dixie" was first used and it appears on the current issue, which began in 1997. The current plate features the slogan "Heart of Dixie" in blue script at the top center with the word "of" on a red heart. "Alabama" is in red script at the bottom and the numbering is black. The background is a graphic that goes from blue to white to red, top to bottom.[1]

ALASKA

Alaska issued its first license plate, which had orange lettering on a black background, in 1922. Plates in a variety of color combinations were issued each year up to 1944, when, for the first time, a validation tab was used on the 1943 plate. New plates were again issued annually until 1954, when the use of validation tabs replaced the yearly issue of plates. New plates were issued sporadically thereafter—in 1956, 1958, 1960, 1962, 1966, 1968, 1970, and 1976. The 1981 plate featured the blue and gold of the Alaska state flag, its depiction in the center, and the slogan "The Last Frontier."[2] The flag graphic had appeared earlier on the 1962 plate. The 1966 gold-on-blue plate displayed a totem pole graphic and the 1976 red-on-white plate a bear graphic.[3] The 1998 plate commemorates the centennial of the Gold Rush. A stream of prospectors is depicted moving from the gold-colored lowlands into the white mountains framed by blue sky. The serials are in black.

ARIZONA

Arizona began issuing passenger license plates when it became a state in 1912. The first plate was actually a four-inch disk made of metal, which was to be placed on the dashboard. The 1913 plate was the type of plate for outside display with which we have become familiar. Like most states, Arizona has used a variety of materials to make the plates, from fiberglass during World War II to the aluminum typical of today's plates. However, during the depression years of 1932–1934, alone among states Arizona issued plates made of copper, which proved too soft, to help its struggling copper industry.[4]

The 1996 graphic-based plate, which replaces the white and maroon 1980 plate, features a white sun rising over maroon mountains in an orange haze that gives way to white and a blue-green sky. "The Grand Canyon State" appears at the lower right.[5]

ARKANSAS

The state of Arkansas began issuing license plates in 1911. During that year, 1,611 of the black-on-white plates were issued. From 1911 to 1949, when the 1948 black-on-aluminum plate was validated for the first time by an aluminum tab, black had been used as one of the two colors in all but nine years. Black was used in combination with white, yellow, light blue, green, silver, orange, aluminum, and light gray. With the white-on-green 1950 plate, white became the most frequently used color.

The 1968 red-on-white plate was the first multiyear, reflectorized plate issued by Arkansas. The 1989 red, white, and blue plate featured the state slogan "The Natural State." The current plate, issued in 1996, retains the slogan and the colors. "Arkansas" appears at the top center, numerals are red, and the slogan is in blue at the bottom, all on a white background.[6]

CALIFORNIA

On March 22, 1905, the state of California began issuing license plates. The plates for the years 1905 through 1913 are known as prestate plates, because the state only assigned numbers—it did not actually manufacture the plates, which were supposed by law to be simple black on white with the words "State of California" on them. But the design law was not always followed strictly and was largely unenforced.

In 1914, the state began to manufacture the plates as it still does today. Until 1943, new issues were produced annually, except for the years 1916 to 1919. In those years symbols were affixed to the basic blue-on-white plates as year validations. The 1916 plate used a bear symbol; the 1917 plate, a poppy; the 1918 plate, a liberty bell; and the 1919 plate, a star. The 1941 plates were replaced in 1945. New plates were issued in the years 1947, 1951, 1956, 1963, 1970, 1982, and 1991. The 1998 plate celebrates California's sesquicentennial in red lettering and blue serials on a white background.[7]

COLORADO

The state of Colorado first issued license plates in 1913. Cities had issued numbers before then when vehicles were registered, and motorists, like those in most states at the time, had to make their own plates to display the registration number. The first plate was black on white and had a porcelain coating. Annual license plate issues were made in various colors except for 1920, 1944, 1952, 1961, and 1976. In 1992, the current month-year plate was issued. Since 1959, however, Colorado has used the dark green and white color combinations, the only exception having been the 1975–1976 red, white, and blue U.S. bicentennial plates. The outline of the Rocky Mountains that appears on the current plate was used first in 1960, and then from 1962 through 1972, and again in 1974. Colorado described itself as "colorful" on the plates of 1950 through 1955, 1958, and 1973. A skier sped through the 1958 plate.[8]

CONNECTICUT

In 1903, the first year registration was required, 1,353 Connecticut citizens paid one dollar to register their automobiles with the state. For those first two years, automobile owners had to make their own plates. Motorists would commonly tack metal numerals preceded by the letter "C" onto pieces of leather. Then from 1905 through 1916, the state issued metal plates covered in porcelain. Painted plates were issued from 1917

through 1919, and then in 1920 the familiar stamped plates were issued for the first time. Steel was used in the manufacture of the plates from 1913 until 1937, when aluminum was used for the first time.

Connecticut issued annual plates until 1937. New multiple-year plates were issued in 1937, 1948, 1957, 1974, and 1975. The current Connecticut plate, which was issued first in 1975, uses white lettering on a deep blue background. At the top left in white is a stamped graphic of a solid outline of the map of the state. The name "Connecticut" is centered at the top and Connecticut's official nickname, "Constitution State," appears across the bottom of the plate, as it has since 1978 by law.[9]

DELAWARE

Although Delaware issued its first license plate in 1910, it had required vehicle registration and assigned numbers to automobile registrations as early as 1907. Thus the 431 automobile owners who registered their vehicles in 1908 had to go to harness makers to get the mandated tag of leather with nickel numbers. The first state-issued plate was white with lettering in black porcelain enamel. The state continued to issue new plates annually through 1939, followed by a blue-on-gold plate in 1941, a gold-on-blue plate on March 31, 1942, and a white-on-black plate on June 30, 1942. A new plate was not issued until 1958. This all-scotchlite gold and blue plate returned to the colors used interchangeably from 1929 to 1937 and had the nickname "The First State" across the top and "Delaware" across the bottom. Gold on blue plates maintaining the same features were issued in aluminum in 1963 and 1970.[10]

FLORIDA

The state of Florida did not issue statewide license plates until 1918. Although the state required the registration of vehicles as early as 1905, motorists received no plate until 1911, when the law was changed to permit licensing by counties. County plates were used until January 1, 1918, when the state comptroller issued the first white-on-black Florida plate. Orange was used on black for the 1919 plate, thus beginning a long love affair with that color, symbolic of one of the state's best-known products. Orange has been used twenty-three times since 1918 in combination with other colors, frequently with blue. Green and white have been used in combination ten times. The current issue combines these traditions as well as the tradition first established in 1923 of placing the outline of the state on the plate. The 1997 plate also includes an orange over the green outline of the state and the slogan "The Sunshine State." Numerals are in green and "Florida" in orange is arched across the top on a white reflectorized background.[11]

GEORGIA

The state of Georgia issued its first license plate in 1910. It was gray on black and undated. Dates were not used on plates until 1914. From 1913 through 1928, the state issued both disks and plates. A host of color combinations were used over the years in the annual issues, including the somewhat unusual combinations of black on green in 1918 and peach on green in 1964. In 1971, a five-year plate was issued, which was blue on white. In 1976 and 1983, seven-year plates were issued. The 1976 red-on-white plate celebrated the U.S. Bicentennial. The 1983 plate was green on white. The 1990 plate was a five-year black-on-white plate. The 1998 plate continues to feature a Georgia peach, this time in the middle of the plate behind black lettering. "Georgia . . . on my mind" graces the top of the plate, which has a white background.[12]

HAWAII

While a 1903 territory-wide law taxed automobiles, four motor vehicles were registered on the main island in 1900. When license plates were first required is a matter of some conjecture, as no certain record exists before 1911. The county of Honolulu did, however, issue a plate in 1914. Plates were issued annually from 1921 to 1942 and again from 1946 to 1952. Multiyear plates were issued thereafter. The current 1991 license plate employs black lettering on a white background. "Hawaii" appears above the license plate number at the center, and "Aloha State," the state's official popular name, appears below the number at the center. A red, yellow, and blue rainbow brightens the plate, stretching from side to side.[13]

IDAHO

The state of Idaho, through the newly created State Highway Commission, issued its first plate, white on blue, to 2,083 people who registered their vehicles in 1913. However, since 1893 Idaho municipalities had had the power to issue local plates, often metal numbers on leather; some cities, like Boise, Twin Falls, Weiser, Hailey, and Payette, issued porcelain-enameled or metal plates. Lewiston actually issued a solid brass engraved plate.

Idaho claims to be the first state to place a slogan on its license plate. The 1928 plate displayed a brown russet potato and the words "Idaho Potatoes." In 1943, the potato again appeared on the Idaho plate and then again in 1948. Since 1957, all Idaho plates have had the slogan "Famous Potatoes." Other slogans also appeared over the years. "Scenic Idaho" was found on the 1941, 1942, 1945, and 1946 plates. "Vacation Wonderland" was proclaimed on 1947 plates. The 1940 plate celebrated "50 Years of Statehood" and an optional plate was issued in 1987 for the 1990 centennial celebration of statehood. The current 1996 issue plate uses a silk-screen graphic in red, white, and blue that depicts a scene of the state's trees and mountains, slightly redesigned from the centennial plate. The slogan "Scenic Idaho" returns on this plate at the top and "Famous Potatoes" remains across the bottom.[14]

ILLINOIS

From 1907, when Illinois adopted its first motor vehicle licensing law, to 1910, motorists were given two-inch round aluminum registration seals rather than plates. Because the registration seal had to be displayed, owners were left to their own devices to have plates made. In 1911, the state issued its first plate, which had black numbers on a white background. Plates were issued annually thereafter until 1978. The blue-on-white 1979 plate was used until 1983, when the current plate was issued. The "Land of Lincoln" slogan on this light blue and white plate with dark blue lettering has been found on Illinois plates since 1954.[15]

INDIANA

From 1905 through 1910, the state of Indiana issued two-inch circular numbered seals to those who registered their automobiles. The vehicle owners were then required to have a plate made with their registration number on it to be placed on the rear of the vehicle. Then in 1911, Indiana issued its first plate, a simple white-on-black design. Plates were issued for most years in a variety of colors until a multiyear license plate program was begun in 1981. Stripes of color have typified these multiyear plates. In 1998, however, the red, gold, and black stripes with a farm scape depiction gave way to a plate that recalls the state flag design on a white background. "Indiana" appears in blue across the top and "The Crossroads of America" across the bottom. To the left center behind blue lettering, the state is depicted in buff with thirteen stars emanating from it. The stars represent the original colonies.[16]

IOWA

In July 1904, the state of Iowa began registering motor vehicles. In that year 155 citizens registered their vehicles for one dollar each. Until 1911, the secretary of state issued two-inch metal disks that were to be displayed on dashboards. There was also a requirement for a plate on the rear of the vehicle, which the state did not supply. These were often the metal numbers on leather plates used in many states at that time. By 1915, the cost of registration had gone to five dollars and the state realized $1,000,000 in revenues from registrations.

Iowa has remained with a plain and simple plate for most of its history. Between 1941 and 1958, plates were black on white or white on black. Only on the 1953 plate did a slogan ever appear: "The Corn State." The use of multiyear plates began first in 1916, for the three-year period of World War I. During World War II, the 1942 plate was used through 1944. Multiyear plates were issued frequently thereafter. The 1997 plate left familiar simplicity for a blue and white graphic-based plate depicting a farm scape. "Iowa" appears across the top in blue and the lettering is in the same blue color.[17]

KANSAS

The state of Kansas began issuing license plates in 1913. Previous to that, municipalities registered vehicles and owners had to find their own way to display their registration numbers. The 1913 plate was black on white with the abbreviation "KAN" descending on the right. That first year 38,680 automobiles were registered.

Until 1976, black was a frequently used color in combination most frequently with white, yellow, and orange. In 1976, with the issue of multiyear plates, blue and white became a familiar color combination. Kansans received an ornamental plate with their white-on-red 1925 plate. It had light blue lettering on a white background and featured the slogan "Kansas the Wheat State" with a small shock of wheat. In 1952, two sunflower decals were used on the plates. "The Wheat State" appeared again on the 1949, 1950, and 1951 plates. In 1965, the slogan "Midway USA" was used on Kansas license plates. Today, no slogan appears on the Kansas plate, but golden wheat dominates the center of the current plate. This 1995 graphic-based plate has blue lettering on a background that moves from cream-yellow to blue.[18]

KENTUCKY

Kentucky issued its first plate, which was undated, in 1914. It was a simple white-on-black plate. For all but ten years since the first plate was issued, white was used either for the numerals or the background in combination with black, red, maroon, green, brown, or blue. Black and yellow combinations were used in 1918, 1935, and 1944. Orange was used as the background for black numerals on the 1922 plate and for numerals against a silver-gray background on the 1948 plate. Black and silver-gray combinations were used on the 1941, 1942, 1946, and 1949 plates. No plates were issued in the years 1943, 1945, 1947, and 1953. Since 1953 up until five-year plates were issued in 1988, blue and white were alternated on the plates. The 1998 issue maintains the slogan "Bluegrass State" beneath "Kentucky" at the top, but gone are the steeples of Churchill Downs. The new plate depicts green mountains in the foreground out to a blue sky. A cloud mass in the shape of Kentucky dominates the center.[19]

LOUISIANA

The state of Louisiana began issuing license plates in 1915. Previous to that time and until 1920, cities authorized plates. The first state plate was white and black. Since the 1930s, the pelican has frequently appeared on the Louisiana plates. The slogan "Sportsman's Paradise" has also frequently been used since the late 1950s.[20] The current plate, in use since 1994, maintains the red, white, and blue theme used since 1989. Numerals are in blue; "Louisiana" appears across the top in red; the slogan "Sportsman's Paradise" is in blue across the bottom, all on a white background.

MAINE

The state of Maine began issuing license plates in 1905. The first iron plates, used until 1911, had white numerals on a red background. Plates were issued annually through 1942. The 1942 plate was validated for 1943 with a windshield decal. Plates were again issued annually for 1944, 1945, and 1946, but validation stickers were used for 1947 and 1949. The 1950 plates were used for five years after the year of issue, which began the pattern now used for multiyear plates. In July of 1999, the famous lobster plate was replaced with the chickadee plate, commemorating the state bird. The chickadee, perched on the branch of the state tree, the white pine, appears at the left. Black numerals are on a white background above a green foreground of north woods.[21]

MARYLAND

Although Maryland began to require motor vehicle registration in 1904, Maryland motorists, like many others all over the country, were responsible for making their own plates. These plates, known as "prestates," were made from a variety of materials including stencils. In 1910, the commissioner of motor vehicles issued the first Maryland plate. It was made of tin, painted black on yellow. In 1934, Maryland issued a tercentenary plate and from December 1975 to February 1977, a special U.S. Bicentennial plate. In 1984, Maryland celebrated its 350th anniversary with the issue of an award-winning plate that featured the state shield. The 1986 issue retained the shield at the center of the plate on a simple black-on-white plate.[22]

MASSACHUSETTS

Automobiles could be found on Massachusetts roads by 1900, but no law governing them was passed until 1902. This law set the speed limit at fifteen miles per hour outside of densely populated areas. By 1903, there were 3,241 automobiles registered with the Massachusetts Highway Commission, and in September of that year it became illegal to operate a vehicle without a license and a registration. So began the issuance of license plates in Massachusetts. Like all the states, Massachusetts has used a variety of colors on its plates. The current issue, however, recalls the importance of this original colony in American history. "Massachusetts" in blue lettering is centered at the top. Beneath the red license plate number, the slogan "The Spirit of America" appears in blue lettering. The background is white, completing the display of patriotic colors.[23]

MICHIGAN

Michigan began registering automobiles in 1906. From 1906 through 1909, vehicle owners received numbered dashboard disks rather than plates to identify their vehicles as registered. Then in 1910 the state issued its first plate, which had black numerals on a white background. Plates issued from 1910 to 1919 included a seal, discontinued with the black-on-orange plate of 1920. For a number of years, Michigan plates bore the slogan "Water-Winter Wonderland." Then the slogan was changed in the late 1960s to "Great Lake State." The current plate bears the slogan "Great Lakes" centered in white at the bottom. "Michigan" is centered at the top in white above the white numerals, all on a field of blue.[24]

MINNESOTA

When Minnesota first began registering motor vehicles in 1903, it was done through the office of the state boiler inspector. License numbers had to be painted on the back of the vehicle. In 1909, the secretary of state was given authority to license vehicles and Minnesota issued its first plate, which had silver lettering on a bright red background. Plates were issued annually until 1912. Three-year plates were issued through 1920. The state went back to annual issues until 1943, when, because of war, multiyear plates were issued. Annual issues occurred again after the war until 1957. Three-year issues were made until 1974 and five-year plates were issued thereafter. The current plate uses a graphic design that depicts Minnesota as the state with "10,000 lakes" and encourages everyone to "explore Minnesota." Above the map of the state that bisects the lettering two persons can be seen canoeing across a blue lake set in the green north woods.[25]

MISSISSIPPI

When the Mississippi legislature passed a bill in 1912 requiring the state auditor to issue annual plates to car owners, the citizens of the state rebelled against it as unfair. Demonstrations ensued in Jackson. When the state supreme court finally declared the 1912 law unconstitutional, car owners were refunded their 1912 and 1913 registration fees, which totalled $28,040. As a consequence, the first black-on-white plate of 1912 was used in 1913, since no plates were issued that year. A new law was passed in 1914, when another black-on-white was issued and used through 1918. Effective January 1, 1919, plates were issued annually. The first annual plate was pea green on black. Over the years, a wide variety of color combinations were used on Mississippi plates, but either black or white frequently appeared with another color. The current Mississippi plate, however, depicts the state flower, the magnolia, at the center of the plate in a diagonal swath of white between yellow and green. Numbering is in green as is "Mississippi" across the top of the plate.[26]

MISSOURI

A 1903 state law made automobile owners register their vehicles at local city or county offices. Owners were required to display a license number, but they had to find a way to do it on their own. In 1907 a new motor vehicle registration law was passed that required the secretary of state to provide for a two-inch circular seal to go to all registrants. Plates displaying the license number were usually made of leather with "house numbers" tacked to it. Finally in 1911, the first Missouri license plate, which had white letters on an orange background, was issued. Plates were issued annually until a multiyear plate program was initiated in 1948 and validation tabs were used for annual validations. Multiyear plates were issued also in 1956 and 1962. Annual plates were then issued for the years 1968 through 1978. Then in 1979, the white-on-maroon multiyear plate displaying the state's nickname, "Show-Me State," was issued. The nickname remains on the green, blue, and white

1996 plate, which features "Missouri" in green at the top floating on a wavy blue line. The numbers are in blue.[27]

MONTANA

Montana began taxing motor vehicles in 1913 to raise money for road construction. Registration of vehicles, therefore, also began that year. In 1914, the state issued its first plate, an unpainted steel plate with black lettering, 4¾ inches by 12 inches. Since the issue of that first rather basic plate, Montana has developed one of the country's most colorful license plates. An outline of Montana first appeared on the 1933 plate, and the bison skull first appeared in 1938. The "Big Sky Country" slogan replaced the "Treasure State" slogan of 1950 in 1967. Then in 1976, a red, white, and blue U.S. Bicentennial plate was issued and used until 1991. In 1987, a Montana centennial plate was issued and will be used through 1996. The "new issue" plate of 1991 combined a number of themes from earlier Montana plates—the "Big Sky," the bison's skull, the outline of the state—with a tricolor mountain graphic on a field of light and sky blue. The 2000 plate keeps the same symbols with rugged purple mountains and vast golden plains depicted on a background of swirling blue and white. "Montana" is in purple across the top.[28]

NEBRASKA

From 1903 to 1915, when the Department of Motor Vehicles first issued plates, license plates of the metal number on leather variety had to be made by the vehicle owners themselves. The 1915 plate was a simple black-on-white plate. Plates were issued annually except for 1920 until 1943. After 1946, revalidation stickers were used in 1947 and 1953. In 1958 a multiyear plate issue program has been used more consistently, with new issues made in 1960, 1962, 1965, 1966, 1969, 1972, 1976, 1984, 1987, 1990, 1993, 1996 and 1999. The 1999 plate incorporates previously used city and prairie themes on a buff, white, and blue background. "Nebraska" appears at the top and the lettering is in red.[29]

NEVADA

The state of Nevada first required motor vehicle registration in 1913. Between 1913 and 1915, a metal disk for display on the dashboard was issued with plates being optional. Beginning in 1916, the state stopped issuing disks and required a license plate. Since 1936, the only exception having been the gold-on-green plate of 1953, Nevada plates have used combinations of cobalt blue and silver, the state colors. Multiyear plates began to be issued in 1960. The current plate was first issued in 1982. Cobalt blue is used for "Nevada" at the center top of the plate, the license number, and the state's nickname, "The Silver State," at the bottom. Against a white background and covering nearly the entire plate is a graphic in silver, which depicts a Nevada mountain scene replete with state symbols: the desert bighorn sheep to the top left, the single-leaf piñon in the center, and the sagebrush to the bottom right.[30]

NEW HAMPSHIRE

New Hampshire's first motor vehicle registration law became effective on March 10, 1905. In that year, five hundred passenger vehicles were issued a pair of green porcelain plates with white numbers. Except for the years 1945 through 1949, New Hampshire plates have had green and white color combinations. In 1926, the Old Man of the Mountains, the state emblem, first appeared on the license plate. This emblem appears on

the 1999 plate in green on the left half of the plate, sky blue on the right. New Hampshire's memorable slogan "Live Free or Die" is written across the top and "New Hampshire" across the bottom. Lettering and numbering are in green.[31]

NEW JERSEY

The state of New Jersey began issuing license plates in 1908, although plates had been required since 1906. For those first two years, New Jersey residents, like automobile owners in many other states, had to have plates made themselves. The first plate featured cream numbers on a blue background. Various background colors—black, yellow, blue, white, gray, red, orange, green, brown—were used, predominantly with white numbers, from 1909 until 1932. Plates with black backgrounds were utilized from 1932 through 1943. From 1944 through 1947, the plates had cream backgrounds with either black or light blue numbers. The 1948 plate first used black-on-straw colors and these colors were repeated from 1959 through 1978, after five years of orange-on-black plates. In 1979, the familiar buff-on-blue plate was first issued. The new plate has black lettering and numbers on a buff background that fades to white from top to bottom. The outline of the state is colored in black and separates the numbers. "Garden State," New Jersey's nickname, appears at the bottom center.[32]

NEW MEXICO

When New Mexico became a state in 1912, only 870 automobiles and 60 trucks were registered. Because plates were numbered consecutively until 1927, the actual numbers on these tags marked with "NM" equalled the number of registrations. The 1927 plate featured the Zia, the sun symbol which appears on the state flag, and "New Mexico" rather than the abbreviation used until then. In 1941, the slogan "The Land of Enchantment" appeared on the plates, replacing the 1932 "Sunshine State" slogan that Florida had appropriated. "USA" was added to "New Mexico" on the 1975 plates, dropped in 1976, and added again in 1987. It remains on the current plate to identify clearly the owner's country. In 1991, all license plates were replaced with what is surely one of the nation's most distinctive plates. Against a bright yellow background, the city name centered at the top, the numerals and "New Mexico USA" stand out in red. An Indian design at the top left and right, the yucca flower at the bottom left, and "Land of Enchantment" centered at the bottom are in blue.[33]

NEW YORK

The state of New York was the first to require motor vehicle registration. In 1901, 954 vehicles were registered. By 1903, registrations had reached 6,412. Vehicle owners had to supply their own rear plates with their initials on them for the first two years of registration. Numbers were assigned beginning in 1903, but owners still had to supply their own plates until August 1, 1910, when the secretary of state issued a white-on-blue plate. In 1966, permanent plates began to be issued. Since that orange-on-blue plate was issued, only two other plates had been issued: the 1973 blue on gold plates and the well-known Lady Liberty plates. In 2000, however, a new plate was issued that depicts New York state scenes across the top in shades of blue and white, a white center with blue lettering divided by the outline of the state, and a blue band across the bottom. "New York" is in white over the scenes at the top and "The Empire State" is in white on the bottom of the plate.[34]

NORTH CAROLINA

The first car registered in the state of North Carolina was John A. Park's Hudson on July 9, 1909. Mr. Park, like all the other car owners, had to manufacture his own front and rear plates until 1913, when the state began to supply the license plates. The first plate was white on black. Various colors were used in the annual issues thereafter. Slogans and mottoes began appearing on the plates in 1956. "Drive Safely" appeared on plates from 1956 through 1964. From 1975 through 1979, "First in Freedom" appeared on the plates. In 1982, the current plate was issued, the design having been mandated by law. This plate has the slogan "First in Flight" in red at the top over a light blue graphic of the Wright brothers' first plane, which was flown at Kitty Hawk. The license plate number is in deep blue at the center. Below, "North Carolina" in red overlays a scene of sea oats in light blue.[35]

NORTH DAKOTA

The state of North Dakota first required vehicle owners to register their vehicles and display plates, front and rear, in 1911. The first plate had gold letters on a black background. Annual plates in various colors were issued except for 1949 until a four-year plate program was begun in 1958. In 1974, a multiyear plate program was begun. The 1988 centennial plate, celebrating one hundred years of North Dakota statehood in 1989, was replaced with the current 1993 issue. This graphic plate, depicting blue sky over the yellow prairie with bronze mountains in the background and beneath the black license plate number, bids everyone to "Discover the Spirit" across the top. Beneath the number, "North Dakota" is centered in white in a band of black, and beneath the state name in brown is the slogan "The Peace Garden State." A buffalo to the bottom left and wheat to the bottom right complete the theme.[36]

OHIO

The state of Ohio issued 10,649 white-on-blue license plates in 1908, the first year for state-supplied plates. By 1909, the number of registered vehicles had more than doubled to 23,003. The same undated porcelain plate of 1908 was used in 1909. From 1910 until 1974, when multiyear plates came into use, with the exceptions only of the years 1943 and 1952, annually issued plates used a variety of color combinations with no particular pattern. Red and white (1910, 1914, 1930, 1934, 1946, 1959, 1965, 1968, 1976) and blue and white (1908, 1909, 1920, 1922, 1924, 1932, 1936, 1939, 1940, 1944, 1945, 1951, 1955, 1958, 1963, 1967, 1969) were, however, frequently used color combinations. Red, white, and blue came back into use in 1991 when the slogan "The Heart of It All" also appeared. A reflectorized graphic-based plate was issued in 1996, which featured the same 1991 slogan and a background of tan and white. The 1997 plate kept the blue numbering on the same background with a new slogan in red: "Birthplace of Aviation." The Wright brothers were natives of Dayton, Ohio.[37]

OKLAHOMA

The state of Oklahoma began issuing license plates in 1915. Annual plates were issued until 1943, when the metal shortage caused by the war yielded a window sticker plate. Again in 1947, a metal validation tab replaced a new plate, but annual issues continued until 1980, when multiyear plates began to be issued. The slogan "Oklahoma Is OK" appeared on all plates until the 1989 issue, when it was changed slightly to "OK!" in buckskin color beneath "Oklahoma" in black at the top. License plates in Oklahoma

have not been without controversy. The experiment with using school colors—Oklahoma State's orange and black in 1968 and the University of Oklahoma's red and white in 1969—resulted in a 1970 law that prohibited school colors from ever being used again. Official state colors of green and white became the standard. The 1994 issue employs green lettering on a white background with the emblem that appears on the state flag in the center of the plate between the license plate numerals. The "OK!" slogan is gone, replaced by "Native America" across the bottom in red.[38]

OREGON

Oregon began issuing license plates in 1911. The first plate featured black numerals on a yellow background. That same color combination was used again in 1915, 1922, 1925, and finally in 1939, when the color was actually light yellow, but never again. Plates in various color combinations were issued annually with the exceptions of 1930, 1943, 1944, and 1945, until five-year permanent plates began to be issued in 1950. Permanent plates, validated with tabs or stickers, were issued in 1956, 1964, and 1974. Since the 1974 blue-on-gold plates, Oregon changed to graphic plates. The first had a light green fir tree at the center with small gray fir trees below on a tan background. The current issue is much the same as the first graphic except that the fir tree through the center of the plate and "Oregon" at the top are dark green; a white outline silhouettes the mountains beneath the light blue sky, and the small forested peaks at the bottom of the plate are, like the numerals, dark blue.[39]

PENNSYLVANIA

Pennsylvania first issued license plates statewide in 1906. The first plate had white lettering on a deep blue background. It was made of porcelain as were all the annual issues through 1915. While the state used a number of color combinations at first, in 1924 yellow and deep blue were chosen, and those colors have been used in alternating combinations ever since. The yellow on blue plate, used since 1984, gave way to a unique new plate in 1999. A blue band across the top includes "Pennsylvania" in white. A large white band in the middle provides the field for blue numbering. A yellow band across the bottom provides the state's website address in blue: WWW.STATE.PA.US.[40]

RHODE ISLAND

In 1904, Rhode Island issued its first plate, which was white on black. This began a series of black and white combination issues that continued uninterrupted for many years. The 1996 plate has blue lettering on a stylized wave graphic base. An anchor, a state symbol used since 1647 on state and colonial seals, appears on the upper right. Anchors could also be seen on the 1980 and 1985 plates. The nickname "Ocean State" appears across the bottom and has been on every plate since 1973.[41]

SOUTH CAROLINA

When the State Highway Department was created in 1917, it issued license plates for statewide use. Previous to that, counties issued plates that were made either of wood or metal. The 1917 plate had black numbers on a white background. Combinations of black, white, green, and yellow were used frequently for the annual issues up to 1943. The 1942 plate was used for 1943 and 1944 to save metal for the war effort. From 1930 through 1933, the slogan "Iodine State" or "Iodine Products State" was found on South Carolina plates. Plates were issued yearly from 1945 until a five-year plate program

was begun in 1976. All the South Carolina plates issued since the program started have had graphic designs. The 1976 red, white, and blue bicentennial plate featured a blue cannon and a red palmetto tree. The blue-on-white 1981 plate featured the state in outline and the state seal. The 1986 plate was again blue on white with "South Carolina" in red. But the 1990 plate brought back the green, yellow, white, and black colors used so often in earlier plates in a graphic design that featured the state flower, yellow jasmine, across the top of the plate and the state bird, the Carolina wren, centered in the jasmine's branches. The 1999 plate sports a new slogan across the top: "Smiling Faces. Beautiful Places." Black lettering, split by an illustration of the state tree, the palmetto, is surrounded by a blue background at the top and on both sides. "South Carolina" appears in blue at the bottom.[42]

SOUTH DAKOTA

James F. Biglow of Flandreau received the small disk stamped "No. 1" when he registered his Oldsmobile in 1905. Following this first vehicle registration, 17,692 South Dakota citizens received stamped disks up until 1912, when they registered their vehicles. In 1913, two license plates were issued for each vehicle and annual issues began. Perhaps the most enduring feature of South Dakota license plates is the depiction of Mount Rushmore on them. It first appeared on the 1939 plate and then in 1952 it became a permanent feature with legislative authorization. On the 1996 plate, the faces of Mount Rushmore, outlined in tan, peer out from behind green lettering in the center of the white background. "South Dakota" is scripted across the top. At the bottom in green the slogan first used on the 1990 plate appears: "Great Faces. Great Places."[43]

TENNESSEE

Although the state of Tennessee first required motor vehicle registration in 1905, it was not until 1915 that the state supplied license plates. Owners had to make their own plates, usually out of leather or enamel. The 1915 plate had white numerals on a blue background. Annual issues of plates occurred until 1943, when a corner tab was used on the 1942 plate. Plates were then issued annually until 1962. Between 1956 and 1976, the plates were either black on white or white on black, colors which in either combination had appeared on Tennessee plates in 1917, 1926, 1932, 1935, 1941, 1942, 1944, 1947, and 1952. From 1977 through 1987, Tennessee used a white plate with blue numerals. The 1987 issue was red, white, and blue. In 1994, a new plate celebrating Tennessee's bicentennial, 1796–1996, was issued employing again red numbering, a white background, and a blue swatch over which the county name appears in white. The numbering is bisected by a depiction of the state capitol and the nickname "Volunteer State" appears in red at the top beneath the word "Bicentennial," which is in red script except for the blue capital letters "TENN."[44]

TEXAS

Although the state of Texas required vehicle registration by county clerks beginning in 1907, it did not issue plates statewide until 1917, when the Highway Department was created. These first plates were good for as long as the vehicle was in operation, but the state also issued radiator seals, in different colors for different years, that validated the registration annually. The 1917 plate was white on black and the round seal was white on red. When new plates were issued in 1920, again white on black but smaller in size than the first plate, the validation disk changed to a seal. Another white on black was issued in 1923 and the last validation plate in 1924. Thus in 1925 began the practice of annual plate issues except for 1943 and 1944 until multiyear plates were introduced in 1975. While a number of color combinations were used over the years, black-gold combinations were frequent (1941–1945, 1948–1956), as were black-white combinations (1917, 1920, 1923, 1931, 1947, 1957–1968), and silver-black combinations (1969, 1971, 1973, 1975, 1977, 1978, 1983). The current Texas plate is red, white, and blue. The state flag is displayed at the top next to "Texas." At the bottom is the state's nickname, "The Lone Star State." All lettering is in blue against a white background. An outline of Texas in red divides the license plate number.[45]

UTAH

Utah did not issue plates statewide until 1915. Previous to that time, motorists had to make their own plates. The first plate was dark green and white. Over the years, various color combinations have been utilized along with various slogans: "Center Scenic America" in the mid-1940s, "This Is the Place" in 1947, and "The Friendly State" in 1948. In the 1970s, a beehive was depicted on Utah plates.[46] The "Ski Utah" plates of 1985 were replaced by the centennial plates, which were first issued in 1994 and became general issue plates in 1997. The year 1996 marked Utah's 100th year as a state. The brightly colored plates depict the desert and a natural rock arch in red fading to orange against white mountains and a blue sky. The numbering is in blue.

VERMONT

By a law enacted in December 1904, Vermont citizens had until May 1, 1905, to register their automobiles. Through 1906, motorists received a single plate for two dollars, which was made of enameled iron bearing white lettering on a blue background. Black-on-white plates were issued from 1907 until 1916. Various colors, including the University of Vermont's yellow and green in 1918 and Norwich University's maroon and tan in 1929, were used until 1949. Dark blue and white were used from 1931 through 1942 and black and white from 1944 through 1947. But in 1949, the familiar white and green colors of Vermont were used and they have been used ever since, reversing colors from issue to issue. The current license plate, issued in 1986, 1985 and again in 1990 depicts a maple tree in white at the upper left and "Vermont" in white at the top center. The license plate numbers in white are surrounded by a white rectangle. The nickname "Green Mountain State" appears in white at the bottom. All of these are against a solid green background.[47]

VIRGINIA

Carl Leroy Armentrout of Staunton was the first Virginian to register his car on June 1, 1906. He received a black and white enamel plate. Over the years, the state experimented with various materials for the manufacture of plates, including fiberplate in 1925 and fiberboard in 1944. Both of these plates were said to be appealing to goats, who happily ate them. Metal plates became the standard, aluminum having been used since 1973. The current regular plate (illustrated) is a simple blue-on-white plate with "Virginia" at the top center in lighter blue than the blue used in the license plate number. However, a host of other plates, including "Heritage" and "Scenic" graphic plates, are available as current issues. The "Heritage" plates depict a cardinal, the state bird, perched on a branch of a flowering dogwood, the state tree, all in

a light background with deep blue numerals and "Virginia" in red across the bottom. The "Scenic" plates show an ocean scene— blue water, shore, green land, and blue mountains—on a light blue background with lettering in dark blue.[48]

WASHINGTON

When S. A. Perkins of Tacoma became the first citizen of Washington to register his Pope-Toledo touring car on May 2, 1905, he did not receive a license plate for his two-dollar fee. Motorists had to make their own plates or stencil their numbers on the back and front of their vehicles. Finally in 1916, Washington issued its first plate, which was white on blue. Blue and white were used in 1923–1925 and 1936–1937; green and white were used in 1926–1927, 1929–1934, 1938, 1940–1946, and 1950–1986. In 1987 Washington celebrated its centennial as a state, and the multiyear plate issued that year used patriotic colors: blue numerals on a white background, with "Washington" in red letters at the top and "Centennial Celebration" in red at the bottom, all overlaying a light blue graphic of Mount Rainier. Plates issued in 1991 keep the same design and colors but eliminated the centennial designation. The 1998 plate kept the design of the 1991 plate and added the nickname "Evergreen State" in red at the bottom.[49]

WEST VIRGINIA

The 1906 white-on-blue West Virginia license plate was the state's first issue. Various color combinations, usually including white, were used until 1931, when yellow and black became the color combination of all West Virginia plates until the 1956 issue. New plates were not issued, however, for 1943 and 1944 owing to wartime shortages. A black-and-white metal tab was used to validate the 1942 plate for 1943, and a windshield sticker was used for 1944. Between 1956 and 1962, various color combinations were used, green and white being used in 1956, 1958, and 1959. In 1963, a series of blue and yellow combinations began. The current issue retains those colors on a field of white. "West Virginia" is in yellow on a blue stripe at the top. Numbering appears on a white background in blue. The slogan "Wild, Wonderful" appears at the bottom of the plate.[50]

WISCONSIN

The cities of Madison and Milwaukee began registering automobiles in 1904, but the state began furnishing license plates only on July 1, 1905. The first plate was undated with aluminum numbers riveted on a black zinc base. These plates were used until 1912 except by new registrants between July 1 and the end of 1911, who were issued aluminum-on-green plates. The new 1912 annual plates were aluminum on red. The 1913 plates were aluminum on blue. Beginning with the black-on-white 1914 plates, aluminum never was used again as a color on Wisconsin plates. A variety of colors was used over the years from olive drab (1917) to polaris maroon (1965) and jonquil yellow (1961). The slogan "America's Dairyland" first appeared on the red-on-white plate of 1940 and remains today. The first graphic plates were issued in 1986. The current issue continues the use of the graphic plate. "Wisconsin" appears in blue letters at the upper left top of the plate. Green and blue lines cross the plate below the name of the state and define the graphic in the upper right of the plate. The blue line becomes water on which a sailboat is defined sailing against an orange sun. Geese fly toward the sun from a farm scene in the extreme upper right of the plate. The numerals are in red.[51]

WYOMING

The first Wyoming license plate was issued in 1913. It had red letters on a white background and was undated. Not until the white-on-brown plate of 1918 were dates used on the plates. Various color combinations were used in the annual issues that continued each year until 1975, when multiyear plates came into use. Plates were then issued in 1978 (brown on white), 1983 (brown on gold), and 1988 (red, white, and blue bicentennial design). The current 1993 plate is a graphic plate that pictures a green-and-sand-colored prairie at the bottom, which runs up to blue foothills and mountains. "Wyoming" appears in dark blue lettering at the top right. The numerals in dark blue are separated by a cowboy on a bucking horse. The bucking horse first was used on the black-on-white 1936 license plate.[52]

DISTRICT OF COLUMBIA

Black and white and yellow and black have been frequently used color combinations for District license plates. The very first District plate was white on black in 1907. The first yellow and black plate was the 1915 plate. In 1975, however, red, white, and blue became the colors used on the license plates for the nation's capital city.[53] The current license plate highlights the blue numerals between horizontal red stripes on a white background. The license plate number is divided by the "stars and bars" in red. "Washington, D.C." is in blue below the second horizontal stripe, and also in blue above the first stripe is the slogan "Celebrate & Discover" or "A Capital City."

AMERICAN SAMOA

There is no record of when the registration of motor vehicles began in American Samoa.

The earliest extant plate dates back to 1933.[54] The current license plate is red on white with a palm tree swaying in the breeze depicted to the left. The words "Motu o Fiafiaga," or "Land of Happiness," are in red across the top of the plate, and "American Samoa" is across the bottom.

COMMONWEALTH OF THE NORTHERN MARIANA ISLANDS

Since the Commonwealth was only recently created, its first license plate was issued in 1978. The first issue was blue on white with "Commonwealth" at the top and "Northern Marianas" at the bottom. A latte stone and a star were depicted to the left of the plate number. In 1988, however, with the redesign of the flag, a new multiyear plate was issued. This plate features the latte stone, on which a star is centered, and surrounding the latte stone is a white, light blue, yellow, and medium orange MarMar. "Hafa Adai," or "hello," is centered in light blue at the top of the plate and "CNMI–USA," also in light blue, is at the bottom center. The license plate numbers are in navy blue and the background is white.[55]

GUAM

In 1924, Guam began to issue license plates every year. Various color combinations were used. In 1965, multiyear plates began to be issued and with these issues came messages. The plates first issued in 1965, 1974, and 1980 contained the message "HAFA ADAI," meaning "hello." The plate issued in 1970 had the words "America's Day Begins in" at the top and "Guam USA" at the bottom. The plate used from 1983 to 1986 displayed the slogan "Hub of the Pacific."[56] The general issue plate of 1993 depicts the island in yellow at the center. Black numbering is superimposed over it. "Guam U.S.A." is centered at the top and "Tano y Chamorro" appears at the bottom. The background of the entire plate is white.

PUERTO RICO

Motor vehicle registrations in Puerto Rico began in 1908, when 188 vehicles were registered. By 1992 that number had grown to 1,650,709. Multiyear plates have been issued since 1959. The current plate, issued since 1985, is black on white with a silk-screen reproduction of a sentry box in the center. These sentry boxes are found in the sixteenth-century Spanish fortresses on the island. "Garita del Diablo" at San Felipe del Morro is the most famous of the sentry boxes. In black lettering at the top appears "Puerto Rico" and at the bottom, the slogan "Isla del Encanto," or "Island of Enchantment."[57]

U.S. VIRGIN ISLANDS

The 1928 license plate of the U.S. Virgin Islands was probably the first plate issued, even though vehicle registrations may have occurred earlier. For ten years beginning in 1952, the slogan "Tropical Playground" appeared on the plates. From 1963 to 1967, the slogan "Vacation Adventure" appeared. In 1968, the multiyear plates carried the new slogan "American Paradise," which remains on the current issue.[58] The current multiyear plates, which were issued first in 1993, depict the islands in light blue at the center behind red numerals on a white background. "U.S. Virgin Islands" dominates the top of the plate in blue and the slogan "American Paradise" is in blue at the bottom.

NOTES

1. Unpublished information provided by State of Alabama, Department of Revenue, Motor Vehicle Division.

2. Alaska Stat. §28.10.161.

3. *Brief History of Alaska License Plates* (Anchorage: State of Alaska, Department of Public Safety, Division of Motor Vehicles, n.d.); information supplied by Alaska Division of Motor Vehicles.

4. Justin Herman, *This Week on Arizona Highways* (Phoenix: Arizona Highway Department, 1968); supplied by Arizona Department of Transportation, Motor Vehicle Division.

5. Unpublished information supplied by Arizona Department of Transportation, Motor Vehicle Division.

6. "Arkansas Office of Motor Vehicle [*sic*]." (Unpublished information provided by the Arkansas State Library.)

7. *California License Plates and Proof of Current Registration, 1991/92* (State of California, Department of Motor Vehicles, 1991), pp. 2–5.

8. *Colorado License Plate History* (n.p., n.d.); information provided by State of Colorado, Department of Revenue.

9. *Historical Notes about Connecticut's Automobile Registration Plates* (Wethersfield: Commissioner, State Motor Vehicle Department, n.d.); information supplied by the Connecticut Department of Motor Vehicles.

10. *Motor Vehicle History* (Dover: State of Delaware, Department of Public Safety, Division of Motor Vehicles, n.d.); information supplied by Delaware Division of Motor Vehicles.

11. "From file located in the Div. of Motor Vehicles Bureau of Registration; Kirtman Bldg., Rm. A-114, Ms. Cindy Britt." (Provided by Florida Department of State, Division of Library and Information Services.)

12. *Georgia Motor Vehicle License Plate Colors, 1910–1994* (Atlanta: Georgia Department of Revenue, Motor Vehicle Division, n.d.); information supplied by Georgia Department of Revenue, Motor Vehicle Division, Correspondence Section.

13. Gerald Boone, "Hawaii Car Plates," *The New Pacific Magazine* 5 (September/October 1981): 37.

14. *History of Idaho License Plates* (n.p., n.d.); supplied by the Idaho Transportation Department.

15. George H. Ryan, Secretary of State, *Time Marches On . . . As Seen in Illinois License Plates* (n.p., n.d.); supplied by Illinois Office of the Secretary of State.

16. *History of Indiana License Plates* (n.p., 1985); information supplied by the Indiana Bureau of Motor Vehicles.

17. Charles C. Sinclair, Director, *History of Motor Vehicle Registration* (Des Moines: Motor Vehicle Registration Division, Iowa Department of Public Safety, January 17, 1972); information supplied by the Iowa Department of Transportation, Office of Vehicle Registration.

18. *Brief History of License Plates* (n.p., n.d.); information provided by Kansas Department of Revenue, Division of Vehicles.

19. *Kentucky Motor Vehicle Registration Plates* (n.p., n.d.); information provided by the Commonwealth of Kentucky, Transportation Cabinet.

20. Neil Parker, *Registration Plates of the World*, 2d ed. (Somerset, Great Britain: Europlate, 1987), pp. 465, 467.

21. *Color Combinations of Plates Issued by Maine* (n.p., n.d.); information supplied by Maine Motor Vehicle Division.

22. *History of Maryland License Plates* (n.p., revised June 18, 1988); information provided by Maryland Department of Transportation, Motor Vehicle Administration.

23. *Registry of Motor Vehicles, Agency Outline, History of the Registry of Motor Vehicles* (n.p., n.d.); information supplied by the Massachusetts Registry of Motor Vehicles.

24. *The Story of Michigan License Plates* (Lansing: Michigan Department of State, 1967); information provided by the Library of Michigan.

25. *History of Minnesota License Plate* (n.p., n.d.); *State of Minnesota Passenger Car Plate Colors* (n.p., n.d.); information supplied by Minnesota Department of Public Safety, Driver and Vehicle Services Division.

26. Unpublished information supplied by the Mississippi Commission.

27. *License Plate History on Passenger Vehicles* (n.p., n.d.); information supplied by Missouri Department of Revenue, Division of Motor Vehicle and Drivers Licensing.

28. *The Montana License Plate* (n.p., n.d.); in-

formation supplied by State of Montana, Department of Justice, Title and Registration Bureau.

29. *License Plate Information* (Lincoln: State of Nebraska, Department of Motor Vehicles, n.d.); *History of Nebraska License Plates* (Lincoln: State of Nebraska, Department of Motor Vehicles, n.d.); information supplied by Nebraska Department of Motor Vehicles.

30. *The Story of the Nevada License Plate* (n.p., n.d.); information supplied by the Nevada Department of Motor Vehicles and Public Safety.

31. Stanley A. Hamel, *A Brief History of New Hampshire License Plates, 1905–1907* (Seabrook: Stanley A. Hamel, published in cooperation with the New Hampshire Automobile Dealers Association, 1977), pp. 2–4, 15.

32. *The New Jersey License Plate Story* (Trenton: Division of Motor Vehicles, n.d.); information supplied by the State of New Jersey, Motor Vehicle Services.

33. Charlotte S. Valdez, *Highlights of New Mexico Motor Vehicle History* (Santa Fe: State of New Mexico, Motor Vehicle Division, n.d.); information supplied by New Mexico Taxation and Revenue Department, Motor Vehicle Division.

34. *Motor Vehicle and Driver Regulation in New York State* (Albany: State of New York, Department of Motor Vehicles, 1986); information supplied by New York Department of Motor Vehicles.

35. *North Carolina License Plate History* (n.p., n.d.); information supplied by State of North Carolina, Division of Motor Vehicles.

36. *North Dakota License Plates (Passenger)* (Bismarck: North Dakota Department of Transportation, Vehicle Services Division, n.d.); information provided by North Dakota Department of Transportation, Motor Vehicle Division.

37. *1980 Ohio License Plates* (Columbus: Bureau of Motor Vehicles, 1980); information supplied by the State of Ohio.

38. *A Brief History of Oklahoma Passenger Plates* (n.p., n.d.); information provided by Oklahoma Tax Commission, Motor Vehicle License Division.

39. *Color of Oregon Passenger License Plates and Tabs* (Salem: Motor Vehicle Division, Department of Transportation, n.d.); information supplied by the Oregon State Library.

40. Commonwealth of Pennsylvania, Department of Transportation, personal letter.

41. Parker, *Registration Plates*, pp. 503–4, 507–8.

42. *Brief Outline History of License Plates* (n.p.: South Carolina Department of Highways and Public Transportation, n.d.); information provided by South Carolina Department of Highways and Public Transportation, Division of Motor Vehicles, Registration-Reciprocity.

43. Bill Farnham, comp., *85 Years of History: A History of Motor Vehicle Registration and Licensing Activities in the State of South Dakota from 1905 until 1990* (Pierre: South Dakota, Department of Revenue, Division of Motor Vehicles, July 1990); information provided by South Dakota Division of Motor Vehicles.

44. *Motor Vehicle History* (n.p., n.d.); *Color Combinations Used on Plates for Passenger Cars, 1915–1991* (n.p., n.d.); information provided by Tennessee Department of Revenue, Motor Vehicle Division.

45. *The History of Texas License Plates* (Austin: Texas Department of Transportation, Motor Vehicle Division, n.d.); information provided by Texas State Department of Highways and Public Transportation, Division of Motor Vehicles.

46. Parker, *Registration Plates*, pp. 503, 517–18.

47. *Vermont Automobile License Plate History* (n.p., n.d.); information provided by State of Vermont, Agency of Transportation, Department of Motor Vehicles.

48. *The Evolution of Virginia's License Plate* (n.p.: Department of Motor Vehicles, February 1991); information provided by Virginia Department of Motor Vehicles.

49. *License Plate History* (Olympia: State of Washington, Department of Licensing, n.d.); information provided by State of Washington, Department of Licensing.

50. Unpublished information provided by the West Virginia State Museum.

51. *Wisconsin Automobile License Plate History* (Madison: Wisconsin Department of Transportation, n.d.); information supplied by the State of Wisconsin, Legislative Reference Bureau.

52. *Wyoming License Plates* (n.p., 1993); information provided by the Wyoming Department of Transportation.

53. Parker, *Registration Plates*, p. 22.

54. Parker, *Registration Plates*, pp. 436, 446.

55. Letter to License Plate Collectors from Gregorio M. Camacho, Director of Public Safety, Commonwealth of the Northern Mariana Islands, Department of Public Safety, n.d.; provided by Pete Torres, Office of the United States Representative of the Commonwealth of the Northern Mariana Islands.

56. Parker, *Registration Plates*, p. 195.

57. Information provided by the Departamento de Transportacion y Obras Publicas, Area Vehiculos de Motor and Directoriade Servicios al Conductor, Division de Servicios Tecnicos.

58. Parker, *Registration Plates*, p. 536.

12

State and Territory Postage Stamps

The United States Postal Service has chronicled and commemorated significant events in state and territorial history through its issuance of postage stamps. Anniversaries of statehood have provided the occasion for numerous issues of stamps. Some stamps, like the 1935 Connecticut and 1934 Maryland commemorative issues, celebrated three hundred years of settlement. A 1933 issue commemorates the founding of the colony of Georgia by James Oglethorpe. State flags, birds, flowers, seals, and trees are often found in these stamp designs. There are also depictions of cityscapes, landscapes, mountains—from Mount Rushmore to the Old Man of the Mountains—seascapes, and coral reefs. U.S. postage stamps are interesting and colorful reminders of our history. One stamp for each state and territory has been selected for illustrative purposes in this book.

ALABAMA

A series of fifty 13-cent stamps depicting the state flags was issued in Washington, D.C., on February 23, 1976. The stamps went on sale in each state capital on the same day. The series was designed by Walt Reed and Peter Cocci. A. Saavedra was the engraver. Of these stamps, 436,005,000 were printed.

ALASKA

Alaska became a state on January 3, 1959. On that date in Juneau, the Postal Service issued the special 7-cent airmail stamp called the Alaska Statehood Commemorative. The stamp, designed by Richard C. Lockwood and V. S. McCloskey, Jr., pictures the shape of Alaska in dark blue, over which is superimposed the Big Dipper capped by the North Star, as depicted also on the state flag. The wooded hills and snow-capped mountains in the background are meant to show the terrain and vastness of the state of Alaska as well as its wealth. A total of 90,055,200 of these stamps were issued. C. A. Brooks engraved the vignette and R. J. Jones the lettering.

ARIZONA

The Arizona Statehood Commemorative was issued in Phoenix on February 14, 1962, in celebration of fifty years of statehood for Arizona. This 4-cent stamp was designed by Jimmie E. Ihms, James M. Chemi, and C. R. Chickering. The vignette was engraved by A. W. Dintaman. The lettering was engraved by G. A. Payne. A total of 121,820,000 stamps were issued.

The stamp is dominated by the saguaro cactus in both the foreground and background. A flowering saguaro in the foreground shows off Arizona's state flower, while the outline of a full-grown saguaro in the background enhances the beauty of a moonlit desert night.

ARKANSAS

The Postal Service issued the Arkansas Centennial Commemorative on June 15, 1936, in Little Rock. A. R. Meissner designed this 3-cent stamp, which was engraved by C. T. Arlt, W. B. Wells, and E. M. Hall. A total of 72,992,650 stamps were printed.

A circular shield depicting the portico of the old state house is centered on the stamp, with the "new" capitol to its right and Arkansas' first settlement to its left. At the top left "Arkansas 1836" is lettered and on the top right "Centennial 1936." The stamp was printed in purple.

CALIFORNIA

The 3-cent California Statehood Commemorative celebrates that state's centennial of statehood, 1850–1950. Issued on September 9, 1950, in Sacramento, this stamp was designed by V. S. McCloskey and engraved by M. D. Fenton and A. W. Christensen. A total of 121,120,000 stamps were printed in yellow.

The design of this stamp includes both symbols of modern California—oil derricks in the right background and citrus fruits on the left—and historical scenes. At the center is a man panning gold. To the right, a pioneer couple stands before their covered wagon, which is pulled by a yoke of oxen. To the bottom left, beneath the citrus fruits, is the *Oregon*, the steamship that carried the news of California's statehood to the territory.

COLORADO

Colorado attained statehood in 1876, which was the one hundredth year of U.S. inde-

pendence. Colorado is known, therefore, as the Centennial State. The Colorado Statehood Centennial that bears this appellation beneath a depiction of the state flower, the columbine, is a 13-cent gravure stamp issued in Denver on May 21, 1977. The green, wooded hills and snow-capped Rocky Mountains of Colorado rise behind the columbine. A total of 189,750,000 of these stamps, designed by V. Jack Ruther, were printed.

CONNECTICUT

The Connecticut Tercentenary Commemorative was issued in Hartford on April 26, 1935. Designed by V. S. McCloskey, Jr., and engraved by J. C. Benzing and W. B. Wells, this 3-cent stamp, printed in lilac, depicts the Charter Oak tree and three hundred years of settlement in Connecticut, from 1635 to 1935. A total of 70,726,800 stamps were issued.

DELAWARE

The U.S. Postal Service issued thirteen stamps, one for each of the original thirteen states, to commemorate the bicentennial of the ratification of the Constitution. The Delaware stamp was issued first, on July 4, 1987, because it had been the first state to ratify the Constitution. This 22-cent stamp, designed by Richard D. Sheaff, is based on the state seal. A farmer with hoe and a frontiersman with rifle hold a banner dominated by an ox. Sheaves of wheat decorate the area above the ox and a banner inscribed with the words "Liberty and Independence" is on the border beneath it. The farmer is also holding aloft a model of a sailing ship. Below this depiction is the date on which Delaware ratified the Constitution: December 7, 1787.

FLORIDA

The Florida Statehood Commemorative stamp was first sold on March 3, 1945, in Tallahassee. This purple 3-cent stamp commemorates one hundred years of statehood for Florida—1845 to 1945. The stamp was designed by William A. Roach. C. A. Brooks engraved the vignette and A. W. Christensen engraved the lettering. A total of 61,617,350 of the stamps were printed.

The stamp is dominated by the circular state seal in the center. This seal remains the same today except for the substitution of the sabal palmetto for the cocoa tree. The gates of St. Augustine are pictured to the left of the seal and the Florida capitol building to its right.

GEORGIA

General James Oglethorpe founded the colony of Georgia in 1733 with a charter from King George II. The 3-cent General Oglethorpe Commemorative, which commemorates Georgia's founding, was first sold in Savannah on February 12, 1933. C. A. Huston designed the stamp, which pictures a bust of General Oglethorpe in armor. J. Eissler, E. M. Hall, and W. B. Wells did the engravings. A total of 61,719,200 stamps were printed in purple.

HAWAII

On August 21, 1959, President Eisenhower welcomed Hawaii into the Union. On that same date, the Hawaii Statehood Commemorative airmail stamp was issued in Honolulu. A Hawaiian warrior welcomes the star symbolizing statehood by offering a lei in his left hand. A map of the islands runs from the bottom right to the top left. This 7-cent stamp was designed by Joseph Feher. The engravers were C. A. Brooks, W. R. Burnell,

and G. A. Payne. A total of 84,815,000 stamps were printed.

IDAHO

In 1940, Idaho celebrated fifty years as a state. The U.S. Postal Service issued the 3-cent Idaho Statehood Commemorative stamp in Boise on July 3, 1940, to commemorate this event. This purple stamp depicts the Idaho capitol, which was completed in 1920 and fashioned after the U.S. Capitol building in Washington. A total of 50,618,150 stamps were printed. The designer was William K. Schrage. J. R. Lowe engraved the vignette and J. S. Edmondson the lettering.

ILLINOIS

The 15-cent windmill series was printed in unlimited numbers of booklets of five. The booklet was issued first in Lubbock, Texas. Depicted in this series designed by Ronald C. Sharp are historic windmills in Virginia, Rhode Island, Massachusetts, Illinois, and the Southwest. The Illinois stamp features the Dutch Mill near Batavia, Illinois. All stamps in the series are printed in brown on an intaglio press.

INDIANA

The Indiana Statehood Commemorative was issued on April 16, 1966, in Corydon, Indiana, the first capital. The design for this 5-cent stamp was made by V. S. McCloskey, Jr., and was based on a commemorative seal designed by Paul Wehr. J. S. Creamer engraved the vignette and K. C. Wiram the lettering. A total of 123,770,000 stamps were printed.

The stamp announces Indiana's sesquicentennial, 1816 to 1966, with an outline in white of the first statehouse and a map of Indiana in blue on which nineteen stars are emblazoned. Indiana was the nineteenth state to enter the Union.

IOWA

Iowa celebrated one hundred years of statehood in 1946. The 3-cent Iowa Statehood Commemorative was issued for the centennial on August 3, 1946, in Iowa City. On each side are stalks of corn. The center of the stamp is a map of Iowa with the state flag upon it. V. S. McCloskey, Jr., designed the stamp. M. D. Fenton and J. S. Edmondson were the engravers. A total of 132,430,000 stamps were printed in blue.

KANSAS

The distinctive 4-cent Kansas Statehood Commemorative stamp, printed on yellow paper, is dominated at the left center by a sunflower, the state flower. Behind a pioneer couple at the lower right are a covered wagon and a wooden fort, all symbols of the settlement of Kansas.

This stamp was occasioned by the centennial of Kansas statehood in 1961. The stamp was issued at Council Grove, Kansas, on May 10, 1961. It was designed by C. R. Chickering. The engravers were R. M. Bower and R. J. Jones. A total of 106,210,000 stamps were issued.

KENTUCKY

The U.S. Postal Service celebrated Kentucky's sesquicentennial by issuing the Kentucky Statehood Commemorative stamp in Frankfort on June 1, 1942. The 3-cent purple stamp was designed by William A. Roach and engraved by C. A. Brooks and A. W. Christensen. The semicircular vignette reproduces a mural by Gilbert White, which is in the Kentucky capitol building. Daniel Boone and three other frontiersmen are looking over the Kentucky River where

Frankfort is now located. Beneath this centerpiece are the dates 1792 and 1942, separated by the words "Sesquicentennial of the Statehood of Kentucky." A total of 63,558,400 stamps were printed.

LOUISIANA

The Battle of New Orleans assured Andrew Jackson of the status of a military hero. The Battle of New Orleans 5-cent Commemorative stamp pictures Jackson charging forward with his troops. To the lower right and left, the Battle of New Orleans Sesquicentennial Medal, sculpted by Angela Gregory, is depicted in this Robert J. Jones design. The engravers were C. A. Brooks, H. F. Sharpless, and K. C. Wiram. The stamp was issued in New Orleans on January 8, 1965. A total of 115,695,000 were printed in red, blue, and black.

MAINE

A total of 436,005,000 of the fifty-state flag series were printed (see entry for Alabama in this chapter). The first were issued simultaneously in Washington, D.C., at the occasion of the National Governors' Conference, and in each state capital. Walt Reed and Peter Cocci designed the stamps. They were engraved by A. Saavedra.

MARYLAND

Maryland celebrated three hundred years of settlement in 1934. The 3-cent Maryland Tercentenary Commemorative stamp recalls the founding of the colony by depicting the *Ark* and the *Dove*, the two ships that first brought European settlers to Maryland in 1634. Designer A. R. Meissner also placed the coat of arms on the right.

This stamp was issued in St. Mary's City, the first settlement in the state, on March 23, 1934. The engravers were J. C. Benzing and

E. M. Hall. A total of 46,258,300 stamps were printed.

MASSACHUSETTS

The Massachusetts Bay Colony stamp was issued on April 10, 1930. This rose-colored 2-cent stamp celebrated the three hundredth anniversary of the colony's founding. The seal of the colony is depicted. A total of 32,680,900 stamps were issued.

MICHIGAN

The Michigan Centennial Commemorative stamp was issued on November 1, 1935, in Lansing. A. R. Meissner designed this light-purple 3-cent stamp around the circular state seal in the center with the U.S. flag to its left and the Michigan state flag to the right. At the lower left, a forest and lake are depicted and at the lower right, a scene representing industry and commerce. L. C. Kauffmann engraved the vignette. E. M. Hall engraved the lettering. A total of 75,823,900 stamps were printed.

MINNESOTA

The Minnesota Statehood Commemorative stamp was issued in St. Paul on May 11, 1958, to celebrate one hundred years of statehood, from 1858 to 1958. Designers Homer Hill and C. R. Chickering created a scene in green depicting the beauty of Minnesota's lakes, islands, hills, and trees of the northern woods. A branch of the state tree, the red pine, dominates the left side of this 3-cent stamp. M. D. Fenton engraved the vignette and G. A. Payne the lettering. A total of 120,805,200 stamps were printed.

MISSISSIPPI

The Mississippi Territory Commemorative was first sold in Natchez on April 7, 1948.

This maroon 3-cent stamp commemorates the sesquicentennial anniversary of the creation of the Mississippi Territory and depicts the growth of the territory from establishment in 1798 to 1804 and to 1812. The original territorial seal is imposed over the map of the territory. Winthrop Sargent, first territorial governor, is depicted at the upper right. William Schrage designed the stamp. M. D. Fenton engraved the vignette and A. W. Christensen the lettering. A total of 122,650,500 stamps were printed.

MISSOURI

The purple 3-cent Gateway to the West-Midwest Centenary Commemorative stamp first went on sale in Kansas City, Missouri, on June 3, 1950. This design of V. S. Mc-Closkey, Jr., divides a depiction of the Kansas City skyline of 1950 at the top and a depiction of the 1850 settlement of Westport Landing with the words "Kansas City, Missouri, Centennial." R. M. Bower and A. W. Christensen were engravers of this stamp. A total of 122,170,000 were printed.

MONTANA

See description of stamp under state of Washington.

NEBRASKA

First placed on sale May 7, 1954, in Nebraska City, the purple 3-cent Nebraska Territorial Commemorative celebrates the passage of a century since the establishment of the Nebraska Territory. "The Sower," which stands atop the dome of the Nebraska capitol building, is depicted against a background of Mitchell Pass with Scotts Bluff to the right. The stamp was designed by C. R. Chickering and engraved by C. A. Brooks and J. S. Edmondson. A total of 115,810,000 were printed.

NEVADA

The 5-cent Nevada Statehood Commemorative stamp was issued in Carson City on July 22, 1964, the anniversary of the adoption of the state seal one hundred years earlier. The design by William K. Schrage is of the ghost town Virginia City, now a tourist attraction. A map of the state with the centennial dates 1864–1964 is on the right side. M. D. Fenton and G. A. Payne were the engravers. A total of 122,825,000 stamps were printed.

NEW HAMPSHIRE

Dartmouth College is one of New Hampshire's premier colleges and the Dartmouth College Case is one of the country's most famous early cases. The 6-cent stamp that commemorates the 150th anniversary of Daniel Webster's successful argument of the case before the Supreme Court was issued in Hanover on September 22, 1969. John Scotford, Jr.'s design is based on the John Pope portrait of Webster, which hangs in Parkhurst Hall. Dartmouth Hall is sketched in the background. A total of 129,540,000 of these green and white stamps were printed.

NEW JERSEY

The issue of the 3-cent Nassau Hall Commemorative stamp at Princeton on September 22, 1956, commemorated the two hundredth anniversary of that building, the first at what was to become Princeton University. V. S. McCloskey, Jr., based his design of the stamp on a 1764 Dawkins engraving of the building. A total of 122,100,000 stamps were printed.

NEW MEXICO

New Mexico celebrated fifty years as a state in 1962. The 4-cent New Mexico Statehood Commemorative stamp was issued in Santa Fe on January 6, 1962, to commemorate this event. The simple design by Robert J. Jones pictures the sacred Navajo mountain, Shiprock. R. M. Bowever and H. F. Sharpless were the engravers. A total of 112,870,000 stamps were printed.

NEW YORK

The 1964 World's Fair was held in New York City. The Postal Service issued this 5-cent stamp, designed by Robert J. Jones, at the World's Fair post office on April 22, 1964. The central mall of the fair is depicted. The Unisphere, which is to the center left, is the only remaining monument to the fair. A. W. Dintaman and H. F. Sharpless were the engravers. A total of 145,700,000 stamps were printed.

NORTH CAROLINA

The Postal Service issued a series of 13-cent stamps depicting the state flags of each state for the U.S. Bicentennial in 1976. Designed by Walt Reed and Peter Cocci from flags provided by the governors, the first-day ceremony of issuing the stamps was held on February 23, 1976, in Washington, D.C., at a meeting of the National Governors' Conference. The stamps were issued in order of admission to statehood. North Carolina was the twelfth colony to become a state.

NORTH DAKOTA

See description of stamp under state of Washington.

OHIO

The 3-cent brown Ohio sesquicentennial stamp was issued on March 2, 1953, in Ohio's first capital city, Chillicothe. A map of Ohio on which is printed the state seal is surrounded going out from the center first by the sesquicentennial dates, 1803–1953, and then by rows of eight stars on each side. The sixteen stars represent the sixteen states that preceded Ohio into the Union. The lone star above the map of Ohio represents the seventeenth state. To the bottom left is a leaf from the Ohio state tree, the buckeye. The stamp was engraved by M. D. Fenton and G. A. Payne. A total of 118,706,000 were issued.

OKLAHOMA

"Arrows to Atoms" is the theme of the 3-cent stamp that was issued in Oklahoma City on June 14, 1957, to commemorate the fiftieth anniversary of Oklahoma statehood. This progressive theme is depicted symbolically by the arrow that pierces the orbital emblem above the deep blue outline of the Oklahoma map. This stamp was designed by William K. Schrage and engraved by M. D. Fenton and G. L. Huber. A total of 102,219,500 stamps were printed.

OREGON

The lone covered wagon, many of which were used by early settlers headed over the Oregon Trail, dominates the foreground of the green 4-cent Oregon Statehood Centennial Commemorative stamp. Mt. Hood is depicted in the background to the right. From the right, the terrain slopes gently to the ocean. This stamp was designed by Robert Hallock and engraved by C. A. Brooks and J. S. Edmondson. It went on sale February 14, 1959, in Astoria, Oregon. Astoria claims to be the oldest settlement west of the Rocky Mountains. A total of 120,740,200 stamps were printed.

PENNSYLVANIA

The U.S. Postal Service issued thirteen stamps, one for each of the original thirteen states, to commemorate the bicentennial of the ratification of the Constitution. The Pennsylvania stamp was the second of the series to be issued because Pennsylvania was the second state that ratified the Constitution. The stamp was issued on August 26, 1987. Designed by Richard D. Sheaff, this 22-cent stamp depicts Independence Hall in Philadelphia, where American independence was formally born. Beneath the vignette is the date on which Pennsylvania ratified the Constitution: December 12, 1787.

RHODE ISLAND

On May 4, 1936, the Rhode Island Tercentenary Commemorative was issued in Providence. The design by A. R. Meissner is based on a statue of Roger Williams, founder of Rhode Island, which stands in Roger Williams Park in Providence. The tercentenary dates 1636–1936 appear at each side toward the top. Beneath to the left is the state seal and to the right the 3-cent denomination in a circular shield. L. C. Kauffmann, F. Pauling, and C. T. Arlt engraved the vignette. W. B. Wells and D. R. McLeod engraved the lettering. A total of 67,127,650 stamps were printed.

SOUTH CAROLINA

This interesting design by George Samerjau appears to be a series of black line drawings on a pine plank. The line drawings were engraved by E. P. Archer. H. F. Sharpless engraved the lettering, which consists of the words "South Carolina" across the top, the tricentennial dates "1670–1970," "U.S. Postage," and the denomination, "6 cents." The drawings depict symbols and scenes of South Carolina's commerce and history: a couple in colonial dress, the state capitol, St. Phillip's church, Carolina Jessamine, the state flag, a palmetto, cannon at Fort Sumter, barrels, tobacco, and cotton. A total of 135,805,000 stamps were printed.

SOUTH DAKOTA

In 1952, the Mount Rushmore National Memorial became twenty-five years old. The Postal Service issued a 3-cent stamp to commemorate this event. William K. Schrage designed this green stamp dominated by Washington, Jefferson, Theodore Roosevelt, and Lincoln. At the lower right, a woman and child are seated looking up the mountain. The sign in front of them reads "Mount Rushmore National Memorial 1927–1952." The words "Black Hills South Dakota" appear at the lower left. A total of 116,255,000 stamps were printed.

TENNESSEE

The purple 3-cent Tennessee Statehood Commemorative stamp was issued in Nashville on June 1, 1946. Designed by V. S. McCloskey, Jr., the state capitol, reminiscent of an Ionic temple, is depicted at the center. A portrait of Andrew Jackson is on an oval panel to the upper left. On the upper right is a portrait on a symmetrical panel of John Sevier, an early governor and founding father of the state. This stamp commemorates the 150th anniversary of Tennessee statehood and identifies Tennessee as the Volunteer State. The engravers were C. A. Brooks, C. T. Arlt, and A. W. Christensen. A total of 132,274,500 stamps were printed.

TEXAS

The flags of the United States and Texas are featured on the blue 3-cent Texas Statehood stamp, which was issued in Austin on December 29, 1945, to commemorate the centennial anniversary of the admission of Texas to the Union. In this stamp designed by James B. Winn, a ray of light coming

from the twenty-eighth star of the U.S. flag illuminates the star on the flag of the Lone Star State. Texas was the twenty-eighth state to join the Union. Beneath the U.S. flag are the centennial dates 1845–1945. E. R. Grove and E. H. Helmuth did the engraving. A total of 170,640,000 stamps were printed.

UTAH

This purple 3-cent stamp was issued on July 24, 1947, in Salt Lake City to commemorate the anniversary of one hundred years of settlement in Utah. Designed by E. R. Chickering and engraved by M. D. Fenton and E. H. Helmuth, the scene, dominated by a covered wagon, is of the first settlers arriving at the valley of the Great Salt Lake. The words "This is the place," attributed to Brigham Young, who led his Mormon followers to Utah, are found to the upper right. A scroll beneath this scene announces the Utah centennial and its dates, 1847–1947. A total of 131,968,000 stamps were printed.

VERMONT

Vermont was the fourteenth state to enter the Union. On March 4, 1941, the purple 3-cent Vermont Statehood Commemorative was issued in Montpelier for that 150th anniversary occasion. The stamp's design by A. R. Meissner pictures the Vermont capitol. A shield to the lower right contains thirteen stars representing the first thirteen states. The star above the shield represents the fourteenth state, Vermont. C. T. Arlt and J. T. Vail did the engraving. A total of 54,574,550 stamps were issued.

VIRGINIA

On February 7, 1980, in Lubbock, Texas, the Postal Service issued a booklet of 15-cent stamps depicting five historic windmills of the United States. An unlimited number of these booklets were printed. Windmills located in Rhode Island, Illinois, Massachusetts, Virginia, and the southwestern United States were depicted on the stamps. The Virginia stamp pictures the Robertson Windmill in Williamsburg. This and the other windmill stamps were designed by Ronald C. Sharpe and engraved by K. Kipperman and A. Saavedra.

WASHINGTON

In 1939, four states—North Dakota, South Dakota, Montana, and Washington—commemorated their fifty-year anniversaries of statehood. The Postal Service issued a purple 3-cent stamp to celebrate these anniversaries with issue dates in each state capital corresponding to the anniversary date for that state's entry to the Union. Thus, for the state of Washington, the stamp was issued on November 11, 1939, in Olympia. In Bismarck, North Dakota, the stamp went on sale on November 2, 1939. And in Helena, Montana, it went on sale on November 8, 1939. A. R. Meissner designed this stamp, which features the four states highlighted on a map of the northwestern United States and the names of the capitals of each state. M. D. Fenton and W. B. Wells were the engravers. A total of 66,835,000 stamps were printed.

WEST VIRGINIA

The series of fifty stamps, all in 13-cent denominations, depicting the state flags went on sale simultaneously in Washington, D.C., and each state capital on February 23, 1976. Walt Reed and Peter Cocci were the designers. A. Saavedra was the engraver. A total of 436,005,000 stamps were printed.

WISCONSIN

On May 29, 1948, the Wisconsin Statehood Commemorative stamp was issued on the one hundredth anniversary of Wisconsin's entrance to the Union. This purple 3-cent stamp, designed by V. S. McCloskey, Jr., and engraved by R. M. Bower and C. A. Smith, has two main features. To the left, a scroll unrolls with the state of Wisconsin in dark outline and the centennial dates 1848–1948. To the right is the state capitol, above which is the word "Forward," which is the state motto. A total of 115,250,000 stamps were printed.

WYOMING

A. R. Meissner designed the Wyoming Statehood Commemorative stamp, which reproduces the state seal in purple. It was issued in Cheyenne on July 10, 1940, the anniversary of fifty years of statehood. C. A. Brooks designed the vignette and E. H. Helmuth the lettering. A total of 50,034,400 stamps were printed.

DISTRICT OF COLUMBIA

The year 1950 marked the sesquicentennial of the nation's capital city. It also marked the issue of four stamps by the Postal Service to commemorate the 150-year anniversary. The themes of the stamps were freedom, executive, judicial, and legislative. The executive stamp, designed by W. K. Shrage, is illustrated. This green 3-cent stamp was issued in Washington, D.C., on June 12, 1950. Above the depiction of the White House is a panel with the sesquicentennial dates 1800–1950, separated by the city's name, "Washington." Below is another panel with the words "National Capital Sesquicentennial." M. D. Fenton and E. H. Helmuth were the engravers. A total of 130,050,000 stamps were printed.

AMERICAN SAMOA

This stamp was issued on August 26, 1980, as a block of four stamps featuring coral reefs in the Virgin Islands, Florida, Hawaii, and American Samoa. The block of stamps was issued in Charlotte Amalie, St. Thomas, the capital of the U.S. Virgin Islands. Elkhorn coral (*Acropora palmata*) is depicted with two porkfish (*Anisotremus virginicus*) swimming through it. Chuck Ripper designed the stamp, of which 205,165,000 were printed.

COMMONWEALTH OF THE NORTHERN MARIANA ISLANDS

The Commonwealth of the Northern Mariana Islands (CNMI) was honored for the first time by the U.S. Postal Service in November 1993, when a 29-cent commemorative went on sale in post offices. In the foreground to the left, a local inhabitant in native dress sits in the green grass by two latte stones, a palm tree swaying in the breeze to her left. Latte stones, thought to have been used originally by early settlers to support the houses of chieftains or perhaps even to support boat houses, have become important symbols that stand for the strength of the family and the enduring culture of the islands. The flag of the Commonwealth is depicted in the background to the right. Appropriate to the islands, the depictions on the stamp are printed on a surrounding sea of light blue.

GUAM

The U.S. Postal Service has not issued a postage stamp dealing specifically with Guam.

PUERTO RICO

The city of San Juan celebrated its 450-year anniversary in 1971. Founded in 1521, it is the oldest of any city in the United States or its possessions. Designer Walter Brooks depicts the El Morro castle on this 8-cent stamp. The stamp was issued on September 12, 1971, in San Juan. The engraving was done by J. S. Creamer and A. Saavedra. A total of 148,755,000 stamps were printed.

U.S. VIRGIN ISLANDS

The Postal Service issued a series of four 3-cent stamps in 1937 to honor outlying U.S. possessions. They included at the time Hawaii, Alaska, Puerto Rico, and the Virgin Islands. The Virgin Islands stamp was issued on December 15, 1937, in Charlotte Amalie, the city depicted on the stamp with a view of its harbor and surrounding islands. V. S. McCloskey, Jr., designed the stamp. C. T. Arlt engraved the vignette and J. T. Vail the lettering. A total of 76,474,550 stamps were printed.

13

Miscellaneous Official State and Territory Designations

Every state in the union has found it desirable to recognize officially some special symbols that have a unique importance. These legislative actions have largely been phenomena of the past thirty years. Often such official designations recognize the importance of an industry to a particular state. Florida, for example, designated orange juice as its official beverage. Tomato juice is Ohio's state beverage and cranberry juice, Massachusetts'. Wisconsin's official domestic animal is the dairy cow. On the other hand, an official designation may also bring with it special protection for an endangered species. Georgia's and Massachusetts' right whale, California's gray whale, Alaska's bowhead whale, and Florida's manatee received protection as officially designated state marine mammals.

Some designated symbols recall the early history of a state. Gold is the state mineral of California and Alaska. Dog mushing is Alaska's state sport. The American buffalo is the state animal of Kansas, and Plymouth Rock is Massachusetts' historical rock. Other symbols cannot be considered without recalling the state with which they have become identified: Alaskan king salmon, the California grizzly bear, Indiana limestone, Louisiana's crawfish, and Maine's moose.

Whether animals, vegetables, or minerals or even reptiles, mammals, or neckwear, each state expresses its unique character through the symbols it chooses.

ALABAMA

Agricultural Museum (1992)	Dothan Landmarks Parks
Barbecue championship (1991)	Demopolis Christmas on the River Barbecue Cook-Off
Butterfly and mascot (1989)	Eastern Tiger Swallowtail
Championship horse show (1988)	Alabama State Championship Horse Show
Championship horseshoe tournament (1992)	Fall tournament in Stockton
Dance (1981)	Square dance
Fossil (1984)	Species *Basilosaurus cetoides*
Freshwater fish (1975)	Largemouth bass, *Micropterus punctulatus*

Gemstone (1990)	Star blue quartz
Historic theater (1993)	Alabama Theatre for the Performing Arts
Horse (1975)	Rocking horse
Insect (1989)	Monarch butterfly
Mineral (1967)	Hematite
Nut (1982)	Pecan
Outdoor drama (1991)	*The Miracle Worker* by William Gibson, performed at Ivy Green
Outdoor musical drama (1993)	*The Incident at Looney's Tavern*
Renaissance faire (1988)	The Renaissance Faire in Florence
Reptile (1990)	Red-bellied turtle, *Pseudemys alabamensis* of the family *Emydidae* of the order *Testudines*
Rock (1969)	Marble
Saltwater fish (1959)	Tarpon
Shell (1990)	*Scaphella junonia johnstoneae*[1]

ALASKA

Fish (1963)	King salmon, *Oncorhynchus tshawytscha*
Fossil (1986)	Woolly mammoth, *Mammuthus primigenius*
Gem (1968)	Jade
Insect (1995)	Four spot skimmer dragonfly
Land mammal (1998)	Moose, *Alces alces*
Language (1998)	English
Marine mammal (1983)	Bowhead whale
Mineral (1968)	Gold
Sport (1972)	Dog mushing[2]

ARIZONA

Amphibian (1986)	Arizona tree frog, *Hyla eximia*
Fish (1986)	Arizona trout, *Salmo apache*
Fossil (1986)	Petrified wood, *Araucarioxylon arizonicum*
Gem (1974)	Turquoise
Mammal (1986)	Ringtail, *Bassariscus astutus*
Neckwear (1973)	Bola tie
Reptile (1986)	Arizona ridgenose rattlesnake, *Crotalus willardi*[3]

ARKANSAS

Beverage (1985)	Milk
Folk dance (1991)	Square dance
Fruit and vegetable (1987)	South Arkansas vine ripe pink tomato
Gem (1967)	Diamond
Insect (1973)	Honeybee
Language (1987)	English
Mammal (1993)	White-tailed deer
Mineral (1967)	Quartz crystal
Musical instrument (1985)	Fiddle
Northwest purple martin capital of Arkansas (1993)	Fort Smith
Rock (1967)	Bauxite
Sod (1997)	Stuttgart soil series
Southeast purple martin capital of Arkansas (1993)	Lake Village
Trout capital of the USA (1993)	Cotter[4]

CALIFORNIA

Animal (1953)	California grizzly bear, *Ursus californicus*[5]
Dance (1988)	West Coast swing dance
Fish (1947)	Golden trout, *Salmo aqua-bonita*[6]
Folk dance (1988)	Square dance
Fossil (1973)	Saber-toothed cat, *Smilodon californicus*
Gemstone (1985)	Benitoite
Insect (1972)	California dog-face butterfly, *Zerene eurydice*
Marine fish (1995)	Garibaldi, *Hypsypops rubicundus*
Marine mammal (1975)	California gray whale, *Eschrichtus robustus*
Mineral (1965)	Native gold
Prehistoric artifact (1991)	Chipped stone bear
Reptile (1972)	California desert tortoise, *Gopherus agassizi*
Rock (1965)	Serpentine
Soil (1997)	San Joaquin soil[7]

COLORADO

Animal (1961)	Rocky Mountain bighorn sheep, *Ovis canadensis*

Gem (1971)	Aquamarine
Insect (1996)	Colorado hairstreak butterfly, *Hypaurotis crysalus*[8]

CONNECTICUT

Animal (1975)	Sperm whale, *Physeter catadon*
Composer (1991)	Charles Edward Ives
Folk dance (1995)	Square dance
Fossil (1991)	*Eubrontes giganteus*
Hero (1985)	Nathan Hale
Heroine (1995)	Prudence Crandall
Insect (1977)	Praying mantis, *Mantis religiosa*
Mineral (1977)	Garnet
Shellfish (1989)	Eastern oyster, *Crassotrea virginica*[9]
Ship (1983)	USS *Nautilus*[10]

DELAWARE

Beverage (1983)	Milk
Bug (1973)	Ladybug
Fish (1981)	Weakfish, genus *Cynoscion*
Fossil (1990)	*Belemnite*
Herb (1984)	Sweet golden rod, *Solidago odora*
Mineral (1975)	Sillimanite[11]

FLORIDA

Air Fair (1976)	Central Florida Air Fair
Animal (1982)	Florida panther
Band (1990)	St. Johns River City Band
Beverage (1967)	Juice from the mature oranges of the species *Citrus sinensis* and hybrids of that species
Butterfly (1996)	Zebra longwing, *Heliconius charitonius*
Festival (1980)	"Calle Ocho-Open House 8"
Fiddle contest (1989)	Annual contest held by the Florida State Fiddlers' Association at the Stephen Foster State Folk Culture Center
Freshwater fish (1975)	Florida largemouth bass, *Micropterus salmoides floridanus*

Gem (1970)	Moonstone
Litter control symbol (1978)	Keep Florida Beautiful Incorporated, service mark
Marine mammal (1975)	Manatee, commonly called the sea cow
Moving image center and archive (1989)	Louis Wolfson II Media History Center, Inc., in Miami
Opera program (1983)	Greater Miami Opera Association, Orlando Opera Company, Florida State University School of Music
Pageant (1979)	"Indian River"
Play (1973)	*Cross and Sword* by Paul Green
Railroad museums (1984)	Orange Blossom Special Railroad Museum; Gold Coast Railroad Museum, Inc., and Gold Coast Railroad, Inc.; Florida Gulf Coast Railroad Museum
Renaissance festival (1994)	Italian Renaissance Festival in Vizcaya
Reptile (1987)	American alligator
Rodeo (1994)	Silver Spurs Rodeo
Saltwater fish (1975)	Atlantic sailfish, *Istiophorus platypterus*
Saltwater mammal (1975)	Porpoise, commonly called the dolphin
Shell (1969)	Horse conch, *Pleuroploca gigantea*, also known as the giant band shell
Soil (1989)	Myakka fine sand
Sports Hall of Fame (1999)	Florida Sports Hall of Fame in Lake City
Stone (1979)	Agatized coral
Transportation museum (1985)	Florida Museum of Transportation and History in Fernandina Beach[12]

GEORGIA

Atlas (1985)	*The Atlas of Georgia*[13]
Beef Barbecue Champion Cookoff (1997)	Hawkinsville Civitan Club's "Shoot the Bull" barbecue championship
Butterfly (1988)	Tiger swallowtail
Crop (1995)	Peanut
Fish (1970)	Largemouth bass
Folk Dance (1996)	Square dancing
Folk Festival (1992)	Georgia Folk Festival
Fossil (1976)	Shark tooth
Fruit (1995)	Peach

Gem (1976)	Quartz
Historic drama (1990)	*The Reach of Song*
Insect (1975)	Honeybee[14]
Language (1996)	English
Marine mammal (1985)	Right whale[15]
Mineral (1976)	Staurolite
Musical Theater (1993)	Jekyll Island Musical Theatre Festival
'Possum (1992)	Pogo 'Possum
Pork Barbeque Champion Cookoff (1997)	Dooly County Chamber of Commerce "Slosheye Trail Big Pig Jig"
Railroad Museum (1996)	Central of Georgia Railroad Shops Complex in Savannah
Reptile (1989)	Gopher tortoise
Seashell (1987)	Knobbed whelk
Tartan (1997)	72 green, 4 black, 6 green, 24 black, 20 azure, 40 red
Theater (1992)	Springer Opera House
Vegetable (1990)	Vidalia sweet onion[16]

HAWAII

Colors (by island):	
Hawaii	Red
Maui	Pink
Molokai	Green
Kahoolawe	Gray
Lanai	Yellow
Oahu	Yellow
Kauai	Purple
Niihau	White
Gem (1987)	Black coral
Individual Sport (1998)	Surfing
Marine mammal (1979)	Humpback whale
Team sport (1986)	Outrigger canoe paddling[17]

IDAHO

Fish (1990)	Cutthroat trout
Fossil (1988)	Hagerman horse fossil, *Equus simplicidens*

Gem (1967)   Star garnet

Horse (1975)   Appaloosa

Insect (1992)   Monarch butterfly [18]

ILLINOIS

Animal (1982)   White-tailed deer

Fish (1987)   Bluegill, *Lepomis macrochirus*

Folk dance (1990)   Square dance

Fossil (1990)   Tully monster, *Tullimonstrum gregarium*

Insect (1975)   Monarch butterfly, *Danaus plexippus*

Language (1969)   English

Mineral (1965)   Fluorite

Prairie grass (1989)   Big bluestem[19]

INDIANA

Language (1984)   English

Poem (1963)   "Indiana" by Arthur Franklin Mapes

River (1996)   Wabash River

Stone (1971)   Limestone[20]

IOWA

Rock (1967)   Geode[21]

KANSAS

Amphibian (1994)   Barred tiger salamander, *Ambystonia tigrinum mavortium*

Animal (1955)   American buffalo, *Bison americanus*

Insect (1976)   Honeybee

Reptile (1986)   Ornate box turtle, *Terrapene ornata, Agassiz*

Soil (1990)   Harney silt loam[22]

KENTUCKY

Arboretum (1994)   Bernheim Arboretum and Research Forest

Butterfly (1990)   Viceroy butterfly

Fossil (1986)   *Brachiopod*

Gemstone (1986)   Freshwater pearl
Horse (1996)   Thoroughbred horse
Language (1984)   English
Mineral (1998)   Coal
Tug-of-war championship (1984)   Nelson County Fair Tug-of-War Championship Contest

Wild game animal species (1968)   Gray squirrel[23]

LOUISIANA

Amphibian (1993)   Green tree frog
"Christmas in the Country" (1990)   "Christmas in the Country" in Elizabeth
Crustacean (1983)   Crawfish
Dog (1979)   Louisiana Catahoula leopard dog
Doughnut (1986)   Beignet
Drink (1983)   Milk
Fossil (1976)   Petrified palmwood
Freshwater fish (1993)   White perch
Gem (1976)   Agate
Insect (1977)   Honeybee
Judicial poem (1995)   "America, We the People" by Sylvia Davidson Lott Buckley

Mammal (1992)   Black bear
Musical instrument (1990)   Diatonic ("Cajun") accordion
Painting (1995)   "Louisiana" by Johnny O. Bell and Johnny F. Bell

Reptile (1983)   Alligator[24]

MAINE

Animal (1979)   Moose
Berry (1991)   Wild blueberry
Cat (1985)   Maine coon cat
Fish (1969)   Landlocked salmon, *Salmo salar sebago*
Fossil (1985)   *Pertica quadrifaria*
Insect (1975)   Honeybee
Language of the Deaf Community (1991)   American Sign Language
Mineral (1971)   Tourmaline
Vessel (1987)   Schooner *Bowdoin*[25]

MARYLAND

Boat (1985)	Skipjack
Crustacean (1989)	Maryland blue crab, *Callinectes sapidus*
Dinosaur (1998)	*Astrodon johnstoni*
Dog (1964)	Chesapeake Bay retriever
Drink (1998)	Milk
Fish (1965)	Striped bass
Folk dance (1994)	Square dance
Fossil shell (1994)	*Ecphoro gardnerae gardnerae* (Wilson)
Insect (1973)	Baltimore checkerspot butterfly, *Euphydryas phaeton*
Reptile and mascot (1994)	Diamondback terrapin, *Malaclmys terrapin*
Sport (1962)	Jousting
Summer theater (1978)	Olney Theatre in Montgomery County
Theater (1978)	Center Stage in Baltimore[26]

MASSACHUSETTS

Bean (1993)	Navy bean
Berry (1994)	Cranberry, *Vaccinium macrocarpon*
Beverage (1970)	Cranberry juice
Building and monument stone (1983)	Granite
Cat (1988)	Tabby cat
Ceremonial march (1985)	"The Road to Boston"
Cookie (1997)	Chocolate chip
Designation of citizens (1990)	Bay Staters
Dessert (1996)	Boston cream pie
Dog (1979)	Boston terrier
Explorer rock (1983)	Dighton Rock
Fish (1974)	Cod
Folk dance (1989)	Square dancing
Folk hero (1996)	Johnny Appleseed
Fossil (1980)	Dinosaur track
Game bird (1991)	Wild turkey
Gem (1979)	Rhodonite
Heroine (1983)	Deborah Samson
Monument for Veterans of Southwest Asia War (1993)	Monument in Worcester by Desert Calm Committee, Inc.

Historical rock (1983)	Plymouth Rock
Horse (1970)	Morgan horse
Insect (1974)	Ladybug
Marine mammal (1980)	Right whale, *Eubalaena glacialis*
Memorial to honor Vietnam War veterans (1990)	Memorial in Worcester
Mineral (1981)	Babingtonite
Muffin (1986)	Corn muffin
Poem (1981)	"Blue Hills of Massachusetts" by Katherine E. Mullen
Rock (1983)	Roxbury pudding stone
Shell (1987)	New England neptune, *Neptunea lyrata decemcostata*
Soil (1990)	Paxton soil series[27]

MICHIGAN

Fish (1988)	Brook trout
Gem (1973)	Chlorastrolite, or greenstone
Mammal (1997)	White-tailed deer
Reptile (1995)	Painted turtle, *Chrysemys picta*
Soil (1990)	Kalkaska soil series
Stone (1966)	Petoskey Stone[28]

MINNESOTA

Drink (1984)	Milk
Fish (1965)	Walleye, *Stizostedion v. vitreum*
Gem (1969)	Lake Superior agate
Grain (1977)	Wild rice, *Zizania aquatica*
Muffin (1988)	Blueberry muffin
Mushroom (1984)	Morel[29]

MISSISSIPPI

American folk dance (1995)	Square dance
Beverage (1984)	Milk
Butterfly (1991)	Spicebush swallowtail, *Pterourus troilus*
Fish (1974)	Largemouth bass, *Micropterus salmoides*[30]
Fossil (1981)	Prehistoric whale[31]

Grand opera house (1993)   Grand Opera House of Meridian

Insect (1980)   Honeybee

Land mammal (1974)   White-tailed deer, *Odocoileus virginianus*

Language (1987)   English

Shell (1974)   Oyster shell

Water mammal (1974)   Bottle-nosed dolphin, *Tursiops truncatus*[32]

MISSOURI

American folk dance (1995)   Square dance

Animal (1995)   Missouri mule

Aquatic animal (1997)   Paddlefish

Fish (1997)   Channel catfish

Fossil (1989)   Crinoidea, *Delocrinus missouriensis*

Insect (1985)   Honeybee

Mineral (1967)   Galena

Musical instrument (1987)   Fiddle

Rock (1967)   Mozarkite

Tree nut (1990)   Black walnut, *Juglans nigra*[33]

MONTANA

Animal (1983)   Grizzly bear, *Ursus arctos horribilis*

Arboretum (1991)   University of Montana, Missoula campus

Fish (1977)   Blackspotted cutthroat trout, *Salmo clarki*

Fossil (1985)   Duck-billed dinosaur, *Maiasaura peeblesorum*

Gem (1969)   Sapphire and Montana agate

Grass (1973)   Bluebunch grass, *Agropyron spicatum (pursh)*

Korean Veterans' Memorial (1997)   Memorial in Butte

Korean War Veterans' Memorial (1999)   Memorial in Missoula

Language (1997)   English

Veterans' Memorial Rose Garden (1999)   Garden in Missoula

Vietnam Veterans' Memorial (1987)   Memorial in Rose Park, Missoula[34]

NEBRASKA

American folk dance (1997)   Square dance

Baseball capital (1997)   Wakefield

Beverage (1998)	Milk
Fish (1997)	Channel catfish, *Ictalurus punctatus*[35]
Fossil (1967)	Mammoth
Gem (1967)	Blue agate
Grass (1969)	Little bluestem grass
Historic baseball capital (1997)	St. Paul
Insect (1975)	Honeybee
Mammal (1981)	White-tailed deer
River (1998)	Platte River
Rock (1967)	Prairie agate
Soft drink (1998)	Kool-Aid
Soil (1979)	Holdrege series, *Typic Argiustolls*
Village of Lights (1997)	Cody[36,37]

NEVADA

Animal (1973)	Desert bighorn sheep, *Oviscanadensis nelsoni*
Colors (1983)	Silver and blue
Fish (1981)	Lohonton cutthroat trout, *Salmo clarki henshawi*
Fossil (1977)	Ichthyosaur
Grass (1977)	Indian rice grass, *Oryzopsis hymenoides*
Metal (1977)	Silver
Precious gemstone (1987)	Virgin Valley black fire opal
Reptile (1989)	Desert tortoise, *Gopherus agassizii*
Rock (1987)	Sandstone
Semiprecious gemstone (1987)	Nevada turquoise[38]

NEW HAMPSHIRE

Amphibian (1985)	Spotted newt, *Notophthalmus viridescens*
Animal (1983)	White-tailed deer
Butterfly (1992)	Karner blue, *Lycaeides melissa*, subspecies *samuelis*
Freshwater game fish (1994)	Brook trout, *Salvelinus fontinalis*
Gem (1985)	Smoky quartz
Insect (1977)	Ladybug
Language (1995)	English

Mineral (1985)	Beryl
Rock (1985)	Granite
Saltwater game fish (1994)	Striped bass, *Roccus saxatlis*
Sport (1998)	Skiing
Tartan (1995)	Green 56, black 2, green 2, black 12, white 2, black 12, purple 2, black 2, purple 8, red 6, purple 28[39]

NEW JERSEY

Animal (1977)	Horse
Dance (1983)	Square dance
Dinosaur (1991)	*Hadrosaurus foulki*
Fish (1991)	Brook trout
Insect (1974)	Honeybee
Shell (1995)	Knobbed whelk, *Busycon carica gmelin*
Tall ship (1998)	*A. J. Meerwald*[40]

NEW MEXICO

Animal (1963)	New Mexico black bear
Cookie (1989)	Bizochito
Fish (1955)	New Mexico cutthroat trout
Fossil (1981)	*Coelophysis*
Gem (1967)	Turquoise
Grass (1973)	Blue grama grass, *Boutelova gracillis*
Insect (1989)	Tarantula hawk wasp, *Pepsis formosa*
Poem (1991)	"A Nuevo Mexico" by Luis Tafoya
Vegetable (1965)	Pinto bean and the chili[41]

NEW YORK

Animal (1975)	American beaver, *Castor canadensis*
Beverage (1981)	Milk
Fish (1975)	Brook or speckled trout, *Salvelinus fontinalis*
Fossil (1984)	*Eurypterus remipes*
Fruit (1976)	Apple
Gem (1969)	Garnet
Insect (1989)	Ladybug, *Coccinella novemnotata*

Muffin (1987)   Apple muffin
Shell (1988)   Bay scallops, *Argopecten irradians*[42]

NORTH CAROLINA

Beverage (1987)   Milk
Colors (1945)   Red and blue
Dog (1989)   Plott hound
Historical boat (1987)   Shad boat
Insect (1973)   Honeybee
Language (1987)   English
Mammal (1969)   Gray squirrel, *Sciurus carolinensis*
Military academy (1991)   Oak Ridge Military Academy
Northeastern North Carolina Watermelon   Hertford County Watermelon Festival
  Festival (1993)

Reptile (1979)   Turtle (the eastern box turtle is the emblem
                                               representing turtles that inhabit North
                                               Carolina)

Rock (1979)   Granite
Saltwater fish (1971)   Channel bass or red drum
Shell (1965)   Scotch bonnet
Southeastern North Carolina Watermelon   Fair Bluff Watermelon Festival
  Festival (1993)

Stone (1973)   Emerald
Tartan (1991)   Carolina tartan
Vegetable (1995)   Sweet potato[43]

NORTH DAKOTA

Art gallery (1981)   University of North Dakota Art Gallery on
                                               the campus in Grand Forks

Beverage (1983)   Milk
Dance (1993)   Square dance
Fossil (1967)   Teredo petrified wood
Grass (1977)   Western wheat grass, *Agropyron smithii*
Honorary equine (1995)   Nakota horse
Language (1987)   English
Railroad museum (1989)   Mandan Railroad Museum[44]

OHIO

Animal (1988)	White-tailed deer, *Odocoileus virginianus*
Beverage (1965)	Tomato juice
Gem (1965)	Ohio flint
Invertebrate fossil (1985)	*Isotelus*
Reptile (1995)	Black racer, *Coluber constrictor constrictor*[45]

OKLAHOMA

Animal (1972)	American buffalo
Beverage (1985)	Milk
Butterfly (1996)	Black swallowtail[46]
Colors (1915)	Green and white
Country & Western song (1988)	"Faded Love"
Fish (1974)	White bass, *Morone chrysops*
Folk Dance (1988)	Square dance
Furbearer (1989)	Raccoon[47]
Grass (1972)	Indian grass, *Sorghastrum nutans*
Musical instrument (1984)	Fiddle[48]
Percussive musical instrument (1993)	Drum[49]
Poem (1973)	"Howdy Folks" by David Randolph Milsten
Reptile (1969)	Collared lizard, *Crotophytus*
Rock (1968)	Barite rose
Soil (1987)	Port silt loam[50]

OREGON

Animal (1969)	Beaver
Beverage (1997)	Milk
Dance (1977)	Square dance
Father of Oregon (1957)	Dr. John McLoughlin
Fish (1961)	Chinook salmon
Gemstone (1987)	Oregon sunstone
Hostess (1969)	Miss Oregon
Insect (1979)	Swallowtail butterfly
Mother of Oregon (1987)	Tabitha Moffatt Brown
Nut (1989)	Hazelnut

Rock (1965)

Shell (1991)

Thunderegg

Oregon hairy triton, *Fusitriton oregonensis*[51]

PENNSYLVANIA

Animal (1959)

Beautification and conservation plant (1982)

Beverage (1982)

Dog (1965)

Fish (1970)

Fossil (1988)

Insect (1974)

White-tailed deer

Penngift crownvetch, *Coronilla varia L. penngift*

Milk

Great Dane

Brook trout, *Salvelinus fontinalis*

Phacops rana

Firefly, *Lampyridae*[52]

RHODE ISLAND

American folk art symbol (1985)

Drink (1993)

Flagship and tall ship ambassador

Fruit (1991)

Mineral (1966)

Rock (1966)

Shell (1987)

Charles I. D. Looff Carousel

Coffee milk

Providence

Rhode Island greening apple[53]

Bowenite

Cumberlandite[54]

Quahaug, *Mercenaria mercenaria*[55]

SOUTH CAROLINA

Amphibian (1999)

Animal (1972)

Beverage (1984)

Botanical garden (1992)

Butterfly (1994)

Dance (1984)

Dog (1985)

Fish (1972)

Folk dance (1994)

Fruit (1984)

Gem (1969)

Hospitality beverage (1995)

Spotted salamander, *Ambystoma masculatum*

White-tailed deer, *Odocoileus virginianus*

Milk

Botanical Garden of Clemson University

Eastern tiger swallowtail

The shag

Boykin spaniel

Striped bass, or rockfish

Square dance

Peach

Amethyst

Tea, *Camellia sinensis*

Insect (1988)   Carolina mantid, or praying mantis
Language (1987)   English
Music (1999)   The Spiritual
Railroad museum (1997)   South Carolina Railroad Museum in Fair-
                                         field County

Reptile (1988)   Loggerhead turtle, *Caretta caretta*
Shell (1984)   Lettered olive
Stone (1969)   Blue granite[56]

SOUTH DAKOTA

Animal (1949)   Coyote
Drink (1986)   Milk
Fish (1982)   Walleye, *Stizostedion vitreum*
Fossil (1988)   *Triceratops*
Gem (1966)   Fairburn agate
Grass (1970)   Western wheat grass, *Agropyron smithii*
Hall of Fame (1996)   South Dakota Hall of Fame
Insect (1978)   Honeybee
Jewelry (1988)   Black Hills gold
Mineral (1966)   Rose quartz
Musical instrument (1989)   Fiddle
Soil (1990)   Houdek soil[57]

TENNESSEE

Agricultural insect (1990)   Honeybee
Amphibian (1995)   Tennessee cave salamander, *Gyrinophilus*
                                         palleucus
Butterfly (1994)   Zebra swallowtail, *Eurytides marcellus*
Commercial fish (1988)   Channel catfish
Fine art (1981)   Porcelain painting
Folk dance (1980)   Square dance
Game bird (1988)   Bobwhite quail
Gem (1979)   Tennessee pearl
Insects (1975)   Firefly and ladybug
Language (1984)   English
Poem of the Tennessee Bicentennial (1997)   "Who We Are" by Margaret Britton

Railroad museum (1978)	Tennessee Valley Railroad Museum in Hamilton County
Reptile (1995)	Eastern box turtle, *Terrapene carolina*
Rock (1979)	Limestone
Sport fish (1988)	Largemouth bass[58]
Wild animal (1972)	Raccoon[59]

TEXAS

Air Force (1989)	Confederate Air Force
Bluebonnet city (1997)	Ennis
Bluebonnet festival (1997)	Ennis
Bluebonnet trail (1997)	Chappell Hill Bluebonnet Festival
Dinosaur (1997)	*Brachiosaur sauropod (pleurocoelus)*
Dish (1977)	Chili
Fiber and fabric (1997)	Cotton
Fish (1989)	Guadalupe bass
Folk dance (1991)	Square dance
Fruit (1993)	Texas red grapefruit
Gem (1969)	Texas blue topaz
Gemstone cut (1977)	Lone star cut
Grass (1971)	Sideoats grama
Insect (1995)	Monarch butterfly
Mammal, flying (1995)	Mexican free-tailed bat
Mammal, large (1995)	Longhorn
Mammal, small (1995)	Armadillo
Musical instrument (1997)	Guitar
Native pepper (1997)	Chiltepin
Pepper (1995)	Jalapeño
Plant (1995)	Prickly pear cactus
Plays (1979)	*The Lone Star*, presented in Galveston Island State Park; *Texas*, presented in Palo Duro Canyon State Park; *Beyond the Sundown*, presented at the Alabama-Coushatta Indian Reservation; and *Fandangle*, presented in Shackleford County
Reptile (1993)	Horned lizard
Shell (1987)	Lightning whelk
Ship (1995)	USS *Texas*

Alabama

Alaska

Arizona

Arkansas

California

Colorado

Connecticut

Delaware

Florida

Georgia

Hawaii

Idaho

Illinois

Iowa

Indiana

Kansas

Louisiana

Kentucky

Maine

Massachusetts

Maryland

Mississippi

Michigan

Minnesota

Montana

Missouri

Nevada

Nebraska

New Hampshire

New Mexico

New Jersey

New York

North Dakota

North Carolina

Ohio

North Carolina

Oregon

Pennsylvania

Oklahoma

South Carolina

Rhode Island

South Dakota

Texas

Tennessee

Utah

Virginia

Vermont

Washington

Wisconsin

West Virginia

Wyoming

District of Columbia

American Samoa

CNMI

Guam

Puerto Rico

U.S. Virgin Islands

Alaska

Alabama

California

Arizona

Arkansas

Delaware

Colorado

Connecticut

Hawaii

Florida

Georgia

Illinois

Idaho

Iowa

Indiana

Kansas

Kentucky

Louisiana

Maine

Maryland

Massachusetts

Michigan

Minnesota

Mississippi

Missouri

Montana

Nevada

Nebraska

New Hampshire

New Mexico

New Jersey

New York

North Dakota

North Carolina

Ohio

Oregon

Oklahoma

Pennsylvania

Rhode Island

South Carolina

Texas

South Dakota

Tennessee

Virginia

Utah

Vermont

Wisconsin

Washington

West Virginia

Wyoming

District of Columbia
(Insignia)

American Samoa

CNMI

Guam

Puerto Rico

U.S. Virgin Islands

Camellia
Alabama

Forget-Me-Not
Alaska

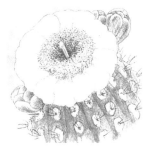

Saguaro
Arizona

Apple Blossom
Arkansas, Michigan

Golden Poppy
California

Columbine
Colorado

Mountain Laurel
Connecticut, Pennsylvania

Peach Blossom
Delaware

Orange Blossom
Florida

Cherokee Rose
Georgia

Hibiscus
Hawaii

Syringa
Idaho

Violet
Illinois, New Jersey, Wisconsin

Peony
Indiana

Wild Rose
Iowa

Wild Native Sunflower
Kansas

Goldenrod
Kentucky, Nebraska

Magnolia
Louisiana, Mississippi

Pine Cone and Tassel
Maine

Black-Eyed Susan
Maryland

Mayflower
Massachusetts

Pink and White Lady Slipper
Minnesota

Red Haw Blossom
Missouri

Bitterroot
Montana

Sagebrush
Nevada

Purple Lilac
New Hampshire

Yucca Flower
New Mexico

Rose
New York

Dogwood
North Carolina, Virginia

Wild Prairie Rose
North Dakota

Scarlet Carnation
Ohio

Mistletoe
Oklahoma

Oregon Grape
Oregon

Wood Violet
Rhode Island

Yellow Jessamine
South Carolina

American Pasque Flower
South Dakota

Iris
Tennessee

Passion Flower
Tennessee

Bluebonnet
Texas

Segolily
Utah

Red Clover
Vermont

Pink Rhododendron
Washington

Rhododendron Maximum
West Virginia

Indian Paintbrush
Wyoming

Southern Pine
Alabama, Arkansas, North Carolina

Sitka Spruce
Alaska

Palo Verde
Arizona

California Redwood
California

Giant Sequoia
California

Blue Spruce
Colorado, Utah

White Oak
Connecticut, Illinois, Iowa,
Maryland

American Holly
Delaware

Sabal Palmetto Palm
Florida, South Carolina

Live Oak
Georgia

Kukui Tree
Hawaii

Western White Pine
Idaho

Tulip Tree
Indiana, Tennessee

Cottonwood
Kansas, Nebraska, Wyoming

Coffeetree
Kentucky

Bald Cypress
Louisiana

Eastern White Pine
Maine, Michigan

American Elm
Massachusetts, North Dakota

Red Pine
Minnesota

Magnolia
Mississippi

Flowering Dogwood
Missouri, Virginia

Ponderosa Pine
Montana

Single-Leaf Pinon
Nevada

White Birch
New Hampshire

Northern Red Oak
New Jersey, Iowa

Nut Pine
New Mexico

Sugar Maple
New York, Vermont, West
Virginia, Wisconsin

Buckeye
Ohio

Redbud Tree
Oklahoma

Douglas Fir
Oregon

Hemlock
Pennsylvania

Red Maple
Rhode Island

Black Hills Spruce
South Dakota

Pecan Tree
Texas

Western Hemlock
Washington

Yellow-Hammer
Alabama

Wild Turkey
Alabama, South Carolina

Willow Ptarmigan
Alaska

Cactus Wren
Arizona

Mockingbird
Arkansas, Florida, Mississippi,
Tennessee, Texas

California Valley Quail
California

Lark Bunting
Colorado

Robin
Connecticut, Michigan, Wisconsin

Blue Hen Chicken
Delaware

Bobwhite Quail
Georgia

Brown Thrasher
Georgia

Nene
Hawaii

Mountain Bluebird
Idaho, Nevada

Cardinal
Illinois, Indiana, Kentucky, North
Carolina, Ohio, Virginia, West
Virginia

Eastern Goldfinch
Iowa, New Jersey

Western Meadowlark
Kansas, Montana, Nebraska,
North Dakota, Oregon, Wyoming

Brown Pelican
Louisiana

Chickadee
Maine, Massachusetts

Baltimore Oriole
Maryland

Loon
Minnesota

Wood Duck
Mississippi

Bluebird
Missouri, New York

Purple Finch
New Hampshire

Chaparral Bird
New Mexico

Scissor-Tailed Flycatcher
Oklahoma

Ruffed Grouse
Pennsylvania

Rhode Island Red
Rhode Island

Carolina Wren
South Carolina

Ring-Neck Pheasant
South Dakota

Sea Gull
Utah

Hermit Thrush
Vermont

Willow Goldfinch
Washington

Scarlet Oak Tree
District of Columbia

American Beauty Rose
District of Columbia

Wood Thrush
District of Columbia

Paogo (Pandanus Tree)
American Samoa

Flame Tree
CNMI

Plumeria
CNMI

Ifit Tree
Guam

Puti-tai-nobio (Bougainvillea)
Guam

Red-Capped Fruit Dove
Guam

Yellow Elder
U.S. Virgin Islands

Bananaquit
U.S. Virgin Islands

Alabama

Alaska

Arizona

Arkansas

California

Colorado

Connecticut

Delaware*

Florida

Georgia

Hawaii

Idaho

Illinois*   Indiana   Iowa

Kansas   Kentucky   Louisiana

Maine   Maryland   Massachusetts

Michigan   Minnesota   Mississippi

Missouri   Nebraska   Nevada

Montana stamp (same as Washington)   * © U.S. Postal Service

New Hampshire   New Jersey   New Mexico

New York   North Carolina   Ohio

North Dakota stamp (same as Washington)

Oklahoma   Oregon   Pennsylvania*

Rhode Island   South Carolina   South Dakota

© U.S. Postal Service

Tennessee

Texas

Utah

Vermont

Virginia*

Washington

West Virginia

Wisconsin

Wyoming

District of Columbia

American Samoa*

CNMI*

Puerto Rico

U.S. Virgin Islands

*© U.S. Postal Service

Alabama

Alaska

Arizona

Arkansas

California

Colorado

Connecticut

Delaware

Florida

Georgia

Hawaii

Idaho

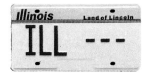

Illinois

Indiana

Iowa

Kansas

Kentucky

Louisiana

Maine

Maryland

Massachusetts

Michigan

Minnesota

Mississippi

Missouri

Montana

Nebraska

Nevada

New Hampshire

New Jersey

New Mexico

New York

North Carolina

North Dakota

Ohio

Oklahoma

Oregon

Pennsylvania

Rhode Island

South Carolina

South Dakota

Tennessee

Texas

Utah

Vermont

Virginia

Washington

West Virginia

Wisconsin

Wyoming

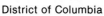

District of Columbia

American Samoa

CNMI

Puerto Rico

U.S. Virgin Islands

Guam

Shrub (1997)	Crape myrtle
Sport (1997)	Rodeo
Stone (1969)	Petrified wood
Tartan (1989)	Texas bluebonnet
Vegetable (1997)	Sweet onion[60]

UTAH

Animal (1971)	Elk
Cooking pot (1997)	Dutch oven
Emblem (1959)	Beehive
Fish (1997)	Bonneville cutthroat trout
Fossil (1988)	*Allosaurus*
Fruit (1997)	Cherry
Gem (1969)	Topaz
Insect (1983)	Honeybee
Railroad museum (1988)	Ogden Union Station
Rock (1991)	Coal[61]

VERMONT

Amphibian (1997)	Northern leopard frog
Animal (1961)	Morgan horse
Beverage (1983)	Milk
Butterfly (1987)	Monarch
Flavor (1993)	Maple
Fossil (1993)	White whale fossilized skeleton
Fruit (1999)	Apple
Gem (1991)	Grossular garnet
Insect (1977)	Honeybee
Mineral (1991)	Talc
Pie (1999)	Apple pie
Rocks (1991)	Marble, granite, and slate
Soil (1985)	Tunbridge soil series[62]

VIRGINIA

Artisans Center (1999)	Virginia Artisans Center in Waynesboro
Beverage (1982)	Milk
Boat (1988)	*Chesapeake Bay Deadrise*

Dog (1966)	American foxhound
Emergency Medical Services Museum (1994)	To the Rescue in Roanoke
Fish (1993)	Brook trout
Folk dance (1991)	Square dancing
Folklore center (1986)	Blue Ridge Institute in Ferrum
Fossil (1993)	*Chesapecten jeffersonius*
Insect (1991)	Tiger swallowtail butterfly, *Papilio glaucus Linne*
Language (1996)	English
Motor sports museum (1995)	Wood Brothers Racing Museum and Virginia Motor Sports Hall of Fame
Outdoor dramas (1994)	*The Trail of the Lonesome Pine Outdoor Drama* and *The Long Way Home*
Shell (1974)	Oyster shell, *Crassoostraea virginica*
Sports hall of fame (1996)	Virginia Sports Hall of Fame in Portsmouth
War memorial museum (1997)	Virginia War Museum in Newport News[63]

WASHINGTON

Arboretum (1995)	Washington Park Arboretum
Dance (1979)	Square dance
Fish (1969)	Steelhead trout, *Salmo gairdnerii*
Fossil (1998)	Columbian mammoth, *Mammuthus columbi*
Fruit (1989)	Apple
Gem (1975)	Petrified wood
Grass (1989)	Bluebunch wheat grass, *Agropyron spicatum*
Insect (1997)	Green darner dragonfly, *Anax junius Drury*
Ship (1983)	*President Washington*
Tartan (1991)	Asett made up of a green background with blue, white, yellow, red, and black stripes[64]

WEST VIRGINIA

Animal (1973)	Black bear, *Euarctos americanus*
Butterfly (1995)	Monarch butterfly

Fish (1973)   Brook trout

Fruit (1972)   Apple[65]

WISCONSIN

Animal (1957)	Badger, *Taxidea taxus*
Beverage (1986)	Milk
Dance (1993)	Polka
Dog (1986)	American water spaniel
Domestic animal (1971)	Dairy cow
Fish (1955)	Muskellunge, *Esox masquinongy masquinongy* Mitchell
Fossil (1988)	Trilobite, *Calymene celebra*
Grain (1991)	Corn, *Zea mays*
Insect (1977)	Honeybee
Mineral (1971)	Galena
Rock (1971)	Red granite
Soil (1983)	Antigo silt loam
Symbol of peace (1971)	Mourning dove
Wildlife animal (1957)	White-tailed deer, *Odocoileus virginianus*[66]

WYOMING

Dinosaur (1994)	Triceratops
Fish (1987)	Cutthoat trout, *Salmo clarki*
Fossil (1987)	Fossilized fish *Knightia*
Gem (1967)	Jade
Mammal (1985)	American bison, *Bison bison*
Reptile (1993)	Eastern short-horned lizard, *Phrynosoma douglassi brevirostre*[67]

DISTRICT OF COLUMBIA

Dinosaur (1998)   Capitalsaurus[68]

AMERICAN SAMOA

Plant (1973)   Kava[69]

COMMONWEALTH OF THE NORTHERN MARIANA ISLANDS

Languages (1985)   Chamorro, Carolinian, English[70]

GUAM

Languages   Chamorro, English[71]

PUERTO RICO

Emblematic Mother's Day flower (1915)   Honeysuckle
Languages (1993)   Spanish and English [72]

NOTES

1. Ala. Code §1–2–30, §1–2–29, §1–2–23, §1–2–22, §1–2–31, §1–2–18, §1–2–20, §1–2–9, §1–2–26, §1–2–32, §1–2–10, §1–2–24, §1–2–13, §1–2–19, §1–2–28, §1–2–33, §1–2–21, §1–2–25, §1–2–14, §1–2–8, §1–2–27.

2. Alaska Stat. §44.09.080, §44.09.120, §44.09.100, §44.09.130, §44.09.078, §44.12.310, §44.09.075, §44.09.110, §44.09.085.

3. Ariz. Rev. Stat. Ann. §41–859, §41–853, §41–858, §41–857.

4. Ark. Rev. Stat. Ann. §41–858, §41–857. Ark. Code Ann. (1987) §1–4–120, §1–4–115, §1–4–117, §1–4–122, §1–4–121, §1–4–124, §1–4–121, §1–4–123.

5. Cal. Govt. Code §425, §421.5 (West).

6. *California's Legislature 1984*, p. 201.

7. Cal. Govt. Code §421.5, §425.7, §425.3, §424.5, §425.5, §425.6, §425.1, §425.8, §422.5, §425.2, §425.9 (West).

8. Colo. Rev. Stat. §24–80–911, §24–80–912, §24–80–913.

9. Conn. Gen. Stat. Ann. §3–109a, §3–109b, §3–100k, §3–110b, §3–109c; §3–100j; *State of Connecticut: Sites, Seals, Symbols* (Hartford: Secretary of the State, n.d.).

10. *State of Connecticut Register and Manual 1983*, p. 904.

11. Del. Code Ann. tit. 29, §312, §309, §311, §314, §313, §310.

12. Fla. Stat. Ann. §15.039, §15.0353, §15.049, §15.032, §15.1382, §15.0395, §15.048, §15.036, §15.034, §15.041, §15.038, §15.0396, §15.044, §15.043, §15.035, §15.045, §15.0445, §15.0385, §15.0391, §15.037, §15.038, §15.033, §15.047, §15.051, §15.0336, §15.046 (West).

13. 1985 Ga. Laws 562.

14. Ga. Code Ann. §50–3–75, §50–3–62, §50–3–72, §50–3–52, §50–3–73, §50–3–67, §50–3–56, §50–3–70, §50–3–57, §50–3–64, §50–3–58, §50–3–100.

15. 1985 Ga. Laws 747; *Georgia's Official Symbols* (Atlanta: Secretary of State, n.d.).

16. Ga. Code Ann. §50–3–59, §50–3–63, §50–3–69, §50–3–68, §50–3–75, §50–3–74, §50–3–76, §50–3–66, §50–3–58.

17. *Hawaii, the Aloha State* (Honolulu: State of Hawaii, Hawaii Visitors Bureau, Chamber of Commerce of Hawaii, n.d.); Haw. Rev. Stat. §5–15, §5–13.5, §5–12, §5–14.

18. Idaho Code §67–4505, §67–4507, §67–4508, §67–4506, §67–4509.

19. Ill. Stat. Ann. ch. 1, §3020, §3031, §3051, §3048, §3004, §3005, §3006, §3041 (Smith-Hurd).

20. Ind. Code Ann. §1–2–10–1, §1–2–5–1, §1–2–11–1, §1–2–9–1 (West).

21. *1985–86 Iowa Official Register*, vol. 61, p. 244.

22. Kan. Stat. Ann. §73–2301, §73–1401, §73–1601, §73–1901, §73–2201.

23. Ky. Rev. Stat. Ann. §2.096, §2.083, §2.082, §2.092, §2.087, §2.013, §2.094, §2.260, §2.085 (Baldwin).

24. La. Rev. Stat. Ann. §49–169.1, §49–170.2, §49–168, §49–165, note preceding §49–

151, §49–170, §49–162, §49–170.4, §49–163, §49–164, §49–155.4, §49–161.1, §49–155.3, §49–170.5, §49–169 (West).

25. Me. Rev. Stat. tit. 1, §215, §219, §216, §212, §216, §214, §219, §213, §218.

26. Md. Ann. Code §13–312, §13–301, §13–316, §13–303, §13–315, §13–304, §13–314, §13–311, §13–301, §13–313, §13–308, §13–309.

27. Mass. Gen. Laws Ann. ch. 2, §38, §39, §10, §25, §30, §27, §41, §35, §40, §14, §24, §13, §32, §36, §17, §37, §15, §26, §23, §11, §12, §16, §34, §18, §28, §21, §22, §29, §33 (West).

28. Mich. Comp. Laws Ann. §2.15, §2.17, §2.71, §2.14, §2.61, §2.16.

29. Minn. Stat. Ann. §1.1495, §1.146, §1.147, §1.148, §1.1496, §1.149 (West).

30. Miss. Code Ann. §3–3–39, §3–3–29, §3–3–33, §3–3–21.

31. *Souvenir of Mississippi* (Jackson: Dick Molpus, n.d.), p. 27.

32. Miss. Code Ann. §3–3–37, §3–3–27, §3–3–17, §3–3–31, §3–3–23, §3–3–19.

33. Mo. Ann. Stat. §10.120, §10.110, §10.130, §10.135, §10–090, §10.070, §10.047, §10.080, §10.045, §10.100 (Vernon).

34. Mont. Code Ann. §1–1–508, §1–1–513, §1–1–507, §1–1–509, §1–1–505, §1–1–506, §1–1–516, §1–1–577, §1–1–510, §1–1–518, §1–1–512.

35. "Nebraska's State Symbols," www.visitnebraska.org/reports/kids-symbols.

36. Neb. Rev. Stat. §90–109, §90–108, §90–112, §90–114, §90–117, §90–110, §90–116.

37. Neb. Rev. Stat. §90–119 allows governor to make official state designations after September 12, 1997. Cites to designations made after that date are to Nebraska's State Symbols, cited above.

38. Nev. Rev. Stat. §235.070, §235.025, §235.075, §235.080, §235.055, §235.090, §235.100, §235.065, §235.120, §235.110.

39. N.H. Rev. Stat. Ann. §3:18, §3:20, §3:16, §3:12, §3–C:1, §3:15, §3:11, §3:14, §3:13, §3:19, §3:22, §3:21.

40. N.J. Stat. Ann. §52:9A–4; N.J. Leg. Joint Res. No. 1, 1983; N.J. Stat. Ann. §52:9A–5, §52:9A–6, §52:9A–3, §52:9A–7, §52:9A–8 (West).

41. N.M. Stat. Ann. §12–3–4, §12–3–11.

42. N.Y. State Law §79, §82, §80, §83, §81, §77, §86, §84, §85 (McKinney).

43. N.C. Gen. Stat. §145–10.1, §145–6, §145–13, §145–11, §145–7, §145–12, §145–5, §145–14, §145–16, §145–9, §145–10, §145–6, §145–4, §145–16, §145–8, §145–15, §145–17.

44. N.D. Cent. Code §54–02–11, §54–02–12, §54–02–16, §54–02–15, §54–02–08, §54–02–10, §54–02–13, §54–02–14.

45. Ohio Rev. Code Ann. §5.032, §5.08, §5.07, §5.071, §5.031 (Page).

46. "Oklahoma State Icons," www.state.ok.us/osfdocs/stinfo; Okla. Stat. Ann. tit. 25, §98.5, §93.

47. "Oklahoma State Icons."

48. §98.2; "Oklahoma State Icons."

49. §98.3; §98.1.

50. "Oklahoma State Icons."

51. Or. Rev. Stat. §186; "1999–2000 Oregon Bluebook," www.bluebook.state.or.us/almanac/almanac.

52. Pa. Stat. Ann. tit. 71, §1007, §1010.2, §1010.1, §1008, §1009, §1010.3, §1010 (Purdon).

53. R.I. Gen. Laws §42–4–11, §42–4–15, §42–4–14, §42–4–13.

54. *The State of Rhode Island and Providence Plantations, 1983–84 Manual.*

55. R.I. Gen. Laws §42–4–12.

56. S.C. Code §1–1–699, §1–1–650, §1–1–690, §1–1–675, §1–1–647, §1–1–665, §1–1–655, §1–1–640, §1–1–680, §1–1–696, §1–1–610, §1–1–692, §1–1–645, §1–1–696, §1–1–688, §1–1–705, §1–1–625, §1–1–695, §1–1–620.

57. S.D. Codified Laws Ann. §1–6–8, §1–6–16, §1–6–15, §1–6–16.1, §1–6–12, §1–6–13, §1–6–16.1, §1–6–14, §1–6–16.2, §1–6–12, §1–6–16.3, §1–6–16.4.

58. Tenn. Code Ann. §4–1–308, §4–1–320, §4–1–319, §4–1–316, §4–1–313, §4–1–312, §4–1–318, §4–1–310, §4–1–308, §4–1–404, §4–1–322, §4–1–303, §4–1–321, §4–1–311, §4–1–309, §4–1–317.

59. *Tennessee Blue Book, 1983–84*, pp. 373–74.

60. "Texas State Library and Archives Commission, Texas State Symbols," www.tsl.state.tx.us/lobby/ref/symbols; Tex. Rev. Civ. Stat. Ann. art. 6143d (Vernon).

61. Utah Code Ann. §63–13–7.2, §63–13–7.6, §63–13–10, §63–13–7.3, §63–13–11.7, §63–13–7.5, §63–13–7.1, §63–13–11.5, §63–13–11.9, §63–13–7.4.

62. Vt. Stat. Ann. tit. 1, §511, §500, §503, §510, §509, §513, §505, §506, §502, §508, §512, §507, §504.

63. Va. Code §7.1–40, §7.1–40.11, §7.1–3, §7.1–39, §7.1–40.4, §7.1.40.2:1, §7.1–40.7, §7.1–40.2, §7.1–40.5, §7.1–40.6, §7.1–42, §7.1–40.2:2, §7.1–40.8, §7.1–40, §7.1–40.9, §7.1–40.10.

64. Wash. Rev. Code Ann. §1.20.120, §1.20.075, §1.20.045, §1.20.042, §1.20.035, §1.20.090, §1.20.025, §1.20.042, §1.20.047, §1.20.110.

65. West Virginia Blue Book, 1980, p. 925; "Fun Facts about West Virginia, Official State Flora and Fauna," www.state.wv.is/tourism/facts/emblems.

66. Wis. Stat. Ann. §1.10.

67. Wyo. Stat. Ann. §8–3–116, §8–3–113, §8–3–112, §8–3–109, §8–3–111, §8–3–115.

68. D.C. Code §1–131.

69. A.S. Code tit. 1, §1104.

70. Amendments to the Constitution of the Northern Mariana Islands (Saipan: Marianas Printing Service, Inc., 1986).

71. Guam USA Fact Sheet (Agana: Guam Visitors Bureau, n.d.).

72. P. R. Laws Ann. tit. 1, §114, §115, §59.

14

State and Territory Fairs and Festivals

There is probably a festival or fair going on every day in the United States. They have many purposes. Famous people and native sons and daughters are remembered and honored. Art, music, and literature of all sorts are celebrated. Ethnic diversity is recognized and appreciated. History and heritage come alive. The fruits of many harvests, of land and sea, are consumed in thanksgiving. Workers from lumberjacks to coal miners are feted. And sometimes a fair or festival has no other purpose than an escape from everyday life and a good time.

The fairs and festivals enumerated below do not represent an exhaustive list by any means. Rather, fairs and festivals in each state and territory have been chosen to illustrate the special character of those areas. State tourism and travel offices may be contacted for exact dates of events. Many colorful publications are available from these offices, and many states and territories provide information on web sites.

ALABAMA

Nature seems to love Alabama and Alabama, in turn, provides many opportunities for citizens and visitors to enjoy all the riches bestowed on it. The sea forms one of Alabama's boundaries. People congregate along or near its edge to enjoy snapper at Orange Beach during the February Red Snapper Festival, shrimp in October at Gulf Shores during the National Shrimp Festival, and oysters at Foley's November Gulf Coast Oyster Festival. Fairhope and Dauphin Island provide places for before, during, and after revelry at the thirty-mile Dauphin Island Race held in late April when over 400 sailboats participate in this colorful event. Bayou la Batre follows in early May with its Annual Blessing of the Fleet. Dauphin Island and Bayou la Batre offer fishing rodeos as entertainment in July with one following the other during weekends from mid-to late July. Throughout the month of October, Orange Beach hosts the Annual Orange Beach Charter Fishing Rodeo. There is also Faunsdale's Alabama Crawfish Festival in mid-April and Lillian's Annual Mullet Festival in early September.

The sea is not the only place where beauty comes naturally. When spring blooms in March and April, dogwood festivals are celebrated at Aliceville and Athens. April also yields strawberries and visitors may get their fill at the Loxley Baldwin County Strawberry Festival and the Castleberry Strawberry Festival, the latter town proclaiming itself the Strawberry Capital of Alabama. Clanton is the home of the late-June Peach Festival, followed by the Henagar Annual Sand Mountain Potato Festival and the Steele Tomato Jubilee, both held in July. August finds Russellville celebrating its Watermelon Festival and Luverne boasts the World's Largest Peanut Boil in September, boiling fourteen tons of peanuts to back up the claim. November supplies plenty of nuts mixed with food, crafts, and music at the annual Alabama Pecan Festival held at Tillman's Corner, coinciding with Dothan's National Peanut Festival. The Kellogg Conference Center at Tuskegee is the site of the annual Peanut Drop on New Year's Eve where a seven-foot peanut is dropped to welcome in the new year.

Variety may be found throughout Alabama from the annual Tuscaloosa Fiddlin' and Bluegrass Contest in February to the Annual Opp Jaycees Rattlesnake Rodeo in March to the March through July Alabama Shakespeare Festival at Montgomery to the Gulf Shores Pleasure Island Festival of Art in mid-March to April's Southeastern Renaissance Festival at Steele to Gadsden's Riverfest in May to Andalusia's Annual World Championship Domino Tournament in July. Fairhope hosts its Annual Arts and Crafts Festival for three days in mid-March. Cullman welcomes the rodeo to town for the Annual World Championship Rodeo in April, followed also in April by Huntsville's Panoply Festival of the Arts, which features dance, theater, and music. Over 30,000 visitors flock to Northport in October for the Kentuck Festival of the Arts to enjoy folk art, quilts, and a wide range of musical genres from gospel to classical to the blues and bluegrass. Perhaps the wildest party is found in Mobile, the birthplace of Mardi Gras in America. An estimated 60,000 visitors attend each of the over twenty parades in February or March with specific carnival dates dependent on the beginning date of the Lentan season. One event covers over 160 miles when visitors are invited to hitch their wagons to the Annual Alabama Wagon Train that travels from Boaz to Montgomery for a week in March. In May, an all-volunteer cast presents Harper Lee's *To Kill a Mockingbird* in Monroeville which was named "Literary Capital of Alabama," by act of the Alabama legislature in 1997. Similarly, Tuscumbia, the birthplace of Helen Keller, presents *The Miracle Worker*, the Official

Outdoor Drama of the State of Alabama, annually at its Helen Keller Festival in June.

Native American heritage celebrations include powwows and festivals in April at Birmingham, in May at Valley Head, in June at Cullman and Mount Vernon, in September at Gadsden and Valley Head, and in October at Boaz. The Black Heritage Festival is held annually in February at Anniston, followed in early March by Selma's Bridge Crossing Jubilee commemorating the Civil Rights march from Selma to Montgomery. Juneteenth celebrations may be found in Birmingham and Prichard in June.[1]

ALASKA

The great outdoors of a great big state provides the setting for many of the festivals and fairs in Alaska. Winter carnivals include such activities as skating, skiing, ice fishing, and snowmobiling, as well as traditional carnival events centered around enjoyment of arts, crafts, and foods of the region. Ketchikan is the home of the Winter Festival held in late January, which also marks the beginning of the two-weekend Winter Festival at Willow. Anchorage welcomes visitors to its Fur Rendezvous for ten days in mid-February, and Homer includes a cook-off and beer-brewing contest as part of its Winter Carnival during mid-February. Wasilla offers its own version of golf on ice during the Iditarod Days Festival. In March, North Pole and Fairbanks host winter carnivals. In many parts of the United States, March brings the beginning of spring thaws but in Fairbanks and Anchorage, ice-sculpturing contests are in full swing at the World Ice Art Championships and the Annual International Ice Carving Competition. Ice bowling joins the lineup of fun winter entertainment at the Snowman Festival held at Valdez in mid-March. The Bering Sea offers plenty of room for golfing enthusiasts during Nome's Bering Sea Ice Golf Classic in late March. This unique golf tournament is followed by another that appeals equally to the adventuresome golfer: the Par 70, a one-hole golf tournament that is played up the 1,400-foot Pillar Mountain at Kodiak. The entire month of December at Trapper Creek is set aside for the Talkeetna Winterfest, a celebration of the Christmas season.

Distance is no barrier and, in fact, is the very point of many competitions. The annual Iditarod Trail Sled Dog Race from Anchorage to Nome in early March is considered one of the most challenging endurance tests in the world. Totalling 1,049 miles, it is preceded in mid-February by the 1,000-mile race from Fairbanks to Whitehorse during the Yukon Quest International Sled Dog Race. In between the two, the Iron Dog Gold Rush Classic in late February pits snowmachines and their riders against the elements and terrain for over 2,000 miles from Wasilla to Fairbanks. In June, riverboats race on the Yukon River from Fairbanks to Galena and back to Fairbanks during the Yukon 800 Race. July finds runners challenging the 3,022-foot Mt. Marathon.

Seafood is the focal point at several derbies and festivals. The King Crab Festival is held at Kodiak in late May, followed by salmon derbies held in Sitka in May and June, in Anchorage in June, and in Seward and Juneau in August. Nature provides cause to celebrate throughout the year, from the Kachemak Bay Shorebird Festival at Homer in early May to the Annual Sitka Whalefest in November to the Moose Dropping Festival at Talkeetna in July. At the latter event, contestants may find reward in tossing a moose nugget the farthest, although others may find more satisfaction in being farthest from a moose nugget being tossed. Nuggets of another variety are celebrated at Gold Rush Days in Juneau during late June and in Valdez in early August. Fairbanks celebrates Golden Days during July as a remembrance of the discovery of gold in this area in 1902.

Music, dance, and ethnic and seasonal celebrations round out Alaskan festivals. These include the early April Native Dance Festival at Bethel, the mid-April Annual Alaska Folk Festival at Juneau, May's Juneau Jazz and Classics Festival, June's Summer Music Festival at Sitka, Palmer's Colony Days also in June, and the Juneteenth Celebration at Anchorage in mid-June. Nome has the distinct honor of celebrating the summer solstice in twenty-four hours of sunlight at its Midnight Sun Festival. Fairbanks is the home of the World Eskimo-Indian Olympics in mid-July. Palmer hosts the late-August and early-September Alaska State Fair which is known for its exhibits of giant vegetables grown in Alaska's rich soil. Also in late August, Kodiak hosts the Kodiak State Fair and Rodeo. Sitka celebrates the Alaska Day Festival in mid-October when reenactments recall the transfer of Alaska from Russia to the United States. Fairbanks is the site of the Athabascan Old Time Fiddling Festival in mid-November.[2,3]

ARIZONA

Rodeos are a staple of western entertainment and Arizona has no shortage of them. They begin in January at Bullhead City with the PRCA Turquoise Circuit Rodeo and continue even into December at the Arizona Stock Show and Rodeo in Phoenix. Between are rodeos in Goodyear, Scottsdale, Yuma, and Buckeye in February, the latter hosting the descriptively named Pioneer Days and Helz-a-Poppin Rodeo. The Copper Dust Stampede Rodeo and Parade is held in March at Globe/Miami. Payson hosts the PRCA Pro Rodeo in May, and Alpine hosts the Alpine Rodeo in June. Frontier Days and the World's Oldest Rodeo are held in Prescott in July, while Payson lays claim to a similar boast as it hosts the Oldest Continuous Rodeo in August. In September, Winslow celebrates Heritage Days and the West's Best Rodeo and Bull Sunday. Phoenix is the home of the Original Coors Rodeo Showdown in October and Parker of November's Parker Rodeo.

The aura and high drama of both present-day and yesterday's western culture are celebrated at several entertaining events. These include the Cochise Cowboy Poetry and Music Gathering in Sierra Vista and the Gold Rush Days at Wickenburg in February; Southwest Days at Camp Verde in April; Cowboy Days and Indian Nights at Page, Wyatt Earp Days at Tombstone, and Rendezvous Days at Williams in May; Old Miners Day at Chloride, Old West Celebration and Bucket of Blood Races at Holbrook, and Territorial Days at Prescott in June; Pioneer Days at St. John's in July; Prescott's Arizona Cowboy Poets Gathering and Tombstone's Vigilante Days in August; and September and October events include Tombstone's Rendezvous of Gunfighters, Benson's Butterfield Overland Stage Days, and Tombstone's Helldorado Days.

Native American culture, arts, and crafts are highlighted at many festivals and pow-wows throughout the year. Litchfield Park hosts the West Valley Native American Invitational Fine Arts Festival and Tucson hosts the Indian America New Years Competition Pow Wow and Indian Craft Market in January. Tucson is home to the Southwest Indian Art Fair in February. Tsaile welcomes visitors to the Navajo Community College Pow Wow in April and Flagstaff celebrates Native American artists in May. The Navajo Culture Conference is held in June, and also in June, San Carlos hosts the Indian Festival. Pinetop/Lakeside hosts the White Mountain Native American Art Festival and Indian Market, and Peach Springs hosts the Hualapai Youth Pow Wow, both in July. In August Chinle hosts the Central Navajo Fair, while Flagstaff hosts the Navajo Market-

place. The Navajo County Rodeo is held in Holbrook, National Indian Days in Parker, and Navajo Nation Fair in Window Rock, all in September. October events include Dilkon's Southwestern Navajo Nation Fair, Globe's Apache Jii Day, Mesa's Native American Pow Wow, Scottsdale's National Indian Rodeo, and Tuba City's Western Navajo Fair.

Arizona also celebrates other cultures. In February, Mesa hosts the Scottish Highland Games and Phoenix celebrates Matsuri: A Festival of Japan. Tucson hosts the Juneteenth Festival in June. Overgaard hosts Oktoberfest in the Pines in September, and Pinetop/Lakeside and Tempe do the same in October. Wickenburg is the site of Fiesta Septiembre, and Phoenix is the site of Dia de los Muertos Festival in October. In November Tucson celebrates La Fiesta de los Chiles.

From chocolate at Glendale in February to the Hava-Salsa Challenge at Lake Havasu City in April to Sizzlin' Salsa Sunday during Cinco de Mayo at Cottonwood in May to barbecue at the Bullhead City County Fair and Burro Barbecue to garlic at Dewey in June, food is cause for celebration or a part of the celebration at many Arizona festivals. Dewey hosts Young's Farm Garlic Festival in June, followed by the Glendale Watermelon Festival and Goodyear's Cool Corn and Melon Celebration. Taylor is the home of the Sweet Corn Festival in September, and also in September, Tucson hosts Some Like It Hot: A Salsa Cook-Off and Dance Party. Dewey is the site of Young's Farm Pumpkin Festival in October. Not to be eaten or beaten, the egg meets a July sidewalk in Oatman's Sidewalk Egg Frying Challenge.[4]

ARKANSAS

Every Saturday evening in January, Salem welcomes visitors to enjoy the music of the mountains at the Annual Ozark Mountain

Music Makers musicals. But silence is part of the pleasure at several eagle watching opportunities from Eagle Awareness Days at Morrilton in mid-January to eagle watches at Bismarck, Eureka Springs, and Mount Ida in January and February. Spring is ushered in with grace and beauty by the early blooming jonquils that are the focus of the Annual Jonquil Festival at Washington in early March. Daffodil festivals are held in Camden, Bigelow, and Conway at the Annual Daffodil Festival, the Annual Wye Mountain Daffodil Festival, and the Annual State Daffodil Show, respectively. Educational wildflower weekends and walks offer visitors a lovely venue for learning about the wildflowers of Arkansas. These events are held throughout April and into May at Morrilton, Star City, Parkin, Bismarck, and Greenbrier.

March and April provide a variety of festivals in addition to those celebrating the natural beauty of the state. From the Annual Wine and Food Celebration at Little Rock, where culinary treats and 350 wines may be enjoyed and taste-tested, to the Annual Creepy Crawly Cold-Blooded Creatures event at Bismarck, there is something for everyone. At the latter event, reptiles and amphibians are to be revered, not feared, and festivalgoers are even coaxed to show such unconventional displays of affection as kissing a frog and petting a toad. If that is too creepy and crawly for the event seeker, Mountain View offers the Annual Arkansas Folk Festival at the same time in mid-April, and earlier in April, Hampton features barbecues, crafts, racing and diving pigs, and carnival events at the Annual Hogskin Holidays. April concludes with the Annual Main Street Crawfish Boil at El Dorado and the Annual Fordyce on the Cotton Belt Festival at Fordyce, which is a celebration of railroad heritage and includes a rodeo.

May events include the Annual State Championship Barbecue Cook-off at De-light, the Annual World Famous Armadillo Festival at Hamburg, Melbourne's Annual Pioneer Days including a rodeo, and the Annual P.R.C.A. Rodeo at Benton. Also in May, Conway hosts the Annual Toad Suck Daze with food, crafts, a carnival, and the Tour De Toad event. Herbs are the focus of festivals at Mammoth Spring and Mountain View in early to mid-May. It may be difficult to decide whether to attend the Dermott Annual Crawfish Festival or the Harrison Annual Crawdad Days Music Festival both held at the same time in mid-May. In late May the Annual Greek Food Festival at Little Rock and the Annual Bream Festival at Felsenthal, which includes a bream tournament and fish fry, are held. Fishing tournaments are numerous and for those of all ages. They include the Annual Tri-Lakes Big Bass Tournament at DeQueen and derbies or tournaments at Morrilton, Lakeview, and Crossett, to name a few.

June begins with music when Bee Branch hosts the Annual Bluegrass Music Festival and Eureka Springs hosts the Annual Blues Festival. The Hot Springs Music Festival includes over twenty concerts and 250 open rehearsals in early to mid-June, followed by the Mountain View String Band Jamboree. Large crowds are drawn to Warren's Annual Bradley County Pink Tomato Festival for the food, arts, crafts, and carnival. Butterflies flutter to the party thrown each June at the Mount Magazine State Park Annual International Butterfly Festival. For some, apparently, bats are beautiful too, with visitors welcomed to the West Fork Bat-O-Rama in mid-June. Malvern claims that it is the "Brick Capital of the World" and celebrates this declaration during the Annual Brickfest with a brick toss and best-dressed brick contest, among other entertainment which includes a pie-baking contest.

Summer continues with rodeos in Lincoln and Springdale, the Annual Bluegrass Music event at Adona, and the Annual Johnson

County Peach Festival at Clarksville in July. Batesville hosts the Annual White River Water Carnival in early August, during the same time as the Annual Great Arkansas Pigout at Morrilton. These are followed by an event over one hundred years old, the Annual Tontitown Grape Festival, which includes arts, crafts, and a farmers' market among other family entertainment. Mid-August events include the Annual Watermelon Festival at Hope when the eating and spitting are not just necessary but become competitive events. Rodeos are held in late August at Crossett and Mount Ida. Bee Branch rounds out the month on a lively note with the Annual Bluegrass Music Festival.

Fall festivals include the Annual Banjo Rally International at Eureka Springs, the Annual Riverfront Blues Festival at Fort Smith, the Annual Jazz Festival at Eureka Springs, the Annual Native American Festival at Fort Smith, and the Annual Southwest District Livestock and Rodeo at Hope, all in September. During October, festivals celebrating the music, arts, crafts, and foods of Arkansas are plentiful. Lincoln serves up apple cider and family entertainment at the Annual Arkansas Apple Festival in early October, followed by the Annual King Biscuit Blues Festival at Helena, DeQueen's Annual Hoo Rah Days Festival, and the Annual Turkey Trot Festival where citizens and visitors, of where else but Yellville, compete in the National Wild Turkey Calling Contest.

Arts and crafts festivals are held in Bentonville, Pocahontas, Bella Vista, War Eagle, Rogers, Hardy, Ashdown, and Fordyce throughout October. Quilt shows may be found at Clinton and Mountain Home in October. Music may be found at the Annual Fiddle and Dance Jamboree at Mountain View in October and in November at the Annual Cowboy Music and Poetry Gathering also at Mountain View. A variety of culinary treats round out the year. In October, Mountain Home hosts the Annual Mountain Mania Barbecue Cook-off and Fall Festival, followed by the Mountain View Annual Bean Fest and Championship Outhouse Race where 1,500 pounds of pinto beans and cornbread are served to visitors at the town square. Chocolate may be sculpted or eaten or both at the mid-December Holiday Chocolate Extravaganza & Arts & Crafts Show at Eureka Springs. Eureka is the right word for chocolate lovers within driving distance of this annual event.[5,6]

CALIFORNIA

California is a state rich in diversity, a fact borne out by the broad range of events that annually celebrate the art, history, crafts, music, and food of many cultures. In early January Sacramento features the Festa de la Befana, a children's Italian Christmas festival, marking the beginning of a year of events paying honor to California's rich heritage. Santa Monica and Davis host Martin Luther King, Jr. celebrations in January followed by the Queen Mary Scottish Festival in Long Beach; Mardi Gras celebrations in Fresno and Los Angeles; Chinese New Year celebrations; the Davis Black History Celebration; the Celtic Music and Arts Festival at San Francisco; Irish Days and other similarly focused events at Murphys, Ventura, and San Diego; and the Bok Kai Festival celebrating the Chinese water god at Marysville, throughout February and March. A sampling of events in April and May includes the Scottish Gathering and Games at Bakersfield; the Scandinavian Festival at Thousand Oaks; the Kernville Indian Powwow; many Cinco de Mayo celebrations in Los Angeles, Dinuba, San Diego, Delano, Calexico, and Oceanside; the Japanese-American Nikkei Matsuri Festival at San Jose; the Mariposa Powwow; the Stanford Powwow at Palo Alto; the Portuguese Festival at Lincoln; the Ethnic Food Fair at San Diego; and the Fandango at Clovis where

Hispanic, African American, and Anglo cultures are all celebrated. Summer events include powwows in Bakersfield, Paradise, Big Bear Lake, and Costa Mesa; the Cajun/Zydeco Festival at Long Beach; the Sacramento Croatian Extravaganza; San Francisco's Ethnic Dance Festival; the Scandinavian Midsummer Festival at Ferndale; the Celtic Festival at Mammoth Lakes; the Lotus Festival at Los Angeles; the Philippine Weekend at Delano; the Latin American Festival at San Diego; Old Spanish Days Fiesta at Santa Barbara; Festa Italiana at Sacramento; and the three-week, late-August to early-September African American festival African Marketplace and Cultural Faire at Los Angeles. Sacramento hosts the early-September Greek Festival. Also in September, Mexican Independence Day Celebrations are held in Los Angeles, Santa Monica, and Calexico; Greek festivals are held in Arcadia and Modesto; and Danish Days is held at Solvang. In September and October a number of Oktoberfests are held at Tahoe City, La Mesa, Torrance, Huntington Beach, Carlsbad, Lakeport, Encinitas, San Diego, Fairfield, Los Osos, and Pasadena.

California is known, of course, for many forms of entertainment, from film to whale watching to appreciation of fine California wines. However, the first, and one of the most famous, events each year is the Tournament of Roses Parade at Pasadena on New Year's Day. Film events include the Nortel International Film Festival at Palm Springs over two weeks in January; the International Film Festival at Santa Clarita in late February; Cinequest, the San Jose Film Festival, and the Best of the Banff Film Festival at Bishop both in March; April's Tahoe International Film Festival and the Yosemite Film Festival; the International Short Film Festival at Palm Springs in August; and the Mill Valley Film Festival held for ten days in mid-October. From January through March Oxnard provides many opportunities for watching the annual migration of the gray whale, and from mid-January to early February, Monterey hosts Whalefest. Dana Point offers coastal cruises in late February and early March during its Festival of Whales; and Ventura and Mendocino provide more chances to observe and appreciate the gray whale in February and March. California wines are big industry and offer visitors many ways to enjoy wine—with art, with beer, with food, with crafts, with credit cards! Santa Cruz County is the site of the Passport to the Wineries of the Santa Cruz Mountains event in mid-January. February through April events are held in Newark, Placerville, Temecula, Monterey, and Santa Ynez Valley. Over fifty wineries and local honey producers are included at the early May Days of Wine and Honey Festival at Livermore, followed by events in Tiburon, Walnut Creek, Foster City, San Anselmo, Mill Valley, Lake Arrowhead, Los Altos, Philo, Rancho Cordova, Cupertino, Monterey, Sebastopol, Millbrae, Livermore, Mountain View, Capitola, Santa Clara, Avalon, Santa Maria, San Diego, San Carlos, and Kelseyville, in order by month, with some cities welcoming visitors more than once throughout the year.

For those with active tastebuds in search of new and flavorful experiences, California serves up carrots and asparagus, strawberries and seafood, lemons, blackberries, and pears. San Francisco celebrates the dungeness crab season and the California fishing industry at the January Crab Festival, followed by the Crabfest at Oceanside and the World Famous Crab Races at Crescent City, both in February. Dinuba continues the feast at the mid-March Crab Feed. Celebrants can begin eating their vegetables early by attending the Holtville Carrot Festival in late January and early February. March brings the Napa Valley Mustard Festival, leaving sinuses and palates ready for the Avocado Festival at Fallbrook, the Stockton Asparagus

Festival, the Santa Maria Strawberry Festival, the Raisin Festival at Selma, and the Artichoke Festival at Castroville in April and May. Cherries, apricots, crawdads, and oysters may be tasted in June at Beaumont, Patterson, Isleton, and Arcata, respectively. July and August bring spice to lives at the Gilroy Garlic Festival and the Oxnard Salsa Festival, with August offering at least a couple of chances to fill up on blackberries at the Lower Lake Blackberry Festival and the Round Valley Blackberry Festival at Covelo. Everyone loves broccoli during the August Broccoli Festival at Greenfield, and Angels Camp hosts the Zucchini Festival and Kelseyville hosts the Pear Festival in mid-September. Other culinary opportunities may be found at the Vacaville Onion Festival, the Carpinteria Avocado Festival, and the Goleta Lemon Festival, ending the year with tart and a pucker.

California is golden and gold rush days are remembered at several events, including Gold Discovery Day on January 24 at Coloma, Gold Nugget Days at Paradise in mid-April, and Old Miners' Days at Big Bear Lake in August. Two California jazz events stand out: the Sacramento Jazz Jubilee in late May and the Monterey Jazz Festival in mid-September, touted respectively as the largest traditional and longest-running jazz festivals in the world. Finally, there is little doubt that the best-known county fair event in the country is the Calaveras County Fair and Jumping Frog Jubilee. Held in mid-May at Angels Camp, the frog-jumping contest has been featured since 1928 and is part of literary history, made famous by Samuel Clemens.[7]

COLORADO

The breathtaking scenery of Colorado is to be celebrated all year long, whether on ski trails, on mountain bikes, along walking trails, or while ice skating. During the last week of January, the Norse god of snow, Ullr, is remembered by Breckenridge at the Ullr Fest parade, concerts, ice-skating parties and other snowy events. Steamboat Springs opens February with the Winter Carnival where the Lighted Man and street events bring entertainment and fun to ski lovers. Denver is a city of lights during the month of December when its Wildlights celebration includes millions of lights and numerous animated animal light sculptures. The holiday season is even more festive when spent taking candlelight walks through Golden, rides on horse-drawn wagons through historic Palisade, or walks on the annual Holiday Home Tour in Colorado Springs.

In January, Greeley hosts the largest agricultural exhibition in Colorado at the Colorado Farm Show. Farm, ranch, home, and garden exhibits, as well as a juried art show, help celebrate spring at the Spring Equinox Festival held in March in Springfield. By mid-April, Grand Junction is ready to celebrate at the Southwest Fest with a chili cook-off, a microbrew festival, and Farm and Ranch Days. During the last week in April, Greeley hosts the weeklong Cinco de Mayo/Semana Latina festival of dancing, music, artwork, and food.

Whitewater rafting and kayaking races help Vail and Dowd Junction usher in summer during the Memorial Day weekend Jeep Whitewater Festival. Each year, cyclists compete at the Durango Iron Horse Bicycle Classic at the end of May when they race the Durango & Silverton Narrow Gauge train to Silverton. Runners and walkers converge each June at the Annual Classic Mountain Race for 5K, 10K, and 18-mile events.

Many summer events celebrate Colorado's beauty and history with activities for the family, arts and crafts exhibits, and a wide variety of food and drink. June events include the annual Fibark Boat Races and Festival in Salida (Chaffee County), Strawberry Days in mid-June in Glenwood Springs,

Central City's Madame Lou Bunch Day on June 19, the Greeley Independence Stampede and rodeos during the last week in June to July 4, the Annual Art Walk in late June in Salida, and the Fort Collins Colorado Brewers' Festival in late June.

During July the fun continues with the largest open rodeo in Colorado, the Brush Rodeo held in early July; the Annual Cowboy Roundup Days and Fourth of July Celebration held in Steamboat Springs; Estes Park's Rooftop Rodeo and Parade, which continues for almost a week in early July; the three-day Annual Carbondale Mountain Fair in mid-July; the Crested Butte Wildflower Festival in mid-July; Golden's Buffalo Bill Days in mid-July; and the Greeley Arts Picnic held for two days in late July.

August events include panning for gold and a lumberjack show at the Breckenridge No Man's Land Celebration; the Frisco Annual Colorado Barbecue Challenge and Frisco Founders Days; Buena Vista's Gold Rush Days held in mid-August; and the weeklong Mushroom Festival, Performing Arts Festival, and Airman's Rendezvous in Telluride. September and October are filled with celebrations of fall, including the Fall Equinox Festival in Springfield; Steamboat Springs' Annual Fall Foliage Festival; and numerous Oktoberfest celebrations in Vail, Breckenridge, Telluride, Woodland Park, and Brush.

Colorado celebrates a wide range of cultures, musical genres, and hobbies. A sampling of these celebrations include the Mountain Film Festival held in Telluride in late May, the scenic Annual Steamboat Marathon held in Steamboat Springs in June, the Telluride Blue Grass Festival in June, the Wool Market held in Estes Park in June, the Glenn Miller Festival held in June in Fort Morgan, and the Silverton Jubilee Folk Music Festival also held in June. Summer entertainment continues with the Rainbow Weekend hot-air balloon exhibition in Steamboat Springs in mid-July and the three-week classical music series, Music in the Mountains, held in Durango in late July and early August. The Telluride Film Festival is in early September. It is followed by the Longs Peak Scottish-Irish Highland Festival held in Estes Park in September, the Telluride Blues and Brews Festival in mid-September, the Council Tree Powwow and Cultural Festival held in Delta in late September, the Durango Cowboy Gathering in late September and early October, and the Continental Divide Hot Air Balloon Festival and Lighting of Breckenridge in early December.[8]

CONNECTICUT

Connecticut begins the year with winter carnivals and festivals at Woodbury, New Britain, and Southington. But there is also quiet fun and inspiration to be found along the Connecticut River as visitors take eagle watching cruises from Essex every weekend from mid-January through mid-March and from Old Saybrook on February weekends.

Spring celebrations and harvest festivals attract visitors who wish to smell the roses and enjoy the simple pleasures that can be found at country fairs. From mid-April through the beginning of May, Hamden celebrates the Annual Goldenbells Festival. The beauty of goldenbells, or forsythia, is appreciated at the event along with crafts, art, concerts, and nature walks. In late April, Meriden hosts the annual Daffodil Festival, and early May brings the Annual Dogwood Festival at Fairfield. The Elizabeth Park Rose Weekend at Hartford is held in mid-June as visitors stroll through the park, all senses alert to the aroma and view provided by 15,000 rosebushes and 900 varieties of award-winning roses. Bristol hosts the Annual Chrysanthemum Festival during the last week of September and into October. Several long-running and well-attended agricultural fairs offer many opportunities for family fun beginning in late August and continuing through September. These include the Annual Brooklyn Fair, the Annual Woodstock Fair, the Annual Hebron Harvest Fair, the Annual Bethlehem Fair, the Annual Durham Fair, and the Four Town Fair at Somers. Southington hosts the Annual Apple Harvest Festival during the first two weekends in October.

The sea yields a variety of tasty seafood and, of course, provides many opportunities to celebrate. Mystic is the home of the Annual Lobsterfest, featuring an outdoor lobster bake and sea chantey music, in late May. Oyster festivals are held in Milford in mid-August and in Norwalk in mid-September, both annual events that include large arts and crafts shows and entertainment for all ages. It is back to Mystic during the second weekend in October for the Annual Chowderfest. The U.S. Navy Submarine Base at Groton is the site of the Annual Subfest held over the Independence Day holiday. Events include a carnival, a boat show, food, family entertainment, and a fireworks display.

Connecticut's culturally diverse population is celebrated at such events as the Grecian Festival at Norwich; the Ridgefield Festival Italiano; Hartford's African-American Parade, Rally and Bazaar; Bristol's Oktoberfest; and Bridgeport's Hungarian Bazaar, all held in or beginning in September. Goshen hosts the Scottish Festival and Scotland hosts the Highland Festival in October. The Harvest Moon Powwow highlights Native American cultural events including storytelling, music, dancing, and food and is held for three days in mid-October at North Stonington.

Goshen welcomes those with their heads in the clouds and their feet firmly planted on the earth to attend the Annual Northwest Connecticut Balloon Festival and Craft Fair in late June. Arts and crafts, while often a part of many festivals, are a large part of the Annual Guilford Handcrafts Exposition in mid-July and at the Annual Mystic Outdoor Art Festival in mid-August. July also offers opportunities for antique boat enthusiasts to converge on Mystic for the Annual Antique and Classic Boat Rendezvous. Finally, statewide celebrations are held as Connecticut honors its state declaration of September 26 as Family Day.[9,10]

DELAWARE

Although Delaware is a small state geographically, it is quite diverse ethnically. The city of Wilmington celebrates its Polish culture at the St. Hedwig Polish Festival in mid-May; its Greek, Italian, and Swedish populations in June at the Holy Trinity Greek Festival, St. Anthony's Italian Festival, and the Swedish Mid-Summer Fest; and Caribbean and African American cultures at the Annual Caribbean Festival and Carnival Parade and Haneef's African Festival and Parade in July. The African-American Festival is held in Dover in late June. Millsboro hosts the Nanticoke Indian Pow-Wow in mid-September. Also in September, Georgetown welcomes visitors to the Hispanic Festival and Newark celebrates Oktoberfest.

It sure is fun at the shore and people in Delaware flock to it in early April for the Annual Great Delaware Kite Festival at Lewes, followed in May by the Cape May–Lewes Ferry Tourism Expo. In July builders of fancy, but ephemeral, real estate head for the Delaware Seashore Sandcastle Contest at Rehoboth Beach. Bethany Beach is the site of the Annual Boardwalk Arts Festival in mid-September, and then it's back to Rehoboth Beach in October for the Annual Autumn Jazz Festival. For those who prefer to stay inland and dream of travel to faraway places, Delaware City celebrates the Annual Old Canal Fest in August in honor of the canal connecting the Delaware and Chesapeake Bays.

In Wilmington, visitors don't need to scream for ice cream at the annual Ice Cream Festival held during the second weekend in July, be crabby for blue crabs at the Arts and Crabs: Blue Claw Crabs and BBQ Chicken Feast also in July, or cry the blues at the Cool Blues and Micro Brews festival in mid-August. Wyoming honors and eats the peach at the Annual Wyoming Peach Festival in early August. Bridgeville welcomes visitors to the Annual Apple-Scrapple Festival in early October.[11]

FLORIDA

In a state with a seemingly endless coastline, it is not surprising that Florida seafood is the center of numerous festivals. The Everglades Seafood Festival held in February in Everglades City offers over 3,000 pounds of locally caught seafood to visitors, who also celebrate Native American arts and crafts. In March, the Port Canaveral Seafest is held. As the northern states are beginning to thaw in April, Fort Walton hosts the Fort Walton Seafood Festival. For three days in May, the Fort Lauderdale Cajun/Zydeco Crawfish Festival is an opportunity to enjoy music, dance, and seafood. For those who would rather have shrimp, Fernandina Beach will be happy to serve ample portions at the Shrimp Festival in May. Volusia County provides more than a week during it's thirteen-day Fish Week in June for bass and flats fishing to be celebrated. In October, Madeira Beach celebrates the John's Pass Seafood Festival, and Destin hosts the monthlong Destin Fishing Rodeo attracting world-class fishing enthusiasts.

The Edison Festival of Light, held in February, includes a parade of lights, a 5K race, and a gala ball to celebrate Fort Myers' famous winter resident, Thomas Edison. In July, Key West is filled with Ernest Hemingway look-alikes during the Hemingway Days Festival, which also includes walking tours and literary contests.

Miami is the site in June of the largest Black heritage festival in America, the Coconut Grove Goombay Festival. Hispanic culture is celebrated during nine days in March at the Carnival Miami/Calle Ocho, concluding with a twenty-three–block street party. Miami Beach has its own unique architecture that is highlighted at the annual Art Deco Weekend Festival in January where visitors are invited to a seven-block street festival.

Music flows throughout Florida from the Havana Music Fest in March—featuring jazz, rhythm and blues, swing, country, gospel and reggae—to the Annual Suwannee River Jam in Live Oak where country music performers delight visitors in April. Jazz fills the air in Sarasota in March at the Sarasota Jazz Festival and in October at the Clearwater Jazz Holiday.

In February, the Florida state mammal, the manatee, is honored at the Crystal River Florida Manatee Festival. The renowned shelling island, Sanibel Island, celebrates the Sanibel Shell Fair in March with shell displays and crafts. Other major Florida festivals include the Annual Florida Citrus Festival and Polk County Fair in Winter Haven, an eleven-day citrus festival in January; the Nationsbank Coconut Grove Arts Festival in February where over a half million people come to view juried art from around the United States; and the Charlotte Harbor International Air Show in March that includes performances by the U.S. Airforce Thunderbirds, the U.S. Army Golden Knights, and wing walkers.[12]

GEORGIA

Georgia abounds with riches and shares them with generosity throughout the year in feasts and festivals when peaches, peanuts, apples, watermelon, and much more are cause for celebration. The world's largest peach cobbler is served at the Georgia Peach Festival held at Fort Valley and Byron in mid-June, the month also celebrating the Blueberry Festival in Alma. From mid-June to mid-July, watermelons are on the menu at the Annual Watermelon Days Festival in Cordele, the Watermelon Capital of the World. The Big Red Apple Festival is celebrated in Cornelia in late September; and during the second and third weekends in October, the Annual Georgia Apple Festival is held in Ellijay. Labor Day is the time and Kingsland is the place for the Annual Labor Day Catfish Festival where southern hospitality joins food, arts and crafts, a parade, and a golf tournament for a special weekend of fun.

For variety, try Mayhaw jelly at the National Mayhaw Festival in Colquitt during the third weekend in April; sign up for the onion-eating contest at the Annual Vidalia Onion Festival at the end of April; and see if you can spot Jimmie and Rosalyn Carter at the Plains Peanut Festival in late September. Buzz on over to the Hahira Honey Bee Festival in early October, before heading to Blairsville in late October for the Annual Sorghum Festival.

In Georgia, February is not too early to celebrate the beauty of nature unfolding with the Camellia Festival in Fort Valley and the annual Forsythia Festival in Forsyth in early March. The Cherry Blossom Festival is held for nine days from the middle to the end of March in Macon, where over 200,000 Yoshino Cherry trees display their beauty and festivalgoers enjoy concerts, parades, arts and crafts, sports events, food, and a hot-air balloonfest. International crafts and foods, games, and a pageant are found at the annual Conyers Cherry Blossom Festival held during the last weekend in March at the Georgia International Horse Park. The forest industry is highlighted an-

nually at the Baxley Tree Fest in mid-April, which also offers arts and crafts, sports events, a cake bake, fireworks, a street dance, concerts, and even chain saw carving. The Mountain Laurel Festival Springtime by the River is held in Clarkesville during mid-May. Winterville celebrates the Marigold Festival in late June.

Native American culture is highlighted at several festivals and powwows, including the Native Way Indian Festival and Pow Wow at the end of July in Perry, the Running Water Pow Wow and Ripe Corn Festival in Rome in early September, and the Native American Festival at Indian Springs in mid-September. The American Indian Festival at Lawrenceville is held in early October, and the Ossahatchee Indian Festival and Pow Wow at Hamilton is held in mid-October.

Some unique Georgia events include the Big Pig Jig Georgia Barbecue Cooking Championship in Vienna in October, where prizes totalling $12,000 are presented to award-winning barbecue cooks as visitors test the entries. Rattlesnakes are rounded up in late January in Whigham and in mid-March in Claxton. Cotton is picked at the Cotton Pickin' Fair held in Gay during the first weekends in May and October and at the Annual Cotton Harvest and Fly-in at Hazlehurst at the end of October. The Georgia Marble Festival at Jasper in early October features tours of marble quarries, marble sculptures, and fine art competitions.

For old-fashioned fun, guests are invited to visit Ellijay's North Georgia mountains throughout the spring and summer for Appalachian Sampler Festivals. These festivals provide samples and full doses of gospel, bluegrass, and mountain music, along with clogging, storytelling, and arts and crafts. For those who wish for the days of horses and buggies, Barnesville hosts the annual Buggy Days Festival in mid-September where guests are treated with a Buggython and arts and crafts. There are many arts and crafts events throughout the year. March festivals include the Calico Arts and Crafts Show in Moultrie, repeated in mid-November, and the Jesup Dogwood Arts and Crafts Festival. Dahlonega is the site of the Wildflower Festival of the Arts in mid-May. September events include the Powers' Crossroads Country Fair and Art Festival at Newnan; the Southern Heartland Arts Festival at Covington; the Annual Yellow Daisy Festival in Stone Mountain, considered one of the South's best craft shows; and the Annual Riverfest Arts and Crafts Festival at Canton. The Georgia Covered Bridge Arts Festival is hosted by Thomaston in mid-October.

History and folklore are highlighted in Georgia with tours, festivals, and storytelling events, such as the Annual Winter Storytelling Festival in Atlanta at the end of January; the Savannah Tour of Homes and Gardens at the end of March; and the Georgia Renaissance Festival held on weekends throughout April, May, June, and October in Fairburn. In mid-May storytellers recall Civil War stories, Native American legends, and ghost stories in a setting certain both to enchant and alarm guests during Georgia Folklore by Moonlight at the Jonesboro Stately Oaks Plantation. Stone Mountain Park's A Tour of Southern Ghosts chills and thrills visitors throughout the Halloween season.[13]

HAWAII

While Aloha Festivals of September and October and the June 11 King Kamehameha Day celebrations are common to all of the main islands, each major island also puts on festivals unique to that island. Oahu's May Day, or Lei Day in Hawaii, is a celebration of flowers. The largest event takes place in Waikiki with music, dances, ethnic food, and lei-making competitions. Also in May is the World Fire-Knife Dance Championship, where, if need be, soothing water is nearby to ease the pain of defeat. Children compete in a hula competition at the November Hula Oni E Keiki Hula Competition. Maui hosts several events unique to the islands of Hawaii, such as the Celebration of Humpback Whales in February, the In Celebration of Canoes event and the Maui Music Festival both in May, and the December Na Mele O Maui celebration of Hawaiian culture including a children's song contest, a hula festival, and an arts and crafts fair.

The Big Island of Hawaii celebrates the Merrie Monarch Hula Festival during the week after Easter, featuring a hula competition along with other cultural events. This festival is a tribute to King David Kalakaua who ruled from 1874 to 1891 and was responsible for bringing back many ancient Hawaiian traditions. Other events on this island include the three-day Dolphin Days event in late June, the July 4th Annual Parker Ranch Rodeo, and the International Festival of the Pacific in August. The Queen Liliuokalani Outrigger Canoe Races find over 2,500 people with paddles making a bid for being the best at what is professed to be the world's longest canoe race. The week-long Kona Coffee Cultural Festival is held in mid-November where there are over thirty events and where one is certain to find a good cup of coffee. On Kauai, the ten days of Koloa Plantation Days get underway in mid-July with canoe races, a parade, food, crafts, and a block party. The mid-September Mokihana Festival celebrates Hawaiian culture and includes men's and women's hula events.

On the fourth of July, Lanai includes food, entertainment, and fireworks at its Pineapple Festival. Finally, traditional Hawaiian games, such as lawn bowling, spear hurling, and wrestling, are the focal points of the January Makahiki Festival on Molokai. The Molokai Ka Hula Piko is a daylong event held on the third Saturday in May and is very popular. Before the sun rises, celebrants begin the "until-the-sun-goes-down" party at the site considered to be the place where hula was first performed in Hawaii.[14]

IDAHO

Idaho's seven regions each provide unique public events. North Idaho has everything from the ten-day Sandpoint Winter Carnival during the third week of January, to the Idaho Draft Horse International in early October, also held in Sandpoint. Hundreds of Native American drummers, horsemen, and dancers from across the United States and Canada join in competitions at the July Pow Wow in Post Falls. Logging is celebrated at the North Idaho Timberfest in Sandpoint in June and at Paul Bunyan Days in St. Maries in September. August provides opportunities to see the Coeur d'Alene Indians' Coming of the Black Robes Ceremony at the Coeur d'Alene Indian Pilgrimage at Cataldo and join in the Mountain Man Rendezvous Pioneer Days at the Old Mission State Park. Moscow, in north central Idaho, presents the Lionel Hampton Jazz Festival for five days in February and the Rendezvous in the Park in mid-July for lovers of all kinds of music including jazz, folk, blues, country, and classical. Moscow's Renaissance Faire takes place during the first part of May. Chief Lookingglass Days in Kamiah in mid-August is a traditional powwow during which the Nez Perce Indians present cultural ceremonies and dancing. Lumberjacks from all over the world gather in Orofino for competition at the Clearwater County Fair and Lumberjack Days during the third weekend in September; and rodeo fans have their choice of the Riggins Rodeo in early May, the Grangeville Border Days Rodeo over the Independence Day holiday, and the Lewiston Roundup in September.

Southwestern Idaho also has its share of rodeos: the Caldwell Night Rodeo in mid-August and the Snake River Stampede in July in Nampa, one of the country's top rodeos. Hot-air balloons grace the skies at the Cherry Festival in Emmett in mid-June and at the Boise River Festival later in June, where they are joined by other festive activities, food, fireworks, and parades. South central Idaho provides ample opportunity to enjoy the present and remember the past during the six-day Cassia County Fair and Rodeo in Burley in mid-August; the Twin Falls County Fair and Rodeo in Twin Falls, in early September; and Western Days at the end of May in Twin Falls where visitors are treated to a Wild West shoot-out, barbecues, dancing, and a parade. In late June, spectators enjoy a picturesque and exciting flat-bottom boat race on the Snake River at the Idaho Regatta at Burley. Mid-August brings the Gooding Basque Festival where festivalgoers enjoy traditional Basque entertainment, arts and crafts, and food.

Southeastern Idaho celebrates the famous Idaho potato in Shelley in mid-September with Idaho Spud Day, and Idaho history in Lava Hot Springs with the Mountain Man Rendezvous–Pioneer Days in July. Rugged mountain men are on center stage at the Massacre Rocks Rendezvous at American Falls in early June where visitors are treated to knife-throwing contests and black powder shoots. Native American culture is celebrated at the Shoshone-Bannock Indian Festival in August at Fort Hall. A rodeo and horse and pig races are just part of the entertainment during the Eastern Idaho State Fair in Blackfoot held during the first week in September. For three days in early August, everyone is enjoying the raspberry at the Raspberry Festival at Bear Lake.

Rexburg, in eastern Idaho, is the site for the Idaho International Folk Dance Festival during the first week in August. Also in August, Driggs hosts three days of musical enjoyment at the Bluegrass Festival. Music rocks in the Tetons for a music and microbrew festival in early July when the Rockin' the Tetons Music Festival attracts blues and brews enthusiasts. The beautiful Grand Teton Mountain Range is the backdrop for the Teton Valley Hot Air Balloon Races in Driggs for the first four days in July.

Sun Valley in central Idaho is the site of the Sun Valley Summer Symphony from the last week in July to mid-August, when free open-air concerts bring enjoyment to visitors. July also provides time for the Sawtooth Mountain Mamas Arts and Crafts Fair in Stanley complete with arts, crafts, fiddlers, a barbecue, and pancakes. The three-day Salmon River Days celebration in early July offers boat and bike races, Kayak and raft races, a rodeo, fireworks, and a fishing derby. In early September, the Ketchum Wagon Days Celebration remembers Idaho's mining history and economic importance with time set aside for some hearty breakfast flapjacks.[15]

ILLINOIS

Illinois yields a rich harvest that is celebrated at a variety of festivals. Strawberry festivals are plentiful, beginning with the Carlinville Strawberry Festival and Eckert's Strawberry Festival and Craft Show in late May, and continuing with the Catlin Strawberry Festival in early June, the Kankakee Valley Strawberry Festival and the Garden Prairie Strawberry Festival in mid-June, and the Long Grove Strawberry Festival in late June. The Amish Farm Market Days at Arcola are held in mid-August where visitors may purchase homemade baked goods and fresh produce, as well as attend a homemade quilt auction. Farmers' markets in Batavia, Frankfort, Park Ridge, Downers Grove, and Glencoe, to name a few, offer many opportunities to enjoy the full range of Illinois produce and homemade goods throughout the summer and autumn. The Annual Sweet Corn Festival at Mendota in mid-August includes a fresh supply of free sweet corn and fun for all ages at a parade, carnival, craft fair, and beer garden. Urbana hosts the late August Sweetcorn Festival, followed by the Hoopeston National Sweetcorn Festival at the end of August (where sweetcorn is eaten by the ton) and the DeKalb Corn Festival, also in late August. Watermelon helps cool hot summer days in August. Hungry visitors may fill up on both sweet corn and watermelon at the Mt. Vernon Southern Illinois Sweet Corn and Watermelon Fest. Early September is not too late for more watermelon at the Thomson Melon Days. Native Americans knew that persimmons must ripen in order to enjoy their full flavor and usefulness. The Icarian Persimmon Festival at Nauvoo in late October and the Persimmon Party at Taylorville in early November provide festivalgoers with a variety of treats from jams and jellies to breads and cookies made with persimmons.

Abraham Lincoln is remembered throughout Illinois at birthday celebrations, reenactments of Lincoln-Douglas debates, historical plays, lectures, and rail-splitting contests. One might even find Abe Lincoln look-alikes in New Salem, at the Lincoln Log Cabin State Historic Site in Lerna, in Springfield, in Danville, or at a number of other locations where Lincoln traveled, tried cases as an attorney, or campaigned for the legislature. The Civil War is reenacted in May where visitors may come across uniformed soldiers in downtown Sycamore. General Ulysses S. Grant was a citizen of the picturesque city of Galena and townspeople remember him while showcasing architectural and historic points of interest during weekly walking tours. It is also the site where two-legged visitors observe winged visitors at numerous Bald Eagle watches and tours along the upper Mississippi River. Eagle-watching opportunities are offered at Grafton, Warsaw, and Rock Island, as well.

Brighton hosts the family-oriented Annual

Olden Days, which offers demonstrations and exhibits of threshing, sawmilling, steam and gas engines, and antique tractors. Arcola welcomes visitors to a similar event during the last three weekends in September when it holds the Horse Farming Days Festival. This festival also includes threshing demonstrations, as well as providing corn-shucking and walking plow contests for those who want to participate in early harvesting activities. Arcola is also the host of the Annual Quilt Celebration from late June through early July, and Decatur hosts the Decatur Quilt Festival in March. Wholesome entertainment can be found at the well-attended Annual Danville Horseshow Club Open in mid-July, at the Illinois Storytelling Festival in Spring Grove in late July, and at the Illinois State Fair in mid-August at Springfield.

Chicago and the Chicago area are alive with all types of festivals and ethnic celebrations too numerous to name in full. Geneva is the site of the annual six-day Swedish Days Festival in late June. The Annual Ethnic Arts Festival is held along the shores of Lake Michigan at Dawes Park during the third weekend in July and celebrates the arts, including music, dance, and poetry, as well as the foods of over sixty-five ethnic groups. Aurora hosts the Puerto Rican Heritage Festival and Parade in early July, and the St. Sophia Greek Festival is held the following week. Evanston celebrates the Armenian Festival in late August, followed by South Elgin's Annual Scandinavian Day Festival and Oktoberfests throughout the Chicago area in September. The famed Magnificent Mile is where the Christmas holiday season is officially opened during the mid-November Annual Magnificent Mile Lights Festival. It is also the site in mid-July of the Annual Chicago Tribune Magnificent Mile Art Festival, a large outdoor juried art show. The 1700s come alive in September at the Annual Illinois and Michigan Canal Rendezvous. Held along the banks of the Des Plaines River, fur trappers, early settlers, and Early American craftspeople reenact history and everyone enjoys Early American foods. Mid-June at Main Street and Chicago Avenue is the place to be for Custer's Last Stand Festival of Arts. There are over 500 arts and crafts exhibits, fifty antique dealers, a Native American Pow Wow, shows, and many opportunities for eating in over fifty area restaurants. Geneva hosts the Folk Music Festival and Storytelling Festival in early September where folk music and storytelling acts are presented on eight stages for two days.

Illinois has a number of unique events. There is a celebration of the dairy farmer at Harvard Milk Days when over 100,000 spectators converge on Harvard in early June. There is a drive across Illinois from Edwardsville to Joliet at the Annual Route 66 Association Car Cruise in June; the Monarch Butterfly Festival at Palos Heights in September; the Annual Morton Pumpkin Festival where the self-proclaimed "Pumpkin Capital of the World" serves pumpkin pancakes and pies to visitors in mid-September; and Cairo's Riverboat Days during the first weekend in October. Nauvoo is the home of the City of Joseph Festival for two weekends in late July and early August when music, dances, and dramas depict the life of the Mormon prophet Joseph Smith who lived in Nauvoo and was martyred in nearby Carthage. Nauvoo also celebrates the Nauvoo Grape Festival with a "Wedding of the Wine and Cheese" and provides plenty of time for grape-stomping fun over four days in early September. The Spoon River Valley and the natural beauty of fall converge during the last two weekends in October for the Spoon River Valley Scenic Drive. Stop at the Lewistown Oak Hill cemetery for a temporary rest along the way and enjoy dramatic poetry readings of the Spoon River Anthology.[16]

INDIANA

The Indianapolis 500 on the Sunday of Memorial Day weekend is perhaps Indiana's single most famous event, but Indy racing is only one event among hundreds every year. Of course, there's the Indiana State Fair, also in Indianapolis, which attracts tens of thousands and showcases national entertainment. But Indiana, a state of many towns and villages, also celebrates gifts of the earth, the pioneer spirit and lifestyle, covered bridges, ethnic diversity, and a wide range of musical interests.

Festivals that highlight a broad range of foods, from maple syrup to hot dogs to turkeys to popcorn, offer a flavor for everyone. Rockville is the home of the Parke County Maple Syrup Festival, one of several Indiana events where there is plenty of maple syrup and some pancakes to keep it company. Other late February and March maple festivals are held in Mansfield, Salem, Evansville, Porter, Hobart, LaGrange, and Wakarusa. April brings mushrooms and mushroom hunts at the Mansfield Mushroom Festival and Car Show. Sassafras Tea accompanies the Vernon Sassafras Tea Festival and Civil War Living History event in late April. Strawberries are the fare at the YWCA Strawberry Festival at Lafayette in June, at Metamora's Strawberry Daze, the Rosedale Strawberry Festival and Bike Tour, the Crawfordsville Strawberry Festival, and the Very Berry Strawberry Fest at Wabash. In July Schererville celebrates the Annual Corn Roast, while Oakland City brings on sweet corn at its early August Sweet Corn Festival. Where else but at Frankfort would one find a hot dog festival. In August, Owensville hosts the Owensville Watermelon Festival, joined later by the Knox County Watermelon Festival at Vincennes. Also in August, Van Buren hosts the Popcorn Festival and Wabash hosts the Wabash Herb Festival. If humans could store up food for the

winter, September would be a very good month to do it in Indiana. The Marshall County Blueberry Festival at Plymouth is held in early September, followed by the Tipton County Pork Festival; the Daviess County Turkey Trot Festival, where turkeys get a chance to trot off a little fat; the Valparaiso Popcorn Festival; Fillmore's Hobbit Gardens Herb Festival; the Nappanee Apple Festival; the Brookston Apple/Popcorn Festival; Terre Haute's Chili Cook-Off; Fort Wayne's Johnny Appleseed Festival; the Western Festival Chili Cookoff at Indianapolis; the Duneland Harvest Festival at Porter; the Owen County Apple Butter Festival at Spencer; the Annual Mitchell Persimmon Festival; the Annual Versailles Pumpkin Show; the Cory Apple Festival; the Apple Festival at Batesville; and the Middlebury Amish Country Harvest Festival. Throughout October apples, sorghum, pumpkins, and other autumn treats are celebrated at Bloomfield, Rockville, Covington, Indianapolis, Kendallville, Danville, Frankton, and Vernon, as well as at other towns and cities.

Music festivals are many and varied. Elkhart's Rhapsody in Green and Woody Turner's Jayland Bluegrass Festival at Portland offer live music and fun during a weekend in mid-June. Also in June, Bean Blossom hosts the Annual Bill Monroe Memorial Bean Blossom Bluegrass Festival, Batesville presents the Batesville Music and Arts Festival, Indianapolis is home to the international Indy Jazz Fest, Petersburg hosts the Official State Pickin' and Fiddlin' Contest, the Indiana Blues Festival is held in Muncie, and the Mansfield Bluegrass Festival is held in Mansfield. Finally, in late June, Battle Ground welcomes fiddlers to the Annual Indiana Fiddlers' Gathering, Elkhart hosts the Elkhart Jazz Festival, and Pendleton welcomes visitors to the Pendleton Art and Jazz Festival. Bloomington is the site of the Bloomington Music and Arts Festival held in July, followed also in July and again in September by the Central Indiana Bluegrass Association Bluegrass Festival at Converse; Derby's Cedar Valley Bluegrass Festival; Westfield's Annual Eagle Creek Bluegrass Festival, which is held in June and again in mid-September; and Leroy's Annual Stoney Run Bluegrass Festival. August finds gospel performances at the Gospel Music Festival at Columbus, and September events include the Jazz Fest at Richmond, the End of Summer Bluegrass Festival at Plymouth, and the Fiddler Fest at Newburgh. The Annual Bill Monroe Hall of Fame and Uncle Pen Festival is held at Bean Blossom in early October, and music is joined by crafts at the Columbus Country Music Festival and Craft show in mid-October.

History, popular culture, and ethnic diversity are all cause for celebration, again far too numerous to mention in full. Movie star James Dean is remembered on February 6 and 7 at the James Dean Birthday Celebration in his hometown of Fairmont, and the life of Wilbur Wright is celebrated in June at his birthplace in Millville. Life for mountain men in the early 1800s is reenacted at the Bridgeton Mountain Men Rendezvous in late April, followed by more frivolous events at the Dillsboro Homecoming Festival in early May where babies are judged, frogs jump, and hospital beds are raced through town. Oswego Trader Days in May offers opportunities for history buffs and those either good at throwing or ducking to participate in a hatchet throw or skillet throw. At the end of May, the Annual Spirit of Vincennes Rendezvous provides an opportunity for the whole family to learn about the Revolutionary War period. Hometowns and midwest living are celebrated at Monticello during the Back Home Again in Indiana Spring Festival in May; the All American Country Hoedown at Campbellsburg, the Hometown Festival Days at Crown Point, and the Blue Jeans Festival at Rising Sun in June; at numerous Fourth of July hometown

events; and at October's Midwest Nostalgia Festival at Bluffton. Indianapolis celebrates the Indianapolis Middle Eastern Festival in mid-June, and the weeklong African-American Summer Celebration in mid-July. Valparaiso is the host of the Gaelic Fest in mid-July; Whiting, the Pierogi Fest in late-July; Berne, Berne Swiss Days at the end of July; Hobart, the Serb Fest at the end of July and beginning of August; Fort Wayne, the Fort Wayne Irish Fest; Evansville, Native American Days in September; and Columbus, Ethnic Expo Festival in October. Nappanee is the site of the Amish Acres Arts and Crafts Festival in mid-August where hundreds of artists participate in the juried art show. Germanfests, Oktoberfests, and other events celebrating German cultural traditions are held at Fort Wayne in mid-June; at Jasper in early August; at Tell City's Swiss-German Schweizer Fest in mid-August; at Michigan City, Terre Haute, New Harmony, Seymour, and Huntingburg in September; and at Lowell in October. No discussion of Indiana festivals would be complete without mentioning covered bridges. Covered bridge festivals are held at Moscow in late June; at Roann, Matthews, and New Harmony in mid-September; and at the ten-day Parke County Covered Bridge Festival in October.[17,18]

IOWA

Towns and cities along the Mississippi River take time out during January to pay homage to the American Bald Eagle. Bellevue, Clinton, Dubuque, Guttenberg, Lake Red Rock, Muscatine, and the Quad Cities welcome visitors, those with feathers and those without, and Keokuk dedicates two days in mid-January to celebrate Annual Bald Eagle Appreciation Days. Hot-air balloons take adventuresome spirits to the sky and provide a dramatic landscape for those who prefer to observe during the National Balloon Classic at Indianola in late July or early August and during the Great Iowa Balloon Race at Storm Lake in early September. The streets are scrubbed at Pella for the early May Tulip Time Festival, followed by the Orange City Tulip Festival in mid-May. The rich Iowa soil is celebrated at fairs, festivals, and threshers' reunions throughout the summer and fall with the Annual Mid-Iowa Antique Power Show at Marshalltown in early August, the Threshermen and Collectors Show at Albert City in mid-August, the Iowa State Fair held at Des Moines during the latter part of August, the Midwest Old Threshers Reunion at Mt. Pleasant in early September, and the Clay County Fair at Spencer in mid-September. Dyersville hosts the National Farm Toy Show in early November where farm toys may be purchased, traded, and/or admired by boys and girls of all ages.

History, nature, sport, and entertainment are found in various combinations and events. The Civil War Reenactment of the Battle of Pea Ridge is held at Keokuk at the end of April. In early June, Fort Dodge is the site of Frontier Days, and Waterloo hosts the My Waterloo Days Festival. During the middle of June, Council Bluffs welcomes visitors to the Renaissance Faire of the Midlands. June is also the month when Burlington celebrates its Steamboat Days/American Music Festival. In early July, Clinton hosts Riverboat Days, and Sac City hosts Chautauqua Days. In mid-July, Sioux City hosts River-Cade over the course of an entire week with carnivals, music, and family entertainment. Amateur sports are the focal point of Iowa Games held at Ames during the middle part of July, when over 15,000 athletes participate in a number of competitions. Muscatine is the site of the Great Rivers Days celebration during mid-August, followed in late August by a historic celebration around the Albia town square during the Albia Restoration Days. Pufferbilly Days at Boone spotlight the railroad during the second weekend

in September. The romance and utility of covered bridges are recalled during the Madison County Covered Bridge Festival at Winterset during the second weekend in October. Cyclists pedal bicycles down crooked streets, across Iowa, and through historic villages at several events from the Snake Alley Criterium at Burlington in late May to the late-July RAGBRAI (Register's Annual Great Bike Ride Across Iowa) to the mid-August Bike Van Buren at Keosauqua. Old-time music festivals are held in Avoca in late August and in Bloomfield during mid-September.

Many ethnic and cultural groups have settled in Iowa and their cultures are kept alive at several events throughout the year. For instance, Elk Horn hosts a Danish celebration of spring at the Tivoli Fest in late May; Story City hosts Scandinavian Days in early June; and Decorah celebrates the Nordic Fest in late July. Czech Days are celebrated in late August at Protivin, and Amana does the polka with gusto at its Oktoberfest held in late September. In mid-August, the Meskwaki Pow Wow is held in Tama where traditional music, dance, and attire are appreciated and enjoyed throughout the four-day event. Cowboys may be found at the Annual Leon Rodeo in early July, as well as at Sidney during the Annual Iowa Championship Rodeo in early August and at Fort Madison in mid-September at the Fort Madison Tri-State Rodeo.

Iowa remembers its many famous sons and daughters, as well as those who have stopped in Iowa along their way. Jesse James Days are held at Corydon in early June, followed also in June by the Glenn Miller Festival at Clarinda, the Felix Adler Clown Festival at Clinton, the Lewis and Clark Festival at Onawa, the Grant Wood Art Festival at Stone City–Anamosa, and the Donna Reed Festival for the Performing Arts at Denison. The Bix Beiderbecke Memorial Jazz Festival is held in late July at Davenport. In early August, West Branch invites visitors to celebrate Hooverfest at the Herbert Hoover Birthplace and Museum. The Annual National Hobo Convention has begun its second century of celebration at Britt where mulligan stew is served and court is held by the hobo king and queen.[19]

KANSAS

Kansas celebrates its first inhabitants and its pioneers, cowboys, cowgirls, and cowpunchers at powwows, rodeos, and old threshers' reunions held throughout the year. From the Haskell Indian Pow Wow at Lawrence in early May to the mid-June Prairie Band Potawatomi Annual Pow Wow at Mayetta to the Wha-Shun-Gah Days at Council Grove also in mid-June to the Lake Shawnee Intertribal Pow Wow at Topeka in early September to the Annual Coffeyville Intertribal Pow Wow in early November, early Native American cultural history is celebrated in song, dance, and the arts. One is certain to find barbecue and many entertainments at rodeos from May to November. May rodeos include the Chisholm Trail Festival and Rodeo at Caldwell, the Abbyville Frontier Days Rodeo and BBQ, the Meade County Rodeo, and the Annual Yates Center Days (which also includes a carnival and a parade). Hutchinson is the site of the mid-July Pretty Prairie Rodeo, Kansas's Largest Night Rodeo, followed later in July by the Franklin County Fair and Rodeo at Ottawa, the Attica Saddle Club Rodeo at Attica, the Kaw Valley Rodeo and Riley County Fair at Manhattan, the Junction City Annual Rodeo, and the late-July to early-August Dodge City Days. In addition to county fairs, Dodge City, Coffeyville, Medicine Lodge, and Kansas City all host rodeos until early November. Sharon Springs welcomes the bravehearted to its May Rattlesnake Roundup. When not taming broncos or rattlesnakes, cowboys may be found tenderly reciting reciting poems and

stories at the May Cowboy Heritage Festival at Dodge City or the June Echoes of the Trail Cowboy Poetry event at Fort Scott. Baxter Springs is the home of the early-August Cowtown Days, and Ellsworth is home to the Ellsworth Cowtown Festival.

A two-legged stampede converges on Manhattan in mid-June for the Country Stampede, where campers can enjoy country music over the course of the three-day festival. Topeka celebrates jazz in May and orchestra and chamber music in June. Dodge City is the host of the Annual Sawlog "N" Strings Bluegrass Festival in mid-August. Arts, music, good barbecue, camping, crafts, and kite flying are the entertainment at the Americana Weekend in late May at Kansas City. Salina hosts the Smokey Hill River Festival, a renowned juried arts and crafts festival in mid-June.

Agriculture and the cattle industry are celebrated at farm and beef expos, such as the early-March Kansas Beef Expo at Hutchinson, the Annual Mid American Farm Expo at Salina, the June Beef Empire Days at Garden City (which also includes a rodeo), the Kansas Wheat Festival at Wellington in mid-July, the Flint Hills Beef Fest at Emporia in mid-August, and the Kansas State Fair in mid-September at Hutchinson. Antique engine expos and shows are held at the Annual Antique Machinery, Threshing, and Power Show at Almena in mid-June; the mid-July Jewell County Threshing Bee at Mankato; the late-July Tri-State Engine and Thresher Show at Bird City; the early-August Goessel Country Threshing Days; and the mid-August Kansas and Oklahoma Steam and Gas Engine Show at Winfield. Lindsborg hosts the Millfest in early May when a flour mill from the late 1800s is operated and pioneer days remembered with arts, crafts, and food. Shawnee, Fort Scott, and Canton celebrate the good old days in early June at the Old Shawnee Days Celebration, the Annual Good Ol' Days festival, and Prairie Days, respectively. Some old settlers prefer to throw cow chips at the September Old Settler's Day, State Cow Chip Throw Contest and Craft Fair at Russell Springs. Fort Scott welcomes visitors in May and September to its Frontier Garrison Life celebration where numerous activities bring history to life. Railroad Days is held at Topeka in early September when railroad enthusiasts can enjoy the past and present, collect memorabilia, and take train rides.

The diverse cultural heritage of Kansas is celebrated at Cinco de Mayo festivals at Hutchinson and Ulysses and during the Celebration of Cultures at Topeka, also held in May. Topeka celebrates the Fiesta Mexicana Week in mid-July, and Garden City hosts the Mexican Fiesta in mid-September. In June, Kansas City is alive with Celtic music and bagpipe bands at its Scottish Highland Games, followed in late September by the Scottish Festival and Highland Games at McPherson. Oktoberfests are held in Hays and Topeka.[20]

KENTUCKY

Kentucky is horse country. Everyone has heard of the Kentucky Derby, which is held on the first Saturday in May and the two-week celebration leading up to the Derby. Over one million visitors converge on Louisville for the main event and the games, parades, concerts, and fun activities for all age groups that precede it. Other horsey events include Equitana USA in mid-June in Louisville; the world-class horse show for Egyptian Arabian horses, the Egyptian Event, in mid-June in Lexington; the Wild Horse Expo hosted in Lexington in late July; the Shelbyville Horse Show Jubilee in early August, which is marked by top competitions, food, and a variety of events; the Festival of the Horse in Georgetown in mid-September; and the Kentucky Fall Classic Saddlebred

Show in Lexington during the second week in October.

Kentucky is the home of the bourbon that goes into the mint juleps drunk on Derby Day. It is celebrated in Bardstown at the Kentucky Bourbon Festival in mid-September. And Kentucky is also a major tobacco producer. Tobacco's importance to the economy of the state is celebrated at the Logan County Tobacco Festival in Russellville during the first week in October and at the Bloomfield Tobacco Festival during mid-October. One of Kentucky's most memorable and successful business characters, Colonel Sanders, opened his first establishment in London where the World Chicken Festival is celebrated at the end of September.

Native American culture is celebrated at several festivals and powwows, such as the Day of the Wolf Traditional Pow Wow in Bardstown in mid-October; the Inter-tribal Indian Festival in Calhoun also in mid-October; and the Trail of Tears Indian Pow Wow at Hopkinsville in mid-September. The latter offers visitors an opportunity to pay tribute to the memories of the Cherokee tribe and its sorrow-filled march to Oklahoma. Events at powwows include storytelling, exhibits of Native American arts and crafts, and tribal dancing.

Music of all varieties is celebrated with vigor at many celebrations throughout the state. There are over twenty-five bluegrass festivals alone. Kentucky is the home of the Father of Bluegrass, Bill Monroe. Just a few of the music festivals in Kentucky include the Kentucky Friends of Bluegrass Music Club's Spring Festival in Clay City in May; the Celebration of Traditional Music in Berea in mid-May; the Yellowbanks Dulcimer Festival in Owensboro in early June; the Festival of the Bluegrass in Lexington in mid-June; the Great American Brass Band Festival in Danville in mid-June; the Kentucky Folk Festival in Bardstown at the end of June; the Northern Kentucky Bluegrass

Festival in Falmouth in mid-July; the Newport Arts and Music Festival held on the riverfront at Newport in mid-July; the Poppy Mt. Bluegrass Festival in Morehead in mid-September; the Great American Dulcimer Convention in Pineville in late September; the Official Kentucky State Championship Old Fiddlers Contest at the Rough River Dam State Resort Park in mid-July where fiddle, mandolin, harmonica, guitar, and banjo music fills the air; and the Big Hill Mountain Family Bluegrass Festival in early August at Morrill.

Appalachian culture and history are celebrated at many festivals. The Jeffersontown Gaslight Festival is a weeklong event in mid-September, which includes juried crafts. Over 400 quilts are exhibited with over $85,000 awarded in prizes at the AQS National Quilt Show and Contest in the self-named "Quilt City USA," Paducah, in late April. Hillbilly Days are celebrated with arts and crafts, food, music, and a parade in Pikesville in April. The Appalachian Family Folk Week is celebrated at the Hindman Settlement School in mid-June. The Pioneer Days Festival celebrates Kentucky's first settlement in Harrodsburg with arts and crafts, food, music, and a truck pull. The Daniel Boone Pioneer Festival is held in Winchester in early September, and Barbourville celebrates the Daniel Boone Festival in early October. The Jenny Wiley Pioneer Festival, held in Prestonsburg the first week in October, honors the pioneer who escaped from the Indians. Last, but not least, Abraham Lincoln's "symbolic birthplace cabin" is the site of his annual birthday celebration in Hodgenville.

A variety of other festivals are held throughout the state celebrating food and nature's beauty. The International BBQ Festival serves tons of barbecue to hungry celebrants in Owensboro in early May. The "Father of the Blues" is celebrated during a week in mid-June at Henderson's W. C. Handy Blues and Barbecue Festival. Chocolate lovers may get their fill at the Chocolate Festival in Mayville at the end of March. May Day in Harrodsburg finds celebrants dancing around the fifteen-foot May pole on May 1. The Buckley Wildlife Sanctuary in Frankfort is the site of the Birdathon in early May and the Wildflower Search at the end of May. Bagdad Days celebrates spring with a pig roast, auctions, and hot-air balloon rides during the first week in May in Bagdad. Also during the first week in May, bird and wildflower hikes and folk dancing are found at the Black Mountain Wildflower Weekend at Pine Mountain. May comes to a close with the Kentucky Mountain Laurel Festival in Pineville.[21,22]

LOUISIANA

Even though officially Mardi Gras lasts only from January 6 until the first day of Lent, it seems that Louisiana is in a constant state of satisfied celebration. The mix of cultures that makes up Louisiana has become almost legendary and certainly unique in America. Natchitoches is the site of the Creole Heritage Day in late January. March events include the Black Heritage Festival at Lake Charles; the Flying Eagle Pow Wow at Prairieville; the Cajun Fun Fest at New Iberia; the Irish/Italian Festival of Southwest Louisiana at Lake Charles; and the Calling of the Tribes Pow Wow at Houma, featuring French-speaking Native Americans. Early April brings the Boggy Bayou Festival at Pine Prairie where Cajun and country music join arts, crafts, a carnival, and magic and comedy shows. In late April, Jeanerette hosts the Creole Festival where visitors may enjoy the fais-do-do, or street dance, along with a cake walk, carnival rides, arts and crafts, and Cabbage Ball Tournament. In May, early French settlers are recalled at the French Festival and Banquet in Crowley and the Fete d'Amerique Francaise, or French Fest, in New Orleans. Marksville provides the venue for the Tunica-Biloxi Pow Wow in mid-May. This annual event pays tribute to the Tunica-Biloxi tribe and other tribes in Louisiana that share their cultural and genealogical heritage with France. Juneteenth celebrations in mid-June are hosted at Opelousas and Donaldsonville. The Cajun Creole Festival at Lafayette and the Cajun Music and Food Festival at Lake Charles provide opportunities to soak in some Cajun country ambience in July. Cajun and Creole food, music, and crafts may be found at the mid-September Festivals Acadiens at Lafayette, and Plaquemine declares that October is a good time for the three-day International Acadian Festival. French West-African folktales of Compair Lapin are cause for rememberin' and tellin' at the Br'er Rabbit Folk Festival and Arts and Crafts Show at Laura Plantation at Vacherie at the end of October.

Louisiana's cultural diversity and gifts from the sea and earth have translated into a fabulous cuisine that can be sampled or shucked and shoveled in from the Amite Oyster Festival and Rodeo in March to the Louisiana Peach Festival at Ruston in June to the Bridge City Gumbo Festival in October. Etouffee anyone? Arnaudville hosts the La Festival de l'Etoufee in mid-April. At the Sorrento Jambalaya Festival cast iron pots meet top-notch cooks and everyone toasts the World Jambalaya Cooking Champion at the end of May. The best seafood and chicken gumbos are served up during the Great Louisiana Gumbo Cookoff at the beginning of May in Oakdale. Louisiana catfish are served at the Louisiana Catfish Festival at Des Allemands in July and at the Annual Franklin Parish Catfish Festival at Winnsboro in April. Fresh Gulf seafood is the fare at the Jean Lafitte Seafood Festival at Lafitte in early August, also the month when Galliano celebrates the South Lafourche Seafood Festival and Delcambre blesses fishermen and their boats at the Shrimp Festival. Morgan City hosts the Louisiana

Shrimp and Petroleum Festival early in September, followed by the Louisiana Shrimp Festival at Meraux. Zydeco and Cajun music aid digestion during the World Championship Gumbo Cookoff at New Iberia in mid-October. Watermelon festivals in July at Farmerville and Franklinton follow such varied celebrations as the Iowa Rabbit Festival in March, the Ponchatoula Strawberry Festival in April, and the Louisiana Corn Festival at Bunkie in June. Colfax celebrates the Louisiana Pecan Festival and Basile celebrates the Louisiana Swine Festival, both in early November. A lot of eggs and people make their way to Abbeville in November for the Giant Omelette Celebration where festivities include the preparation of a giant omelette, Cajun singing and dancing, and arts and crafts exhibits.

Louisiana swings, sings the blues, and, in general, jazzes up the lives of festivalgoers at a number of events throughout the year. As if there weren't enough opportunities during the Mardi Gras festivities to party, New Orleans revs up again in early April for a free community event called the French Quarter Festival where New Orleans jazz and food combine for the touted "world's largest jazz brunch." Zydeco and blues tunes may be found in July at the Lebeau Zydeco Festival; at the late-August Zydeco Dance-Off, Pageant, and Parade at Opelousas; at the St. Martinville Annual Zydeco Festival in early September where one may also enjoy Creole cooking; at the Annual Southwest Louisiana Zydeco Music Festival also in early September and accompanied by good Creole cooking; the Lake Charles Bayou Blues and Zydeco Festival in mid-September; and at the Mamou Zydeco and Blues Festival in early October where alligator and turtle Creole dishes are served. New Orleans hosts the Swamp Festival over two weekends in October as a salute to Louisiana's bayou country, featuring Cajun food, music, and crafts. At the same time in mid-October, Houma welcomes visitors to Downtown on the Bayou, and in late October Opelousas hosts the Louisiana Yambilee Festival.

The beautiful azalea is the adornment at the Hammond Azalea Festival in late March. Covington hosts the Great Louisiana Bird Fest at St. Tammany Parish in mid-April. Old goats and young goats join in the fun and the feast at the Louisiana International Goat Festival at Opelousas in mid-April with a youth market goat show, breeders show, and goat meat cook-off.[23]

MAINE

What is the plural of moose? Visitors might find the answer to that puzzling question at the monthlong Moosemainea event held in Greenville and Rockwood from mid-May to mid-June. Tour De Moose Mountain bike events are part of the fun, which also includes a parade, a canoe race, and craft fairs. Houlton features snowmobiling and a wild game buffet at its Moose Stompers Weekend in February. Speaking of snow, Maine celebrates snow by throwing a party at several events in January and February. Carnivals and festivals are held at Bethel in January and at Kennebunk, Millinocket, Oxford, and Greenville in February and March.

Spring and summer find celebrants near the sea—at Boothbay Harbor at the end of March and first of April for the Fisherman's Festival, again at Boothbay Harbor in June for the Annual Windjammer Days, and at Rockland in June and July enjoying the Annual Great Schooner Race and Schooner Days, respectively. Rockland is also the site, in early August, of what may be Maine's best-known festival, the Maine Lobster Festival. Thousands of lobster dinners are prepared and eaten each day amid such events as the Great Lobster Crate Race, the Maine Seafood Cooking contest, and a lobster-eating contest. For those still possessing a taste for lobster, Winter Harbor

and Biddeford also host lobster festivals in mid-August. Yarmouth hosts the Yarmouth Clam Festival annually in mid-July. Still more foods and flavors provide reasons to celebrate, such as strawberries at festivals in June and July at Wiscasset, Oquossoc, and South Berwick; blueberries at festivals in Wilton, Machias, and Rangeley; and maple syrup at the statewide celebration of Maine Maple Sunday on the last Sunday in March. The long-standing Annual Maine Potato Blossom Festival is held in Fort Fairfield in mid-July for one week, joined later in the summer in late August by the Houlton Potato Feast Days. Applefests, harvest fests, and Oktoberfests are held in October in such places as Nobleboro, Rangeley, Camden, Southwest Harbor, Boothbay, York, and Rumford.

A sampling of other festivals includes the Old Time Fiddler's Contest in Rangeley in early July; the Bar Harbor Downeast Dulcimer and Folk Harp Festival in mid-July; the Annual Maine Festival in early August at Brunswick; and the Annual Topsham Fair in mid-August where high-wire acts and agricultural exhibits provide entertainment and education to celebrants. Maine celebrates French-American culture in late June at the Acadian Festival at Madawaska and at La Kermese Festival at Biddeford. Fiddlers fiddle while folks mingle at the Annual Fiddle Contest and Folk Festival in mid-September at Kennebunk. And finally, Paul Bunyon is alive, well, and tall at the Paul Bunyon Festival Days at Bangor for three days in mid-September.[24]

MARYLAND

Maryland's state sport is jousting and real combat jousting it is at the Maryland Renaissance Festival held from late August to mid-October in Annapolis. The Calvert County Jousting Tournament is an annual event of Port Republic in late August, followed in late September by the Eastern Shore Fall Festival Championship Jousting Tournament in Ridgely.

History and diversity are celebrated at many festivals throughout Maryland, including the Native American Heritage Festival and Pow Wow in early May in Crisfield; the American Indian Inter-Tribal Cultural Organization Pow Wow in Frederick in late June; and the Nause Waiwash Native American Festival in Cambridge in mid-September. Baltimore celebrates Juneteenth with the national sweet potato pie contest, Civil War lectures, blues singers, and underground railroad tours; and Berlin hosts the African-American Heritage Festival during the second week in September. In late April, Celtic music, highland dancing, and storytelling define fun at the Celtic Festival of Southern Maryland held in St. Leonard. For more Celtic music and dancing, the annual McHenry Highland Festival in early June delivers vocal and harp music, bagpipe bands, and highland dancing. Baltimore celebrates the Latino Festival in late June and the St. Demetrios Greek Festival in early October; and Adelphi celebrates the Hispanic Festival in mid-September. Oktoberfests are held in Ocean City, Frederick, and Thurmont; but first, warm up your most comfortable shoes for four days of continuous dancing to polka music in September at the Polkamotion-By-The-Ocean in Ocean City.

Seafood is served up fresh, fried, and steamed as Maryland celebrates the rich bounty of the sea. To name only a few, in August, Crab Days is held in St. Michaels and the Dorchester Chamber Seafood Feast-i-val is held in Cambridge; the entertainment is served at the National Hard Crab Derby and Fair in September in Crisfield when crab racing consumes spectators as crabs are consumed in large quantities. The Preakness Crab Derby in Baltimore in mid-May provides fun and laughter for charity. The Annapolis Rotary Annual Crab Feast is held in early August in Annapolis, where the annual Maryland Seafood Festival is held in September. And oysters are served in November at the OysterFest held in St. Michaels.

The earth yields many gifts celebrated at many festivals. Maryland maple syrup is celebrated in March at the Annual Maple Syrup Heritage Festival where tree tapping, sap boiling, and storytelling accompany maple syrup testing with pancakes and sausages. Colesville, New Market, Sandy Spring, Sykesville, and Thurmont offer tasty strawberries and strawberry wine in May and June celebrations. Maryland wines are celebrated at several wine-tasting festivals, such as the Maryland Wine Festival in Westminster in September, Wine in the Woods in Columbia in mid-May, and the Chesapeake Wine and All That Jazz Celebration in Essex in late June.

The skies are cause for celebration as birders gaze skyward during the Delmarva Birding Weekend held throughout the Eastern Shore in April. At the famous Waterfowl Festival in November, paintings, wood carvings, decoys, sculptures, food, and contests draw visitors each year to Easton, also located on Maryland's Eastern Shore. The annual Decoy, Wildlife Art and Sportsman Festival is held in Havre de Grace in early May.[25]

MASSACHUSETTS

Massachusetts is the place to experience Early American colonial and revolutionary history. In early March, the Boston Massacre is reenacted at the Old State House. The Indian House Memorial 1704 Weekend in Old Deerfield in late February re-creates the early New England cultures represented by Native Americans, French soldiers, and English Puritans. In Boston, the Annual Lantern Celebration on April 18 at the Old North Church recalls Paul Revere's signal to ride. On the next day, Paul Revere's ride is reenacted, as is the Battle of Lexington and Concord. Bunker Hill Day Weekend, a military encampment, takes place in mid-June in Charlestown. The Boston Tea Party is reenacted on December 12.

When the sap rises in late February and early March, the eighteen Massachusetts Audubon Sanctuaries invite visitors to demonstrations on processing sap into syrup. For three days in mid-February craftspeople and cooks invite visitors to a nineteenth-century Shaker village at the Pittsfield Hancock Shaker Village Winter Weekend. Boston, Lowell, and Holyoke celebrate the rich Irish heritage of Massachusetts at parades and at a variety of cultural events during mid-March. The Boston Marathon is the oldest marathon in the United States, stretching over 26.2 miles and attracting spectators and participants to a bracing mid-April race through eight cities and towns. With spring in bloom, Nantucket celebrates its Daffodil Festival toward the end of April, soon followed by a blooming Brewster when houses are open and hot-air balloons take visitors above the spring countryside at the Brewster in Bloom festival. Sandwich celebrates the Dexter Rhododendron Festival at the Heritage Plantation in late May through mid-June.

Many summer and fall events are found near the sea or in celebration of the sea's many bounties. In early June, Hyannis hosts a Blessing of the Fleet at the Hyannis Harbor Festival, and Martha's Vineyard celebrates the Oak Bluffs Harbor Festival. At June's end and into July, Gloucester, Provincetown, Boston, Salem, North Quincy, and Plymouth pay tribute to fishing, sailing, and boating at numerous festivals. For almost a week in mid-August, Fall River welcomes visitors to the Fall River Celebrates America activities that include a Parade of Ships, arts, antiques, food, speed boat races, and fireworks. Gloucester serves up yummy food and entertainment at the Gloucester Waterfront

Festival in mid-August. Treats include a Yankee lobster bake, a pancake breakfast, and entertainment including whale watches. In September, Gloucester is also the site of the Gloucester Schooner Festival where 100-foot schooners compete and everyone enjoys a parade and a fireworks display. In mid-September, Bourne hosts the Bourne Scallop Fest; Essex, the Essex Clamfest; and Martha's Vineyard, the Striped Bass and Bluefish Derby.

Dancing, musical, theatrical, and other cultural events are offered throughout the summer at the Hatch Shell and Harborlights Pavilion in Boston; at Boardinghouse Park in Lowell; at the Great Woods Center for the Performing Arts in Mansfield; at Jacob's Pillow Dance Festival in Becket; at the Williamstown Theatre Festival; and at the Berkshire Theatre Festival in Stockbridge. Italian street festivals are held throughout the summer in Boston and at North Adams during the latter part of June. The Feast of Blessed Sacrament is a large Portuguese feast held in New Bedford at the end of July and into the beginning of August; and Fall River hosts the Great New England Feast of the Holy Ghost, also devoted to the celebration of Portuguese food and culture.

Cranberries are harvested in September and October and celebrated at the Harwich Cranberry Harvest Festival, the Cranberry Harvest Festival at South Carver, and Nantucket's Cranberry Harvest Festival with bog tours and plenty of cranberry treats. Fall is celebrated at festivals throughout Massachusetts including the "Big E," New England's Great Fall Festival in West Springfield; the Westport Harvest Festival; and Thanksgiving Day reenactments.[26]

MICHIGAN

Michigan celebrates its ethnic diversity, major industries, lush flora, and foods in countless events throughout the year. March is a good month for the Clare Irish Festival where celebrants may choose to be warmed by some hearty Irish stew or by dancing an Irish jig. Bagpipes and drums call visitors to Alma for the Alma Highland Festival and Games, which are held every Memorial Day weekend, followed in June by the well-attended Bavarian Festival in Frankenmuth where 50,000 celebrants polka with abandon. Native American powwows, Irish music, and Hispanic, African American, Mexican, Swedish, Polish, and Italian events all mark the Michigan festival landscape. One festival even combines ethnic culture with one of Michigan's primary natural resources at the Paul Bunyon Days and Oktoberfest at Oscoda in mid-September.

Food and industry blend at events such as the late June National Baby Food Festival held in Fremont, the home of the Gerber Products Company. The World's Longest Breakfast Table is set during the second weekend in June at Battle Creek, the self-proclaimed Cereal Capital of the World, when, at least for that day, 60,000 people eat a good breakfast. The Annual Greenfield Village Motor Muster is held in mid-June when over 10,000 car enthusiasts converge on Dearborn, a western suburb of Detroit, to share a love of antique and classic cars and to take in the exhibits at the Henry Ford Museum. Michigan gives thanks at a wide variety of harvests, including the long-running Vermontville Maple Syrup Festival at the end of April and many other similar events in Mason, Lansing, White Lake, Milford, and Kalamazoo. Visitors get their just (strawberry) desserts at the St. Florian Strawberry Festival at Hamtramck in early May. Boyne City gives festivalgoers a chance to exercise and forage for food during the mid-May National Morel Mushroom-Hunting Festival, and Shelby hosts the National Asparagus Festival in mid-June. Michigan cherries are on the menu at the National Cherry Festival in Traverse City

during the first week of July. A no-hands pie-eating contest joins parades, sporting activities, and fireworks at this very popular annual event. For those who wonder what happens with all of those cherry pits, they are in Eau Claire at the International Cherry Pit Spitting Championship. As of 1998, the pit that has been spit the farthest traveled 72 feet, 11 inches. During the second week in August, South Haven hosts the National Blueberry Festival, and in early September, Fairgrove welcomes visitors to the Michigan Bean Festival. Fall harvest celebrations are plentiful and include scarecrow festivals, apple festivals, cider festivals, pumpkin festivals, and even the Appleumpkin Festival in mid-October at Tecumseh. The Great Lakes offer food and entertainment at events such as fishing derbies held in summer and winter alike, the National Trout Festival at Kalkaska held at the end of April, and the Bay Port Fish Sandwich Festival when 10,000 fried fish sandwiches are served along the shores of Lake Huron.

The beauty of Michigan is honored in May during the Tulip Time Festival held in Holland as visitors are treated to spotless streets through which costumed adults and children march in the Volksparade and Kinder Parade. Literally millions of red, yellow, and pink tulip blooms adorn the town and environs for this joyous ten-day event. Muskegon hosts the annual Trillium Festival also in early May, and lilacs welcome summer at the Mackinac Island Lilac Festival. Planted 200 years ago by French missionaries, the lavender and white lilac bushes have grown to tree-size.

Mackinac Bridge is a marvel, spanning five miles between Michigan's Lower and Upper Peninsulas, and every September walkers make a trek across it from St. Ignace to Mackinac City. At the same time, Detroit is jazzing it up at the Ford Montreux Detroit Jazz Festival, considered the largest free jazz festival on the continent. Michigan wine is celebrated at the mid-September Michigan Wine and Harvest Festival at Kalamazoo and Paw Paw. The Red Flannel Festival offers an excellent opportunity to suit up for winter in early October. Once home of the manufacturer of red union suits, Cedar Springs welcomes visitors to compete in the bed race through town.[27,28]

MINNESOTA

Minnesota in January and February may bring to mind many activities but with one theme—the cold winter weather and how to make the best of it. From Duluth to International Falls, winter festivals and winter carnivals are held and include such activities as lutefisk-eating contests, dog sled races, ice dances, ice-carving contests, skiing competitions, and even a beach party. Perhaps the most unusual name for an event is the Freeze Yer Gizzard 10K race held during Icebox Days at International Falls in mid-January. Some of the towns and cities holding winter events are Breezy Point, Red Wing, St. Paul, Cannon Falls, Hibbing, Chisholm, Ely, Palisade, Aurora, Winona, Zimmerman, Apple Valley, Nisswa, and Detroit Lakes.

Festivals celebrating the rich and diverse ethnic populations of Minnesota are numerous. Scandinavian festivals include the celebration of the Finnish St. Urho's Day in March at Finlayson, and Norwegian festivals in May at Hendricks, Milan, Wahkon, Spring Grove, Willmar, and Starbuck. Scandinavian festivals held in June, including midsummer festivals, include the Nisswa Scandinavian Fiddling Festival, the Embarrass Summer Finnish Festival, the Minneapolis Midsommar Celebration, the Bemidji Swedish Midsummer Festival, the Moorhead Scandinavian Hjemkomst Festival, the Scandia Midsommar Dag, and the Minneapolis Svenskarnas Dag. Chisholm celebrates the Festival Finlandia in late July, and Elbow Lake is the home of the early August Flek-

kefest. For those with the taste and fortitude for it, Madison offers an excellent opportunity for eating one's fill of lutefisk at the mid-November Norsefest Celebration. But many ethnic backgrounds are celebrated throughout the year. These festivals include the early-May Festival of Nations at St. Paul; the Winona Pow-Wow, which is a traditional American Indian gathering; the Cinco de Mayo Fiesta held at St. Paul; and the mid-May World Festival at Rochester. June events include the White Earth Pow-Wow, the International Polka Fest at Chisholm, and Sauerkraut Days at Henderson. In July, Seaforth hosts the Polka Fest-Plus, Montgomery welcomes visitors to the Czech Kolacky Days, and New Ulm hosts the German Heritagefest. Continuing into late July and throughout August a variety of cultures are recalled including the Viennese Sommerfest at Minneapolis, the Rosemount Leprechaun Days, Silver Lake's Pola-Czesky Days, Berne's Swissfest, Ivanhoe's Polska Kielbasa Days, McGregor's Polka Fest, the St. Paul Minnesota Irish Heritage Fair, and Chisholm's All Slav Days. In July and September, Red Wing and Mankato, respectively, host powwows. For over a week in mid-September, Bloomington hosts the Experience India Event. Oktoberfests are held in Baudette, Frazee, Lanesboro, and Madison. In late December, the American Swedish Institute at Minneapolis hosts the Julgladje Christmas Celebration.

The culture of the Wild West is the focal point of the Zimmerman Wild West Days and rodeo held in late May. Fur trader rendezvous events are held in May at Jackson's Fort Belmont, in September at Rochester, at Albert Lea in early October, and at Onamia in late November. The land and the harvesting of the land are reasons to come together and learn about the agriculture and lumber industries. Stillwater celebrates Lumberjack Days in late July. In early August, Grand Rapids celebrates the Tall Timber

Days Festival with lumberjack shows and chain saw–carving demonstrations, followed also in August by the Hanley Falls Pioneer Power Threshing Show, Miltona's Rose City Threshing Festival, and Nowthen's Threshing Show. Logging and threshing shows are held later in August and in September at Elk River, Rollag, Finlayson, Strathcona, Atwater, Butterfield, Verndale, Donnelly, and Argyle. The dairy industry is highlighted during the Pine Island Cheese Festival, the Waseca Spring Festival and Dairy Days, and the New Ulm Dairy Day, all in June. Many festivals are centered on corn where visitors are provided with corn on the cob and buttered corn including Moose Lake's Crazy Corn Days, Cokato's Corn Festival, the Backus Corn Fest, Plainview's Corn on the Cob Festival, and Sleepy Eye's Buttered Corn Day, all in August. In July, Olivia hosts Corn Capital Days, and in September, Shakopee hosts the Green Giant Annual Corn Feast. Potato golf, potato billiards, and mashed potato–wrestling events are held and, hopefully, a lot of potatoes are consumed at the Barnesville Potato Days held in late August. Wild rice festivals are held in September at Tower and Onamia. Minnesota Lake is the home of the Festag Festival of Agriculture in mid-July. Maple-sugaring events are held in March in St. Paul, Richfield, Albert Lea, Chanhassen, and in May in Pine City.

Art, music, and dance are central to many festivals in Minnesota. St. Paul hosts the mid-February Scottish Ramble Highland dance competition. At July's end, Ely is the site of the Blueberry Art Festival, and in August, Minneapolis plays host to a large juried art show called the Uptown Art Fair. Also in August, Zimmerman hosts the Bluegrass and Old-Time Music Festival. Minnesota celebrates its famous at the Judy Garland Festival held in late June at her hometown of Grand Rapids and at the Pioneer Festival held in July at the Laura Ingalls Wilder home-

site on the banks of Plum Creek. Finally, visitors are encouraged to look to the skies at the Winona Eagle Watch in early March and, throughout May, at the Odessa Big Stone Bird Festival, the Detroit Lakes Festival of Birds, and the International Falls Birder's Spring Rendezvous. In June Gunflint Trail hosts the Boreal Birding Days event.[29–31]

MISSISSIPPI

Mississippi recalls its early history with two events in April at Ocean Springs. In early April, the Fort Maurepas Living History Weekend delivers many events and reenactments of the early lives of settlers and Native Americans. For three days in late April, the beach landing of French explorer Pierre Lemoyne Sieur d'Iberville in 1699 is reenacted. At the end of October, the 1830 Treaty of Dancing Rabbit Creek is recalled in Macon at the Dancing Rabbit Festival. This treaty opened Choctaw lands to white settlers. Beauvoir, Jefferson Davis's last home in Biloxi, is the scene of the Fall Muster in mid-October, in which Mississippi's role in preparing for the Civil War is emphasized. Antebellum architecture remains resplendent in Natchez and other Mississippi towns and cities. Homes, gardens, and historic landmarks are all part of many pilgrimages throughout March, April, and September when visitors are often greeted by costumed guides at Natchez, Vicksburg, Brookhaven, Port Gibson, Columbus, Aberdeen, Holly Springs, and all along the Mississippi Gulf Coast. The Civil War Battle of Corinth is reenacted in early October when over 2,000 visitors participate in this two-day event on foot, in wagons, and on horses. Native American culture is celebrated in late March at the Natchez Powwow at the Grand Village of the Natchez Indians, at the Choctaw Indian Fair in mid-July at Philadelphia, and at the Pioneer and Indian Festival in Ridgeland in mid-October. The Vaiden/Kosciusko

Spring Roundup and Fall Trail Ride provide plenty of fresh air, cookouts, and entertainment along the trail.

Music is one of Mississippi's enduring legacies with some festivals celebrated twice a year. To name a few, Kosciusko is the site of the Natchez Trace Festival and Fiddler's Jamboree in mid-April; Meridian invites guests to the Jimmie Rodgers Memorial Country Music Festival in late May; and Smithville honors Grand Ole Opry star Rod Brasfield in late August at the festival that bears his name. Bluegrass is enjoyed at the Magnolia State Bluegrass Festival in Wiggins in both the spring and the fall. Meridian is the home of the Sandy Ridge Spring and Fall Bluegrass Festivals held in May and September. At the end of May, the Atwood Music Festival in Monticello includes a variety of musical genres including bluegrass, gospel, and country, as well as opportunities to enjoy arts and crafts, hot-air balloon races, and fireworks. The Longhorn Bluegrass Festival is held in mid-September at Bay Springs. But Mississippi's claim to being the "Birthplace of the Blues" is remembered at several special events, such as the Natchez Bluff Blues Fest in mid-April; the Mississippi Gulf Coast Blues Festival in mid-September at Biloxi; the Sunflower River Blues and Gospel Festival in Clarksdale in early August; and the Mississippi Delta Blues and Heritage Festival, which is touted as one of the largest music festivals in the South held in Greenville in September.

Mississippi has its share of food extravaganzas where it feasts on the riches of the land and sea. Broilers are broiled, fried, barbecued, and shish-kabobed at the Mississippi Broiler Festival in Forest in early June. The Mississippi Pecan Festival, held in Richton in late September, includes a beauty contest, a mule pull, a talent show, and bluegrass and gospel music. The Biloxi Oyster Festival is held in mid-March, and Greenville hosts the Leland Crawfish Festival in early May where cajun food and crawfish are on the menu. The Fourth of July Crab Festival is held in Bay St. Louis. For three days in September, Biloxi hosts the Biloxi Seafood Festival, and Gautier hosts its Mullet Festival in mid-October with a special-event mullet toss. If barbecue is your poison or your passion, Jackson invites you to go Hog Wild in mid-June; Columbus provides ample barbecue and storytelling at its September Possum Town Pigfest; and the Clarksdale Delta Jubilee and Mississippi State Championship Pork Barbecue delivers three days of barbecue, cooking contests, and music to chew to in early June. Watermelons are celebrated at the Water Valley Watermelon Festival in early August and at the Mize Watermelon Festival at the end of July with a number of wacky competitions involving seed spitting and greased watermelons. Other edible causes for celebration include the Blueberry Festival in Poplarville in mid-June, the Muscadine Jubilee in Pelahatchie in mid-September, and the Crystal Springs Tomato Festival at the end of June.

Diverse ethnic and cultural backgrounds are highlighted at several festivals. The Scottish Heritage Festival is held in Jackson in mid-August, where the Celtic Fest is held in mid-September. Oktoberfests are held in Heidelberg, Olive Branch, and Biloxi; and Biloxi hosts its Highlands and Islands Scottish Games and Celtic Festival during the first weekend in October. African American culture is celebrated at the Juneteenth Celebration in Biloxi, and Dr. Martin Luther King, Jr.'s life is celebrated in mid-January in Jackson and Biloxi.

For the serious party goers, Mardi Gras parades and balls abound in Gautier, Natchez, Long Beach, Ocean Springs, and Biloxi. Cajun and zydeco music, country music, and crawfish bring enjoyment to visitors of the Biloxi Coliseum Country Cajun Crawfish Festival in mid-April. Numerous hot-air balloon festivals and contests are held in Mississippi, including the Balloon Fest in Greenwood during the early part of June, the Mississippi International Balloon Classic and Airshow in Greenville in late June, and the annual Great Mississippi River Balloon Race in Natchez in mid-October.

William Faulkner fans can soak in southern culture during a week of lectures, discussions, and dramatic readings at the Annual Faulkner and Yoknapatawpha Conference in Oxford during the last week in July, while Tennessee Williams fans converge on Clarksville for similar activities in mid-October at the Tennessee Williams Festival. Can't have Faulkner and Williams without kudzu. During three hot days in July, Holly Springs celebrates at the Kudzu Festival with a carnival, talent shows, and a barbecue cooking contest.[32]

MISSOURI

Missouri celebrates its history and heritage by remembering its days as the gateway to the West with Santa-Cali-Gon Days in Independence early in September, which celebrates the Santa Fe, California, and Oregon trails. Many events throughout the year create a classroom for the whole family with reenactments, demonstrations, and exhibits, such as the Lexington Heritage Days in late June, the 1800's Trade Show and Pioneer Days in Defiance, and the Annual Frisco Days Historical Festival at Springfield in April. Lewis and Clark Heritage Days takes place in St. Charles in mid-May. The Civil War Battle of Athens Reenactment occurs at Revere in early August, and Trails West! is held at St. Joseph in mid-August. Native American celebrations include the Annual American Indian Center Pow Wow in St. Louis in late March, the Missouri State Pow Wow in Sedalia in mid-July, and the Native American Pow Wow at Moberly in mid-September, to name a few. Learning continues as summertime brings chautaquas in

Lexington, Columbia, Carthage, and Chillicothe.

Rodeos and horse shows are frequent in Missouri, starting with the Longhorn World Championship Rodeo in Cape Girardeau at the end of February and continuing with rodeos in June and July at Kirksville, Carrollton, Odessa, Caledonia, Kennett, Perry, Kansas City, Warsaw, and Savannah. The Annual Western Horse Show at Farmington is held in May, and the Missouri State Championship Racking Horse Show is held at Dexter in early June.

The arts are the highlight of festivals throughout the state. A sampling includes Artsfest at the beginning of May in Springfield, the Annual Mayfest Arts and Crafts Fair at Mountain Grove in mid-May, the River Arts Festival in Hannibal in late May, the Annual Fulton Art Festival in mid-June, the Missouri River Festival of the Arts held during two weekends in mid-August at Boonville, and Watercolor USA from early in June through July when over 1,000 watercolors are entered into competition at Springfield.

Fishing is big business and big sport to countless participants in competitions and at festivals, including Osage Beach's Operation Bass, a four-day fishing tournament in March; the Opening Day celebration in March at Roaring River in Cassville where men, women, and youth are awarded prizes for the largest fish caught; the Spring Fishing Classic and Tracker Legends Tournament where top fishermen and women compete for a grand prize of $150,000 at Springfield in mid-March; and the Spring Trout Derby in Cassville in early April.

The earth yields beauty and food, both celebrated at shows and festivals. The Annual St. Louis Flower Show is held in early January, followed by the Flower, Lawn and Garden Show in early February at Kansas City. West Plains hosts the Home and Garden Show in early March. Camdenton celebrates the Annual Dogwood Festival in mid-April, and over 2,500 varieties of iris are showcased at the Iris Festival in May at Gower. Independence celebrates the Annual Farm and Flower Festival on the first of May; Bridgeton, the Annual Strawberry Festival in early June; and East Prairie, the Annual Sweet Corn Festival and Fourth of July Celebration in June and early July.

Missouri loves music, all types and in many places throughout the year. It is celebrated at the Winter Bluegrass Festival at Hannibal in mid-February; at the Big Muddy Folk Festival at Boonville in April; in Kirksville and Steelville at bluegrass festivals in mid-May; and at the Mid-American Old Time Fiddling Championship at Bethel, the St. Louis Ragtime Festival, the Springfield Country Music Festival, the Heart of the Ozarks Bluegrass Association Festival at West Plains, and the Old-Time Music Ozark Heritage Festival at West Plains, all in June. July musical festivals include the Kansas City Blues and Jazz Festival in mid-July and the Annual Sam A. Baker Bluegrass Festival in late July at Patterson. St. Louis is the home of the Annual Big Muddy Blues and Roots Festival in September.

Missouri offers something for almost everyone. For the young at heart, Hannibal offers the Annual Farm Toy Show in late February. Groundhog Day finds Kansas City hosting underground 10K and 5K runs at the Ground Hog Run. Hot-air balloon races are held in September at Brookfield and St. Louis. The Springfield Symphony offers a synchronized performance with the Fire Fall fireworks show in late June. At the end of June, over 15,000 Honda Gold Wing motorcycle riders roar into Springfield for a four-day Gold Wing Road Riders Association Annual "Wing Ding." Steamboats race the Mississippi at Cape Girardeau in early July at the Great Steamboat Race. Mark Twain would not approve. But he might approve of the National Tom Sawyer Days

in Hannibal from July 1 to July 4 when the competitions involve fence painting and frog jumping. Other festivals unique to Missouri include the St. Joseph Pony Express–Jesse James Weekend in early April, the Emmett Kelly Clown Festival at Houston in late April and early May, the Scott Joplin Ragtime Festival during the first week in June at Sedalia, and the world-famous barbecue of Kansas City at the Annual Royal BBQ Contest in early October.

Ethnicity is celebrated throughout Missouri at German, Latin American, Japanese, Hispanic, African American, and Polish festivals, including the International Folkfest held in St. Louis in mid-October when seventy ethnic groups are celebrated with food, dance, costumes, and crafts. St. Louis hosts a number of such festivals in June and September, and Kansas City plays host in August and September.[33]

MONTANA

Other than the Perch Derby at Townsend in late January and the Northern Rodeo Association Finals at Billings in early February, Montana's winter months are taken up for the most part by winter carnivals. Participants can play snow volleyball, ice skate, compete in snowboard contests, take free bobsled and sleigh rides, ice fish, or even run in sled dog races from January to March. Such events include the Whitefish Winter Carnival, the Frost Fever Winterfest at Missoula, the Snowboard Jams at Missoula and Neihart, the Lakeside Annual Winterfest, the Glasgow Ice Fishing Tournament, the Race to the Sky Sled Dog Race at Helena, the Winter Carnival at Red Lodge, and the Annual Snow Rodeo and Spring Ski Race at Essex.

Rodeos dominate the summer season when they are either the main attraction or part of other fairs. Culbertson's Frontier Days, Forsyth's Rodeo Days, Livingston's

Western Days and Rodeo, and the Upper Yellowstone Roundup Gardiner Rodeo are just a few held in June, with others in Wilsall, Roy, Big Timber, Augusta, and Opheim. Fourth of July celebrations are just some of the places where rodeos are held in July. Towns and cities from Ennis to Hinsdale, Big Sky, Butte, Drummond, Three Forks, Hamilton, Richey, Eureka, East Helena, Hardin, Polson, and Lewistown roll out the red carpet with a wide array of activities such as bullriding, barrel racing, and calf roping. August rodeos and county fairs are held in Sidney, Boulder, Dillon, Plains, Superior, Twin Bridges, Ronan, Missoula, Havre, Broadus, and Townsend. It is bull that is found at the NILE Bull Riders Invitational at Billings in early April and at the Annual Big Timber Bull-a-Rama at Big Timber in mid-May. Horses are featured at the Horse Fair in Bozeman in April, at the Hamilton Bitterroot Horse and Mule Expo in early May, and at the Big Sky Classic and Derby at Billings in June. Yet another equine event is held in June when Drummond hosts Montana Mule Days.

Old-timer's festivals, Wild West days, western heritage days, historical reenactments, and pioneer days are plentiful throughout June, July, and August. Events might include threshing machine exhibits, shoot-outs and gun-slinging contests, rodeos, barbecues, gold panning, storytelling, and western dancing, to name just a few. In April, Cut Bank hosts the Annual Story Telling Roundup. In June, Malta welcomes visitors to the Lewis and Clark Encampment, followed by the Homesteader Days Celebration at Hot Springs; Virginia City's Gold Rush Fever Day; Lewistown's Pioneer Power Day Threshing Bee; the Fort Union Rendezvous; Custer's Last Stand Reenactment at Hardin; Poplar's Wild West Days; Stevensville's Western Days; and the Lewis and Clark Festival at Great Falls. In July, Scobey, Deer Lodge, Jackson, Columbia Falls, Huntley, Bannack, and Virginia City all host festivals celebrating western culture. Western events continue from late July into August and September with such events as Cut Bank's Lewis and Clark Days Festival, the Red Lodge Mountain Man Rendezvous, Bigfork's Wild West Day, and Chinook's Western Days. Threshing bees are held in Huntley, Choteau, and Culbertson. Considered the largest event in Montana, the MontanaFair, held at Billings for a week in mid-August, entertains over 225,000 visitors annually with concerts, food, rodeos, and a carnival.

Native American activities include many powwows and rodeos, such as the Buffalo Feast and Pow-wow at St. Ignatius in mid-May; the Annual Northern American Indian Days at Browning in early July, where Blackfeet Tribal culture is celebrated; and the Standing Arrow Pow Wow at Elmo and Fort Belknap's Milk River Indian Days also in July. In August, Rocky Boy's Annual Pow Wow is held. September events include Poplar's Indian Days in early September and the North American Indian Alliance Pow Wow at Butte in mid-September. Other cultural and ethnic celebrations in Montana include the Germanfest at Missoula and the Laurel Herbstfest in mid-September, as well as Oktoberfests in Livingston, Polson, Superior, and Anaconda. In early August, Billings plays host to the two-day Annual Hispanic Fiesta.

Montana celebrates nature with sport, food, and fun at many diverse events throughout the year. Walleye tournaments are held at Big Sandy in June, Townsend in July, and Fort Peck and Lewistown in August. Seeley Lake and Bigfork are the sites of the Loon and Fish Festival and the Bigfork Whitewater Festival in late June. Logging is spotlighted at Stumptown Days in mid-May and at Libby Logger Days in mid-July. Moiese holds the annual National Bison Range Birthday Celebration to commemorate the establishment of the National Bison Range on May 23, 1908. In July, the great blue skies of Montana are the venue for hot-air balloons at the Billings Big Skyfest and for skydiving in Marion at the Skydive Lost Prairie Annual Jump Meet. The state flower of Montana, the bitterroot, is cause for celebration at the Annual Bitterroot Days in late June at Hamilton. Huckleberry festivals are held in August at Trout Creek, Swan Lake, and Whitefish, followed by the Montana State Chokecherry Festival at Lewistown in mid-September. Perhaps not appetizing to think about but apparently tasty to some, Rocky Mountain oysters are on the menu at the Mission Mountain Testicle Festival at Charlo in June and at the Clinton Testicle Festival in September. Beginning in late October and continuing into December, Helena is visited by bald eagles, there to feed on spawning salmon. This is a prime opportunity for visitors to appreciate this great natural resource and symbol of national pride.

Arts and music round out the kaleidoscope of Montana activities. Miles City is the home of the Annual Juried Exhibit in late February through mid-March; the Billings Annual Art Auction is held in mid-March; and the Annual Spring Art and Craft Show is held at Helena in mid-April. The International Wildlife Film Festival is held for one week in mid-April at Missoula. Hamilton invites bluegrass lovers to the mid-July Bitterroot Valley Bluegrass Festival. The Annual Festival of the Arts is held in Bigfork in early August, followed in mid-August by poetry and western music at the Montana Cowboy Poetry Gathering at Lewistown.[34]

NEBRASKA

Nebraska is proud of its early settlers, and many of the festivals and fairs celebrated throughout the year feature some aspect of early life in the state. These include a wide range and number of ethnic events, rodeos, barbecues, pioneer days, powwows, old threshers' reunions, and quilt shows. In late February, the World's Toughest Rodeo at Lincoln begins a year of rodeos. The Mexican Rodeo is held in Kearney in early April, as well as mid-June. Also in mid-June, North Platte hosts the Buffalo Bill Rodeo and Norfolk hosts the Norfolk Rodeo. Nebraska's Big Rodeo in Burwell in late July boasts a professional rodeo, as well as chuck wagon races, a dinner bell derby, and clown bullfighting. During July and August and into September, many rodeos are held as part of county fairs. These include fairs in Madison, Pawnee City, David City, Stockville, Albion, North Platte, Kearney, Sidney, Ogallala, and Valentine.

Fairmont is the site of the Old Settler's Picnic at the end of May. Pioneer days and similar events are held in Palisade, Callaway, Winside, and North Bend in June. The state tree of Nebraska, the cottonwood, provides the cause for celebration at the mid-June Cottonwood Prairie Festival at Hastings. The Annual Old Settler's Picnic is held at Western in early July, followed by the Pawnee Pioneer Panorama at Pawnee City, the Camp Creek Threshers Show at Waverly, and Wagon Train Days at Benkelman, all in July. Minden hosts Pioneer Farming Days in late August. Gothenburg and Petersburg host antique tractor shows and related events in late August highlighting early pioneer days and early harvests. In mid-September, the Old Time Threshers Bee is celebrated at Pierce. Cowboys may shed a tear or two during poetry readings at the Valentine Old West Days, powwow, quilt show, and barbecue held during the end of September and into mid-October. Old Man River Days at Peru provide such entertainment as face painting and a carnival, while a quilt show, rodeo, and cowboy poetry readings may be found during Nebraskaland Days at North Platte; both celebrations are held in June. Chili and barbecue may be enjoyed at chili cook-offs at Arapahoe in February, at Arnold in March, and at Lincoln at the Annual Capital City Ribfest in mid-August.

Quilt shows are frequent in Nebraska. To name a few, Vogie's Annual Quilt Show is held in Dodge for almost a week at the beginning of February, the Clay Center Annual Quilt Show is held over two weekends in early February; the Bellevue Quilt Show is held in June and July; the Seasons of Our Lives Quilt Show is held at Lincoln in mid-June; and the Annual Nimble Thimble Quilt Show is hosted at Aurora in late June.

Arts and craft fairs begin in the spring and continue throughout the year. The Omaha Spring Festival: An Arts and Crafts Affair is held in early April, followed later in April by the Annual Art and Craft Show at Lincoln and in May by the Spring Festival of Crafts at Norfolk.

Among Nebraska's many ethnic festivals are the Annual Irish Festival at Norfolk in late March; Czech festivals from May through August in Lincoln, Hastings, Clarkson, and Wilber; and Swedish festivals in June at Stromsburg and Holdrege. Loup City celebrates Polish Days in mid-June. Danneborg hosts the Danish festival, Grundlovsfest, in early June. Germanfests are held in Fairbury, Syracuse, and Grand Island; and an Oktoberfest is held at Sidney. One last chance to engage in an energetic polka can be had at the Annual Czechlanders Polka Fest at Grand Island in mid-October.

From the serene to the silly to the romantic, other Nebraska events include January's Grand Island Bald Eagle Tour and Avoca's Quack-off when festivalgoers race ducks on ice. In late February the Annual Spring Orchid Show is held at Omaha, and the Crane Watch and Spring Migration is observed at Kearney in March and April. Wildflower Days is celebrated at Hastings from mid-May to late-May, and the Valentine's Day Celebration is held in Valentine, of course, where the King and Queen of Hearts are crowned. Madison offers Days of Swine and Roses in early June, and a divot takes on a whole new meaning at Lawrence during the annual Cow Chip Open golf tournament in mid-June.[35,36]

NEVADA

Nevada's fairs, festivals, and events celebrate the history, cultural heritage, and natural resources of the state. A wide variety of rodeos, powwows, competitions, and carnivals offer plenty of opportunities to learn about the many cultures that built and comprise the special essence of the state of Nevada. In late January events get underway with the Cowboy Poetry Gathering in Elko. Hawthorne is the site of the Walker Lake Fishing Derby in mid-February, and March brings the Snowfest Winter Carnival where numerous outdoor activities include a chilling polar bear swim, ice-carving, and snow-sculpting activities. March ends and April begins with the Invitational Native American Arts Festival in Henderson, followed by the Clark County Fair and Rodeo in Logandale. The Annual Henderson Heritage Days include a picnic, talent show, chili cook-off, carnival, and recreational activities for over a week in mid-April. Other April events include the Topaz Lake Chili Cook-Off and Craft Fair, the Annual Fly Fishing Festival at Minden, and the Loon Festival at Walker Lake. During May, Wendover and Virginia City host Cinco de Mayo celebrations with arts and crafts, music, and a chili cook-off. The Silver State Square and Round Dance Festival is held at Reno in early May, and May concludes with the Snow Mountain Powwow at the Paiute Indian Reservation and the Portuguese Festival and Parade at Lovelock. Railroad Days in Beatty, the Yerington Portuguese Celebration, Ely's Model Train Expo and Long Steel Rail Festival, and the Quinn River Father's Day Open Rodeo bring spring to a close.

Rodeos continue in full swing with the Reno Rodeo in mid-June, the Fourth of July Powwow and Rodeo in Owyhee, and the Silver State International Rodeo and the Fallon All-Indian Rodeo and Powwow both at Fallon in mid-July. The National Basque Festival in late June and early July at Elko includes games, dances, and skill and strength competitions. July concludes with the Lovelock Frontier Days, the Valhalla Brews and Blues Festival, and the Goldfield Days, the latter including gold panning, a parade, a 10K run, and a chili cook-off. Historical and cultural themes continue in August with the Northern Nevada Living History Festival at Fernley that includes a Civil War encampment, rodeo, powwow, and mountain man rendevous. In mid-August, Yerington hosts the Lyon County Fair and Rodeo and the Spirit of Wovoka Days Powwow in late August.

Good eating marks the beginning of September at Fallon's Hearts of Gold Cantaloupe Festival, the Best in the West Nugget Rib Cook-Off at Sparks, and the Annual Corn Feed at Jarbidge. The wide-open skies above Reno's Rancho San Rafael Park are home to the Great Reno Balloon Race, an event that attracts over 100,000 spectators. Reno is the site, also in September, for the National Championship Air Races and the Sierra Folklife Festival. Mid-September provides other opportunities for entertainment including the Dayton Valley Days and Rodeo, the Pahrump Harvest Festival and Rodeo, and the Las Vegas Street Fair/San Gennaro Feast. September concludes with the Annual Tahoe Donner International Wheelchair Tennis Sectional Championship. October events include the Great Italian Festival at Reno, the Las Vegas Basque Festival, the Elko Te-Moak Powwow, and Beatty's Burro Races where packing for vacation is nothing compared to packing and unpacking

an unmotivated burro. North Las Vegas is the gathering place for aspiring cowboy poets, Western music entertainers, hot-air balloonists, artists, and craftspeople in early November. At the same time, Minden provides a chance to perform tales of the early West at the Rhymer's Rodeer Cowboy Poetry event. Overton, home of the Anasazi Indians, hosts Festival Americana in early November where crafts of Native Americans and pioneers are part of the celebration. The National Finals Rodeo is held in Las Vegas for over a week in early December, a fitting conclusion to a year about to begin all over again with the Elko Cowboy Poetry Gathering.[37]

NEW HAMPSHIRE

New Hampshire is premier ski country with numerous winter events that include activities for skiers and non-skiers alike. During January and February at Bretton Woods, New London, North Sutton, Lincoln, Sandwich, Berlin, Grantham, East Madison, Franconia, and Tamworth, snow and ice become the instruments of fun at ice harvests, winterfests, winter carnivals, snowshoe fests, sled dog races, ice-sculpting competitions, sleigh rides, and other events. When the first hint of spring is in the air, Littleton welcomes folks to Cabin Fever Weekend for an auction, chili cook-off, and celebrity pancake breakfast, and Gorham springs for an annual Spring Fever BBQ at the end of March. March also brings maple-sugaring festivals at Tamworth, Barrington, and Lincoln. Long winter months also yield a strong appreciation for crafts and quilts. There is the Salem Spring Craft Festival in mid-March, the Annual New England Craft and Specialty Food Fair in Farmington also in mid-March, the July Bow Street Fair at Portsmouth, and numerous quilt shows. May finds lilacs blooming during Lisbon's New Hampshire Annual Lilac Festival. June brings catamarans and their energetic owners out for the Annual Hampton Beach Hobie Cat Regatta; and later in June, trout fishing is on the agenda during a three-day fishing tournament on the Moore Dam Lake at Littleton. In July, visitors look to the skies during the Hillsborough Balloon Festival and Fair. It's back to Hampton Beach in mid-September for the Annual Seafood Festival and Sidewalk Sales.

Antique fairs are plentiful, such as the Annual Wolfeboro Antiques Fair in late July and the early-August New England Antique and Collectible Festival at Hopkinton, which is considered the largest antique fair in New Hampshire. In mid-August, Manchester hosts the New Hampshire Antique Dealers Association Annual Show. Folk music and woodworking are combined during Wood Days at Canterbury during late June, and Newbury hosts the Annual League of New Hampshire Craftsmen Fair in early to mid-August. County and agricultural fairs highlight the importance of agriculture to the economy of the state and the state's diversity. For two days in mid-May, New Boston celebrates the New Hampshire Sheep and Wool Festival with sheepdog trials and a lamb barbecue. Cornish hosts the Cornish Fair in mid-August, and Sandwich hosts a country fair for three days in mid-October.

New Hampshire's history, diversity, and love of music are celebrated at many events. In mid-February, North Conway hosts a large indoor powwow and gathering during the Annual Mountain Valley Mall Pow Wow. Keene hosts the Annual Monadnock Valley Indian Festival and Pow Wow in mid-June. The Exeter Revolutionary War Festival in mid-July includes reenactments, music, and food. Campton is the site of the Pemi Valley Bluegrass Festival in early August, and Portsmouth is home to the mid-August Portsmouth Blues Festival. Waterville Valley hosts the Italian Fest and Duck Race annually in early September.[38,39]

NEW JERSEY

The warmth of spring takes citizens of the Garden State outside to celebrate. In mid-April, Morristown hosts the New Jersey Daffodil Show, followed in late April by the Cape May Tulip and Garden Festival. In late May, Bordentown welcomes guests to the Annual Iris Festival and Art Show. Ocean City plays host to the Ocean City Flower Show during early June. During the fall, the New Jersey State Chrysanthemum Society's Annual Show and Sale is held at Morris Township. The dead of winter is alive at Edison, when in February the Flower and Garden Show of New Jersey brings visitors inside, and it all begins again in the spring.

Foods of all types are cause for jubilation with some produced from the soil and some from the sea. In June, there are strawberries at Bridgeton and Chester, and in August Bridgeton offers peaches to visitors. Chatsworth celebrates the Cranberry Festival with food, family entertainment, and bog tours in October. Hayrides and pumpkin picking provide entertainment at the Windsor Farm Pumpkin Festival at West Windsor in mid-October. New Jersey wines may be sampled at Stanhope in late May during the Spring Wine Festival and again in the fall at the Garden State Wine Grower's Fall Wine and Cheese Classic. Seafood festivals are plentiful from late spring to early fall at such places as Atlantic City, North Wildwood, Belman, and Tuckerton in June; at Brant Beach in July; and at Point Pleasant and Beach Haven in September and October. In early August, Ocean City hosts a special treat for hermit crabs and their fans when it hosts the Miss Crustacean Hermit Crab Beauty Pageant. Not only beauty, but speed, are rewarded at the hermit crab beauty contest and the hermit crab races.

Back on land, Augusta is the home of the Garden State Horse Show in May, where in August it also hosts the Sussex County Farm and Horse Show. In between is the New Jersey State Fair at Cherry Hill held in late July and early August. Crafts, antique, and art shows are numerous. To mention a few, Stanhope hosts the late-May Waterloo Antiques Fair, followed in June by the Tom's River Summer Sampler of Arts and Crafts, the Allentown Annual Antiques and Collectible Auction, and Cranford's Spring Fine Art and Crafts at Nomahegan Park event. Stone Harbor welcomes around 350 artists and crafters to its annual Art and Crafts Show in early August, and also in early August, Bay Head hosts St. Paul's Annual Antiques Show and Sale. Other events featuring the handiwork of crafters are held in North Wildwood, Cape May, Chester, Burlington, Morristown, and Nutley.

Music is the focal point at several popular events with several towns and cities presenting concerts throughout the summer. Jazz brings lively entertainment to festivalgoers at the Cape May Jazz Festival in mid-April and at the Annual Asbury Park Jazz Festival in late June. Also in late June is the Metuchen Street Fair and Jazz Festival. Summer concerts may be enjoyed at Sandy Hook, North Wildwood, Red Bank, Long Beach, Jersey City, and Eastampton. The Riverfest is held in June at Red Bank where jazz, food, crafts, and river cruises provide a little something for everyone.

New Jersey celebrates its rich ethnic and cultural diversity at many festivals throughout the year. In May, Bridgeton and East Rutherford celebrate Cinco de Mayo. African American festivals are held at Middletown in January, at Montclair and Lincroft in June, at Trenton in August, and at Holmdel in September. Italian festivals are held in Holmdel and North Wildwood in June and at East Rutherford and Hoboken in September. Irish festivals are held at Holmdel in June and at North Wildwood and Stanhope in September. Jersey City hosts the Annual Chinese Culture Day in mid-May. The Fes-

tival Latino Americano is hosted by Atlantic City in mid-September. The American Pow Wow and Western Festival is held in August at Budd Lake, and the American Indian Arts Festival is held in Westampton. Holmdel celebrates the New Jersey Ethnic and Diversity Festival in late September when annually it recognizes the many ethnic and diverse groups that make New Jersey a culturally rich state.

Finally, several additional events draw visitors for all kinds of nourishment of the body and soul. Tom's River provides some spice at the Annual New Jersey State Chili and Salsa Cook Off in May, and North Wildwood offers good eating at the New Jersey State Barbecue Championship in early July. Atlantic City provides the cooling sea breezes required to deliver maximum pleasure at concerts, sporting events, dances, and meals during the Beach Fest in mid-June. Readington welcomes balloonists and spectators to the QuickChek New Jersey Festival of Ballooning in late July.[40–42]

NEW MEXICO

New Mexico offers a wide variety of carnivals, festivals, and events, from powwows to balloon rallies to wine festivals to lizard races. From the ridiculous to the sublime and inspirational, visitors to these events find fun and enrichment throughout the year. Beginning in January, balloonists and balloon watchers may attend the Mesilla Valley Balloon Rally at Las Cruces, followed in late February by the Hot-Air Balloon Festival and Snowmobile Chase at Chama, and the St. Patrick's Day Balloon Rally in March at Los Lunas. The world-renowned Kodak Albuquerque International Balloon Fiesta during the first week in October attracts over 900 balloonists and enthusiastic observers of many events and competitions. For those unsure of what they see in the evening skies, the UFO Encounter in Roswell in early July provides opportunities to dress like aliens, attend a UFO lecture series, attend concerts, and enjoy laser light shows. Several events feature food and drink, including the Winter Wine Festival held for a week in mid-January at Taos Ski Valley, the New Mexico Wine and Chile War Festival at the end of May in Las Cruces, and the New Mexico Wine Festival in Bernalillo in early September. Early September is a good time to eat chili and lots of it at the Annual Bean Day at Wagon Mound and the Hatch Chile Festival where games, contests, and arts and crafts are enjoyed along with a variety of chili concoctions. The United Way CASI Chili Cook-off in Hobbs in early October provides yet another opportunity for good eating.

Musical concerts, stargazing, wildlife festivals, and winter carnivals represent a range of activities New Mexicans and their visitors enjoy. To name a few events, February begins with the Winter Carnival at Taos Ski Valley, followed by Mardi Gras in the Mountains at Red River. Cinco de Mayo fiestas are celebrated in Hobbs, Old Mesilla, Belén, Artesia, Bernalillo, and Las Vegas in early May. Wildlife West Nature Park in Albuquerque is the site of Celebrate Wildlife New Mexico at the end of May and the Madrid Blues Festival is held from May to September. Old Man Gloom is burned during the Aztec Fiesta Days at Aztec in early June, and the World's Greatest Lizard Race is the highlight of Lovington's Lizard Week in early July. The Deming "Duck Downs" is the spot where the Great American Duck Race is held at the end of August, and Socorro throws the Enchanted Skies Star Party in mid-October.

New Mexico offers unique opportunities to learn about and observe Native American culture. During American Indian Week in Albuquerque at the end of April, there is the Gathering of the Nations Powwow. The Red Rock State Park at Gallup is the site of the Inter-Tribal Indian Ceremonial Song and Dance Competition in mid-July, as well as the home of the Annual Inter-Tribal Indian Ceremonial in mid-August. Activities at these events include an all-Indian rodeo, parades, arts and crafts exhibits, food, and ceremonies. Perhaps one of the most interesting ways to observe Native American cultural events is to visit the pueblos themselves on special feast days of the saints. On these feast days, various dances—harvest, elk, buffalo, deer, corn, Comanche—may take place, depending on the occasion.

These special feast days begin at most pueblos on January 1 with dances and the Transfer of Canes. On January 23, the San Ildefonso Pueblo Feast Day and Animal Dance Feast Day is celebrated. Laguna Pueblo holds its St. Joseph's Feast Day on March 19. The St. Phillip's Feast Day is held at the San Felipe Pueblo on May 1. The Taos Pueblo is the site of the Feast of the Santa Cruz footrace and Corn Dance on May 3. The St. Anthony Feast Day and Comanche Dance is held at the Santa Clara, San Juan, and Taos Pueblos on June 13. On June 24, the San Juan Pueblo Feast Day is held at the San Juan Pueblo, and the Feast of San Juan is held at the Taos Pueblo. On June 29, corn dances are held at the San Felipe, Santa Ana, and Santo Domingo Pueblos for San Pedro Feast Day, and the Ácoma Pueblo celebrates the St. Peter and Paul's Feast Day. On July 25 and 26, the Feast of Santa Ana and Santiago is celebrated at the Taos Pueblo. July 26 is the St. Ann's Feast Day celebrated at the Laguna Pueblo.

In August, the Ácoma Pueblo, Picuris, and the Cochití Pueblo celebrate the San Lorenzo Feast Day on the tenth. The Zia Pueblo celebrates Feast Day on August 15, also the date of The Assumption of Our Blessed Mother's Feast Day at Laguna Pueblo. September 2 is the San Esteban Feast Day and Harvest Dance at Ácoma Pueblo. The Nativity of the Blessed Virgin Mary's Feast Day is celebrated on September 8 at the Laguna Pueblo, where the St. Joseph's Feast Day is celebrated on September 19. The Feast of San Geronimo is celebrated on September 29 and 30 at the Taos Pueblo with a footrace, pole climbing, and a Sunset Dance. The Nambé Pueblo celebrates the St. Francis of Assisi Feast Day on October 4. The Tesuque Pueblo celebrates San Diego Feast Day on November 12 with flag, buffalo, corn, Comanche, and deer dances. The year ends with the celebration of the Nuestra Senora Guadalupe Feast Day at the Pojoaque and Tesuque Pueblos.[43]

NEW YORK

New York is a state of many regions and landscapes. From New York City to Niagara Falls to the Adirondacks, New Yorkers gather to celebrate in song and dance and to enjoy nature and food at many festivals throughout the year. The Hudson Valley is the home of Rhinebeck where the Great Hudson Valley Balloon Race is held in mid-June, followed two weeks later by Crafts at Rhinebeck when over 350 artisans display and sell a wide variety of arts and crafts. The Dutchess County Fair is also held in Rhinebeck during the latter part of August. Tarrytown hosts Spring Crafts at Lyndhurst in early May, and Fall Crafts at Lyndhurst in mid-September, both large craft fairs with other 300 participants. Yonkers is the site of the Westchester County Fair for over two weeks in late May through mid-June. The Hudson Valley Wine and Food Festival is celebrated in mid-June at Annandale-on-Hudson, also the home of the mid-October Harvest Fair. The Hudson River Arts Festival is held in mid-September at Beacon and Poughkeepsie. Ancramdale is the home of the Winterhawk Bluegrass Festival in mid-July. Tuxedo spends its weekends in costume from late July through mid-September for the Annual New York Renaissance Faire.

The Adirondacks provide a lovely backdrop to the Glens Falls Adirondack Balloon Festival for four days in mid-September. But solitude will not be found a month later in Glens Falls at the Adirondack Stampede Championship Rodeo. Tupper Lake welcomes lumberjacks in mid-July to the Woodsmen's Field Days, followed in mid-August by the Tupper Lake Adirondack Fair. North Creek hosts the Annual White Water Derby in mid-May for those who enjoy canoeing, kayaking, and camping. Lake Placid hosts the Lake Placid Horse Show over two weekends in early July. East Durham, located in the Catskills region, hosts the Annual East Durham Irish Festival in late May complete with bagpipers, dancers, and food, while at the same time Woodstock celebrates its Annual Renaissance Faire and the Woodstock/New Paltz Art and Crafts Fair. The German Alps Festival is held in Hunter in early August, soon followed by its International Celtic Festival. A stray member of the Woodstock generation might be found at Bethel in mid-August to celebrate A Day in the Garden.

The Thousand Island and Seaway region is the natural place for boating and outdoor events, including the Clayton 1000 Islands Annual Spring Boat Show in early April and the Lake Ontario Bird Festival at Mexico in early May. Three flags (British, French, and American) flew over Fort Ontario from 1755–1946, a fact that Oswego commemorates annually at the Flags Over Fort Ontario celebration on June 12. Sackets Harbor hosts the War of 1812 Can Am Festival annually in late June with reenactments and a tall ships parade. In mid-July the French Festival is held annually at Cape Vincent. The Jefferson County Fair is held annually at Watertown in mid-July, followed in late July by the Oswego Harborfest. The Finger Lakes region celebrates its famous wineries in mid-July at the Watkins Glen Finger Lakes Wine Festival. Prior to that, beginning in mid-May, Rochester hosts the Lilac Festival. Syracuse brings music to jazz and blues lovers at its June Jazz Fest and July Blues Festival. Syracuse is also the home of the New York State Fair, considered the largest fair in New York, from the end of August through the first week in September. LaFayette hosts its annual Apple Festival in mid-October.

The Greater Niagara area is home to Niagara Falls' Spring Festival of Gold during April when over two million daffodils bloom. The Youngstown French and Indian War Encampment, which is a reenactment of the 1759 Siege of Niagara, and the Italian Heritage and Food Festival at Buffalo are both held in July. Lewiston is the home of the Niagara County Peach Festival in mid-September. Central New York and the Leatherstocking area welcome visitors to celebrate the Erie Canal with food, music, and exhibits at Fort Hunter's Canal Days in mid-June. The New York State Woodsmen's Field Day at Boonville is held in mid-August, at the same time as the Madison and Bouckville Annual Antiques Show where over 1,100 antique dealers converge from around the country and present their treasures to eager antique hunters. The Capital-Saratoga area celebrates the Tulip Festival at Albany in mid-May, the Saratoga Springs Saratoga Equine Family Festival in late May, the Johnstown Market Faire in mid-June, the Altamont Fair (including a circus and horse shows) in mid-August, and the Altamont Capital District Apple Festival and Craft Show in early October.

The Chautauqua-Allegheny region celebrates the Jazz Festival at Ellicottville in late May. The Chautauqua Institution Season is from late June through late August. Many cultural events in the fine and performing arts, as well as programs in education, recreation, and religion, are held at the Chautauqua Institution, where visitors may also enjoy a wide range of outdoor recreational activities. In early August, Gerry hosts the Gerry Rodeo, which it promotes as the oldest consecutively running rodeo east of the Mississippi. It is impossible to present a single snapshot of events at the undisputed entertainment capital of the world, New York City. The city from Manhattan to Long Island, celebrates year-round. During the second and third weekends in June, Manhattan hosts the American Crafts Festival where over 400 crafters present wares. In mid-September, Manhattan also welcomes visitors to the San Gennaro Feast, a twelve-block festival in Little Italy. Of course, everyone comes running in early November for the New York City Marathon. Brooklyn is home to the West Indian–American Day Carnival in early September, and Long Island says shucks to oyster lovers at the Oyster Bay Oyster Festival in mid-October.[44]

NORTH CAROLINA

North Carolina hums with festivals that are sure to strike a chord with people fond of blues, bluegrass, jazz, and folk music. A lively pace is set early in the year as Wilmington hosts the Annual North Carolina Jazz Festival in February. The Annual Yadkinville Bluegrass Contest and Fiddlers' Convention is held in mid-April, followed by the Ole Time Fiddler's and Bluegrass Festival at Union Grove, the Gold Hill Bluegrass Festival, and Asheville's Black Mountain Music Festival in May. The Bluegrass and Old Time Fiddlers Convention is held at Mount Airy in June, the Annual Denton Bluegrass Festival at Mocksville is held in early July, and the Annual Cape Fear Blues Festival is hosted by Wilmington in late July. Also in July is the internationally known Folkmoot USA where dancers, musicians, and craftspeople entertain and educate as the world comes to the mountains of western North Carolina where events are spread across ten counties. Every Friday from mid-May through August, Stecoah Valley hosts Bluegrass Music and Clogging events. Blues performers and blues fans flock to Durham in mid-September for two days at the Bull Durham Blues Festival, and Littleton celebrates the Butterwood Bluegrass Festival in early October.

Cultural diversity and heritage festivals are celebrated in Banner Elk, Huntersville, Fayetteville, Raleigh, Chapel Hill, and many other places throughout North Carolina. Events include the Loch Norman Highland Games in mid-April, the Annual Grandfather Mountain Highland Games in mid-July, Greek festivals in May at Fayetteville and Wilmington, the Banner Elk Oktoberfest, and international festivals in Fayetteville and Raleigh in September and October, respectively. Native American culture is the focus of many events held throughout the year. The Annual Native-American Pow Wow is held in Durham in mid-February, and Hollister hosts the Haliwa-Saponi Annual Indian Tribe Pow-Wow in mid-April. Hillsborough hosts the Occaneechi-Saponi Spring Festival and Pow Wow in mid-June, and Ahoskie is the site of the Meherrin Indian Tribe Pow Wow in late October.

The natural beauty of North Carolina and the created beauty of North Carolinians are the subjects of a variety of flora and arts and crafts festivals, beginning as early as April with the Annual North Carolina Azalea Festival in Wilmington. Dogwood festivals are held in Fayetteville, Lake Lure, and Farmville in April, followed by more nature celebrations at the Annual Spring Wildflower and Bird Pilgrimage in Asheville in early May, the Dogwood and Wildflower Festival at Stecoah Valley at the end of May, and the Annual Rhododendron Festival at Bakersville in mid-June. Arts and crafts events are plentiful and far too many to mention in full. From January events in Fayetteville to March and April events in Elizabeth City,

Hendersonville, Lenoir, Cary, and Greensboro to May events in Blowing Rock and Fayetteville, visitors can enjoy everything from juried art shows to exhibits on quilting, pottery, woodturning, wood carving, jewelry-making, and photography. Blowing Rock provides a venue for over 100 crafters on many Saturdays from May through October. Summer and fall events are held in Sparta, Fayetteville, Asheville, Banner Elk, Southern Pines, Burnsville, Cary, Hertford, Angier, Aberdeen, Long Beach, Black Mountain, Maggie Valley, Durham, Edenton, and Williamston. Wilmington is the site of the Piney Woods Festival in early September where visitors have been congregating annually for over two decades to enjoy arts, recreation, ethnic food, and crafts. Finally, the Wings Over Water Festival at Manteo in November provides a forum for study and appreciation of the natural wildlife and lands of northeastern North Carolina.

From strawberries to watermelon to pickles to peanuts, there is a festival for all kinds of tastebuds. Strawberries are on the menu at the weeklong Annual Strawberry Festival at Chadbourn in late April and at Conover in mid-May. Pickles are cause for celebration at the North Carolina Pickle Festival at Mount Olive in late April. Bridgeton hosts the Blueberry Festival in mid-June, and watermelon festivals are held at Fair Bluff at the end of July and at South Mills in mid-August. Enfield hosts the Peanut Festival in mid-September, followed by the Mount Airy Sonker (deep-dish pie) Festival in early October. Yams and hams are the fare at the Ham and Yam Festival at Smithfield in mid-April and at the Tabor City North Carolina Yam Festival in mid-October. Seafood is offered in April at the Grifton Shad Festival and the Blowing Rock Trout Derby, the Sneads Ferry Annual Shrimp Festival in mid-August, and at the Annual North Carolina Oyster Festival at Shallotte and the North Carolina Seafood Festival in Morehead City, both in October. Maggie Valley hosts the Chili Challenge in mid-February, followed by the Chicken Fest at Ahoskie in late April, the Annual Blue Ridge Barbeque Festival at Tryon in mid-June, and the North Carolina Turkey Festival at Raeford in mid-September.

Variety is the spice of life, and it can be found while flying a kite at the Carolina Kite Festival at Atlantic Beach in mid-October or while fishing in the Annual Carolina Beach Fall Surf Fishing Tournament at Carolina Beach also in mid-October. Durham is the host of the American Dance Festival in June, Weldon of August's Ducky Derby/Rockfish Festival, and Benson of the Annual Benson Mule Days in September. Woolly worms and unwoolly heads are raced and watched, respectively, at the Annual Woolly Worm Festival in Banner Elk and the "Bald is Beautiful" Convention in Morehead City.[45,46]

NORTH DAKOTA

Rodeos, barbecues, powwows, pioneer and old settlers days, and lighthearted polka festivals offer many opportunities for entertainment and appreciation of North Dakota's cultural heritage. Roughrider Days and PRCA Rodeo at Dickinson are held from late June through July 4, at the same time as the July 3–4 Towner Roughrider Rodeo. In early August, the Champions Ride Rodeo is held at Sentinel Butte. The NDRA Rodeo Finals competition is in Dickinson in early September, and Minot hosts the Y's Men's Rodeo in early October. Native American culture is celebrated at several events throughout the year. The Time Out Waccipi and Powwow is held at Grand Forks in early March, followed by the Northern Plains Indian Culture Fest at Stanton in late July, the Little Shell Pow Wow at New Town in mid-August, and the United Tribes International Pow Wow at Bismarck in mid-September.

Early settlers and early agricultural techniques are remembered at many events during the year. In June, Wolford hosts the Antique Farm Show, and Center invites history buffs to the Old Settlers Celebration. Also in June, Lansford holds Threshing Days, followed in July by Fort Ransom's Sodbuster Days and McCluskey's Mid-Summer Fest and Old Settler's Day. August events include Pioneer Days in West Fargo and Heritage Days in East Grand Forks. Old Settler's Day in early September at Alexander includes a rodeo, and Cavalier hosts the Annual Pioneer Machinery Show in mid-September. Early fur traders and pioneers may be seen at Cavalier during the Rendezvous Festival in mid-June, and early frontier days are recalled during the Fort Stevenson Frontier Military Days in late June at Garrison. Lewis and Clark still scout along the Missouri River in late July when those with an imagination and a hunger for history and wagon train grub may join the Lewis and Clark Wagon Train.

Speaking of food, barbecue is found in abundance at several festivals, with a few events making barbecue the main attraction. Fargo hosts the RibFest and More festival in early June, followed a week later by the Annual Lakota Turkey Barbeque. Hebron in early July serves plenty of barbecue and watermelon, and entertains with turtle races, an egg toss, a dance, and a carnival.

The land of North Dakota and the skies above it are appreciated not only during Pioneer Days events but also as valuable natural resources of today's North Dakota. For instance, the late-July North Dakota State Fair at Minot includes a wide range of agriculture exhibits, and Fargo hosts the North Dakota Ag Show for three days in late November. Fort Totten welcomes nature lovers to the early-May North Dakota Chautauqua Bird Watch and Lecture, as well as to the late-July Sully's Hill Birding and Nature Festival.

With the heavy population of German and

Scandinavian descendants, polka festivals can be found throughout the state. They include the Stump Lake Polka Fest at Lakota in late June and the Eagles Polkafest at Dickinson in early October, and it is certain that a polka band can also be found at the New Leipzig German Festival in July. Scandinavian festivals include the late-June Scandinavian Hjemkomst Festival at Moorhead, the North Dakota Chautauqua Scandiafest at Devil's Lake in late July, and the mid-October Norsk Hostfest at Minot. Dickinson hosts the North Dakota Ukrainian Festival in mid-July.

A few unique festivals include Cabin Fever Days at Jamestown in early February where housebound North Dakotans can find company and entertainment at cook-offs and dances; the Big Chill at Cooperstown in mid-February that includes a Mr. Big Chill pageant, snow volleyball, and broom ball; and the Dunseith Annual International Old-Time Fiddler's Contest and Workshop in mid-June. Bismarck hosts the September Folkfest and Kenmare, the six-day Goosefest hunting festival in mid-October. Enderlin celebrates the Annual Sunflower Festival in mid-September with a tractor pull, a quilt show, a parade, and an opportunity for spitting sunflower seeds the farthest and getting rewarded for it.[47]

OHIO

Oh, how Ohioans celebrate the many fruits of the rich soil, air, and water of Ohio—from Chardon's Geauga County Maple Festival and Bellbrook's Sugar Maple Festival in April to the North Ridgeville Corn Festival, the Sweet Corn Festival, Inc., at Millersport, and the Fairborn Sweet Corn Festival in mid- to late August where visitors may eat their fill of Amish-style, roasted corn or hot buttered corn. An estimated 25,000 people attend the Norwalk Jaycees' Strawberry Fest in late May, while at the same time a com-

parable number may be found at Utica at the Old Fashion Ice Cream Festival. The Eldorado Zucchini Festival in late July and the Obetz Zucchinifest in late August provide opportunities to enjoy a broad range of foods made with zucchini, such as zucchini burgers, fudge, and breads. Tons of bratwurst are served at the Bucyrus Bratwurst Festival in mid-August when the blends made by local butchers make Bucyrus bratwurst a new experience every time. Milan is the site of the annual Milan Melon Festival in early September, followed shortly thereafter by the Reynoldsburg Tomato Festival when festivalgoers may enjoy fried green tomatoes, free tomato juice, and entertainment such as the Grand Champion Tomato Contest. The Marion Popcorn Festival is held during the first weekend after Labor Day and includes musical entertainment, a variety of sports tournaments and competitions, a parade, arts, crafts, and lots of popcorn. Beavercreek likewise hosts a well-attended festival highlighting the popcorn industry in mid-September. Mantua celebrates potatoes annually at its mid-September Potato Festival, and also in mid-September, Amanda celebrates soybeans at its American Soya Festival.

Apple cider, apple pies, apple butter, and candy apples are served at the Jackson County Apple Festival Inc. in Jackson during mid-September. Oxford celebrates the sweetness of honey at the Ohio Honey Festival, Inc., when homemade honey ice cream is served and spectators are entertained by a trained beekeeper who creates a beard of live bees. In late September, Geneva celebrates the grape harvest at the Geneva Area Grape Jamboree. Fresh grape juice, wines, and other grape products may be tasted, and entertainment includes arts and crafts shows, dancing, carnival rides, and, of course, grape stomping. During the first weekend in October, Mt. Gilead welcomes visitors to the annual Ohio Gourd Show, and later in October, Circleville hosts the Circleville Pumpkin Show, now in its ninth decade, with parades, pumpkin foods, and competitions. Seafood and the sport of fishing are celebrated in May and June during the Port Clinton Walleye Festival and the Festival of the Fish at Vermilion.

There are many opportunities to show, purchase, and enjoy arts and crafts in Ohio. Some festivals are centered on arts or crafts and others include arts and crafts as part of the overall entertainment. A few of these events include the Pike County Dogwood Festival in late April and the Adams County Redbud Fest of Arts and Crafts in West Union also in late April. May festivals include the annual Dogwood Festival in Coshocton; Hartville's Quail Hollow Craft and Herb Fair, attended by approximately 100,000 visitors; Delaware's annual Delaware Arts Festival; Gahanna's Herb and Craft Festival; and Miamisburg's Spring Fling. The Columbus Arts Festival attacts a half million arts and crafts lovers in early June, at the same time as Cleveland's annual June Art Walk, Van Wert's Peony Festival, Troy's Strawberry Festival, and Toledo's Old West End Fest Art Show. Bedford hosts the annual Strawberry Festival in mid-June that includes an arts and crafts show, ethnic foods, and, of course, plenty of strawberry foods. Other June events include the Cleveland Clifton Arts & Musicfest, Beachwood's Festival of the Arts, a celebration of Latin culture during the Festival Latino at Columbus, the Worthington Art Festival, Toledo's Crosby Festival of the Arts, and Peninsula's Boston Mills Artfest. Kent hosts the Heritage Festival in early July, quickly followed by Home Days at Garfield Heights, Toledo's Lagrange Street Polish Fest, and Westerville's Music & Arts Fest. Willard is the site of the Festival in the Park and Cleveland is the site of the Cain Park Arts Festival, both held in mid-July. Lakeside welcomes artists to its well-attended Lakeside Annual Art Show in late July and early August; Akron hosts its annual Akron Arts Expo in late July; Celina is home to the Celina Lake Festival; and music joins art during the Cuyahoga Falls Crooked River Jazz, Blues and Art Fest at the end of July.

It is estimated that one million visitors attend the Handmade Heritage Crafts event during the Ohio State Fair held in Columbus for almost three weeks in early August. The celebration of multiple births, as well as of city founders, is reason enough for over 60,000 festivalgoers to converge on Twinsburg in early August for the annual Twins Day Festival. Berlin Heights hosts the Basket Festival in early August, and a variety of arts and crafts events follow throughout August in such locations as Chardon, Vermilion, Lima, Kettering, and Columbus.

The Slavic Village Harvest Fest at Cleveland in late August is followed by Oktoberfests in September and October at Vandalia, Columbus, Dayton, Bremen, Minster, Cuyahoga Falls, Boardman, and Zanesville. Pioneer crafts, foods, and lifestyles are remembered at the mid-September Pioneer Days Festival at Brownhelm. Starving artists are provided an opportunity to sell arts and crafts at the Miamisburg Starving Artists Show in mid-September. Also in mid-September, Utica hosts the Buckeye Tree Festival, Sylvania hosts the Sylvania Arts and Crafts Festival, and Xenia hosts the Old Fashioned Days Fest. Tipp City is not mum during its annual Tipp City Mum Festival in mid-September when 50,000 people converge on this normally tranquil, historic city. Germantown is host of the late-September annual Germantown Pretzel Festival that includes crafts, music, and other entertainment. Swiss heritage is the focal point of the Sugarcreek Ohio Swiss Festival held annually in late September. Coshocton and Delphos welcome visitors to their celebrations that recognize the importance of canals in the history of the settlement of

Ohio. Coshocton hosts its Canal Festival in mid-August, and Delphos hosts its annual Old Fashioned Canal Days in mid-September.[48,49]

OKLAHOMA

Oklahoma celebrates its history and Native American heritage with a variety of gatherings and competitions, from tribal powwows to international rodeos. Pioneer Days are held at Okemah and Guymon in late April and early May, although many events throughout the year bring history to life in the form of gunfight reenactments and demonstrations of the music, entertainment, crafts, and harvesting equipment of the early pioneers. There are '89er Day Celebrations in El Reno, Guthrie, and Norman that recall the 1889 Oklahoma Land Run in late April. Oklahoma City hosts the Chuckwagon Gathering and Children's Cowboy Festival in late May. Several Old Settlers Days, reunions, and picnics are held at Checotah, Perkins, Keota, Buffalo, Skiatook, and Arnet from May to September. Native American powwows and gatherings are plentiful and include the Choctaw Intertribal Powwow in mid-April at Durant, Spavinaw Days and Powwow in late May, the Red Earth Native American Cultural Festival at Oklahoma City in mid-June, and the Iowa Tribal Powwow at Perkins also in mid-June. The Pawnee Indian Veterans Homecoming and Powwow is in late June, the Sac and Fox Nation Annual Powwow at Stroud in early July, the Tonkawa Tribal Powwow also in early July, and the Comanche Homecoming Powwow at Walters in mid-July. September events include the Cheyenne-Arapaho Labor Day Celebration at Colony, the Chickasaw Annual Festival at Tishomingo, and the Standing Bear Powwow at Ponca City.

The International Finals Rodeo runs in Oklahoma City in mid-January and offers over $275,000 in prize money. However, this is just the beginning of a year filled with rodeos and the many events that accompany them, such as steer wrestling, barrel racing, calf roping, bareback and saddle bronc riding, and chuck wagon meals. Later in January, Tulsa hosts the Longhorn World Championship Rodeo, followed by rodeos in March at Enid, in April at Oktaha and Guthrie, and in May at Guymon, Idabel, Pryor, and Boley. There are no fewer than ten rodeos in June and July held at such places as Sulphur, Hugo, Checotah, Muskogee, Miami, Hinton, Oktaha, Wynnewood, Woodward, and Ada. August rodeos include the Annual Rodeo and Old Cowhand Reunion in Freedom where old cowhands may enjoy a chuck wagon dinner and dance into the evening to the music of Country Western tunes. Other August rodeos are held at Holdenville, Clearview, Lawton, Ponca, and Buffalo. September rodeos include those held at Arnett, Elk City, and Mustang. For those bullish about rodeos, Bullnanza's are held in February at Guthrie and in August at Oklahoma City. For the truly devoted tamers of the wild, Mangum and Okeene host rattlesnake roundups in April and May, respectively. But for really gritty characters, the Cimarron Territory Celebration and World Cow Chip Throwing Championship offer good clean fun, a chili cook-off, and a western arts and crafts show at Beaver in mid-April.

For food lovers, Muskogee in April and Stilwell in May are the places to be for strawberry festivals. Okmulgee hosts the Pecan Festival in mid-June, followed by the Stratford Peach Festival in mid-July and watermelon festivals in Terral and Rush Springs in July and August, respectively. Arnett hosts the Ardmoredillo Chili Cookoff in early April where festivities include a jalapeno-eating contest, a rodeo, and cowboy poetry readings. Whole Hawg Days in July at Eufaula and Hog-Wild Day at Holdenville in

October provide opportunities for pigging out and for competing in a greased pig contest at the latter event. Hollis is the home of the Blackeyed Pea Festival in August where visitors may enjoy a parade, arts and crafts, black-eyed pea meals, watermelon, and an event of perhaps uncertain pleasure, Cow Patty Bingo. Checotah celebrates the Okrafest in September with a variety of activities including an okra cookoff, music, and arts and crafts. Foods from many cultures may be found at festivals such as the Scottish Heritage Festival at Midwest City in March; the Italian Festival at McAlester, the Kolache Festival at Prague, and the Harrah Polish Festival all in May; and the Czech Festival at Yukon and Oktoberfests at Oklahoma City, Roff, and Ponca City in September and October. The State Fair of Oklahoma is held each September in Oklahoma City, and the Tulsa State Fair is held in late September through the first week in October.

Festivals spotlighting Oklahoma industry and industrious Oklahomans include the Gusher Days at Seminole in early June, and Will Rogers Days and Parade at Claremore in November. Ponca City and Drumright pay tribute to early oil boom days at the Oil Boom Day in May and the Oil Patch Jamboree in September. The wide open spaces of Oklahoma provide a canvas of blue sky where hot-air balloons play and compete in August at the Gatesway International Balloon Festival at Tulsa, followed by the Oklahoma City Balloon Fest and the Illinois River Balloon Fest at Tahlequah. The nationally regarded Bok/Williams Jazz on Greenwood festival at Tulsa is held over two weekends in early August, and Guthrie hosts the Oklahoma International Bluegrass Festival in early October. Artists and artisans converge on Bartlesville in mid-September for the Indian Summer Festival, a celebration of the arts and dances of Native Americans.[50]

OREGON

Oregon is comprised of several distinctive geographic areas, each with its own brand of celebration. The Oregon coast area includes 400 miles of beaches and plenty of room for seafood festivals year-round. Annual Crab Feeds in Warrenton and Charleston in mid-February are quickly followed by the Newport Seafood and Wine Festival in late February. Festivals in March and April include the Southcoast Dixieland Clambake Jazz Festival in Coos Bay and North Bend, the Chowder Challenge in Lincoln City, the Sea-Side Chowder Cook-Off in Seaside, and the three-day Astoria/Warrenton Crab and Seafood Festival in Hammond. Gold Beach combines seafood with flowers and art at the Clam Chowder Festival, Flower and Art Show beginning May 1, and Bandon concludes May with the Annual Seafood and Wine Festival. Summer brings the Wheeler Crab Fest, numerous Fourth of July celebrations, the Yachats Annual Smelt Fry, Charleston's Annual Salmon BBQ, and the Annual Depoe Bay Salmon Bake. Florence welcomes the fall season with Chowder, Brews and Blues in late September. Other coastal festivals include the mid-May Annual Rhododendron Festival in Florence where flower shows are joined by a carnival, a parade, and slug races; the Annual Azalea Festival in Brookings in late May; June's Annual Sandcastle Day Festival in Cannon Beach; the Southern Oregon Kite Festival in Brookings and the Oregon Coast Music Festival in Coos Bay in July; and Lincoln City's Annual Sandcastle Building Contest and Newport's Jazz on the Water Festival in August. The Bandon Cranberry Festival in mid-September delivers barbecue, bog tours, a parade, and an outdoor market, and the Annual Fall International Kite Festival is held in Lincoln City in early October.

The Portland area loves roses and June brings many events connected with the Port-

land Rose Festival, including parades, a jur-
ied art show, an airshow, fireworks, and the
Rose Festival Queen's coronation and re-
lated events. There is a Junior Rose Festival
Parade, a celebration of the Rose Festival
Fleet Week, Dragon Boat Races, and the Ro-
tary Rose Festival Ducky Derby when
rubber duckies race on the Willamette River.
Other popular events in Portland are the
Portland International Film Festival held
over two weeks in February, the Annual
Spring Beer Fest in mid-April, the Cinco de
Mayo festival in early May, the Waterfront
Blues Festival over the Independence Day
holiday, and the Homowo Festival of African Arts in August. Don't forget the Annual
Elephant Garlic Festival in North Plains in
mid-August or to add spice to October Sherwood offers the Great Annual Onion
Festival and Canby offers the Chili Cookoff
and Harvest Festival. Gresham boasts that
its Mt. Hood Festival of Jazz in August is
one of the West's top jazz events.

Mt. Hood and the Columbia River Gorge
provide a scenic backdrop to a number of
outdoor events. Families who kayak, wind
surf, snowboard, and/or mountain bike together can find amusement and sport in July
at the weeklong Gorge Games at the Hood
River and Mt. Hood. Nature's adornments
and nourishments provide cause for celebration at the Northwest Cherry Festival in
mid-April at The Dalles, the Hood River
Valley Blossom Festival at Hood River also
in mid-April, the Cherry Harvest in Hood
River during the first two weeks in July, and
the Gravenstein Apple Days at the Hood
River Valley in late August. The Salmon
Shuffle takes place in mid-September at Cascade Locks and the Salmon/Mushroom Festival takes place in Welches in early October.
The Troutdale Salmon Festival is in mid-
October, the Annual Hood River Valley
Harvest Fest and Odell Fruit and Craft Fair
at Hood River is also in mid-October, and
the Resort at the Mountain's Annual Wine

and Art Festival is in mid-November at
Welches.

The Willamette Valley area includes Eugene where the Oregon Asian Celebration is
held in mid-February and the aptly named
Eugene Celebration provides three days in
September for a party, art shows, and a
wacky parade. Festival excitement grows in
the Willamette Valley with the March Annual Daffodil Drive in Junction City and the
Woodburn Tulip Festival from mid-March
to mid-April. The Lebanon Strawberry Festival begins in early June, and in July there
is the World Championship Timber Carnival
in Albany where visitors can participate in
such mild entertainment as ax throwing, log
rolling, and tree climbing. Veneta hosts the
Oregon Country Fair in early July. Art, science, and technology are celebrated at the da
Vinci Days in Corvallis for three days in
mid-July, and at the same time Salem hosts
the Annual Salem Art Fair and Festival. The
Oregon Jamboree at Sweet Home is a large
country music and camping festival in early
August, followed by the Scandinavian Festival in Junction City in August and the Mt.
Angel Oktoberfest in mid-September.

Southern Oregon is the home of the
Oregon Shakespeare Festival at Ashland beginning in mid-February and spanning much
of the year to the end of October. April
events include the Pear Blossom Festival and
10 Mile Run at Medford and the Wildflower
Show in Glide. The Boatnik Festival is a
whitewater adventure held on the Rogue
River in late May. Graffiti Week in Roseburg in mid-July provides a neat opportunity
to recall the 1950s at car shows and ice
cream socials. Crescent Lake is the venue for
the Annual Pioneer Cup Canoe and Kayak
Races and BBQ in late July. In late August
and during the first week in September,
Grants Pass is the site of the Jedediah Smith
Mountain Man Rendevous. The Roseburg
Oktoberfest Microbrew Festival is held in
late September, and October offers the Med-

ford Jazz Festival and the Merrill Potato Festival.

Events in Central Oregon include the mid-May Collage of Culture in Madras, the Sisters Rodeo in Sisters in June, the Prineville Crooked River Rodeo also in June, Bend's Cascade Cycling Classic and Redmond's Walk the Art Beat in July; and the Sunriver Music Festival and Bend's Cascade Festival of Music in August and September. Eastern Oregon provides a rodeo every weekend from May to mid-September, as well as many celebrations in which history is brought to life for those interested in the Native American culture and the pioneer experience. To name a few, the Chief Joseph Days Rodeo and Encampment is held in July at Joseph, shortly after the Miners' Jubilee in Baker City. Oregon Trail Days is celebrated in La Grande in late August with Dutch-oven cooking, crafts, and an Old-Time Fiddle Contest. The Pendleton Round-Up in mid-September is a famous rodeo and Indian powwow. Barbecue is served in July when visitors nibble on it and mosquitos nibble on visitors as everyone celebrates the Mosquito Festival at Paisley.[51,52]

PENNSYLVANIA

On February 2, about two weeks after Somerset's Fire and Ice Festival, Punxsutawney Phil, the great seer of seers revered for his age and his ability to forecast the coming of spring, emerges from his official home on Gobbler's Knob. It's Groundhog Day. Phil can be seen at the Punxsutawney Groundhog Festival, as well, held during the week of the Fourth of July, when he resides at the Groundhog Zoo. The legend of groundhog prognostication on Candlemas Day was brought to Pennsylvania by early German settlers. From Punxsutawney, one may wish to journey to Pittsburgh where unique entertainment may also be found. Pittsburgh is the home of the Greater Pittsburgh Renais-

sance Festival where sixteenth-century armored jousting demonstrations, food, entertainment, and games are found in late August and throughout September. Pittsburgh is also host to many other celebrations such as the Three Rivers Art Festival, the Three Rivers Rib and Music Festival, and the Pittsburgh Three Rivers Regatta.

Pennsylvania was the stopping point for many early settlers whose heritage and culture are still celebrated today. Irish, Scottish, and Welsh cultures are the focus at several Celtic and Highland games festivals including the Ligonier Highland Games at Bethel Park and the Celtic Classic Highland Games and Festival at Bethlehem, both in September. Festivals with a Pennsylvania Dutch and German flavor include the Kutztown Pennsylvania German Festival in early July where one will find apple dumplings, Pennsylvania Dutch dinners, folk art and crafts, and a renowned quilt display; the Goschenhoppen Historical Annual Authentic Pennsylvania Folk Festival at East Greenville in August; the Annual Pennsylvania Dutch Folk Festival at Summit Station in late June; and folkfests and fairs, polkafests, and Oktoberfests in such places as Johnstown, Pittsburgh, York, and Philadelphia. Italians, Greeks, Hispanics, Ukrainians, Irish, Germans, and many other nationalities and ethnic groups are celebrated around the state throughout the year from Blakeslee in the Pocono's to Penn's Landing along the Delaware River at Philadelphia to Pittsburgh, Bradford, Scranton, Uniontown, and Mt. Jewett. The Native American culture is highlighted at powwows and festivals such as the Indian Pow Wow at the Samuel S. Lewis State Park in York County in mid-May, the Native American Pow Wow at Forksville in mid-June, the Annual Authentic Indian Pow Wow at Shartlesville in mid-August, and the Native American Fall Festival at Airville in late September.

Pennsylvania's natural beauty and resources provide the backdrop at many events where festival goers may sample local foods and enjoy a variety of entertainment and exhibits. For instance, Meyersdale and Asbury Woods celebrate maple festivals in March and April, followed by the Grove City Strawberry Days Arts and Music Festival and the Finleyville Strawberry Festival, both held in June. Large agricultural and county fairs are held in Irwin, York, Allentown, Shippensburg, and many other communities throughout the summer season. Cooksburg is the site of the June Herb Festival, and Kennett Square celebrates the Annual Mushroom Festival in mid-September with farm tours, a street festival and parade, and a cook-off. Apples, apple harvests, apple dumplings, and apple blossoms are celebrated at festivals from May to October. Eagles Mere provides beautiful mountain scenery for the August Eagles Mere Arts and Crafts Festival and the September Eagles Mere Fall Festival. With its extensive forests, it is not surprising to find Pennsylvania the home of the Black Moshannon Lumber Day Contest at the Black Moshannon State Park at Phillipsburg in late July and the Annual Woodsman's Show at Galeton in early August. The Black Cherry Festival at Kane in mid-July celebrates the beauty and importance of the black cherry hardwood in building Pennsylvania. Flowers and gardens, both inside and out, bring many gardening enthusiasts to the York Garden and Flower Show at York in February and to the largest indoor flower show in the world, the Philadelphia Flower Show, in early spring.

In Pennsylvania, American history comes to life. French Alliance Day is celebrated at Valley Forge Historical Park early in May. Also in May, the National Road Festival takes place along ninety miles of historic landscape around Farmington where visitors can enjoy wagon train reenactments, encampments, food, and entertainment. On Christmas Day at Washington Crossing, the Reenactment of Washington Crossing the Delaware takes place. Gettysburg Civil War Heritage Days runs from the end of June to July 4, and then on November 19, the Anniversary Celebration of the Gettysburg Address honors Abraham Lincoln.[53-60]

RHODE ISLAND

Rhode Island has a long and rich history and heritage that is celebrated in its fairs and festivals. Gaspee Days in Warwick remembers June 9, 1772, when Rhode Island patriots burned the HMS *Gaspee*, a British revenue ship. In fact, celebration of this event begins in late May when Warwick welcomes vendors and visitors to its Gaspee Days Arts and Crafts Festival. Annually, Warwick recreates a colonial militia encampment in late May. Rhode Island Navy Day in East Greenwich commemorates the founding of the Rhode Island Navy on June 12, 1775. Providence holds its Festival of Historic Houses early in June.

Celebrations of heritage include the Annual East Providence Heritage Festival in late July, the Annual Narragansett Heritage Days in early August, and the Rhode Island Labor and Ethnic Heritage Festival in Pawtucket early in September. The Black Ships Festival at Newport toward the end of July is a Japanese celebration commemorating Rhode Island son Admiral Perry and the Treaty of Kanagawa. Newport is the site of the Annual Newport Waterfront Irish Festival in early September. Newport also celebrates an annual Oktoberfest over three days in October when enthusiastic partakers of traditional German food and drink may dance away the calories to the tune of lively German bands.

Music, art, and crafts are featured in numerous fairs and festivals, such as the Newport International Film Festival held in early June, the Annual Newport Outdoor Art Festival in mid-June, Newport's Annual Sunset

Music Festival in late June, the Newport Music Festival during the middle two weeks of July, the Wickford Art Festival on the second weekend of July, and Newport's Folk Festival early in August. In mid-August, Woonsocket hosts the Rhode Island International Film Festival that celebrates the independent filmmaker and provides the opportunity to watch many films over the course of the five-day event. Also in mid-August Newport hosts the renowned Newport JVC Jazz Festival preceded by the Providence Jazz and Blues Festival in late July.

The sea plays a large part in the recreational lives of Rhode Islanders. Clambakes and regattas are held at such places as Newport and Jamestown where visitors can unwind under the summer sun. Seafood is on the plate or in the bowl at the Annual Schweppes Great Chowder Cook-Off in Newport in early June, the late-July Annual Clambake at Rose Island Lighthouse in Newport during late July, and the Block Island Clam Bake & Cook Out in early September. Narragansett holds its Blessing of the Fleet ceremonies toward the end of July. Wickford's International Quahog Festival gives tribute to the official Rhode Island shellfish in late August. The jubilation continues into the fall at the Newport Harvest-by-the-Sea Festival held during the entire month of October, as apple cider and hay-rides join whale watching as entertainment. Wakefield hosts the Annual Snug Harbor Bass and Bluefish Boogie in mid-October where fishing competitions continue for three days.[61]

SOUTH CAROLINA

Perhaps one of the most well-known South Carolina events is the Spoleto Festival USA held from the end of May into mid-June. Annually, visitors converge on Charleston for total immersion in the performing arts,

including dance, theater, and music. The grand finale event includes a fireworks display over the butterfly lakes at Middleton Place Gardens. The arts are celebrated throughout South Carolina at a number of events, such as the Carolina Craftsmen's Spring Classic held for three days in early March at Columbia; the mid-July Art in the Park festival held in North Myrtle Beach, where over one hundred artisans participate in the juried art show; and Sumter's Fall for the Arts in mid-October.

From grits to okra, peaches, watermelon, and seafood, there are many opportunities to taste-test good food in South Carolina. The South Carolina Oyster Festival is held in Columbia in mid-March, followed by the World Grits Festival at St. George in April where there are plenty of grits for everyone to eat and, for those in a competitive spirit, to experience more fully by joining in the Rolling-in-the-Grits contest. Walterboro's Colleton County Rice Festival and Hemingway's Barbecue Shag Festival arrive in late April, followed by the South Carolina Poultry Festival at Leesville in early May. Succulent juices flow in June and July at the Hampton County Watermelon Festival in Hampton, the Pageland Watermelon Festival, the Ridge Peach Festival at Trenton, and the Lexington County Peach Festival at Gilbert. It would not be South Carolina without okra, and okra it is at the Okra Strut Festival held at Irmo in late September. Salley struts too at the end of November during the Chitlin' Strut where visitors can eat chitterlings or not and enjoy a carnival, crafts, and dances.

South Carolina's natural beauty is celebrated during the Johnston Peach Blossom Festival, the Dogwood Festival at Denmark, the Southern Plant and Flower Festival at Florence, and the South Carolina Festival of Roses at Orangeburg, all held in April. The iris is celebrated in May at the Iris Festival held at Sumter, followed by the South Carolina Festival of Flowers in mid-June at Greenwood. The latter event includes jazz, bluegrass, and beach music, as well as arts and crafts and an opportunity for visitors to see 1,500 varieties of flowers and vegetables.

Diverse cultures are celebrated throughout the year with games, powwows, arts and crafts, and a wide variety foods and events. To name a few of the celebrations that pay honor to South Carolina's history and heritage, Columbia hosts the Columbia International Festival in mid-March; powwows and Civil and Revolutionary War reenactments are held in Cowpens, Ehrhardt, Aiken, Ladson, Ninety Six, Georgetown, Pickens, Andrews, Camden, and Rock Hill; and Charleston hosts the Festival Hispano and the Scottish Games and Highland Gathering in mid-September. The Schuetzenfest and Oktoberfests are held at Ehrhardt, Myrtle Beach, Walhalla, Sumter, and Columbia. Southern hospitality is the focus, along with the Low Country chicken-bog dish, at the Bog-Off Festival at Loris in October. African American festivals include the Africa Alive Festival in late February at Rock Hill, the Gullah Festival at the end of May in Beaufort, the Juneteenth Festival at Timmonsville in mid-June when the end of African American slavery is celebrated, and Jubilee: Festival of Heritage held at Columbia in mid-August. The African American and Caribbean cultures of the Low Country are highlighted at the Moja Arts Festival in early October at Charleston. Low Country cooking, wildlife paintings, carvings, sculptures, and conservation exhibits are enjoyed at the Southeastern Wildlife Exposition at Charleston in mid-February, the home and month also of the Lowcountry Blues Bash where blues of all types are heard for over a week. Charleston hosts yet another festival in April when food and entertainment are enjoyed at the Lowcountry Cajun Festival. Authentic creole and cajun dishes provide Charleston with an opportunity to put its own stamp on South Louisiana cuisine. Crawfish races provide another distinctive and fun reason to remember this event. Too numerous to mention are the many historical tours in Charleston, Beaufort, Georgetown, Pendleton, Columbia, and Hartsville, where homes, gardens, and plantations are toured throughout the spring and fall.

Some other unique South Carolina festivals include the Stone Soup Storytelling Festival at Woodruff in mid-April, when youngsters of all ages gather around bonfires to hear yarns and ghost stories; the Spring Fling at Spartanburg and Mayfest at Columbia in April and May; and the Hell Hole Swamp Festival in early May in Jamestown where visitors are encouraged to stand back or join in at the adult spitting contest, climb greased poles, and enjoy a variety of games and contests.[62]

SOUTH DAKOTA

South Dakota celebrates its first residents at Mammoth Days in Hot Springs in late June, when visitors can view a mammoth collection of Columbian and woolly mammoth bones. Buffalo still roam the plains and are rounded up at the Custer State Park Buffalo Roundup each year in October for sale in November. Custer State Park is also the site in early October for the Buffalo Roundup Arts Festival and Annual Buffalo Wallow Chili Cook-off. Rodeos and roundups are plentiful in South Dakota, far too many to name in full. Most of the rodeos take place in late June and into October. July starts out with a bang at Independence Day holiday festivities such as the Sitting Bull Stampede Rodeo and Celebration at Mobridge, the Faulkton Rodeo and Wild West Days, the Black Hills Roundup at Belle Fourche, and the Fort Pierre Rodeo. July continues in full swing with rodeos at Sturgis, Burke, Mitchell, Buffalo Gap, and Winner. August rodeos are held in Selby, Watertown, Scotland, Aberdeen, White River, and Rosebud, the latter the site of the Annual Rosebud Fair and All-Indian Rodeo. Eagle Butte hosts the Cheyenne River Sioux Tribe Fair and Rodeo in early September, and Sioux Falls and Rapid City rodeos are held in October.

Summer months bring powwows almost weekly, and in some cases, two or three powwows are held per week. The Ring Thunder Traditional Powwow is held at Mission in mid-June, followed by the Native American Heritage International Powwow in Rapid City and the St. Francis Indian Day Celebration at St. Francis. July begins with the Sisseton–Wahpeton Dakota Nation's Annual Wacipi and the Antelope Community Powwow at Mission, followed by the Annual Corn Creek Traditional Wacipi, the Santee Sioux Wacipi at Flandreau and Milk's Camp Traditional Powwow at St. Charles/Bonesteel. August powwows are held in Lake Andes, Pine Ridge, Parmalee, Martin, Lower Brule, Bear Creek, Kyle, White River, Cherry Creek, and Faith. Chamberlain and Rapid City are the sites for powwows in September and October, the latter hosting the Annual Black Hills Powwow and Art Expo, which includes juried art shows and intertribal competitive powwows.

Discovery and settlement are strong themes at many historical festivals such as the Fort Sisseton Historical Festival in early June; the Old Timer's Day Celebration at Volga and the Sturgis Cavalry Days, both in mid-June; and the Lewis and Clark Historic Festival and Rendezvous at Chamberlain and Gold Discovery Days at Custer in July. The Southeastern South Dakota Threshing Show is at Lennox, the Annual Fur Traders Days at Geddes, the Black Hills Steam and Gas Threshing Bee at Sturgis, the Prairie Village Steam Threshing Jamboree at Madison, and the Yankton Lewis and Clark Festival all in August. Andover hosts the James Valley Threshing Show in mid-September.

Laura Ingalls Wilder, who wrote about her childhood as a pioneer, is one of South Dakota's most-loved authors. She is remembered over three weekends in late June and continuing into July during pageants at De Smet.

German culture is celebrated at several events, beginning with the Schmeckfest at Freeman in mid-March and continuing with the Dakota German Fest at Hill City, the Dakota Polka Festival at Rapid City, the Germanfest at Sioux Falls, and the German Russian Schmeckfest at Eureka in September. Deadwood hosts Oktoberfest in early October.

Visual and performing arts, crafts, dance, quilts, and tasty foods are highlighted at many events, including Salem's Annual Arts in the Park in May and the Red Cloud Indian Art Show at Pine Ridge held throughout June and into August. The John Morrell Sioux Empire Ribfest at Sioux Falls, the Black Hills Quilters Guild Annual Show at Rapid City, the All Dakota Fine Arts Festival at Groton, the Black Hills Folk Festival at Spearfish, the Aberdeen Arts Festival, the Summer Solstice Arts Festival at Mitchell, the Main Street Arts and Crafts Festival at Hot Springs, and the Black Hills Bluegrass Festival at Rapid City are all held in June. July and August events include the Annual Black Hills Square and Round Dance Festival at Rapid City in late July, the Annual Sioux River Folk Festival at Canton in early August, and the Eastern South Dakota Bluegrass Jamboree at Astoria in mid-August. The Autumn Fest offers fine homemade arts and crafts for sale to visitors at Sioux Falls in mid-October.

Nature lovers may look above the Big Stone Lake to find nature at the Big Stone Birding Festival in early May. They may look also into the Big Stone Lake in mid-June and gamely participate in the Annual Big Stone Walleye Classic. Walleye tournaments throughout June and July provide ample opportunity for competing and enjoying nature. Lake Preston, Mobridge, Gettysburg, and Pierre all host events. If neither fish nor fowl appeal to festival seekers, a fresh-air hike beginning at the Crazy Horse Memorial may be found in early June at the Crazy Horse Hike Up the Mountain. Stories told around the campfire and during long winter evenings may be recalled during the Northern Prairie Storytelling Festival at Sioux Falls in early June and the Dakota Storytelling Festival at Aberdeen in mid-September. Enjoy manly prose and say a sad farewell to summer at the Badger Clark Hometown Cowboy Poetry Gathering at Hot Springs in late September. Also in late September, Canadian geese migrate south above appreciative crowds at the Goosefest at Pierre. The Goosefest includes Lewis and Clark reenactments and arts and crafts.[63]

TENNESSEE

The Reelfoot Lake State Park hosts the Eagle Watch Tours in early January through mid-March. But eagles are not the only attraction for nature lovers. Pigeon Forge celebrates the Wilderness Wildlife Week of Nature in early January. The Annual Spring Wildflower Pilgrimage begins on the first day of spring and continues for three days in Gatlinburg. For two weeks in April, Maryville celebrates the Blount County Dogwood Arts Festival. The iris, the state flower of Tennessee, is celebrated in Greeneville in late May at the Iris Festival. Beautiful rhododendron flowers cover Roan Mountain in a brilliant blanket of pinks and reds during the Annual Rhododendron Festival in late June. Fall is celebrated at the Annual Roan Mountain State Park's Fall Festival in mid-September with crafts, music, dancing, demonstrations, apple butter, and coal-baked cornbread. Fall colors are enjoyed on cruises at the Reelfoot Lake State Park in mid-October and at the end of October in Chattanooga. The Smoky

Mountain Harvest Festival is held for six weeks beginning in mid-September at Gatlinburg, Pigeon Forge, and Sevierville, three communities located near the Tennessee entrance to the Great Smoky Mountains National Park. The Smoky Mountain Winterfest begins in mid-November and continues through February in the same three towns. The graceful Tennessee Walking Horse is the focus of attention at the Tennessee Walking Horse National Celebration beginning at August's end in Shelbyville.

Nature can be edible too and it is at strawberry festivals in Dayton, Humboldt, and Portland in May, and at the Scott County Sorghum Festival in Oneida in mid-September. Nature's restorative powers are celebrated at the Folk Medicine Festival at the end of July in Red Boiling Springs.

Who hasn't heard of Tennessee folk and country music? Visitors may select from several musical events such as the Annual Dulcimer and Harp Festival in mid-June at Cosby, the International Country Music Fan Fair in Nashville during the second week in June, the Official State and National Championship Fiddlers' Jamboree and Crafts Festival in Smithville in early July, and the Annual Smoky Mountain Fiddlers Convention in late August at London. Tennessee also celebrates blues at the Brownsville Bluesfest in late September and jazz at the Franklin Jazz Festival in early August.

Tennessee crafts, history, and culture are highlighted at several events throughout the state. These include the Tennessee Craft Fair at the end of April and the first part of May at Nashville and the Gatlinburg Scottish Festival and Games and the Festival of British and Appalachian Culture in Rugby both in May. Chattanooga's Riverbend Festival is held for one week in mid-June. The celebration of the oldest city in Tennessee takes place at Historic Jonesborough Days from July 3 to 5. The Annual Gatlinburg Craftsmen Fair is held during the last week in July, for several days in September, and for two weeks in October; the Cherokee Days of Recognition is in early August at the Red Clay State Historic Park in Cleveland; and the well-known National Storytelling Festival is in October at Jonesborough.

A summary of Tennessee events would not be complete without mention of Elvis. The Graceland Mansion in Memphis hosts events in remembrance of "the King." Celebrate at the Elvis Presley Birthday Celebration in January or end the year with Christmas at Graceland.[64]

TEXAS

It seems that Texans love to round 'em up year-round at rodeos, roundups, fairs, and county and livestock shows. There is the Houston Livestock Show Rodeo in early March, followed by the Stock Show and Rodeo Classic at San Angelo also in March. In fact, rodeos are almost continuous throughout the spring and summer in such places as Sulpher Springs, Austin, Mercedes, Goliad, Boerne, Lubbock, Huntsville, Sweetwater, Athens, Mesquite, Beaumont, Longview, Vernon, Taylor, Whitesboro, Clifton, and Odessa, and the list goes on and on. Though individual events vary, common activities include country-western entertainment, chili and barbecue cook-offs, parades, trail rides, and, of course, roping competitions and bronc riding. Texans don't stop with cattle, however. At the Rattlesnake Roundup, held annually in Sweetwater during the second weekend in March, they round up over 12,000 pounds of live western diamondback rattlesnakes. Festivities at the event include snake handling, snake milking, plenty of rattlesnake meat, performance of the Rattlesnake Dance, and the Miss Snake Charmer Queen contest. Similar events are held in Jacksboro and Big Spring in mid-and late March, and in Freer in late April.

The sea bordering the abundant Texas coastline offers many opportunities for celebration. Fulton hosts the annual Oysterfest, which includes oyster-shucking and -eating contests for four days in early March. This event is followed in late March by the Saltwater Crawfish and Crab Festival at Orange, the Crawfish Festival at Mauriceville in mid-April, and the Texas Crab Festival at Crystal Beach in mid-May where Miss Crab Legs and her subjects enjoy fresh gulf seafood and crab. Over two weekends in mid-May, the Texas Crawfish Festival is held at Spring. Midland hosts the Shrimp Festival in mid-June.

Texas offers a broad range of rich culinary experiences celebrated throughout the year at fiestas, festivals, and cook-offs. Kingsville features cactus cuisine at its Texas Cactus Festival in early March, followed in Cotulla by the Wild Hog Cookoff and County Fair. Festivalgoers might want to learn more about the subtleties in the name of the mid-May Beaumont Annual Cookoff and Cow Dump prior to partaking of the food, but barbecued beef is sure to be included. Vidor hosts the Texas Barbecue Festival in late May. Throughout the spring and summer, hungry festivalgoers are likely to find turnip greens in Easton; tomatoes in Jacksonville; blueberries in Nacogdoches; onions in Noonday; watermelon in Stockdale, Luling, Naples, and Knox City; and peaches in Stonewall. The Corn Festival is held in mid-June at Holland, and Hallettsville is the site of the South Texas Polka and Sausage Fest in March. The Oldtime Cowboy Gathering & Chuckwagon Cookoff is held at Weatherford in mid-April. Chili cook-offs combine fun, the competitive spirit, and good eating during several events. For instance, the Texas Open Chili Cookoff at Lewisville includes music and arts and crafts and offers a venue for over 250 chili cooks to compete. The Cowtown CASI (Chili Appreciation Society, International) Chili Cookoff is held at Grand Prairie in mid-June.

A miscellany of other festivals round out the big way Texans celebrate their history, culture, music, flora, leisure activities, and even pests such as mosquitos. In late March Denton welcomes visitors to its Texas Storytelling Festival. Round Rock is proud of its daffodils during the Daffodil Days Festival in early March, which is followed by dogwood festivals at Palestine (Dogwood Trails Festival) and Woodville (Tyler County Dogwood Festival). The Bluebonnet Festival of Texas follows in early April at Chappell Hill. Wills Point is the home of the mid-April Bluebird Festival, and Fredericksburg is the home of the Herb Fest. Viking Fest at Georgetown celebrates the achievements of early Swedes, Norwegians, Danes, Finns, Estonians, and Icelanders in the settlement of Texas. Ennis does the polka during the National Polka Festival in late May. Cinco de Mayo celebrations are held in early May at Alvin, Houston, Huntsville, San Antonio, Grand Prairie, Tyler, Odessa, Dallas, and Corpus Christi, to name a few. Fiesta San Antonio, is held for a week in April, when millions of celebrants enjoy a lighthearted spring fling and carnival. July is a good time to be thoroughly aggravated and enjoy it at the Great Texas Mosquito Festival at Clute.[65]

UTAH

Utah begins the year with the perfect remedy for cabin fever: the Salt Lake City Sundance Film Festival, held annually in Park City for ten days beginning in mid-January. The festival offers an opportunity for independent filmmakers to develop and showcase their work and at the same time provides rich entertainment to thousands of filmgoers. Winter sporting events and celebrations dominate the winter months, from snowmobiling and skiing to the January Hof Winter Carnival in Ogden and the SnowShine Festival in Park City from late March to mid-April, which features spring skiing events.

Celebrations of the arts and western and international cultures begin with the Arts Festival and Annual Folk Arts and Crafters Market in St. George at the end of March. The Moab Arts Festival is held at the end of May, and the Annual Music in the Mountains celebration is held from June through September in Park City. Perhaps the most famous artistic celebration is the Utah Shakespearean Festival, held from the end of June to the middle of October. Here, six Shakespearean dramas are performed in rotation for over 100,000 visitors annually. A sampling of summer folk art and western heritage festivals includes the Western Heritage Festival at Tremonton, the West Valley City West Fest International, the Utah Arts Festival at Salt Lake City, the Springville World Folkfest, the Park City Arts Festival, and the Southern Utah Folklife Festival at Springdale. In addition to festivals, the Wild West is celebrated at rodeos held in June in Morgan (Morgala Days Rodeo); in July at Oakley (Oakley Rodeo), Nephi (Ute Stampede PRCA Rodeo), and Ogden (Pioneer Days and Rodeo); in August (Bear Lake Raspberry Days and Rodeo), and in September at Bluff (Utah Navajo Fair and Rodeo). Pioneer Days are held in Hanksville, Levan, Logan, and Monroe.

Ogden hosts the Mountain Man Rendezvous in early April, followed by similar events in May at Logan, in June at Kanab, in late June to early July at Escalante, and in September at Bear Lake State Park. Heber City is the site of the Heber Valley Annual Indian Pow Wow at the end of June. In late October and into early November, the Antelope Island State Park is home for the Annual Bison Roundup. Cowboys and adventurers will find excitement at Moab in June at the Butch Cassidy Days Celebration and at summer's end at Grantsville during Donner Days. Oktoberfests are held in Snowbird, Price, and Ogden. The Scandinavian Festival is held at Ephraim in mid-May. The Swedish Midsummer Festival is held at Salt Lake City in mid-June. In early September, Salt Lake City also hosts the Greek Festival.

Harvest festivals begin with Strawberry Days in June at Pleasant Grove, followed by Cherry Days at North Ogden City in July, Onion Days at Payson and the Corn Festival at Enterprise in August, and Annual Peach Days in Brigham City and Peach Days and Horse Races at Ferron, both in September. Green River invites visitors to the Melon Days Celebration in mid-September. The Utah State Fair is held at Salt Lake City from early to mid-September. The Castle Valley Pageant in early August is held at Castle Dale in tribute to the settlement of the valley.[66]

VERMONT

Vermont celebrates and luxuriates in its great natural beauty year-round. Beginning in January with the Harriman Reservoir Ice Fishing Derby at Whitingham, and with ice-sculpturing and ice-cutting competitions at the Brookfield Ice Harvest, winter is only getting started. A number of carnivals offer opportunities to skate, ski, create snow sculptures, take sleigh rides, compete in sled dog and snowmobile races, snowboard, play snow golf, and enjoy Vermont foods and crafts. Some of the winter carnivals include the Burke Mountain Resort Winter Carnival and the Stowe Winter Carnival in January, and the Mad River Valley Winter Carnival, the Brattleboro Winter Carnival, and the Middlebury College Winter Carnival in February.

Nature bears many gifts in Vermont. The sugar maple is the official state tree of Vermont, an honor remembered throughout the spring at maple festivals such as the three-day Vermont Maple Festival in April in St. Albans and the Whitingham Sugar Festival in late March. Strawberry suppers and festivals are held in Dummerston Center, East Bethel, South Londonderry, and Cornwall in late June, in North Pomfret in early July, and in Wells in late July. The state beverage is milk so it is no surprise that Vermont hosts an annual Dairy Festival in early June in Enosburg Falls and an Annual Cow Appreciation Day in Woodstock in mid-July. These events are sure to be crowd pleasers, especially for ice cream lovers.

History is celebrated statewide during the Vermont Heritage Weekend and Historical Society Open House in mid-June. Sites throughout the state offer glimpses into Vermont's role in the Revolutionary and Civil Wars, including a Revolutionary War encampment and weapons demonstration in Arlington and at the Civil War Underground Railroad Station in Barnet. Events include guided tours of eighteenth- and nineteenth-century homes, historic buildings, and museums; ice cream socials; walking tours of historic cemeteries; dairy and creamery exhibits; farm tool and other agricultural exhibits; quilt exhibits; and various food tastings. Similarly, Vermont's Northeast Kingdom Fall Foliage Festival in late September provides a number of towns the opportunity to welcome visitors to enjoy special events, foods, and crafts along with fall colors throughout the countryside. The Underhill Old Fashioned Harvest Market in late September welcomes thousands to taste Vermont's harvest including apple cider and baked goods.

Quilting and arts and crafts offer Vermonters some indoor activities that have both practical and creative results. There are many festivals celebrating these creative efforts, including Northfield's Annual Vermont Quilt Festival in mid-July; the Annual Quilt Exhibition in Woodstock beginning at the end of July and continuing through much of August; the Annual Summer Craft Show at Killington at the end of July; and the Vermont Festival of the Arts, a ten-day festival in the Mad River Valley beginning in mid-August.

Though music is often a part of many festivals, some festivals highlight music and musical genres, such as the Discover Jazz Festival in early to mid-June at Burlington, the Annual Weeklong Festival on the Green in Middlebury in mid-July, and the Champlain Valley Folk Festival in early August in Burlington. At the Annual Basin Bluegrass Festival in Brandon in mid-July guests are invited to join in with their own instruments. The Vermont Bach Festival is held in mid-October.

The Morgan, the state horse of Vermont, is the focus of several events in which spectators attend demonstrations on a wide variety of riding styles. One such event is the Annual Morgan Horse Demonstrations held in Shelburne in mid-August. Shelburne also celebrates the Vermont Morgan Field Day in late June with demonstrations on dressage, driving, sidesaddle, jumping, racing, and English and Western pleasure styles. At this event, spectators can also enjoy log-rolling demonstrations and meet Vermontica, the official State Calf of Vermont. In July, Vermont Morgan Heritage Days are celebrated at the Tunbridge Fairgrounds.[67–69]

VIRGINIA

Virginia's rich history is celebrated at the Jamestown Founders' Weekend in mid-May at Jamestown Island; and Landing Day, the reenactment of the landing of the first colonists, is held on May 15 at the Yorktown Victory Center and Jamestown Settlement. Yorktown, Jamestown, and Williamsburg celebrate colonial life during the Thanksgiving season with feasts and festivals. Native Americans, early settlers, builders of colonial

America, and immigrants of diverse nationality are celebrated at many events, including the Native American Powwow in Roanoke in mid-May and the Native American Occoneechee State Park Heritage Festival and Powwow in Clarksville in early May. The Juneteenth Commemoration in Alexandria's African American Heritage Park is held in mid-June, and the African American Festival of Pride is held in October in Virginia Beach. The Annual Virginia Scottish Games are in Alexandria in late July. The International Scottish Highland Games and Irish Festival is in mid-June in Fredericksburg, the Potomac Celtic Festival is in mid-June in Leesburg, and the Greek Festival of Fredericksburg is in September. Oktoberfest celebrations take place in Virginia Beach and throughout the state in mid-October.

A Civil War reenactment is held in early August in Leesburg, along with other reenactments held throughout the state throughout the year to keep history alive. Civil War weekends are held in late July and late August in Manassas and in Yorktown in May. The Battle of New Market is reenacted at the New Market Re-enactment and Living History Weekend in mid-May. The Reenactment of the Battle of Fredericksburg is held at Kenmore Plantation and Gardens in December.

A number of parades, celebrations, and parties are held in February in honor of George Washington's birthday: in Alexandria, Fredericksburg, and at his birthplace in Westmoreland County. Thomas Jefferson's birthday is celebrated in April at Monticello, and President John Tyler's life is celebrated at his Annual Birthday celebration in Williamsburg in late March. Virginia celebrates Historic Garden Week in mid-April by opening homes, gardens, and historic landmarks throughout the entire state.

The natural beauty and bounty of the earth are causes for celebration at the Delaplane Strawberry Festival at the end of May and the Strawberry Festival at the end of April in Roanoke. The Annual Vinton Dogwood Festival and the International Azalea Festival held in Norfolk are in mid-April. Winchester's Shenandoah Apple Blossom Festival is at the end of April. The Sorghum Molasses Festival is in early October in Clifford (Amherst County); the Whitetop Mountain maple and molasses festivals are in March and October, respectively; and the Virginia Garlic Festival is hosted in mid-October in Amherst County. Let us not forget wine tastings and festivals in mid-May at Mount Vernon at the Wine Tasting and Sunset Tour; the Annual Festival of Virginia Wines in mid-August at The Plains; Wine Down with Jazz weekends held on September weekends in Portsmouth; and the Annual Virginia Wine Festival in Charlottesville in late May.

The sea yields many opportunities to give thanks and enjoy an abundance of seafood at the mid-September Annual Bay Seafood Festival held along the banks of Fleets Bay in Lancaster County. There is also the Annual Northern Neck Seafood Extravaganza at Ingleside in Oak Grove in September, the Seafood Fling at Fort Monroe in Hampton at the end of July, the Annual Chincoteague Oyster Festival in early October, and at the Urbanna Annual Oyster Festival in early November, to name a few.

Music plays throughout Virginia at jazz festivals, fiddler's conventions, and bluegrass events. Hampton hosts the Hampton Jazz Festival in late June, Danville hosts the Annual Southern Virginia Jazz and Blues Festival also in June, Vinton celebrates bluegrass at the Annual Vinton Old-time Bluegrass Festival and Competition in mid-August, and fiddlers converge on Buena Vista in mid-June at the annual Maury River Fiddlers' Convention.

Chincoteague and Assateague Islands welcome visitors during the last week in July to the Annual Pony Swim and Auction. Chin-

coteague is also the site of the Decoy Carvers Association Decoy Show in early September and the Annual Deborah Waterfowl Show and Auction in late November. Roanoke is the site of the New River Rodeo in late April, and Salem hosts the Roanoke Valley Horse Show in June. Warrenton invites visitors to the Warrenton Horse Show in early September.[70]

WASHINGTON

Chili and hot chocolate await polar bears and penguins of the human variety after the January 1 Birch Bay Polar Bear Swim and the Grayland Penguin Plunge on January 2. In fact, there are several opportunities to put another log on the fire as Washingtonians celebrate winter. In addition to festivities in Conconully, Mazama, Republic, and Chelan, the Deer Park Winter Festival offers visitors ice sculptures, outhouse races, a chili cook-off, dogsled pulls, fireworks, and a bonfire over three days in mid-January. The Leavenworth Bavarian Ice Fest, also in mid-January, includes a regional dogsled-pulling competition, sleigh rides, and an ice cube hunt for children.

A sure remedy for winter blues is chocolate, and lots of it is available at the Red Wine and Chocolate event at Yakima Valley. Timed over the Valentine's Day holiday, this event and the Fudge Mountain Mania festival at Zillah may tide chocolate lover's over until the Yakima Chocolate Fantasy in March. Spokane keeps visitors happily supplied by throwing a Chocolate and Champagne Gala in mid-April. Mellow musical tunes may be heard across Washington at over thirty musical events. Festivals range from the Viking Jazz Festival held in Poulsbo in early February to bluegrass festivals in Puyallup, Darrington, Stevenson, Olalla, Kingston, and Port Angeles to folk and fiddling festivals in Shelton, Cashmere, Stanwood, Greenbank, and Republic.

The sea and, of course, salmon are the focal points at many celebrations. In mid-April, Westport hosts the World Class Crab Races and Crab Feed, followed by the Fathers Day Salmon Bake at Manchester in mid-June, the Allyn Days Salmon Bake and the Salmon Bake at Steilacoom in July, and the Pacific Beach Perch Fishing Derby and Salmon Bar-B-Que at Anacortes in late August. Leavenworth hosts the Wenatchee River Salmon Festival in mid-September, which follows the Salmon BBQ at Waitsburg and the Seafood Festival at Westport. Issaquah and Shelton are the sites for the Salmon Days Festival and Oysterfest, respectively, both held in early October.

Over twenty rodeos and powwows are held in Washington each year beginning with the January Columbia River Circuit Rodeo Finals at Yakima and continuing until the Labor Day Rodeo at Winthrop. In between are events at such places as Spokane, Tonasket, Glenwood, Newport, Long Beach, Walla Walla, and Ellensburg. History comes alive at numerous Civil War reenactments in Spokane, Lakewood, Tacoma, Cle Elum, Roslyn, Ferndale, and Pasco. The Lewis and Clark Festival at Walla Walla is held for two days in early June.

Many other festivals celebrate the beauty, commerce, and lifestyles found in the state. At the end of January, eagle-watching tours are offered at the Upper Skagit Bald Eagle Festival. For ten days in late April, visitors enjoy the Washington State Apple Blossom Festival at Wenatchee. The Yakima Valley wine country hosts the Spring Barrel Tasting in late April, and in early May, Spokane hosts the annual Lilac Festival. Poulsbo celebrates Scandinavian culture during its Viking Fest later in May and Seattle holds the Northwest Folklife Festival, also in May. Loggers and the logging industry are celebrated at the Loggerodeo at Sedro-Woolley in late June and early July, as well as at the Loggers Jubilee at Morton in early August.

In July, lovers of exotic food can sample bear meat and bear stew at the McCleary Bear Festival. Wild blackberries are served at the Joyce Daze Wild Blackberry Festival in early August, followed by the Bremerton Blackberry Festival and the Bingen Huckleberry Festival in September. Port Townsend hosts the Wooden Boat Festival in mid-September, followed by the Odessa Deutschesfest. Ilwaco and Grayland conduct tours of cranberry bogs during their cranberry festivals in October, and many harvest festivals celebrate the Washington apple industry.[71]

WEST VIRGINIA

From the small towns of the Mid-Ohio Valley to mountain country and the lakes in the central part of the state, West Virginia's festivals capture its many interests and industries. Canoe and raft races, gospel singing, and a $5,000 rubber ducky race are just some of the events at the Ronceverte River Festival held in mid-June at Ronceverte. Arts and crafts are showcased in many festivals including the Appalachian Weekend at Pipestem in late March, the Dogwood Arts and Crafts Festival at Huntington in late April, the Mountain State Art and Craft Fair at Ripley in early July, the Appalachian Arts and Crafts Festival at Beckley in late August, the Mountain Heritage Arts and Crafts Festivals at Charles Town in June and September, the Harvest Moon Arts and Crafts Festival at Parkersburg in mid-September, and the Weirton Arts and Crafts Festival in early November.

Music is the theme of several events. Glenville hosts the West Virginia State Folk Festival in mid-June when folk musicians and visitors immerse themselves in the music of the pre-1930s with such instruments as mandolins, autoharps, dulcimers, fiddles, and banjos. Other musical events include the Augusta Spring Dulcimer Week in mid-April at Elkins, the Bluegrass Country Music Festival at Summersville in late June, and Clifftop's Appalachian String Band Music Festival and Salem's Dulcimer Weekend both in August. The Mountain State Forest Festival is held in late September and early October at Elkins, which provides something for everyone in mountain arts including crafts, sports, and music. The late October Old Time Week and Fiddlers Reunion is at Elkins, and a festival with two themes expressed in the name, the Lumberjackin' Bluegrassin' Jamboree, is at Mullens in mid-October.

Life is sweet and especially so at the West Virginia Maple Syrup Festival in mid-March at Pickens. More sugar may be found during the West Virginia Honey Festival in mid-September at Mineral Wells, where the sting is taken out of beekeeping with bee-handling demonstrations, candlemaking, and a honey bake contest. Nature yields many unique treats to be savored and celebrated such as strawberries at the West Virginia Strawberry Festival at Buckhannon in late May; blackberries at the Nutter Fort Blackberry Festival in early August; and wild scallions or ramson, which turn up at cook-offs and in stews during April's International Ramp Cook-off at Elkins and at the Feast of the Ramson at Richwood. Dandelion greens and wine are consumed in late May at the West Virginia Dandelion Festival held in White Sulphur Springs. Summersville sees nothing but spuds at the Nicholas County Potato Festival in September.

With the approach of fall, sorghum cane, pumpkins, walnuts, and apples are ready for harvest. With a harvest comes celebration. Arnoldsburg hosts the West Virginia Molasses Festival in late September. Apple harvest festivals and apple butter festivals are held in Salem, Berkeley Springs, Martinsburg, and Burlington throughout October. The West Virginia Pumpkin Festival is held at Milton in early October, and Spencer is the site of the West Virginia Black Walnut Festival in mid-October.

Civil War reenactments may be found from March to November for Civil War history buffs. Hurricane is the site of an encampment and reenactment in late March, followed in early June by the Blue and Gray Reunion at Philippi and the mid-July Battle of Laurel Hill Reenactment at Belington. In mid-August, the Battle of Dry Creek is reenacted at the Greenbrier State Forest in White Sulphur Springs. The Battle of Carnifex Ferry is the focal point of the Civil War Weekend in mid-September at Summersville. Guyandotte hosts the Guyandotte Civil War Days in late October and early November.

The ethnic diversity of West Virginia is celebrated at numerous festivals throughout the year. In March, Wheeling hosts the Celtic Celebration, where Irish and Scottish music, dancing, food, and crafts are highlighted. The Native American Pow Wow is held in South Charleston in mid-May. Wheeling hosts the Upper Ohio Valley Italian Festival in late July. August events include the Multi-Fest at Charleston and the West Virginia Highland Games at South Charleston. In late August, Weirton hosts the Greek Bazaar, followed in September by the West Virginia Italian Heritage Festival at Clarksburg and the Black Heritage Festival also in Clarksburg. Oktoberfests are held in September and October at Wheeling, Weston, and Barboursville.

Finally, entertainment comes in many forms, from fishing to exhibiting prize-winning farm projects at the State Fair to telling stories at day's end. The West Virginia Bass Festival at St. Mary's on the second full weekend in June includes an Ohio River bass catching tournament, crafts, and nightly musical entertainment. In mid-August, the State Fair of West Virginia is underway at Lewisburg. This fair's origin dates back to 1858, when General Robert E. Lee's warhorse, Traveller, was exhibited as a yearling. The West Virginia Oil and Gas Festival in Sistersville in mid-September celebrates antique engines of the 1890s, as well as rides on the Ohio River's last ferry. Weston welcomes folks with yarns to delight crowds at the Storytelling Festival Voices of the Mountains in early October.[72]

WISCONSIN

When given ice and snow, make ice sculptures and snow angels. And while visitors to the many winter events in Wisconsin are enjoying the ice and snow, they are invited to yodel, make chili, play ice golf, ice fish, dance a polka or two, figure skate, enjoy pancakes, take sleigh rides, join in fishing competitions, participate in sled dog races, and gaze at hot-air balloon tableaus. To name a few celebrations of Wisconsin winters held during January, there is the Little Switzerland Winter Festival at New Glarus, the Winter Carnival at Merrill, the Winter Janboree at Waukesha, the annual Flake Out Festival at the Wisconsin Dells, the Dodgeville Winterfest, the Beloit Winterfest, Clintonville's Winter Whirl; Burlington's Chilly Chocolate Days, Sherwood's Winterfest, and Milwaukee's U.S. International Snow Sculpting Competition. In February, La Crosse welcomes visitors to the Winter Rec-Fest, Kiel to Winter Carnival, Cedarburg to the Winter Festival, Hayward to Winterfest, Nekoosa to Snoblast, Minocqua to Snowfest, Green Lake to Winterfest, and Neillsville to Winter Carnival. Sled dog races include the January Empire 130 Sled Dog Races from Solon Springs to Amnicon Lake and the Nicolet Sprint Sled Dog Race at Eagle River. In February, Bowler hosts the Many Trails Sled Dog Races and Land O' Lakes hosts the Headwaters Classic Sled Dog Races. Ice fishing competitions include the Fisharama at Lake Nebagamon, the Lake Isadore Ice Fishing Contest at Medford, the Lions Ice Fishing Contest at Minong, and the Brice Prairie Ice-Fishing Derby at Onalaska. In early March, Cable claims

to offer the longest weenie roast in the world as over 1,000 people line up to roast weenies at the Winter Festival and Weenie Roast.

Fish as sport and food is celebrated at the Nekoosa Walleye Days held from the end of March through mid-April, at Baileys Harbor Brown Trout Tournament in April, and at Racine's Salmon-a-rama in mid-July. Wisconsin enjoys culinary delicacies throughout the year from chocolate at the Burlington Chocolate Festival and mushrooms at the Muscoda Morel Mushroom Festival, both in May, to mustard at Mount Horeb's National Mustard Day and sweet corn at Sun Prairie's Sweet Corn Festival, both held in August. Cranberry and apple festivals are held in Eagle River, Warrens, Waukesha, and Gays Mill in September and October. Franksville is the site of the June Kraut Festival. However, no discussion of Wisconsin festivals that include food would be complete without mention of the dairy industry. Little Chute offers cheese curds to contestants until they have their fill, followed by a cheese-carving competition at its Great Wisconsin Cheese Festival in early June. West Salem hosts June Dairy Days, Marshfield the Dairyfest, and Sparta the Butterfest, all in June. In September, Monroe welcomes visitors to Cheese Days. Touted as the largest agricultural fair in Wisconsin, Fond du Lac hosts Farm Progress Days in mid-July, and the Wisconsin State Fair is held at West Allis from early to mid-August.

Wisconsin has a rich ethnic heritage that is celebrated frequently throughout the state throughout the year. Events celebrating Scandinavian heritage include Ashland's Scandinavian Heritage Day, Sister Bay's Taste of Scandinavia Festival, Racine's Scandinavian Festival, and Superior's Scandinavian Festival. The Spring Polka Fest is held in early April at the Wisconsin Dells, followed by the West Allis Cinco De Mayo celebration, the Concord Wisconsin Polkafest, and Germantown's Mai Fest, all held in

May. June events include the New Glarus Swiss Polkafest, Milwaukee's Asian Moon Festival, the Czechoslovakian Community Festival at Phillips, the Juneteenth Day Celebration at Milwaukee, the Fiesta Waukesha at Waukesha, the Polish Fest at Milwaukee, the African-American Homecoming at Eagle, and the Black Creek Polkafest.

July begins with the Ellsworth Polka Fest, followed by the Bear River Pow Wow at Lac du Flambeau, Belgian Days at Brussels, Festa Italiana at Milwaukee, Polka Day at Pulaski, and the Milwaukee German Fest. August events include the Keshena Menominee Pow-Wow, Baldwin's Let's Go Dutch Days, Milwaukee's African World Festival, Milwaukee's Irish Fest, Mount Horeb's Annual Norwegian American Fest, and Milwaukee's Mexican Fiesta. The fall brings Oktoberfests at Milwaukee, Appleton, La Crosse, Brodhead, and Omro, to name a few.

A number of festivals celebrate fur trading and life on the frontier such as Eagle River's Klondike Days. The Saukville Crossroads Rendezvous competitions include tomahawk-and knife-throwing contests. The Fort Atkinson Buckskinner Rendezvous, the Saukville French and Indian Encampment, the Baraboo River Rendezvous, and Hartford's Buckskinners Encampment also celebrate times past. Lumberjacks converge on Hayward in July for the Lumberjack World Championship when victors take home $50,000 in prize money. Life is grand in Wisconsin whether celebrants are at Hudson in February for the Hot Air Affair or at Madison for the Kites on Ice festival, at Fond du Lac in April at the Jazz Festival, or at the Sheboygan Falls Ducktona 500, when 2,000 plastic ducks race on the Sheyboygan River.[73,74]

WYOMING

The new year gets off to a chilly beginning in January with ice fishing derbies in Lara-mie, Saratoga, and Meeteetse, and sled dog races at Dubois and Jackson Hole. In early February Lander hosts the Annual Wyoming State Winter Fair, followed by the Ice Fishing Derby at Cheyenne's Curt Gowdy State Park, the Rawlins Annual Carbon County Winterfest, and Riverside's Annual Sierra Madre Winter Carnival. A variety of outdoor activities continue with events such as the March Ice Fishing Derby at Rawlins and the Pole-Peddle-Paddle competitions, held on April 1st, where the emphasis is on having fun skiing, biking, and boating at Jackson Hole. The Woodchoppers Jamboree and Rodeo in mid-June combines two types of entertainment for energetic competitors.

The old days of the West come to life during the Annual Cowboy Songs and Range Ballads event at Cody in early April, Old West Days in late May at Jackson, and almost daily from Memorial Day to Labor Day at the Jackson Hole Shootout Gang reenactments. The Green River Rendezvous Pagent is held in July at Pinedale where many mountain men and fur traders encamped in the early to mid-1800s. September provides another opportunity to learn about the past at the Mountain Man Rendezvous held at Fort Bridger. In addition to black powder shoots, mountain men and women competitions, and western food and music, Native American dancing is performed at this annual event. Native American powwows and festivals include the Northwest College Pow Wow at Powell in April, the Northern Arapahoe Spring Pow Wow and Yellow Calf Memorial Pow Wow in May, the Fort Fetterman Pow Wow Days and the Fort Washakie Eastern Shoshone Indian Days in June, and the Ethete Pow Wow in July.

The rodeo season provides plenty of entertainment in such events as the Biggest Little Rodeo at Hulett in June, and July's Jubilee Days at Laramie. Other events held in July include the Annual Cody Stampede

Rodeo; the Sheridan WYO Rodeo; the Rendezvous Rodeo at Riverton; Wyoming's Big Show at Rock Springs, where the entertainment includes a downtown cattle drive; Lander's Pioneer Days Rodeo; the Annual Cheyenne Frontier Days event; and the Red Desert Roundup Rodeo at Rock Springs. Riverton, Douglas, Glenrock, Cheyenne, and Gillette host rodeos in August. Douglas is also the site of the Wyoming State Fair and Rodeo held in mid-August. The western experience would not be complete without red hot chili, and in late August, plenty is found at the Saratoga Chili Cookoff.

September celebrates the arts with the Jackson Hole Fall Arts Festival and the Cheyenne Western Film Festival. Winter comes early with Jackson hosting the Winterfest in early October, and continuing into the season in Sheridan at the late-October Winter Snow Show and in Riverton at the Winter Art Fair in November. Oktoberfests are held at Dubois, Wheatland, Rock Springs, Rawlins, and Powell.[75,76]

DISTRICT OF COLUMBIA

Many visitors to the District of Columbia will visit the museums and national landmarks, but the District is much more than famous national institutions. It is also home to a diverse population of people who celebrate their diversity in fairs and festivals throughout the year. The Chinese Lunar New Year Celebration gets underway in late January. Two weeks after the St. Patrick's Day Parade on March 17, the Cherry Blossom Festival begins and runs into April. Perhaps the most popular and well-known festival held in the District of Columbia is sponsored by the Smithsonian Institute Center for Folklife and Cultural Heritage when the Folklife Festival features regions, states, ethnic and cultural groups, nations of the world, or occupations with music, demon-

strations, and a variety of other activities in late June and early July.

In early May the Asian Pacific American Heritage Festival is held. Malcolm X Day is celebrated on May 16. The Philippine Independence Day is celebrated in early June. The Latin-American Festival takes place in late July and early August on Pennsylvania Avenue. The African-American Family Day Summerfest is in early August, the Thai Heritage Festival is in mid-August, and the African Cultural Festival and Black Family Reunion are in September after Labor Day. October 2 is the United Nations Celebration.

The District swings when Duke Ellington's Birthday is celebrated on April 24. Dance Africa, D.C., is in mid-June, and the D.C. Free Jazz Festival is held around July 4. The Mambo USA Festival takes place in early August and the D.C. Blues Festival in early September.[77]

AMERICAN SAMOA

April 17 is American Samoa Flag Day, celebrating the first day that the flag of the United States was raised over the Samoan Islands in 1900. The celebration features singing, dancing, and longboat races, as well as basket-weaving, coconut-husking, spear-throwing, and fire-making contests. Tourism Week is in May and features cultural awareness programs along with various other activities. White Sunday occurs on the second Sunday in October. White Sunday, a children's celebration introduced by English missionaries, is quite a special day for the children of American Samoa. They lead church services and receive special foods and clothing. The Palolo Festival takes place in October and November when the tides and lunar conditions are just right. Sometimes called the Caviar of the Pacific, palolo are marine worms that emerge from the reefs annually to reproduce. Thousands of people wade out to the reef to scoop them up and often eat them raw. Christmas Week is a special time in American Samoa, with festivities that go on the full week before Christmas.[78]

COMMONWEALTH OF THE NORTHERN MARIANA ISLANDS

Free Chamorro food—coconut crab, lobster, fish, taro and sweet potatoes, fruit bat, roast pig, deer kelaquin, breadfruit—is a main attraction at Commonwealth fiestas. The fiestas are held around feast days of the saints and the church calendar. On the island of Rota, San Francisco De Borja is honored on October 10. On the island of Tinian, St. Joseph is honored on May 6. Saipan, the largest of the islands, holds six fiestas throughout the year. Saipan hosts the Annual Flame Tree Arts Festival in April when visitors can enjoy a wide array of cultural treasures including dance, music, art, and food.[79]

GUAM

Festivals are a way of life on Guam. Many of them are centered around the church calendar and village celebrations of patron saints. In January, there is a nationwide novena for the Celebration of the Holy Family. Village fiestas are held in Asan, Tumon, Chalan Pago, Tamuning, Maina, Yigo, Mongmong, Inarajan, Barrigada, Merizo, Agafa Gumas, Malojloj, Santa Rita, Ordot, Toto, Agat, Piti, Anigua, Talofofo, Yona, Umatac, Sinajana, Mangilao, Hagatna Heights, and Dededo.

Chamorro Week, held during the last week in February and the first week in March, celebrates Chamorro culture with singing, dancing, weaving, carving, and a variety of cultural displays. Chamorro Week concludes with a reenactment and carnival on Discovery Day, commemorating the landing at Umatac Bay of Ferdinand Magel-

lan on March 6, 1521. In May, the Guam-Micronesia Island Fair is held at Tumon, when Micronesian Island culture is highlighted with dances, songs, food, and goods. Liberation Day, held on July 21 at Tumon, offers visitors an opportunity to pay tribute to the thousands who gave their lives while liberating Guam from Japanese control during World War II. Festivities include a parade, carnival rides, and a fireworks display. All Souls Day, celebrated on November 2, is a day when masses in remembrance of loved ones are held at cemeteries throughout the island.[80]

PUERTO RICO

Fiestas seem to occur daily somewhere in Puerto Rico. Each town celebrates the *fiestas patronales* in honor of its patron saint in a ten-day festival that often mixes local and African elements in a series of processions, games, dances, and musical events around the town plaza. These festivals are held in the evenings during the week and all day on weekends. In January there are four such festivals, in February there are five, in March there are eight, and in May there are seven. June festivals include three honoring St. John the Baptist held in Maricao, Orocovis, and San Juan. July is the most celebrated month with fifteen festivals; but festivals continue throughout the entire year. Carnival festivities, which include the traditional coastal burial of the sardine, are also celebrated in many towns.

The Casals Festival, founded by cellist Pablo Casals in 1957, is a highly respected international music festival. It is held from early to mid-June. Another festival of interest in June is the Aibonito Flower Festival, held from late June into July, featuring popular varieties of tropical plants for sale and exhibit. Loiza hosts the Loiza Carnival throughout the month of July, when African culture and heritage are celebrated with a carnival, parade, masks, and bomba dancing. The World Salsa Congress is held at Isla Verde for almost a week at the end of July when visitors are welcome to listen to, dance to, and learn about salsa music. The Festival of Puerto Rican Music is held annually at San Juan from mid-November through early December and features classical and folk music. The music, art, food, entertainment, and traditions of Puerto Rico's Taino Indians are celebrated at the Jayuya Indian Festival at Jayuya held in mid-November.

Unique foods and beverages are highlighted at several festivals. In early September, Juana Diaz hosts the Mavi Carnival where many festive activities, such as a parade, music, and a carnival, are accompanied by food and mavi. Mavi is a fermented drink made from ironwood tree bark. The annual National Plantain Festival at Corozal held during the latter part of October features dishes made from plantains, which are starchy relatives of the banana. The ceti, or sardine fish, found in northern coastal waters, are on the minds and palates of visitors at the Ceti Festival at Arecibo in mid-November. Foods and beverages made with coconuts are on the menu at the Festival of Typical Dishes held at Luquillo in late November.[81,82]

U.S. VIRGIN ISLANDS

Regattas feature prominently on the calendar of events for the U.S Virgin Islands, from the Annual St. Croix Race in late February to the June Royak Regatta at St. Croix to the Mid-Summer Race in late July also at St. Croix. The Hugo Memorial Day Regatta is held in mid-September, followed by the Mumm's Cup Tune-Up Regatta in October, the International Match Race at St. Thomas in December, and the Boxing Day Regatta at the St. Croix Yacht Club on December 26. The beautiful sea surrounding the U.S. Virgin Islands is the venue for several notable fishing tournaments, including the July Open Tournament in early July, the United States Virgin Islands Open Blue Marlin Tournament in late August, and the Wahoo Tournament in late November all in St. Thomas.

Throughout the year, a variety of festivals are held that reflect diverse interests and ways to have fun. In January, St. Croix hosts the Anatomy of Latin Jazz Festival and it also hosts the February Annual Agriculture and Fair. St. Thomas Carnival events include talent shows, pageants, parades, water sport activities, and musical performances held throughout April. St. John hosts the St. John Festival during the month of June ending in early July. St. Thomas invites hungry guests to the mid-September Annual Chili Cook-off. In mid-November, the St. Thomas Arts Alive Arts and Crafts Festival is held.

The celebrations of special historical events are recurring reminders of the past. Organic Act Day in June commemorates the Organic Act of 1936 that granted local government to the Islands. The Slaves Rebellion of 1733 is remembered on St. John at the end of June. In the first mass resistance ever displayed in the Islands' history, slaves took control of St. John for six months before the revolt was crushed. July 3 is Virgin Islands Emancipation Day, marking the end of slavery in the former Danish West Indies in 1848. Fireburn recalls an 1878 revolt in Frederiksted led by a slave named Queen Mary of St. Croix, who led women and children in the razing of homes and stores in a protest against slavery. D. Hamilton Jackson Day on November 1 commemorates the man who won the right to a free press and other reforms from Denmark on a 1915 mission there.[83]

NOTES

1. *Calendar of Events, Alabama Bureau of Tourism and Travel* (Url: www.touralabama. org).

2. *2000 Official State of Alaska Vacation Planner* (n.p.: Alaska Visitors Association, 1999).

3. *Travel Alaska Trip Planner, Statewide Event Calendar* (Url: www.travelalaska.com/planner).

4. *Arizona Journeys* (Phoenix: Arizona Office of Tourism, 1999).

5. *The 2000 Spring and Summer Arkansas Calendar of Events* (Arkansas Department of Parks and Tourism, n.d.).

6. *The 1999/2000 Fall and Winter Arkansas Calendar of Events* (Arkansas Department of Parks and Tourism, n.d.).

7. *California Celebrations 1999* (Sacramento: State of California Trade and Commerce Agency, Division of Tourism, 1999).

8. *Colorado 1999 Official State Vacation Guide* (Denver: Colorado Travel and Tourism Authority, 1999).

9. *Connecticut Vacation Guide 1999* (Hartford: Connecticut Department of Economic and Community Development, Office of Tourism, n.d.).

10. *Connecticut Special Events Calendar: Fall/Winter 1999/2000* (n.p.: Connecticut Department of Economic and Community Development, Office of Tourism, n.d.).

11. *1999 Delaware Calendar of Events* (Dover: Delaware Tourism Office, n.d.).

12. *1999 Official Florida Vacation Guide* (Sarasota: Miles Media Group, n.d.).

13. *Georgia Department of Industry, Trade, and Tourism: Calendar of Events* (Url: www2.ganet.org/visitga/tour_event.html).

14. *The Islands of Aloha: The 1999 Official Travel Guide of the Hawaii Visitors and Convention Bureau, Spring/Summer Edition 1999* (Santa Monica, Calif.: Plan B for Hawaii Visitors and Convention Bureau, n.d.).

15. *Idaho: Official State Travel Guide* (Boise: Idaho Department of Commerce, Idaho Travel Council, n.d.).

16. *Illinois Bureau of Tourism Events Search: Trip Planner* (Url: www.enjoyillinois.com).

17. *Indiana 1999 Festival Guide* (Url: www.state.in.us/tourism/html/fest99).

18. *1999 Travel Guide* (Indianapolis: Indiana Department of Commerce, Tourism Division, 1999).

19. *Iowa: Come Be Our Guest. 2000 Travel Guide* (Des Moines: Iowa Department of Economic Development, Division of Tourism, n.d.).

20. *Kansas Travel and Event Guide* (Topeka: Kansas Department of Commerce and Housing, Travel and Tourism Division, 1999).

21. *1999 Great Kentucky Getaway Guide* (Frankfort: Kentucky Department of Travel, 1999).

22. *1999 Kentucky Calendar of Events* (Frankfort: Kentucky Department of Travel, 1999).

23. *Francofete: 1999 Events and Attractions* (Baton Rouge: State of Louisiana Department of Culture, Recreation, and Tourism, n.d.).

24. *1999 Maine Invites You: The Official Travel Planner* (Hallowell: The Maine Publicity Bureau, Inc., 1999).

25. *Maryland Celebrates* (Baltimore: Maryland Office of Tourism and Development, n.d.).

26. *Massachusetts 1999 Getaway Guide* (Boston: Massachusetts Office of Travel and Tourism, n.d.).

27. *Michigan Travel Ideas* (n.p.: Midwest Living Magazine, n.d.).

28. *1999–2000 Michigan Fall/Winter Calendar of Events and Travel Guide* (Flint: Travel Michigan, n.d.).

29. *Minnesota Explorer: Winter 1999–2000* (St. Paul: Minnesota Office of Tourism, 1999).

30. *Minnesota Explorer: Fall 1999* (St. Paul: Minnesota Office of Tourism, 1999).

31. *Minnesota Explorer: Spring/Summer 2000* (St. Paul: Minnesota Office of Tourism, 1999).

32. *1999 Calendar of Events* (Jackson: Mississippi Department of Economic and Community Development, n.d.).

33. *Missouri: Where the Rivers Run. 1999 Calendar of Events* (St. Louis: Missouri Division of Tourism in cooperation with Preprint Publishing, n.d.).

34. *Travel Montana* (Url: visitmt.com/tripplanner/events).

35. *1999 Nebraska Catalog of Events, August–December* (Lincoln: Nebraska Department of Economic Development, Division of Travel and Tourism, n.d.).

36. *Visit Nebraska Travel Planner: Events* (Url: www.visitnebraska.org/planner/eventlist.asp).

37. *Millennium Countdown Calendar of Nevada Events and Shows: A Section of Nevada Magazine* (n.p.: Nevada Magazine, n.d.).

38. *1999–2000 Official New Hampshire Guidebook* (Concord: New Hampshire Department of Resources and Economic Development, 1999).

39. *Events in New Hampshire* (Url: www.visitnh.gov).

40. *New Jersey Calendar of Events, October 1999–March 2000* (Trenton: New Jersey Commerce and Economic Growth Commission, 1999).

41. *1999 Travel Guide* (Url: www.state.nj.us/travel).

42. *Online State New Jersey Calendar* (Url: www.state.nj.us/travel).

43. *New Mexico Calendar of Events* (Url: www.newmexico.org/calendar).

44. *I Love New York Travel Guide* (New York: New York State Department of Economic Development, 1999).

45. *Calendar of Events, January–December 1999* (Raleigh: North Carolina Division of Tourism, n.d.)

46. *North Carolina Division of Tourism web site* (Url: www.visitnc.com).

47. *Events in North Dakota* (Url: www.ndtourism.com).

48. *2000 Ohio Arts Festivals and Competitions Directory* (Columbus: Ohio Arts Council, 1999).

49. *2000 Ohio Festivals and Events Association* (n.p.: Ohio Festivals and Events Association, n.d.)

50. *Events and Festivals* (Url: www.travelok.com).

51. *The Official Oregon Travel Guide* (Salem: Oregon Tourism Commission, 1999).

52. *The 1999 Oregon Events Calendar* (Tigard, Oreg.: Community Newspapers Contract Publishing Division, n.d.).

53. *Brandywine Country* (Media, Pa.: Brandywine Conference and Visitors Bureau, Summer 2000).

54. *Johnstown and Cambria County Pennsylvania* (Johnstown: Greater Johnstown/Cambria County Convention and Visitors Bureau, n.d.).

55. *Laurel Highlands of Southwestern Pennsylvania: 2000 Visitors Guide* (Ligonier, Pa.: Laurel Highlands Visitors Bureau, n.d.).

56. *Lehigh Valley 1999 Map and Guide* (Lehigh Valley, Pa.: Lehigh Valley Convention and Visitors Bureau, n.d.).

57. *Pennsylvania Rainbow Region: 2000 Visitors' Guide* (n.p.: The Barash Group and the PA Rainbow Region Vacation Bureau, 2000).

58. *Pittsburgh Events Calendar: May thru August 2000* (Greater Pittsburgh Convention and Visitors Bureau, n.d.).

59. *Where and When, Pennsylvania's Travel Guide* (State College, Pa.: The Barash Group, Summer 2000).

60. *York County Gateway to Central Pennsylvania* (York: York County Convention and Visitors Bureau and Genesis Publishing, 2000).

61. *Visit Rhode Island: Official Rhode Island Tourism Division Site* (Url: visitrhodeisland.com).

62. *South Carolina Smiling Faces. Beautiful Places* (Columbia: South Carolina Department of Parks, Recreation, and Tourism, 1999).

63. *South Dakota Vacation Guide, 1999–2000* (published by the South Dakota Department of Tourism; Southeast South Dakota Visitors Association; Glacial Lakes and Prairies Tourism Association; Greak Lakes of South Dakota Association; and Black Hills, Badlands, and Lakes Association, n.d.).

64. *Official 1999 Vacation Guide* (Franklin, Tenn.: Journal Communications Inc., for the Tennessee Department of Tourist Development, 1998).

65. *Travel Tex* (Texas Department of Economic Development) (Url: www.traveltex.com).

66. *Utah Travel Guide* (Salt Lake City: Utah Travel Council, 1997).

67. *Vermont Life Explorer 1999* (Montpelier: Vermont Life Magazine, 1999).

68. *Vermont Traveler's Guidebook* (n.p.: Vermont Chamber of Commerce, 1999).

69. *Vermont's Summer Events 1999* (n.p., n.d.).

70. *1999 Virginia Travel Guide* (n.p., n.d.).

71. *Washington State Calendar of Events 1999* (n.p.: Washington State Department of Community, Trade, and Economic Development, Tourism Office, n.d.).

72. *1999 West Virginia Wild and Wonderful: The State's Official Travel Guide* (n.p.: Bell Atlantic, 1999).

73. *Wisconsin 1999/2000 Fall/Winter Event and Recreation Guide* (Madison: Wisconsin Department of Tourism, 1999).

74. *Wisconsin 2000 Spring/Summer Event & Recreation Guide* (Madison: Wisconsin Department of Tourism, 2000).

75. *Wyoming Vacation Directory* (Cheyenne: Wyoming Division of Tourism, n.d.)

76. *Wyoming Electronic Scout Events* (Url: www.wyomingtourism.org).

77. *Washington DC: The Official Tourism Site of Washington, DC* (Url: www. washington.org).

78. *American Samoa Office of Tourism 1998 Events* (Url: www.samoanet.com).

79. *Northern Mariana Islands* (Url: www. mariana-islands.gov.mp/tourism.htm).

80. *Festivals (Fiestas) and Events* (Url: www. visitguam.org).

81. *Puerto Rico Festivals* (Url: Welcome. toPuertoRico.org).

82. *Puerto Rico Tourism Company Activity Calendar* (Url: www.prtourism.com).

83. *U.S. Virgin Islands Calendar of Events* (Url: www.usvi-info.com).

15

State and Territory Universities

There are nearly 600 public four-year institutions of higher education in the United States and its territories. This chapter provides a brief history of the development of the major state universities, including land grant institutions and historically black institutions, and the location of the main and other campuses. The universities' symbols as denoted by official colors, nicknames, and fight songs are also listed.[1]

ALABAMA

Alabama State University (1867)

The Lincoln Normal School, which later became Alabama State University, was originally founded in Marion, Alabama, as a private school for Negroes. [2]

Campuses: Main campus in Montgomery
Colors: Black and Gold
Nickname: Hornets
Song: "Hail Alabama!"[3]

Auburn University (1856)

Auburn was chartered by the state of Alabama in 1856 as a private school called East Alabama Male College. Closed because of the Civil War from 1861 to 1866, the Methodist Church, by 1872, transferred title of the college to the state due to financial constraints. Thus was born the land grant college known as the Agricultural and Mechanical College of Alabama. From 1899 until 1960, when another name change created Auburn University, the college was called the Alabama Polytechnic Institute.[4]

Campuses: Auburn; Auburn University at Montgomery
Colors: Burnt Orange and Navy Blue
Nickname: Tigers
Song: "War Eagle;" "Tiger Rag;" "Thumb Cheer/War Eagle"[5]

University of Alabama (1831)

Tuscaloosa, which had been Alabama's capital in 1827, was chosen to be the home of the University of Alabama. The land on which the university was built had been donated in 1819 by the U.S. government for an institution of learning. Four years later, the university enrolled its first students. It became a military university in 1860 and all but four of its buildings were burned to the ground by Union troops in 1864. Today, the University of Alabama is one of three autonomous universities making up the University of Alabama System, which was formed in 1969.[6]

Campuses: Tuscaloosa
Colors: Crimson and White

Nickname: Crimson Tide

Song: "Yea Alabama"[7]

University of Alabama at Birmingham (1966)

The Birmingham campus began as an extension center of the University of Alabama in 1936. The medical school was moved to Birmingham from Tuscaloosa in 1945 and the School of Dentistry opened in 1948. In 1966 the extension center became the University of Alabama in Birmingham, and in 1984 the University underwent a slight name change to its current form.[8]

Campuses: Birmingham

Colors: Green, Gold, and White

Nickname: Blazers

Song: "UAB Fight Song"[9]

University of Alabama in Huntsville (1950)

Classes were first held at the Huntsville campus in 1950, with master's courses added in 1963 and baccalaureate level courses the next year. In 1971 doctoral programs in physics and engineering as well as the School of Nursing were begun. In 1969 the Huntsville campus became part of the University of Alabama system as an independent university.[10]

Campuses: Huntsville

Colors: Blue and White

Nickname: Chargers

Song: "UAH Fight Song" by Jon Hand[11]

ALASKA

University of Alaska

Opening its doors in 1922 as the Alaska Agricultural College and School of Mines on land near Fairbanks set aside by the U.S. Congress in 1915 for a land-grant college, the University of Alaska was so named in 1935. Today, the university system consists of three universities each with a number of colleges or campuses.[12]

University of Alaska Anchorage (1976)

Campuses: Anchorage Campus; Kenai Peninsula College; Kodiak College; Matanuska-Susitna Campus; Chugiak-Eagle River Campus; Prince William Sound Community College

Colors: Green and Gold

Nickname: Seawolves

Song: "U.A.A., The Seawolves Song," music by Cal Scott, lyrics by Cal Scott and Dan Cox[13]

University of Alaska Fairbanks (1917)

Campuses: Fairbanks Campus; Chukchi Campus; Kuskokwim Campus; Northwest Campus; Bristol Bay Campus; Interior Aleutians Campus; Tanana Campus; College of Rural Alaska

Colors: Royal Blue and Sunflower Gold

Nickname: Nanooks

Song: "University of Alaska Fight Song," music by Carl M. Franklin, lyrics by Mary J. Walker and Carl M. Franklin[14]

University of Alaska Southeast (1956)

Campuses: Juneau Campus; Sitka Campus; Ketchikan Campus

Colors: Royal Blue and Silver
Nickname: Humpback whale
Song: None[15]

ARIZONA

Arizona State University (1885)

Arizona State University was founded as a normal school in 1885 by an act of the Arizona Territory Legislative Assembly and classes were first held in the following year. Before becoming Arizona State University, the school was known as the Normal School of Arizona and then the Arizona State Teachers College. Today, it is a major research institution.[16]

Campuses: ASU Main in Tempe; ASU West in Phoenix; ASU East in Mesa
Colors: Maroon and Gold
Nickname: Sun Devils
Song: "Fight, Devils Down the Field"[17]

University of Arizona (1885)

Although founded by an act of the territorial legislature in 1885, the University of Arizona did not admit its first class until 1891 for want of land on which to build. As Arizona's land-grant institution, the University continues the tradition of teaching and research in agriculture and science.[18]

Campuses: Tucson
Colors: Red and Blue
Nickname: Wildcats
Song: "Bear Down, Arizona!" by Jack K. Lee[19]

ARKANSAS

Arkansas State University (1909)

Arkansas State began as an agricultural training school, offering its first two-year college courses in 1918. In 1925 the school's name was changed to First District Agricultural and Mechanical College; and in 1933, after commencing a four-year collegiate program in 1930, its name was changed again to Arkansas State College. The college attained university status in 1967.[20]

Campuses: Main Campus in State University; Beebe Campus and Newport Campus; Mountain Home Campus
Colors: Scarlet and Black
Nickname: Indians
Song: "ASU Loyalty Song"[21]

University of Arkansas (1871)

The Arkansas Industrial Institution was founded by the Arkansas legislature in 1871 in accordance with the Federal Land Grant Act of 1862. Students began taking classes the next year. In 1899 the Institution's name was changed to the University of Arkansas, and in 1969 the University of Arkansas System was created.[22] In addition to the campuses listed below, the system includes the University of Arkansas for Medical Sciences in Little Rock.

Campuses: Main Campus in Fayetteville; Pine Bluff; Little Rock; Monticello
Colors: Cardinal and White
Nickname: Razorbacks
Song: "Hit That Line"[23]

CALIFORNIA

The California State University (1857)

The California state colleges were brought together into a system by a 1960 act. In 1972 the system was called the California State University and Colleges. In 1982 it became known as the California State University.[24]

Campuses: Bakersfield; California Maritime Academy; Channel Islands; Chico; Coachella Valley; Dominguez Hills; Fresno; Fullerton; Hayward; Humboldt; Long Beach; Los Angeles; Monterey Bay; Northridge; Pomona (Cal Poly); Sacramento; San Bernardino; San Diego; San Francisco; San Jose; San Luis Obispo (Cal Poly); San Marcos; Sonoma; Stanislaus[25]

San Jose State University (1857)

SJSU is the oldest campus of The California State University. It was founded in 1857 in San Francisco, established as California State Normal School in 1862, and moved to San Jose in 1871. In 1974, after several name changes, it became San Jose State University.[26]

Campuses: Main campus in San Jose
Colors: Blue and Gold
Nickname: Spartans
Song: "Spartan Fight Song"[27]

University of California (1868)

The University of California was chartered in 1868 as California's only land-grant institution. Now one of the largest universities in the world, UC first opened its doors in Oakland to thirty-eight students and ten faculty members.

Campuses: Berkeley; Davis; Irvine; Los Angeles; Riverside; San Diego; San Francisco; Santa Narnara; Santa Cruz.[28]

University of California, Berkeley (1868)

The merger of the private College of California in Oakland and the land-grant Agricultural, Mining, and Mechanical Arts College created the University of California, which moved to Berkeley in 1873.[29]

Colors: Blue and Gold
Nickname: Golden Bears
Songs: "All Hail Blue and Gold" by Harold W. Bingham; "The Golden Bear" by Charles Mills Gayley; "Palms of Victory" by Stuart L. Rawlings; "Sons of California" by Clinton R. Morse[30]

COLORADO

Colorado State University (1870)

Colorado's land-grant university, Colorado State first opened its doors as the Agricultural College of Colorado. It gained university status in 1957.[31]

Campuses: Main campus in Fort Collins; the CSU system includes Fort Lewis College and the University of Southern Colorado in Pueblo
Colors: Green and Gold
Nickname: Rams

Song: "Fight On, You Stalwart Ram Team"[32]

University of Colorado (1876)

In 1861 the Colorado legislature passed an act providing for a university in Boulder, but the founding of the University of Colorado was delayed by the Civil War. Students first attended classes in the fall of 1877.[33]

Campuses: Main campus in Boulder; the system also includes the University of Colorado at Denver, the University of Colorado at Colorado Springs, and the Health Sciences Center in Denver
Colors: Silver, Gold, and Black
Nickname: Buffaloes
Songs: "Fight CU Down the Field"; "Glory, Glory Colorado"[34]

CONNECTICUT

Central Connecticut State University (1849)

Central Connecticut State is Connecticut's oldest public higher educational institution. It was founded as a normal school in 1849. Today, the CSU system includes Western Connecticut State University, Southern Connecticut University, and Eastern Connecticut University.[35]

Campuses: Main campus in New Britain
Colors: Blue and White
Nickname: Blue Devils
Song: None[36]

Eastern Connecticut State University (1889)

Eastern is the second oldest institution in the Connecticut State University System. It, like the others, was founded as a normal school.[37]

Campuses: Main campus in Willimantic
Colors: Blue and White
Nickname: Warriors
Song: None[38]

Southern Connecticut State University (1893)

Southern began in 1893 as the New Haven State Normal School. It became the New Haven State Teachers College after four-year classes were introduced in 1937. In 1959 another name change created Southern Connecticut State College. The college became a university in March 1983.[39]

Campuses: Main campus in New Haven
Colors: Blue and White
Nickname: Owls
Song: "SCSU Fight Song"[40]

University of Connecticut (1881)

The Storrs Agricultural School was chartered on April 21, 1881. In 1893 the school was designated the state's land-grant institution and it became a college. Two more name changes (Connecticut Agricultural College in 1899 and Connecticut State College in 1933) occurred before the current name was adopted in 1939.

Campuses: Main campus in Storrs; regional campuses in Avery Point, Greater Hartford, Stamford, Torrington, and Waterbury
Colors: Navy and White
Nickname: Huskies

Song: "UConn Husky" or "The Fight Song" by Herbert France[41]

Western Connecticut State University (1903)

Western Connecticut State was founded in 1903 and located in the heart of downtown Danbury.

Campuses: Midtown Campus; Westside Campus[42]

Colors: Red, Blue, and White

Nickname: Colonials

Song: None[43]

DELAWARE

Delaware State University (1891)

The Delaware General Assembly established Delaware State College on May 15, 1891, under provisions of the 1890 Morrill Act. This act created land-grant colleges for blacks in states where racial separation had been practiced in educational institutions. On July 1, 1993, a state law changed the name of the college to Delaware State University.[44]

Campuses: Main campus in Dover

Colors: Columbia Blue and Red

Nickname: Hornets[45]

Song: "The Fight Song," words by Dorian Allen, music by Ivory Brock[46]

University of Delaware (1833)

The state of Delaware chartered the Academy of Newark in 1833 and renamed it Delaware College in 1843. In 1921 the College was combined with a women's college that had been established in 1914 and named the University of Delaware. The university is a land-, sea-, space-, and urban-grant institution.[47]

Campuses: Main campus in Newark

Colors: Blue and Gold

Nickname: Blue Hens

Song: "Delaware Fight Song" by George F. Kelly[48]

FLORIDA

The Florida State University System includes ten universities.

Florida Agricultural and Mechanical University (1887)

The State Normal College for Colored Students was founded on October 3, 1887. In 1891, with the passage of the second Morrill Act the previous year, it was renamed the State Normal and Industrial College for Colored Students. In 1909 the college achieved higher education status and the name Florida Agricultural and Mechanical College for Negroes. In 1953, university status was achieved.

Campuses: Main campus in Tallahassee

Colors: Orange and Green

Nickname: Rattlers[49]

Song: None[50]

Florida Atlantic University (1961)

FAU became the fifth university in the Florida State University System in 1961. The Boca Raton campus had been the site of a U.S. Army airfield.[51]

Campuses: Main campus in Boca Raton; Commercial Boulevard Campus, Fort Lauderdale; Davie Campus; John D. MacArthur Campus, Jupiter; SeaTech Campus, Dania Beach; Reubin O'D. Askew Tower, Fort Lauderdale; Treasure Coast Campus, Port St. Lucie[52]

Colors: Gray and Blue

Nickname: Owls

Song: None[53]

Florida Gulf Coast University (1991)

In May 1991 Governor Chiles signed the bill creating the university, which was officially named in a 1991 law. The first student was admitted in January 1997.[54]

Campuses: Main campus in Ft. Myers

Colors: Cobalt Blue and Forest Green

Nickname: Eagles

Song: None[55]

Florida International University (1965)

The Florida legislature established Florida International University in 1965, but classes were not held until September 1972.[56]

Campuses: University Park, Miami; North Campus, Key Biscayne; academic sites in Davie, Fort Lauderdale, and Homestead

Colors: Blue and Gold

Nickname: Golden Panthers

Song: None[57]

Florida State University (1851)

The property of the Florida Institute in Tallahassee was offered to the state in 1851 as the home of the state-supported Seminary West of the Suwannee, which opened for classes in 1857. In 1863 the legislature changed the name of the Seminary to the Florida Military and Collegiate Institute. After the Civil War, it was renamed The West Florida Seminary and then in 1901, Florida State College. When the state of Florida reorganized higher education in 1905, Florida State became Florida Female College and then Florida State College for Women in 1909. The name of Forida State University was not adopted until 1947, when the legislature allowed coeducational campuses in the system.[58]

Campuses: Main campus in Tallahassee; programs in Panama City and Sarasota

Colors: Garnet and Gold

Nickname: Seminoles

Song: "War Chant"[59]

University of Central Florida (1963)

Florida Technological University was founded in 1963 and received its current name on December 6, 1978.[60]

Campuses: Main campus in Orlando; UCF Brevard Area Campus; UCF Daytona Beach Area Campus; UCF Downtown Academic Center

Colors: Gold and Black

Nickname: Golden Knights

Song: "The UCF Fight Song"[61]

University of Florida (1853)

When East Florida Seminary, funded by the state, took over Kingsbury Academy in

1853, the University of Florida was born. It was moved to Gainesville in the 1860s and then consolidated with Florida Agricultural College in Lake City before receiving its current name and being moved back to Gainesville by legislative mandate in 1905.[62]

Campuses:	Main campus in Gainesville
Colors:	Orange and Blue
Nickname:	Gators
Songs:	"Gator Spell Out"; "Orange and Blue"[63]

University of North Florida (1965)

Chartered in 1965, UNF opened its doors to juniors and seniors in 1972 and to its first freshman class in 1984.[64]

Campuses:	Main campus in Jacksonville
Colors:	Blue and Gray
Nickname:	Ospreys
Song:	"UNF Fight Song"[65]

University of South Florida (1956)

What had been Henderson Air Field during World War II became the site of the University of South Florida when the State Board of Education established it in 1956. Classes first began in 1960.

Campuses:	Main campus in Tampa; USF–St. Petersburg campus; USF–Lakeland campus; USF–Sarasota campus[66]
Colors:	Green and Gold
Nickname:	Bulls
Songs:	"USF Fight Song"; "USF March Victorious"[67]

University of West Florida (1963)

The University of West Florida was authorized by the Florida Legislature as one of the ten state system universities in 1963. Classes first began in the fall of 1967.

Campuses:	Main campus in Pensacola; Fort Walton Beach Campus; Eglin Center[68]
Colors:	Blue and Green
Nickname:	Argonauts
Song:	None[69]

GEORGIA

The University System of Georgia is comprised of four universities including the Medical College of Georgia, two regional universities, thirteen four-year colleges, and fifteen two-year colleges. The three comprehensive universities are listed below.[70]

Georgia Institute of Technology (1885)

Georgia Tech was founded in 1885, but classes were not held until 1888. It received its current name in 1948.[71]

Campuses:	Main campus in Atlanta; Lorraine, France
Colors:	Old Gold and White
Nickname:	Yellow Jackets
Song:	"Up with the White and Gold" and "Ramblin Wreck" by Frank Roman[72]

Georgia State University (1913)

Georgia State University was so named in 1969. It began in 1913 as a night school for the Georgia Institute of Technology and has become Georgia's second-largest institution of higher learning.[73]

Campuses:	Main campus in Atlanta
Colors:	Crimson and Royal Blue
Nickname:	Panthers
Song:	None[74]

University of Georgia (1785)

Georgia was the first state to charter a state supported university in 1785. A site for it was not selected, however, until 1801. The first class graduated in 1804.[75]

Campuses:	Main campus in Athens
Colors:	Red and Black
Nickname:	Bulldogs
Song:	"Glory, Glory," arranged by Hugh Hodgson[76]

HAWAII

University of Hawaii at Manoa (1907)

The Manoa campus is the oldest and flagship campus in the University of Hawaii system, having opened on 1907 as a land-grant institution. In 1920 it attained university status as the University of Hawaii. As the system added campuses, the University of Hawaii at Manoa became the campus's official name in 1972.[77]

Campuses:	Main campus in Manoa; University of Hawaii at Hilo; University of Hawaii–West Oahu
Colors:	Green and White
Nickname:	Rainbows[78]

| Song: | "Co-ed," written by J. S. Zamecnik, arranged by William Kaneda[79] |

IDAHO

Idaho State University (1901)

The Academy of Idaho opened in 1901, but in 1915 it was renamed the Idaho Technical Institute. In 1927, it was reorganized as the Southern Branch of the University of Idaho, but then in 1947 it was established as Idaho State College. It became a university in 1963.[80]

Campuses:	Main campus in Pocatello
Colors:	Orange and Black
Nickname:	Bengals
Song:	"Growl Bengals Growl" by Del Slaughter and Jay Slaughter[81]

University of Idaho (1889)

Idaho's land-grant university was chartered on January 30, 1889, while Idaho was still a territory. Classes did not begin until October of 1892.

Campuses:	Main campus in Moscow; resident instructional centers in Boise, Coeur d'Alene, Idaho Falls, Twin Falls[82]
Colors:	Silver and Gold
Nickname:	Vandals
Song:	"Go Vandals Go," words and music by J. Morris O'Donnel[83]

ILLINOIS

Chicago State University (1867)

Chicago State was founded as an experimental teacher training school in 1867 and is today a comprehensive institution of higher learning.[84]

Campuses: Main campus in Chicago
Colors: Green and White
Nickname: Cougars[85]
Song: "CTC-CSU Fight Song," arranged by Bruno Paige[86]

Eastern Illinois University (1895)

Eastern was founded in 1895 and its first building, Old Main, was constructed in 1899. It is a regional university in the Illinois system.[87]

Campuses: Main campus in Charleston
Colors: Blue and Gray
Nickname: Panthers[88]
Song: "We Are Loyal EIU"[89]

Illinois State University (1857)

Illinois State was the first public university in the state of Illinois. Abraham Lincoln drafted the documents that established the school, whose purpose was to educate teachers. Today, it is a multipurpose institution.[90]

Campuses: Main campus in Normal
Colors: Red and White
Nickname: Redbirds
Song: "ISU Fight Song" composed by Kenyon S. Fletcher[91]

Northeastern Illinois University (1961)

NIEU is a comprehensive university located on the northwest side of Chicago whose population reflects the diversity of the Chicago metropolitan area.[92]

Campuses: Main campus in Chicago
Colors: Royal Blue and Gold
Nickname: Golden Eagles
Song: None[93]

Northern Illinois University (1895)

Northern Illinois was chartered in 1895 and it has become a comprehensive teaching and research institution.

Campuses: Main campus in De Kalb; regional sites in Rockford, Hoffman Estates, Oregon, Naperville[94]
Colors: Cardinal and Black
Nickname: Huskies
Song: "Huskie Fight Song," composed and written by Neil Annas and Francis Stroup[95]

Southern Illinois University (1869)

Southern Illinois University is comprised of two institutions: SIU at Carbondale and SIU at Edwardsville. From the time of its charter in 1869 until 1947, Southern Illinois was called Southern Illinois Normal University. Having offered courses off-campus near East St. Louis since 1949, a separate campus at Edwardsville eventually developed.[96]

Southern Illinois University at Carbondale (1869)

Campuses: Main campus in Carbondale; School of Medicine in Springfield; Niigata, Japan, campus
Colors: Maroon and White

Nickname: Salukis

Songs: "Go Southern Go"; "Go You Salukis"[97]

Southern Illinois University at Edwardsville (1957)

Campuses: Main campus in Edwardsville; School of Dental Medicine in Alton; center in East St. Louis

Colors: Red and White

Nickname: Cougars

Song: "Cougar Courage"[98]

University of Illinois at Urbana–Champaign (1867)

The University of Illinois at Urbana–Champaign was chartered in 1867 as a land-grant institution.[99]

Campuses: Main campus in Urbana–Champaign; University of Illinois at Chicago; University of Illinois at Springfield

Colors: Orange and Navy Blue
Nickname: Fighting Illini

Songs: "Illinois Loyalty;" "Oskee-Wow-Wow;" "March of the Illini;" "Hail to the Orange"[100]

Western Illinois University (1899)

Western Illinois was chartered on April 24, 1899, but classes did not begin until September 23, 1902.

Campuses: Main campus in Macomb; WIU Regional Center in Moline[101]

Colors: Pantone Violet and Gold

Nickname: Fighting Leathernecks (men) Westerwinds (women)[102]

Song: "We're Marching On," written by Walter H. Eller[103]

INDIANA

Ball State University (1918)

The eastern division of the Indiana State Normal School at Muncie opened on June 17, 1918. It was rechristened Ball Teachers College in 1922 and then Ball State Teachers College in 1929. In 1965 it became Ball State University.[104]

Campuses: Main campus in Muncie

Colors: Cardinal and White

Nickname: Cardinals

Song: "Fight Team, Fight for Ball State"[105]

Indiana State University (1865)

The General Assembly created the Indiana State Normal School by an 1865 act and the school opened its doors to students in 1870. The education of teachers was its primary purpose. In 1929 the Assembly changed the Normal School's name to Indiana State Teachers College, and then in 1961 to Indiana State College. Finally, in 1965 Indiana State received university status.[106]

Campuses: Main campus in Terre Haute

Colors: Royal Blue and White

Nickname: Sycamores

Song: "On You Fighting Sycamores" by Joseph A. Gremelspacher[107]

Indiana University Bloomington (1820)

IU was founded four years after Indiana became a state, making it one of the oldest public universities in the United States.[108]

Campuses:	Main campus in Bloomington; Indiana University–Purdue University–Indianapolis; Indiana University East in Richmond; Indiana University–Purdue University at Fort Wayne; Indiana University at Kokomo; Indiana University Northwest in Gary; Indiana University at South Bend; Indiana University Southeast in Albany[109]
Colors:	Cream and Crimson
Nickname:	Hoosiers
Song:	"Indiana, Our Indiana," from the melody of "The Viking March"[110]

Purdue University (1869)

The Morrill Act of 1862, the Indiana General Assembly's decision to participate in it, and gifts of land from local residents, $50,000 from the county, and $150,000 from John Purdue combined to create Purdue University. Classes were first held in 1874.[111]

Campuses:	Main campus in West Lafayette; Indiana University–Purdue University–Indianapolis; Indiana University–Purdue University at Fort Wayne; Purdue University Calumet in Hammond; Purdue University North Central Campus in Westville

Colors:	Gold and Black
Nickname:	Boilermakers
Song:	"Hail Purdue," music by Edward S. Wotawa, words by James R. Morrison[112]

IOWA

Iowa State University (1858)

Iowa Agricultural College and Model Farm was created in March 1858 with the governor's signature. In 1864 land-grant funds from the 1862 Morrill Act were applied to the college. In 1891 a name change was effected to the Iowa State College of Agriculture and Mechanical Arts. University status was granted as part of the 1958 centennial celebration and the official name of the university was eventually modernized to Iowa State University of Science and Technology.[113]

Campuses:	Main campus in Ames; seven extension areas
Colors:	Cardinal and Gold
Nickname:	Cyclones
Song:	"ISU Fights"[114]

University of Iowa (1847)

Founded on February 25, 1847, the university's doors opened to students in March 1855. When the capital was moved to Des Moines in 1857, the Old Capitol became the university's first permanent home.

Campuses:	Main campus in Iowa City
Colors:	Black and Gold
Nickname:	Hawkeyes
Songs:	"On Iowa;" "Iowa Fight Song," "Roll Along, Iowa"[115]

University of Northern Iowa (1876)

The Iowa State Normal School opened for classes on September 6, 1876. It became the Iowa State Teachers College in 1909. The General Assembly renamed the school in 1961, when it became the State College of Iowa. In 1967 the General Assembly gave the college university status and its current name.[116]

Campuses: Main campus in Cedar Falls; UNI Center for Urban Education in Waterloo
Colors: Purple and Old Gold
Nickname: Panthers
Song: "UNI Fight"[117]

KANSAS

The Kansas Board of Regents governs six public universities in the state of Kansas.[118]

Emporia State University (1863)

The Kansas State Normal School was founded by an 1863 legislative act. In 1867 its first two students graduated. In February 1923 the school was renamed Kansas State Teachers College, and in July 1974 another name change created Emporia Kansas State College. Then, in April 1977 the college became Emporia State University.[119]

Campuses: Main campus in Emporia
Colors: Black and Gold
Nickname: Hornets
Song: "Fight On, Emporia," composed by Alfred Thompson[120]

Fort Hays State University (1902)

When the university was established in 1902, its first location was on the site of Old Fort Hays. When the first building was constructed in 1904, the university was moved to its current location.[121]

Campuses: Main campus in Hays
Colors: Black and Gold
Nickname: Tigers
Song: "Northwestern University Fight Song"[122]

Kansas State University (1863)

The campus of Bluemont Central College, chartered in 1858, became the home of Kansas State University when it was founded on February 16, 1863. It is the land-grant institution of Kansas.[123]

Campuses: Main campus in Manhattan; KSU–Salina College of Technology and Aviation
Colors: Purple and White
Nickname: Wildcats
Song: "Wildcat Victory"[124]

Pittsburg State University (1903)

Pittsburg State was founded in 1903 as a coeducational college.[125]

Campuses: Main campus in Pittsburg
Colors: Crimson and Gold
Nickname: Gorillas
Song: "Pittsburg State Team, Fight for Your College!"[126]

University of Kansas (1864)

The University of Kansas was founded on March 1, 1864. Classes were first held on September 12, 1866.

Campuses: Main campus in Lawrence; Medical Center campus in Kansas City; School of Medicine Clinical Branch in Wichita; Regents Center (Edwards campus) in Overland Park; Capitol Complex Center in Topeka[127]

Colors: Maize and Blue

Nickname: Jayhawks

Song: "I'm a Jayhawk" by George Bowls[128]

Wichita State University (1892)

When Fairmont College opened in 1895, it was affiliated with the Congregational Church. In 1926 The Municipal University of Wichita was opened when Fairmont became publicly funded. In 1963 the legislature approved a new state university, and since 1964 the current name has been in use.[129]

Campuses: Main campus in Wichita

Colors: Yellow and Black

Nickname: Shockers

Song: "WSU Fight Song"[130]

KENTUCKY

Eastern Kentucky University (1906)

Eastern Kentucky State Normal School became a reality on the old campus of Central University on March 21, 1906. The name was changed to Eastern Kentucky State Normal School and Teachers College in 1922 when the college introduced a four-year curriculum. In 1930 another name change created Eastern Kentucky State Teachers College. In 1948 the word "Teachers" was dropped, and in 1966 the current name was adopted.[131]

Campuses: Main campus in Richmond

Colors: Maroon and White

Nickname: Colonels

Songs: "Hail, Hail"; "Yea Eastern"[132]

Kentucky State University (1886)

Kentucky State is one of the seventeen land-grant institutions that came out of the 1890 Morrill Act, which mandated educational opportunity for blacks.[133]

Campuses: Main campus in Frankfort

Colors: Kelly Green and Gold

Nickname: Thorobreds and Thorobrettes

Song: "The Kentucky State University Fight Song" by Robert Townsend[134]

Morehead State University (1922)

Morehead State Normal School was chartered in 1922. By 1926 it received a new name: Morehead State Normal School and Teachers College. In 1930 the name was shortened to Morehead State Teachers College. The name was shortened further in 1948 when the word "Teachers" was dropped. University status was obtained in 1966.[135]

Campuses: Main campus in Morehead

Colors: Blue and Gold

Nickname: Eagles

Song: "Morehead Fight Song" by Earl K. Senff[136]

Murray State University (1922)

Murray State began classes in September 1923 as a normal school. By 1926 it had become a normal school and teachers college. The current name was adopted in 1966.[137]

Campuses: Main campus in Murray; Centers in Paducah, Madison-ville, Henderson, Hopkins-ville, Fort Campbell[138]
Colors: Blue and Gold
Nickname: Racers; Thoroughbreds (Base-ball)
Song: "MSU Fight Song"[139]

Northern Kentucky University (1968)

NKU is the youngest of the state's eight universities, having awarded its first bachelor's degrees in 1973 as Northern Kentucky State College. In 1976 it became a university.

Campuses: Main campus in Highland Heights; Covington Campus[140]
Colors: Black, Gold, and White
Nickname: Norse
Song: "Fight Song" by T. Ruddick; "Go Norse" by Wes Flinn[141]

University of Kentucky (1865)

This university was the vision of John Bowman who combined private donations with funding from the Morrill Act to begin this land-grant institution. Before receiving its current name, the University was known as the Kentucky Agricultural and Mechanical College.[142]

Campuses: Main campus in Lexington
Colors: Blue and White
Nickname: Wildcats

Songs: "On, On U of K," "My Old Kentucky Home"[143]

University of Louisville (1798)

In 1844 the Louisville Collegiate Institute took over the land that had belonged to the defunct Jefferson Seminary, which had been founded in 1798. In 1846 the state combined the Collegiate Institute with the Louisville Medical Institute. In 1950–1951 the all-black Louisville Municipal College was incorporated into the university. By the mid-1960s state support of the university became a reality.[144]

Campuses: Main Belknap campus in Louisville; Health Science Center; Shelby Campus[145]
Colors: Red, Black, and White
Nickname: Cardinals
Song: "Fight! U of L," words and music by R. B. Griffith[146]

Western Kentucky University (1906)

Western Kentucky State Normal School was established on March 21, 1906. In 1911 it moved to its current location, and in 1922 it was renamed the Western Kentucky State Normal School and Teachers College. Having absorbed Ogden College in 1927, the college's name was shortened in 1930 to Western State Teachers College. In 1948 another name change resulted in Western Kentucky State College. The current name was adopted in 1966.[147]

Campuses: Main campus in Bowling Green
Colors: Red and White
Nickname: Hilltoppers
Song: "Stand Up and Cheer"[148]

LOUISIANA

Grambling State University (1901)

The private Colored Industrial and Agricultural School opened on November 1, 1901. In 1905 it relocated to its current setting and became the North Louisiana Agricultural and Industrial School. In 1919, it became the Lincoln Parish Training School, and in 1928, now with state support, it became the Louisiana Negro Normal and Industrial Institute. Grambling College became the new name in 1946 and university status was achieved twenty years later.[149]

Campuses:	Main campus in Grambling
Colors:	Black and Gold
Nickname:	Tigers
Song:	"Fight for Dear Old Grambling"[150]

Louisiana State University–Baton Rouge (1853)

The main campus of LSU opened for classes on January 2, 1860. LSU is both a land-grant and a sea-grant institution.[151]

Campuses:	Main campus in Baton Rouge; LSU–Alexandria; LSU–Eunice; LSU–Shreveport; LSU Medical Center; LSU Medical Center–Shreveport; University of New Orleans[152]
Colors:	Purple and Gold
Nickname:	Fighting Tigers
Songs:	"Hey Fighting Tigers" and "Tiger Rag"[153]

Louisiana Tech University (1894)

The Industrial Institute and College of Louisiana opened its doors in 1895. It became the Louisiana Polytechnic Institute in 1921 and the current name was adopted in 1970.

Campuses:	Main campus in Ruston; degree program at Barksdale Air Force Base[154]
Colors:	Red and Columbia Blue
Nickname:	Bulldogs; Lady Techsters
Song:	"The LaTech Fight Song" and "Go Bulldogs Go"[155]

McNeese State University (1939)

McNeese State began as a division of LSU, but only a year after its founding it was named John McNeese Junior College. McNeese State College was the new name of the institution when it became independent in 1950. In 1970 university status was achieved.[156]

Campuses:	Main campus in Lake Charles
Colors:	Blue and Gold
Nickname:	Cowboys; Cowgirls
Song:	"On McNeese"[157]

Nicholls State University (1948)

On September 23, 1948, the John T. Nicholls Junior College opened as a campus of LSU. In 1956 it separated from LSU and the current name was adopted in 1970.[158]

Campuses:	Main campus in Thibodaux
Colors:	Red and Gray
Nickname:	Colonels
Song:	"Fight for NSU," arranged by Paul Prado[159]

Northwestern State University (1884)

Northwestern State began in 1884 as the Louisiana State Normal School. Today, it includes the state's designated liberal arts honors college.[160]

Campuses: Main campus in Natchitoches
Colors: Purple and White
Nickname: Demons
Song: "Demon Fight Song" by Seitz (to the tune of the trio of "British 8")[161]

Southeastern Louisiana University (1925)

The year 2000 marked the 75th anniversary of SLU.[162]

Campuses: Main campus in Hammond
Colors: Green and Gold
Nickname: Lions
Song: None[163]

Southern University and A & M College (1880)

Founded by legislative act in 1880, the historically black university was reorganized to receive funds from the 1890 Morrill Act. In 1912 the University in New Orleans was closed and reborn in Baton Rouge in 1914. In 1974 campuses in New Orleans and Shreveport were authorized.

Campuses: Main campus in Baton Rouge; Southern University at New Orleans; Southern University at Shreveport; A. A. Lenoir Law School[164]
Colors: Columbia Blue and Gold
Nickname: Jaguars
Song: "Southern University Fight Song" by Huel D. Perkins[165]

University of Louisiana at Lafayette (1898)

UL Lafayette opened in 1898 as the Southwestern Louisiana Industrial Institute. In 1921 the word Industrial was dropped, and in 1960 the University of Southwestern Louisiana emerged. In 1999 the current name was adopted.[166]

Campuses: Main campus in Lafayette
Colors: Vermillion and White
Nickname: Ragin' Cajuns; Lady Cajuns
Song: "Ragin' Cajuns Fight Song" by Miss Hilma LaBauve[167]

University of Louisiana at Monroe (1931)

The Ouachita Parish Junior College opened in 1931. Three years later it became the Northeast Center of Louisiana State University, and in 1939 it became Northeast Junior College. 1950 brought another name, Northeast Louisiana State College, as did 1970, Northeast Louisiana University. The current name was adopted in 1999.[168]

Campuses: Main campus in Monroe
Colors: Maroon and Gold
Nickname: Indians
Song: "ULM Fite" by Bob Cotter[169]

MAINE

University of Maine (1865)

The State College of Agriculture and Mechanic Arts was founded as a land-grant college in 1865 under the Morrill Act of 1862. Classes were first held in September 1868. A name change in 1897 created the University of Maine. In 1980 the University also became a sea-grant college.[170]

Campuses: Main campus in Orono; University of Maine at Augusta; University of Maine at Farmington; University of Maine at Fort Kent; University of Maine at Machias; University of Maine at Presque Isle; University of Southern Maine

Colors: Blue and White

Nickname: Black Bears

Song: "The Maine Stein Song," words by Lincoln Colcord, music by E. A. Fenstad, arranged by Rudy Vallee[171]

MARYLAND

Morgan State University (1867)

Morgan State was founded in 1867 as the Centenary Biblical Institute. In recognition of a donor, it was renamed Morgan College in 1890. The college was purchased by the state in 1939 to provide new opportunities for black students. It was designated a university in 1975 and designated Maryland's public urban university in 1988.[172]

Campuses: Main campus in Baltimore

Colors: Blue and Orange

Nickname: Bears[173]

Song: "The Grizzlies"[174]

University of Maryland, College Park (1856)

The College Park campus was founded in 1856 as the Maryland State College of Agriculture. It was merged with the professional schools in Baltimore to form the University in 1920. In 1865 the University became a land-grant institution and in 1983 a sea-grant institution.

Campuses: The University of Maryland System includes eleven institutions in addition to the College Park campus: University of Maryland, Baltimore; University of Maryland, Baltimore County; University of Maryland, Eastern Shore; University of Maryland, University College; University of Baltimore; Bowie State University; Coppin State University; Frostburg State University; Salisbury State University; Towson University[175]

Colors: Red, White, Black, and Gold

Nickname: Terrapins

Song: "Maryland Victory Song"[176]

MASSACHUSETTS

University of Massachusetts Amherst (1863)

UMASS Amherst was established in 1863 under the first Morrill Act as the state's land-grant institution.

Campuses: Main campus in Amherst; Campuses in Boston, Dartmouth, Lowell, Worcester[177]

Colors: Maroon and White

Nickname: Minutemen, Minutewomen

Song: "Fight Mass"[178]

MICHIGAN

Central Michigan University (1892)

Central Michigan Normal School opened on September 13, 1892. In 1927 it became Central State Teacher's College and in 1941, Central Michigan College of Education. In 1955 another name change created Central Michigan College and four years later university status was granted.[179]

Campuses:	Main campus in Mount Pleasant
Colors:	Maroon and Gold
Nickname:	Chippewas
Song:	"CMU Fight Song" by Howdy Loomis[180]

Eastern Michigan University (1849)

EMU was chartered by the state in 1849 as the Michigan State Normal School. It became a university in 1959.[181]

Campuses:	Main campus in Ypsilanti
Colors:	Green and White
Nickname:	Eagles[182]
Song:	"Eagles Fight Song" by Larry Livingston[183]

Ferris State University (1884)

Ferris State was founded in 1884 by Woodbridge N. Ferris as a private industrial school. It became part of the Michigan higher education system in 1950.[184]

Campuses:	Main campus in Big Rapids
Colors:	Crimson and Gold
Nickname:	Bulldogs
Song:	"Bulldog Fight Song"[185]

Grand Valley State University (1960)

GVSU was chartered in 1960 and accepted its first class in 1963.

Campuses:	Main campus in Allendale; courses offered in Muskegon, Scottville, Grand Rapids, Holland, Traverse City, Petoskey[186]
Colors:	Black, White, and Blue
Nickname:	Lakers
Song:	"Grand Valley Victory," music by William Root, lyrics by Kathy Ure and Maris Tracy[187]

Lake Superior State University (1946)

Lake Superior State began in 1946 as a satellite campus for the Michigan Technological University in Houghton. It is located on the former site of U.S. Army Fort Brady, which was purchased by the state for $1 after World War II.[188]

Campuses:	Main campus in Sault Sainte Marie
Colors:	Royal Blue and Gold
Nickname:	Lakers
Song:	None[189]

Michigan State University (1855)

Michigan State claims to be the nation's first land-grant institution and a model for the sixty-nine others that followed under the 1862 Morrill Act.[190]

Campuses:	Main campus in East Lansing
Colors:	Green and White
Nickname:	Spartans
Song:	"On the Banks of the Red Cedar"[191]

Michigan Technological University (1885)

Michigan Tech opened in 1885 as the Michigan Mining School. By 1896 it had become the Michigan College of Mines and by 1926, the Michigan College of Mining and Technology. The current name was adopted in 1964 to better reflect the university's programs.[192]

Campuses: Main campus in Houghton
Colors: Silver and Gold
Nickname: Huskies
Song: "Fight Tech Fight"[193]

Northern Michigan University (1899)

Northern State Normal School opened in 1899 to train teachers. Its curriculum diversified over the years, and in 1963 Northern as well as the other Michigan public institutions received university status.[194]

Campuses: Main campus in Marquette
Colors: Old Gold and Olive Green
Nickname: Wildcats
Song: "Northern Michigan University Fight Song," arranged by Lorin Richtmeyer[195]

Oakland University (1957)

Founded in 1957, Oakland University has developed institutes and centers in wellness, eye research, robotics, technology, and international studies.

Campuses: Main campus in Rochester
Colors: Black and Gold
Nickname: Golden Grizzlies [196]
Song: "OU Fight" by Michael A. Mitchell, D.M.A.[197]

Saginaw Valley State University (1963)

Saginaw Valley, as one of the fifteen public universities in Michigan, is a comprehensive institution serving the east central portion of the state.[198]

Campuses: Main campus in University Center
Colors: Red, White, and Blue
Nickname: Cardinals
Song: "Cardinal Fight" by Tom Root[199]

University of Michigan (1817)

Founded in Detroit in 1817 on land ceded by three Native American tribes for a college, the institution moved to Ann Arbor in 1837. By 1866 it had become the largest university in the country.[200]

Campuses: Main campus in Ann Arbor; campuses in Dearborn and Flint
Colors: Maize and Blue
Nickname: Wolverines
Song: "The Victors" [201]

Wayne State University (1868)

Wayne State began in 1868 as the Detroit Medical College. Colleges of education and liberal arts were added in 1881 and 1917, which began a long development of curricula that led to Wayne State's development as a comprehensive university.[202]

Campuses: Main campus in Detroit
Colors: Forest Green and Old Gold
Nickname: Tartars

Songs: "War March of the Tartars"
by Karl L. King, march and
words by Paul Schuster; "Victory Song" by Don Gragg[203]

Western Michigan University (1903)

Western State College was founded in 1903.
It was designated as the state's fourth public
university.[204]

Campuses: Main campus in Kalamazoo;
sites in Holland and Traverse
City; Centers in Battle Creek;
Grand Rapids; Lansing; Muskegon; Benton Harbor/St. Joseph[205]

Colors: Brown and Gold

Nickname: Broncos

Song: "Western Michigan University
Fight Song" by Walter Gilbert[206]

MINNESOTA

Bemidji State University (1919)

Bemidji State Normal School opened in
1919 and two years later it was renamed Bemidji State Teachers College. In 1957 another name change produced Bemidji State
College and in 1975 university status was
achieved.[207]

Campuses: Main campus in Bemidji

Colors: Green and White

Nickname: Beavers

Song: "Go, Bemidji Beavers," words
and tune by the Advanced
Harmony Class of 1947, pi-
ano arrangement by D. Patterson[208]

Metropolitan State University (1971)

Metro State was founded as an upper-
division institution for working adults. It
now offers a full array of programs.[209]

Campuses: Main campus in Minneapolis

Colors: Blue and White

Nickname: None

Song: None[210]

Minnesota State University, Mankato (1866)

Mankato Normal School opened its doors in
October 1868. It has since gone through
these name changes: Mankato State Teachers College (1921); Mankato State College
(1957); Mankato State University (1975);
and Minnesota State University (1998).[211]

Campuses: Main campus in Mankato

Colors: Purple and Gold

Nickname: Mavericks

Song: "Minnesota State Rouser" by
Kenneth Pinckney[212]

Moorhead State University (1887)

The idea for a college in northwest Minnesota was born out of an 1885 bill stating
that it would be a good idea for a normal
school to be established there. In the fall of
1888 classes began, and in 1921 the college
became Moorhead State Teachers College.
Again renamed in 1957, Moorhead State
College was given university status in
1975.[213]

Campuses: Main campus in Moorhead

Colors: Scarlet and White

Nickname: Dragons

Song: "MSU Fight Song," arranged
by Brekke[214]

Southwest State University (1963)

Southwest is a four-year college. The majority of its students comes from Southwest Minnesota.[215]

Campuses:	Main campus in Marshall
Colors:	Gold and Brown
Nickname:	Golden Mustangs
Song:	"SU Fight Song"[216]

St. Cloud State University (1869)

St. Cloud State is Minnesota's second-largest university. It began in 1869 as a normal school.[217]

Campuses:	Main campus in St. Cloud
Colors:	Cardinal and Black
Nickname:	Huskies
Song:	"Oh Hear We Are, the Gang and All"[218]

University of Minnesota (1851)

The University of Minnesota began in 1851 as a preparatory school. Closed during the Civil War due to financial difficulties, it reopened in 1867 in part with the assistance of the Morrill Act. The University is Minnesota's land-grant institution.[219]

Campuses:	Main campus in Minneapolis–St. Paul; campuses in Duluth, Crookston, Morris
Colors:	Maroon and Gold
Nickname:	Golden Gophers
Songs:	"The Minnesota Rouser," "Minnesota March," "Go Gopher Victory," "Our Minnesota," "Minnesota Fight," "Hail Minnesota"[220]

Winona State University (1858)

Winona State claims to be the first institution west of the Mississippi established for the training of teachers. Today, it is one of seven of the state's universities.

Campuses:	Main campus in Winona; WSU Rochester Center[221]
Colors:	Purple and White
Nickname:	Warriors
Song:	"Winona State University Rouser" by J. Neville[222]

MISSISSIPPI

Alcorn State University (1871)

Alcorn University was established on May 13, 1871, on the site of the defunct Oakland College, a Presbyterian school for whites. It became a school exclusive for black men until 1895, when women were admitted. With a change in name to Alcorn Agricultural and Mechanical College in 1878 came the designation of a land-grant college under the 1862 Morrill Act. It later received land-grant status under the 1890 Morrill Act. In 1974 the current name was adopted.[223]

Campuses:	Main campus in Lorman
Colors:	Purple and Gold
Nickname:	Braves
Song:	"Cherokee" by Ray Noble[224]

Delta State University (1924)

Delta State Teachers College opened for classes on September 15, 1925. In 1955 the name was changed to Delta State College. University status was granted in 1974.[225]

Campuses:	Main campus in Cleveland
Colors:	Green and White

Nickname: Statesmen

Song: "Orange and Blue" by Thornton W. Allen, arranged by Reid Poole[226]

Jackson State University (1877)

Jackson State is the urban university of Mississippi. It is a historically black, comprehensive university.[227]

Campuses: Main campus in Jackson

Colors: Royal Blue and White

Nickname: Tigers

Song: "Cheer Boys for Jackson" by William Brown[228]

Mississippi State University (1878)

The Agricultural and Mechanical College of the State of Mississippi was chartered by the state in 1878 as a land-grant college and opened for classes in 1880. The college was renamed Mississippi State College in 1932 and became a university in 1958.[229]

Campuses: Main campus in Mississippi State (Starkville); centers in Meridian and the Stennis Space Center

Colors: Maroon and White

Nickname: Bulldogs

Song: "Hail State"[230]

Mississippi Valley State University (1946)

The Mississippi Vocational College was founded in 1946 but did not open until the summer of 1950. In 1964 the name was changed to Mississippi Valley State College,

and in 1974 university status was granted by the state.[231]

Campuses: Main campus in Itta Beena

Colors: Green and White

Nickname: Delta Devils

Song: "Devil's Gun," words by Agusta White[232]

University of Mississippi (1844)

"Ole Miss" first held classes four years after its 1844 state charter. It is the state's oldest higher education institution.

Campuses: Main campus in University City (Oxford); campuses in Southhaven and Tupelo; Medical Center in Jackson

Colors: Red and Blue

Nickname: Rebels

Song: "Forward, Rebels, March to Fame"[233]

University of Southern Mississippi (1910)

USM was founded by the state as a Normal School, a school for training teachers. It became a comprehensive university in 1962.

Campuses: Main campus in Hattiesburg; USM Gulf Coast at Long Beach; teaching centers at the Jackson County Center in Gautier and the Keesler Center in Biloxi[234]

Colors: Black and Gold

Nickname: Golden Eagles

Song: "Southern to the Top" by Robert Hayes[235]

MISSOURI

Central Missouri State University (1871)

One of Missouri's regional universities, CMSU was designated as the state's lead university for professional technology.[236]

Campuses: Main campus in Warrensburg
Colors: Cardinal and Black
Nickname: Mules (Men), Jennies (Women)
Song: "Go Mules" by Clifton Burmeister[237]

Lincoln University (1866)

Lincoln Institute was established on January 14, 1866, for the benefit of freed blacks by members of the 62nd and 65th Colored Infantry. In 1879 the Institute began to receive funds from the state, and it was named a land-grant institution under the 1890 Morrill Act. The name was changed by the legislature to Lincoln University in 1921.[238]

Campuses: Main campus in Jefferson City
Colors: Navy, Blue, and White
Nickname: Blue Tigers
Song: "LU Fight Song," word adaptation by Mildred Robertson, Richard A. McCall, Sr., and Robert L. Mitchell, Sr. (to the tune of the "Washington and Lee Swing")[239]

Northwest Missouri State University (1905)

Founded in 1905, Northwest Missouri State is a regional university governed by a state appointed Board of Regents.[240]

Campuses: Main campus in Maryville
Colors: Green and White
Nickname: Bearcats
Song: "NWMSU Fight Song"[241]

Southeast Missouri State University (1873)

The Southeast Missouri Normal School was chartered in 1873. In 1919 it was renamed Southeast Missouri State Teachers College and began granting degrees. Then, in 1946 it was renamed Southeast Missouri State College. In 1972 university status was achieved.[242]

Campuses: Main campus in Cape Girardeau; Crisp Bootheel Education Center; Sikeston Area Higher Education Center; Kennet Area Higher Education Center; Sereno Education Center, Perryville.[243]
Colors: Red and Black
Nickname: Indians (Men), Otahkians (Women)
Song: None[244]

Southwest Missouri State University (1906)

The Fourth District Normal School became Southwest Missouri State Teachers College in 1919. In 1945 the name was changed to Southwest Missouri State College. University status was achieved in 1972.[245]

Campuses: Main campus in Springfield; SMSU–West Plain; SMSU–Mountain Grove[246]
Colors: Maroon and White
Nickname: Bears
Song: "The Scotchman"[247]

Truman State University (1878)

North Missouri Normal School and Commercial College opened as a private school on September 2, 1867. In 1870, it received state support as the First District Normal School. 1919 brought a name change to Northeast Missouri State Teachers College, but in 1967, the word "Teachers" was dropped. University status was received in 1972, and in 1996, the current name was adopted.

Campuses:	Main campus in Kirksville
Colors:	Purple and White
Nickname:	Bulldogs
Song:	"The Purple and White" by Basil Brewer[248]

University of Missouri (1839)

The Geyer Act of 1839 created the University of Missouri. Superior fund-rasing in Boone County landed the university in Columbia. It became Missouri's land-grant institution in 1870.[249]

Campuses:	Main campus in Columbia; University of Missouri–Kansas City; University of Missouri–Rolla; University of Missouri–St. Louis[250]
Colors:	Black and Old Gold
Nickname:	Tigers
Songs:	"Fight Tigers," "Every True Son/Daughter"[251]

MONTANA

Montana State University-Bozeman (1893)

Montana State University is Montana's land-grant institution. It was chartered on February 16, 1893, as the Agricultural College of the State of Montana, and classes were first held on April 17 of the same year.[252]

Campuses:	Main campus in Bozeman; Montana State University College of Technology–Great Falls; Montana State University–Billings; Montana State University–Billings College of Technology; Montana State University–Northern[253]
Colors:	Royal Blue and Gold
Nickname:	Bobcats
Song:	"Stand Up and Cheer"[254]

University of Montana (1893)

Since its charter was received in 1893, the Missoula campus of the University of Montana has developed into a comprehensive university with exclusive responsibility in the system for specific curricula.[255]

Campuses:	Main campus in Missoula; University of Montana–Missoula College of Technology; Helena College of Technology of the University of Montana; Montana Tech of the University of Montana in Butte; Western Montana College of the University of Montana in Dillon[256]
Colors:	Copper, Silver, and Gold
Nickname:	Grizzlies
Song:	"Up with Montana"[257]

NEBRASKA

University of Nebraska–Lincoln (1869)

The University of Nebraska, with its campuses, is Nebraska's only public university. It was founded as a land-grant university.

Campuses: Main campus in Lincoln; University of Nebraska at Omaha; University of Nebraska Medical Center; University of Nebraska at Kearney[258]

Colors: Scarlet and Cream

Nickname: Cornhuskers[259]

Song: "Hail Varsity"[260]

NEVADA

University of Nevada–Las Vegas (1955)

Once a satellite campus of the University of Nevada, UNLV was named Nevada Southern University in 1965. In 1969, it received its current name.

Campuses: Main Campus in Las Vegas

Colors: Scarlet and Gray

Nickname: Rebels

Song: "Win with the Rebels"[261]

University of Nevada–Reno (1874)

Nevada's land-grant university opened originally in Elko in 1874. It moved to Reno in 1885.

Campuses: Main campus in Reno; Redfield campus and Stead campus

Colors: Silver and Blue

Nickname: Wolf Pack [262]

Song: "Hail to Our Sturdy Men" (to the tune of the "Yale Fight Song")[263]

NEW HAMPSHIRE

University of New Hampshire (1866)

The New Hampshire College of Agriculture and Mechanical Arts was founded in 1866 as a land-grant college in Hanover. In 1893 the college moved to Durham, and in 1923 it was rechartered as the University of New Hampshire. UNH is also a sea-and space-grant institution.

Campuses: Main campus in Durham; Manchester; Keene State College and Plymouth State College are also part of the University System[264]

Colors: Blue and White

Nickname: Wildcats

Song: "On to Victory" by George W. Dahlquist[265]

NEW JERSEY

Kean University (1855)

Although founded in 1855, Kean College did not move from Newark to Union until 1958. The college became a university on September 26, 1997.

Campuses: Main campus in Union

Colors: Royal Blue and Silver

Nickname: Cougars[266]

Song: None[267]

Montclair State University (1908)

Montclair State was founded as a normal school and became Montclair State Teachers College in 1927. In 1958 the name was changed to Montclair State College. In 1994 Montclair State, a comprehensive institution since 1966, was designated a teaching university.[268]

Campuses:	Main campus in Upper Montclair
Colors:	Scarlet and White
Nickname:	Redhawks
Song:	None[269]

New Jersey City University (1927)

The New Jersey State Normal School opened for classes on September 12, 1929. Only six years later it became the Jersey City State Teachers College and then in 1958, Jersey City State College. The current name was adopted in 1998.[270]

Campuses:	Main campus in Jersey City
Colors:	Green and Gold
Nickname:	Gothic Knights
Song:	"Green and Gold" by William Hayes and Aubrey Kemper[271]

New Jersey Institute of Technology (1881)

The Newark Technical School opened for classes in 1884 thanks to the donations of local industrialists and private citizens. The current name was adopted in 1975 because the Newark College of Engineering, which the Technical had become, did not adequately express the breadth of academic programs.

Campuses:	Main campus in Newark; NJIT in Mt. Laurel[272]
Colors:	Red and White
Nickname:	Highlanders
Song:	None[273]

Rowan University (1923)

Glassboro Normal School opened on September 4, 1923. In 1935, it became the New Jersey State Teachers College at Glassboro and in 1958, Glassboro State College. With a $100 million gift from Henry and Betty Rowan in 1992, the name was changed to Rowan College of New Jersey. The current name was adopted in 1997.[274]

Campuses:	Main campus in Glassboro
Colors:	Brown and Gold
Nickname:	Profs
Song:	None[275]

Rutgers, The State University of New Jersey (1766)

Rutgers is the eighth-oldest collegiate institution in the United States, having been chartered in 1766 as Queen's College. Its doors opened in 1771. Changing its name in 1825 to honor Colonel Henry Rutgers, Rutgers College became a land-grant institution in 1864 and a university in 1924.

Campuses:	Main campus in New Brunswick; Camden; Newark
Color:	Scarlet
Nickname:	Knights
Songs:	"Nobody Died for Dear Old Rutgers," "In a Quaint Old Jersey Town," "A Hymn to Queens," "The Rutgers History Lesson," "The Bells Must Ring"[276]

The William Paterson University of New Jersey (1855)

Paterson City Normal School opened in 1855 and was taken over by the state in 1923 as the New Jersey State Normal School at Paterson. In 1937 it became a teacher's college, and in 1958 another name change created Paterson State College. 1971 brought another name change to The William Paterson College of New Jersey. University status was achieved in 1997.[277]

Campuses:	Main campus in Paterson
Colors:	Orange and Black
Nickname:	Pioneers
Song:	None[278]

NEW MEXICO

Eastern New Mexico University (1927)

Although chartered in 1927, classes did not begin on campus until 1934. ENMU was a two-year college until 1940.

Campuses:	Main campus in Portales; Roswell; Ruidoso (Instruction Center)[279]
Colors:	Silver and Green
Nicknames:	Greyhounds; Zias[280]
Song:	"O Hail ENMU" (to the trio section of "Stars and Stripes Forever")[281]

New Mexico State University (1888)

The New Mexico College of Agriculture and Mechanical Arts, later to become NMSU, opened its doors in 1888 with a primary emphasis on agricultural education.

Campuses:	Main campus in Las Cruces; Alamogordo; Carlsbad; Grants
Colors:	Crimson and White
Nickname:	Aggies
Song:	"The Aggie Fight Song"[282]

University of New Mexico (1889)

Although founded in 1889, the university did not hold classes until June of 1892, when twenty-five students began studies.

Campuses:	Main campus in Albuquerque; Gallup; Los Alamos; Graduate Center in Santa Fe; Taos; Valencia[283]
Colors:	Cherry and Silver
Nickname:	Lobos
Song:	"Hail to Thee New Mexico," music by Dean Lena Clauve, lyrics by Dr. George St. Clair[284]

Western New Mexico University (1893)

New Mexico's territorial legislature passed a bill in 1893 that provided for a normal school in Silver City. The next year, the cornerstone was laid for the New Mexico Normal School, which became New Mexico State Teachers' College in the 1920s, and Western New Mexico University in 1963.

Campuses:	Main campus in Silver City[285]
Colors:	Purple and Gold
Nickname:	Mustangs
Song:	"Rally 'Round You Mustangs," words by Ross Capshaw, music by Abramo Parotti, arranged by Dennis Hayslett[286]

NEW YORK

The State University of New York is comprised of sixty-four campuses, with university centers in Albany, Binghamton, Buffalo, and Stony Brook.[287]

The University at Albany (1844)

Until becoming New York State College for Teachers in 1914, the Normal School had been a two-year college for most of its existence. It is New York's oldest state chartered higher education institution. In 1962 it became a university, and in 1976 it received its current name.[288]

Campuses: Main campus in Albany

Colors: Purple and Gold

Nickname: Great Danes

Song: "Purple and Gold" by John Regan and Jon Hansen[289]

The University at Binghamton (1946)

Binghamton University began as a branch of Syracuse University called Triple Cities College. In 1950 it was renamed Harpur College. In 1965 the college was renamed the State University of New York at Binghamton.[290]

Campuses: Main campus in Binghamton

Colors: Green and White

Nickname: Colonials

Song: "Binghamton University Fight Song" by Mike Boxer[291]

The University at Buffalo (1846)

The University of Buffalo was chartered as a private institution on May 11, 1846. On September 1, 1962, the University merged into the New York State System as one of its major universities.[292]

Campuses: Main campus in Buffalo

Colors: Blue and White

Nickname: Bulls

Song: "Victory March" by Robert Mols[293]

The University at Stony Brook (1957)

Classes were held from 1957 to 1962 at the former Oyster Bay estate of William R. Coe until the university moved to Stony Brook. In 1960 Stony Brook was designated to become a major research university.[294]

Campuses: Main campus in Stony Brook

Colors: Scarlet and Gray

Nickname: Seawolves

Song: None[295]

NORTH CAROLINA

The University of North Carolina System includes sixteen universities. The system's oldest and largest institutions are noted below.[296]

North Carolina Agricultural and Technical State University (1891)

North Carolina A and T was chartered in 1891 as a college for "the Colored Race" so that the state could take advantage of the 1890 Morrill Act. In 1915 it was named The Agricultural and Technical College of North Carolina, and in 1967 it became a regional university.[297]

Campuses: Main campus in Greensboro

Colors: Blue and Gold

Nickname: Aggies

Song: "Aggie Bad"[298]

North Carolina State University (1887)

The North Carolina College of Agriculture and Mechanic Arts was created by the legislature on March 7, 1887. Land-grant status was moved from the University of North Carolina to this institution, which opened its doors in October 1889. In 1917 a name change created the North Carolina State College of Agriculture and Engineering, and in 1965 the current name was adopted.[299]

Campuses: Main campus in Raleigh

Colors: Red and White

Nickname: Wolfpack

Song: "NC State Fight Song," words by Hardy M. Ray, separate arrangements by Edward L. Gruber and Douglas R. Overmier; "Red and White" by J. Perry Watson[300]

University of North Carolina (1789)

North Carolina's first constitution in 1776 envisioned the establishment of state universities, but it was not until 1789 that the University of North Carolina was chartered. And it was not until January of 1795 that the university opened to students.[301]

Campuses: Main campus in Chapel Hill; UNC at Asheville; UNC at Charlotte; UNC at Greensboro; UNC at Pembroke; UNC at Wilmington

Colors: Light Blue and White

Nickname: Tar Heels

Song: "I'm a Tar Heel Born"[302]

NORTH DAKOTA

The North Dakota University System includes eleven campuses. The University of North Dakota is the largest university in the Dakotas, and North Dakota State University is the state's land-grant institution.

North Dakota State University (1890)

An 1890 act created the North Dakota Agricultural College, whose purpose was to educate the common person by combining technical and academic subjects in the spirit of the 1862 Morrill Act.[303]

Campuses: Main campus in Fargo

Colors: Green and Yellow

Nickname: Bison, Thundering Herd[304]

Song: "On Bison!"; "We Are the Pride"[305]

University of North Dakota (1883)

The Dakota Territorial Assembly founded the University of North Dakota six years before North Dakota attained statehood. Classes opened on September 8, 1884. The University began as a college of arts and sciences with a normal school attached to it.[306]

Campuses: Main campus in Grand Forks; branch campuses in Williston and Devil's Lake[307]

Colors: Green and White

Nickname: Fighting Sioux

Songs: "Fight On Sioux," "Stand Up and Cheer," "It's for You North Dakota U"[308]

OHIO

Bowling Green State University (1910)

Bowling Green began as a normal school in 1910. Classes were first held in 1914. Four-year programs were initiated in 1929, and university status was attained in 1935.

Campuses: Main campus in Bowling Green; Firelands College[309]

Colors: Brown and Orange

Nickname: Falcons

Song: "Forward Falcons," words and music by Dr. Wayne Bohrnstedt[310]

Central State University (1887)

Central State was founded on March 19, 1887, as a normal and industrial department of Wilberforce University with its own board. In 1941 four-year programs began, and six years later the department began to operate separately from Wilberforce University. In 1951 Central State College emerged, and in 1965 the college became a university in the Ohio state system.[311]

Campuses: Main campus in Wilberforce

Colors: Maroon and Gold

Nickname: Marauders

Song: None[312]

Cleveland State University (1964)

Cleveland State was officially chartered in 1964, but its origin can be traced back to the Association Institute, which was reorganized out of a Cleveland YMCA program. The Institute gave way to Fenn College in 1929, and then, in 1964 Cleveland State became a university in the Ohio system.[313]

Campuses: Main campus in Cleveland

Colors: Forest Green and White

Nickname: Vikings

Song: None[314]

Kent State University (1910)

Kent Normal School opened in 1913 on land donated by William S. Kent for a teachers school. By 1919 it had become Kent State College and, in 1935, Kent State University.

Campuses: Main campus in Kent; Ashtabula Campus; East Liverpool Campus; Geauga Campus; Salem Campus; Stark Campus; Trumbull Campus; Tuscarawas Campus[315]

Colors: Blue and Gold

Nickname: Golden Flashes

Song: "Fight On for KSU" by Ed Siennicki[316]

Miami University (1809)

George Washington signed a law in 1792 that granted a township in the Miami Valley to be held in trust for a higher education institution. Ohio became a state in 1803, and the Ohio General Assembly chartered Miami University in 1809. Miami did not begin college-level classes until 1824 due in part to the War of 1812.[317]

Campuses: Main campus in Oxford; Miami University Hamilton; Miami University Middletown; Miami University Dolibois European Center in Luxembourg[318]

Colors: Red and White
Nickname: Red Hawks
Song: "Love and Honor to Mi-
             ami"[319]

The Ohio State University (1870)

Ohio State was established as a land-grant institution under the provisions of the Morrill Act in 1870. It opened its doors under the name of the Ohio Agricultural and Mechanical College in 1873. In 1878 the college became The Ohio State University.

Campuses: Main campus in Columbus;
             Lima; Mansfield; Marion;
             Newark[320]
Colors: Scarlet and Gray
Nickname: Buckeyes
Song: "Across the Field," "Buckeye
             Battlecry," "Carmen
             Ohio"[321]

Ohio University (1804)

Ohio University was chartered by the state of Ohio in 1804 and opened for classes in 1808. It is the oldest university in the Northwest Territory.

Campuses: Main campus in Athens; East-
             ern campus (St. Clairsville);
             Zanesville; Lancaster;
             Southern campus (Ironton);
             Chillicothe[322]
Colors: Kelly Green and White
Nickname: Bobcats
Song: "Stand Up and Cheer"[323]

Shawnee State University (1975)

The newest university in the Ohio system grew out of the Shawnee State General

and Technical College, formed in 1975, and the Shawnee State Community College, named in 1977. In 1986 it became a university.[324]

Campuses: Main campus in Portsmouth
Colors: Royal Blue and Dove Gray
Nickname: Bears
Song: "Onward and Upward Shaw-
             nee" by Shirley Crothers[325]

University of Akron (1870)

The university traces its origin back to the denominational Buchtel College, founded in 1870. By 1913 the college had come on hard times and the city took its assets, renaming it The Municipal University of Akron. In 1963 the state started to assist the university, and in 1967 it became a state university.[326]

Campuses: Main campus in Akron
Colors: Blue and Gold
Nickname: Zips
Song: "The Akron Blue and Gold"
             by Fred Waring and Pat Bal-
             lard[327]

University of Cincinnati (1819)

Cincinnati College and the Medical College of Ohio were founded in 1819. Both were absorbed into the University of Cincinnati in 1870, which was established by the city. In 1977 UC officially became one of Ohio's state universities.[328]

Campuses: Main campus in Cincinnati;
             off-campus sites at Clermont
             College; West Chester and UC
             centers in Western Hills and
             Warren County[329]
Colors: Red and Black

Nickname: Bearcats

Song: "Cheer, Cincinnati"[330]

University of Toledo (1872)

The Toledo University of Arts and Trades was born out of a gift of land by Jesup W. Scott in 1872. The city of Toledo supported the university from 1883 until 1967, when it joined the state university system.[331]

Campuses: Main campus in Toledo

Colors: Midnight Blue and Gold

Nickname: Rockets

Song: "U of Toledo," written by Dave Connelly, arranged by David Jex[332]

Wright State University (1964)

Wright State opened in 1964 as the Dayton academic center of Miami University and a graduate center for Ohio State University. Three million dollars was raised by the community of Dayton to fund a public university. In 1965 the Ohio General Assembly approved the Wright State name to honor the Wright brothers of Dayton, and in 1967 Wright State became an independent institution.[333]

Campuses: Main campus in Dayton; Lake Campus between Celina and St. Mary's[334]

Colors: Green and Gold

Nickname: Raiders

Song: "We Are Tough! We Are Great!"[335]

Youngstown State University (1908)

Youngstown State began when the School of Law of the Youngstown Association School sponsored by the YMCA opened in 1908. In 1921 the Youngstown Institute of Technology was offering four-year curricula. In 1928 the Institute was renamed Youngstown College. The YMCA transferred control to the college itself in 1944, and in 1955 the college was recharted as The Youngstown University. The University joined the Ohio state system in 1967.[336]

Campuses: Main campus in Youngstown

Colors: Red and White

Nickname: Penguins

Song: "YSU Fight Song," composer anonymous, arranged by Robert Fleming[337]

OKLAHOMA

The Oklahoma State System of Higher Education was created in 1941. Twenty-five colleges and universities are part of the system. Oklahoma State and the University of Oklahoma are the largest universities in the system.[338]

Oklahoma State University (1890)

The Oklahoma Agricultural and Mechanical College was founded on Christmas Day in 1890. A year later, when classes commenced, there were still no facilities, a condition that was maintained until 1894. Oklahoma's land-grant institution received its current name in 1957.

Campuses: Main campus in Stillwater; OSU–Tulsa; OSU College of Osteopathic Medicine, Tulsa; OSU Technical Branch–Oklahoma City; OSU Technical Branch–Okmulgee[339]

Colors: Orange and Black

Nickname: Cowboys

Song: "Ride 'Em Cowboys!"[340]

University of Oklahoma (1890)

The University of Oklahoma was chartered in 1890 when Oklahoma was still a territory.

Campuses: Main campus in Norman; University of Oklahoma Health Sciences Center, Oklahoma City; University of Oklahoma Health Sciences Center, Tulsa[341]

Colors: Red and White

Nickname: Sooners

Song: "Boomer Sooner" [342]

OREGON

The Oregon University System includes seven colleges and universities, three of which are statewide universities: Oregon State University, Portland State, and the University of Oregon.[343]

Oregon State University (1868)

In 1868 Corvallis College, which had not given college-level instruction, became the land-grant institution of Corvallis College and Agricultural College of Oregon. In 1937, after nine name changes, the college finally was called Oregon State College. In 1961 Oregon State became a university.[344]

Campuses: Main campus in Corvallis

Colors: Orange and Black (Orange is the official color)

Nickname: Beavers

Song: "OSU Fight Song"[345]

Portland State University (1946)

An urban university, Portland State began in 1946 as The Vanport Extension Center of the Oregon State System of Higher Education. It became Portland State College in 1955 and received university status in 1969.[346]

Campuses: Main campus in Portland

Colors: Green and White

Nickname: Vikings

Song: "Men of Ohio"[347]

University of Oregon (1876)

The Oregon legislature created the university in 1872. Students first registered for classes on October 16, 1876, and the first building was completed the next year.[348]

Campuses: Main campus in Eugene

Colors: Yellow and Green

Nickname: Ducks

Song: "Mighty Oregon"[349]

PENNSYLVANIA

The State System of Higher Education of the Commonwealth of Pennsylvania is comprised of fourteen universities. The largest campuses in the system are Indiana University of Pennsylvania and West Chester University of Pennsylvania.

Indiana University of Pennsylvania (1875)

In April 1920 the Commonwealth took ownership of an existing school and called it The State Normal School. In 1927 the school became the State Teachers College at Indiana. In 1959 another name change produced Indiana State College. In December 1965 the current name came into use.[350]

Campuses: Main campus in Indiana; branch campuses in Punxsutawney and Armstrong[351]

Colors: Crimson and Gray

Nickname: Indians

Song: "Cherokee" by Ray Noble[352]

The Pennsylvania State University (1855)

Penn State was founded in 1855 with the goal of applying science to farming. In 1863 the Agricultural College of Pennsylvania became a land-grant college, and by the mid-1880s was renamed The Pennsylvania State College. In 1953 The Pennsylvania State University was so named.[355]

Campuses: Main campus in University Park; Abington; Altoona; Beaver; Berks; Delaware County; Dickinson; Dubois; Erie/Behrend; Fayette; Great Valley; Harrisburg; Hazelton; Hershey (College of Medicine); McKeesport; Mont Alto; New Kensington; Lehigh Valley; Pennsylvania College of Technology; Shenango; Schuylkill; Wilkes-Barre; Worthington-Scranton; York[356]

Colors: Blue and White

Nickname: Nittany Lions

Song: "Fight On, State"[357]

West Chester University of Pennsylvania (1871)

The West Chester Normal School, which dated back to 1812 as the West Chester Academy, was privately owned when it opened in 1871 and remained so until 1913. As a commonwealth school, West Chester State Teachers College was born in 1927 and West Chester State College in 1960. The current name was adopted on July 1, 1983.[353]

Campuses: Main campus in West Chester

Colors: Purple and Gold

Nickname: Golden Rams

Song: "Rams Fight" by Earl Mayes; "The Buglers' Dream" by Leo Arnaud[354]

RHODE ISLAND

University of Rhode Island (1888)

Chartered as an agricultural school and a land-grant college, the Rhode Island College of Agriculture and Mechanic Arts accepted its first class in 1892, four years after it was chartered. The name was changed to Rhode Island State College in 1909 and then in 1951 to the University of Rhode Island. Rhode Island is also a sea-grant institution.[358]

Campuses: Main campus in Kingston; Narragansett Bay; Providence; W. Alton Jones campus[359]

Colors: Blue and White

Nickname: Rams

Song: "URI Fight Song"[360]

SOUTH CAROLINA

The Citadel (1842)

The Citadel became an educational institution on December 20, 1842, when the state established the South Carolina Military Academy by combining The Citadel in Charleston and The Arsenal in Columbia. The Academy was closed from 1865 until 1882 because of the Civil War, and in 1910 the Academy was renamed The Citadel.[361]

Campuses:	Main campus in Charleston
Colors:	Citadel Blue and White
Nickname:	Bulldogs[362]
Song:	"The Citadel Forever," "The Fighting Light Brigade," "As the Cadets Go Rolling Along," "All Hail to the Bulldogs" by Lee M. Glaze; "The Citadel Ramble," "Goodbye Carolina"[363]

Clemson University (1889)

Clemson Agricultural College came into being in November of 1889 when the governor signed a bill accepting Thomas Clemson's gift of funds and his Fort Hill plantation. Clemson College, a land-grant institution, opened for classes in July 1893 as an all-male military school. The current name was adopted in 1964.[364]

Campuses:	Main campus in Clemson
Colors:	Purple and Burnt Orange
Nickname:	Tigers
Songs:	"Sock It to 'Em/Orange Bowl March," "Tiger Rag," "Tiger Roar"[365]

South Carolina State University (1896)

Supported in part by funds from the 1890 Morrill Land Grant Act, the Colored Normal, Industrial, Agricultural, and Mechanical College of South Carolina was born in 1896. In 1954 a name change created South Carolina State College, and in 1992 the college was made a university by the legislature.[366]

Campuses:	Main campus in Orangeburg
Colors:	Blue and Garnet
Nickname:	Bulldogs
Song:	"Bulldog Fight Song" by Ronald Serjeant[367]

University of South Carolina (1801)

South Carolina was the first state to charter and fund, by itself, a college known as South Carolina College. Closed from 1862 to 1865 and having struggled until 1906, the college was rechartered a third time as the University of South Carolina.[368]

Campuses:	Main campus in Columbia; Aiken; Beaufort; Lancaster; Salkehatchie; Spartanburg; Sumter; Union[369]
Colors:	Garnet and Black
Nickname:	Fighting Gamecocks
Song:	"Carolina Fight Song" by C. Leigh and E. Bernstein[370]

SOUTH DAKOTA

South Dakota State University (1881)

Dakota Agricultural College, a land-grant college, first accepted students three years after its 1881 charter, but college classes did not begin until one year later. The College attained university status and its current name in 1964.[371]

Campuses: Main campus in Brookings

Colors: Yellow and Blue

Nickname: Jackrabbits

Song: "Ring the Bells"; "Yellow and Blue"[372]

University of South Dakota (1862)

The University of Dakota, which preceded USD, began as an academy. Today, USD houses the state's only law and medical schools.[373]

Campuses: Main campus in Vermillion

Colors: Red and White

Nickname: Coyotes

Song: "South Dakota Victory," "Hail South Dakota," "Get Along Coyotes" by Fred Waring[374]

TENNESSEE

Austin Peay State University (1927)

After Southwestern Presbyterian University closed in 1925, the state created the Austin Peay State Normal School in its place. In 1943 the School became a college and in 1967, a university.[375]

Campuses: Main campus in Clarksville

Colors: Red and White

Nickname: Governors; Lady Govs

Song: "Smash Bang" by Charles Gary[376]

East Tennessee State University (1911)

The East Tennessee State Normal School opened in 1911, and its name was changed to State Teachers College, Johnson City, in 1930. The current name was adopted in 1963 when university status was achieved.

Campuses: Main campus in Johnson City; ETSU at Bristol; ETSU at Greeneville; ETSU at Kingsport[377]

Colors: Navy Blue and Old Gold

Nickname: Buccaneers

Song: "ETSU Fight Song"[378]

Middle Tennessee State University (1911)

Middle Tennessee State Normal School opened in 1911. It became a state college in 1943 and a university in 1965.[379]

Campuses: Main campus in Murfreesboro

Colors: Royal Blue and White

Nickname: Blue Raiders; Lady Raiders

Song: "MTSU Fight Song" by Gary Ingle, lyrics by Mike and Lori Casteel[380]

Tennessee State University (1912)

On June 12, 1912, the Agricultural and Industrial State Normal School opened, and ten years later was named a normal college. In 1951 land-grant status under the 1890 law was approved for the college, and then in 1958 university status was granted. Due to litigation about dual educational systems for blacks and whites, Tennessee State University was merged with the University of Tennessee at Nashville on July 1, 1979.[381]

Campuses: Main campus Nashville

Colors: Blue and White

Nickname: Tigers

Song: "I'm So Glad That I Go to
             TSU"[382]

Tennessee Technological University (1915)

The Tennessee Polytechnic Institute opened in 1916 on the former campus of Dixie College. In 1965 university status was achieved and the current name came into being.[383]

Campuses: Main campus in Cookeville
Colors: Purple and Gold
Nickname: Golden Eagles; Golden Eaglettes
Song: "Tennessee Tech Fight Song" by Paul Yoder; "Tennessee Tech Hymn" by Joan Derryberry[384]

University of Memphis (1912)

The West Tennessee State Normal School was established on September 12, 1912. It became a state teachers college in 1929 and then Memphis State College in 1941. University status was achieved in 1957 and on July 1, 1994, the current name was adopted.[385]

Campuses: Main campus in Memphis
Colors: Royal Blue and Gray
Nickname: Tigers
Song: "Go Tigers Go"[386]

University of Tennessee, Knoxville (1794)

Blount College, which was all-male until 1892, was chartered by the southwest territory's legislature in 1794. The College was renamed East Tennessee College in 1807 and made a university in 1840. In 1869 the university was designated a land-grant institu-tion, and in 1879 the current name was selected.

Campuses: Main campus in Knoxville; UT Chattanooga; UT Martin; UT Memphis; UT Space Institute, Tullahoma[387]
Colors: Orange and White
Nickname: Volunteers/Vols
Song: "Rocky Top!"[388]

TEXAS

Southwest Texas State University (1899)

Southwest Texas State Normal School opened in 1903. Until it became a university in 1969, it had been a normal college, a teachers college, and a college. It has since become one of the largest universities in Texas.[389]

Campuses: Main campus in San Marcos
Colors: Maroon and Gold
Nickname: Bobcats
Song: "Fight Song" or "Go Bobcats" by Paul Yoder[390]

Texas A & M University (1876)

The Agricultural and Mechanical College of Texas opened on October 4, 1876, as a land-grant institution. It received its current name in 1963. Texas A & M is also a sea-grant and a space-grant institution.[391]

Campuses: Main campus in College Station; Texas A & M University at Galveston; Texas A & M University–Commerce; Texas A & M University–Corpus Christi; Texas A & M University–Kingsville; Texas A & M University–Texarkana[392]

Colors: Maroon and White

Nickname: Aggies

Song: "The Aggie War Hymn"[393]

Texas Tech University (1923)

Chartered on February 10, 1923, Texas Technological College opened in the fall of 1925. Graduate instruction began two years later. The current name was adopted in 1969.[394]

Campuses: Main campus in Lubbock; educational facility in Junction; regional health sciences centers in Amarillo, El Paso, and Odessa

Colors: Scarlet and Black

Nickname: Red Raiders; Lady Raiders

Song: "Matador Song" by Harry and R. C. Marshall[395]

University of Houston (1927)

Houston Junior College began in 1927 under the operation of the Houston Independent School District. In 1934 it became a university, and eleven years later it separated from the district and became a private university. In 1963 the university began receiving support from the state.[396]

Campuses: Main campus in Houston; UH–Clear Lake; UH–Downtown; UH–Victoria[397]

Colors: Scarlet and White

Nickname: Cougars

Song: "Cougars Fight for Dear Old U of H," music by Marion Ford, lyrics by Forest Fountain[398]

University of North Texas (1890)

Texas Normal College and Teacher Training Institute has undergone five name changes since 1890: North Texas Normal College (1894), North Texas State Normal College (1901), North Texas State Teachers College (1923), North Texas State College (1949), North Texas State University (1961), and University of North Texas in 1988.[399]

Campuses: Main campus in Denton

Colors: Green and White

Nickname: Eagles

Song: "Fight Song" by Francis Stroup[400]

University of Texas (1883)

UT Austin was chartered in 1883 and located at that time on forty acres. Today, it is the flagship campus of a fifteen-unit system with a main campus of 357 acres. UT Austin is proud of being the largest single campus in the nation.[401]

Campuses: Main campus in Austin; UT at Arlington; UT at Brownsville; UT at Dallas; UT at El Paso; UT at San Antonio; UT at Tyler; UT of the Permian Basin; UT–Pan American[402]

Colors: Burnt Orange and White

Nickname: Longhorns

Song: "Texas Fight" or "TAPS" by Colonel Walter S. Honnicutt, in collaboration with James E. King[403]

UTAH

University of Utah (1850)

The University of Deseret was chartered in 1850, but having suspended operations in

1853, it did not grant its first degrees until 1886. The Territorial Legislature changed the name of the university to the current one on February 17, 1892.[404]

Campuses:	Main campus in Salt Lake City
Colors:	Crimson and White
Nickname:	Utes
Song:	"Utah Man"[405]

Utah State University (1888)

Utah State Agricultural College, which later became Utah State University, was founded in 1888 as the state's land-grant institution.

Campuses:	Main campus in Logan; Brigham City; Moab; Ogden; Richfield; Roosevelt; Salt Lake City; Tooele; Vernal[406]
Colors:	Navy and White
Nickname:	Aggies
Song:	"Hail, Utah Aggies"[407]

VERMONT

University of Vermont (1791)

The date of the charter of the University of Vermont and Vermont's entering statehood is the same. The legal name of the university, which pertains today, was changed in 1865 following the Morrill Act of 1862 to The University of Vermont and State Agricultural College.

Campuses:	Main campus in Burlington; off-campus offices in Berlin, Morrisville, Randolph Center, Guildhall, Newport, St. Johnsbury, Middlebury, South Burlington, St. Albans, Bennington, Brattleboro, Rutland, and White River Junction

Colors:	Green and Gold
Nickname:	Catamounts[408]
Song:	None[409]

VIRGINIA

College of William and Mary (1693)

King William III and Queen Mary II chartered the College in 1693. It became the second college in the colonies. In 1906 it became a state supported institution and received university status in 1967.[410]

Campuses:	Main campus in Williamsburg; Richard Bland College
Colors:	Green, Gold, and Silver
Nickname:	Tribe
Song:	"Fight, Fight, Fight for the Indians"[411]

George Mason University (1957)

George Mason College opened in 1957 as a branch of the University of Virginia. It became a four-year college in 1966. It became an independent institution and a university in 1972.

Campuses:	Main campus in Fairfax; Arlington Campus; Prince William Campus[412]
Colors:	Dark Green and Gold
Nickname:	Patriots
Song:	"The GMU Fight Song" by Anthony Maiello[413]

Old Dominion University (1930)

Old Dominion opened as a branch of the College of William and Mary, offering two-year programs. In 1962 it became an independent, state-supported institution called Old Dominion College. In 1969 it became a university.[414]

Campuses:	Main campus in Norfolk; Peninsula Higher Education Center; Virginia Beach Higher Education Center[415]
Colors:	Slate Blue and Silver
Nickname:	Monarchs
Song:	"ODU Fight Song"[416]

University of Virginia (1819)

The University of Virginia was founded by Thomas Jefferson, who designed the original campus and was its first rector. Classes were first held in 1825.[417]

Campuses:	Main campus in Charlottesville; UVA's College at Wise
Colors:	Orange and Blue
Nickname:	Cavaliers; Wahoos; Hoos
Song:	"The Good Old Song," words by Edward H. Craighill, Jr.[418]

Virginia Commonwealth University (1837)

Virginia Commonwealth University is the result of the 1968 merger of the Medical College of Virginia and the Richmond Professional Institute.

Campuses:	Main campus in Richmond; Medical College of Virginia Campus[419]
Colors:	Black and Gold
Nickname:	Rams
Song:	"VCU Fight Song," composer unknown[420]

Virginia Polytechnic Institute and State University (1872)

Better known as Virginia Tech, this university is Virginia's land-grant institution under the first Morrill Act. It is also Virginia's largest university.[421]

Campuses:	Main campus in Blacksburg; Northern Virginia Graduate Center; Hotel Roanoake and Conference Center; Roanoke Valley Graduate Center; Center for European Studies and Architecture (Switzerland); Virginia Tech Hampton Roads Center; Marion duPont Scott Equine Medical Center (Leesburg); Washington-Alexandria Center[422]
Colors:	Maroon and Orange
Nickname:	Hokies
Songs:	"Tech Triumph," "VPI Victory March," "Hokie Pokie"[423]

Virginia State University (1882)

Founded on March 6, 1882, and opened on October 1, 1883, the Virginia Normal and Collegiate Institute lost its collegiate status in 1902 when it became the Virginia Normal and Industrial Institute. In 1920 the Institute received land-grant designation under the second Morrill Act. In 1923 collegiate programs were renewed, and in 1930 the name was changed to Virginia State College for Negroes. In 1946 another name change created Virginia State College. In 1979 university status was achieved.[424]

Campuses:	Main campus in Petersburg
Colors:	Orange and Blue

Nickname: Trojans
Song: None[425]

WASHINGTON

University of Washington (1861)

The Territorial University of Washington opened on November 4, 1861, in downtown Seattle, twenty-seven years before Washington became a state.

Campuses: Main campus in Seattle; Tacoma; Bothell
Colors: Purple and Gold
Nickname: Huskies
Song: "Bow Down to Washington"[426]

Washington State University (1890)

Washington State is a land-grant institution founded in 1890. It has grown since then to include branch campuses, extension offices in thirty-nine counties, and learning centers in eleven counties.[427]

Campuses: Main campus in Pullman; Spokane; Tri-Cities; Vancouver; College of Nursing
Colors: Crimson and Gray
Nickname: Cougars
Song: "The Fight Song," words by Zella Melcher, music by Phyllis Sayles[428]

WEST VIRGINIA

West Virginia University (1867)

West Virginia University was founded in 1967 as West Virginia's land-grant institution under the first Morrill Act.

Campuses: Main campus in Morgantown; Potomac State College of West Virginia University (Keyser); West Virginia University, Charleston Division; West Virginia University at Parkersburg; West Virginia Institute of Technology (Montgomery)[429]
Colors: Old Gold and Blue
Nickname: Mountaineers
Songs: "Fight Mountaineers" and "Hail West Virginia"[430]

WISCONSIN

University of Wisconsin (1848)

Wisconsin's first governor, Nelson Dewey, approved the university's act of incorporation in 1848. The first class met the next year. The University of Wisconsin system was established in 1971.[431]

Campuses: Main campus in Madison; four-year campuses: UW–Eau Claire; UW–Green Bay; UW–LaCrosse; UW–Milwaukee; UW–Oshkosh; UW–Parkside; UW–Platteville; UW–River Falls; UW–Stevens Point; UW–Stout; UW–Superior; UW–Whitewater
Colors: Cardinal and White
Nickname: Badgers
Song: "On Wisconsin," words by Carl Beck, music by William Purdy, adapted by Michael Leckrone[432]

WYOMING

University of Wyoming (1886)

UW is the only university established by the state of Wyoming with a bill signed by Governor Francis E. Warren in 1886. It is a land-grant university.[433]

Campuses:	Main campus in Laramie; UW/Casper College Center
Colors:	Brown and Yellow
Nickname:	Cowboys
Song:	"Ragtime Cowboy Joe"[434]

DISTRICT OF COLUMBIA

University of the District of Columbia (1974)

UDC was chartered as an urban land-grant institution in 1974. It is the District's only public institution of higher learning. UDC was born out of the consolidation in 1977 of the District of Columbia Teachers College, the Washington Technical Institute, and the Federal City College.[435]

Campuses:	Main campus in Washington, D.C.
Colors:	Red and Gold
Nickname:	Firebirds
Song:	None[436]

GUAM

University of Guam (1952)

The University is a land-grant institution chartered in 1952. It began as a two-year school called the Territorial College of Guam whose purpose was to train teachers.

In 1968, with the addition of four-year programs, the college became the University of Guam.[437]

Campuses:	Main campus in Mangilao
Colors:	Green and White
Nickname:	Tritons
Song:	"The University Anthem" by R. Mannoni[438]

PUERTO RICO

University of Puerto Rico (1903)

The University is the public system of higher education in Puerto Rico. It consists of eleven educational units.[439]

Campuses:	Main campus in Rio Piedras; Aguadilla; Arecibo; Bayamón; Carolina; Cayey; Ciecias Médicas; Humacao; Mayagüez; Ponce; Utuado[440]
Colors:	Red and White
Nickname:	Gallitos; Roosters
Song:	"The Official Hymn of the University of Puerto Rico"[441]

U.S. VIRGIN ISLANDS

University of the Virgin Islands (1962)

The University was chartered on March 16, 1962, as the College of the Virgin Islands. It opened in July 1963. In 1972 the College received land-grant status by the United States Congress. In 1986 university status was achieved.[442]

Campuses: Main campus in St. Thomas; St. Croix.

Colors: Caribbean Blue, White, and Yellow

Nickname: Buccaneers[443]

Song: None[444]

NOTES

1. Unless otherwise noted, the source used for university colors and nicknames, with the permission of the author, is Roy E. Yarbrough's *The History of Senior College and University Mascots/Nicknames* (Lynchburg, Va.: Bluff University Publications, 1998).

2. "Office of Institutional Research, Alabama State University," www.alasu.edu/factbook/fact99.

3. Telephone conversation with Miss Adams, Office of the Dean, 9/6/00.

4. "The University," www.auburn.edu/student_info/bulletin/university.

5. "Sounds of the AU Band," www.auburn.edu/auband/sounds.

6. "A Brief History of the University of Alabama," faq.ua.edu/history.html.

7. "Alabama Athletics," www.rolltide.com/local/tradition.

8. "UAB Significant Dates," www.iss.uab.edu/f&f1997–1998/sigdate.

9. Personal e-mail correspondence from Richard H. Harrison, II, 9/28/00.

10. "About UAH," www.uah.edu/html/About/index.

11. Personal e-mail correspondence from Robin Douglass, 9/5/00.

12. University of Alaska, www.alaska.edu/info

13. Sheet music provided by Kristi Palmer, Assistant Sports Information Director, University of Alaska Anchorage.

14. Personal e-mail correspondence from Sharon Burke, 9/5/00.

15. Personal e-mail correspondence from Tish Giffin, 9/6/00.

16. Arizona State University, www.asu.edu/aad/catalogs/general/general-information.

17. "Official Athletic Site of Arizona State University: Traditions," www.thesundevils.com/trads/asu-trads-song.

18. "A Brief History and Description," www.queenb.opi.arizona.edu/facts/briefhistory.

19. "The University of Arizona, Traditions," www.tour.arizona.edu/new/traditions/traditions 11.

20. "Arkansas State University," www.astate.edu/docs/asu_news/intro.

21. "Arkansas State University SoundZone," www.astate.edu/docs/cards/sounds/soundzone.

22. "Your U of A Briefing Book," www.pigtrail.uark.edu/info/briefing_book/Dates.

23. "Official Razorback Colors," "Arkansas Fight Song," www.HogWired.com.

24. "About the CSU," www.calstate.edu/tier3/PubAffairs/info/System.

25. "Historic Milestones," www.calstate.edu/tier3/PubAffairs/info/milestones.

26. "SJSU History at a Glance," www.sjsu.edu/pres/sjsuhist.

27. "Official Web Site of San Jose State University Athletics," www.sjsuspartans.com/local/interactive.

28. University of California, Profile of the University," www.ucop.edu/ucophome/commserv/profile.

29. "About UC Berkeley: A Brief History of the University," www.berkeley.edu/about_documents/history.

30. "Cal Traditions, Songs of California," www.fansonly.com/schools/cal/trads/cal-m-fb-songs.

31. "History of Colorado State University," www.colostate.edu/history.

32. "Recognizing CSU," www.colostate.edu/Level12/csulogos.

33. "University of Colorado System," www.cu.edu/About_CU/CU_System

34. "University of Colorado Athletic Dept. Official Site, Traditions," www.cu-sports.com/multimedia/audio/school/fightsong.

35. "What is CSU?" www.csu.ctstateu.edu/whatiscsu.

36. Telephone conversation with Joan Packer, CSU Library, 10/12/00.

37. "Connecticut State University System: What Is CSU?" www.ctstateu.edu/whatiscsu.

38. Personal e-mail correspondence from Bill Gamzon, 10/10/00.

39. "Southern Connecticut State University—Undergraduate Studies, Undergraduate Catalog; University Information," www.SouthernCT.edu/catalogue/undergrad/univinfo.

40. Telephone conversation.

41. "Uconn '99 Fact Sheet," www.uconn.edu/uconn/Facts.

42. "Welcome to Western," www.wcsu.ctstateu.edu/welcomme/university.

43. Personal e-mail correspondence from Tim Sohn, 4/27/00.

44. "Delaware State University—History," www.dsc.edu/p0012.

45. "Delaware State University at a Glance," www.dsc.edu/p0011.

46. Words provided by R. Batson, Delaware State University Library, 10/31/00.

47. "Tradition and Innovation—Our History and Future," www.udel.edu/catalog/current/univer.

48. Personal e-mail correspondence from Scott Selheimer, 4/18/00.

49. "FAMU History," www.famu2.famu.edu/future/visitor/history; "Athletics," www.famu2.famu.edu/athletics/facts.

50. Personal e-mail correspondence from FAMU Library Reference Department, 10/9/00.

51. "University History," www.fau.edu/about/history.

52. "Florida Atlantic University 1999–2000 Facts," www.fau.edu/academic/iea/inst/facts.

53. Personal e-mail correspondence from Katrina McCormack, 3/4/00.

54. "Florida Gulf Coast University, University Overview," www.fgcu.edu/catalog/Overview.

55. Personal e-mail correspondence from Jeff Bluestein, 3/4/00.

56. "The University," www.fiu.edu/fiufacts.

57. Personal e-mail correspondence from Richard J. Kelch, 3/21/00.

58. "A Brief History of the State of Florida and the University," www.fsu.edu/~rsect/factbook99/History.

59. "FSU Traditions," www.fansonly.com/schools/fsu/trads/fsu/trads.

60. "University of Central Florida," www.ucf.edu/catalog/9900/UCF_Section/home.

61. "UCF Marching Knights—History," www.oir.ucf.edu/mk/history2.

62. "UF Facts and Rankings," www.ufl.edu/facts.

63. "University of Florida Bands—Sound Clips," www.ufbands.ufl.edu/band/sounds.

64. "University of North Florida Undergraduate Catalog, 1999–2000," www.unf.edu.

65. "The University of North Florida Department of Music Home Page," www.unf.edu/coas/music/.

66. "USF History: Timeline of Events," www.usf.edu/History/timeline.

67. "USF Fight Song" and "USF March Victorious," www.usf.edu.

68. "Welcome to UWF," www.uwf.edu/catalog/welcome.

69. Personal e-mail correspondence from Richard T. Glaze, 9/4/00.

70. "University System of Georgia, Degrees and Majors Approved," www.peachnet.edu/admin/accaff/degapp.

71. "Georgia Institute of Technology," www.peachnet.edu/inst/about/gatech.; "Georgia Institute of Technology: Visitor Information," www.gatech.edu/techhome/subpgs/visitor.

72. Personal e-mail correspondence from Christopher Neill, 4/25/00.

73. "Georgia State University," www.peachnet.edu/inst/about/gastate.

74. Personal e-mail correspondence from Virginia A. Brown, 9/26/00.

75. "Undergraduate Catalog," www.bulletin.uga.edu/bulletin/univ/history.

76. "University of Georgia Athletic Association, Traditions," www.georgiadogs.com/traditions/index.

77. "General Information; The University of Hawaii System," www.hawaii.edu/welcome/general-info.

78. "Rainbow Athletics: Tradition," www.uhathletics.hawaii.edu/tradition.

79. Personal e-mail correspondence from Gwen Nakamura, 4/20/00.

80. "About Idaho State University," www.isu.edu/aboutisu/aboutisu.

81. Personal e-mail correspondence from Dan Kalantarian, 4/20/00.

82. "University of Idaho—Fact Book 99," www.uidaho.edu/UIcommunications/factbook99.

83. "Vandal Fight Song," www.its.uidaho.edu/athletics/fightsong.

84. "General Information: The University," www.csu.edu/catalogs/graduate/02GEN.

85. "Intercollegiate Athletics; Home of the Chicago State University Cougars," www.csu.edu/athletics/facts.

86. Telephone conversation with Public Affairs Office, Chicago State University, 9/6/00.

87. "Eastern Virtual Tour," www.eiu.edu/vr/oldmain.

88. "Panthers, Athletic Quick Facts," www.eiu.edu/~sportinfo/quickfacts.

89. "Eastern Athletic Traditions, EIU School Songs," www.eiu.edu/~sprtinfo/gopanthers/scl_sngs.

90. "Illinois State: Mission and Profile," www.ppsis.ilstu.edu/facts/current/book/Profile-Mission.

91. Personal e-mail correspondence from Kenny Mossman, 3/7/00.

92. "Northeastern Illinois University, About Northeastern," www.neiu.edu/About.

93. Personal e-mail correspondence from Tony Courier, 3/15/00.

94. "Northern Illinois University General Information," www.niu.edu/geninfo.

95. "Huskie Bands—Sights and Sounds," www.niu.edu/band/archive.

96. "SIU, About Our University," www.siu.edu/hp/aboutsiu.

97. "Marching Salukis," www.siu.edu/departments/cola/music001/music002/marsal.

98. Personal e-mail correspondence from Marjorie Baier, 9/12/00.

99. "Illinois at a Glance," www.uiuc.edu/admin2/about.

100. "Illinois, Traditions," www.fansonly.com/schools/ill/trads/ill-trads-songs.

101. "Graduate Catalog 1999–2000 Overview," www.wiu.edu/users/miprov/ugcat99/overview.

102. "Western Illinois Athletics," www.wiu.edu/textver/athletics.

103. Personal e-mail correspondence from Rodney Schueller, 3/7/00.

104. "Ball State University, BSU Athletics History," www.bsu.edu/sports/program/bsu/bsuhistory.

105. "Ball State University, Ball State Fight Song," www.bsu.edu/sports/programs/newweb/fightsong.

106. "Indiana State University Historical Development," www.indstate.edu/isuorg/history.

107. "Indiana State University Intercollegiate Athletics/Tradition," web.indstate.edu/athletics/tradition/home2.html.

108. "Indiana University: About IU," www.indiana.edu/iu/iuinfo/aboutiu.

109. "About IU Campuses," www.indiana.edu/campuses/index.

110. Personal e-mail correspondence from Kit Klingelhoffer, 3/6/00.

111. "History, University Founding," www.purdue.edu/OOP/facts/frames/history.

112. "Traditions," www.purdue.edu/OOP/facts/frames/traditions.

113. " 'From Prairie to Prominence': A Brief History of Iowa State University," www.lib.iastate.edu/arch/isuhist.

114. "ISUCF 'V'MB," www.music.iastate.edu/org/marching/ss.

115. "Overview, Brief History," www.uiowa.edu/~our/fact.book.

116. "University of Northern Iowa Catalog, 1998–2000: General Information," www.uni.edu/pubrel/catalog/gen-info.

117. "University of Northern Iowa "Panther" Marching Band Background," www.uni.edu/maucker/sordir/sorg492/main.

118. "The Kansas Board of Regents," www.kansasregents.org.

119. "University Information," www.emporia.edu/regist/instudy/information.

120. Personal e-mail correspondence from Barb Robins, 10/12/00.

121. "Welcome to Fort Hays State University," www.fhsu.edu/campus.

122. Personal e-mail correspondence from Dr. Michael C. Robinson, 3/14/00.

123. "Kansas State University: About K-State," www.ksu.edu/Welcome/background.

124. "KSUMB-Sound: School Songs," www.ksu.edu/band/KSUMB/schoolsongs.

125. "Pittsburg State University: Quick Facts," www.pittstate.edu/admit/ugfacts.

126. "School Songs," www.pittstate.edu/pubs/stuhbook/songs.

127. "The University of Kansas: Facts, 1999," www.urc.ukans.edu/About/Facts/universityfacts.

128. "KU," www.jayhawks.org/left.

129. "WSU History," www.wichita.edu/online/history.

130. Personal e-mail correspondence from John Barker, 6/23/00.

131. "About EKU—Some Details," www.eku.edu/about/abouteku.

132. Personal e-mail correspondence from Christopher Hayes, 3/8/00.

133. "Kentucky State University: Land Grant Mission," www.kysu.edu/landgrant/default2.

134. Personal e-mail correspondence from Ann Sullivan, 9/18/00.

135. "Morehead State University History and Mission," www.morehead-st.edu/visitors/history.

136. Personal e-mail correspondence from Susan D. Creasap, 9/15/00.

137. "Brief History of Murray State University," www.muruky.edu/rainey.

138. "Murray State University Extended Campus Programs," www.murraystate.edu/ec/excamp.

139. Telephone conversation, Murray State Music Department, 10/27/00.

140. "Northern Kentucky University Information," www.nku.edu/www/about_nku.

141. Personal e-mail correspondence from Carol Dunevant, 4/24/00.

142. "University of Kentucky, History," www.uky.edu/newhome/submain/about1.

143. "University of Kentucky, Traditions," www.uky.edu/newhome/submain/about2.

144. "U of L—A Brief History," www.louisville.edu/ur/onpi/history.

145. "U of L—University Profile," www.louisville.edu/ur/onpi/profile.

146. Personal e-mail correspondence from Kathy Tronzo, 3/13/00.

147. "History of Western Kentucky University," www2.wku.edu/www/library/dlsc/ua/wkuhist/wkuhist.

148. "Fight Song," www.wku.edu/Athletics/tradition/fight.

149. "History of Grambling State University," www.gram.edu/htm_files/history_of_grambling.

150. "Fight Song," www.gram.edu/htm_files/fight_song_page.

151. "Louisiana State University System Information," www.webserv.regents.state.la.us/lsusys.

152. "About LSU," www.lsu.edu/center/about.

153. Personal e-mail correspondence from LSU webmaster, 3/7/00.

154. "Louisiana Tech University—University Bulletin (Catalog), General Information," www.atech.edu/tech/admissions/bulletin/1999_2000/general.

155. "Louisiana Tech University Band of Pride," www.latech.edu/music/band/sites/mp3/index.

156. "McNeese—History," www.mcneese.edu/information/history.

157. "The Pride of McNeese," www.mcneese.edu/org/band/onmcneese.

158. "Nicholls State University—About Nicholls State University, History," www.nich.edu/about.history.

159. Telephone conversation with Eric Gueniot, Band director, 10/9/00.

160. "About NSU," www.nsula.edu/about SU1.

161. Personal e-mail correspondence from Bill Brent.

162. "Southeastern Louisiana University: A Message from the President," www.selu.edu/PresidentMsg.

163. Personal e-mail correspondence from Glen J. Hemberger, 4/26/00.

164. "Southern University and A & M College, Facts," www.subr.edu/sufacts.

165. Telephone conversation, Southern University and A & M College Archives, 10/12/00.

166. "University of Louisiana at Lafayette: About the University: Introduction," www.usl.edu/About/introduction.

167. Telephone conversation with Bruce Turn, 10/10/00.

168. "NLU Is Now The University of Louisiana at Monroe," www.ulm.edu/ulmannounce.

169. Telephone conversation, ULM Band Department, 10/13/00.

170. "Campus History," www.umaine.edu/Administration/history.

171. Personal e-mail correspondence from Karen Cole, 9/5/00.

172. "A Brief History of Morgan State University," www.morgan.edu/welcome/history.

173. "Sportszone, Department of Athletics," www.morgan.edu/welcome/athletic/sports.

174. Personal e-mail correspondence from Melvin Miles, 4/20/00.

175. "University System of Maryland: Origin and Functions," www.mdarchives.state.md/us/msa/mdmanual/25ind/html/74systf.

176. "Maryland Victory Song," www.fansonly.com / schools / md / trads / md-m-fb-victorysong.

177. "University of Massachusetts Amherst, News and Information," www.umass.edu/umhome/about.

178. "University of Massachusetts Minuteman Marching Band: Music," www.umass.edu/band/music.

179. "Central Michigan University: Fast Facts," www.cmich.edu/HISTORY.

180. Personal e-mail correspondence from Tammi Schafer, 3/6/00.

181. "Eastern Michigan University, 1999–2000 Online Catalog, Undergraduate Edition: University Profile," www.emich.edu/public/catalogs/current/ugradinfo/profile.

182. "Eastern Athletics," www.emich.edu/public/admissions/fastfact/athletics.

183. Personal e-mail correspondence from Max Plank, 4/24/00.

184. "College Catalog, Ferris State University: Introduction," www.ferris.edu/htmls/fsucatalg/geninfo/fsumission/introduction.

185. "Ferris State University Fight Song," www.ferris.edu/HTMLS/alumni/fight.

186. "Grand Valley State University, 1999–2000 Catalog," www.gvsu.edu/catalog/catalog 99–00/opening.

187. Personal e-mail correspondence from Kent Fisher, 4/26/00.

188. "Welcome to Lake Superior State University," www.lssu.edu/tour/photo/lowres.

189. Telephone conversation, KJS Library, Reference Department, 10/9/00.

190. "Michigan State University," www.msu.edu/dig/facts/FIB.

191. "Michigan State, the Fight Song and Alma Mater," www.fansonly.com/schools/msu/trads/msu-trads-colors, nickname, songs.

192. "Michigan Tech: What's It All About?" www.admin.mtu.edu/urel/catalogs/ugrad/mtu.

193. Personal e-mail correspondence from Dave Fischer, 4/25/00.

194. "Northern's History," www.nmu.edu/facts/history.

195. Telephone conversation with Stephen Grugin, Band Department.

196. "Oakland University, Profile of OU," www.oakland.edu/admissions/profile.

197. "OU Fight Song," www.ou.sv3.com/athletics/athletics_fightsong.

198. "About SVSU," www.svsu.edu/transfer/about.

199. Personal e-mail correspondence from Anita Dey, 9/14/00.

200. "University of Michigan Campus Information Centers, History of UM," www.umich.edu/~info/aboutum.

201. "The Victors," www.umich.edu/UM-Lyrics.

202. "About Wayne State University," www.wayne.edu/about_profile.

203. Personal e-mail correspondence from Doug Bianchi, 9/5/00.

204. "Western Michigan University, Profile of WMU," www.wmich.edu/wmu/profile/index.

205. "Western Michigan University, 1999–2000 WMU Facts," www.wmich.edu/wmu/facts/index.

206. Personal e-mail correspondence from Bill Pease, 3/13/00.

207. "BSU History," www.bemidji.msus.edu/BSUCatalog/FRONTPAGES/SectionI?History.

208. Personal e-mail correspondence from Meredith Brown, 5/1/00.

209. "Metropolitan State University," History, www.metrostate.edu/about/AMhistory.

210. Personal e-mail correspondence from Sue Amos Parker, 5/24/00.

211. "Minnesota State University, Mankato—A Brief History and Profile," www.mankato.msus.edu/dept/univops/history.

212. Personal e-mail correspondence from Rose Blumenshein, 3/21/00.

213. "Moorhead State University's History," www.moorhead.msus.edu/publications/history.

214. Telephone conversation with John Tesch, Band Department, 10/13/00.

215. "Southwest at a Glance," www.southwest.msus.edu/Admission/SouthwestataGlance/default.

216. Sheet music provided by Mary Jane Striegel, Southwest State University Library.

217. "St. Cloud State University: The Tradition," www.stcloudstate.edu/about/tradition.

218. "St. Cloud State University Huskies: A Tradition of Excellence," www.stcloudstate.edu/~sports/tradition.

219. "University of Minnesota: About the U of M," www1.umn.edu/systemwide/facthistory.

220. "Songs of the University of Minnesota," www.music.umn.edu/marchingband/songs.

221. "Winona State University, Welcome," www.winona.msus.edu/catalog/homepg.

222. Personal e-mail correspondence from Gloria Miller, 4/25/00.

223. "ASU—A History of Greatness," www.alcorn.edu/history.

224. Telephone conversation, Band Department, 10/12/00.

225. "Delta State University, History of Delta State University," www.deltast.edu/pubinfo/history.

226. Telephone conversation, Music Department, Delta State University, 10/9/00.

227. "JSU—University Profile," www.ccaix.jsums.edu/~www/profile.

228. Personal e-mail correspondence from Jimmie James, Jr., 9/18/00.

229. "Mississippi State University: General Information," www.msstate.edu/web/gen_info.

230. "University Athletics . . . traditions," www.msstate.edu/athletics/Traditions/traditions.

231. "History of Mississippi Valley State University," www.mvsu.edu/history.

232. Personal e-mail correspondence from Lawrence Horn, 4/24/00.

233. "About Ole Miss: The University of Mississippi," www.olemiss.edu/hospitality/about/history, traditions.

234. "Welcome to the USM Campus," www.usm.edu/usmweb/welcome/aboutusm.

235. Personal e-mail correspondence from Steven Moser, 4/25/00.

236. "Central at a Glance," www.cmsu.edu/about/cmglance.

237. Personal e-mail correspondence from Patrick Casey, 4/27/00.

238. "University Profile," www.lincolnu.edu/uni-info/profile.

239. Personal e-mail correspondence from Debra Walker, 9/13/00.

240. "Northwest Missouri State University, Northwest Profile," www.nwmissouri.edu/home/PROFILE.html.

241. "College Fight Songs," www.fightsongs.com.

242. "Overview of Southeast Missouri State University," www2.semo.edu/registrar/bulletin/overview.

243. "Southeast Missouri State Education Centers," www.semo.edu/edcenters.

244. Personal e-mail correspondence from Janice Miller, 9/11/00.

245. "History, Mission and Accreditation," www.smsu.edu/OIR/factbook/general_information.

246. "About SMSU," www.smsu.edu/aboutsmu.

247. Personal e-mail correspondence from Sara M. Clark, 4/25/00.

248. "University History," www.truman.edu/about/univhistory.

249. "Archives of the University of Missouri at Columbia: A History of the University of Missouri–Columbia and the University of Missouri System," www.system.missouri.edu/archives/um-hist.

250. "The University of Missouri System," www.system.missouri.edu.

251. "University of Missouri, Official Athletic Site of the MU Tigers," www.fansonly.com/schools/miss/trads/miss-trads-schoolsongs.

252. "A Brief History," www.montana.edu/misc/history.

253. "Montana University System," www.montana.edu/wwoche/docs/campuses.

254. Personal e-mail correspondence from Brad Fuster, 4/24/00.

255. "The University of Montana—Administration," www.umt.edu/catalog/97–98/admin.

256. "Montana University System," www.montana.edu/wwoche/docs/campuses.

257. "Grizzly Athletics," www.grizzly.umt.edu/athlet.

258. "Welcome to the University of Nebraska," www.uneb.edu.

259. "University of Nebraska Fact Book 1998," www.uneb.edu/planreport/factunl.

260. "UNL Band—120 Years of Nebraska Band History," www.unl.edu/band/history.

261. "UNLV Athletics, Traditions," www.fansonly.com/schools/unlv/trads/unlv/trads.

262. "About Our University . . . ," www.unr.edu/about.

263. Telephone conversation with Dr. A. G. McGrannahan, II, Music Department, 10/9/00.

264. "About UNH," www.unh.edu/aboutunh; "University of New Hampshire Athletics, UNH Information," www.unhwildcats.com/info/index.

265. Personal e-mail correspondence from Tom Keck, 9/18/00.

266. "Welcome to Kean University," www.kean.edu/General_Info/GenInfo.

267. Personal e-mail correspondence from Caroline Jolly, Alumni Director, 10/6/00.

268. "Montclair State University, MSU History," www.montclair.edu/welcome/history.

269. Telephone conversation, Sports Information Department, 10/12/00.

270. "New Jersey City University, A Brief History of the University," www.njcu.edu/aboutNJCU/NJCUhistory.

271. Telephone conversation, NJCU Department of Student Services, 10/23/00.

272. "NJIT History," www.njit.edu/Overview/About/Profile/history.

273. Telephone conversation with Robert Van Houten, Library Reference Department, 10/13/00.

274. "From Normal to Extraordinary: A History of Rowan University," www.rowan.edu/news_happenings/history_rowan.

275. Personal e-mail correspondence from Sheila Stevenson, 4/19/00.

276. "Rutgers, A Brief History," www.rutgers.edu/menus/brief-history.

277. "WPUNJ: About Us: History," www.wpunj.edu/aboutus/history.cfm.

278. Telephone conversation with WPU Music Department, 10/25/00.

279. "Eastern New Mexico University: ENMU History," www.enmu.edu/aboutenmu/history.

280. "ENMU Athletics, Mascots," www.enmu.edu/athletics/mascots.

281. Personal e-mail correspondence from Dustin D. Seifert, 9/10/00.

282. "New Mexico State University, NMSU at a Glance," www.nmsu.edu/General/NMSU-At-a-Glance; "What Is an Aggie?" www.nmsu.edu/aggieland/aggies.

283. "UNM Facts at a Glance," www.unm.edu/yo_facts.

284. Personal e-mail correspondence from Greg S. Remington, 3/28/00.

285. "Introducung Western New Mexico University," www.wnmu.edu/univ/intrwnmu.

286. Personal e-mail correspondence from Dennis Hayslett, 10/5/00.

287. "State University of New York Campuses," www.suny.edu/campuses/CampusInfo.

288. "Back to the Future," www.albany.edu/uahistory/text.

289. Personal e-mail correspondence from Vincent Reda, 9/11/00.

290. "Binghamton University: An Overview," www.binghamton.edu/home/about/overview.

291. Telephone conversation, Binghamton University Library Reference Department, 10/13/00.

292. "Fronting the Future: Yesterday . . . ," www.buffalo.edu/UB/main_frame1.

293. Personal e-mail correspondence from John A. Zaepfel, 8/28/00.

294. "Who Are We?" www.sunysb.edu/whoarewe.

295. Personal e-mail correspondence from Peter Bellino, 5/7/00.

296. University of North Carolina: A 16-Campus University, www.northcarolina.edu/campusesmap.cfm.

297. "Historical Statement," www.nct.edu/bulletin/disk1/history.

298. Telephone conversation, Aggie Athletics Sports Information, 10/23/00.

299. "North Carolina State University Historical Sketch," www.ncsu.edu/provost/ugcat/acadadmi/mcsuhist.

300. Personal e-mail correspondence from Dr. John A. Fuller, 4/24/00.

301. "Carolina—A Brief History," www.unc.edu/about/history.

302. "Tar Heel Traditions," www.unc.edu/about/traditions; "UNC Bands: UNC's Official Fight Song," www.unc.edu/student/orgs/uncbands/tag.

303. "NDSU in Perspective," www.ndsu.nodak.edu/oair/ins . . . university_related/perspective.

304. "North Dakota State University: Intercollegiate Athletics," www.ndsu.nodak.edu/oair/ins . . . b/university_related/athletic.

305. Personal correspondence from George A. Ellis, 3/11/00.

306. "Brief History of the University of North Dakota," www.und.edu/history.

307. "The Scope of the University," www.und.edu/dept/Admisinfo/Year9901/Geninfo/scope.

308. "University of North Dakota School Songs," www.und.edu/prospective/multimedia/schoolsong.

309. "History and Setting of the University," www.bgsu.edu/catalog/front/intro/theu.

310. "Bowling Green State University, Official Athletic Site—Traditions," www.fansonly.com/schools/bgu/trads/songs.

311. "The CSU Legacy: About Central State University," www.centralstate.edu/legacy/about.

312. Personal e-mail correspondence from Marianne Nolan, 9/19/00.

313. "A Tour of the Cleveland State University Campus," www.csuohio.edu/admissions/campus_tour/csu.

314. Telephone conversation, CSU Library Multi-Media Department, 10/23/00.

315. "Kent State University: History," www.kent.edu/ksuHistory/index.

316. Telephone conversation, Kent State University Library Reference Center, 10/27/00.

317. "Miami Milestones," www.muohio.edu/~hstcwis/miamimiles.

318. "Miami University Regional Campuses," www.muohio.edu/campuses.

319. "Athletic Tradition," www.muredhawks.com/local/tradition.

320. "Points of Pride, Ohio State University, University Profile," www.osu.edu/units/ucomm/points/uprofile.

321. "The Ohio State University: History and Traditions," www.osu.edu/units/ucomm/history.

322. "A Brief History of Ohio University," www.ohiou.edu/factbook/99/history.

323. "Ohio University Marching Band History," www.ohiou.edu/marching110/oumb100.

324. "Visitors: Facts about SSU," www.shawnee.edu/visitors/facts.

325. Personal e-mail correspondence from Tess Midkiff, 9/19/00.

326. "University of Akron," www.uakron.edu.

327. Personal e-mail correspondence from Bob Jorgenson, 9/19/00.

328. "University of Cincinnati, History in Brief," www.uc.edu/ucinfo/history.

329. "University of Cincinnati, Additional Off-Campus Sites for Classes," www.uc.edu/cece/offcsites.

330. Personal e-mail correspondence from Barb Rink, 9/18/00.

331. "History of the University of Toledo," www.utoledo.edu/_campus-info/_UNIVERSITY-OF-TOLEDO-history.

332. "Official Athletic Site of the University of Toledo Rockets—Traditions," www.fansonly.com/schools/tol/trads.

333. "Historical Timeline of WSU Happenings," www.wright.edu/founders/timeline/timeline.

334. "WSU—About Lake Campus," www.wright.edu/lake/index.

335. "Wright State University Spirit Unit: Fight Song and Alma Mater," www.wright.edu/athletics/spirit/spirit.

336. "General Information about YSU," www.ysu.edu/admfinad/catalog/geninfo.

337. Personal e-mail correspondence from Jean A. Romeo, 10/9/00.

338. "Oklahoma Higher Education: State System," www.okhighered.org/stsystm2.

339. "About OSU," www.okstate.edu/visitors/history.

340. "Traditions: OSU Songs," www.fansonly.com/schools/okst/trads/okst-trads-songs.

341. "The University of Oklahoma: The University," www.ou.edu/web/about.

342. "The University of Oklahoma," www.ou.edu/visitorcenter/traditions.

343. "Higher Education in Oregon," www.bluebook.state.or.us/education/education04.

344. "Chronological History of Oregon State University," www.osu.orst.edu/dept/budgets/IR/FB99/9chronhs.

345. "Traditions," www.fansonly.com/schools/orst/trads/orst-trads.

346. "Profile: Portland State University," www.pdx.edu/psuprofile.

347. Personal e-mail correspondence from Mike Lund, 4/10/00.

348. "A Brief History of the University of Oregon," www.comm.uoregon.edu/newsreleases/facts/history.

349. "UO Song Lyrics," www.uoregon.edu/vis_lyrics2.html.

350. "Indiana University of Pennsylvania: The University; History of the University," www.iup.edu/schedu/catalog/university/history.

351. "Indiana University of Pennsylvania: The University; Buildings and Grounds," www.iup.edu/schedu/catalog/university/buildings.

352. Personal e-mail correspondence from Jennifer Watson, 4/10/00.

353. "West Chester University," www.wcupa.edu.

354. Telephone conversation with Nick Russo, 10/26/00.

355. "A Brief History of Penn State," www.psu.edu/ur/history.

356. "Penn State Maps," www.psu.edu/ur/PROFILE/pennstatemaps.

357. "Pennsylvania State University Marching Blue Band: Gallery," www.music.psu.edu/blueband/gallery.

358. "University of Rhode Island, About the University," www.uri.edu/home/about/history.

359. "University of Rhode Island—Campuses," www.uri.edu/home/campus/index.

360. "University of Rhode Island Official Athletic Site," gorhody.fansonly.com/genrel/061600aab.

361. "The Citadel: Origins, Civil War Period, Reopening, Name Change," www.citadel.edu/history.

362. "Citadel Quick Facts," www.citadelsports.com/quick/default.asp.

363. Personal e-mail correspondence from Herb Nath, 9/18/00.

364. "Clemson Quickly: History," www.clemson.edu/welcome/history/index.

365. "Traditions; Clemson Fight Songs," www.fansonly.com/schools/clem/trads/clem-trads-songs.

366. "South Carolina State University: A Century of Progress," www.scsu.edu/welcome/history.

367. Personal e-mail correspondence from SCSU Library Reference Department, 10/11/00.

368. "Carolina—A Historical Note; 'Faithful Index to the Ambitions and Fortunes of the State,' " www.president.sc.edu/history.

369. "University of South Carolina, Information About Campuses," www.sc.edu/campuses.

370. "1998 Carolina Band Repertoire," www.music.sc.edu/Departments/MarchingBand/CBRepertoire.

371. "History of SDSU," www.sdstate.edu/wbhp/http/camptour/history.

372. Telephone conversation, SDSU Sports Information Department, 10/30/00.

373. "About the University," www.usd.edu/aboutU.

374. Personal e-mail correspondence from Rolf Olson, 5/16/00.

375. "Austin Peay State University, Vision Statement," www.apsu.edu/records/bulletin/9899/MISSVIS.

376. Personal e-mail cooorespondence from Brad Kirtley, 4/10/00.

377. "ETSU's Historical Highlights," www.etsu.edu/univrel/etsuhist.

378. Personal e-mail correspondence from Paul R. Hinman, 10/11/00.

379. "Middle Tennessee State University Undergraduate Catalog: The History of the University," www.mtsu.edu/ucat/intro/uh.

380. Personal e-mail correspondence from Terry Jolley, 9/27/00.

381. "Tennessee State University: Historical Statement," www.tnstate.edu/hismsnmem.

382. Telephone conversation, TSU Library Reference Department, 10/12/00.

383. "Establishment and History—TTU," www.tntech.edu/www/admin/ugcat/history.

384. Personal e-mail correspondence from Joseph W. Hermann, 4/26/00.

385. "Description of the University," www.people.memphis.edu/~acadafflib/bulletin/descrip.

386. "Official Athletic Site of the University of Memphis—Traditions," www.fansonly.com/schools/mem/trads.

387. "University of Tennessee: Historical Background," www.utenn.edu/undergrad/B-Univ.

388. "A Short History of the "Pride of the Southland," web.utk.edu/~utband/rockytop.

389. "Southwest Texas State University: About SWT," www.swt.edu/swt/aboutswt.

390. Personal e-mail correspondence from Margaret Vaverek, 9/18/00.

391. "Texas A & M University: Facts and Figures," www.tamu.edu/new/facts.

392. "Texas Institutions of Higher Education: Public Universities," www.thecb.state.tx.us/UHRI.

393. "Aggie Band Fact Sheet," www.aggieband.com/info/factsheet.

394. "UGTTU: Texas Tech University," www.ttu.edu/~offpub/UGTTU.

395. "Official Athletic Site, Texas Tech University," www.fansonly.com/schools/text/trads/text-m-fb-band.

396. "UH at a Glance: General Information," www.uh.edu/news/uh_glance/general.

397. "Texas Institutions of Higher Education: Public Universities," www.thecb.state.tx.us/UHRI.

398. Personal e-mail correspondence from Jill Butler, 4/17/00.

399. "1998–99 UNT Undergraduate Catalog: The University," www.unt.edu/catalogs/98–99/university.

400. Personal e-mail correspondence from Brad Genevro, 9/15/00.

401. "The University of Texas at Austin: Facts," www.utexas.edu/admin/opa/facts/facts.

402. "Texas Institutions of Higher Education: Public Universities," www.thecb.state.tx.us/UHRI.

403. "History of School and Fight Songs," www.utexas.edu/students/lhbsa/history/songs.

404. "University of Utah Sesquicentennial Exhibition: Deseret University, 1850–1892," www.lib.utah.edu/150/01.

405. "Utah Fight Song," www.fansonly.com/schools/utah/trads/ute-trads-songs.

406. "Utah State University, USU in Fact 1998," www.usu.edu/About/infact98.

407. Personal e-mail correspondence from Thomas P. Rohrer, Ph.D., 9/6/00.

408. "Symbols of the University of Vermont," www.uvm.edu.

409. Telephone conversation, University of Vermont Sports Information Department, 10/13/00.

410. "William and Mary at a Glance," www.wm.edu/about/glance.

411. Personal e-mail correspondence from Gina C. Woodward, 9/22/00.

412. "George Mason University, A Brief History of George Mason University," www.gmu.edu/vcenter/history.

413. Personal e-mail correspondence from Andrew D. Ruge, 4/25/00.

414. "Old Dominion University: History," www.odu.edu / ~affairs / catalogs / new_catalog / history.

415. "Old Dominion University: Higher Education Centers," www.odu.edu/webroot/FrontEnd.nsf/pages/about_higher.

416. Telephone conversation with Michelle Griggs, Sports Information Department, 10/13/00.

417. "The University of Virginia," www.fansonly.com / schools / va / school-bio-va-school-bio.

418. "Traditions/School Info," www.fansonly.com/schools/va/trads/va.

419. "Brief History of VCU," www.vcu.edu/ireweb/factcardtabs.AboutVCU.

420. Personal e-mail correspondence from Terry Austin, 5/17/00.

421. "Virginia Tech—University Profile," www.unirel.vt.edu/profile/VTProfile.

422. "Virginia Tech Campus Overview," www.unirel.vt.edu/view/campus.overview.

423. "The Marching Virginians—The Spirit of Tech," www.music.vt.edu/ensembles/mv/mvinfo/mvcd.

424. "Virginia State University—History," www.vsu.edu/history.

425. Telephone conversation, VSU Office of Student Activities, 10/31/00.

426. "University of Washington: About the University," www.washington.edu/home/profile.

427. "Washington State University: Welcome from President Samuel H. Smith," www.wsu.edu/president/Welcome.

428. Personal e-mail correspondence from Lou Vyhnanek, 10/3/00.

429. "West Virginia University at a Glance," www.wvu.edu/~instadv/maps.

430. "The Pride of West Virginia—The Mountaineer Marching Band," www.themarchingpride.org/multimedia/audio/sounds.

431. "UW-Madison History—Timeline," www.news.wisc.edu/welcome/odyssey/History/index.

432. "Wisconsin: UW Band Songs," www.wisc.edu/ath/athdep/songs.

433. "University of Wyoming, History," www.uwyo.edu / OM / UNIREL / HTM / Facts / History.

434. "University of Wyoming, Official Athletic Site," www.wyomingathletics.com/wyo-body.

435. "About UDC," www.udc2.org/news/about; "History of the University of the District of Columbia," www.udc2.org/history.

436. Telephone conversation, UDC Athletic Department, 10/31/00.

437. "Welcome to the University of Guam," www.uog2.uog.edu/welcome/index.

438. Richard H. J. Wyttenbach-Santos, Vice President for Student Affairs, University of Guam, private electronic correspondence, 1/19/00.

439. "President's Message," www.upr.clu.edu/upri/presidents_office/message/message.

440. "System's Units," www.upr.clu.edu/upri/system_units.

441. Telephone conversations with Maricelle Ruiz Calderon and Krystall Molina, Puerto Rico Federal Affairs Administration, 11/9/00.

442. "The University: History," www.uvi.edu/pub-relations/caty2khis.

443. "About Playing UVI," www.uvi.edu/pub-relations/athletics/playinguvi/html.

444. Personal conversation with Chrystal Wilson, 9/23/00.

16

State and Territory Governors

The lists of governors of the states provide a quick summary of political party ups and downs and disappearances. They also chart the political progress of many national figures, including presidents, who came to prominence out of state government. Each list of state governors begins with the date of statehood. Each entry notes the governor's political party and years served as governor. The lists of territory governors begin with the first elected governor.[1]

ALABAMA

William Wyatt Bibb	Democrat	1819–1820
Thomas Bibb	Democrat	1820–1821
Israel Pickens	Democrat	1821–1825
John Murphy	Democrat	1825–1829
Gabriel Moore	Democrat	1829–1831
Samuel B. Moore	Democrat	1831
John Gayle	Democrat-Whig	1831–1835
Clement Comer Clay	Democrat	1835–1837
Hugh McVay	Democrat	1837
Arthur Pendleton Bagby	Democrat	1837–1841
Benjamin Fitzpatrick	Democrat	1841–1845
Joshua Lanier Martin	Democrat	1845–1847
Reuben Chapman	Democrat	1847–1849
Henry Watkins Collier	Democrat	1849–1853
John Anthony Winston	Democrat	1853–1857
Andrew Barry Moore	Democrat	1857–1861
John Gill Shorter	Democrat	1861–1863
Thomas Hill Watts	Democrat	1863–1865
Lewis E. Parsons	Democrat	1865 (Provisional Governor)
Robert Patton	Pre–War Whig	1865–1868
William H. Smith	Republican	1868–1870

Robert Burns Lindsay	Democrat	1870–1872
David P. Lewis	Republican	1872–1874
George Smith Houston	Democrat	1874–1878
Rufus W. Cobb	Democrat	1878–1882
Edward Asbury O'Neal	Democrat	1882–1886
Thomas Seay	Democrat	1886–1890
Thomas Goode Jones	Democrat	1890–1894
William C. Oates	Democrat	1894–1896
Joseph Forney Johnston	Democrat	1896–1900
William D. Jelks	Democrat	1900 (Acting)
William J. Samford	Democrat	1900–1901
William D. Jelks	Democrat	1901–1904
Russell McWhorter Cunningham	Democrat	1904–1905 (Acting)
William D. Jelks	Democrat	1905–1907
Braxton Bragg Comer	Democrat	1907–1911
Emmett O'Neal	Democrat	1911–1915
Charles Henderson	Democrat	1915–1919
Thomas Erby Kilby	Democrat	1919–1923
William Woodward Brandon	Democrat	1923–1927
Bibb Graves	Democrat	1927–1931
Benjamin Meek Miller	Democrat	1931–1935
Bibb Graves	Democrat	1935–1939
Frank Murray Dixon	Democrat	1939–1943
Chauncey M. Sparks	Democrat	1943–1947
James Elisha Folsom	Democrat	1947–1951
Gordon Persons	Democrat	1951–1955
James Elisha Folsom	Democrat	1955–1959
John Patterson	Democrat	1959–1963
George Corley Wallace	Democrat	1963–1967
Lurleen B. Wallace	Democrat	1967–1968
Albert P. Brewer	Democrat	1968–1971
George Corley Wallace	Democrat	1971–1979
Forrest (Fob) James, Jr.	Democrat	1979–1983
George Corley Wallace	Democrat	1983–1987
Guy Hunt	Republican	1987–1993
James E. Folsom	Democrat	1993–1995

Forrest (Fob) James	Republican	1995–1999
Don Siegelman	Democrat	1999–2003

ALASKA

William Allen Egan	Democrat	1959–1966
Walter Joseph Hickel	Republican	1966–1969
Keith H. Miller	Republican	1969–1970
William Allen Egan	Republican	1970–1974
Jay S. Hammond	Republican	1974–1982
Bill Sheffield	Democrat	1982–1986
Steve Cowper	Democrat	1986–1990
Walter J. Hickel	Alaskan Independent	1990–1994
Tony Knowles	Democrat	1994–2002

ARIZONA

George W. P. Hunt	Democrat	1912–1917; 1917–1919; 1923–1929; 1931–1933
Thomas E. Campbell	Republican	1917; 1919–1923
John C. Phillips	Republican	1929–1931
Benjamin B. Moeur	Democrat	1933–1937
Rawghlie C. Stanford	Democrat	1937–1939
Robert T. Jones	Democrat	1939–1941
Sidney P. Osborn	Democrat	1941–1948
Dan E. Garvey	Democrat	1948–1951
John Howard Pyle	Republican	1951–1955
Ernest W. McFarland	Democrat	1955–1959
Paul J. Fannin	Republican	1959–1965
Samuel P. Goddard	Democrat	1965–1967
John R. "Jack" Williams	Republican	1967–1975
Raul H. Castro	Democrat	1975–1977
Harvey Wesley Bolin	Democrat	1977–1978
Bruce Babbitt	Democrat	1978–1987
Evan Mecham	Republican	1987–1988
Rose Mofford	Democrat	1988–1991
Fife Symington	Republican	1991–1997
Jane Hull	Republican	1997–2003

ARKANSAS

James S. Conway	Democrat	1836–1840
Archibald Yell	Democrat	1840–1844
Thomas S. Drew	Democrat	1844–1849
John S. Roane	Democrat	1849–1852
Elias N. Conway	Democrat	1852–1860
Henry M. Rector	Democrat	1860–1862
Harris Flannigan	Democrat	1862–1864
Isaac Murphy	Union	1864–1868
Powell Clayton	Republican	1868–1871
Ozra Hadley	Republican	1871–1873
Elisha Baxter	Republican	1873–1874
Aug. H. Garland	Democrat	1874–1877
William R. Miller	Democrat	1877–1881
Thomas J. Churchill	Democrat	1881–1883
James H. Berry	Democrat	1883–1885
Simon P. Hughes	Democrat	1885–1889
J. P. Eagle	Democrat	1889–1893
W. M. Fishback	Democrat	1893–1895
J. P. Clarke	Democrat	1895–1897
Dan W. Jones	Democrat	1897–1901
Jefferson Davis	Democrat	1901–1907
John Sebastion Little	Democrat	1907
John I. Moore	Democrat	1907 (Acting)
Xenophon Overton Pindall	Democrat	1907–1909
George W. Donaghey	Democrat	1909–1913
Joseph Taylor Robinson	Democrat	1913
William K. Oldham	Democrat	1913 (Acting)
Junius Marion Futrell	Democrat	1913 (Acting)
George Washington Hays	Democrat	1913–1917
Charles Hilman Brough	Democrat	1917–1921
Thomas Chipman McRae	Democrat	1921–1925
Thomas J. Terral	Democrat	1925–1927
John Ellis Martineau	Democrat	1927–1928
Harvey Parnell	Democrat	1928–1933
Junius Marion Futrell	Democrat	1933–1937
Carl Edward Bailey	Democrat	1937–1941

Homer Martin Adkins	Democrat	1941–1945
Benjamin T. Laney	Democrat	1945–1949
Sidney Sanders McMath	Democrat	1949–1953
Frances Adams Cherry	Democrat	1953–1955
Orval Eugene Faubus	Democrat	1955–1967
Winthrop Rockefeller	Republican	1967–1971
Dale Bumpers	Democrat	1971–1975
Bob Riley	Democrat	1975
David Pryor	Democrat	1975–1979
Joe Purcell	Democrat	1979
Bill Clinton	Democrat	1979–1981
Frank D. White	Republican	1981–1983
Bill Clinton	Democrat	1983–1992
Jim Guy Tucker	Democrat	1992–1996
Mike Huckabee	Republican	1996–2003

CALIFORNIA

Peter H. Burnett	Democrat	1849–1851
John McDougal	Democrat	1851–1852
John Bigler	Democrat	1852–1856
J. Neely Johnson	American	1856–1858
John B. Weller	Democrat	1858–1860
Milton S. Latham	Democrat	1860
John G. Downey	Democrat	1860–1862
Leland Stanford	Republican	1862–1863
Frederick F. Low	Union Republican	1863–1867
Henry H. Haight	Democrat	1867–1871
Newton Booth	Republican	1871–1875
Romualdo Pacheco	Republican	1875
William Irwin	Democrat	1875–1880
George C. Perkins	Republican	1880–1883
George Stoneman	Democrat	1883–1887
Washington Bartlett	Democrat	1887
Robert W. Waterman	Republican	1887–1891
Henry H. Markham	Democrat	1891–1895
James H. Budd	Democrat	1895–1899
Henry Tifft Gage	Republican	1899–1903

George Cooper Pardee	Republican	1903–1907
James Norris Gillett	Republican	1907–1911
Hiram Warren Johnson	Republican	1911–1917
William Dennison Stephens	Republican	1917–1923
Friend William Richardson	Republican	1923–1927
Clement Calhoun Young	Republican	1927–1931
James Rolph, Jr.	Republican	1931–1934
Frank Finley Merriam	Republican	1934–1939
Culbert Levy Olson	Democrat	1939–1943
Earl Warren	Republican	1943–1953
Goodwin Jess Knight	Republican	1953–1959
Edmund G. Brown	Democrat	1959–1967
Ronald Reagan	Republican	1967–1975
Edmund G. Brown Jr.	Democrat	1975–1983
George Deukmejian	Republican	1983–1991
Pete Wilson	Republican	1991–1999
Gray Davis	Democrat	1999–2003

COLORADO

John L. Routt	Republican	1876–1879
F. W. Pitkin	Republican	1879–1883
James B. Grant	Democrat	1883–1885
Benjamin H. Eaton	Republican	1885–1887
Alva Adams	Democrat	1887–1889
Job A. Cooper	Republican	1889–1891
John L. Routt	Republican	1891–1893
Davis H. Waite	Populist	1893–1895
Albert W. McIntire	Republican	1895–1897
Alva Adams	Democrat	1897–1899
Charles S. Thomas	Democrat	1899–1901
James B. Orman	Democrat	1901–1903
James H. Peabody	Republican	1903–1905
Alva Adams	Democrat	1905
James H. Peabody	Republican	1905
Jesse F. McDonald	Republican	1905–1907
Henry A. Buchtel	Republican	1907–1909
John F. Shafroth	Democrat	1909–1913

Elias M. Ammons	Democrat	1913–1915
George A. Carlson	Republican	1915–1917
Julius C. Gunter	Democrat	1917–1919
Oliver H. Shoup	Republican	1919–1923
William H. Sweet	Democrat	1923–1925
Clarence J. Morley	Republican	1925–1927
William H. Adams	Democrat	1927–1933
Edwin C. Johnson	Democrat	1933–1937
Ray H. Talbot	Democrat	1937
Teller Ammons	Democrat	1937–1939
Ralph L. Carr	Republican	1939–1943
John C. Vivian	Republican	1943–1947
William L. Knous	Democrat	1947–1950
Walter W. Johnson	Democrat	1950–1951
Daniel I. J. Thornton	Republican	1951–1955
Edwin C. Johnson	Democrat	1955–1957
Stephen L. R. McNichols	Democrat	1957–1963
John A. Love	Republican	1963–1973
John D. Vanderhoof	Republican	1973–1975
Richard D. Lamm	Democrat	1975–1987
Roy R. Romer	Democrat	1987–1999
Bill Owens	Republican	1999–2003

CONNECTICUT

Samuel Huntington		1787–1796
Oliver Wolcott	Federalist	1796–1797
Jonathan Trumbull	Federalist	1797–1809
John Treadwell	Federalist	1809–1811
Roger Griswold	Federalist	1811–1812
John Cotton Smith	Federalist	1812–1817
Oliver Wolcott	Democratic-Republican	1817–1827
Gideon Tomlinson	Democratic-Republican; National Republican	1827–1831
John S. Peters	National Republican	1831–1833
Henry W. Edwards	Democrat	1833–1834
Samuel A. Foot	National Republican	1834–1835
Henry W. Edwards	Democrat	1835–1838

William W. Ellsworth	Whig	1838–1842
Chauncey F. Cleveland	Democrat	1842–1844
Roger S. Baldwin	Whig	1844–1846
Isaac Toucey	Democrat	1846–1847
Clark Bissell	Whig	1847–1849
Joseph Trumbull	Whig	1849–1850
Thomas H. Seymour	Democrat	1850–1853
Charles H. Pond	Democrat	1853–1854 (Acting)
Henry Dutton	Whig	1854–1855
William T. Minor	American	1855–1857
Alexander H. Holley	Republican	1857–1858
William A. Buckingham	Republican	1858–1866
Joseph R. Hawley	Republican	1866–1867
James E. English	Democrat	1867–1869
Marshall Jewell	Republican	1869–1870
James E. English	Democrat	1870–1871
Marshall Jewell	Republican	1871–1873
Charles R. Ingersoll	Democrat	1873–1877
Richard D. Hubbard	Democrat	1877–1879
Charles B. Andrews	Republican	1879–1881
Hobart B. Bigelow	Republican	1881–1883
Thomas M. Waller	Democrat	1883–1885
Henry B. Harrison	Republican	1885–1887
Phineas C. Lounsbury	Republican	1887–1889
Morgan G. Bulkeley	Republican	1889–1893
Luzon B. Morris	Democrat	1893–1895
O. Vincent Coffin	Republican	1895–1897
Lorrin A. Cook	Republican	1897–1899
George E. Lounsbury	Republican	1899–1901
George Payne McLean	Republican	1901–1903
Abiram Chamberlain	Republican	1903–1905
Henry Roberts	Republican	1905–1907
Rollin Simmons Woodruff	Republican	1907–1909
George Leavens Lilley	Republican	1909
Frank Bentley Weeks	Republican	1909–1911
Simeon Eben Baldwin	Democrat	1911–1915
Marcus Hensey Holcomb	Republican	1915–1921

Everett John Lake	Republican	1921–1923
Charles Augustus Templeton	Republican	1923–1925
Hiram Bingham	Republican	1925
John Harper Trumbull	Republican	1925–1931
Wilbur Lucius Cross	Democrat	1931–1939
Raymond Earl Baldwin	Republican	1939–1941
Robert Augustine Hurley	Democrat	1941–1943
Raymond Earl Baldwin	Republican	1943–1946
Charles Wilbert Snow	Democrat	1946–1947
James Lukens McConaughy	Republican	1947–1948
James Coughlin Shannon	Republican	1948–1949
Chester Bowles	Democrat	1949–1951
John Davis Lodge	Republican	1951–1955
Abraham Ribicoff	Democrat	1955–1961
John Dempsey	Democrat	1961–1971
Thomas J. Meskill	Republican	1971–1975
Ella T. Grasso	Democrat	1975–1980
William O'Neill	Democrat	1980–1991
Lowell P. Weicker, Jr.	Independent	1991–1995
John G. Rowland	Republican	1995–2003

DELAWARE

Joshua Clayton	Federalist	1789–1796
Gunning Bedford	Federalist	1796–1797
Daniel Rogers	Federalist	1797–1799 (Acting)
Richard Bassett	Federalist	1799–1801
James Sykes	Federalist	1801–1802 (Acting)
David Hall	Democratic-Republican	1802–1805
Nathaniel Mitchell	Federalist	1805–1808
George Truitt	Federalist	1808–1811
Joseph Haslet	Democratic-Republican	1811–1814
Daniel Rodney	Federalist	1814–1817
John Clark	Federalist	1817–1820
Jacob Stout	Federalist	1820–1821 (Acting)
John Collins	Democratic-Republican	1821–1822
Caleb Rodney	Democratic-Republican	1822–1823 (Acting)
Joseph Haslet	Democratic-Republican	1823

Charles Thomas	Democratic-Republican	1823–1824 (Acting)
Samuel Paynter	Federalist	1824–1827
Charles Polk	Federalist	1827–1830
David Hazzard	Democrat	1830–1833
Caleb P. Bennett	Democrat	1833–1836
Charles Polk		1836–1837 (Acting)
Cornelius P. Comegys	Whig	1837–1841
William B. Cooper	Whig	1841–1845
Thomas Stockton	Whig	1845–1846
Joseph Maull	Whig	1846 (Acting)
William Temple	Whig	1846–1847 (Acting)
William Tharp	Democrat	1847–1851
William H. Ross	Democrat	1851–1855
Peter F. Causey	American	1855–1859
William Burton	Democrat	1859–1863
William Cannon	Union	1863–1865
Gove Saulsbury	Democrat	1865–1871
James Ponder	Democrat	1871–1875
John P. Cochran	Democrat	1875–1879
John W. Hall	Democrat	1879–1883
Charles C. Stockley	Democrat	1883–1887
Benjamin T. Biggs	Democrat	1887–1891
Robert J. Reynolds	Democrat	1891–1895
Joshua H. Marvel	Republican	1895
William T. Watson	Democrat	1895–1897 (Acting)
Ebe W. Tunnell	Democrat	1897–1901
John Hunn	Republican	1901–1905
Preston Lea	Republican	1905–1909
Simeon Selby Pennewill	Republican	1909–1913
Charles R. Miller	Republican	1913–1917
John Gillis Townsend, Jr.	Republican	1917–1921
William DuHamel Denney	Republican	1921–1925
Robert P. Robinson	Republican	1925–1929
C. Douglass Buck	Republican	1929–1937
Richard Cann McMullen	Democrat	1937–1941
Walter W. Bacon	Republican	1941–1949
Elbert N. Carvel	Democrat	1949–1953

James Caleb Boggs	Republican	1953–1960
David P. Buckson	Republican	1960–1961
Elbert Nostrand Carvel	Democrat	1961–1965
Charles Laymen Terry, Jr.	Democrat	1965–1969
Russell Wilbur Peterson	Republican	1969–1973
Sherman Willard Tribbitt	Democrat	1973–1977
Pierre Du Pont	Republican	1977–1985
Michael N. Castle	Republican	1985–1992
Dale E. Wolf	Republican	1993
Thomas Carper	Democrat	1993–2001
Ruth Ann Minner	Democrat	2001–2005

FLORIDA

William D. Moseley	Democrat	1845–1849
Thomas Brown	Whig	1849–1853
James E. Broome	Democrat	1853–1857
Madison S. Perry	Democrat	1857–1861
John Milton	Democrat	1861–1865
A. K. Allison		1865–1868
Harrison Reed	Republican	1868–1873
Ossian B. Hart	Republican	1873–1874
Marcellus L. Stearns	Republican	1874–1877
George F. Drew	Democrat	1877–1881
William D. Bloxham	Democrat	1881–1885
Edward A. Perry	Democrat	1885–1889
Francis P. Fleming	Democrat	1889–1893
Henry L. Mitchell	Democrat	1893–1897
William D. Bloxham	Democrat	1897–1901
William S. Jennings	Democrat	1901–1905
Napoleon B. Broward	Democrat	1905–1909
Albert W. Gilchrist	Democrat	1909–1913
Park Trammell	Democrat	1913–1917
Sidney J. Catts	Independent Party–Prohibition	1917–1921
Cary A. Hardee	Democrat	1921–1925
John W. Martin	Democrat	1925–1929
Doyle E. Carlton	Democrat	1929–1933

David Sholtz	Democrat	1933–1937
Frederick P. Cone	Democrat	1937–1941
Spessard L. Holland	Democrat	1941–1945
Millard F. Caldwell	Democrat	1945–1949
Fuller Warren	Democrat	1949–1953
Daniel T. McCarty	Democrat	1953
Charley E. Johns	Democrat	1953–1955
LeRoy Collins	Democrat	1955–1961
Farris Bryant	Democrat	1961–1965
Haydon Burns	Democrat	1965–1967
Claude R. Kirk, Jr.	Republican	1967–1971
Reubin Askew	Democrat	1971–1979
Robert Graham	Democrat	1979–1987
John W. Mixon	Democrat	1987
Robert Martinez	Republican	1987–1991
Lawton Chiles	Democrat	1991–1998
Kenneth H. (Buddy) McKay, Jr.	Democrat	1998–1999
John E. (Jeb) Bush	Republican	1999–2003

GEORGIA

George Mathews		1787–1788
George Handley		1788–1789
George Walton	Democratic-Republican	1789–1790
Edward Telfair	Democratic-Republican	1790–1793
George Mathews	Democratic-Republican	1793–1796
Jared Irwin	Democratic-Republican	1796–1798
James Jackson	Democratic-Republican	1798–1801
David Emanuel	Democratic-Republican	1801 (President of Senate)
Josiah Tattnall, Jr.	Democratic-Republican	1801–1802
John Milledge	Democratic-Republican	1802–1806
Jared Irwin	Democratic-Republican	1806–1809 (President of Senate)
David B. Mitchell	Democratic-Republican	1809–1813
Peter Earley	Democratic-Republican	1813–1815
David B. Mitchell	Democratic-Republican	1815–1817
William Rabun	Democratic-Republican	1817–1819 (President of Senate)

Matthew Talbot	Democratic-Republican	1819 (President of Senate)
John Clark	Democratic-Republican	1819–1823
George M. Troup	Democratic-Republican	1823–1827
John Forsyth	Democratic-Republican	1827–1829
George R. Gilmer	Democrat	1829–1831
Wilson Lumpkin	Union Democrat	1831–1835
William Schley	Democrat	1835–1837
George R. Gilmer	Whig	1837–1839
Charles J. McDonald	Democrat	1839–1843
George W. Crawford	Whig	1843–1847
George W. Towns	Democrat	1847–1851
Howell Cobb	Union Democrat	1851–1853
Herschel V. Johnson	Democrat	1853–1857
Joseph E. Brown	Democrat	1857–1865
James Johnson	Democrat	1865 (Provisional Governor)
Charles J. Jenkins	Democrat	1865–1868
General T. H. Ruger	Republican	1868 (Provisional Governor)
Rufus B. Bullock	Republican	1868 (Provisional Governor)
Rufus B. Bullock	Republican	1868–1871
Benjamin Conley	Republican	1871–1872 (President of Senate)
James M. Smith	Liberal Republican	1872–1877
Alfred H. Colquitt	Democrat	1877–1882
Alexander H. Stephens	Democrat	1882–1883
James S. Boynton	Democrat	1883 (President of Senate)
Henry D. McDaniel	Democrat	1883–1886
John B. Gordon	Democrat	1886–1890
William J. Northen	Democrat	1890–1894
William Y. Atkinson	Democrat	1894–1898
Allen D. Candler	Democrat	1898–1902
Joseph M. Terrell	Democrat	1902–1907
Hoke Smith	Democrat	1907–1909
Joseph M. Brown	Democrat	1909–1911
Hoke Smith	Democrat	1911
John M. Slaton	Democrat	1911–1912 (Acting)
Joseph M. Brown	Democrat	1912–1913
John M. Slaton	Democrat	1913–1915

Nathaniel E. Harris	Democrat	1915–1917
Hugh M. Dorsey	Democrat	1917–1921
Thomas W. Hardwick	Democrat	1921–1923
Clifford M. Walker	Democrat	1923–1927
Lamartine G. Hardman	Democrat	1927–1931
Richard B. Russell, Jr.	Democrat	1931–1933
Eugene Talmadge	Democrat	1933–1937
Eurith D. Rivers	Democrat	1937–1941
Eugene Talmadge	Democrat	1941–1943
Ellis G. Arnall	Democrat	1943–1947
Eugene Talmadge	Democrat	(Died before taking office)
Herman E. Talmadge	Democrat	1947
Melvin E. Thompson	Democrat	1947–1948 (Acting)
Herman E. Talmadge	Democrat	1948–1955
S. Marvin Griffin	Democrat	1955–1959
Samuel Ernest Vandiver, Jr.	Democrat	1959–1963
Carl Edward Sanders	Democrat	1963–1967
Lester G. Maddox	Democrat	1967–1971
Jimmy Carter	Democrat	1971–1975
George Busbee	Democrat	1975–1983
Joe Frank Harris	Democrat	1983–1991
Zell Miller	Democrat	1991–1999
Roy E. Barnes	Democrat	1999–2003

HAWAII

William Francis Quinn	Republican	1959–1962
John Anthony Burns	Democrat	1962–1974
George R. Ariyoshi	Democrat	1974–1986
John Waihee	Democrat	1986–1994
Benjamin J. Cayetano	Democrat	1994–2002

IDAHO

George L. Shoup	Republican	1890
N. B. Wiley	Republican	1891–1893
William J. McConnell	Republican	1893–1897
Frank Steunenberg	Democrat	1897–1901

Frank Williams Hunt	Democrat	1901–1903
John Tracy Morrison	Republican	1903–1905
Frank Robert Gooding	Republican	1905–1909
James Henry Brady	Republican	1909–1911
James Henry Hawley	Democrat	1911–1913
John Michener Haines	Republican	1913–1915
Moses Alexander	Democrat	1915–1919
David William Davis	Republican	1919–1923
Charles Calvin Moore	Republican	1923–1927
H. Clarence Baldridge	Republican	1927–1931
Charles Ben Ross	Democrat	1931–1937
Barzilla Worth Clark	Democrat	1937–1939
Clarence Alfred Bottolfsen	Republican	1939–1941
Chase Addison Clark	Democrat	1941–1943
Clarence Alfred Bottolfsen	Republican	1943–1945
Charles Clinton Gossett	Democrat	1945
Arnold Williams	Democrat	1945–1947
Charles A. Robbins	Republican	1947–1951
Leonard Beck Jordan	Republican	1951–1955
Robert Eben Smylie	Republican	1955–1967
Don W. Samuelson	Republican	1967–1971
Cecil D. Andrus	Democrat	1971–1977
John V. Evans	Democrat	1977–1987
Cecil D. Andrus	Democrat	1987–1995
Phillip E. Batt	Republican	1995–1999
Dirk Kempthorne	Republican	1999–2003

ILLINOIS

Edward Coles	Democratic-Republican	1822–1826
Ninian Edwards	National Republican	1826–1830
John Reynolds	National Republican	1830–1834
William L. D. Ewing		1834
Joseph Duncan	Whig	1834–1838
Thomas Carlin	Democrat	1838–1842
Thomas Ford	Democrat	1842–1846
Augustus C. French	Democrat	1846–1853
Joel A. Matteson	Democrat	1853–1857

William H. Bissell	Republican	1857–1860
John Wood	Republican	1860–1861
Richard Yates	Republican	1861–1865
Richard J. Oglesby	Republican	1865–1869
John M. Palmer	Republican	1869–1873
Richard J. Oglesby	Republican	1873
John L. Beveridge	Republican	1873–1877
Shelby M. Cullom	Republican	1877–1883
John M. Hamilton	Republican	1883–1885
Richard J. Oglesby	Republican	1885–1889
Joseph W. Fifer	Republican	1889–1893
John P. Altgeld	Democrat	1893–1897
John Riley Tanner	Republican	1897–1901
Richard Yates	Republican	1901–1905
Charles Samuel Deneen	Republican	1905–1913
Edward F. Dunne	Democrat	1913–1917
Frank Orren Lowden	Republican	1917–1921
Len(nington) Small	Republican	1921–1929
Louis L. Emmerson	Republican	1929–1933
Henry Horner	Democrat	1933–1940
John H. Stelle	Democrat	1940–1941
Dwight H. Green	Republican	1941–1949
Adlai Ewing Stevenson	Democrat	1949–1953
William Grant Stratton	Republican	1953–1961
Otto Kerner	Democrat	1961–1968
Samuel Henry Shapiro	Democrat	1968–1969
Richard B. Ogilvie	Republican	1969–1973
Daniel Walker	Democrat	1973–1977
James R. Thompson	Republican	1977–1991
Jim Edgar	Republican	1991–1999
George H. Ryan	Democrat	1999–2003

INDIANA

Jonathan Jennings	Democratic Republican	1816–1822
Ratliff Boon	Democratic Republican	1822
William Hendricks	Democratic Republican	1822–1825
James B. Ray	Clay Republican	1825–1831

Noah Noble	National Republican–Whig	1831–1837
David Wallace	Whig	1837–1840
Samuel Bigger	Whig	1840–1843
James Whitcomb	Democrat	1843–1848
Paris C. Dunning	Democrat	1848–1849 (Acting)
Joseph A. Wright	Democrat	1849–1857
Ashbel P. Willard	Democrat	1857–1860
Abram A. Hammond	Democrat	1860–1861 (Acting)
Henry S. Lane	Republican	1861
Oliver P. Morton	Republican	1861–1867
Conrad Baker	Republican	1867–1873
Thomas A. Hendricks	Democrat	1873–1877
James D. Williams	Democrat	1877–1880
Isaac P. Gray	Democrat	1880–1881 (Acting)
Albert G. Porter	Republican	1881–1885
Isaac P. Gray	Democrat	1885–1889
Alvin P. Hovey	Republican	1889–1891
Ira J. Chase	Republican	1891–1893 (Acting)
Claude Matthews	Democrat	1893–1897
James A. Mount	Republican	1897–1901
Winfield T. Durbin	Republican	1901–1905
J. Frank Hanly	Republican	1905–1909
Thomas R. Marshall	Democrat	1909–1913
Samuel M. Ralston	Democrat	1913–1917
James Putnam Goodrich	Republican	1917–1921
Warren T. McCray	Republican	1921–1924
Emmett F. Branch	Republican	1924–1925
Edward L. Jackson	Republican	1925–1929
Harry G. Leslie	Republican	1929–1933
Paul V. McNutt	Democrat	1933–1937
Maurice Clifford Townsend	Democrat	1937–1941
Henry F. Schricker	Democrat	1941–1945
Ralph F. Gates	Republican	1945–1949
Henry F. Schricker	Democrat	1949–1953
George N. Craig	Republican	1953–1957
Harold W. Handley	Republican	1957–1961
Matthew E. Welsh	Democrat	1961–1965

Roger D. Branigin	Democrat	1965–1969
Edgar D. Whitcomb	Republican	1969–1973
Otis R. Bowen	Republican	1973–1981
Robert D. Orr	Republican	1981–1989
Evan Bayh	Democrat	1989–1997
Frank O'Bannon	Democrat	1997–2005

IOWA

Ansel Briggs	Democrat	1846–1850
Stephen Hempstead	Democrat	1850–1854
James W. Grimes	Whig	1854–1858
Ralph P. Lowe	Republican	1858–1860
Samuel J. Kirkwood	Republican	1860–1864
William M. Stone	Republican	1864–1868
Samuel Merrill	Republican	1868–1872
Cyrus C. Carpenter	Republican	1872–1876
Samuel J. Kirkwood	Republican	1876–1877
Joshua F. Newbold	Republican	1877–1878
John H. Gear	Republican	1878–1882
Buren R. Sherman	Republican	1882–1886
William Larrabee	Republican	1886–1890
Horace Boies	Democrat	1890–1894
Frank D. Jackson	Republican	1894–1896
Francis M. Drake	Republican	1896–1898
Leslie M. Shaw	Republican	1898–1902
Albert B. Cummins	Republican	1902–1908
Warren Garst	Republican	1908–1909
Beryl F. Carroll	Republican	1909–1913
George W. Clarke	Republican	1913–1917
William L. Harding	Republican	1917–1921
Nathan E. Kendall	Republican	1921–1925
John Hammill	Republican	1925–1931
Daniel W. Turner	Republican	1931–1933
Clyde L. Herring	Democrat	1933–1937
Nelson G. Kraschel	Democrat	1937–1939
George A. Wilson	Republican	1939–1943
Bourke B. Hickenlooper	Republican	1943–1945

Robert D. Blue	Republican	1945–1949
William S. Beardsley	Republican	1949–1954
Leo Elthon	Republican	1954–1955
Leo Arthur Hoegh	Republican	1955–1957
Herschel C. Loveless	Democrat	1957–1961
Norman A. Erbe	Republican	1961–1963
Harold E. Hughes	Democrat	1963–1969
Robert D. Fulton	Democrat	1969
Robert D. Ray	Republican	1969–1983
Terry E. Branstad	Republican	1983–1999
Tom Vilsack	Democrat	1999–2003

KANSAS

Charles Lawrence Robinson	Republican	1861–1863
Thomas Carney	Republican	1863–1865
Samuel J. Crawford	Republican	1865–1868
Nehemiah Green	Republican	1868–1869
James M. Harvey	Republican	1869–1873
Thomas A. Osborn	Republican	1873–1877
George T. Anthony	Republican	1877–1879
John Pierce St. John	Republican	1879–1883
George W. Glick	Democrat	1883–1885
John Alexander Martin	Republican	1885–1889
Lyman Underwood Hum-phrey	Republican	1889–1893
Lorenzo D. Lewelling	Populist	1893–1895
Edmund Needham Morrill	Republican	1895–1897
John W. Leedy	Democrat-Peoples	1897–1899
William Eugene Stanley	Republican	1899–1903
Willis Joshua Bailey	Republican	1903–1905
Edward Wallis Hoch	Republican	1905–1909
Walter Roscoe Stubbs	Republican	1909–1913
George H. Hodges	Democrat	1913–1915
Arthur Capper	Republican	1915–1919
Henry Justin Allen	Republican	1919–1923
Jonathan McMillan Davis	Democrat	1923–1925
Ben Sanford Paulen	Republican	1925–1929

Clyde Martin Reed	Republican	1929–1931
Harry Hines Woodring	Democrat	1931–1933
Alfred M. Landon	Republican	1933–1937
Walter August Huxman	Democrat	1937–1939
Payne Harry Ratner	Republican	1939–1943
Andrew F. Schoeppel	Republican	1943–1947
Frank Carlson	Republican	1947–1950
Frank Lester Hagaman	Republican	1950–1951
Edward F. Arn	Republican	1951–1955
Frederick L. Hall	Republican	1955–1957
John McCuish	Republican	1957
George Docking	Democrat	1957–1961
John Anderson, Jr.	Republican	1961–1965
William H. Avery	Republican	1965–1967
Robert B. Docking	Democrat	1967–1975
Robert Bennett	Republican	1975–1979
John Carlin	Democrat	1979–1987
Mike Hayden	Republican	1987–1991
Joan Finney	Democrat	1991–1995
Bill Graves	Republican	1995–2003

KENTUCKY

Isaac Shelby	Democratic-Republican	1792–1796
James Garrard	Democratic-Republican	1796–1804
Christopher Greenup	Democratic-Republican	1804–1808
Charles Scott	Democratic-Republican	1808–1812
Isaac Shelby	Democratic-Republican	1812–1816
George Madison	Democratic-Republican	1816–1819
Gabriel Slaughter	Democratic-Republican	1819–1820
John Adair	Democratic-Republican	1820–1824
Joseph Desha	Democratic-Republican	1824–1828
Thomas Metcalfe	National Republican	1828–1832
John Breathitt	Democrat	1832–1834
James T. Morehead	National Republican	1834–1836
James Clark	Whig	1836–1839
Charles A. Wickliffe	Whig	1839–1840
Robert P. Letcher	Whig	1840–1844

William Owsley	Whig	1844–1848
John J. Crittenden	Whig	1848–1850
John L. Helm	Whig	1850–1851
Lazarus W. Powell	Democrat	1851–1855
Charles S. Morehead	American	1855–1859
Beriah Magoffin	Democrat	1859–1862
James F. Robinson	Union	1862–1863
Thomas E. Bramlette	Union	1863–1867
John L. Helm	Democrat	1867
John W. Stevenson	Democrat	1867–1871
Preston H. Leslie	Democrat	1871–1875
James B. McCreary	Democrat	1875–1879
Luke P. Blackburn	Democrat	1879–1883
J. Procter Knott	Democrat	1883–1887
Simon B. Buckner	Democrat	1887–1891
John Young Brown	Democrat	1891–1895
William O. Bradley	Republican	1895–1899
William S. Taylor	Republican	1899–1900
William Goebel	Democrat	1900
J. C. W. Beckham	Democrat	1900–1907
Augustus E. Willson	Republican	1907–1911
James Bennett McCreary	Democrat	1911–1915
Augustus Owsley Stanley	Democrat	1915–1919
James Dixon Black	Democrat	1919
Edwin Porch Morrow	Republican	1919–1923
William Jason Fields	Democrat	1923–1927
Flem D. Sampson	Republican	1927–1931
Ruby Lafoon	Democrat	1931–1935
Albert Benjamin Chandler	Democrat	1935–1939
Keen Johnson	Democrat	1939–1943
Simeon S. Willis	Republican	1943–1947
Earle C. Clements	Democrat	1947–1950
Lawrence Winchester Wetherby	Democrat	1950–1955
Albert Benjamin Chandler	Democrat	1955–1959
Bert Thomas Combs	Democrat	1959–1963
Edward T. Breathitt	Democrat	1963–1967

Louie B. Nunn	Republican	1967–1971
Wendell H. Ford	Democrat	1971–1974
Julian Carroll	Democrat	1974–1979
John Y. Brown, Jr.	Democrat	1979–1983
Martha Layne Collins	Democrat	1983–1987
Wallace Wilkinson	Democrat	1987–1991
Brereton Jones	Democrat	1991–1995
Paul E. Patton	Democrat	1995–2003

LOUISIANA

W. C. C. Claiborne		1812–1816
Jacques Villere		1816–1820
Thomas B. Robertson		1820–1822
Harry S. Thibodaux		1822–1824 (Acting)
Harry Johnson	American Faction	1824–1828
Pierre Derbigny	National Republican	1828–1829
A. Beauvais		1829–1830 (Acting)
Jacques Dupre		1830–1831
Andre Bienvenu Roman	National Republican	1831–1835
Edward White	Whig	1835–1839
Andre Bienvenu Roman	Whig	1839–1843
Alexandre Mouton	Democrat	1843–1846
Isaac Johnson	Democrat	1846–1850
Joseph Walker	Democrat	1850–1853
Paul O. Hebert	Democrat	1853–1856
Robert C. Wickliffe	Democrat	1856–1860
Thomas O. Moore	Democrat	1860–1864
Gen. G. Shepley		1862–1863 (Military Governor)
Henry W. Allen		1864 (Confederate Government)
Michael Hahn		1864 (Federal Government)
James Madison Wells	Democrat	1864–1867
Benjamin Flanders	Military	1867–1868 (Military Governor)
Joshua Baker	Military	1868 (Military Governor)
Henry C. Warmoth	Republican	1868–1873
P. B. S. Pinchback		1873 (Acting)

William P. Kellogg	Republican	1873–1877
Francis T. Nicholls	Democrat	1877–1880
Louis Alfred Wiltz	Democrat	1880–1881
Samuel D. McEnery	Democrat	1881–1888
Francis T. Nicholls	Democrat	1888–1892
Murphy J. Foster	Anti-Lottery Democrat	1892–1900
William Wright Heard	Democrat	1900–1904
Newton Crain Blanchard	Democrat	1904–1908
Jared Young Sanders	Democrat	1908–1912
Luther Egbert Hall	Democrat	1912–1916
Ruffin Golson Pleasant	Democrat	1916–1920
John Milliken Parker	Democrat	1920–1924
Henry Luce Fuqua	Democrat	1924–1926
Oramel Hinckley Simpson	Democrat	1926–1928
Huey P. Long, Jr.	Democrat	1928–1932
Alvin Olin King	Democrat	1932
Oscar Kelly Allen	Democrat	1932–1936
James Albert Noe	Democrat	1936
Richard Webster Leche	Democrat	1936–1939
Earl K. Long	Democrat	1939–1940
Sam Houston Jones	Democrat	1940–1944
James Houston Davis	Democrat	1944–1948
Earl K. Long	Democrat	1948–1952
Robert F. Kennon	Democrat	1952–1956
Earl K. Long	Democrat	1956–1960
James Houston Davis	Democrat	1960–1964
John J. McKeithen	Democrat	1964–1972
Edwin W. Edwards	Democrat	1972–1980
David C. Treen	Republican	1980–1984
Edwin W. Edwards	Democrat	1984–1988
Charles Roemer	Democrat; Republican	1988–1992
Edwin W. Edwards	Democrat	1992–1996
Mike Foster	Republican	1996–2004

MAINE

William King	Democratic-Republican	1820–1821
W. D. Williamson	Democratic-Republican	1821 (Acting)

Benjamin Ames	Democratic-Republican	1821–1822 (Acting)
Daniel Rose	Democratic-Republican	1822
Albion K. Parris	Democratic-Republican	1822–1827
Enoch Lincoln	Democratic-Republican	1827–1829
Nathan Cutler	Democratic-Republican	1829–1830 (Acting)
Joshua Hall	National Republican	1830 (Acting)
Jonathan G. Hunton	National Republican	1830–1831
Samual E. Smith	Democratic-Republican	1831–1834
Robert P. Dunlap	Democrat	1834–1838
Edward Kent	Whig	1838–1839
John Fairfield	Democrat	1839–1841
Richard H. Vose		1841 (Acting)
Edward Kent	Whig	1841–1842
John Fairfield	Democrat	1842–1843
Edward Kavanagh	Democrat	1843–1844 (Acting)
David Dunn	Democrat	1844 (Acting)
Hugh J. Anderson	Democrat	1844–1847
John W. Dana	Democrat	1847–1850
John Hubbard	Democrat	1850–1853
William G. Crosby	Whig	1853–1855
Anson P. Morrill	Know-Nothing	1855–1856
Samuel Wells	Democrat	1856–1857
Hannibal Hamlin	Republican	1857
Joseph H. Williams	Republican	1857–1858 (Acting)
Lot M. Morrill	Republican	1858–1861
Israel Washburn, Jr.	Republican	1861–1863
Abner Coburn	Republican	1863–1864
Samuel Cony	Republican	1864–1867
Joshua L. Chamberlain	Republican	1867–1871
Sidney Perham	Republican	1871–1874
Nelson Dingley, Jr.	Republican	1874–1876
Selden Connor	Republican	1876–1879
Alonzo Garcelon	Democrat	1879–1880
Daniel F. Davis	Republican	1880–1881
Harris M. Plaisted	Fusion	1881–1883
Frederick Robie	Republican	1883–1887
Joseph R. Bodwell	Republican	1887

S. S. Marble	Republican	1887–1889 (Acting)
Edwin C. Burleigh	Republican	1889–1893
Henry B. Cleaves	Republican	1893–1897
Llewellyn Powers	Republican	1897–1901
John Fremont Hill	Republican	1901–1905
William T. Cobb	Republican	1905–1909
Bert M. Fernald	Republican	1909–1911
Frederick W. Plaisted	Democrat	1911–1913
William T. Haines	Republican	1913–1915
Oakley C. Curtis	Democrat	1915–1917
Carl E. Milliken	Republican	1917–1921
Frederick H. Parkhurst	Republican	1921
Percival P. Baxter	Republican	1921–1925
Ralph O. Brewster	Republican	1925–1929
William T. Gardiner	Republican	1929–1933
Louis J. Brann	Democrat	1933–1937
Lewis O. Barrows	Republican	1937–1941
Sumner Sewall	Republican	1941–1945
Horace A. Hildreth	Republican	1945–1949
Frederick G. Payne	Republican	1949–1952
Burton M. Cross	Republican	1952–1955
Nathaniel M. Haskell	Republican	1953 (Acting)
Edmund S. Muskie	Democrat	1955–1959
Robert N. Haskell	Republican	1959
Clinton A. Clauson	Democrat	1959
John H. Reed	Republican	1959–1967
Kenneth M. Curtis	Democrat	1967–1975
James B. Longley	Independent	1975–1979
Joseph E. Brennan	Democrat	1979–1987
John R. McKernan, Jr	Republican	1987–1995
Angus King, Jr.	Independent	1995–2003

MARYLAND

John Eager Howard	Federalist	1788–1791
George Plater	Federalist	1791–1792
James Brice	Federalist	1792
Thomas Sim Lee	Federalist	1792–1794

John H. Stone	Federalist	1794–1797
John Henry	Federalist	1797–1798
Benjamin Ogle	Federalist	1798–1801
John Francis Mercer	Democratic-Republican	1801–1803
Robert Bowie	Democratic-Republican	1803–1806
Robert Wright	Democratic-Republican	1806–1808
James Butcher	Democratic-Republican	1808–1809 (Acting)
Edward Lloyd	Democratic-Republican	1809–1811
Robert Bowie	Democratic-Republican	1811–1812
Levin Winder	Federalist	1812–1816
Charles Ridgely	Federalist	1816–1819
Charles Goldsborough	Federalist	1819
Samuel Sprigg	Democratic-Republican	1819–1822
Samuel Stevens, Jr.	Democratic-Republican	1822–1826
Joseph Kent	Democratic-Republican	1826–1829
Daniel Martin	Anti-Jackson Democrat	1829–1830
Thomas King Carroll	Democrat	1830–1831
Daniel Martin	Anti-Jackson Democrat	1831
George Howard	Anti-Jackson Democrat	1831–1833
James Thomas	Anti-Jackson Democrat	1833–1836
Thomas W. Veazey	Whig	1836–1839
William Grason	Democrat	1839–1842
Francis Thomas	Democrat	1842–1845
Thomas G. Pratt	Whig	1845–1848
Philip F. Thomas	Democrat	1848–1851
Enoch Louis Lowe	Democrat	1851–1854
Thomas Watkins Ligon	Democrat	1854–1858
Thomas Holliday Hicks	American	1858–1862
Augustus W. Bradford	Union Republican	1862–1866
Thomas Swann	Union Republican	1866–1869
Oden Bowie	Democrat	1869–1872
William Pinkney Whyte	Democrat	1872–1874
James Black Groome	Democrat	1874–1876
John Lee Carroll	Democrat	1876–1880
William T. Hamilton	Democrat	1880–1884
Robert M. McLane	Democrat	1884–1885
Henry Lloyd	Democrat	1885–1888

Elihu E. Jackson	Democrat	1888–1892
Frank Brown	Democrat	1892–1896
Lloyd Lowndes	Republican	1896–1900
John Walter Smith	Democrat	1900–1904
Edwin Warfield	Democrat	1904–1908
Austin L. Crothers	Democrat	1908–1912
Phillips L. Goldsborough	Republican	1912–1916
Emerson C. Harrington	Democrat	1916–1920
Albert C. Ritchie	Democrat	1920–1935
Harry W. Nice	Republican	1935–1939
Herbert R. O'Conor	Democrat	1939–1947
William Preston Lane, Jr.	Democrat	1947–1951
Theodore R. McKeldin	Republican	1951–1959
J. Millard Tawes	Democrat	1959–1967
Spiro T. Agnew	Republican	1967–1969
Marvin Mandel	Democrat	1969–1979
Blair Lee	Democrat	1977–1979 (Acting)
Harry R. Hughes	Democrat	1979–1987
William D. Schaefer	Democrat	1987–1995
Parris N. Glendening	Democrat	1995–2003

MASSACHUSETTS

John Hancock		1787–1793
Samuel Adams		1793–1797
Increase Sumner	Federalist	1797–1799
Caleb Strong	Federalist	1799–1807
James Sullivan	Democratic-Republican	1807–1808
Christopher Gore	Federalist	1809–1810
Elbridge Gerry	Democratic Republican	1810–1812
Caleb Strong	Federalist	1812–1816
John Brooks	Federalist	1816–1823
William Eustis	Democratic Republican	1823–1825
Levi Lincoln	Adams and National Republican	1825–1834
John Davis	National Republican–Whig	1834–1835
Edward Everett	Whig	1835–1840
Marcus Morton	Democrat	1840–1841

John Davis	Whig	1841–1843
Marcus Morton	Democrat	1843–1844
George N. Briggs	Whig	1844–1851
George S. Boutwell	Democrat	1851–1853
John H. Clifford	Whig	1853–1854
Emory Washburn	Whig	1854–1855
Henry J. Gardner	American	1855–1858
Nathaniel P. Banks	Republican	1858–1861
John A. Andrew	Republican	1861–1866
Alexander H. Bullock	Union	1866–1869
William Claflin	Republican	1869–1872
William B. Washburn	Republican	1872–1874
William Gaston	Democrat	1875–1876
Alexander H. Rice	Republican	1876–1879
Thomas Talbot	Republican	1879–1880
John Davis Long	Republican	1880–1883
Benjamin F. Butler	Democrat	1883–1884
George D. Robinson	Republican	1884–1887
Oliver Ames	Republican	1887–1890
John Q. A. Brackett	Republican	1890–1891
William E. Russell	Democrat	1891–1894
Frederic T. Greenhalge	Republican	1894–1896
Roger Wolcott	Republican	1896–1900
Winthrop Murray Crane	Republican	1900–1903
John Lewis Bates	Republican	1903–1905
William Lewis Douglas	Democrat	1905–1906
Curtis Guild, Jr.	Republican	1906–1909
Eban Sumner Draper	Republican	1909–1911
Eugene Noble Foss	Democrat	1911–1914
David I. Walsh	Democrat	1914–1916
Samuel Walker McCall	Republican	1916–1919
Calvin Coolidge	Republican	1919–1921
Channing Harris Cox	Republican	1921–1925
Alvan Tufts Fuller	Republican	1925–1929
Frank Gilman Allen	Republican	1929–1931
Joseph Buell Ely	Democrat	1931–1935
James Michael Curley	Democrat	1935–1937

Charles Francis Hurley	Democrat	1937–1939
Leverett Saltonstall	Republican	1939–1945
Maurice J. Tobin	Democrat	1945–1947
Robert Fiske Bradford	Republican	1947–1949
Paul Andrew Dever	Democrat	1949–1953
Christian A. Herter	Republican	1953–1957
Foster John Furcolo	Democrat	1957–1961
John A. Volpe	Republican	1961–1963
Endicott Peabody	Democrat	1963–1965
John A. Volpe	Republican	1965–1969
Francis Williams Sargent	Republican	1969–1975
Michael S. Dukakis	Democrat	1975–1979
Edward King	Democrat	1979–1983
Michael S. Dukakis	Democrat	1983–1991
William Weld	Republican	1991–1997
Argeo Paul Cellucci	Republican	1997–2003

MICHIGAN

Stevens Thompson Mason	Democrat	1835–1840
Edward Mundy	Democrat	1838 (Acting)
William Woodbridge	Whig	1840–1841
James Wright Gordon	Whig	1841–1842 (Acting)
John S. Barry	Democrat	1842–1846
Alpheus Felch	Democrat	1846–1847
William L. Greenly	Democrat	1847–1848 (Acting)
Epaphroditus Ransom	Democrat	1848–1850
John S. Barry	Democrat	1850–1851
Robert McClelland	Democrat	1851–1853
Andrew Parsons	Democrat	1853–1855
Kinsley S. Bingham	Republican	1855–1859
Moses Wisner	Republican	1859–1861
Austin Blair	Republican	1861–1865
Henry H. Crapo	Union Republican	1865–1869
Henry P. Baldwin	Republican	1869–1873
John J. Bagley	Republican	1873–1877
Charles M. Croswell	Republican	1877–1881
David H. Jerome	Republican	1881–1883

Josiah W. Begole	Democrat	1883–1885
Russell A. Agler	Republican	1885–1887
Cyrus G. Luce	Republican	1887–1891
Edward B. Winans	Democrat	1891–1893
John T. Rich	Republican	1893–1897
Hazen S. Pingree	Republican	1897–1901
Aaron Thomas Bliss	Republican	1901–1905
Fred Maltby Warner	Republican	1905–1911
Chase Salmon Osborn	Republican	1911–1913
Woodbridge N. Ferris	Democrat	1913–1917
Albert E. Sleeper	Republican	1917–1921
Alexander J. Groesbeck	Republican	1921–1927
Fred Warren Green	Republican	1927–1931
Wilber Marion Brucker	Republican	1931–1933
William A. Comstock	Democrat	1933–1935
Frank Dwight Fitzgerald	Republican	1935–1937
Frank Murphy	Democrat	1937–1939
Frank Dwight Fitzgerald	Republican	1939
Luren D. Dickinson	Republican	1939–1941
Murray Delos Van Wagoner	Democrat	1941–1943
Harry Francis Kelly	Republican	1943–1947
Kim Sigler	Republican	1947–1949
G. Mennen Williams	Democrat	1949–1961
John Burley Swainson	Democrat	1961–1963
George W. Romney	Republican	1963–1969
William G. Milliken	Republican	1969–1983
James Blanchard	Democrat	1983–1991
John Engler	Republican	1991–2003

MINNESOTA

Henry H. Sibley	Democrat	1858–1860
Alexander Ramsey	Republican	1860–1863
Henry A. Swift	Republican	1863–1864
Stephen Miller	Union	1864–1866
William R. Marshall	Republican	1866–1870
Horace Austin	Republican	1870–1874
Cushman K. Davis	Republican	1874–1876

John S. Pillsbury	Republican	1876–1882
Lucius F. Hubbard	Republican	1882–1887
A. R. McGill	Republican	1887–1889
William R. Merriam	Republican	1889–1893
Knute Nelson	Republican	1893–1895
David M. Clough	Republican	1895–1899
John Lind	Democrat-Populist	1899–1901
Samuel Rinnah Van Sant	Republican	1901–1905
John A. Johnson	Democrat	1905–1909
Adolph Olson Eberhart	Republican	1909–1915
Winfield Scott Hammond	Democrat	1915
Joseph A. A. Burnquist	Republican	1915–1921
Jacob A. O. Preuss	Republican	1921–1925
Theodore Christianson	Republican	1925–1931
Floyd Bjornsterne Olson	Farmer-Labor	1931–1936
Hjalmar Petersen	Farmer-Labor	1936–1937
Elmer Austin Benson	Farmer-Labor	1937–1939
Harold E. Stassen	Republican	1939–1943
Edward John Thye	Republican	1943–1947
Luther Wallace Youngdahl	Republican	1947–1951
Clyde Elmer Anderson	Republican	1951–1955
Orville L. Freeman	Democrat–Farmer-Labor	1955–1961
Elmer Lee Andersen	Republican	1961–1963
Karl Fritjof Rolvaag	Democrat–Farmer-Labor	1963–1967
Harold LeVander	Republican	1967–1971
Wendell R. Anderson	Democrat–Farmer-Labor	1971–1976
Rudy Perpich	Democrat–Farmer-Labor	1976–1979
Albert H. Quie	Independent-Republican	1979–1983
Rudy Perpich	Democrat–Farmer-Labor	1983–1991
Arne Carlson	Independent-Republican	1991–1999
Jesse Ventura	Reform Party	1999–2003

MISSISSIPPI

David Holmes	Democratic-Republican	1817–1820
George Poindexter	Democratic-Republican	1820–1822
Walter Leake	Democratic-Republican	1822–1825
Gerard C. Brandon	Democratic-Republican	1825–1826

David Holmes	Democratic-Republican	1826
Gerard C. Brandon	Democrat	1826–1832
Abram M. Scott	National Republican	1832–1833
Charles Lynch	National Republican	1833
Hiram G. Runnels	Democrat	1833–1835
John A. Quitman	Whig	1835–1836
Charles Lynch	Whig	1836–1838
Alexander G. McNutt	Democrat	1838–1842
Tilgham M. Tucker	Democrat	1842–1844
Albert G. Brown	Democrat	1844–1848
Joseph M. Matthews	Democrat	1848–1850
John A. Quitman	Democrat	1850–1851
John I. Guion	Democrat	1851
James Whitfield	Democrat	1851–1852
Henry S. Foote	Union	1852–1854
John J. Pettus	Democrat	1854
John A. McRae	Democrat	1854–1857
William McWillie	Democrat	1857–1859
John J. Pettus	Democrat	1859–1863
Charles Clark	Democrat	1863–1865
William L. Sharkey		1865
Benjamin G. Humphreys		1865–1868
Adelbert Ames		1868–1870
James L. Alcorn	Republican	1870–1871
Ridgley C. Powers	Republican	1871–1874
Adelbert Ames	Republican	1874–1876
John M. Stone	Democrat	1876–1882
Robert Lowry	Democrat	1882–1890
John M. Stone	Democrat	1890–1896
Anselm J. McLaurin	Democrat	1896–1900
Andrew Houston Longino	Democrat	1900–1904
James Kimble Vardaman	Democrat	1904–1908
Edmond Favor Noel	Democrat	1908–1912
Earl LeRoy Brewer	Democrat	1912–1916
Theodore Gilmore Bilbo	Democrat	1916–1920
Lee Maurice Russell	Democrat	1920–1924
Henry Lewis Whitfield	Democrat	1924–1927

Dennis Murphree	Democrat	1927–1928
Theodore Gilmore Bilbo	Democrat	1928–1932
Martin Sennett Conner	Democrat	1932–1936
Hugh Lawson White	Democrat	1936–1940
Paul Burney Johnson	Democrat	1940–1943
Dennis Murphree	Democrat	1943–1944
Thomas L. Bailey	Democrat	1944–1946
Fielding Lewis Wright	Democrat	1946–1952
Hugh L. White	Democrat	1952–1956
James P. Coleman	Democrat	1956–1960
Ross R. Barnett	Democrat	1960–1964
Paul Burney Johnson, Jr.	Democrat	1964–1968
John Bell Williams	Democrat	1968–1972
William Lowe Waller	Democrat	1972–1976
Cliff Finch	Democrat	1976–1980
William Winter	Democrat	1980–1984
Bill Allain	Democrat	1984–1988
Ray Mabus	Democrat	1988–1992
Kirk Fordice	Republican	1992–2000
Ronnie Musgrove	Democrat	2000–2004

MISSOURI

Alexander McNair	Democratic-Republican	1820–1824
Frederick Bates	Adams Republican	1824–1825
Abraham J. Williams	Democratic-Republican	1825–1826
John Miller	Jackson Democrat	1826–1832
Daniel Dunklin	Democrat	1832–1836
Lilburn W. Boggs	Democrat	1836–1840
Thomas Reynolds	Democrat	1840–1844
Meredith M. Marmaduke	Democrat	1844 (Acting)
John C. Edwards	Democrat	1844–1848
Austin A. King	Democrat	1848–1853
Sterling Price	Democrat	1853–1857
Trusten Polk	Democrat	1857
Hancock Lee Jackson	Democrat	1857
Robert M. Stewart	Democrat	1857–1861
Claiborne Fox Jackson	Democrat	1861

Hamilton R. Gamble	Union	1861–1864
Willard P. Hall	Union	1864–1865
Thomas C. Fletcher	Union Republican	1865–1869
Joseph W. McClurg	Republican	1869–1871
B. Gratz Brown	Republican	1871–1873
Silas Woodson	Democrat	1873–1875
Charles H. Hardin	Democrat	1875–1877
John S. Phelps	Democrat	1877–1881
Thomas T. Crittenden	Democrat	1881–1885
John S. Marmaduke	Democrat	1885–1887
Albert P. Morehouse	Democrat	1887–1889
David R. Francis	Democrat	1889–1893
William Joel Stone	Democrat	1893–1897
Lawrence Vest Stephens	Democrat	1897–1901
Alexander Monroe Dockery	Democrat	1901–1905
Joseph Wingate Folk	Democrat	1905–1909
Herbert Spencer Hadley	Republican	1909–1913
Elliot Woolfolk Major	Democrat	1913–1917
Frederick Dozier Gardner	Democrat	1917–1921
Arthur Mastick Hyde	Republican	1921–1925
Samuel Aaron Baker	Republican	1925–1929
Henry Stewart Caulfield	Republican	1929–1933
Guy Brasfield Park	Democrat	1933–1937
Lloyd Crow Stark	Democrat	1937–1941
Forrest C. Donnell	Republican	1941–1945
Phil M. Donnelly	Democrat	1945–1949
Forrest Smith	Democrat	1949–1953
Phil M. Donnelly	Democrat	1953–1957
James Thomas Blair, Jr.	Democrat	1957–1961
John Montgomery Dalton	Democrat	1961–1965
Warren Eastman Hearnes	Democrat	1965–1973
Christopher S. Bond	Republican	1973–1977
Joseph P. Teasdale	Democrat	1977–1981
Christopher S. Bond	Republican	1981–1985
John Ashcroft	Republican	1985–1993
Mel Carnahan	Democrat	1993–2000

Roger B. Wilson	Democrat	2000–2001
Bob Holden	Democrat	2001–2005

MONTANA

Joseph K. Toole	Democrat	1868–1893
John E. Richards	Republican	1893–1897
Robert Burns Smith	Democrat	1897–1901
Joseph Kemp Toole	Democrat	1901–1908
Edwin Lee Norris	Democrat	1908–1913
Samuel Vernon Stewart	Democrat	1913–1921
Joseph Moore Dixon	Republican	1921–1925
John Edward Erickson	Democrat	1925–1933
Frank H. Cooney	Democrat	1933–1935
William Elmer Holt	Democrat	1935–1937
Roy E. Ayers	Democrat	1937–1941
Samuel C. Ford	Republican	1941–1949
John Woodrow Bonner	Democrat	1949–1953
John Hugo Aronson	Republican	1953–1961
Donald Grant Nutter	Republican	1961–1962
Tim M. Babcock	Republican	1962–1969
Forrest Howard Anderson	Democrat	1969–1973
Thomas Lee Judge	Democrat	1973–1981
Ted Schwinden	Democrat	1981–1989
Stan Stephens	Republican	1989–1993
Marc Racicot	Republican	1993–2001
Judy Martz	Republican	2001–2005

NEBRASKA

David Butler	Republican	1867–1871
W. H. James	Republican	1871–1873
Robert W. Furnas	Republican	1873–1875
Silas Garber	Republican	1875–1879
Albinus Nance	Republican	1879–1883
James W. Dawes	Republican	1883–1887
John M. Thayer	Republican	1887–1891
James E. Boyd	Democrat	1891–1893

Lorenzo Crounse	Republican	1893–1895
Silas A. Holcomb	Democrat–People's Independent	1895–1899
William Amos Poynter	Fusion	1899–1901
Charles H. Dietrich	Republican	1901
Ezra Perin Savage	Republican	1901–1903
John Hopwood Mickey	Republican	1903–1907
George Lawson Sheldon	Republican	1907–1909
Ashton C. Shallenberger	Democrat	1909–1911
Chester Hardy Aldrich	Republican	1911–1913
John Henry Morehead	Democrat	1913–1917
Keith Neville	Democrat	1917–1919
Samuel Roy McKelvie	Republican	1919–1923
Charles Wayland Bryan	Democrat	1923–1925
Adam McMullen	Republican	1925–1929
Arthur J. Weaver	Republican	1929–1931
Charles Wayland Bryan	Democrat	1931–1935
Robert Leroy Cochran	Democrat	1935–1941
Dwight Palmer Griswold	Republican	1941–1947
Val Peterson	Republican	1947–1953
Robert Berkey Crosby	Republican	1953–1955
Victor Emanuel Anderson	Republican	1955–1959
Ralph Gilmour Brooks	Democrat	1959–1960
Dwight Willard Burney	Republican	1960–1961
Frank Brenner Morrison	Democrat	1961–1967
Norbert T. Tiemann	Republican	1967–1971
J. James Exon	Democrat	1971–1979
Charles Thone	Republican	1979–1983
Bob Kerrey	Democrat	1983–1987
Kay A. Orr	Republican	1987–1991
Ben Nelson	Democrat	1991–1999
Mike Johanns	Republican	1999–2003

NEVADA

H. G. Blasdel	Union Republican	1865–1871
L. R. Bradley	Democrat	1871–1879
John H. Kinkead	Republican	1879–1883

Jewett Adams	Democrat	1883–1887
C. C. Stevenson	Republican	1887–1890
Frank Bell	Republican	1890–1891 (Acting)
R. K. Colcord	Republican	1891–1895
John E. Jones	Democrat (Silver)	1895–1896
Reinhold Sadler	Silver Republican	1896–1903
John Sparks	Silver & Democrat	1903–1908
Denver S. Dickerson	Silver & Democrat	1908–1911
Tasker Lowndes Oddie	Republican	1911–1915
Emmet Derby Boyle	Democrat	1915–1923
James Graves Scrugham	Democrat	1923–1927
Frederick Bennett Balzar	Republican	1927–1934
Morley Isaac Griswold	Republican	1934–1935
Richard Kirman, Sr.	Democrat	1935–1939
Edward Peter Carville	Democrat	1939–1945
Vail Montgomery Pittman	Democrat	1945–1951
Charles Hinton Russell	Republican	1951–1959
Frank Grant Sawyer	Democrat	1959–1967
Paul D. Laxalt	Republican	1967–1971
Mike O'Callaghan	Democrat	1971–1979
Robert F. List	Republican	1979–1983
Richard H. Bryan	Democrat	1983–1989
Bob J. Miller	Democrat	1989–1999
Kenny Guinn	Republican	1999–2001

NEW HAMPSHIRE

John Langdon		1788–1789
John Sullivan	Federalist	1789–1790
Josiah Bartlett	Democratic-Republican	1790–1794
John Taylor Gilman	Federalist	1794–1805
John Langdon	Democratic-Republican	1805–1809
Jeremiah Smith	Federalist	1809–1810
John Langdon	Democratic-Republican	1810–1812
William Plumer	Democratic-Republican	1812–1813
John Taylor Gilman	Federalist	1813–1816
William Plumer	Democratic-Republican	1816–1819
Samuel Bell	Democratic-Republican	1819–1823

Levi Woodbury	Democratic-Republican	1823–1824
David L. Morrill	Democratic-Republican	1824–1827
Benjamin Pierce	Democratic-Republican	1827–1828
John Bell	National Republican	1828–1829
Benjamin Pierce	Jackson Democrat	1829–1830
Matthew Harvey	Jackson Democrat	1830–1831
Joseph M. Harper	Democrat	1831
Samuel Dinsmoor	Jackson Democrat	1831–1834
William Badger	Democrat	1834–1836
Isaac Hill	Democrat	1836–1839
John Page	Democrat	1839–1842
Henry Hubbard	Democrat	1842–1844
John H. Steele	Democrat	1844–1846
Anthony Colby	Whig	1846–1847
Jared W. Williams	Democrat	1847–1849
Samuel Dinsmoor	Democrat	1849–1852
Noah Martin	Democrat	1852–1854
Nathaniel B. Baker	Democrat	1854–1855
Ralph Metcalf	American	1855–1857
William Haile	Republican	1857–1859
Ichabod Goodwin	Republican	1859–1861
Nathaniel S. Berry	Republican	1861–1863
Joseph A. Gilmore	Republican	1863–1865
Frederick Smyth	Union	1865–1867
Walter Harriman	Republican	1867–1869
Onslow Stearns	Republican	1869–1871
James A. Weston	Democrat	1871–1872
Ezekial A. Straw	Republican	1872–1874
James A. Weston	Democrat	1874–1875
Person C. Cheney	Republican	1875–1877
Benjamin F. Prescott	Republican	1877–1879
Natt Head	Republican	1879–1881
Charles H. Bell	Republican	1881–1883
Samuel W. Hale	Republican	1883–1885
Moody Currier	Republican	1885–1887
Charles H. Sawyer	Republican	1887–1889
David H. Goodell	Republican	1889–1891
Hiram A. Tuttle	Republican	1891–1893

John B. Smith	Republican	1893–1895
Charles A. Busiel	Republican	1895–1897
George A. Ramsdell	Republican	1897–1899
Frank W. Rollins	Republican	1899–1901
Chester B. Jordan	Republican	1901–1903
Nahum J. Bachelder	Republican	1903–1905
John McLane	Republican	1905–1907
Charles M. Floyd	Republican	1907–1909
Henry B. Quinby	Republican	1909–1911
Robert P. Bass	Republican	1911–1913
Samuel D. Felker	Democrat	1913–1915
Rolland H. Spaulding	Republican	1915–1917
Henry Wilder Keyes	Republican	1917–1919
John H. Bartlett	Republican	1919–1921
Albert O. Brown	Republican	1921–1923
Fred H. Brown	Democrat	1923–1925
John G. Winant	Republican	1925–1927
Huntley N. Spaulding	Republican	1927–1929
Charles W. Tobey	Republican	1929–1931
John G. Winant	Republican	1931–1935
Henry Styles Bridges	Republican	1935–1937
Francis P. Murphy	Republican	1937–1941
Robert O. Blood	Republican	1941–1945
Charles M. Dale	Republican	1945–1949
Sherman Adams	Republican	1949–1953
Hugh Gregg	Republican	1953–1955
Lane Dwinell	Republican	1955–1959
Wesley Powell	Republican	1959–1963
John W. King	Democrat	1963–1969
Walter Peterson	Republican	1969–1973
Meldrim Thomson, Jr.	Republican	1973–1979
Hugh J. Gallen	Democrat	1979–1982
Vesta M. Roy	Democrat	1982–1983
John H. Sununu	Republican	1983–1989
Judd Gregg	Republican	1989–1993
Stephen E. Merrill	Republican	1993–1997
Jeanne Shaheen	Democrat	1997–2003

NEW JERSEY

William Livingston	Federalist	1776–1790
Elisha Lawrence	Federalist	1790
William Paterson	Federalist	1790–1792
Richard Howell	Federalist	1792–1801
Joseph Bloomfield	Democratic-Republican	1801–1802
John Lambert	Democratic-Republican	1802–1803 (Acting)
Joseph Bloomfield	Democratic-Republican	1803–1812
Aaron Ogden	Federalist	1813
William S. Pennington	Democratic-Republican	1813–1815
William Kennedy	Democratic-Republican	1815
Mahlon Dickerson	Democratic-Republican	1815–1817
Isaac H. Williamson	Federalist	1817–1829
Peter D. Vroom	Democrat	1829–1832
Samuel L. Southard	Whig	1832–1833
Elias P. Seeley	Whig	1833
Peter D. Vroom	Democrat	1833–1836
Philemon Dickerson	Democrat	1836–1837
William Pennington	Whig	1837–1843
Daniel Haines	Democrat	1843–1845
Charles C. Stratton	Whig	1845–1848
Daniel Haines	Democrat	1848–1851
George F. Fort	Democrat	1851–1854
Rodman M. Price	Democrat	1854–1857
William A. Newell	Fusion	1857–1860
Charles S. Olden	Republican	1860–1863
Joel Parker	Democrat	1863–1866
Marcus L. Ward	Union	1866–1869
Theodore F. Randolph	Democrat	1869–1872
Joel Parker	Democrat	1872–1875
Joseph D. Bedle	Democrat	1875–1878
George B. McClellan	Democrat	1878–1881
George C. Ludlow	Democrat	1881–1884
Leon Abbett	Democrat	1884–1887
Robert S. Green	Democrat	1887–1890
Leon Abbett	Democrat	1890–1893
George T. Werts	Democrat	1893–1896
John W. Griggs	Republican	1896–1898

Foster M. Voorhees	Republican	1898 (Acting)
David O. Watkins	Republican	1898–1899 (Acting)
Foster M. Voorhees	Republican	1899–1902
Franklin Murphy	Republican	1902–1905
Edward C. Stokes	Republican	1905–1908
John Franklin Fort	Republican	1908–1911
Woodrow Wilson	Democrat	1911–1913
James Fairman Fielder	Democrat	1913
Leon R. Taylor	Democrat	1913–1914 (Acting)
James Fairman Fielder	Democrat	1914–1917
Walter Evans Edge	Republican	1917–1919
William Nelson Runyon	Republican	1919–1920 (Acting)
Clarence Edwards Case	Republican	1920 (Acting)
Edward Irving Edwards	Democrat	1920–1923
George S. Silzer	Democrat	1923–1926
Arthur Harry Moore	Democrat	1926–1929
Morgan F. Larson	Republican	1929–1932
Arthur Harry Moore	Democrat	1932–1935
Clifford R. Powell	Republican	1935
Horace G. Prall	Republican	1935 (Acting)
Harold Giles Hoffman	Republican	1935–1938
Arthur Harry Moore	Democrat	1938–1941
Charles Edison	Democrat	1941–1944
Walter Evans Edge	Republican	1944–1947
Alfred Eastlack Driscoll	Republican	1947–1954
Robert Baumle Meyner	Democrat	1954–1962
Richard J. Hughes	Democrat	1962–1970
William T. Cahill	Republican	1970–1974
Brendan T. Byrne	Democrat	1974–1982
Thomas H. Kean	Republican	1982–1990
James J. Florio	Democrat	1990–1994
Christine Todd Whitman	Republican	1994–2001
Donald T. DiFrancesco	Republican	2001–2002 (Acting)

NEW MEXICO

William C. McDonald	Democrat	1912–1917
Ezequiel Cabeza de Baca	Democrat	1917

Washington Ellsworth Lindsey	Republican	1917–1919
Octaviano A. Larrazolo	Republican	1919–1921
Merritt Cramer Mechem	Republican	1921–1923
James Fielding Hinkle	Democrat	1923–1925
Arthur T. Hannett	Democrat	1925–1927
Richard C. Dillon	Republican	1927–1931
Arthur Seligman	Democrat	1931–1933
Andrew W. Hockenhull	Democrat	1933–1935
Clyde Tingley	Democrat	1935–1939
John Esten Miles	Democrat	1939–1943
John J. Dempsey	Democrat	1943–1947
Thomas Jewett Mabry	Democrat	1947–1951
Edwin Leard Mechem	Republican	1951–1955
John F. Simms	Democrat	1955–1957
Edwin Leard Mechem	Republican	1957–1959
John Burroughs	Democrat	1959–1961
Edwin Leard Mechem	Republican	1961–1962
Tom Bolack	Republican	1962–1963
Jack M. Campbell	Democrat	1963–1967
David Francis Cargo	Republican	1967–1971
Bruce King	Democrat	1971–1975
Jerry Apodaca	Democrat	1975–1979
Bruce King	Democrat	1979–1983
Toney Anaya	Democrat	1983–1987
Garrey Carruthers	Republican	1987–1991
Bruce King	Democrat	1991–1995
Gary E. Johnson	Republican	1995–2003

NEW YORK

George Clinton	Democratic-Republican	1777–1795
John Jay	Federalist	1795–1801
George Clinton	Democratic-Republican	1801–1804
Morgan Lewis	Democratic-Republican	1804–1807
Daniel D. Tompkins	Democratic-Republican	1807–1817
John Tayler	Democratic-Republican	1817 (Acting)
De Witt Clinton	Democratic-Republican	1817–1822

Joseph C. Yates	Democratic-Republican	1822–1824
De Witt Clinton	Clinton Republican	1824–1828
Nathaniel Pitcher	Democratic-Republican	1828 (Acting)
Martin Van Buren	Jackson Democrat	1828–1829
Enos T. Throop	Jackson Democrat	1829–1833
William L. Marcy	Democrat	1833–1839
William H. Seward	Whig	1839–1843
William C. Bouck	Democrat	1843–1845
Silas Wright	Democrat	1845–1847
John Young	Whig	1847–1849
Hamilton Fish	Whig	1849–1851
Washington Hunt	Whig Anti-Rent	1851–1853
Horatio Seymour	Democrat	1853–1855
Myron H. Clark	Fusion Republican	1855–1857
John A. King	Republican	1857–1859
Edwin D. Morgan	Republican	1859–1863
Horatio Seymour	Democrat	1863–1865
Reuben E. Fenton	Union	1865–1869
John T. Hoffman	Democrat	1869–1873
John A. Dix	Republican	1873–1875
Samuel J. Tilden	Democrat	1875–1877
Lucius Robinson	Democrat	1877–1880
Alonzo B. Cornell	Republican	1880–1883
Grover Cleveland	Democrat	1883–1885
David B. Hill	Democrat	1885–1891
Roswell P. Flower	Democrat	1891–1895
Levi P. Morton	Republican	1895–1897
Frank S. Black	Republican	1897–1899
Theodore Roosevelt	Republican	1899–1901
Benjamin Barker Odell, Jr.	Republican	1901–1905
Frank Wayland Higgins	Republican	1905–1907
Charles Evans Hughes	Republican	1907–1910
Horace White	Republican	1910–1911
John Alden Dix	Democrat	1911–1913
William Sulzer	Democrat	1913
Martin H. Glynn	Democrat	1913–1915
Charles Seymour Whitman	Republican	1915–1919

Alfred E. Smith	Democrat	1919–1921
Nathan L. Miller	Republican	1921–1923
Alfred E. Smith	Democrat	1923–1929
Franklin D. Roosevelt	Democrat	1929–1933
Herbert H. Lehman	Democrat	1933–1942
Charles Poletti	Democrat	1942–1943
Thomas E. Dewey	Republican	1943–1955
W. Averell Harriman	Democrat	1955–1959
Nelson A. Rockefeller	Republican	1959–1973
Malcolm Wilson	Republican	1973–1975
Hugh Carey	Democrat	1975–1983
Mario M. Cuomo	Democrat	1983–1995
George E. Pataki	Republican	1995–2003

NORTH CAROLINA

Samuel Johnston		1787–1789
Alexander Martin	Federalist	1789–1792
R. D. Spaight	Democratic-Republican	1792–1795
Samuel Ashe	Democratic-Republican	1795–1798
W. R. Davie	Federalist	1798–1799
Benjamin Williams	Democratic-Republican	1799–1802
James Turner	Democratic-Republican	1802–1805
Nathaniel Alexander	Democratic-Republican	1805–1807
Benjamin Williams	Democratic-Republican	1807–1808
David Stone	Democratic-Republican	1808–1810
Benjamin Smith	Democratic-Republican	1810–1811
William Hawkins	Democratic-Republican	1811–1814
William Miller	Democratic-Republican	1814–1817
John Branch	Democratic-Republican	1817–1820
Jesse Franklin	Democratic-Republican	1820–1821
Gabriel Holmes	Democratic-Republican	1821–1824
H. G. Burton	Democratic-Republican	1824–1827
James Iredell	Democratic-Republican	1827–1828
John Owen	Democrat	1828–1830
Montfort Stokes	Democrat	1830–1832
D. L. Swain	Democrat	1832–1835
R. D. Spaight, Jr.	Democrat	1835–1836

E. B. Dudley	Whig	1836–1841
J. M. Morehead	Whig	1841–1845
W. A. Graham	Whig	1845–1849
Charles Manly	Whig	1849–1851
D. S. Reid	Democrat	1851–1854
Warren Winslow	Democrat	1854–1855
Thomas Bragg	Democrat	1855–1859
John W. Ellis	Democrat	1859–1861
Henry T. Clark	Democrat	1861–1862
Z. B. Vance	Conservative	1862–1865
W. W. Holden	Republican	1865
Jonathan Worth	Conservative	1865–1868
W. W. Holden	Republican	1868–1870
T. R. Caldwell	Republican	1870–1874
C. H. Brogden	Republican	1874–1877
Z. B. Vance	Democrat	1877–1879
T. J. Jarvis	Democrat	1879–1885
A. M. Scales	Democrat	1885–1889
D. G. Fowle	Democrat	1889–1891
Thomas M. Holt	Democrat	1891–1893
Elias Carr	Democrat	1893–1897
Daniel L. Russell	Republican	1897–1901
Charles Brantley Aycock	Democrat	1901–1905
Robert B. Glenn	Democrat	1905–1909
William W. Kitchin	Democrat	1909–1913
Locke Craig	Democrat	1913–1917
Thomas W. Bickett	Democrat	1917–1921
Carmeron A. Morrison	Democrat	1921–1925
Angus Wilton McLean	Democrat	1925–1929
Oliver Max Gardner	Democrat	1929–1933
John C. B. Ehringhaus	Democrat	1933–1937
Clyde Roark Hoey	Democrat	1937–1941
Joseph Melville Broughton	Democrat	1941–1945
Robert Gregg Cherry	Democrat	1945–1949
William Kerr Scott	Democrat	1949–1953
William B. Umstead	Democrat	1953–1954
Luther H. Hodges	Democrat	1954–1961

Terry Sanford	Democrat	1961–1965
Dan Killian Moore	Democrat	1965–1969
Robert W. Scott	Democrat	1969–1973
James E. Holshouser, Jr.	Republican	1973–1977
James B. Hunt Jr.	Democrat	1977–1985
James G. Martin	Republican	1985–1993
James B. Hunt, Jr.	Democrat	1993–2001
Mike Easley	Democrat	2001–2005

NORTH DAKOTA

John Miller	Republican	1889–1891
Andrew H. Burke	Republican	1891–1893
Eli C. D. Shortridge	Fusion	1893–1895
Roger Allin	Republican	1895–1897
Frank A. Briggs	Republican	1897–1898
Joseph M. Devine	Republican	1898–1899
Frederick B. Fancher	Republican	1899–1901
Frank White	Republican	1901–1905
Elmore Y. Sarles	Republican	1905–1907
John Burke	Democrat	1907–1913
Louis B. Hanna	Republican	1913–1917
Lynn J. Frazier	Republican	1917–1921
Ragnvald A. Nestos	Republican	1921–1925
Arthur Gustav Sorlie	Republican	1925–1928
Walter J. Maddock	Republican	1928–1929
George F. Shafer	Republican	1929–1932
William Langer	Republican	1932–1934
Ole H. Olson	Republican	1934–1935
Thomas Hilliard Moodie	Democrat	1935
Walter Welford	Republican	1935–1937
William Langer	Independent	1937–1939
John Moses	Democrat	1939–1945
Fred G. Aandahl	Republican	1945–1951
Clarence Norman Brunsdale	Republican	1951–1957
John E. Davis	Republican	1957–1961
William L. Guy	Democrat	1961–1973

Arthur A. Link	Democrat	1973–1981
Allen Olson	Republican	1981–1985
George Sinner	Democrat	1985–1993
Edward T. Schafer	Republican	1993–2001
John Hoeven	Republican	2001–2004

OHIO

Edward Tiffin	Democratic-Republican	1803–1807
Thomas Kirker	Democratic-Republican	1807–1808
Samuel Huntington	Democratic-Republican	1808–1810
Return Jonathan Meigs	Democratic-Republican	1810–1814
Othneil Looker	Democratic-Republican	1814
Thomas Worthington	Democratic-Republican	1814–1818
Ethan Allen Brown	Democratic-Republican	1818–1822
Allen Trimble	Democratic-Republican	1822
Jeremiah Morrow	Jackson Democrat	1822–1826
Allen Trimble	National Republican	1826–1830
Duncan McArthur	National Republican	1830–1832
Robert Lucas	Democrat	1832–1836
Joseph Vance	Whig	1836–1838
Wilson Shannon	Democrat	1838–1840
Thomas Corwin	Whig	1840–1842
Wilson Shannon	Democrat	1842–1844
Thomas W. Bartley	Democrat	1844
Mordecai Bartley	Whig	1844–1846
William Bebb	Whig	1846–1849
Seabury Ford	Whig	1849–1850
Reuben Wood	Democrat	1850–1853
William Medill	Democrat	1853–1856
Salmon P. Chase	Republican	1856–1860
William Dennison	Republican	1860–1862
David Tod	Union	1862–1864
John Brough	Union	1864–1865
Charles Anderson	Union	1865–1866
Jacob D. Cox	Union	1866–1868
Rutherford B. Hayes	Republican	1868–1872

Edward F. Noyes	Republican	1872–1874
William Allen	Democrat	1874–1876
Rutherford B. Hayes	Republican	1876–1877
Thomas L. Young	Republican	1877–1878
Richard M. Bishop	Democrat	1878–1880
Charles Foster	Republican	1880–1884
George Hoadly	Democrat	1884–1886
Joseph B. Foraker	Republican	1886–1890
James E. Campbell	Democrat	1890–1892
William McKinley	Republican	1892–1896
Asa Smith Bushnell	Republican	1896–1900
George Kilbon Nash	Republican	1900–1904
Myron T. Herrick	Republican	1904–1906
John M. Pattison	Democrat	1906
Andrew Lintner Harris	Republican	1906–1909
Judson Harmon	Democrat	1909–1913
James M. Cox	Democrat	1913–1915
Frank B. Willis	Republican	1915–1917
James M. Cox	Democrat	1917–1921
Harry Lyman Davis	Republican	1921–1923
Alvin Victor Donahey	Democrat	1923–1929
Myers Young Cooper	Republican	1929–1931
George White	Democrat	1931–1935
Martin Luther Davey	Democrat	1935–1939
John W. Bricker	Republican	1939–1945
Frank J. Lausche	Democrat	1945–1947
Thomas J. Herbert	Republican	1947–1949
Frank J. Lausche	Democrat	1949–1957
John W. Brown	Republican	1957
C. William O'Neill	Republican	1957–1959
Michael Vincent DiSalle	Democrat	1959–1963
James A. Rhodes	Republican	1963–1971
John J. Gilligan	Democrat	1971–1975
James A. Rhodes	Republican	1975–1983
Richard F. Celeste	Democrat	1983–1991
George V. Voinovich	Republican	1991–1999
Bob Taft	Republican	1999–2003

OKLAHOMA

Charles N. Haskell	Democrat	1907–1911
Lee Cruce	Democrat	1911–1915
Robert L. Wiliams	Democrat	1915–1919
James Brooks Ayers Robert-son	Democrat	1919–1923
James (Jack) C. Walton	Democrat	1923
Martin E. Trapp	Democrat	1923–1927
Henry S. Johnston	Democrat	1927–1929
William Judson Holloway	Democrat	1929–1931
William H. Murray	Democrat	1931–1935
Ernest Whitworth Marland	Democrat	1935–1939
Leon C. Phillips	Democrat	1939–1943
Robert S. Kerr	Democrat	1943–1947
Roy J. Turner	Democrat	1947–1951
Johnston Murray	Democrat	1951–1955
Raymond D. Gary	Democrat	1955–1959
James Howard Edmondson	Democrat	1959–1963
George P. Nigh	Democrat	1963
Henry Louis Bellmon	Republican	1963–1967
Dewey Follette Bartlett	Republican	1967–1971
David Hall	Democrat	1971–1975
David L. Boren	Democrat	1975–1979
George Nigh	Democrat	1979–1987
Henry Louis Bellmon	Republican	1987–1991
David Walters	Democrat	1991–1995
Frank Keating	Republican	1995–2003

OREGON

John Whiteaker	Democrat	1859–1862
A. C. Gibbs	Union Republican	1862–1866
George L. Woods	Republican	1866–1870
Lafayette Grover	Democrat	1870–1877
Stephen F. Chadwick	Democrat	1877–1878
W. W. Thayer	Democrat	1878–1882
Z. F. Moody	Republican	1882–1887

Sylvester Pennoyer	Democrat	1887–1895
William Paine Lord	Republican	1895–1899
Theodore Thurston Geer	Republican	1899–1903
George E. Chamberlain	Democrat	1903–1909
Frank Williamson Benson	Republican	1909–1910
Jay Bowerman	Republican	1910–1911
Oswald West	Democrat	1911–1915
James Withycombe	Republican	1915–1919
Ben Wilson Olcott	Republican	1919–1923
Walter M. Pierce	Democrat	1923–1927
Isaac L. Patterson	Republican	1927–1929
Albin W. Norblad	Republican	1929–1931
Julius L. Meier	Independent	1931–1935
Charles H. Martin	Democrat	1935–1939
Charles A. Sprague	Republican	1939–1943
Earl W. Snell	Republican	1943–1947
John H. Hall	Republican	1947–1949
Douglas McKay	Republican	1949–1952
Paul L. Patterson	Republican	1952–1956
Elmo Smith	Republican	1956–1957
Robert D. Holmes	Democrat	1957–1959
Mark O. Hatfield	Republican	1959–1967
Tom McCall	Republican	1967–1975
Robert W. Straub	Democrat	1975–1979
Victor Atiyeh	Republican	1979–1987
Neil Goldschmidt	Democrat	1987–1991
Barbara Roberts	Democrat	1991–1995
John Kitzhaber	Democrat	1995–2003

PENNSYLVANIA

Thomas Mifflin		1790–1799
Thomas McKean	Democratic-Republican	1799–1808
Simon Snyder	Democratic-Republican	1808–1817
William Findlay	Democratic-Republican	1817–1820
Joseph Hiester	Democratic-Republican	1820–1823
John Andrew Shulze	Jackson Democrat	1823–1829

George Wolfe	Jackson Democrat	1829–1835
Joseph Ritner	Democrat	1835–1839
David Rittenhouse Porter	Democrat	1839–1845
Francis Rawn Shunk	Democrat	1845–1848
William F. Johnston	Whig	1848–1852
William Bigler	Democrat	1852–1855
James Pollock	Whig	1855–1858
William Fisher Packer	Democrat	1858–1861
Andrew Gregg Curtin	Republican	1861–1867
John White Geary	Republican	1867–1873
John Frederick Hartranft	Republican	1873–1879
Henry Martyn Hoyt	Republican	1879–1883
Robert Emory Pattison	Democrat	1883–1887
James A. Beaver	Republican	1887–1891
Robert Emory Pattison	Democrat	1891–1895
Daniel Hartman Hastings	Republican	1895–1899
William Alexis Stone	Republican	1899–1903
Samuel Whitaker Penny-packer	Republican	1903–1907
Edwin Syndney Stuart	Republican	1907–1911
John Kinley Tener	Republican	1911–1915
Martin Grove Brumbaugh	Republican	1915–1919
William Cameron Sproul	Republican	1919–1923
Gifford Pinchot	Republican	1923–1927
John Stuchell Fisher	Republican	1927–1931
Gifford Pinchot	Republican	1931–1935
George H. Earle	Democrat	1935–1939
Arthur H. James	Republican	1939–1943
Edward Martin	Republican	1943–1947
John C. Bell, Jr.	Republican	1947
James Henderson Duff	Republican	1947–1951
John Sydney Fine	Republican	1951–1955
George M. Leader	Democrat	1955–1959
David L. Lawrence	Democrat	1959–1963
William Warren Scranton	Republican	1963–1967
Raymond P. Shafer	Republican	1967–1971
Milton J. Shapp	Democrat	1971–1979

Richard L. Thornburgh	Republican	1979–1987
Robert P. Casey	Democrat	1987–1995
Tom Ridge	Republican	1995–2003

RHODE ISLAND

Arthur Fenner	Democratic-Republican	1790–1805
Henry Smith	Democratic-Republican	1805–1806
Isaac Wilbour	Democratic-Republican	1806–1807
James Fenner	Democratic-Republican	1807–1811
William Jones	Federalist	1811–1817
Nehemiah R. Knight	Democratic-Republican	1817–1821
William C. Gibbs	Democratic-Republican	1821–1824
James Fenner	Democratic-Republican	1824–1831
Lemuel H. Arnold	Democrat	1831–1833
John Brown Francis	Democrat	1833–1838
William Sprague	Whig	1838–1839
Samuel Ward King	Whig	1839–1843
James Fenner	Law and Order Whig	1843–1845
Charles Jackson	Liberation Whig	1845–1846
Byron Diman	Law and Order Whig	1846–1847
Elisha Harris	Whig	1847–1849
Henry B. Anthony	Whig	1849–1851
Philip Allen	Democrat	1851–1853
Francis M. Dimond	Democrat	1853–1854
William Warner Hoppin	Whig-Republican	1854–1857
Elisha Dyer	Republican	1857–1859
Thomas G. Turner		1859–1860
William Sprague	Fusion-Union	1860–1863
William C. Cozzens		1863
James Y. Smith	Union Republican	1863–1866
Ambrose E. Burnside	Republican	1866–1869
Seth Padelford	Republican	1869–1873
Henry Howard	Republican	1873–1875
Henry Lippitt	Republican	1875–1877
Charles C. Van Zandt	Republican-Temperance	1877–1880
Alfred H. Littlefield	Republican	1880–1883

Augustus O. Bourn	Republican	1883–1885
George P. Wetmore	Republican	1885–1887
John W. Davis	Democrat	1887–1888
Royal C. Taft	Republican	1888–1889
Herbert W. Ladd	Republican	1889–1890
John W. Davis	Democrat	1890–1891
Herbert W. Ladd	Republican	1891–1892
D. Russell Brown	Republican	1892–1895
Charles W. Lippitt	Republican	1895–1897
Elisha Dyer	Republican	1897–1900
William Gregory	Republican	1900–1901
Charles Dean Kimball	Republican	1901–1903
Lucius F. C. Garvin	Democrat	1903–1905
George H. Utter	Republican	1905–1907
James H. Higgins	Democrat	1907–1909
Aram J. Pothier	Republican	1909–1915
R. Livingston Beeckman	Republican	1915–1921
Emery J. San Souci	Republican	1921–1923
William Smith Flynn	Democrat	1923–1925
Aram J. Pothier	Republican	1925–1928
Norman S. Case	Republican	1928–1933
Theodore F. Green	Democrat	1933–1937
Robert E. Quinn	Democrat	1937–1939
William H. Vanderbilt	Republican	1939–1941
J. Howard McGrath	Democrat	1941–1945
John O. Pastore	Democrat	1945–1950
John Sammon McKiernan	Democrat	1950–1951
Dennis J. Roberts	Democrat	1951–1959
Christopher Del Sesto	Republican	1959–1961
John A. Notte, Jr.	Democrat	1961–1963
John H. Chafee	Republican	1963–1969
Frank Licht	Democrat	1969–1973
Phillip W. Noel	Democrat	1973–1977
Joseph J. Garrahy	Democrat	1977–1985
Edward D. DiPrete	Republican	1985–1991
Bruce Sundlun	Democrat	1991–1995
Lincoln C. Almond	Republican	1995–2003

SOUTH CAROLINA

Charles Pinckney		1789–1792
William Moultrie	Federalist	1792–1794
Arnoldus Vander Horst	Federalist	1794–1796
Charles Pinckney	Democratic-Republican	1796–1798
Edward Rutledge	Federalist	1798–1800
John Drayton	Democratic-Republican	1800–1802
James Burchell Richardson	Democratic-Republican	1802–1804
Paul Hamilton	Democratic-Republican	1804–1806
Charles Pinckney	Democratic-Republican	1806–1808
John Drayton	Democratic-Republican	1808–1810
Henry Middleton	Democratic-Republican	1810–1812
Joseph Alston	Democratic-Republican	1812–1814
David Rogerson Williams	Democratic-Republican	1814–1816
Andrew Pickens	Democratic-Republican	1816–1818
John Geddes	Democratic-Republican	1818–1820
Thomas Bennett	Democratic-Republican	1820–1822
John Lyde Wilson	Democratic-Republican	1822–1824
Richard Irvine Manning	Democratic-Republican	1824–1826
John Taylor	Democratic-Republican	1826–1828
Stephen D. Miller	Democrat	1828–1830
James Hamilton, Jr.	Democrat	1830–1832
Robert Young Hayne	Democrat	1832–1834
George McDuffie	Democrat	1834–1836
Pierce Mason Butler	Democrat	1836–1838
Patrick Noble	Democrat	1838–1840
B. K. Henagan	Democrat	1840
John Peter Richardson	Democrat	1840–1842
James Henry Hammond	Democrat	1842–1844
William Aiken	Democrat	1844–1846
David Johnson	Democrat	1846–1848
Whitemarsh B. Seabrook	Democrat	1848–1850
John Hugh Means	Democrat	1850–1852
John Laurence Manning	Democrat	1852–1854
James Hopkins Adams	Democrat	1854–1856
Robert Francis Withers Alston	Democrat	1856–1858

William H. Gist	Democrat	1858–1860
Francis Wilkinson Pickens	Democrat	1860–1862
Milledge Luke Bonham	Democrat	1862–1864
Andrew Gordon Magrath	Democrat	1864–1865
Benjamin F. Perry		1865
James Lawrence Orr	Conservative	1865–1868
Robert K. Scott	Republican	1868–1872
Franklin J. Mose, Jr.	Republican	1872–1874
Daniel H. Chamberlain	Republican	1874–1876
Wade Hampton	Democrat	1876–1879
William Dunlap Simpson	Democrat	1879–1880
Thomas Bothwell Jeter	Democrat	1880
Johnson Hagood	Democrat	1880–1882
Hugh Smith Thompson	Democrat	1882–1886
John C. Sheppard	Democrat	1886
John Peter Richardson	Democrat	1886–1890
Benjamin Ryan Tillman	Democrat	1890–1894
John Gary Evans	Democrat	1894–1897
William Haselden Ellerbe	Democrat	1897–1899
Miles B. McSweeney	Democrat	1899–1903
Duncan Clinch Heyward	Democrat	1903–1907
Martin F. Ansel	Democrat	1907–1911
Coleman Livingston Blease	Democrat	1911–1915
Charles A. Smith	Democrat	1915
Richard Irvine Manning	Democrat	1915–1919
Robert Archer Cooper	Democrat	1919–1922
Wilson Godfrey Harvey	Democrat	1922–1923
Thomas Gordon McLeod	Democrat	1923–1927
John Gardiner Richards	Democrat	1927–1931
Ibra C. Blackwood	Democrat	1931–1935
Olin Dewitt Johnston	Democrat	1935–1939
Burnet Rhett Maybank	Democrat	1939–1941
Joseph E. Harley	Democrat	1941–1942
Richard Manning Jeffries	Democrat	1942–1943
Olin D. Johnston	Democrat	1943–1945
Ransome Judson Williams	Democrat	1945–1947
James Strom Thurmond	Democrat	1947–1951

James F. Byrnes	Democrat	1951–1955
George Bell Timmerman, Jr.	Democrat	1955–1959
Ernest F. Hollings	Democrat	1959–1963
Donald S. Russell	Democrat	1963–1965
Robert E. McNair	Democrat	1965–1971
John C. West	Democrat	1971–1975
James Edwards	Republican	1975–1979
Richard Riley	Democrat	1979–1987
Carroll Ashmore Campbell, Jr.	Republican	1987–1995
David Beasley	Republican	1995–1999
James H. Hodges	Democrat	1999–2003

SOUTH DAKOTA

Arthur C. Melette	Republican	1889–1893
Charles H. Sheldon	Republican	1893–1897
Andrew E. Lee	Populist	1897–1901
Charles N. Herreid	Republican	1901–1905
Samuel H. Elrod	Republican	1905–1907
Coe I. Crawford	Republican	1907–1909
Robert Scadden Vessey	Republican	1909–1913
Frank M. Byrne	Republican	1913–1917
Peter Norbeck	Republican	1917–1921
William H. McMaster	Republican	1921–1925
Carl Gunderson	Republican	1925–1927
William J. Bulow	Democrat	1927–1931
Warren E. Green	Republican	1931–1933
Tom Berry	Democrat	1933–1937
Leslie Jensen	Republican	1937–1939
Harlan J. Bushfield	Republican	1939–1943
Merrell Q. Sharpe	Republican	1943–1947
George T. Mickelson	Republican	1947–1951
Sigurd Anderson	Republican	1951–1955
Joseph J. Foss	Republican	1955–1959
Ralph E. Herseth	Democrat	1959–1961
Archie M. Gubbrud	Republican	1961–1965
Nils A. Boe	Republican	1965–1969

Frank L. Farrar	Republican	1969–1971
Richard F. Kneip	Democrat	1971–1978
Harvey L. Wollman	Democrat	1978–1979
William J. Janklow	Republican	1979–1987
George S. Mickelson	Republican	1987–1993
Walter D. Miller	Republican	1993–1995
William J. Janklow	Republican	1995–2003

TENNESSEE

John Sevier	Democrat	1796–1801
Archibald Roane	Democrat	1801–1803
John Sevier	Democrat	1803–1809
Willie Blount	Democrat	1809–1815
Joseph McMinn	Democrat	1815–1821
William Carroll	Democrat	1821–1827
Sam Houston	Democrat	1827–1829
William Hall	Democrat	1829
William Carroll	Democrat	1829–1835
Newton Cannon	Whig	1835–1839
James K. Polk	Democrat	1839–1841
James C. Jones	Whig	1841–1845
Aaron V. Brown	Democrat	1845–1847
Neill S. Brown	Whig	1847–1849
William Trousdale	Democrat	1849–1851
William B. Campbell	Whig	1851–1853
Andrew Johnson	Democrat	1853–1857
Isham G. Harris	Democrat	1857–1862
Andrew Johnson	Democrat	1862–1865
William G. Brownlow	Whig-Republican	1865–1867
Dewitt Clinton Senter	Whig-Republican	1867–1871
John C. Brown	Whig-Democrat	1871–1875
James D. Porter	Democrat	1875–1879
Albert S. Marks	Democrat	1879–1881
Alvin Hawkins	Republican	1881–1883
William B. Bate	Democrat	1883–1887
Robert L. Taylor	Democrat	1887–1891
John P. Buchanan	Farmer-Labor	1891–1893

Peter Turney	Democrat	1893–1897
Robert L. Taylor	Democrat	1897–1899
Benton McMillin	Democrat	1899–1903
James B. Frazier	Democrat	1903–1905
John I. Cox	Democrat	1905–1907
Malcolm R. Patterson	Democrat	1907–1911
Ben W. Hooper	Republican	1911–1915
Thomas C. Rye	Democrat	1915–1919
Albert H. Roberts	Democrat	1919–1921
Alfred A. Taylor	Republican	1921–1923
Austin Peay	Democrat	1923–1927
Henry H. Horton	Democrat	1927–1933
Hill McAlister	Democrat	1933–1937
Gordon W. Browning	Democrat	1937–1939
W. Prentice Cooper	Democrat	1939–1945
James N. McCord	Democrat	1945–1949
Gordon Browning	Democrat	1949–1953
Frank G. Clement	Democrat	1953–1959
Buford Ellington	Democrat	1959–1963
Frank G. Clement	Democrat	1963–1967
Buford Ellington	Democrat	1967–1971
Winfield Dunn	Republican	1971–1975
Ray Blanton	Democrat	1975–1979
Lamar Alexander	Republican	1979–1987
Ned R. McWherter	Democrat	1987–1995
Don Sundquist	Republican	1995–2003

TEXAS

J. Pinckney Henderson	Democrat	1846–1847
George T. Wood	Democrat	1847–1849
P. Hansbrough Bell	Democrat	1849–1853
James W. Henderson	Democrat	1853
Elisha M. Pease	Democrat	1853–1857
Hardin R. Runnels	Democrat	1857–1859
Sam Houston	Independent Democrat	1859–1861
Edward Clark	Democrat	1861
Francis R. Lubbock	Democrat	1861–1863

Pendleton Murrah	Democrat	1863–1865
Andrew J. Hamilton	Conservative	1865–1866
James Webb Throckmorton	Conservative	1866–1867
Elisha M. Pease	Republican	1867–1869
Edmund J. Davis	Republican	1870–1874
Richard Coke	Democrat	1874–1876
Richard B. Hubbard	Democrat	1876–1879
Oran M. Roberts	Democrat	1879–1883
John Ireland	Democrat	1883–1887
Lawrence S. Ross	Democrat	1887–1891
James S. Hogg	Democrat	1891–1895
Charles A. Culberson	Democrat	1895–1899
Joseph D. Sayers	Democrat	1899–1903
Samuel Willis Tucker Lanham	Democrat	1903–1907
Thomas M. Campbell	Democrat	1907–1911
Oscar B. Colquitt	Democrat	1911–1915
James E. Ferguson, Jr.	Democrat	1915–1917
William P. Hobby	Democrat	1917–1921
Pat M. Neff	Democrat	1921–1925
Miriam A. Ferguson	Democrat	1925–1927
Daniel James Moody, Jr.	Democrat	1927–1931
Ross Shaw Sterling	Democrat	1931–1933
Miriam A. Ferguson	Democrat	1933–1935
James V. Allred	Democrat	1935–1939
Wilbert Lee O'Daniel	Democrat	1939–1941
Coke R. Stevenson	Democrat	1941–1947
Beauford H. Jester	Democrat	1947–1949
Robert Allan Shivers	Democrat	1949–1957
Marion Price Daniel	Democrat	1957–1963
John B. Connally, Jr.	Democrat	1963–1969
Preston Smith	Democrat	1969–1973
Dolph Briscoe, Jr.	Democrat	1973–1979
William P. Clements	Republican	1979–1983
Mark Wells White	Democrat	1983–1987
William P. Clements	Republican	1987–1991
Ann W. Richards	Democrat	1991–1995

George W. Bush	Republican	1995–2000
Rick Perry	Republican	2000–2003

UTAH

Heber Manning Wells	Republican	1896–1905
John Christopher Cutler	Republican	1905–1909
William Spry	Republican	1909–1917
Simon Bamberger	Democrat	1917–1921
Charles R. Mabey	Republican	1921–1925
George H. Dern	Democrat	1925–1933
Henry Hooper Blood	Democrat	1933–1941
Herbert B. Maw	Democrat	1941–1949
Joseph Bracken Lee	Republican	1949–1957
George Dewey Clyde	Republican	1957–1965
Calvin L. Rampton	Democrat	1965–1977
Scott M. Matheson	Democrat	1977–1985
Norman H. Bangerter	Republican	1985–1993
Michael O. Leavitt	Republican	1993–2005

VERMONT

Thomas Chittenden		1790–1797
Paul Brigham		1797
Isaac Tichenor	Federalist	1797–1807
Israel Smith	Democratic-Republican	1807–1808
Isaac Tichenor	Federalist	1808–1809
Jonas Galusha	Democratic-Republican	1809–1813
Martin Chittenden	Federalist	1813–1815
Jonas Galusha	Democratic-Republican	1815–1820
Richard Skinner	Democratic-Republican	1820–1823
C. P. Van Ness	Democratic-Republican	1823–1826
Ezra Butler	Democratic-Republican	1826–1828
Samuel C. Crafts	National Republican	1828–1831
William A. Palmer	Anti-Mason	1831–1835
Silas H. Jennison	Whig	1835–1841
Charles Paine	Whig	1841–1843
John Mattocks	Whig	1843–1844

William Slade	Whig	1844–1846
Horace Eaton	Whig	1846–1848
Carlos Coolidge	Whig	1848–1850
Charles K. Wiliams	Whig	1850–1852
Erastus Fairbanks	Whig	1852–1853
John S. Robinson	Democrat	1853–1854
Stephen Royce	Whig-Republican	1854–1856
Ryland Fletcher	Republican	1856–1858
Hiland Hall	Republican	1858–1860
Erastus Fairbanks	Republican	1860–1861
Frederick Holbrook	Republican	1861–1863
J. Gregory Smith	Republican	1863–1865
Paul Dillingham	Republican	1865–1867
John B. Page	Republican	1867–1869
Peter T. Washburn	Republican	1869–1870
George W. Hendee	Republican	1870
John W. Stewart	Republican	1870–1872
Julius Converse	Republican	1872–1874
Asahel Peck	Republican	1874–1876
Horace Fairbanks	Republican	1876–1878
Redfield Proctor	Republican	1878–1880
Roswell Farnham	Republican	1880–1882
John L. Barstow	Republican	1882–1884
Samuel E. Pingree	Republican	1884–1886
Ebenezer J. Ormsbee	Republican	1886–1888
William P. Dillingham	Republican	1888–1890
Carroll S. Page	Republican	1890–1892
Levi K. Fuller	Republican	1892–1894
Urban A. Woodbury	Republican	1894–1896
Josiah Grout	Republican	1896–1898
Edward C. Smith	Republican	1898–1900
William Wallace Stickney	Republican	1900–1902
John Griffith McCullough	Republican	1902–1904
Charles J. Bell	Republican	1904–1906
Fletcher Dutton Proctor	Republican	1906–1908
George H. Prouty	Republican	1908–1910
John A. Mead	Republican	1910–1912

Allen Miller Fletcher	Republican	1912–1915
Charles Winslow Gates	Republican	1915–1917
Horace French Graham	Republican	1917–1919
Percival Wood Clement	Republican	1919–1921
James Hartness	Republican	1921–1923
Redfield Proctor	Republican	1923–1925
Franklin Swift Billings	Republican	1925–1927
John Eliakim Weeks	Republican	1927–1931
Stanley C. Wilson	Republican	1931–1935
Charles Manley Smith	Republican	1935–1937
George D. Aiken	Republican	1937–1941
William H. Wills	Republican	1941–1945
Mortimer Robinson Proctor	Republican	1945–1947
Ernest W. Gibson	Republican	1947–1950
Harold J. Arthur	Republican	1950–1951
Lee E. Emerson	Republican	1951–1955
Joseph Blaine Johnson	Republican	1955–1959
Robert T. Stafford	Republican	1959–1961
Frank Ray Keyser, Jr.	Republican	1961–1963
Philip H. Hoff	Democrat	1963–1969
Deane Chandler Davis	Republican	1969–1973
Thomas P. Salmon	Democrat	1973–1977
Richard A. Snelling	Republican	1977–1985
Madeleine M. Kunin	Democrat	1985–1991
Richard A. Snelling	Republican	1991
Howard Dean	Democrat	1991–2005

VIRGINIA

Beverley Randolph		1788–1791
Henry Lee		1791–1794
Robert Brooke		1794–1796
James Wood	Democratic-Republican	1796–1799
James Monroe	Democratic-Republican	1799–1802
John Page	Democratic-Republican	1802–1805
William H. Cabell	Democratic-Republican	1805–1808
John Tyler, Sr.	Democratic-Republican	1808–1811
James Monroe	Democratic-Republican	1811

George William Smith	Democratic-Republican	1811 (Acting)
Peyton Randolph	Democratic-Republican	1811–1812 (Acting)
James Barbour	Democratic-Republican	1812–1814
Wilson Carey Nicholas	Democratic-Republican	1814–1816
James P. Preston	Democratic-Republican	1816–1819
Thomas M. Randolph	Democratic-Republican	1819–1822
James Pleasants, Jr.	Democratic-Republican	1822–1825
John Tyler, Jr.	Democratic-Republican	1825–1827
William B. Giles	Democrat	1827–1830
John Floyd	Democrat	1830–1834
Littleton W. Tazewell	Democrat	1834–1836
Wyndham Robertson	Democrat	1836–1837 (Acting)
David Campbell	Democrat	1837–1840
Thomas W. Gilmer	Whig	1840–1841
John Mercer Patton	Whig	1841 (Acting)
John Rutherford	Whig	1841–1842 (Acting)
John M. Gregory	Whig	1842–1843 (Acting)
James McDowell	Whig	1843–1846
William Smith	Democrat	1846–1849
John B. Floyd	Democrat	1849–1852
Joseph Johnson	Democrat	1852–1856
Henry A. Wise	Democrat	1856–1860
John Letcher	Democrat	1860–1864
William Smith	Democrat	1864–1865
Francis H. Pierpont		1861–1868 (Provisional)
Henry H. Wells		1868–1869 (Provisional)
Gilbert C. Walker	Conservative	1869–1874 (Provisional)
James Lawson Kemper	Democrat	1874–1878
Frederick W. M. Holliday	Democrat	1878–1882
William E. Cameron	Readjuster	1882–1886
Fitzhugh Lee	Democrat	1886–1890
Philip W. McKinney	Democrat	1890–1894
Charles T. O'Ferrall	Democrat	1894–1898
James Hoge Tyler	Democrat	1898–1902
Andrew J. Montague	Democrat	1902–1906
Claude A. Swanson	Democrat	1906–1910
William H. Mann	Democrat	1910–1914

Henry C. Stuart	Democrat	1914–1918
Westmoreland Davis	Democrat	1918–1922
E. Lee Trinkle	Democrat	1922–1926
Harry F. Byrd	Democrat	1926–1930
John G. Pollard	Democrat	1930–1934
George C. Peery	Democrat	1934–1938
James H. Price	Democrat	1938–1942
Colgate W. Darden, Jr.	Democrat	1942–1946
William M. Tuck	Democrat	1946–1950
John S. Battle	Democrat	1950–1954
Thomas B. Stanley	Democrat	1954–1958
J. Lindsay Almond, Jr.	Democrat	1958–1962
Albertis S. Harrison, Jr.	Democrat	1962–1966
Mills E. Godwin, Jr.	Democrat	1966–1970
Linwood Holton	Republican	1970–1974
Milles E. Godwin, Jr.	Republican	1974–1978
John Dalton	Republican	1978–1982
Charles S. Robb	Democrat	1982–1986
Gerald L. Baliles	Democrat	1986–1990
Lawrence Douglas Wilder	Democrat	1990–1994
George Allen	Republican	1994–1998
James S. Gilmore III	Republican	1998–2002

WASHINGTON

Elisha P. Ferry	Republican	1889–1893
John H. McGraw	Republican	1893–1897
John R. Rogers	People's-Democrat	1897–1901
Henry McBride	Republican	1901–1905
Albert E. Mead	Republican	1905–1909
Samuel G. Cosgrove	Republican	1909
Marion E. Hay	Republican	1909–1913
Ernest Lister	Democrat	1913–1919
Louis Folwell Hart	Republican	1919–1925
Roland Hill Hartley	Republican	1925–1933
Clarence D. Martin	Democrat	1933–1941
Arthur B. Langlie	Republican	1941–1945
Monrad C. Wallgren	Democrat	1945–1949

Arthur B. Langlie	Republican	1949–1957
Albert D. Rosellini	Democrat	1957–1965
Daniel J. Evans	Republican	1965–1977
Dixy Lee Ray	Democrat	1977–1981
John D. Spellman	Republican	1981–1985
Booth Gardner	Democrat	1985–1993
Mike Lowry	Democrat	1993–1997
Gary Locke	Democrat	1997–2005

WEST VIRGINIA

Arthur I. Boreman	Union Republican–Republic	1863–1869
Daniel Duane Tompkins Farnsworth	Republican	1869
William E. Stevenson	Republican	1869–1871
John Jeremiah Jacob	Democrat-Independent	1871–1877
Henry Mason Mathews	Democrat	1877–1881
Jacob B. Jackson	Democrat	1881–1885
Emanuel Willis Wilson	Democrat	1885–1890
Aretas Brooks Fleming	Democrat	1890–1893
William A. MacCorkle	Democrat	1893–1897
George W. Atkinson	Republican	1897–1901
Albert B. White	Republican	1901–1905
William Mercer Owens Dawson	Republican	1905–1909
William E. Glasscock	Republican	1909–1913
Henry D. Hatfield	Republican	1913–1917
John J. Cornwell	Democrat	1917–1921
Ephraim F. Morgan	Republican	1921–1925
Howard M. Gore	Republican	1925–1929
William G. Conley	Republican	1929–1933
Herman G. Kump	Democrat	1933–1937
Homer A. Holt	Democrat	1937–1941
Matthew M. Neely	Democrat	1941–1945
Clarence W. Meadows	Democrat	1945–1949
Okey L. Patteson	Democrat	1949–1953
William C. Marland	Democrat	1953–1957
Cecil H. Underwood	Republican	1957–1961

William W. Barron	Democrat	1961–1965
Hulett C. Smith	Democrat	1965–1969
Arch A. Moore, Jr.	Republican	1969–1977
John D. Rockefeller IV	Democrat	1977–1985
Arch A. Moore, Jr.	Republican	1985–1989
William Gaston Caperton III	Democrat	1989–1997
Cecil H. Underwood	Republican	1997–2001
Bob Wise	Democrat	2001–2005

WISCONSIN

Nelson Dewey	Democrat	1848–1852
Leonard J. Farwell	Whig	1852–1854
William A. Barstow	Democrat	1854–1856
Arthur McArthur	Democrat	1856
Coles Bashford	Republican	1856–1858
Alex W. Randall	Republican	1858–1862
Louis P. Harvey	Republican	1862
Edward Salomon	Republican	1862–1864
James T. Lewis	Republican	1864–1866
Lucius Fairchild	Republican	1866–1872
C. C. Washburn	Republican	1872–1874
William R. Taylor	Democrat	1874–1876
Harrison Ludington	Republican	1876–1878
William E. Smith	Republican	1878–1882
Jeremiah M. Rusk	Republican	1882–1889
William D. Hoard	Republican	1889–1891
George W. Peck	Democrat	1891–1895
William H. Upham	Republican	1895–1897
Edward Scofield	Republican	1897–1901
Robert M. LaFollette	Republican	1901–1906
James O. Davidson	Republican	1906–1911
Francis E. McGovern	Republican	1911–1915
Emanuel Lorenz Philipp	Republican	1915–1921
John J. Blaine	Republican	1921–1927
Fred R. Zimmerman	Republican	1927–1929
Walter Jodok Kohler, Sr.	Republican	1929–1931

Philip Fox LaFollette	Republican	1931–1933
Albert G. Schmedeman	Democrat	1933–1935
Philip Fox LaFollette	Progressive	1935–1939
Julius P. Heil	Republican	1939–1943
Orland S. Loomis	Progressive	(Died before taking office)
Walter S. Goodland	Republican	1943–1947
Oscar Rennebohm	Republican	1947–1951
Walter J. Kohler, Jr.	Republican	1951–1957
Vernon W. Thomson	Republican	1957–1959
Gaylord A. Nelson	Democrat	1959–1963
John W. Reynolds	Democrat	1963–1965
Warren Perley Knowles	Republican	1965–1971
Patrick J. Lucey	Democrat	1971–1977
M. J. Schreiber	Democrat	1977–1979
Lee S. Dreyfus	Republican	1979–1983
Anthony S. Earl	Democrat	1983–1987
Tommy G. Thompson	Republican	1987–2003

WYOMING

Francis E. Warren	Republican	1890
Amos W. Barber	Republican	1890–1893
John E. Osborne	Democrat	1893–1895
W. A. Richards	Republican	1895–1899
DeForest Richards	Republican	1899–1903
Fenimore C. Chatterton	Republican	1903–1905
Bryant Butler Brooks	Republican	1905–1911
Joseph Maull Carey	Democrat	1911–1915
John B. Kendrick	Democrat	1915–1917
Frank L. Houx	Democrat	1917–1919
Robert D. Carey	Republican	1919–1923
William Bradford Ross	Democrat	1923–1924
Frank E. Lucas	Republican	1924–1925
Nellie Tayloe Ross	Democrat	1925–1927
Frank C. Emerson	Republican	1927–1931
Alonzo M. Clark	Republican	1931–1933
Leslie A. Miller	Democrat	1933–1939
Nels Hanson Smith	Republican	1939–1943

Lester C. Hunt	Democrat	1943–1949
Arthur Griswold Crane	Republican	1949–1951
Frank A. Barrett	Republican	1951–1953
Clifford Joy "Doc" Rogers	Republican	1953–1955
Milward L. Simpson	Republican	1955–1959
John J. Hickey	Democrat	1959–1961
Jack Robert Gage	Democrat	1961–1963
Clifford P. Hansen	Republican	1963–1967
Stanley Knapp Hathaway	Republican	1967–1975
Ed Herschler	Democrat	1975–1987
Michael J. Sullivan	Democrat	1987–1995
Jim Geringer	Republican	1995–2003

AMERICAN SAMOA

Peter Tali Coleman	Republican	1977–1985
A. P. Lutali	Democrat	1985–1989
Peter Tali Coleman	Republican	1989–1997
Tauese P. F. Sunia	Democrat	1997–2001

COMMONWEALTH OF THE NORTHERN MARIANA ISLANDS

Carlos Camacho	Democrat*	1978–1982
Pedro P. Tenorio	Republican*	1982–1986
Lorenzo Deleon Guerrero	Republican*	1986–1990
Froilan Tenorio	Democrat*	1990–1998
Pedro P. Tenorio	Republican*	1998–2002

*Parties are not affiliated with U.S. political parties of the same name.

GUAM

Carlos Camacho	Republican	1971–1974
Ricardo J. Bordallo	Democrat	1975–1978
Paul M. Cavo	Republican	1979–1982
Ricardo J. Bordallo	Democrat	1983–1986
Joseph F. Ada	Republican	1987–1994
Carl T. C. Gutierrez	Democrat	1995–

PUERTO RICO

Luis Muñoz Marín	Popular Democratic	1948–1964
Roberto Sánchez Vilella	Popular Democratic	1964–1968
Luis A Ferré Aguayo	New Progressive	1968–1972
Rafael Hernández Colón	Popular Democratic	1972–1976
Carlos Romero Barceló	New Progressive	1976–1984
Rafael Hernández Colón	Popular Democratic	1984–1992
Pedro Rosselló González	New Progressive	1992–2000

U.S. VIRGIN ISLANDS

Melvin H. Evans, M.D.	Republican	1971–1975
Cyril Emmanual King	Independent	1975–1978
Juan Francisco Luis	Independent	1978–1987
Alexander A. Farrelly	Democrat	1987–1993
Roy L. Schneider, M.D.	Independent	1993–1999
Charles Wesley Turnbull	Democrat	1999–

NOTE

1. Primary sources for this chapter include *The Book of Governors*, compiled by William Welch Hunt (Los Angeles: Washington Typographers, 1935), for information about state governors prior to 1900. Congressional Quarterly's *Guide to U.S. Elections* was used with permission to supplement Hunt's compilation with political party information for the same period. *The Governors of the States, 1900–74*, compiled by Samuel R. Solomon (Lexington, Ky.: The Council of State Governments), was used with permission for information on state governors from 1900–1974. The Council of State Governments', *Book of the States* was used for later data. In addition, a number of websites provided by the states and territories themselves were consulted. These include: "Alabama Governors" (www.archives.state.al.us/govslist.html); "Arizona's Governors" (www.governor.state.az.us / kids / govs.html); "Governors of California—Biographies" (www.governor.ca.gov/govgallery/h/biography/index); "Colorado Governors" (www.archives.state.co.us/offic/gov.html); "Florida Governors Portraits" (www.dhr.dos. state.fl.us/governors);

"Georgia Governors" (www.cviog.uga.edu/Projects/gainfo/gagovs.htm); "Governors of the Great State of Idaho" (www.state.id.us/gov/pastgov.htm); "Indiana Governors: Sequential List of Indiana Governors" (www.statelib.in.us/WWW/ihb/govlist.html); "Governors" (www.sos.state.ia.us/register/r7/r7hgov.htm); "Governors of Maine" (www.state.me.us/legis/lawlib/govs.htm); "Maryland State Archives, Governors of Maryland 1634–1689" (www.mdarchives.state.md.us/ . . . ccol/sc2600/sc2685/html); "New Hampshire Almanac—Governors" (www.state.nh.us/nhinfo/gov.html); "North Carolina Governors" (www.itpi.dpi.state.nc.us/governors/gov1.html); "Past Governors of Tennessee" (www.state.tn.us/sos/bluebook/formgov.htm); "Governors of the State of Texas" (isadore.tsl.state.tx.us/dir/ref_faq.dir/.files/governor.txt); "The Governors of Virginia" (www.state.va.us/home/vagov/governor5.html); "West Virginia's Governors" (www.wvlc.wvnet.edu/history/govmenu.html); "The Government of the U.S. Virgin Islands—Past Governors" (www.gov.vi/html/pastgov.html).

The American Samoa list was provided by

Marty Yerick, Delegate's Office, Washington, D.C. The Commonwealth of the Northern Mariana Islands (CNMI) list was provided by Bob Schwalbach of the CNMI Resident Representative's Office. The list of Guam's elected governors was provided by the Governor of Guam's Office.

The list of governors of Puerto Rico was supplied by Krystall Molino, Communications and Press Division, Puerto Rico Federal Affairs Administration, Office of the Governor, from "Governors of Puerto Rico, 1948–2000" (http://eleccionespuertorico.org/archivo/1948–88.html).

17

State Professional Sports Teams

Professional sports are a big and constantly changing business. Twenty-nine states and the District of Columbia are now homes to 172 teams in nine professional leagues: the Arena Football League, Major League Baseball, Major League Soccer, the National Basketball Association, the National Football League, the National Hockey League, the National Professional Soccer League, the Women's National Basketball Association, and the Women's Professional Softball League. Some franchises claim a very old history. The Cincinnati Reds trace their roots back to 1869 and the St. Louis Cardinals to 1881. But an old history does not mean things remained constant. The Atlanta Braves, for example, trace their history to 1871 in Boston, where they were known over the years there as the Redstockings, Red Caps, Beaneaters, Doves, Pilgrims, Bees, and Braves. Then the team moved to Milwaukee before landing in Atlanta. Many professional teams are of very recent vintage. The new millennium introduced the National Hockey League's Minnesota Wild and the Arena Football League's Detroit Fury, as well as the Women's National Basketball Association's Miami Sol, to name just a few.

WEB SITES FOR PROFESSIONAL LEAGUES

Arena Football League: www.arenafootball. com

Major League Baseball: www. majorleaguebaseball.com

Major League Soccer: www.mlsnet.com

National Basketball Association: www.nba. com

National Football League: www.nfl.com

National Hockey League: www.nhl.com

National Professional Soccer League: www. npsl.com

Women's National Basketball Association: www.wnba.com

Women's Professional Softball League: www.prosoftball.com

In the list that follows the date in parentheses following the team name is the year in which the team was founded. Following the current name of the team is the league in which it plays and the former name or names of the team, if applicable.

ARIZONA

Arizona Cardinals (1920)
   National Football League
   Previous Names: Racine Cardinals, Chicago Cardinals, St. Louis Cardinals, Phoenix Cardinals

Arizona Diamondbacks (1998)
   Major League Baseball
   Previous Names: None

Arizona Rattlers (1992)
Arena Football League
Previous Names: None

Phoenix Coyotes (1979)
National Hockey League
Previous Names: Winnipeg Jets

Phoenix Mercury (1997)
Women's National Basketball Association
Previous Names: None

Phoenix Suns (1968)
National Basketball Association
Previous Names: None

CALIFORNIA

Anaheim Angels (1961)
Major League Baseball
Previous Names: Los Angeles Angels, California Angels

Golden State Warriors (1946)
National Basketball Association
Previous Names: Philadelphia Warriors, San Francisco Warriors

Los Angeles Avengers (2000)
Arena Football League
Previous Names: None

Los Angeles Clippers (1970)
National Basketball Association
Previous Names: Buffalo Braves, San Diego Clippers

Los Angeles Dodgers (1884)
Major League Baseball
Previous Names: Brooklyn Bridegrooms, Brooklyn Superbas, Brooklyn Robins, Brooklyn Dodgers

Los Angeles Galaxy (1996)
Major League Soccer
Previous Names: None

Los Angeles Kings (1967)
National Hockey League
Previous Names: None

Los Angeles Lakers (1947)
National Basketball Association
Previous Names: Minneapolis Lakers

Los Angeles Sparks (1997)
Women's National Basketball Association
Previous Names: None

Mighty Ducks of Anaheim (1993)
National Hockey League
Previous Names: None

Oakland Athletics (1901)
Major League Baseball
Previous Names: Philadelphia Athletics, Kansas City Athletics

Oakland Raiders (1960)
National Football League
Previous Names: Los Angeles Raiders

Sacramento Kings (1948)
National Basketball Association
Previous Names: Rochester Royals, Cincinnati Royals, Kansas City–Omaha Kings, Kansas City Kings

Sacramento Monarchs (1997)
Women's National Basketball Association
Previous Names: None

San Diego Chargers (1960)
National Football League
Previous Names: Los Angeles Chargers

San Diego Padres (1969)
Major League Baseball
Previous Names: None

San Francisco 49ers (1946)
National Football League
Previous Names: None

San Francisco Giants (1883)
Major League Baseball
Previous Names: New York Gothams,
New York Giants

San Jose Clash (1996)
Major League Soccer
Previous Names: None

San Jose SaberCats (1995)
Arena Football League
Previous Names: None

San Jose Sharks (1990)
National Hockey League
Previous Names: None

COLORADO

Colorado Avalanche (1979)
National Hockey League
Previous Names: Quebec Nordiques

Colorado Rapids (1996)
Major League Soccer
Previous Names: None

Colorado Rockies (1993)
Major League Baseball
Previous Names: None

Denver Broncos (1960)
National Football League
Previous Names: None

Denver Nuggets (1976)
National Basketball Association
Previous Names: None

CONNECTICUT

New England Sea Wolves (1997)
Arena Football League
Previous Names: New York City Hawks

FLORIDA

Florida Bobcats (1992)
Arena Football League
Previous Names: Sacramento Attack, Miami Hooters

Florida Marlins (1993)
Major League Baseball
Previous Names: None

Florida Panthers (1993)
National Hockey League
Previous Names: None

Jacksonville Jaguars (1995)
National Football League
Previous Names: None

Miami Dolphins (1966)
National Football League
Previous Names: None

Miami Fusion (1998)
Major League Soccer
Previous Names: None

Miami Heat (1988)
National Basketball Association
Previous Names: None

Miami Sol (2000)
Women's National Basketball Association
Previous Names: None

Orlando Magic (1989)
National Basketball Association
Previous Names: None

Orlando Miracle (1999)
Women's National Basketball Association
Previous Names: None

Orlando Predators (1991)
Arena Football League
Previous Names: None

Tampa Bay Buccaneers (1976)
National Football League
Previous Names: None

Tampa Bay Devil Rays (1998)
Major League Baseball
Previous Names: None

Tampa Bay Firestix (1997)
Women's Professional Softball League
Previous Names: None

Tampa Bay Lightning (1991)
National Hockey League
Previous Names: None

Tampa Bay Mutiny (1996)
Major League Soccer
Previous Names: None

Tampa Bay Storm (1987)
Arena Football League
Previous Names: Pittsburgh Gladiators.

GEORGIA

Atlanta Braves (1871)
Major League Baseball
Previous Names: Boston Redstockings, Boston Red Caps, Boston Beaneaters, Boston Doves, Boston Pilgrims, Boston Bees, Boston Braves, Milwaukee Braves

Atlanta Falcons (1966)
National Football League
Previous Names: None

Atlanta Hawks (1949)
National Basketball Association
Previous Names: Tri-Cities Blackhawks, Milwaukee Hawks, St. Louis Hawks

Atlanta Thrashers (1997)
National Hockey League
Previous Names: None

Georgia Pride (1997)
Women's Professional Softball League
Previous Names: None.

ILLINOIS

Chicago Bears (1920)
National Football League
Previous Names: Decatur Staleys, Chicago Staleys

Chicago Blackhawks (1926)
National Hockey League
Previous Names: None

Chicago Bulls (1966)
National Basketball Association
Previous Names: None

Chicago Cubs (1871)
Major League Baseball
Previous Names: Chicago White Stockings, Chicago Colts, Chicago Orphans

Chicago Fire (1998)
Major League Soccer
Previous Names: None

Chicago White Sox (1901)
Major League Baseball
Previous Names: None.

INDIANA

Indiana Colts (1953)
National Football League
Previous Names: Baltimore Colts

Indiana Fever (2000)
Women's National Basketball Association
Previous Names: None

Indiana Pacers (1967)
National Basketball Association
Previous Names: None.

IOWA

Iowa Barnstormers (1995)
Arena Football League
Previous Names: None

KANSAS

Wichita Wings (1992)
National Professional Soccer League
Previous Names: None

LOUISIANA

New Orleans Saints (1967)
National Football League
Previous Names: None

MARYLAND

Baltimore Blast (1992)
National Professional Soccer League
Previous Names: Baltimore Spirit

Baltimore Orioles (1901)
Major League Baseball
Previous Names: Milwaukee Brewers, St.
Louis Browns

Baltimore Ravens (1996)
National Football League
Previous Names: None.

MASSACHUSETTS

Boston Bruins (1924)
National Hockey League
Previous Names: None

Boston Celtics (1946)
National Basketball Association
Previous Names: None

Boston Red Sox (1871)
Major League Baseball
Previous Names: Boston Red Stockings,

Boston Somersets, Boston Pilgrims, Boston Puritans

New England Patriots (1960)
National Football League
Previous Names: Boston Patriots

New England Revolution (1996)
Major League Soccer
Previous Names: None

MICHIGAN

Detroit Fury (2000)
Arena Football League
Previous Names: None

Detroit Lions (1930)
National Football League
Previous Names: Portsmouth Spartans

Detroit Pistons (1941)
National Basketball Association
Previous Names: Fort Wayne Zollner Pistons; Fort Wayne Pistons

Detroit Red Wings (1926)
National Hockey League
Previous Names: None

Detroit Rockers (1990)
National Professional Soccer League
Previous Names: None

Detroit Shock (1998)
Women's National Basketball Association
Previous Names: None

Detroit Tigers (1901)
Major League Baseball
Previous Names: None

Grand Rapids Rampage (1998)
Arena Football League
Previous Names: None

MINNESOTA

Minneapolis Timberwolves (1989)
  National Basketball Association
  Previous Names: None

Minnesota Lynx (1999)
  Women's National Basketball Association
  Previous Names: None

Minnesota Twins (1901)
  Major League Baseball
  Previous Names: Washington Senators

Minnesota Vikings (1961)
  National Football League
  Previous Names: None

Minnesota Wild (2000)
  National Hockey League
  Previous Names: None

MISSOURI

Kansas City Attack (1989)
  National Professional Soccer League
  Previous Names: Atlanta Attack

Kansas City Chiefs (1960)
  National Football League
  Previous Names: Dallas Texans

Kansas City Royals (1969)
  Major League Baseball
  Previous Names: None

Kansas City Wizards (1996)
  Major League Soccer
  Previous Names: Kansas City Wiz

St. Louis Ambush (1991)
  National Professional Soccer League
  Previous Names: Tulsa Ambush

St. Louis Blues (1967)
  National Hockey League
  Previous Names: None

St. Louis Cardinals (1881)
  Major League Baseball
  Previous Names: St. Louis Brown Stock-
    ings, St. Louis Browns, St. Louis Perfec-
    tos

St. Louis Rams (1937)
  National Football League
  Previous Names: Cleveland Rams, Los
    Angeles Rams

NEW JERSEY

New Jersey Devils (1972)
  National Hockey League
  Previous Names: Kansas City Scouts, Col-
    orado Rockies

New Jersey Nets (1967)
  National Basketball Association
  Previous Names: New Jersey Americans,
    New York Nets

New Jersey Red Dogs (1997)
  Arena Football League
  Previous Names: None

NEW YORK

Albany Firebirds (1990)
  Arena Football League
  Previous Names: None

Buffalo Bills (1960)
  National Football League
  Previous Names: None

Buffalo Blizzards (1992)
  National Professional Soccer League
  Previous Names: None

Buffalo Destroyers (1999)
Arena Football League
Previous Names: None

Buffalo Sabres (1970)
National Hockey League
Previous Names: None

MetroStars (1996)
Major League Soccer
Previous Names: None

New York Giants (1925)
National Football League
Previous Names: None

New York Islanders (1972)
National Hockey League
Previous Names: None

New York Jets (1960)
National Football League
Previous Names: New York Titans

New York Liberty (1997)
Women's National Basketball Association
Previous Names: None

New York Mets (1962)
Major League Baseball
Previous Names: None

New York Rangers (1926)
National Hockey League
Previous Names: None

New York Yankees (1901)
Major League Baseball
Previous Names: Baltimore Orioles, New
York Highlanders

NORTH CAROLINA

Carolina Cobras (2000)
Arena Football League
Previous Names: None

Carolina Diamonds (1997)
Women's Professional Softball League
Previous Names: None

Carolina Hurricanes (1979)
National Hockey League
Previous Names: Hartford Whalers

Carolina Panthers (1995)
National Football League
Previous Names: None

Charlotte Hornets (1988)
National Basketball Association
Previous Names: None

Charlotte Sting (1997)
Women's National Basketball Association
Previous Names: None

Durham Dragons (1997)
Women's Professional Softball League
Previous Names: None

OHIO

Akron Racers (1999)
Women's Professional Softball League
Previous Names: None

Cincinnati Bengals (1968)
National Football League
Previous Names: None

Cincinnati Reds (1869)
Major League Baseball
Previous Names: Cincinnati Red Stock-
ings, Cincinnati Red Legs

Cleveland Browns (1999)
National Football League
Previous Names: None

Cleveland Cavaliers (1970)
National Basketball Association
Previous Names: None

Cleveland Crunch (1992)
National Professional Soccer League
Previous Names: None

Cleveland Indians (1901)
Major League Baseball
Previous Names: Cleveland Blues, Cleveland Broncos, Cleveland Naps

Cleveland Rockers (1997)
Women's National Basketball Association
Previous Names: None

Columbus Blue Jackets (1997)
National Hockey League
Previous Names: None

Columbus Crew (1996)
Major League Soccer
Previous Names: None

OKLAHOMA

Oklahoma City Wranglers (1995)
Arena Football League
Previous Names: Portland Forest Dragons

OREGON

Portland Fire (2000)
Women's National Basketball Association
Previous Names: None

Portland Trailblazers (1970)
National Basketball Association
Previous Names: None

PENNSYLVANIA

Harrisburg Heat (1991)
National Professional Soccer League
Previous Names: None

Philadelphia Eagles (1933)
National Football League
Previous Names: None

Philadelphia Flyers (1967)
National Hockey League
Previous Names: None

Philadelphia Kixx (1996)
National Professional Soccer League
Previous Names: None

Philadelphia Phillies (1880)
Major League Baseball
Previous Names: Worcester, Philadelphia Blue Jays

Philadelphia 76ers (1946)
National Basketball Association
Previous Names: None

Pittsburgh Penguins (1967)
National Hockey League
Previous Names: None

Pittsburgh Pirates (1882)
Major League Baseball
Previous Names: Pittsburgh Alleghenys, Pittsburgh Innocents

Pittsburgh Steelers (1933)
National Football League
Previous Names: Pittsburgh Pirates

TENNESSEE

Nashville Kats (1997)
Arena Football League
Previous Names: None

Nashville Predators (1997)
National Hockey League
Previous Names: None

Tennessee Titans (1960)
National Football League
Previous Names: Houston Oilers, Tennessee Oilers

TEXAS

Dallas Burn (1996)
Major League Soccer
Previous Names: None

Dallas Cowboys (1960)
National Football League
Previous Names: None

Dallas Mavericks (1980)
National Basketball Association
Previous Names: None

Dallas Stars (1967)
National Hockey League
Previous Names: Minnesota Northstars

Houston Astros (1962)
Major League Baseball
Previous Names: Houston Colt 45's

Houston Comets (1997)
Women's National Basketball Association
Previous Names: None

Houston Rockets (1967)
National Basketball Association
Previous Names: San Diego Rockets

Houston ThunderBears (1996)
Arena Football League
Previous Names: None

San Antonio Spurs (1967)
National Basketball Association
Previous Names: Dallas Chaparrals, Texas
Chaparrals

Texas Rangers (1961)
Major League Baseball
Previous Names: Washington Senators

UTAH

Utah Jazz (1974)
National Basketball Association
Previous Names: New Orleans Jazz

Utah Starzz (1997)
Women's Basketball Association
Previous Names: None

VIRGINIA

Virginia Roadsters (1997)
Women's Professional Softball League
Previous Names: None

WASHINGTON

Seattle Mariners (1977)
Major League Baseball
Previous Names: None

Seattle Seahawks (1976)
National Football League
Previous Names: None

Seattle Storm (2000)
Women's National Basketball Association
Previous Names: None

Seattle SuperSonics (1967)
National Basketball Association
Previous Names: None

WISCONSIN

Green Bay Packers (1921)
National Football League
Previous Names: None

Milwaukee Brewers (1969)
Major League Baseball
Previous Names: Seattle Pilots

Milwaukee Bucks (1968)
National Basketball Association
Previous Names: None

Milwaukee Mustangs (1994)
Arena Football League
Previous Names: None

Milwaukee Wave (1984)
National Professional Soccer Association
Previous Names: None

DISTRICT OF COLUMBIA

D.C. United (1996)
Major League Soccer
Previous Names: None

Washington Capitals (1974)
National Hockey League
Previous Names: None

Washington Mystics (1998)
Women's National Basketball Association
Previous Names: None

Washington Redskins (1932)
National Football League
Previous Names: Boston Braves, Boston Redskins

Washington Wizards (1961)
National Basketball Association
Previous Names: Chicago Packers, Chicago Zephyrs, Baltimore Bullets, Capitol Bullets, Washington Bullets

Selected Bibliography of State and Territory Histories

ALABAMA

Du Bose, Joel C. *Alabama History*. Richmond: B. F. Johnson, 1908.

Griffith, Lucille B. *Alabama: A Documentary History*. Rev. and enl. ed. Tuscaloosa: University of Alabama Press, 1972.

Hamilton, Virginia V. *Alabama, A History*. New York: Norton; Nashville: American Association for State and Local History, 1984.

Moore, Albert B. *History of Alabama and Her People*. 3 vols. Chicago: American Historical Society, 1927.

Owen, Marie B. *The Story of Alabama; A History of the State*. 5 vols. New York: Lewis Historical Publishing Company, 1949.

Owen, Thomas M. *History of Alabama and Dictionary of Alabama Biography*. 4 vols. Chicago: S. J. Clarke, 1921.

Rogers, William W. et al. *Alabama, the History of a Deep South State*. Tuscaloosa: University of Alabama Press, 1994.

ALASKA

Andrews, Clarence L. *The Story of Alaska*. Seattle: Lowman & Hanford, 1931.

Gruening, Ernest H. *The State of Alaska*. New York: Random House, 1968.

Mangusso, Mary C., and Stephen W. Haycox, eds. *Interpreting Alaska's History*. Seattle: University of Seattle Press, 1995.

Naske, Claus-M., and Herman E. Slotnick. *Alaska, a History of the 49th State*. 2d ed. Norman: University of Oklahoma Press, 1987.

Nichols, Jeannette P. *Alaska*. New York: Russell & Russell, 1963.

Ritter, Harry. *Alaska's History: The People, Land, and Events of the North Country*. Anchorage: Alaska Northwest Books, 1993.

Wold, Jo Anne. *The Way It Was: Of People, Places, and Things in Pioneer Interior Alaska*. Anchorage: Alaska Northwest Publishing Company, 1988.

ARIZONA

Farish, Thomas E. *History of Arizona*. 8 vols. Phoenix: State of Arizona, 1915–1918.

Goff, John S. *Arizona, An Illustrated History of the Grand Canyon State*. Northridge, Calif.: Windsor Publications, 1988.

Leshy, John D. *The Arizona State Constitution: A Reference Guide*. Westport, Conn.: Greenwood Press, 1993.

Miller, Joseph. *Arizona; The Grand Canyon State; A State Guide*. 4th completely rev. ed. New York: Hastings House, 1966.

Officer, James E. *Hispanic Arizona, 1536–1856*. Tucson: University of Arizona Press, 1987.

Peplow, Edward H. *History of Arizona*. 3 vols. New York: Lewis Historical Publishing Company, 1958.

Sheridan, Thomas E. *Arizona: A History*. Tucson: University of Arizona Press, 1995.

Sloan, Richard E., and Ward R. Adams. *History of Arizona*. 4 vols. Phoenix: Record Publishing Company, 1930.

Walker, Henry P., and Don Bufkin. *Historical Atlas of Arizona*. 2d ed. Norman and London: University of Oklahoma Press, 1986.

Wyllys, Rufus K. *Arizona: The History of a Frontier State*. Phoenix: Hobson & Herr, 1950.

ARKANSAS

Ashmore, Harry S. *Arkansas, A History*. New York: Norton; Nashville: American Association for State and Local History, 1984.

Berry, Fred, and John Novak. *The History of Arkansas*. Little Rock: Rose Publishing Company, 1987.

Fletcher, John G. *Arkansas*. Chapel Hill: University of North Carolina Press, 1947.

Goss, Kay Collett. *The Arkansas State Constitution: A Reference Guide*. Westport, Conn.: Greenwood Press, 1993.

Hanson, Gerald T., and Carl H. Moneyhon. *Historical Atlas of Arkansas*. Norman and London: University of Oklahoma Press, 1989.

Herndon, Dallas T. *Centennial History of Arkansas*. Easley, S.C.: Southern Historical Press, 1984; originally published in 1922.

McNutt, Walter S., et al. *A History of Arkansas*. Little Rock: Democrat Printing and Lithographing, 1932.

Thomas, David Y. *Arkansas and Its People, A History, 1541–1930*. 4 vols. New York: American Historical Society, 1930.

Williams, C. Fred, and Starr Mitchell. *Arkansas, An Illustrated History of the Land of Opportunity*. Northridge, Calif.: Windsor Publications, 1986.

CALIFORNIA

Bancroft, Hubert H. *California*. 7 vols. San Francisco: A. L. Bancroft, 1884–1890.

Boule, Mary Null. *The Missions: California's Heritage*. 21 vols. Vashon, Wash.: Merryant Publishers, 1988.

Chapman, Charles E. *A History of California: The Spanish Period*. New York: Macmillan, 1921.

Cleland, Robert G. *A History of California: The American Period*. Westport, Conn.: Greenwood Press, 1975; reprint of 1922 edition.

Fehrenbacher, Don E. *A Basic History of California*. Princeton, N.J.: Van Nostrand, 1964.

Grodin, Joseph R., Calvin R. Massey, and Richard B. Cunningham. *The California State Constitution: A Reference Guide*. Westport, Conn.: Greenwood Press, 1993.

Hutchinson, William H. *California; Two Centuries of Man, Land, and Growth in the Golden State*. Palo Alto: American West Publishing Company, 1969.

Lavender, David S. *California, a History*. New York: Norton; Nashville: American Association for State and Local History, 1985.

Rawls, James J. and Walton Bean. *California: An Interpretive History*. 7th ed. New York: McGraw-Hill, 1998.

Rice, Richard B., et al. *The Elusive Eden: A New History of California*. 2d ed. New York: McGraw-Hill, 1996.

Rolle, Andrew F. *California: A History*. 5th ed., rev. and exp. Wheeling, Ill.: Harlan Davidson, 1998.

Wheeler, B. Gordon. *Black California: The History of African-Americans in the Golden State*. New York: Hippocrene Books, 1992.

COLORADO

Abbott, Carl, et al. *Colorado: A History of the Centennial State*. 3d ed. Niwot: University Press of Colorado, 1994.

Echevarria, Evelio, and Jose Otero, eds. *Hispanic Colorado: Four Centuries of History and Heritage*. Fort Collins, Colo.: Centennial Publications, 1976.

Ellis, Richard N., and Duane A. Smith. *Colorado: A History in Photographs*. Niwot: University Press of Colorado, 1991.

Hafen, LeRoy R., ed. *Colorado and Its People; A Narrative and Topical History of the Centennial State*. 4 vols. New York: Lewis Historical Publishing Company, 1948.

Hall, Frank. *History of the State of Colorado . . .* 4 vols. Chicago: Blakely Printing Company, 1889–1895.

May, Stephen. *Pilgrimage: A Journey through Colorado's History and Culture*. Athens: Swallow Press/Ohio University Press, 1987.

Schmidt, Cynthia. *Colorado: Grassroots*. Phoenix: Cloud Publishing, 1984.

Sprague, Marshall. *Colorado: A Bicentennial History*. New York: Norton, 1976.

———. *Colorado, A History*. New York: Norton; Nashville: American Association for State and Local History, 1984.

Stone, Wilbur F. *History of Colorado*. 6 vols. Chicago: S. J. Clarke, 1918–1919.

Ubbelohde, Carl, et al. *A Colorado History*. 7th ed. Boulder: Pruett Publishing Company, 1995.

CONNECTICUT

Bingham, Harold J. *History of Connecticut*. 4 vols. New York: Lewis Historical Publishing Company, 1962.

Grant, Ellsworth S., and Oliver O. Jensen. *The Miracle of Connecticut*. Hartford: Connecticut Historical Society and Fenwick Productions, 1992.

Horton, Wesley W. *The Connecticut State Constitution: A Reference Guide*. Westport, Conn.: Greenwood Press, 1993.

Morgan, Forrest, ed. *Connecticut As a Colony and As a State, or One of the Original Thirteen*. 4 vols. Hartford: Publishing Society of Connecticut, 1904.

Osborn, Norris G. *History of Connecticut in Monographic Form*. 5 vols. New York: The States History Company, 1925.

Roth, David M. *Connecticut, a History*. New York: Norton; Nashville: American Association for State and Local History, 1985.

Sherer, Thomas E. *The Connecticut Atlas*. 2d ed. Old Lyme, Conn.: Kilderatlas Publishing Company, 1992.

Trumbull, Benjamin. *A Complete History of Connecticut*. New York: Arno Press, 1972; reprint of 1818 edition.

DELAWARE

Conrad, Henry C. *History of the State of Delaware*. 3 vols. Wilmington: The Author, 1908.

Eckman, Jeannette, et al., eds. *Delaware: A Guide to the First State*. New and rev. ed. St. Clair Shores, Mich.: Scholarly Press, 1976; reprint of 1955 edition.

Munroe, John A. *History of Delaware*. 3d ed. Newark: University of Delaware Press; London: Associated University Presses, 1993.

Reed, H. C. Roy, ed. *Delaware: A History of the First State*. 3 vols. New York: Lewis Historical Publishing Company, 1947.

Scharf, John T. *History of Delaware, 1609–1888*. 2 vols. Philadelphia: L. J. Richards, 1888.

FLORIDA

Brevard, Caroline M., and James A. Robertson. *A History of Florida from the Treaty of 1763 to Our Own Times*. 2 vols. Deland, Fla.: Florida State Historical Society, 1924–1925.

Coker, William S., et al. *Florida: From the Beginning to 1992: A Columbus Jubilee Commemorative*. Houston: Pioneer Publications, 1991.

D'Alemberte, Talbot. *The Florida State Constitution: A Reference Guide*. Westport, Conn.: Greenwood Press, 1991.

Dovell, Junius E. *Florida: Historic, Dramatic, Contemporary*. 4 vols. New York: Lewis Historical Publishing Company, 1952.

Gannon, Michael, ed. *The New History of Florida*. Gainesville: University of Florida Press, 1996.

George, Paul S., ed. *A Guide to the History of Florida*. Westport, Conn.: Greenwood Press, 1989.

Horgan, James J., and Lewis N. Wynne, eds. *Florida Decades: A Sesquicentennial History, 1845–1995*. Saint Leo: Saint Leo College Press, 1995.

Jahoda, Gloria. *Florida, a History*. New York: Norton; Nashville: American Association for State and Local History, 1984.

Keuchel, Edward F., and Judy Moore. *Florida, Enterprise under the Sun: An Illustrated History*. Chatsworth, Calif.: Windsor Publications, 1990.

Milanich, Jerald T. *Florida Indians and the Invasion from Europe*. Gainesville: University of Florida Press, 1995.

Patrick, Rembert W., and Allen Morris. *Florida under Five Flags*. 4th ed. Gainesville: University of Florida Press, 1967.

GEORGIA

Bonner, James C., and Lucien E. Roberts. *Georgia History and Government*. Spartanburg,

S.C.: Reprint Company, 1974; reprint of 1940 edition.

Clements, John. *Georgia Facts: A Comprehensive Look at Georgia Today, County by County.* Dallas: Clements Research, Inc., 1989.

Coleman, Kenneth, ed. *A History of Georgia.* 2d ed. Athens: University of Georgia Press, 1991.

Coulter, E. Merton. *Georgia; A Short History.* Chapel Hill: University of North Carolina Press, 1947.

Jones, Charles C. *The History of Georgia.* 2 vols. Boston: Houghton Mifflin, 1883.

Lane, Mills. *The People of Georgia: An Illustrated History.* 2d ed. Savannah: Library of Georgia, 1992.

——, ed. *Georgia: History Written by Those Who Lived It.* Savannah: Beehive Foundation, 1995.

London, Bonnie. *A History of Georgia.* Montgomery, Ala.: Clairmont Press, 1992.

Rice, Bradley R., and Harvey H. Jackson. *Georgia: Empire State of the South.* Northridge, Calif.: Windsor Publications, 1988.

Scott, Thomas A., ed. *Cornerstones of Georgia History: Documents That Formed the State.* Athens: University of Georgia Press, 1995.

HAWAII

Day, A. Grove. *Hawaii and Its People.* Rev. ed. New York: Meredith Press, 1968.

Kuykendall, Ralph S. *The Hawaiian Kingdom.* 3 vols. Honolulu: University of Hawaii, 1966–1968.

Kuykendall, Ralph S., and A. Grove Day. *Hawaii: A History, From Polynesian Kingdom to American State.* Rev. ed. Englewood Cliffs, N.J.: Prentice-Hall, 1961.

Lee, Anne Feder. *The Hawaii State Constitution: A Reference Guide.* Westport, Conn.: Greenwood Press, 1993.

Melendy, H. Brett. *Hawaii: America's Sugar Territory, 1898–1959.* Lewiston, N.Y.: Edwin Mellen Press, 1999.

Tabrah, Ruth M. *Hawaii, a History.* New York: Norton; Nashville: American Association for State and Local History, 1984.

Withington, Antoinette. *The Golden Cloak: An Informal History of Hawaiian Royalty and of the Development of the Government during Each Reign under Steadily Increasing Foreign Influence.* Honolulu: Mutual Publishing, 1986.

IDAHO

Arrington, Leonard J. *History of Idaho.* Moscow: University of Idaho Press; Boise: Idaho State Historical Society, 1993.

Beal, Merrill D., and Merle W. Wells. *History of Idaho.* 3 vols. New York: Lewis Historical Publishing Company, 1959.

Crowley, Donald, and Florence Heffron. *The Idaho State Constitution: A Reference Guide.* Westport, Conn.: Greenwood Press, 1994.

Hailey, John. *The History of Idaho.* Boise: Press of Syms-York Company, 1910.

Hawley, James H. *History of Idaho, The Gem of the Mountains.* 4 vols. Chicago: S. J. Clarke, 1920.

Schwantes, Carlos A. *In Mountain Shadows: A History of Idaho.* Lincoln: University of Nebraska Press, 1991.

Wells, Merle W., and Arthur A. Hart. *Idaho, Gem of the Mountains.* Northridge, Calif.: Windsor Publications, 1985.

ILLINOIS

Alvord, Clarence W., ed. *Centennial History of Illinois.* 5 vols. Chicago: A. C. McClurg, 1922, c 1918–1920.

Bridges, Roger D., and Rodney O. Davis. *Illinois, Its History and Legacy.* St. Louis: River City Publishers, 1984.

Carrier, Lois. *Illinois: Crossroads of a Continent.* Urbana: University of Illinois Press, 1993.

Clements, John. *Illinois Facts: A Comprehensive Look at Illinois Today, County by County.* Dallas: Clements Research, Inc., 1989.

Davis, James E. *Frontier Illinois.* Bloomington: Indiana University Press, 1998.

Hoffmann, John, ed. *A Guide to the History of Illinois.* Westport, Conn.: Greenwood Press, 1991.

Pease, Theodore C. *The Story of Illinois.* 3d ed.,

rev. by Marguerite J. Pease. Chicago: University of Chicago Press, 1965.

INDIANA

Barnhart, John D., and Donald Carmony. *Indiana from Frontier to Industrial Commonwealth*. 4 vols. New York: Lewis Historical Publishing Company, 1954.

Cayton, Andrew R. L. *Frontier Indiana*. Bloomington: Indiana University Press, 1996.

Esarey, Logan. *A History of Indiana*. 2 vols. in one. Indianapolis: Hoosier Heritage Press, 1970; reprint of 1915 and 1918 editions.

Hoover, Dwight W. *A Pictorial History of Indiana*. Bloomington: Indiana University Press, 1998.

Madison, James H. *The Indiana Way: A State History*. Bloomington: Indiana University Press; Indianapolis: Indiana Historical Society, 1990.

Taylor, Robert M., ed. *Indiana: A New Historical Guide*. Indianapolis: Indiana Historical Society, 1989.

Taylor, Robert M., et al., eds. *Peopling Indiana: The Ethnic Experience*. Indianapolis: Indiana Historical Society, 1996.

Wilson, William E. *Indiana: A History*. Bloomington: Indiana University Press, 1966.

IOWA

Bennett, Mary. *An Iowa Album: A Photographic History, 1860–1920*. Iowa City: University of Iowa Press, 1990.

Brigham, Johnson. *Iowa: Its History and Its Foremost Citizens*. 3 vols. Chicago: S. J. Clarke, 1915.

Carpenter, Allan, et al. *Between Two Rivers: Iowa Year by Year*. 3d ed. Ames: Iowa State University Press, 1997.

Cole, Cyrenus. *A History of the People of Iowa*. Cedar Rapids: Torch Press, 1921.

———. *Iowa through the Years*. Iowa City: State Historical Society of Iowa, 1940.

Gue, Benjamin T. *History of Iowa from the Earliest Times to the Beginning of the Twentieth Century*. 4 vols. New York: Century History Company, 1903.

Harlan, Edgar R. *A Narrative History of the People of Iowa*. 5 vols. Chicago: American Historical Society, 1931.

Kimball, Donald L. *A History of Iowa*. 2 vols. Fayette, Iowa: Historic Publications (division of the Trends and Events Publishing Company), 1987.

Sabin, Henry, and Edwin L. Sabin. *The Making of Iowa*. Chicago: A. Flanagan, 1916.

Sage, Leland L. *A History of Iowa*. Ames: Iowa State University Press, 1987.

Schwieder, Dorothy. *Iowa: The Middle Land*. Ames: Iowa State University Press, 1996.

Stark, Jack. *The Iowa Constitution: A Reference Guide*. Westport, Conn.: Greenwood Press, 1998.

KANSAS

Blackmar, Frank W., ed. *Kansas: A Cyclopedia of State History . . .* in four vols. Chicago: Standard Publishing Company, 1912.

Bright, John D., ed. *Kansas: The First Century*. 4 vols. New York: Lewis Publishing Company, 1956.

Clements, John. *Kansas Facts: A Comprehensive Look at Kansas Today, County by County*. Dallas: Clements Research, Inc., 1990.

Connelley, William E. *History of Kansas, State and People*. 5 vols. Chicago: American Historical Society, 1928.

Davis, Kenneth S. *Kansas, a History*. New York: Norton; Nashville: American Association for State and Local History, 1984.

Heller, Francis H. *The Kansas State Constitution: A Reference Guide*. Westport, Conn.: Greenwood Press, 1992.

Isern, Thomas D., and Raymond Wilson. *Kansas Land*. 2d ed. Salt Lake City: Peregrine Smith Books, 1992.

Richmond, Robert W. *Kansas, a Land of Contrasts*. 4th ed. Wheeling, Ill.: Harlan Davidson, 1999.

———. *Kansas, a Pictorial History*. Rev. ed. Lawrence: University Press of Kansas, 1992.

Shortridge, James R. *Peopling the Plains: Who Settled Where in Frontier Kansas*. Lawrence: University Press of Kansas, 1995.

KENTUCKY

Clark, Thomas D. *A History of Kentucky*. Revised edition, 6th printing. Lexington: John Bradford Press, 1977.

Connelley, William E., and E. Merton Coulter. *History of Kentucky*. 5 vols. Chicago: American Historical Society, 1922.

Harrison, Lowell H., and James C. Klotter. *A New History of Kentucky*. Lexington: University Press of Kentucky, 1997.

Ireland, Robert M. *The Kentucky State Constitution: A Reference Guide*. Westport, Conn.: Greenwood Press, 1999.

Klotter, James C., ed. *Our Kentucky: A Study of the Bluegrass State*. Lexington: University Press of Kentucky, 2000.

Rice, Otis K. *Frontier Kentucky*. Lexington: University Press of Kentucky, 1993.

Schmidt, Martin F., ed. *Kentucky Illustrated: The First Hundred Years*. Lexington: University Press of Kentucky, 1992.

Smith, Zachariah F. *History of Kentucky, From Its Earliest Discovery and Settlement, to the Present Date*. Louisville: Prentice Press, 1895.

Wallis, Frederick A., and Hambleton Tapp. *A Sesqui-Centennial History of Kentucky*. 4 vols. Hopkinsville: Historical Record Association, 1945.

LOUISIANA

Castle, Joseph D. *Louisiana: Exploration and Early Settlement, 1584–1803*. New Orleans: Louisiana State Museum, 1989.

Chambers, Henry E. *A History of Louisiana, Wilderness-Colony-Province-Territory-State-People*. 3 vols. Chicago: American Historical Society, 1925.

Conrad, Glenn R., ed. *The French Experience in Louisiana*. Lafayette: Center for Louisiana Studies, University of Southwestern Louisiana, 1995.

Cummins, Light Townsend, and Glen Jeansonne, eds. *A Guide to the History of Louisiana*. Westport, Conn.: Greenwood Press, 1982.

Davis, Edwin A. *The Story of Louisiana*. 4 vols. New Orleans: Hyer, 1960–1963.

Davis, Edwin A., et al. *Louisiana, the Pelican State*. Rev. ed. Baton Rouge: Louisiana State University Press, 1985.

Dethloff, Henry C., and Allen E. Begnaud. *Louisiana, a Study in Diversity*. Austin, Tex.: Steck-Vaughn Company, 1992.

Eakin, Sue L., et al. *Louisiana: The Land and Its People*. 3d ed. Gretna, La.: Pelican, 1991.

Fortier, Alcee. *Louisiana*. 2 vols. Atlanta: Southern Historical Association, 1933.

Gayarre, Charles. *History of Louisiana*. 4 vols. 4th ed. New Orleans: Pelican, 1965; reprint of 1903 edition.

Giraud, Marcel. *A History of French Louisiana*. Trans. Joseph C. Lambert. Baton Rouge: Louisiana State University Press, 1974–.

Hargrave, Lee. *The Louisiana State Constitution: A Reference Guide*. Westport, Conn.: Greenwood Press, 1991.

Kein, Sybil, ed. *Creole: The History and Legacy of Louisiana's Free People of Color*. Baton Rouge: Louisiana State University Press, 2000.

Taylor, Joe Gray. *Louisiana, a History*. New York: Norton; Nashville: American Association for State and Local History, 1984.

Wall, Bennett H., and Light Townsend Cummins, eds. *Louisiana, a History*. 3d ed. Wheeling, Ill.: Harlan Davidson, 1997.

MAINE

Abbott, John S. *The History of Maine*. Boston: B. B. Russell, 1875.

Clark, Charles E. *Maine, a History*. New York: Norton; Nashville: American Association for State and Local History, 1985.

Hatch, Louis C. *Maine: A History*. 5 vols. New York: American Historical Society, 1919.

Judd, Richard W., et al., eds. *Maine: The Pine Tree State from Prehistory to the Present*. Orono: University of Maine Press, 1995.

Rich, Louise Dickinson. *State o' Maine*. Camden, Me.: Down East Books, 1987.

Rolde, Neil. *Maine: A Narrative History*. Gardiner, Me.: Harpswell Press, 1990.

Smith, David C., and Edward O. Schriver. *Maine: A History through Selected Readings*. Dubuque: Kendall/Hunt, 1985.

Smith, Marion J. *A History of Maine from Wilderness to Statehood*. Portland: Falmouth Publishing House, 1949.

Tinkle, Marshall J. *The Maine State Constitution: A Reference Guide.* Westport, Conn.: Greenwood Press, 1992.

Williamson, William D. *The History of the State of Maine.* 2 vols. Freeport, Maine: Cumberland Press, 1966; reprint of 1832 edition.

MARYLAND

Andrews, Matthew P. *History of Maryland: Province and State.* Hatboro, Pa.: Tradition Press, 1965; reprint of 1929 edition.

Bozman, John L. *The History of Maryland: From the Settlement in 1633, to Restoration, in 1660.* 3 vols. Bowie, Md.: Heritage Books, 1990; published originally in 1837.

Brugger, Robert J. *Maryland: A Middle Temperament, 1634–1980.* Baltimore and London: Johns Hopkins University Press in association with the Maryland Historical Society, 1988.

Marck, John T. *Maryland, the Seventh State: A History.* Glen Arm, Md.: Creative Impressions, 1995.

Richardson, Hester D. *Side-lights on Maryland History, with Sketches of Early Maryland Families.* 2 vols. in one. Cambridge, Md.: Tidewater Publishers, 1967; reprint of 1913 edition.

Rollo, Vera A. Foster. *Your Maryland: A History.* 5th rev. ed. Lanham: Maryland Historical Press, 1993.

Russo, Jean B., ed. *Unlocking the Secrets of Time: Maryland's Hidden Heritage.* Baltimore: Maryland Historical Society, 1991.

Scharf, John T. *History of Maryland from the Earliest Period to the Present Day.* 3 vols. Hatboro, Pa.: Tradition Press, 1967; reprint of 1879 edition.

Walsh, Richard, and William L. Fox. *Maryland, a History.* Annapolis: Hall of Records Commission, Department of General Services, 1983.

MASSACHUSETTS

Brown, Richard D. and Jack Trager. *Massachusetts: A Concise History.* Rev and exp. ed. Amherst: University of Massachusetts Press, 2000.

Clark, Judith Freeman, and David Horn. *Massachusetts from Colony to Commonwealth: An Illustrated History.* Northridge, Calif.: Windsor Publications, 1987.

Clements, John. *Massachusetts Facts: A Comprehensive Look at Massachusetts Today, County by County.* Dallas: Clements Research, 1987.

Hart, Albert B., ed., *Commonwealth History of Massachusetts.* 5 vols. New York: Russell & Russell, 1966; reprint of 1930 edition.

Kaufman, Martin, et al., eds. *A Guide to the History of Massachusetts.* Westport, Conn.: Greenwood Press, 1988.

Marsh, Daniel L., and William H. Clark. *The Story of Massachusetts.* 4 vols. New York: American Historical Society, 1938.

Wilkie, Richard W., et al., eds. *Historical Atlas of Massachusetts.* Amherst: University of Massachusetts Press, 1991.

MICHIGAN

Bald, F. Clever. *Michigan in Four Centuries.* Rev. and enl. ed. New York: Harper & Row, 1961.

Catton, Bruce. *Michigan, a History.* New York: Norton; Nashville: American Association for State and Local History, 1984.

Deur, Lynne, and Sara Michel. *The Making of Michigan.* Spring Lake, Mich.: River Road Publications, 1989.

Dunbar, Willis F. *Michigan, a History of the Wolverine State.* 3d rev. ed. by George S. May. Grand Rapids, Mich.: W. B. Eerdmans Publishing Company, 1995.

Fino, Susan P. *The Michigan State Constitution: A Reference Guide.* Westport, Conn.: Greenwood Press, 1996.

Fuller, George N. *Michigan: A Centennial History of the State and Its People . . .* 5 vols. Chicago: Lewis Publishing Company, 1939.

Grimm, Joe, ed. *Michigan Voices: Our State's History in the Words of the People Who Lived It.* Detroit: Detroit Free Press and Wayne State University Press, 1987.

Hathaway, Richard J., ed. *Michigan: Visions of Our Past.* East Lansing: Michigan State University Press, 1989.

Quaife, Milo M., and Sidney Glazer. *Michigan:*

From Primitive Wilderness to Industrial Commonwealth. New York: Prentice-Hall, 1948.

Rubinstein, Bruce A., and Lawrence E. Ziewacz. *Michigan: A History of the Great Lakes State*. 2d ed. Wheeling, Ill.: Harlan Davidson, 1995.

Utley, Henry M., and Byron M. Cutcheon. *Michigan As a Province, Territory and State*. 4 vols. New York: Publishing Society of Michigan, 1906.

MINNESOTA

Blegen, Theodore C. *Minnesota: A History of the State*. Minneapolis: University of Minnesota Press, 1975.

Clark, Clifford E., ed. *Minnesota in a Century of Change: The State and Its People since 1900*. St. Paul: Minnesota Historical Society Press, 1989.

Folwell, William W. *A History of Minnesota*. 4 vols. St. Paul: Minnesota Historical Society, 1921–1930.

Hubbard, Lucius F., et al. *Minnesota in Three Centuries, 1655–1908*. 4 vols. New York: Publishing Society of Minnesota, 1908.

Kaplan, Anne R. and Marilyn Ziebarth, eds. *Making Minnesota Territory, 1849–1858*. St. Paul: Minnesota Historical Society, 1999.

Lass, William E. *Minnesota, a History*. 2d ed. New York: Norton, 1998.

MISSISSIPPI

Akin, Edward N., and Roger Walker. *Mississippi, an Illustrated History*. Northridge, Calif.: Windsor Publications, produced in cooperation with Mississippi Historical Society, 1987.

Banks, Sarah J., et al., ed. *Mississippi's Spanish Heritage: Selected Writings, 1492–1798*. Jackson: Mississippi State Department of Education and Mississippi Institutions of Higher Learning, 1992.

Buzhardt, Gail A., and Margaret Hawthorne, eds. *Mississippi's French Heritage: Selected Writings, 1682–1763*. Jackson: Mississippi

State Department of Education and Mississippi Institutions of Higher Learning, 1992.

Carpenter, Barbara, ed. *Ethnic Heritage in Mississippi*. Jackson: Published for the Mississippi Humanities Council by the University Press of Mississippi, 1992.

Lowry, Robert, and W. H. McCardle. *A History of Mississippi*. Spartanburg, S.C.: Reprint Company, 1978; reprint of 1891 edition.

Rowland, Dunbar. *Encyclopedia of Mississippi History*. 2 vols. Madison, Wis.: S. A. Brant, 1907.

———. *History of Mississippi, the Heart of the South*. 2 vols. Spartanburg, S.C.: Reprint Company, 1978; reprint of Chicago: S. J. Clarke, 1925.

Skates, John R. *Mississippi, a History*. New York: Norton; Nashville: American Association for State and Local History, 1985.

Wells, Mary Ann. *Native Land: Mississippi, 1540–1789*. Jackson: University Press of Mississippi, 1994.

Winkle III, John W. *The Mississippi State Constitution: A Reference Guide*. Westport, Conn.: Greenwood Press, 1993.

Yates, Gayle G. *Mississippi Mind: A Personal Cultural History of an American State*. Knoxville: University of Tennessee Press, 1990.

MISSOURI

Conard, Howard L. *Encyclopedia of the History of Missouri*. 6 vols. New York: Southern History Company, 1901.

Culmer, Frederic A. *A New History of Missouri*. Mexico, Mo.: McIntyre Publishing Company, 1938.

Foley, William E. *The Genesis of Missouri: From Wilderness Outpost to Statehood*. Columbia and London: University of Missouri Press, 1990.

———. *History of Missouri, Volume 1: 1673 to 1820*. (The Missouri Sesquicentennial Edition.) Columbia: University of Missouri Press, 1971.

Houck, Lewis. *A History of Missouri, from the Earliest Explorations and Settlements Until the Admission of the State into the Union*. 3 vols. Chicago: R. R. Donnelley, 1908.

March, David D. *The History of Missouri.* 4 vols. New York: Lewis Historical Publishing Company, 1967.

McCandless, Perry. *A History of Missouri, Volume 2: 1820 to 1860.* (The Missouri Sesquicentennial Edition.) Columbia: University of Missouri Press, 1972.

Meyer, Duane G. *The Heritage of Missouri.* 3d ed. St. Louis: River City Publishers, 1982.

Nagel, Paul C. *Missouri: A History.* Lawrence and London: University Press of Kansas, 1989.

Parrish, William E., ed. *A History of Missouri.* (The Missouri Sesquicentennial Edition). Columbia: University of Missouri Press, 1971–.

Parrish, William E., et al. *Missouri, the Heart of the Nation.* 2d ed. Arlington Heights, Ill.: H. Davidson, 1992.

Shoemaker, Floyd C. *Missouri and Missourians: Land of Contrasts and People of Achievements.* 5 vols. Chicago: Lewis Publishing Company, 1943.

Stevens, Walter B. *Centennial History of Missouri: One Hundred Years in the Union, 1820–1921.* 5 vols. St. Louis: S. J. Clarke, 1921.

Violette, Eugene M., and Forrest Wolverton. *A History of Missouri.* Cape Girardeau: Ramfre Press, 1960; reprint of 1918 edition.

Williams, Walter, and Floyd C. Shoemaker. *Missouri, Mother of the West.* 5 vols. Chicago: American Historical Society, 1930.

MONTANA

Burlingame, Merrill G., and K. Ross Toole. *History of Montana.* 3 vols. New York: Lewis Historical Publishing Company, 1957.

Elison, Larry M. and Fritz Snyder. *The Montana State Constitution: A Reference Guide.* Westport, Conn.: Greenwood Press, 2000.

Hamilton, James M. *History of Montana, From Wilderness to Statehood.* 2d ed. Ed. Merrill G. Burlingame. Portland, Oreg.: Binfords & Mort, 1970.

Leeson, Michael A. *History of Montana, 1739–1885.* Chicago: Warner, Beers & Company, 1885.

Malone, Michael P. *Montana: A History of Two Centuries.* Rev. ed. Seattle: University of Washington Press, 1991.

——, ed. *Montana Century: 100 Years in Pictures and Words.* Helena: Falcon Publishing Co., 1999.

Raymer, Robert G. *Montana, the Land and the People.* 3 vols. Chicago: Lewis Publishing Company, 1930.

Sanders, Helen F. *A History of Montana.* 3 vols. Chicago: Lewis Publishing Company, 1913.

Stout, Tom. *Montana: Its Story and Biography.* 2 vols. Chicago: American Historical Society, 1921.

Toole, K. Ross. *Montana: An Uncommon Land.* Norman: University of Oklahoma Press, 1959.

NEBRASKA

Brown, Elinor L. *Maps Tell Nebraska's History.* Ceresco, Nebr.: Midwest Publishing, 1991.

History of the State of Nebraska. Chicago: Western Historical Company (A. T. Andreas, proprietor), 1882.

Luebke, Frederick C. *Nebraska: An Illustrated History.* Lincoln: University of Nebraska Press, 1995.

Miewald, Robert S., and Peter J. Longo. *The Nebraska State Constitution: A Reference Guide.* Westport, Conn.: Greenwood Press, 1993.

Morton, Julius S., et al. *Illustrated History of Nebraska.* 3 vols. Lincoln: J. North, 1905–1913.

Nebraska History. Lincoln: State of Nebraska Historical Society, 1989.

Olson, James C. *History of Nebraska.* 3d ed. Lincoln: University of Nebraska Press, 1997.

Sheldon, Addison E. *Nebraska: The Land and the People.* 3 vols. Chicago: Lewis Publishing Company, 1931.

NEVADA

Angel, Myron, ed. *History of Nevada.* New York: Arno Press, 1973; reprint of 1881 edition.

Bowers, Michael W. *The Nevada State Consti-*

tution: A Reference Guide. Westport, Conn.: Greenwood Press, 1993.

———. *The Sagebrush State: Nevada's History, Government, and Politics.* Reno: University of Nevada Press, 1996.

Davis, Samuel P. *The History of Nevada.* 2 vols. Las Vegas: Nevada Publications, 1984; reprint of 1913 edition.

Earl, Phillip I. *This Was Nevada.* Reno: Nevada Historical Society, 1986.

Elliott, Russell R., and William D. Rowley. *History of Nevada.* 2d ed., rev. Lincoln: University of Nebraska Press, 1987.

Hulse, James W. *The Nevada Adventure: A History.* 6th ed. Reno: University of Nevada Press, 1990.

———. *The Silver State: Nevada's Heritage Reinterpreted.* 2d ed. Reno: University of Nevada Press, 1998.

Mack, Effie M. *Nevada: A History of the State from the Earliest Times through the Civil War.* Glendale, Calif.: Arthur H. Clark Company, 1936.

NEW HAMPSHIRE

Belknap, Jeremy. *The History of New Hampshire.* 3 vols. New York: Arno Press, 1972; reprint of 1791–92 edition.

Heffernan, Nancy C., and Ann P. Stecker. *New Hampshire—Crosscurrents in Its Development.* Updated ed. Hanover, N.H.: University Press of New England, 1996.

Jager, Ronald, and Grace Jager. *New Hampshire, an Illustrated History of the Granite State.* Woodland Hills, Calif.: Windsor Publications, 1983.

McClintock, John N. *Colony, Province, State, 1623–1888: History of New Hampshire.* Boston: B. B. Russell, 1889.

Morison, Elizabeth F., and Elting E. Morison. *New Hampshire, a History.* New York: Norton; Nashville: American Association for State and Local History, 1985.

Pillsbury, Hobart. *New Hampshire; Resources, Attractions, and Its People; a History.* 5 vols. New York: Lewis Historical Publishing Company, 1927.

Sanborn, Edwin D. *History of New Hampshire . . .* Manchester, N.H.: J. B. Clarke, 1875.

Squires, James D. *The Granite State of the United States.* 4 vols. New York: American Historical Company, 1956.

Stackpole, Everett S. *History of New Hampshire.* 4 vols. New York: American Historical Society, 1916.

NEW JERSEY

Fleming, Thomas J. *New Jersey, a History.* New York: Norton; Nashville: American Association for State and Local History, 1984.

Johnson, James P. *New Jersey: History of Ingenuity and Industry.* Northridge, Calif.: Windsor Publications, 1987.

Kross, Peter, *New Jersey History.* Wilmington, Del.: Middle Atlantic Press, 1987.

Kull, Irving S., ed. *New Jersey, a History.* 6 vols. New York: American Historical Society, 1930–32.

Lee, Francis B. *New Jersey As a Colony and a State; One of the Original Thirteen.* 4 vols. New York: Publishing Society of New Jersey, 1902.

McCormick, Richard P. *New Jersey from Colony to State, 1609–1789.* Rev. ed. Newark: New Jersey Historical Society, 1981.

Myers, William S., ed. *The Story of New Jersey.* 5 vols. New York: Lewis Historical Publishing Company, 1945.

Stockton, Frank R. *Stories of New Jersey.* New Brunswick, N.J.: Rutgers University Press, 1987; published originally in 1961.

Williams, Robert F. *The New Jersey State Constitution: A Reference Guide.* Westport, Conn.: Greenwood Press, 1990.

NEW MEXICO

Beck, Warren A. *New Mexico; A History of Four Centuries.* Norman: University of Oklahoma Press, 1962.

Chavez, Thomas E. *An Illustrated History of New Mexico.* Niwot: University Press of Colorado, 1992.

Jaramillo, Nash. *A History of New Mexico.* Rev. ed. Santa Fe: Distributed by La Villa Real, Southwest Books Materials, 1986; text originally published in 1973.

Murphy, Dan. *New Mexico, the Distant Land; An Illustrated History*. Northridge, Calif.: Windsor Publications, 1985.

Nostrand, Richard L. *The Hispano Homeland*. Norman: University of Oklahoma Press, 1992.

Roberts, Calvin A., and Susan A. Roberts. *New Mexico*. Albuquerque: University of New Mexico Press, 1988.

Simmons, Marc. *New Mexico!* Rev., enl. ed. Albuquerque: University of New Mexico Press, 1991.

Twitchell, Ralph E. *The Leading Facts of New Mexican History*. 5 vols. Cedar Rapids, Iowa: Torch Press, 1911–1917.

NEW YORK

Brodhead, John R. *History of the State of New York*. 2 vols. New York: Harper, 1853–1871.

Ellis, David M. *A History of New York State*. Ithaca, N.Y.: Cornell University Press, 1967.

———. *New York State: Gateway to America*. Northridge, Calif.: Windsor Publications, 1988.

Flick, Alexander C., ed. *History of the State of New York*. 10 vols. New York: Columbia University Press, 1933–1937.

Galie, Peter. *The New York State Constitution: A Reference Guide*. Westport, Conn.: Greenwood Press, 1991.

Schoener, Allon. *New York: An Illustrated History of the People*. New York: Norton, 1998.

NORTH CAROLINA

Ashe, Samuel A. *History of North Carolina*. 2 vols. Spartanburg, S.C.: Reprint Company, 1971; reprint of 1908–1925 edition.

Bell, John L., and Jeffrey J. Crow. *North Carolina: The History of an American State*. Montgomery, Ala.: Clairmont Press, 1992.

Clements, John. *North Carolina Facts: A Comprehensive Look at North Carolina Today, County by County*. Dallas: Clements Research, Inc., 1988.

Henderson, Archibald. *North Carolina: The Old*
North State and the New. 5 vols. Chicago: Lewis Publishing Company, 1941.

Lefler, Hugh T., and Albert R. Newsome. *North Carolina*. Rev. ed. Chapel Hill: University of North Carolina Press, 1963.

Orth, John V. *The North Carolina State Constitution: A Reference Guide*. Westport, Conn.: Greenwood Press, 1993.

Powell, William S. *North Carolina, a History*. New York: Norton; Nashville: American Association for State and Local History, 1985.

———. *North Carolina through Four Centuries*. Chapel Hill: University of North Carolina Press, 1989.

Smith, Margaret S., and Emily H. Wilson. *North Carolina Women: Making History*. Chapel Hill: University of North Carolina Press, 1999.

Waggoner, Sara M. *North Carolina, the Tar Heel State*. Bryn Mawr, Pa.: Dorrance, 1988.

Williamson, Hugh. *The History of North Carolina*. 2 vols. Spartanburg, S.C.: Reprint Company, 1973; reprint of 1812 edition.

NORTH DAKOTA

Compendium of History and Biography of North Dakota. Chicago: George A. Ogle and Company, 1900.

Crawford, Lewis F. *History of North Dakota*. 3 vols. Chicago: American Historical Society, 1931.

Dill, Christopher L., and Brian Austin. *Early Peoples of North Dakota*. 2d ed. Bismarck: State Historical Society of North Dakota, North Dakota Heritage Center, 1990.

Gray, David P., and Gerald G. Newborg. *North Dakota: A Pictorial History*. Norfolk, Va.: Donning Company, 1988.

Hennessy, William B. *History of North Dakota . . . Including the Biographies of the Builders of the Commonwealth*. Bismarck: Bismarck Tribune Company, 1910.

Lounsberry, Clement A. *Early History of North Dakota: Essential Outlines of American History*. Washington: Liberty Press, 1919.

Rezatto, Helen. *The Making of the Two Dakotas*. Lincoln, Nebr.: Media Publishing, 1989.

Robinson, Elwyn B. *History of North Dakota*. Lincoln: University of Nebraska Press, 1966.

Rolfsrud, Erling N. *Story of the Peace Garden State.* Farwell, Minn.: Lantern Books, 1990.

Schlasinger, Ethel, ed. *North Dakota: A Guide to the Northern Prairie State.* 2d ed. New York: Oxford University Press, 1950.

OHIO

Knepper, George W. *Ohio and Its People.* 2d ed. Kent: Kent State University Press, 1997.

Randall, E. O., and Daniel J. Ryan. *History of Ohio; the Rise and Progress of an American State.* 5 vols. New York: Century History Company, 1912.

Roseboom, Eugene H., et al. *A History of Ohio.* 2d ed. Columbus: Ohio Historical Society, 1986; originally published in 1967.

Wittke, Carl F., ed. *The History of the State of Ohio.* 6 vols. Columbus: printed under the auspices of the Ohio State Archaeological and Historical Society, 1941–1944.

OKLAHOMA

Dale, Edward E., and Morris L. Wardell. *History of Oklahoma.* New York: Prentice-Hall, 1948.

Foreman, Grant. *A History of Oklahoma.* Norman: University of Oklahoma Press, 1942.

Gibson, Arrell M. *Oklahoma, a History of Five Centuries.* 2d ed. Norman: University of Oklahoma Press, 1981.

Gibson, Arrell M., and Victor E. Harlow. *The History of Oklahoma.* New ed. Norman: University of Oklahoma Press, 1984.

Morgan, Howard W., and Anne H. Morgan. *Oklahoma, a History.* New York: Norton; Nashville: American Association for State and Local History, 1984.

Morris, John W., et al. *Historical Atlas of Oklahoma.* 3d ed. Norman: University of Oklahoma Press, 1986.

Thoburn, Joseph B., and Muriel H. Wright. *Oklahoma; A History of the State and Its People.* 4 vols. New York: Lewis Historical Publishing Company, 1929.

OREGON

Bancroft, Hubert H. *History of Oregon.* 2 vols. New York: Arno, 1967; reprint of 1886 edition.

Carey, Charles H. *A General History of Oregon Prior to 1861.* 2 vols. Portland: Metropolitan Press, 1935.

———. *History of Oregon.* Chicago: Pioneer Historical Publishing Company, 1922.

Corning, Howard M. *Dictionary of Oregon History.* 2d ed. Portland: Binford & Mort Publishing, 1989.

Lyman, Horace S. *History of Oregon: The Growth of an American State.* 4 vols. New York: North Pacific Publishing Society, 1903.

O'Donnell, Terence. *That Balance So Rare: The Story of Oregon.* Portland: Oregon Historical Society Press, 1988.

Scott, Harvey W. *History of the Oregon Country.* Comp. Leslie M. Scott. 6 vols. Cambridge: Riverside Press, 1924.

PENNSYLVANIA

Clements, John. *Pennsylvania Facts: A Comprehensive Look at Pennsylvania Today, County by County.* Dallas: Clements Research, 1987.

Donehoo, George P., ed. *Pennsylvania, a History.* 7 vols. New York: Lewis Historical Publishing Company, 1926.

Downey, Dennis B., and Francis J. Bremer, eds. *A Guide to the History of Pennsylvania.* Westport, Conn.: Greenwood Press, 1993.

Dunaway, Wayland F. *A History of Pennsylvania.* 2d ed. New York: Prentice-Hall, 1961.

Jenkins, Howard M. *Pennsylvania, Colonial and Federal; A History, 1608–1903.* 3 vols. Philadelphia: Pennsylvania Historical Publishing Association, 1903.

Stevens, Sylvester K. *Pennsylvania, Birthplace of a Nation.* New York: Random House, 1964.

———. *Pennsylvania: Keystone State.* 2 vols. New York: American Historical Company, 1956.

RHODE ISLAND

Arnold, Samuel G. *History of the State of Rhode Island and Providence Plantations*. 2 vols. New York: Appleton, 1859–60.

Bicknell, Thomas W. *The History of the State of Rhode Island and Providence Plantations*. 5 vols. New York: American Historical Society, 1920.

Carroll, Charles. *Rhode Island: Three Centuries of Democracy*. 4 vols. New York: Lewis Historical Publishing Company, 1932.

Conley, Patrick T. *An Album of Rhode Island History, 1636–1986*. Norfolk: Donning Company, 1986.

Davis, Hadassah, and Natalie Robinson. *History You Can See*. Providence: Rhode Island Publications Society, 1986.

Field, Edward. *State of Rhode Island and Providence Plantations and the End of the Century: A History*. 3 vols. Boston: Mason, 1902.

McLoughlin, William G. *Rhode Island, a History*. New York: Norton; Nashville: American Association for State and Local History, 1985.

Tanner, Earl C. *Rhode Island: A Brief History*. Providence: Rhode Island State Board of Education, 1954.

SOUTH CAROLINA

Edgar, Walter B. *South Carolina, a History*. Columbia: University of South Carolina Press, 1998.

Lander, Ernest M. *A History of South Carolina, 1865–1960*. 2d ed. Columbia: University of South Carolina Press, 1970.

———. *South Carolina: An Illustrated History of the Palmetto State*. Northridge, Calif.: Windsor Publications, 1988.

McCrady, Edward. *The History of South Carolina*. 4 vols. New York: Paladin Press, 1969; reprint of 1897–1902 editions.

Rogers, George C., Jr., and C. James Taylor. *A South Carolina Chronology, 1492–1992*. 2d ed. Columbia: University of South Carolina Press, 1994.

Wallace, David D. *South Carolina, a Short History, 1520–1948*. Columbia: University of South Carolina Press, 1966; reprint of 1951 edition.

SOUTH DAKOTA

Karolevitz, Robert F., and Bernie Hunhoff. *Uniquely South Dakota*. Norfolk, Va.: Donning Company, 1988.

Milton, John R. *South Dakota: A Bicentennial History*. New York: Norton; Nashville: American Association for State and Local History, 1988; published originally in 1977.

Robinson, Doane. *History of South Dakota*. 2 vols. Logansport, Ind.: B. F. Bowen, 1904.

Schell, Herbert S. *History of South Dakota*. 3d ed., rev. Lincoln: University of Nebraska Press, 1975.

Smith, George M. *South Dakota: Its History and Its People*. 5 vols. Chicago: S. J. Clarke, 1914.

Van Balen, John. *South Dakota Chronology, from Prehistoric Times to 1899*. Vermillion: I. D. Weeks Library, University of South Dakota, 1998.

TENNESSEE

Bergeron, Paul H., et al. *Tennesseans and Their History*. Knoxville: University of Tennessee Press, 1999.

Corlew, Robert E., and James A. Hoobler. *Tennessee: The Volunteer State*. Northridge, Calif.: Windsor, 1989.

Corlew, Robert E., et al. *Tennessee, a Short History*. 2d ed., updated through 1989. Knoxville: University of Tennessee Press, 1990.

Dykeman, Wilma. *Tennessee, a History*. New York: Norton; Nashville: American Association for State and Local History, 1984.

Folmsbee, Stanley J., et al. *History of Tennessee*. 4 vols. New York: Lewis Publishing Company, 1960.

Hale, William T., and Dixon L. Merritt. *History of Tennessee and Tennesseans*. 8 vols. Chicago: Lewis Publishing Company, 1913.

Hamer, Philip M., ed. *Tennessee: A History, 1673–1932*. 4 vols. New York: American Historical Society, 1933.

Jones, James B. *Every Day in Tennessee History.* Winston–Salem, N.C.: John F. Blair, 1996.

Laska, Lewis L. *The Tennessee State Constitution: A Reference Guide.* Westport, Conn.: Greenwood Press, 1990.

Moore, John T., and A. P. Foster. *Tennessee: The Volunteer State, 1769–1923.* 5 vols. Chicago: S. J. Clarke, 1923.

Van West, Carroll, ed. *The Tennessee Encyclopedia of History and Culture.* Nashville: Tennessee Historical Society; Rutledge Hill Press, 1998.

TEXAS

Calvert, Robert A., and Arnoldo De Leon. *The History of Texas.* 2d ed. Wheeling, Ill.: Harlan Davidson, 1996.

Cummins, Light Townsend, and Alvin R. Bailey, eds. *A Guide to the History of Texas.* Westport, Conn.: Greenwood Press, 1988.

Fehrenbach, T. R. *Lone Star: A History of Texas and the Texans.* New York: Da Capo Press, 2000.

Frantz, Joe B. *Texas, A History.* New York: Norton; Nashville: American Association for State and Local History, 1984.

Haley, James L. *Texas: From the Frontier to Spindletop.* New York: St. Martin's Press, 1991.

———. *Texas: From Spindletop through World War II.* New York: St. Martin's Press, 1993.

Johnson, Francis W. *A History of Texas and Texans.* 5 vols. Chicago: American Historical Society, 1916.

McDonald, Archie P. *Historic Texas: An Illustrated Chronicle of Texas' Past.* San Antonio: Historical Pub. Network, 1996.

McDonald, Archie P., and Richard Dillard. *In Celebration of Texas: An Illustrated History.* Northridge, Calif.: Windsor Publications, 1986.

Procter, Ben H., and Archie P. McDonald, eds. *The Texas Heritage.* 3d ed. Wheeling, Ill.: Harlan Davidson, 1998.

Richardson, Rupert N., et al. *Texas: The Lone Star State.* 7th ed. Upper Saddle River, N.J.: Prentice-Hall, 1997.

Wallace, Ernest, et al., eds. *Documents of Texas History.* 2d ed. Austin: State House Press, 1994.

Webb, Walter P., et al., eds. *The Handbook of Texas.* 3 vols. Austin: Texas State Historical Association, 1952–1976.

Wooten, Dudley G., ed. *A Comprehensive History of Texas, 1685–1897.* 2 vols. Dallas: W. G. Scarff, 1898.

UTAH

Alexander, Thomas G. *Utah, the Right Place: The Official Centennial History.* Rev.ed. Salt Lake City: Gibbs Smith, 1996.

Alter, J. Cecil. *Utah, the Storied Domain.* 3 vols. Chicago: American Historical Society, 1932.

Hunter, Milton R. *Utah: The Story of Her People, 1540–1947; A Centennial History of Utah.* Salt Lake City: Desert News Press, 1946.

May, Dean L. *Utah: A People's History.* Salt Lake City: University of Utah Press, 1987.

McCormick, John S. and John R. Sillito, eds. *A World We Thought We Knew: Readings in Utah History.* Salt Lake City: University of Utah Press, 1995.

Neff, Andrew L. *History of Utah, 1847 to 1869.* Ed. and annot. Leland H. Creer. Salt Lake City: Deseret News Press, 1940.

Peterson, Charles S. *Utah, a History.* New York: Norton; Nashville: American Association for State and Local History, 1984.

Powell, Allan K., ed. *Utah History Encyclopedia.* Salt Lake City: University of Utah Press, 1994.

Warrum, Noble, ed. *Utah since Statehood, Historical and Biographical.* 4 vols. Chicago: S. J. Clarke, 1919.

Whitney, Orson F. *History of Utah . . .* 4 vols. Salt Lake City: Cannon, 1892–1904.

VERMONT

Crockett, Walter H. *Vermont, the Green Mountain State.* 4 vols. New York: Century History Company, 1921.

Graffagnino, J. Kevin, et al., eds. *Vermont Voices, 1609 through the 1990s: A Documentary History of the Green Mountain State.* Montpelier: Vermont Historical Society, 1999.

Hall, Hiland. *The History of Vermont, From Its Discovery to Its Admission into the Union in 1791*. Albany, N.Y.: Munsell, 1868.

Hill, William C. *The Vermont State Constitution: A Reference Guide*. Westport, Conn.: Greenwood Press, 1992.

Klyza, Christopher M., and Stephen C. Trombulak. *The Story of Vermont: A Natural and Cultural History*. Hanover, N.H.: University Press of New England, 1999.

Morissey, Charles T. *Vermont, a History*. New York: Norton; Nashville: American Association for State and Local History, 1984.

Newton, Earle W. *The Vermont Story: A History of the People of the Green Mountain State*. Montpelier: Vermont Historical Society, 1983–.

Sherman, Michael, and Jennie G. Versteeg, eds. *We Vermonters: Perspectives on the Past*. Montpelier: Vermont Historical Society, 1992.

VIRGINIA

Beverley, Robert. *The History and Present State of Virginia*. Ed. Louis B. Wright. Published for the Institute of Early American History and Culture at Williamsburg, Va. Chapel Hill: University of North Carolina Press, 1947.

Billings, Warren M., et al. *Colonial Virginia: A History*. White Plains, N.Y.: KTO Press, 1986.

Rubin, Louis D. *Virginia, a History*. New York: Norton; Nashville: American Association for State and Local History, 1984.

WASHINGTON

Avery, Mary W. *Washington: A History of the Evergreen State*. Seattle: University of Washington Press, 1965.

Barto, Harold E., and Catharine Bullard. *History of the State of Washington*. 2d ed. Boston: Heath, 1953.

Beckett, Paul L. *From Wilderness to Enabling Act: Evolution of the State of Washington*. Pullman: Washington State University Press, 1968.

Clements, John. *Washington Facts: A Comprehensive Look at Washington Today, County by County*. Dallas: Clements Research II, Inc., 1989.

Ficken, Robert E., and Charles P. LeWarne. *Washington: A Centennial History*. Seattle: University of Washington Press, 1988.

Gulick, Bill. *A Traveler's History of Washington*. Caldwell, Wa.: Caxton Printers, 1996.

LeWarne, Charles P. *Washington State*. Seattle: University of Washington Press, 1986.

Meany, Edmond S. *History of the State of Washington*. New York: Macmillan, 1924.

Pollard, Lancaster. *A History of the State of Washington*. New ed., rev. 1951. Portland, Oreg.: Binfords & Mort, 1954.

Snowden, Clinton A. *History of Washington; the Rise and Progress of an American State*. 4 vols. New York: Century History Company, 1909.

Stratton, David H., ed. *Washington Comes of Age: The State in the National Experience*. Pullman: Washington State University Press, 1992.

White, Sid, and S. E. Solberg, eds. *Peoples of Washington: Perspectives on Cultural Diversity*. Pullman: Washington State University Press, 1989.

WEST VIRGINIA

Ambler, Charles H., and Festus P. Summers. *West Virginia, the Mountain State*. 2d ed. Englewood Cliffs, N.J.: Prentice-Hall, 1958.

Callahan, James M. *History of West Virginia, Old and New*. 3 vols. Chicago: American Historical Society, 1923.

Conley, Philip, and Boyd B. Stutler. *West Virginia, Yesterday and Today*. 4th ed., Rev. and rewritten. Charleston, W.V.: Education Foundation, 1966.

Hall, Granville D. *The Rending of Virginia: A History*. Knoxville: University of Tennessee Press, 2000.

Lewis, Ronald L., and John Hennen, eds. *West Virginia: Documents in the History of a Rural-Industrial State*. Dubuque, Iowa: Kendall/Hunt Publishing Company, 1991.

Miller, Thomas C., and Hu Maxwell. *West Vir-*

ginia and Its People. 3 vols. New York: Lewis Historical Publishing Company, 1913.

Myers, Sylvester. *Myers' History of West Virginia*. 2 vols. Wheeling: The Wheeling News Lithograph Company, 1915.

Rice, Otis K. *West Virginia, a History*. Lexington: University of Kentucky, 1985.

Shawkey, Morris P. *West Virginia in History, Life, Literature and Industry*. 5 vols. Chicago: Lewis Publishing Company, 1928.

Williams, John A. *West Virginia, a History*. New York: Norton; Nashville: American Association for State and Local History, 1984.

WISCONSIN

Austin, H. Russell. *The Wisconsin Story: The Building of a Vanguard State*. 3d ed. Milwaukee: Milwaukee Journal, 1964.

Campbell, Henry C., ed. *Wisconsin in Three Centuries, 1634–1905*. 4 vols. New York: Century History Company, 1906.

Gara, Larry. *A Short History of Wisconsin*. Madison: State Historical Society of Wisconsin, 1962.

Nesbit, Robert C., and William Fletcher Thompson. *Wisconsin: A History*. 2d ed., rev. and updated. Madison: University of Wisconsin Press, 1989.

Raney, William F. *Wisconsin, a Story of Progress*. Appleton: Perin Press, 1963.

WYOMING

Bartlett, Ichabod S. *History of Wyoming*. 3 vols. Chicago: S. J. Clarke, 1918.

Beard, Frances B., ed. *Wyoming from Territorial Days to the Present*. 3 vols. Chicago: American Historical Society, 1933.

Coutant, Charles G. *History of Wyoming and the Far West*. Published for University Microfilms. New York: Argonaut Press, 1966; reprint of 1899 edition.

Junge, Mark. *Wyoming, a Pictorial History*. Norfolk: Donning Company, 1989.

Keiter, Robert S., and Tim Newcomb. *The Wyoming State Constitution: A Reference Guide*. Westport, Conn.: Greenwood Press, 1992.

Larson, Taft A. *History of Wyoming*. Lincoln: University of Nebraska Press, 1965.

———. *Wyoming, a History*. New York: Norton; Nashville: American Association for State and Local History, 1984.

Sodaro, Craig, and Randy Adams. *Frontier Spirit: The Story of Wyoming*. Rev. and updated. Boulder: Johnson Books, 1996.

DISTRICT OF COLUMBIA

Bowling, Kenneth R. *The Creation of Washington, D.C.: The Idea and Location of the American Capital*. Fairfax, Va., and Lanham, Md.: George Mason University Press; distributed by arrangement with University Publishing Associates, 1991.

Bryan, W. B. *A History of the National Capital from Its Foundation through the Period of the Adoption of the Organic Act*. 2 vols. New York: Macmillan, 1914, 1916.

Fogle, Jeanne. *Two Hundred Years: Stories of the Nation's Capital*. Arlington, Va.: Vandamere Press, 1991.

Green, Constance McLaughlin. *Washington: A History of the Capital, 1800–1950*. Princeton, N.J.: Princeton University Press, 1977; first published in 1962.

Gutheim, Frederick A., and Wilcomb E. Washburn. *The Federal City, Plans and Realities: The History*. 2nd print. Washington, D.C.: published in cooperation with the National Capital Planning Commission by the Smithsonian Institution Press, 1981, 1976.

Howard, George W. *The Monumental City: Its Past History and Present Resources*. 2 vols in one. Baltimore: J. D. Ehlers & Company, 1873, 1880.

Lewis, David L. *District of Columbia: A Bicentennial History*. New York: Norton, 1976.

Melder, Keith, et al., eds. *City of Magnificent Intentions: A History of the District of Columbia*. Washington, D.C.: Published for Associates for Renewal in Education by Intac, Inc., 1983.

Porter, John Addison. *The City of Washington, Its Origin and Administration*. New York: Johnson Reprint Corporation, 1973, 1885.

Tindall, William. *Origin and Government of the*

District of Columbia. Washington, D.C.: Government Printing Office, 1903.

Wilson, Rufus R. *Washington, the Capital City, and Its Part in the History of the Nation.* 2d ed. 2 vols. Philadelphia and London: J. B. Lippincott Company, 1902.

AMERICAN SAMOA

The Cyclopedia of Samoa (Illustrated). Western Samoa: Commercial Printers, 1984, 1907.

Gilson, Richard P. *Samoa 1830 to 1900: The Politics of a Multi-cultural Community.* Melbourne and New York: Oxford University Press, 1970.

Gray, J.A.C. *Amerika Samoa: A History of American Samoa and Its United States Naval Administration.* Annapolis, Md.: United States Naval Institute, 1960.

Henry, Fred, and Tofa Pula. *Samoa, an Early History.* Pago Pago: Department of Education, American Samoa, 1980.

Masterman, Sylvia. *An Outline of Samoan History.* Apia, Western Samoa: Commercial Printers, 1980.

Moors, H. J. *Some Recollections of Early Samoa.* Apia, Western Samoa: Western Samoa Historical and Cultural Trust, 1986, 1924–1926.

Rowe, Newton A. *Samoa under the Sailing Gods.* New York: AMS Press, 1978, 1930.

Runeborg, Ruth E. *Western Samoa and American Samoa: History, Culture and Communication.* Honolulu: East-West Communication Institute, East-West Center, 1980.

Watson, Robert M. *History of Samoa.* Wellington, New Zealand: Whitcombe and Tombs, Ltd., 1918.

COMMONWEALTH OF THE NORTHERN MARIANA ISLANDS

Del Valle, Maria Teresa. *The Marianas Islands in the Early Nineteenth Century.* Agana: Micronesian Area Research Center, University of Guam, 1980.

Farrell, Don A., and Phyllis Koontz. *History of the Northern Mariana Islands.* Saipan: Public School System, Commonwealth of the Northern Mariana Islands, 1991.

Fritz, Georg. *The Chamorros: A History and Ethnography of the Marianas.* Mangilao, Guam: Micronesian Area Research Center, University of Guam, 1984.

Hezel, Francis X. *From Conquest to Colonization: Spain in the Mariana Islands, 1690–1740.* Saipan: Division of Historic Preservation, 1989.

Hoyt, Edwin P. *To the Marianas: War in the Central Pacific, 1944.* New York: Avon, 1983, 1980.

Johnson, James B. *Land Ownership in the Northern Mariana Islands: An Outline History.* Saipan: Mariana Islands District, Trust Territory of the Pacific Islands, 1969.

Thompson, Laura. *The Native Culture of the Mariana Islands.* New York: Kraus Reprint Company, 1971, 1945.

GUAM

Beaty, Janice J. *Guam: Today and Yesterday.* Agana, Guam: Department of Education, Government of Guam, 1968.

Blaz, Ben. *Bisita Guam: A Special Place in the Sun.* Fairfax Station, Va.: Evers Press, 1998.

Carano, Paul, and Pedro C. Sanchez. *A Complete History of Guam.* Rutland, Vt.: C. E. Tuttle, 1965.

Farrell, Don A., and Phyllis Koontz. *The Pictorial History of Guam.* 2d ed. Tamuning, Guam: Micronesian Productions, 1986.

Holmes, Joseph R. *This Is Guam.* Agana, Guam: Pacific Press, 1953.

Maga, Timothy P. *Defending Paradise: The United States and Guam, 1898–1950.* New York: Garland Publishing, 1988.

Nelson, Evelyn G., and Frederick J. Nelson. *The Island of Guam: Description and History from a 1934 Perspective.* Washington, D.C.: Ana Publications, 1992.

Perez, Remedios Leon-Guerrero. *Guam, Past and Present.* 3 vols. Guam: Department of Education, 1946, 1950.

Rogers, Robert F. *Destiny's Landfall: A History of Guam.* Honolulu: University of Hawaii Press, 1995.

Sanchez, Pedro C. *Guahan Guam: The History of Our Island.* Agana, Guam: Sanchez Publishing House [1988?].

PUERTO RICO

Cardona, Luis A. *A History of the Puerto Ricans in the Unitied States of America.* Rev. and enl. ed. Bethesda, Md.: Carreta Press, 1995–.

Dietz, James L. *Economic History of Puerto Rico: Institutional Change and Capitalist Development.* Princeton, N.J.: Princeton University Press, 1987.

Figueroa, Loida. *History of Puerto Rico from the Beginning to 1892.* New York: L. A. Publishers, Neografis, 1978.

Morales Carrion, Arturo, and Maria Teresa Babin. *Puerto Rico, a Political and Cultural History.* New York: Norton; Nashville: American Association for State and Local History, 1983.

Phelps de Cordova, Loretta. *Five Centuries in Puerto Rico: Portraits and Eras.* San German: Interamerican University Press, 1988.

Ribes Tovar, Federico. *A Chronological History of Puerto Rico.* New York: Plus Ultra Educational Publishers, 1973.

Van Middeldyk, Rudolph A., and Martin G. Brumbaugh. *The History of Puerto Rico, from the Spanish Discovery to the American Occupation.* New York: D. Appleton and Company, 1915.

Wagenheim, Kal, and Olga Jimenez Wagenheim, eds. *The Puerto Ricans: A Documentary His-*

tory. Princeton, N.J.: M. Wiener Publishers, 1994.

U.S. VIRGIN ISLANDS

Anderson, Lillian S. *Up and Down the Virgin Islands.* Orford, N.H.: Equity Publishing Corporation, 1963.

Boyer, William W. *America's Virgin Islands: A History of Human Rights and Wrongs.* Durham, N.C.: Carolina Academic Press, 1983.

Cochran, Hamilton. *These Are the Virgin Islands.* New York: Prentice-Hall, 1937.

Creque, Darwin D. *The U.S. Virgins and the Eastern Caribbean.* Philadelphia: Whitmore Publishing Company, 1968.

Dookhan, Isaac. *A History of the Virgin Islands of the United States.* Epping, England: Caribbean Universities Press for the College of the Virgin Islands, 1974.

Harrigan, Norwell, and Pearl Varlack. *The Virgin Islands Story.* Kingston, Jamaica: Caribbean Universities Press; Epping, England: Bowker, 1975.

Hill, Valdemar A. *Rise to Recognition: An Account of Virgin Islanders from Slavery to Self-Government.* St. Thomas, V.I.: n.p., 1971.

Jarvis, Jose A. *Brief History of the Virgin Islands.* St. Thomas, V.I.: Art Shop, 1980, 1938.

Larsen, Jens P. M. *Virgin Islands Story. . . .* Philadelphia: Muhlenberg Press, 1950.

Leary, Paul M., ed. *Major Political and Constitutional Documents of the United States Virgin Islands, 1671–1991.* St. Thomas, V.I.: University of the Virgin Islands, 1992.

Index

A. J. Meerwald (ship), 237
"A nuevo Mexico" (poem), 237
Academic classical architecture, 83, 85–86
Acer rubrum Linn., 119
Acer saccharum Marsh, 117, 121
Ad Astra per Aspera (motto), 19
Adams, Alton A., 153
Aesculus glabra Willd., 118
Agana, Guam, 14, 92
Agate, 232
Agatized coral, 229
"Agriculture and Commerce" (motto), 18, 22
Agropyron smithii, 238, 241
Agropyron spicatum (pursh), 235, 244
Aix sponsa, 136–37
Alabama: agricultural museum, 225; barbecue championship, 225; bird, 126–27; butterfly and mascot, 225; capitol, 77; championship horseshoe tournament, 225; championship horseshow, 225; coat of arms, 27–28; dance, 225; fairs & festivals, 259–50; flag, 53; flower, 97; fossil, 225; freshwater fish, 225; game bird, 126–27; gemstone, 226; governor's flag, 53; governors, 373–75; historic theater, 226; histories of state, 453; horse, 226; insect, 226; legal holidays, 155; license plates, 195; mineral, 226; motto, 17; name, 1; nicknames, 1; nut, 226; outdoor drama, 226; postage stamp, 215; Renaissance Faire, 226; reptile, 226; rock, 226; saltwater fish, 226; seal, 27–28; shell, 226; song, 147; tree, 109; universities, 319–20
"Alabama" (song), 147
Alaska: bird, 127; capitol, 77–78; fairs & festivals, 250–51; fish, 226; flag, 53; flower, 97; fossil, 226; gem, 226; governors, 375; histories of state, 453; land mammal, 226; legal holidays, 156; license plates, 196; marine animal, 226; mineral, 226; motto, 17; name, 1–2; nicknames, 1–2; observances, 156; postage stamp, 215; seal, 28; song, 147; sport, 226; tree, 110; universities, 320–21
Alaska pine, 120
"Alaska's Flag" (song), 147
Albany, New York, 86
Aleurites moluccana (L.) Willd., 112–13
Alis volat Propriis (motto), 22
Alki (motto), 23
"All for Our Country" (motto), 21
"All Hail to Massachusetts" (song), 149
Allen, Ira, 23
Alligator, 229, 232
Alligator State (Florida), 3
Allosaurus, 243
Aloha State (Hawaii), 4, 198
American Beauty rose, 105
American beaver, 237
American bison, 245
American buffalo, 231, 239
American dogwood, 104
American elm, 114–15, 118
American foxhound, 244
American holly, 111–12
American horse chestnut, 118
American pasque flower, 103
American Samoa: bird, 144; capitol, 91–92; fairs & festivals, 312–13; flag, 72–73; flower, 105; governors, 440; histories, 469; legal holidays, 186; license plates, 209–10; motto, 23; name, 13; plant, 245; postage stamp, 223–24; seal, 49–50; song, 153; tree, 121
American sign language, 232
American water spaniel, 245
America's Last Frontier (Alaska), 2

America's Paradise (U.S. Virgin Islands), 14, 210

America's Paradise in the Pacific (Guam), 14

"Amerika Samoa" (song), 153

Amethyst, 240

Ancient Dominion (Virginia), 12

Andrews, Frank M., 84

Animis Opibusque Parati (motto), 22

Annapolis, Maryland, 83

Antelope State (Nebraska), 8

Antigo silt loam, 245

Apache State (Arizona), 2

Appaloosa, 231

Apple, 237, 244, 245

Apple blossom, 98, 101

Apple muffin, 328

Apple pie, 243

April-fools, 103

Aquamarine, 228

Arizona: amphibian, 226; bird, 127–28; capitol, 78; fairs & festivals, 251–52; fish, 226; flag, 54; flower, 98; fossil, 226; gem, 226; governors, 375; histories of state, 453; legal holidays, 156; license plates, 196; mammal, 226; motto, 17; name, 2; neckwear, 226; nicknames, 2; observances, 157; postage stamp, 215–16; reptile, 226; seal, 28; song, 147; sports teams, 443–44; tree, 110; universities, 321

"Arizona March Song" (song), 147

Arizona ridgenose rattlesnake, 226

Arizona tree frog, 226

Arizona trout, 226

Arkansas: beverage, 227; bird, 128; capitol, 78, 216; fairs & festivals, 252–54; flag, 54; flower, 98; folk dance, 227; fruit & vegetable, 227; gem, 227; governors, 376–77; histories of state, 454; insect, 227; language, 227; legal holidays, 157; license plates, 196; mammal, 227; mineral, 227; motto, 18; musical instrument, 227; name, 2; nicknames, 2; observances, 157; postage stamp, 216; rock, 227; salute to flag, 54; seal, 28; slogan, 2; sod, 227; songs, 147–48; tree, 110; trout capital of the USA, 227; universities, 321

"Arkansas" (song), 147–48

"Arkansas (You Run Deep in Me)" (song), 147–48

"The Arkansas Traveler" (song), 147–48

Armadillo, 242

Armentrout, Carl L., 208

Art Moderne architecture, 82

Artemisia tridentata, 102

Artemisia trifida, 102

Artesian State (South Dakota), 11

"Asi Es Nuevo Mejico" (song), 151

Astragalinus tristis salicamans, 143–44

Astrodon johnstoni, 233

Atlanta, Georgia, 80

Atlantic sailfish, 229

Atlas of Georgia, 229

Audemus Jura Nostra Defendere (motto), 17

Augusta, Maine, 83

Austin, Texas, 89

Auto State (Michigan), 7

Azalea, 99

Babingtonite, 234

Badger, 13, 245

Badger State (Wisconsin), 13

Baked Bean State (Massachusetts), 6

Bald cypress, 114

Balsam, 111

Baltimore, Lord, 6, 135

Baltimore checkerspot butterfly, 233

Baltimore oriole, 135

Bananaquit, 145

Bank's palmetto, 112

Banner State (Texas), 12

Barite rose, 239

Barnett, Eva Ware, 147–48

Barred tiger salamander, 231

Barrett, Martha Kemm, 151

Basilosaurus cetoides, 225

Basswood, 113

Baton Rouge, Louisiana, 82

Batterson, James G., 79

Battle Born State (Nevada), 8

Battle of New Orleans, 11, 218

Bat-tree, 115

Bauxite, 227

Bay scallops, 238

Bay State (Massachusetts), 6

Bay Staters, 233

Bayou State (Louisiana), 6

Bayou State (Mississippi), 7

Beach heliotrope, 99

"Beautiful Nebraska" (song), 150

"Beautiful Ohio" (song), 151

Beaux arts classical architecture, 84

Beaver, 10, 237, 239
Beaver State (Oregon), 10
Beef State (Texas), 12
Beehive, 12, 243
Beehive State (Utah), 12
Beignet, 232
Belemnite, 228
Bell, Charles Emlen, 84, 89
Bell, Iris, 153
Belt, Lemmon & Lo (architects), 80
Benicia, California, 78
Benitoite, 227
Benson, Benny, 53
Benton, Thomas Hart, 7
Berberis aquifolium, 103
Berkeley, Sir John, 8
Bernicata sandwicensis, 132
Beryl, 237
Betula papyrifera Marsh., 116–17
"Beyond the Sundown" (play), 242
Big Bend State (Tennessee), 11
Big Bluestem grass, 231
Big cottonwood, 113–14
Big laurel, 104, 115
Big pine, 116
Big Sky Country (Montana), 8, 202
Big Wyoming, 13
Biglow, James F., 206
Bigtree, 110–11
Bismarck, North Dakota, 87
Bison americanus, 231
Bitterroot, 101
Bizochito, 237
Black bear, 232, 244
Black coral, 230
Black cypress, 114
Black Hawk, Chief, 5
Black Hills gold, 241
Black Hills spruce, 119–20
Black maple, 117
Black oak, 117
Black racer, 239
Black swallowtail butterfly, 239
Black walnut, 235
Black-capped chickadee, 135
Black-eyed susan, 101
Blackspotted cutthroat trout, 235
Black-eyed susan, 101
Bland, James B., 152
Bleeding Kansas, 5

Bley, J. Earl, 150
Blizzard State (South Dakota), 11
Block, Adrian, 11
Bloody warrior, 105
Blue, 236, 238
Blue agate, 236
Blue grama grass, 237
Blue granite, 241
Blue hen chicken, 130
"Blue Hills of Massachusetts" (poem), 234
"Blue Moon of Kentucky" (song), 149
Blue poplar, 113
Blue spruce, 111, 120
Blueberry muffin, 234
Bluebonnet, 104
"Bluebonnets" (song), 152
Bluebunch grass, 235, 244
Bluegill, 231
Bluegrass State (Kentucky), 5–6
Blumenthal, Maurice, 147
Bobwhite quail, 131–32, 142, 241
Bog spruce, 119–20
Boise, Idaho, 80
Bola tie, 226
Bonanza State (Montana), 8
Bonasa umbellus, 140
Bonner, Ronnie, 151
Boomer's Paradise (Oklahoma), 10
Boone, Daniel, 6
Booth, Julia D., 152
Border State (Maine), 6
Border-Eagle State (Mississippi), 7
Borinquen, 14
"La Borinquena" (song), 153
"Born to Run" (song), 151
Boston, Massachusetts, 83
Boston cream pie, 233
Boston terrier, 233
Bottlenosed dolphin, 235
Bougainvillea, 105
Bouteloua gracillis, 237
Bowenite, 240
Bowhead whale, 226
Boxwood, 104, 111–12, 115
Boykin spaniel, 240
Brachiopod, 231
Bread and Butter State (Minnesota), 7
Bristlecone pine, 116
Britton, Margaret, 241

Brook trout, 234, 236, 237, 240, 244, 245
Broom, Lewis, 85–86
Brown, T. Clarke, 151
Brown, Tabitha Moffatt, 239
Brown, Will M. S., 148
Brown pelican, 134–35
Brown pine, 109
Brown thrasher, 131–32
Bryant, Boudleaux, 152
Bryant, Felice, 152
Bryant, Gridley J. F., 85
Buchanan, J. A., 151
Buckeye State (Ohio), 10
Buckeye tree, 118
Buffalo, American, 231, 239
Bug-eating State (Nebraska), 8
Bulfinch, Charles, 83
Bull bay, 115
Bull Pen, 86
Bull pine, 116
Bullion State (Missouri), 7
Burch, James B., 148
Burgess, Anne Custis, 152
Bushnell Memorial Park, 79
Butler, M. F., 78
Buzzard State (Georgia), 4
Byers, S.H.M., 149

Cabbage palmetto, 112
Cactus State (New Mexico), 9
Cactus wren, 127–28
Cahaba, Alabama, 77
Calamospiza melancorys stejneger, 129–30
Calico bush, 98
California: animal, 227; bird, 128–29; capitol, 78–79; dance, 227; fairs & festivals, 254–56; fish, 227; flag, 54–55; flower, 98; folk dance, 227; fossil, 227; gemstone, 227; governors, 377–78; histories of state, 454; insect, 227; legal holidays, 157–58; license plates, 196–97; marine fish, 227; marine mammal, 227; mineral, 227; motto, 18; name, 2–3; nicknames, 2–3; observances, 158; postage stamp, 216; prehistoric artifact, 227; reptile, 227; rock, 227; seal, 28–29; soil, 227; song, 148; sports teams, 444–45; trees, 110–11; universities, 322
California desert tortoise, 227
California dog-face butterfly, 227
California gray whale, 227

California grizzly bear, 227
California hemlock spruce, 120
California redwood, 110–11
California valley quail, 128–29
Calochortus nuttalli, 104
Camden, Harriet Parker, 151
Camden and Amboy State (New Jersey), 9
Camellia, 97
Canadian hemlock, 119
Canadian Judas tree, 118
Canadian red pine, 115
Candlenut tree, 112–13
Canoe birch, 116–17
Capitalsaurus, 245
Cardinal, 133, 134, 139, 143, 144
Cardinalis cardinalis, 133, 134, 139, 143, 144
Carmichael, Hoagy, 148
Carmoega, Rafael, 92
Carnagiea gigantea, 98
Carnation, 99, 103
"Carolina" (song), 152
Carolina mantid, 241
Carolina poplar, 113–14
Carolina tartan, 238
Carolina wren, 141
Carolinian language, 246
Carpodacus purpureus, 137–38
"Carry Me Back to Old Virginia" (song), 152
Carson City, Nevada, 85
Carteret, Sir George, 8
Carya illinoensis (Wangenh.) K. Koch, 120
Cass, Lewis, 20
Castilleja linariaefolia, 105
Castor canadensis, 237
Cat spruce, 119–20
Cavalier State (Virginia), 12
Cave State (Missouri), 7
Centennial State (Colorado), 3
Cercidium torreyanum (Wats.) Sargent., 110
Cercis canadensis Linn., 118
Chamberlain, C. H., 148
Chamorro architecture, 92
Chamorro language, 246
Chamorros, 13, 23
Champlain, Samuel de, 12
Channel bass, 238
Channel catfish, 235, 236, 241
Chaparral bird, 138–39
Charles I, King of England, 6, 9, 11
Charles II, King of England, 9–12, 111

Charles IX, King of France, 9, 11
Charles I. D. Looff Carousel, 240
Charleston, West Virginia, 90–91
Charlotte Amalie, St. Thomas, 93, 224
Charter Oak, 111, 224
Chene Vert, 112
Cherokee rose, 99
Cherry (fruit), 243
Chesapeake Bay Deadrise, 233
Chesapeake Bay retriever, 233
Chesapecten jeffersonius, 244
Chester, Kathryn, 152
Cheyenne, Wyoming, 91
Chickadee, 135, 136
Child of the Mississippi (Louisiana), 6
Chili, 242
Chillicothe, Ohio, 87
Chiltepin, 242
Chinook salmon, 239
Chinook State (Washington), 12
Chipped Stone Bear, 227
Chlorastrolite, 234
Chocolate chip, 233
Cicero, 20, 21
Citrus sinensis, 228
Clam State (New Jersey), 9
Clark, Joseph, 83
Classical Renaissance architecture, 80, 82, 84, 89, 91
Clerisseau, Charles Louis, 90
Clifford, Margaret Rowe, 147
Clint, H. O'Reilly, 150
Coal, 232, 243
Coast redwood, 110–11
Coast spruce, 110
Coat of arms: Alabama, 27–28; Connecticut, 29–30; Guam, 50; Massachusetts, 35; Michigan, 35–36; New Hampshire, 39; Ohio, 41; Puerto Rico, 51; Rhode Island, 43; Vermont, 46; West Virginia, 47–48; Wisconsin, 48
Coburn, Harold G., 61
Cochrane, John C., 81
Cockspur thorn, 101
Cod, 233
Coelophysis, 237
Coereba flaveola, 145
Coffee milk, 240
Coffee tree, 114
Cohan, Charles C., 150
Colaptes auratus, 126

Colinus virginianus, 131–32
Collared lizard, 239
Colonial style architecture, 79, 85
Colorado: animal, 227; bird, 129–30; capitol, 79; fairs & festivals, 256–57; flag, 55; flower, 98; gem, 228; governors, 378–79; histories of state, 454–55; insect, 228; legal holidays, 158; license plates, 197; motto, 18; name, 3; nicknames, 3; observances, 158; postage stamp, 216; seal, 29; song, 148; sports teams, 445; tree, 111; universities, 322–23
Colorado blue spruce, 111
Colorado hairstreak butterfly (*Hypaurotis crysalus*), 228
Colorado pinyon pine, 117
Colorado spruce, 111
Columbia, South Carolina, 88
Columbia River, 4, 10
Columbine, 98
Columbine aquilegia caerulea, 98
Columbus, Christopher, 14
Columbus, Ohio, 87
Commonwealth of the Northern Mariana Islands: bird, 144; capitol, 92; fairs & festivals, 313; flag, 73; flower, 105; governors, 440; histories, 469; legal holidays, 186–87; languages, 246; license plates, 210; motto, 23; name, 13; nicknames, 13; observances, 187; postage stamp, 224; seal, 50; song, 153; tree, 121
Concord, New Hampshire, 85
Confederate Air Force, 242
Connecticut: animal, 228; bird, 130; capitol, 79; coat of arms, 29–30; composer, 228; fairs & festivals, 257–58; flag, 55; flower, 98; folk dance, 228; fossil, 228; governors, 379–81; hero, 228; heroine, 228; histories of state, 455; insect, 228; legal holidays, 158–59; license plates, 197; mineral, 228; motto, 18; name, 3; nicknames, 3; observances, 159; postage stamp, 216; seal, 29; shellfish, 228; ship, 228; song, 148; sports teams, 445; tree, 111; universities, 323–24
Connecticut River, 3
Constitution State (Connecticut), 3
Cook, Captain James, 4
Cook, Don, 151
Copa de Oro, 98
Copper State (Arizona), 2
Copper State (Wisconsin), 13

Coreopsis, 98–99
Cork-barked Douglas spruce, 118
Corn, 245
Corn muffin, 234
Corn State (Illinois), 5
Cornel, 115–16
Cornhusker State (Nebraska), 8
Cornus florida, 104, 115–16
Coronilla varia L. penngift, 240
Cortez, Hernando, 2
Corydon, Indiana, 81
Cotter, Arkansas, 227
Cotton, 242
Cotton tree, 113–14
Cottonwood tree, 113–14, 116, 121
Coues' cactus wren, 127
Cowboy State (Wyoming), 13
Cowgrass, 104
Cow-plant, 104
Coyote, 11, 241
Coyote State (South Dakota), 13
Cracker State (Georgia), 4
Cranberry, 233
Cranberry juice, 233
Crandall, Prudence, 227
Crassoostraea virginica, 228
Crataegus, 101
Crawfish, 232
Crepe myrtle, 243
Crescit Eundo (motto), 21
Crinoidea, 235
Crockett, Lora C., 152
"Cross and Sword" (play), 229
"Crossroads of America" (motto), 5, 19
Crotophytus, 239
Cucumber tree, 113
Cumberlandite, 240
Cup of gold, 98
Curry, John Stewart, 82
Cutthroat trout, 230, 243, 245
Cyclone State (Kansas), 5
Cynoscion, 228
Cypripedium acaule, 102
Cypripedium reginae, 101

Dairy cow, 245
Danaus plexippus, 231
Dark and Bloody Ground (Kentucky), 6
David W. Gibbs and Co. (architects), 91
Davidson, Bernard, 149

Davis, Alexander Jackson, 86
Davis, Helen, 152
Davis, Houston, 150
Davis, Jimmy H., 149
Day, Maria, 152
De Remer, Joseph Bell, 87
Debar, Joseph H. D., 23
Deciduous cypress, 114
Deer-laurel, 104
Delaware: beverage, 228; bird, 130; bug, 228; capitol, 79; fairs & festivals, 258–59; fish, 228; flag, 55–56; flower, 98; fossil, 228: governor's flag, 55–56; governors, 381–83; herb, 228; histories of state, 455; legal holidays, 159–60; license plates, 197; mineral, 228; motto, 18; name, 3; nicknames, 3; observances, 160; postage stamp, 216; seal, 30; song, 148; tree, 111–12; universities, 324
Delaware River, 3
Delonix regia, 121
Denver, Colorado, 3, 79
Des Moines, Iowa, 81
Desert bighorn sheep, 236
Desert tortoise, 236
Detroit, Michigan, 7, 83
Diamond, 2, 227
Diamond State (Delaware), 3
Diamondback terrapin, 233
Diatonic (Cajun) accordion, 232
Dickinson, John, 19
Dighton Rock, 233
Dinosaur track, 233
Dirigo (motto), 6, 19–20
Diss, Joseph H., 23
District of Columbia: bird, 144; capitol, 91; fairs & festivals, 312; flag, 72; flower, 105; histories, 468–69; legal holidays, 186; license plates, 209; motto, 23; name, 13; nicknames, 13; postage stamp, 223; seal, 49; song, 153; sports teams, 452; tree, 121; university, 361
Ditat Deus (motto), 17
Doanne, Jonathan, 85
Dog mushing, 226
Dogwood, 102, 104, 115, 117, 120
Dolphin, 229
Double spruce, 119–20
Douglas, Sallie Hume, 148
Douglas fir, 118
Douglas spruce, 118
Douglas tree, 118

Dover, Delaware, 79
Dragonfly, four spot skimmer, 226
Dragonfly, green darner, 244
Drake, Marie, 147
Drayton, William H., 43
Dresser, Paul, 149
Drum, 239
Duck-billed dinosaur, 235
Dum Spiro Spero (motto), 22
Duncan, Lt. J. K., 23
Dusenbury, Elinor, 147
Dutch oven, 243
Dutton, Stephen D., 77
Dwarf lake iris, 101

Eagle State (Mississippi), 7
Earl, Mary, 151
Early blue violet, 103
Eastern bluebird, 137, 139
Eastern box turtle, 238, 242
Eastern cottonwood, 113–14
Eastern goldfinch, 133–34, 138
Eastern hemlock, 119
Eastern Oyster, 228
Eastern poplar, 113–14
Eastern short-horned lizard, 245
Eastern tiger swallowtail, 225, 229, 240
Eastern white pine, 114
Ecphora quadricostata, 233
Ecphoro gardnerae gardnerae (Wilson), 233
Edbrooke and Burnham (architects), 80
Edwards, Harry, 45
Edwards, James G., 5
Eidlitz, Leopold, 86
Elizabeth I, Queen of England, 12
Elk, 243
Emerald, 238
Empire State (New York), 9
Empire State of the South (Georgia), 4
Engle, H. E., 153
English language, 226, 227, 230, 231, 232, 235, 236, 238, 241, 244, 245
Ense petit placidam sub libertate quietem (motto), 20
Epigea repens, 101
Eppel, John Valentine, 150
"Equal Rights" (motto), 23
"Equality Before the Law" (motto), 21
Equality State (Wyoming), 13
Erable, 119

Eschrichtius robustus, 227
Eschscholtzia californica, 98
Esox masquinongy Masquinongy Mitchell, 245
Esse Quam Videri (motto), 21
Esto Perpetua (motto), 19
Euarctos americanus, 244
Eubalaena glacialis, 234
Eubrontes giganteus, 227
Euphydryas phaeton, 233
Eureka (motto), 18
Eurypterus remipes, 237
Everglades State (Florida), 3
Evergreen holly, 111–12
Evergreen magnolia, 101, 115
Evergreen State (Washington), 12
Exselsior (motto), 9, 21
Exselsior State (New York), 9

F. M. Andrews & Co. (architects), 82
"Faded Love" (song), 239
Fairburn agate, 241
False Box-dogwood, 115–16
"Fandangle" (play), 242
Fat pine, 109
Fatti maschii parole femine (motto), 20
Ferdinand, King of Spain, 24
Fernandez Juncos, Don Miguel, 153
Fetid buckeye, 118
Fiddle, 227, 235, 239, 241
Finger-cone pine, 113
Fir tree, 118
Firefly, 240, 241
First State (Delaware), 3, 197
Fisherman's Paradise (Lousiana), 6
Flagg, Ernest, 90
Flame tree, 121
Flicker, 126
"Flickertail March" (song), 151
Flickertail State (North Carolina), 10
Flores Mayo, 105
Florida: air fair, 228; animal, 228; band, 228; beverage, 228; bird, 131; butterfly, 228; capitol, 79–80; fairs & festivals, 228, 229, 259; fiddle contest, 228; flag, 56; flower, 98–99; freshwater fish, 228; gem, 229; governors, 383–84; histories of state, 455; legal holidays, 160; license plates, 197–98; litter control symbol, 229; marine mammal, 229; motto, 18; moving image center and archive, 229; name, 3; nicknames, 3; observances, 160–61;

opera program, 229; pageant, 229; play, 229; postage stamp, 217; railroad museums, 229; Renaissance festival, 229; reptile, 229; saltwater fish, 229; saltwater mammal, 229; seal, 30; shell, 229; soil, 229; song, 148; sports hall of fame, 229; sports teams, 445–46; stone, 229; transportation museum, 229; tree, 112; universities, 324–26; wildflower, 98–99

Florida largemouth bass, 228

Florida panther, 228

Flowering cornel, 115–16

Flowering dogwood, 104, 115, 120

Flower-of-gold, 100

Fluorite, 231

Flycatcher, scissor-tailed, 139–40

Flynn, A. J., 148

Foley, James W., 151

Fontane, Doralice, 149

Foothills yellow pine, 116

Forget-me-not, 97

Fort Smith, Arkansas, 227

"Forward" (motto), 23, 223

Foster, Stephen Collins, 148, 149

Frankenstein, A. F., 148

Frankfort, Kentucky, 82

Fras, Jim, 150

Free State (Maryland), 6

"Freedom and Unity" (motto), 23

Freeman, Legh Richmond, 13

Fremont, Charles, 8

French, Daniel Chester, 91

French Renaissance architecture, 82, 85

"Friendship" (motto), 22

Fuller, Thomas, 86

Fusitriton oregonensis, 240

Gaillardia pulthella, 103

Galena, 235, 245

Garden, Mary, 148

"Garden of Paradise" (song), 148

Garden State (New Jersey), 8–9, 203

Garibaldi (fish), 227

Garnet, 228, 231, 237, 243

Garrett, Elizabeth, 151

Gavia immer, 136

Gebhardt, Dixie Cornell, 58

Gem of the Mountains (Idaho), 4

Gem State (Idaho), 4

Geode, 231

George II, King of England, 3

George B. Post and Sons (architects), 91

Georgia: atlas, 229; beef barbeque champion cookoff, 229; bird, 131–32; butterfly, 229; capitol, 80; fairs & festivals, 259–61; fish, 229; flag, 56–57; flower, 99; folk dance, 229; folk festival, 229; fossil, 229; fruit, 229; game bird, 131–32; gem, 230; governors, 384–86; historic drama, 230; histories of state, 455–56; insect, 230; language, 230; legal holidays, 161; license plates, 198; marine mammal, 230; mineral, 230; mottoes, 18; musical theater, 230; name, 3–4; nicknames, 3–4; observances, 161; pledge of allegiance to flag, 57; 'possum, 230; postage stamp, 217; railroad museum, 230; reptile, 230; seal, 30–31; seashell, 230; song, 148; sports teams, 446; tartan, 230; theater, 230; tree, 112; universities, 326–27; vegetable, 230; waltz, 148; wild flower, 99

"Georgia" (song), 148

"Georgia on My Mind" (song), 148

Giant band shell, 229

Giant sequoia, 110–11

"The Gifts of Earth" (song), 149

Giganticaerulea, 100

Gilbert, Cass, 78, 84, 91

Gilman, Arthur D., 86

Gilpin, William, 18

"Give Me Louisiana" (song), 149

"Go Mississippi" (song), 150

Gold, 226, 227, 241

Golden poppy, 98

Golden State (California), 2

Golden trout, 227

Goldenrod, 97, 100

Goldenrod, late, 101

Goldenrod, sweet, 228

Goldfinch, eastern, 133, 138

Gomulka, Jenny, 150

Goober State (Georgia), 4

Goodhue, Bertram, 85

Gopher State (Minnesota), 7

Gopher tortoise, 230

Gopherus agassizi, 227, 236

Gordon, James Riely, 78

Gorrell, Stuart, 148

Gosling, Joseph, 85

Governor's flag: Alabama, 53; Delaware, 56; Massachusetts, 61; Michigan, 61; Ohio, 66; Rhode Island, 68; Utah, 70

Grand Canyon State (Arizona), 2

Grand Trianon Palace, 82
The Grange, 19
Granite, 233, 237, 238, 243
Granite State (New Hampshire), 8
Gray, 230
Gray elm, 114–15
Gray pine, 116
Gray squirrel, 232, 238
Great dane, 240
Great laurel magnolia, 115
"The Great State of Massachusetts" (song), 149–50
Greek revival architecture, 77, 80–91
Green, 230, 239
Green, Emma Edwards, 31–32
Green barked Acacia, 110
Green Mountain State (Vermont), 12, 207–8
Greenstone, 234
Grizzly bear, 235
Grossular garnet, 243
Ground laurel, 101
Guadalupe bass, 242
Guam: bird, 144–45; capitol, 92; coat of arms, 50; fairs & festivals, 313; flag, 73; flower, 105; governors, 440; histories, 469–70; languages, 246; legal holidays, 187; license plates, 210; march, 153; motto, 24; name, 13–14; nicknames, 13–14; observances, 187; postage stamp, 224; seal, 50; song, 153; tree, 121; university, 361
"Guam Hymn" (song), 153
"Guam March" (song), 153
Guitar, 242
Gulf cypress, 114
Gussen, Edna Gockel, 147
Guthrie, Arlo, 149
Guthrie, Woody, 152

Hadley, Paul, 58
Hadrosaurus foulki, 237
Hagerman horse fossil (Equus simplicidens), 230
"Hail! Minnesota" (song), 150
"Hail! South Dakota" (song), 152
"Hail, Vermont!" (song), 152
Haire, Charles S., 84
Hale, Nathan, 227
Hall, Charlie, 152
Hamilton, George, 149
Hammerstein, Oscar, 151

Hammitt, Deecort, 152
Hancock, John, 83
Hard maple, 117
Hard pine, 109, 115
Hard-case State (Oregon), 10
Harney silt loam, 231
Harrisburg, Pennsylvania, 88
Hartford, Connecticut, 79
Harvey, Carleen, 150
Harvey, LeGrande, 150
Hawaii: bird, 132; capitol, 80; colors, 230; fairs & festivals, 261–62; flag, 57; flower, 99; gem, 230; governors, 386; histories of state, 456; individual sport, 230; legal holidays, 161–62; license plates, 198; marine mammal, 230; motto, 18–19; name, 4; nicknames, 4; observances, 162; postage stamp, 217; seal, 31; song, 148; team sport, 230; tree, 112–13; universities, 327
Hawaii Island: color, 230; flower, 99
Hawaii Loa, 4
"Hawaii Ponoi" (song), 148
Hawaiian goose, 132
Hawkeye State (Iowa), 5
Hawthorn, 101
Heard, William W., 33
Hearne, Colonel Julian G., 153
Heart of Dixie (Alabama), 1, 195
Heart pine, 109
Heavy pine, 116
Heavy-wooded pine, 116
Helena, Montana, 84
Heleodytes brunneicapillus couesi (Sharpe), 127
Helianthus, 100
Heliconius charitonius, 228
Helm, McKinley, 148
Hematite, 226
Hemlock spruce, 119, 120–21
Hemp State (Kentucky), 6
Hennepin, Louis, 13
Henrietta Maria, Queen, 6
"Here We Have Idaho" (song), 148
Hermit thrush, 143
Hetuck, 118
Hibiscus, 99
Hickory poplar, 113
Highest State (Colorado), 3
Higley, Dr. Brewster, 149
Hinahina, 99
Hocker, Willie K., 54

Hoffmann, Maurice, 150
Hog and Hominy State (Tennessee), 11
Holabird and Root (architects), 87
Holdrege soil series, 236
Holly, 111–12
Holly-leaf barberry, 103
Holmes, Dr. John F., 150
Holt, Barachias, 77
Holyfield, Wayland, 147
"Home Means Nevada" (song), 150
"Home on the Range" (song), 149
Honeybee, 227, 230, 231, 235–38, 241, 243
Honeysuckle, 246
Honeysuckle clover, 104
Honolulu, Hawaii, 80
Hooker, Philip, 86
Hoosier State (Indiana), 5
"Hope" (motto), 22
Horned lizard, 242
Horse, 232, 237
Horse conch, 229
Hot Water State (Arkansas), 2
Houdek soil, 241
Houston, Joseph M., 88
Howard, Joseph E., 150
"Howdy Folks" (poem), 239
Humpback whale, 230
Huntsville, Alabama, 77, 126
Hylocichia mustelina, 144
Hylocichla guttata faxoni, 143
Hynson, George B., 148
Hypsypops rubicundus, 227

"I Love You, California" (song), 148
Ichthyosaur, 236
Icterus galbula, 135
Idaho: bird, 132–33; capitol, 80, 217; fairs &
    festivals, 262–63; fish, 230; flag, 57; flower,
    99; fossil, 230; gem, 231; governors, 386–87;
    histories of state, 456; horse, 231; insect, 231;
    legal holidays, 162; license plates, 198–99;
    motto, 19; name, 4; nicknames, 4; obser-
    vances, 162; postage stamp, 217; seal, 31–32;
    song, 148; tree, 113; universities, 327
Idaho Springs, 4
Idaho white pine, 113
Ifit, 121
Ilex opaca Ait., 111–12
Ilima, 99
Illinois: animal, 231; bird, 133; capitol, 81; fairs

& festivals, 263–64; fish, 231; flag, 57–58;
    flower, 99; folk dance, 231; fossil, 231; gov-
    ernors, 387–88; histories of state, 456–57; in-
    sect, 231; language, 231; legal holidays, 162–
    63; license plates, 199; mineral, 231; motto,
    19; name, 4–5; nicknames, 4–5; observances,
    163; postage stamp, 217; prairie grass, 231;
    seal, 32; song, 148; sports teams, 446; tree,
    113; universities, 327–29
"Illinois" (song), 148
"In God We Trust" (motto), 18
Indian arrowwood, 104
Indian blanket, 103
Indian grass, 239
Indian paintbrush, 105
Indian rice grass, 236
Indiana: bird, 133; capitol, 81; fairs & festivals,
    265–66; flag, 58; flower, 99–100; governors,
    388–90; histories of state, 457; language, 231;
    legal holidays, 163; license plates, 199; motto,
    19; name, 5; nicknames, 5; observances, 163;
    poem, 231; postage stamp, 217–18; river,
    231; seal, 32; song, 148–49; sports teams,
    446; stone, 231; tree, 113; universities, 329–
    30
"Indiana" (poem), 231
Indianapolis, Indiana, 81
"Industry" (motto), 22
Ingalls, John J., 19
Ingham Township, Michigan, 83
Inodes palmetto, 119
Intsia bijuga, 121
Iodine State (South Carolina), 11, 206
Iowa: bird, 133–34; capitol, 81; fairs & festi-
    vals, 266–68; flag, 58; flower, 100; governors,
    390–91; histories of state, 457; legal holidays,
    164; license plates, 199; motto, 19; name, 5;
    nickname, 5; observances, 164; postage
    stamp, 218; rock, 231; seal, 33; song, 149;
    sports teams, 447; tree, 113; universities, 330–
    31
Iowa City, Iowa, 81
"Iowa Corn Song" (song), 149
Iowa River, 5
Iris, 104
Iris lacustrus, 101
Isotelus, 239
Istiophorus platypterus, 229
Italian Renaissance architecture, 86, 88
Ives, Charles Edward, 227

Jackson, Andrew, 11, 218, 222
Jackson, Mississippi, 84
Jade, 226, 245
Jalapeño, 242
James II, King of England, 111
Jamestown, Virginia, 90
Jayhawk State (Kansas), 5
Jefferson, Thomas, 3, 90
Jefferson City, Missouri, 84
Jersey Blue State (New Jersey), 9
Joannes Est Nomen Ejus (motto), 24
John Carl Warnecke and Associates (architects), 80
Johnny Appleseed, 233
Johnny-jump-up, 103
Johnston, Archibald, 148
Jousting, 233
Judas tree, 118
Juneau, Alaska, 77
Justitia Omnibus (motto), 23

Kahoolawe: color, 230; flower, 99
Kalkaska soil series, 234
Kalm, Peter, 98
Kalmia latifolia, 98, 103
Kamehameha I, King of Hawaii, 4
Kamehameha III, King of Hawaii, 19
Kansas: amphibian, 231; animal, 231; banner, 58–59; bird, 134; capitol, 81–82; fairs & festivals, 268–69; flag, 58–59; flower, 100; governors, 391–92; histories of state, 457; insect, 231; legal holidays, 164; license plates, 199–200; march, 149; motto, 19; name, 2, 5; nicknames, 5; observances, 164; postage stamp, 218; reptile, 231; seal, 33; soil, 231; song, 149; sports teams, 447; tree, 113–14; universities, 331–32
"The Kansas March" (song), 149
Kansas River, 5
Karner blue, 236
Kaskaskia, Illinois, 81
Kaul, Hugh, 110
Kaumaoa, 99
Kava, 245
Kavanagh, Giles, 150
Keally, Francis, 88
Kelly, Dan, 149
Kelly, N. B., 87
Kent, John Hackett, 84

Kentucky: arboretum, 231; bird, 134; bluegrass song, 149; butterfly, 231; capitol, 82, 218; fairs & festivals, 269–70; flag, 59; flower, 100; fossil, 231; gemstone, 232; governors, 392–94; histories of state, 458; horse, 232; language, 232; legal holidays, 164–65; license plates, 200; mineral, 232; motto, 19; name, 5–6; nicknames, 5–6; observances, 165; postage stamp, 218; seal, 33; song, 149; tree, 114; tug-of-war championship, 232; universities, 332–33; wild animal game species, 232
Kentucky cardinal, 134
Keyes, Mrs. A. C., 71
Keystone of the South Atlantic Seaboard (South Carolina), 11
Keystone State (Pennsylvania), 10–11, 205–6
Khoury, Eddie, 151
King, David, 153
King, Ellen, 153
King, Pee Wee, 152
King salmon, 226
Klaff, Gary, 147
Kletting, Richard K. A., 89
Knapp, George E., 153
Knickerbocker State (New York), 9
Knightia, 245
Knobbed whelk, 230, 237
Kochtitzsky, Mary, 62
Kool-Aid, 236
Kukui tree, 112–13
Kurke, William F., 87

La Salle, Robert Cavalier, Sieur de, 4, 6, 7, 10
Labor Omnia Vincit (motto), 22
Lady of the Lake (Michigan), 7
Ladybug, 228, 234, 236, 237, 241
Lagopus lagopus alascensis Swarth, 127
Lake State (Michigan), 7
Lake Superior agate, 234
Lake Village, Arkansas, 227
Lampyridae, 240
Lanai: color, 230; flower, 99
Lancaster, Pennsylvania, 88
Land of Enchantment (New Mexico), 9, 203–4
"Land of Enchantment—New Mexico" (song), 151
Land of Lincoln (Illinois), 4, 199
Land of Midnight Sun (Alaska), 2
Land of Opportunity (Arkansas), 2
Land of Roger Williams (Rhode Island), 11

Land of 10,000 Lakes (Minnesota), 7
Land of the Dakotas (North Dakota), 10
Land of the Saints (Utah), 12
Landlocked salmon, 232
Lanier, Sidney, 112
Lansing, Michigan, 83
Large white birch, 116–17
Large-flowered magnolia, 115
Largemouth bass, 225, 229, 234, 242
Lark bunting, 129–30
Larus californicus, 142–43
Late goldenrod, 101
Lathrop, John H., 23
Laurel bay, 115
Laurel-leaved magnolia, 115
"Lauriger Horatius" (song), 149
Lawrence, William, 241
Lawrie, Lee, 85
Layton-Smith (architects), 87
Lead State (Missouri), 7–8
LeBeau, Frances, 149
L'Etoile du Nord (motto), 20
Lettered olive, 241
Lewis, Meriwether, 137
Lewisia rediviva, 101–2
"Liberty and Independence" (motto), 18, 216
"Liberty and Prosperity" (motto), 21
"Liberty and Union Now and Forever, One and
    Inseparable" (motto), 21
Lightning whelk, 242
Limestone, 231, 242
Lincoln, Abraham, 4, 81
Lincoln, Nebraska, 85
Link, John G., 84
Link, Theodore C., 84
Liriodendron tulipifera, 113, 120
Little blue stem grass, 236
Little Rhody (Rhode Island), 11
Little Rock, Arkansas, 78
Little sugar pine, 113
Little Tennessee River, 11
"Live Free or Die" (motto), 21, 203
Live oak, 112
Lockwood, Frank, 77
Logan, Frederick Knight, 150
Loggerhead turtle, 241
Lohonton cutthroat trout, 236
Lokelani, 99
"The Lone Star" (play), 242
Lone Star cut, 242

Lone Star State (Texas), 12, 207
Long, Huey, 82
Longhorn, 242
Longleaf pitch pine, 109
Longleaf yellow pine, 109
Long-leaved pine, 116
Longstraw pine, 109
Loon, 136
Lopez de Legaspi, Miguel, 13–14
Lophortyx californica, 128
Louis XIV, King of France, 6
Louisiana: amphibian, 232; bird, 134–35; capi-
    tol, 82; "Christmas in the Country," 232;
    crustacean, 232; dog, 232; doughnut, 232;
    drink, 232; fairs & festivals, 270–72; flag, 59–
    60; flower, 100; fossil, 232; gem, 232; gover-
    nors, 394–95; histories of state, 458; insect,
    232; judicial poem, 232; legal holidays, 165;
    license plates, 200; motto, 19; musical instru-
    ment, 232; name, 6; nicknames, 6; obser-
    vances, 165–66; pledge of allegiance, 60;
    postage stamp, 218; reptile, 232; seal, 33;
    songs, 149; sports teams, 447; tree, 114; uni-
    versities, 334–35; wildflower, 100
Louisiana Catahoula leopard dog, 232
Louisiana Iris, 100
Louisville, Georgia, 80
Loveman, Robert, 148
Lownes, Caleb, 22
Lucero, Amadeo, 151
Lumber State (Maine), 6
Lupinus subcarnosis, 104

MacDonald, Ballard, 151
Macon, Georgia, 80
Madison, Wisconsin, 91
Magellan, Ferdinand, 13
Magnolia, 100, 101, 115
Magnolia grandiflora, 101, 105
Magnolia State (Mississippi), 7
Maine: animal, 232; berry, 232; bird, 135; capi-
    tol, 83; cat, 232; fairs & festivals, 272; fish,
    232; flag, 60; flower, 100; fossil, 232;
    governors, 395–97; histories of state, 458–59;
    insect, 232; language of the deaf community,
    232; legal holidays, 166; license plates, 200;
    merchant and marine flag, 60; mineral, 232;
    motto, 6, 19–20; name, 6; nicknames, 6; ob-
    servances, 166; postage stamp, 218; seal, 34;

song, 149; tree, 114; universities, 335–36; vessel, 232

Maine coon cat, 232

Mammoth, 226, 236

Mammoth tree, 110–11

Manatee, 229

Mangravatti, Pepino, 93

Mann, George R., 78

Mantis religiosa, 228

Mapes, Arthur Franklin, 231

Maple (flavor), 243

Marble, 226, 243

Margaretta, 101

Mariana, Queen of Austria, 13–14

Mariana fruit dove, 144

Mariana Islands, 13–14

Marquette, Jacques, 2, 7

Marsh, Arthur J., 149

Marsh, William J., 152

Maryland: bird, 135; boat, 233; capitol, 83; crustacean, 233; dinosaur, 233; dog, 233; drink, 233; fairs & festivals, 272–73; fish, 233; flag, 60; flower, 101; folk dance, 233; fossil shell, 233; governors, 397–99; histories of state, 459; insect, 233; legal holidays, 166–67; license plates, 200–201; mottoes, 20; name, 6; nicknames, 6; observances, 167; postage stamp, 218–19; reptile & mascot, 233; seal, 34–35; song, 149; sport, 233; sports teams, 447; summer theater, 233; theater, 233; tree, 114; universities, 336

"Maryland! My Maryland" (song), 149

Maryland blue crab, 233

Mason, Captain John, 8

Massachusetts: bean, 233; berry, 233; beverage, 233; bird, 135–36; building and monument stone, 233; capitol, 83; cat, 233; ceremonial march, 233; coat of arms, 35; designation of citizens, 233; dessert, 233; dog, 233; explorer rock, 233; fairs & festivals, 273–74; fish, 233; flag, 60–61; flower, 101; folk dance, 233; folk hero, 233; folk song, 149–50; fossil, 233; game bird, 136, 233; gem, 233; glee club song, 150; governor's flag, 60–61; governors, 399–401; heroine, 233; historical rock, 233; histories of state, 459; horse, 234; insect, 234; legal holidays, 167; license plates, 201; marine mammal, 234; memorial to honor Vietnam War veterans, 234; mineral, 234; motto, 20; muffin, 234; name, 6; nicknames, 6; ob-

servances, 167–70; poem, 234; postage stamp, 219; rock, 234; seal, 35; shell, 234; soil, 234; songs, 149–50; sports teams, 447; tree, 114–15; university, 336

"Massachusetts" (song), 149–50

"Massachusetts (Because of You Our Land Is Free)" (song), 149–50

Maui: color, 230; flower, 99

May, Edwin, 81

May Day flower, 103

Mayflower, 101

Maypop, 104

McCormick, Richard C., 18

McDonald Brothers (architects), 82

McKim, Charles Follen, 88

McKinley, William, 103

McLoughlin, Dr. John, 239

Meadow violet, 102

Meadowlark, 129, 139, 144

Meadowlark, western, 144

Meiere, Hildreth, 85

Meleagris gallopavo, 126, 136, 141

Menzies' spruce, 110

Mera, Harry, 63

Mercenaria mercenaria, 240

Merchant and marine flag (Maine), 60

Mexican free-tailed bat, 242

Michigan: bird, 136; capitol, 83; coat of arms, 35–36; fairs & festivals, 274–75; fish, 234; flag, 61; flower, 101; gem, 234; governor's flag, 61; governors, 401–2; histories of state, 459–60; legal holidays, 170; license plates, 201; motto, 20; name, 7; nicknames, 7; observances, 170; pledge of allegiance, 61; postage stamp, 219; reptile, 234; seal, 35–36; soil, 234; song, 150; sports teams, 447; stone, 234; tree, 115; universities, 336–39; wild flower, 101

Micronesia's Sunbelt, 13

Micropterus punctulatus, 225

Micropterus salmoides, 228, 234

Middleton, Arthur, 43

Middleton, Duff E., 149

Midway USA, 5

Milburn, Frank P., 88

Milk, 227, 228, 232–34, 236–40, 243, 245

Milledgeville, Georgia, 80

Milsten, David Randolph, 239

Mimus polyglottos, 128, 142

Mining State (Nevada), 8

Minnesota: bird, 136; capitol, 84; drink, 234; fairs & festivals, 276–77; fish, 234; flag, 61; flower, 101; gem, 234; governors, 402–3; grain, 234; histories of state, 460; legal holidays, 170; license plates, 201; motto, 20; muffin, 234; mushroom, 234; name, 7; nicknames, 7; observances, 171; postage stamp, 219; seal, 36–37; song, 150; sports teams, 448; tree, 115; universities, 339–40

Minnesota River, 7

Miss Oregon, 239

Mississippi: American folk dance, 234; beverage, 234; bird, 136–37; butterfly, 234; capitol, 84; fairs & festivals, 277–79; fish, 234; flag, 61–62; flower, 101; fossil, 234; governors, 403–5; grand opera house, 235; histories of state, 460; insect, 235; land mammal, 235; languages, 235; legal holidays, 171; license plates, 201–2; motto, 20; name, 7; nicknames, 7; observances, 171; pledge of allegiance, 62; postage stamp, 219; seal, 37; shell, 235; song, 150; tree, 115; universities, 340–41; water mammal, 235; waterfowl, 136–37

Mississippi River, 7

Missouri: American folk dance, 235; animal, 235; aquatic animal, 235; bird, 137; capitol, 84; fairs & festivals, 279–80; fish, 235; flag, 62; flower, 101; fossil, 235; governors, 405–7; histories of state, 460–61; insect, 235; legal holidays, 171; license plates, 202; mineral, 235; motto, 20; musical instrument, 235; name, 7–8; nicknames, 7–8; observances, 171; postage stamp, 219; rock, 235; seal, 37; song, 150; sports teams, 448; tree, 115–16; tree nut, 235; universities, 342–43

Missouri mule, 235

Missouri River, 7

"Missouri Waltz" (song), 150

Mistletoe, 103

Mitchell, Charles, 149

Mockingbird, 128, 131, 136, 141, 1420

Modern American architecture, 85, 87

Modern Renaissance architecture, 81

Mokihana, 99

Molokai: color, 230; flower, 99

Monahan, Robert S., 137–38

Monarch butterfly, 226, 231, 242–44

Monroe, Bill, 149

Montalvo, Garcia Ordonez de, 2–3

Montana: animal, 235; arboretum, 235; ballad, 150; bird, 137; capitol, 84–85, 89; fairs & festivals, 280–82; fish, 235; flag, 62; flower, 101–2; fossil, 235; gems, 235; governors, 407; grass, 235; histories of state, 461; Korean Veterans' Memorial, 235; language, 235; legal holidays, 171–72; license plates, 202; motto, 20–21; name, 4, 8; nicknames, 8; observances, 172; postage stamp, 219; seal, 38; song, 150; tree, 116; universities, 343; Veterans' Memorial Rose Garden, 235; Vietnam Veterans' Memorial, 235

"Montana" (song), 150

Montana agate, 235

Montana black pine, 116

"Montana Melody" (song), 150

Montani Semper Liberi (motto), 23

Montgomery, Alabama, 77

Montpelier, Vermont, 90

Moonstone, 229

Moose, 226, 232

Morehouse, George P., 100

Morel, 234

Morgan horse, 234, 243

Mormon State (Utah), 12

Morone chrysops, 239

Morris, George P., 19

Mother of Modern Presidents (Ohio), 10

Mother of Presidents (Virginia), 12

Mother of Rivers (New Hampshire), 8

Mother of Southwestern Statesmen (Tennessee), 11

Mother of States (Virginia), 12

Mother of Statesmen (Virginia), 12

Moultrie, Colonel William, 68

Mount Rushmore State (South Dakota), 11

Mountain bluebird, 129, 132–33, 137

Mountain laurel, 98, 103

Mountain pine, 113

Mountain State (West Virginia), 12

Mountain Weymouth pine, 113

Mourning dove, 245

Mozarkite, 235

Mud-cat State (Mississippi), 7

Mullen, Katherine E., 234

Murphy, Martin, 151

Murtagh, Henry B., 151

Muscivora forticata, 139–40

Muskellunge, 245

"My Homeland, Tennessee" (song), 152

"My Maryland" (song), 149
"My Michigan" (song), 150
"My Old Kentucky Home" (song), 149
"My Tennessee" (song), 152
"My Western Home" (song), 149
Myaaka fine sand, 229
Myers, Ekijah E., 79, 83, 89
Myosotis alpestris Schmidt Boraginaceae, 97

Nakota horse, 238
Nashville, Tennessee, 89
Natchez, Mississippi, 84
Native gold, 227
Native violet, 99
The Natural State, 2
Nature's mistake, 104
Navy bean, 233
Nebraska: Ameican folk dance, 235; baseball capital, 235; beverage, 235; bird, 137; capitol, 85; fairs & festivals, 282–83; fish, 236; flag, 62; flower, 102; fossil, 236; gem, 236; governors, 407–8; grass, 236; historic baseball capital, 236; histories of state, 461; insect, 236; legal holidays, 172; license plates, 202–3; mammal, 236; motto, 21; name, 8; nicknames, 8; observances, 172; postage stamp, 219; river, 236; rock, 236; seal, 38; soft drink, 236; soil, 236; song, 150; tree, 116; universities, 344; village of lights, 236
Necklace poplar, 113–14
Neilson, J. Crawford, 88
Nene, 132
Neo-Gothic architecture, 82, 86
Nesochen sandwicensis, 132
Nevada: animal, 236; bird, 137; capitol, 85; colors, 236; fairs & festivals, 283–84; fish, 236; flag, 63; flower, 102; fossil, 236; governors, 408–9; grass, 236; histories of state, 461–62; legal holidays, 172–73; license plates, 203; metal, 236; motto, 21; name, 8; nicknames, 8; observances, 173; postage stamp, 220; precious gemstone, 236; reptile, 236; rock, 236; seal, 38; semiprecious gemstone, 236; song, 150; tree, 116; universities, 344
Nevada nut pine, 116
New England boxwood, 115–16
New England hemlock, 119
New England neptune, 234
New Hampshire: amphibian, 236; animal, 236; bird, 137–38; butterfly, 236; capitol, 85; coat of arms, 39; emblem, 39; fairs & festivals, 284–85; flag, 63; flower, 102; freshwater game fish, 236; gem, 236; governors, 409–12; histories of state, 462; insect, 236; language, 236; legal holidays, 173; license plates, 203; mineral, 237; motto, 21; name, 8; nicknames, 8; observances, 173; postage stamp, 220; rock, 237; saltwater game fish, 237; seal, 39; song, 150; sport, 237; tartan, 237; tree, 116–17; university, 344; wildflower, 102
"New Hampshire, My New Hampshire" (song), 150
New Jersey: animal, 237; bird, 138; capitol, 85–86; dance, 237; dinosaur, 237; fairs & festivals, 285–86; fish, 237; flag, 63; flower, 102; governors, 412–13; histories of state, 462; insect, 237; legal holidays, 173–74; license plates, 203; memorial tree, 117; motto, 21; name, 8–9; nicknames, 8–9; observances, 174; postage stamp, 220; rock song, 151; seal, 39–40; shell, 237; song, 151; sports teams, 448; tall ship, 237; tree, 117; universities, 344–46; wildflower, 102
New Mexico: animal, 237; ballad, 151; bird, 138–39; capitol, 86; cookie, 237; fairs & festivals, 286–88; fish, 237; flag, 63–64; flower, 102; fossil, 237; gem, 237; governors, 413–14; grass, 237; histories of state, 462–63; insect, 237; legal holidays, 174; license plates, 203–4; motto, 21; name, 9; nicknames, 9; observances, 174–75; poem, 237; postage stamp, 220; salute to flag, English, 64; salute to flag, Spanish, 64; seal, 40; song, English, 151; song, Spanish, 151; tree, 117; universities, 346; vegetable, 237
New Mexico black bear, 237
New Mexico cutthroat trout, 237
New Mexico piñon, 117
New Mexico Territorial architecture, 86
New Orleans Territory, 6
New York: animal, 237; beverage, 237; bird, 139; capitol, 86; fairs & festivals, 288–89; fish, 237; flag, 64; flower, 102; fossil, 237; fruit, 237; gem, 237; governors, 414–16; histories of state, 463; insect, 237; legal holidays, 175; license plates, 204; motto, 9, 21; muffin, 238; name, 9; nicknames, 9; observances, 175; postage stamp, 220; seal, 40; shell, 238; song, 151; sports teams, 448–49; tree, 117; universities, 347

Nichols, William, 86
Niernsee, Frank, 88
Niernsee, Major John R., 88
Niihau: color, 230; flower, 99
Nil Sine Numine (motto), 18
North Carolina: beverage, 238; bird, 139; capitol, 86–87; colors, 238; dog, 238; fairs & festivals, 289–91; flag, 65; flower, 102; governors, 416–18; historical boat, 238; histories of state, 463; insect, 238; language, 238; legal holidays, 175–76; license plates, 204; mammal, 238; military academy, 238; motto, 21; name, 9; nicknames, 9; observances, 176; postage stamp, 220; reptile, 238; rock, 238; saltwater fish, 238; seal, 40–41; shell, 238; song, 151; sports teams, 449; stone, 238; tartan, 238; toast, 151; tree, 118; universities, 347–48; vegetable, 238
North Dakota: art gallery, 238; beverage, 238; bird, 139; capitol, 87; dance, 238; fairs & festivals, 291–92; flag, 65; flower, 102–3; fossil, 238; governors, 418–19; grass, 238; histories of state, 463–64; honorary equine, 238; language, 238; legal holidays, 176; license plates, 204–5; march, 151; motto, 21; name, 9–10; nicknames, 9–10; observances, 176; postage stamp, 220; railroad museum, 238; seal, 41; song, 151; tree, 118; universities, 348
"North Dakota Hymn" (song), 151
North Star State (Minnesota), 7, 20
"North to the Future" (motto), 17
Northern red oak, 117
Northern white pine, 114
Norway pine, 115
Nosebleed, 105
Notman, John, 85
Nut pine, 116, 117
Nutmeg State (Connecticut), 3

"O, Fair New Mexico" (song), 151
"O Tannenbaum" (song), 149
Oahu: color, 230; flower, 99
Oak, 113
Ocean State (Rhode Island), 11, 206
Ocoee, 104
Odocoileus virginianus, 235, 239, 240, 245
Oglethorpe, James, 3, 112, 217
"Oh Arkansas" (song), 147
"Oh Tennessee, My Tennessee" (poem), 241

Ohio: animal, 239; beverage, 239; bird, 139; capitol, 87; coat of arms, 41; fairs & festivals, 292–94; flag, 65–66; flower, 103; gem, 239; governor's flag, 65–66; governors, 419–20; histories of state, 464; invertebrate fossil, 239; legal holidays, 176–77; license plates, 205; motto, 21–22; name, 10; nicknames, 10; observances, 177; postage stamp, 220–21; seal, 41; song, 151; sports teams, 449–50; tree, 118; universities, 349–51; wildflower, 103
Ohio buckeye, 118
Ohio flint, 239
Ohio River, 10
Oklahoma: animal, 239; beverage, 239; bird, 139–40; butterfly, 239; capitol, 87–88; children's song, 151; colors, 239; country and western song, 239; fairs & festivals, 294–95; fish, 239; flag, 66; flower, 103; folk dance, 239; furbearer, 239; governor's flag, 66; governors, 421; grass, 239; histories of state, 464; legal holidays, 177; license plates, 205; motto, 22; name, 10; nicknames, 10; observances, 177–78; percussive musical instrument, 239; poem, 239; postage stamp, 221; reptile, 239; rock, 239; salute to flag, 67; seal, 41–42; soil, 239; song, 151; sports teams, 450; tree, 118; universities, 351–52; wildflower, 103
"Oklahoma" (song), 151
"Oklahoma (A Toast)" (song), 151
"Oklahoma, My Native Land" (song), 151
Oklahoma City, Oklahoma, 87
Old Bay State (Massachusetts), 6
Old Colony State (Massachusetts), 6
Old Dirigo State (Maine), 6
Old Dominion (Virginia), 12
"Old Folks at Home" (song), 148
Old Line State (Maryland), 6
"Old New Hampshire" (song), 150
"The Old North State" (North Carolina), 9, 151
Old-wife's-shirt-tree, 113
Oliver, Marie E., 62
Olmstead, Frederick Law, 86
Olympia, Washington, 90
"On the Banks of the Wabash, Far Away" (song), 148–49
"On Wisconsin" (song), 153
Oncorhynchus tshawytscha, 226
Orange blossom, 98

Orange juice, 228

Orange State (Florida), 3

Oregon: animal, 239; beverage, 239; bird, 140; capitol, 88; dance, 239; fairs & festivals, 295–97; father of Oregon, 239; fish, 239; flag, 67; flower, 103; gemstone, 239; governors, 421–22; histories of state, 464; hostess, 239; insect, 239; legal holidays, 178; license plates, 205; mother of Oregon, 239; motto, 22; name, 10; nicknames, 10; nut, 239; observances, 178; postage stamp, 221; rock, 240; seal, 42; shell, 240; song, 151; sports teams, 450; tree, 118–19; universities, 352

"Oregon, My Oregon" (song), 151

Oregon grape, 103

Oregon hairy triton, 240

Oregon pine, 118

Oregon sunstone, 239

Orme Maigre, 114–15

Ornate box turtle, 231

Oro y Plata (motto), 20

Oryzopsis hymenoides, 236

"Our Delaware" (song), 148

"Our Georgia" (song), 148

"Our Liberties We Prize, and Our Rights We Will Maintain" (motto), 19

Overmyer, David H., 82

Ovis canadensis, 227, 236

Owen, Marie Bankhead, 17

Owens, Hamilton, 6

Oyster shell, 235, 244

Ozark State (Missouri), 8

Pacific hemlock, 120

Paddlefish, 235

Paeonia, 99

Painted turtle, 234

El Palacio, 86

Palmetto, 112, 119

Palmetto State (South Carolina), 11

Paloverde, 110

Paluman tottut, 144

Pandanus tree, 121

Panhandle State (West Virginia), 12

Paogo, 105, 121

Paper birch, 116–17

Paradise of the Pacific (Hawaii), 4

Park, John A., 204

Park, Stuart, 85

Parry's spruce, 111

Parthenon, 86–87

Partridge, 131–32

Passiflora incarnata, 103

Passion flower, 103

Pathway of the Revolution (New Jersey), 9–10

Paton, David, 86

Paxton soil series, 234

Peabody and Stearns (architects), 85

Peace Garden State (North Dakota), 9

Peach, 229, 240

Peach blossom, 98

Peach State (Georgia), 4

Peanut, 229

Pecan, 226

Pecan (hickory), 120

Pecan nut, 120

Pecan tree, 120

Pecanier, 120

Pelican, brown, 134–35

Pelican State (Louisiana), 6

Pelecanus occidentalis occidentalis, 134–35

Penn, William, 10

Penngift crownvetch, 240

Pennsylvania: animal, 240; beautification and conservation plant, 240; beverage, 240; capitol, 88; dog, 240; fairs & festivals, 297–98; fish, 240; flag, 67; flower, 103; fossil, 240; game bird, 140; governors, 422–24; histories of state, 464; insect, 240; legal holidays, 178–79; license plates, 205–6; motto, 22; name, 10–11; nicknames, 10–11; observances, 179; postage stamp, 221; seal, 42; song, 151; sports teams, 450; tree, 119; universities, 352–53

"Pennsylvania" (song), 151

Penthestes artricapillus, 135, 136

Peony, 99

Perry, Josephine Hovey, 152

Pertica quadrifaria, 232

Peter, Richard, 17

Petoskey stone, 234

Petrified palmwood, 232

Petrified wood, 226, 243, 244

Phacops rana, 240

Phasianus colchicus, 141–42

Pheasant, ring-necked, 141–42

Philadelphia, Pennsylvania, 88

Philadelphus lewissii, 99

Phoenix, Arizona, 78

Phoradendron serotinum, 103

Physeter catadon, 227
Picea glauca (Moench) Voss., 119–20
Picea pungens Engelm., 111
Picea sitchenis (Bong.) Carr., 110
Pierre, South Dakota, 89
Pilgrim State (Massachusetts), 6
Pine cone and tassel, 100
Pine tree, 110, 118, 119–20
Pine Tree State (Maine), 6
Pineapple State (Hawaii), 4
Pink, 230
Pink and white lady slipper, 101
Pink cottage rose, 100
Pink lady's slipper, 102
Pink rhododendron, 104
Pinto bean and the chili, 237
Pinus aristata, 116
Pinus edulis Engelm., 117
Pinus longaeva, 116
Pinus monophylla Torr. and Frem., 116
Pinus monticola Dougl., 113
Pinus palustris Mill., 109
Pinus ponderose Laws., 116
Pinus resinosa Ait., 115
Pinus strobus Linnaeus, 100, 114, 115
Pinyon, 116, 117
Pinyon pine, 117
Pioneer Space Capitol of the World (Alabama), 1
Piquenard, A. H., 81
Pitch pine, 109, 116
Plains cottonwood, 121
Plains poplar, 121
Plantation State (Rhode Island), 11
Platte River, 8, 236
Pledge of allegiance to flag: Arkansas, 54; Georgia, 57; Louisiana, 60; Michigan, 61; Mississippi, 66; New Mexico, 64; Oklahoma, 67; Puerto Rico, 73; South Carolina, 68; South Dakota, 68–69; Texas, 70
Pleuroploca gigantea, 229
Plott hound, 238
Ployhar, James D., 151
Plumeria acuminata, 105
Plymouth Rock, 234
Pogo 'possum, 230
Polka, 245
Ponce de Leon, Juan, 3
Ponderosa pine, 116
Poplar, 113

Populus deltoides Bartr., 113–14
Populus deltoides var. occidentalis Ryb., 121
Populus sargentii Dode, 121
Porcelain painting, 241
Porpoise, 229
Port silt loam, 239
Post, Bill, 149
Poston, Charles D., 2
Prairie agate, 236
Prairie fire, 105
Prairie State (Illinois), 4
Praying mantis, 228, 241
Prehistoric whale, 234
Prescott, Arizona, 78
President Washington (ship), 244
Preston, James R., 20
Prickly pear cactus, 242
Prickly spruce, 111
Prince Albert's fir, 120
Providence (ship), 240
Providence, Rhode Island, 88
Providence Plantation, 11
Pseudotsuga menziessi (Mirb.) Franco, 118
Ptilinopus roseicapilla, 144–45
Pua Aloala, 99
Puerto Rico: bird, 145; capitol, 92; coat of arms, 51; emblematic Mother's Day flower, 246; fairs & festivals, 313–14; flag, 73; flower, 105; governors, 441; histories, 470; languages, 246; legal holidays, 187–88; license plates, 210; motto, 24; name, 14; observances, 188–89; postage stamp, 224; salute to flag, 73; seal, 50–51; song, 153; tree, 122; university, 361
Puget Sound pine, 118
Pulsatilla hirsutissima, 103
Purdy, William T., 153
Puritan State (Massachusetts), 6
Purple, 230
Purple finch, 137–38
Purple lilac, 102
Puti tai nobio, 105
Putnam, Dr. C. S., 151
Pyrus coronaria, 101
Pyrus malus, 98

Quahaug, 240
Quaker State (Pennsylvania), 10
Quartz, 230
Quartz crystal, 227

Quercus alba, 111, 114
Quercus rubra Linn., 117
Quercus spp., 113
Quercus virginiana Mill., 112
Qui transtulit sustinet (motto), 18

Raccoon, 239, 242
Raffetto, Bertha, 150
Rainbow trout, 243
Raines, Chick, 151
Raleigh, North Carolina, 86
Randall, James Ryder, 149
The Reach of Song, 230
Red, 230, 238
Red bird, 133, 134
Red clover, 104
Red cypress, 114
Red drum, 238
Red fir, 118
Red granite, 245
Red haw, 101
Red Judas tree, 118
Red Lehua (Ohia), 99
Red maple, 119
Red oak, 113, 117
Red pine, 115, 116, 118, 219
Red-bellied turtle, 226
Redbud tree, 118
Redwood, 110–11
Reeves, LeRoy, 69
Regnat Populus (motto), 18
Revere, Paul, 83
Reynolds, Smith & Hills (architects), 80
Rhode Island: American folk art symbol, 240;
    bird, 140; capitol, 88; coat of arms, 43;
    drink, 240; fairs & festivals, 298–99; flag, 67–
    68; flagship and tall ship ambassador, 240;
    flower, 103; fruit, 240; governor's flag, 67–68;
    governors, 424–25; histories of state, 465; le-
    gal holidays, 179; license plates, 206; march,
    151–52; mineral, 240; motto, 22; name, 11;
    nicknames, 11; observances, 179–80; postage
    stamp, 221; rock, 240; seal, 43; shell, 240;
    song, 151–52; tree, 119; university, 353
"Rhode Island" (song), 151–52
Rhode Island greening apple, 240
Rhode Island Red, 140
"Rhode Island's It for Me" (song), 151–52
Rhododendron macrophyllum, 104
Rhododendron maximum, 104

Rhodonite, 233
Rice State (South Carolina), 11
Richardson, H. H., 86
Richelson, Julius, 150
Richmond, Virginia, 90
Richmondena cardinalis, 133, 144
Rickard, Truman E., 150
Right whale, 230, 234
Ring-necked pheasant, 141–42
Ringtail, 226
Rio Grande River, 9
"The Road to Boston" (march), 233
Roadrunner, 138–39
Robin, 130, 136, 139, 143, 144
Rock elm, 114–15
Rock lilly, 103
Rock maple, 117
Rockfish, 240
Rocking horse, 226
Rocky Mountain bighorn sheep, 227
Rocky Mountain grape, 103
"Rocky Top" (song), 152
Rogers, Isaiah, 87
Rogers, Richard, 151
Roggeveen, Jacob, 13
"Roll On Columbia, Roll On" (song), 152
Roman Corinthian architecture, 78, 85, 89
Roman Renaissance architecture, 90
Romanesque architecture, 84, 86
Roosevelt, Theodore, 88
Rosa arkansana, 102
Rosa blanda, 102
Rosa pratincola, 100
Rosa sinica, 99
Rose, 102, 105
Rose, Terry, 147
Rose bay, 104
Rose quartz, 241
Rosemary pine, 109
Roughrider State (North Dakota), 10
Round House, 86
Roxbury pudding stone, 234
Rudbeckia hirta, 101
Ruffed grouse, 140
Russian America (Alaska), 2
Ryan, Edward, 23

Sabal palmetto palm, 112
Saber-toothed cat, 227
Sablan, Ramon M., 153

Sacramento, California, 78
Saffold, W. B., 17
Sage State (Nevada), 8
Sagebrush, 102
Sagebrush State (Nevada), 8
Saguaro, 98, 215–16
St. Charles, Missouri, 84
St. Croix, 92–93
St. John the Baptist, 14, 24
St. Louis, Missouri, 84
St. Paul, Minnesota, 84
St. Paul, Nebraska, 236
St. Paul's Cathedral, 30, 78
St. Ursula, 14
Saipan, 92
Salad-tree, 118
Salem, Oregon, 88
Salmo aqua-bonita, 227
Salmo clarki, 235, 236, 245
Salmo gairdnerii, 244
Salmo salar sebago, 232
Salt Lake City, Utah, 89
Salt Lake State (Utah), 12
Salus populi suprema lex esto (motto), 20
Salvelinus fontinalis, 236, 237, 240
Samoa—Muamua le Atua (motto), 23
Samoan architecture, 91–92
Samson, Deborah, 233
San Francisco, Fray Jacinto de, 9
San Joaquin soil, 227
San Jose, California, 78
San Juan, 14, 92
Sandstone, 236
Sandwich Islands, 4
Santa Fe, New Mexico, 86
Sapphire, 235
Sarpi, Pietro, 19
"Say Hello to Massachusetts" (song), 150
Scaphella junonia johnstoneae, 226
Scarlet carnation, 103
Scarlet maple, 119
Scarlet oak, 121
Schaum, John W., 149
Schooner *Bowdoin*, 232
Scissor-tailed flycatcher, 139–40
Sciurus carolinensis, 238
Scotch bonnet, 238
Scott, Peter, 132
Scuto bonae voluntatis tuae coronasti nos (motto), 20

Sea cow, 229
Sea gull, 142–43
Sego lilly, 104
Sequoia sempervirens (D. Don) Endl., 110–11
Sequoiadendron giganteum (Lindl.) Buchholz., 110–11
Serpentine, 227
Sevier, John, 222
Seward, William, 2
Seward's Folly (Alaska), 2
Seward's Ice Box (Alaska), 2
Shad boat, 238
The Shag (dance), 240
Shannon, J. R., 150
Shark tooth, 229
Shipman, Herbert, 132
Shoe-peg maple, 119
Show Me State (Missouri), 7, 202
Si quaeris peninsulam amoenam circumspice (motto), 20
Sialia arctica, 132–33
Sialia currocoides, 132–33, 137
Sialia sialis, 137, 139
Sic Semper Tyrannis (motto), 23
Sideoats grama, 242
Sierra brownbark pine, 116
Sierra Nevada Mountains, 8, 111
Sierra redwood, 110–11
Sillimanite, 228
Silver, 236
Silver birch, 116–17
Silver spruce, 110, 111
Silver State (Nevada), 8, 203
Silverwood, F. B., 148
Single spruce, 119–20
Singleleaf pinyon pine, 116
Sioux State (North Dakota), 10
Sitka spruce, 110
Skiing, 237
Skipjack, 233
Skunk spruce, 119–20
Slate, 243
Smallest State (Rhode Island), 11
Smilodon californicus, 227
Smith, Roy Lamont, 152
Smith, Walter, P., 150
Smoky quartz, 236
Snow, Roger Vinton, 149
Soft elm, 114–15
Soft maple, 119

Soft pine, 114
Solidago odora, 228
Solidago serotina, 102
"The Song of Iowa" (song), 149
Sooner State (Oklahoma), 10
Sorghastrum nutans, 239
South Carolina: amphibian, 240; animal, 240; beverage, 240; bird, 141; botanical garden, 240; butterfly, 240; capitol, 88–89; dance, 240; dog, 240; fairs & festivals, 299–300; fish, 240; flag, 68; flower, 103; folk dance, 240; fruit, 240; gem, 240; governors, 426–28; histories of state, 465; hospitality beverage, 240; insect, 241; language, 241; legal holidays, 180–81; license plates, 206; mottoes, 22; name, 9, 11; nicknames, 11; observances, 181; pledge to flag, 68; postage stamp, 221–22; railroad museum, 241; reptile, 241; seal, 43; shell, 241; songs, 152; stone, 241; tree, 119; universities, 354; wild game bird, 141
"South Carolina on My Mind" (song), 152
South Dakota: animal, 241; bird, 141–42; capitol, 89; drink, 241; fairs & festivals, 300–302; fish, 241; flag, 68; flower, 103; fossil, 241; gem, 241; governors, 428–29; grass, 241; hall of fame, 241; histories of state, 465; insect, 241; jewelry, 241; legal holidays, 181; license plates, 206; mineral, 241; motto, 22; musical instrument, 241; name, 11; nicknames, 11; observances, 181; pledge of allegiance to flag, 68–69; postage stamp, 222; seal, 43–44; soil, 241; song, 152; tree, 119–20; universities, 354–55
Southern cypress, 114
Southern pine, 109
Southernmost State (Florida), 3
Spanish language, 246
Spanish oak, 117
Spanish State (New Mexico), 9
Speckled trout, 237
Sperm whale, 227
Spicebush swallowtail, 234
Spinus tristis tristis, 133–34
Spiritual (music), 241
Spollett, Doris M., 138
Spoon-hutch, 104
Spoonwood, 98
Spotted newt, 236
Spotted salamander, 240
Springer Opera House, 230

Springfield, Illinois, 81
Sproat, Colonel, 10
Spruce, 118, 119
Spruce pine, 114, 119
Square dance, 225, 227, 229, 231, 233–35, 237–42, 244
Squatter State (Kansas), 5
Star blue quartz, 226
Star garnet, 231
"Star Spangled Banner" (song), 153
Stark, General John, 21
"State of Maine Song" (song), 149
"State Sovereignty, National Union" (motto), 19
Staurolite, 230
Stave oak, 111
Steelhead trout, 244
Stephens, Evan, 152
Stewart, Redd, 152
Stinking buckeye, 118
Stizostedion vitreum, 234, 241
Stone, Edward Durell, 80
Strickland, William, 89
Striped bass, 233, 237, 240
Stub Toe State (Montana), 8
Sturnella neglecta, 134, 137, 139, 140
Stuttgart soil series, 227
Sugar maple, 117, 120, 121
Sugar plum, 104
Sugar State (Louisiana), 6
Sullivan's Island, 119–20
Summer duck, 136–37
Sunflower, 100, 218
Sunflower State (Kansas), 5
Sunshine State (Florida), 3
Sunshine State (South Dakota), 11
Surfing, 230
Swallowtail butterfly, 239
Swamp cypress, 114
Swamp elm, 114–15
Swamp maple, 119
Swamp State (South Carolina), 11
"The Swanee River" (song), 148
Sweet onion, 243
Sweet potato, 238
Switzerland of America (Colorado), 3
Switzerland of America (New Hampshire), 8
Switzerland of America (West Virginia), 12
Sydney, Algernon, 20

Syringa, 99
Syringa vulgaris, 102

Tabby cat, 233
Tack, Vincent, 85
Talc, 243
Tallahassee, Florida, 79
Tarantula hawk wasp, 237
Tarheel State (North Carolina), 9
Tarpon, 226
Taxidea taxus, 245
Taxodium distichum (L.) Rich., 114
Taylor, Nell Grayson, 152
Tea (*Camellia sinensis*), 240
Tecoma stans, 105
Tennessee: agricultural insect, 241; amphibian, 241; bird, 142; butterfly, 241; capitol, 89; commercial fish, 241; cultivated flower, 103–4; fairs & festivals, 302–3; fine art, 241; flag, 69; folk dance, 241; game bird, 241; gem, 241; governors, 429–30; histories of state, 465–66; insects, 241; language, 241; legal holidays, 181–82; license plates, 207; motto, 22; name, 11; nicknames, 11; observances, 182; poem, 241; postage stamp, 222; railroad museum, 242; reptile, 242; rock, 242; seal, 44–45; songs, 152; sport fish, 242; sports teams, 450; tree, 120; universities, 355–56; wild animal, 242; wildflower, 103–4
Tennessee cave salamander, 241
Tennessee pearl, 241
Tennessee River, 11
"The Tennessee Waltz" (song), 152
Teredo petrified wood, 238
Texas: Air Force, 242; bird, 142; bluebonnet city, 242; bluebonnet festival, 242; bluebonnet trail, 242; capitol, 89; dinosaur, 242; dish, 242; fairs & festivals, 303–4; fiber and fabric, 242; flag, 69–70; flower, 104; flower song, 152; flying mammal, 242; folk dance, 242; fruit, 242; gem, 242; gemstone cut, 242; governors, 430–32; grass, 242; histories of state, 466; insect, 242; large mammal, 242; legal holidays, 182; license plates, 207; motto, 22; musical instrument, 242; name, 11–12; native pepper, 242; nicknames, 12; observances, 182; pepper, 242; plant, 242; plays, 242; postage stamp, 222; reptile, 242; salute to flag, 70; seal, 45; shell, 242; ship, 242; shrub, 243; small mammal, 242; song, 152;

sport, 243; sports teams, 451; stone, 243; tartan, 243; tree, 120; universities, 356–57; vegetable, 243
"Texas" (play), 242
"Texas, Our Texas" (song), 152
Texas blue topaz, 242
Texas bluebonnet, 243
Texas red grapefruit, 242
"This Is My West Virginia" (song), 153
Thoroughbred horse, 232
Thrasher, 131–32
Thryothorus ludovicianus, 141
Thunderegg, 240
Tideland spruce, 110
Tidewater red cypress, 114
Tieman, B. J., 17
Tiger swallowtail butterfly, 229, 244
Timrod, Henry, 152
"A Toast to North Carolina" (song), 151
Tobacco State (Kentucky), 6
Tomato, 227
Tomato juice, 239
Tompkins, Albert J., 148
Toothpick State (Arkansas), 2
Topaz, 243
Topeka, Kansas, 81
Torres, Jose Martinez, 153
Totot, 144–45
Tourmaline, 232
Tourtellette and Hummell (architects), 80
Town, Ithiel, 86
Toxostoma rufum, 131–32
Tracy and Swartwout (architects), 84
Tranum, Francis Hannah, 152
Treasure State (Montana), 8
Tree frog, green, 232
Tree palmetto, 112
Tree Planters' State (Nebraska), 8
Trenton, New Jersey, 85
Triceratops, 241, 245
Trifolium pratense, 104
Trillium grandiflorum, 103
Trilobite, 245
Trongkon Atbot, 121
Tsuga canadensis (Linn.) Carr., 119
Tsuga heterophylla (Raf.) Sargent, 120
Tucson, Arizona, 78
Tulip poplar, 114, 120
Tulip tree, 99, 113
Tulipwood, 113

Tullimonstrum gregarium, 231
Tully monster, 231
Tunbridge soil series, 243
Turdus migratorius, 130, 144
Turkey apple, 101
Turpentine pine, 109
Turpentine State (North Carolina), 9
Turquoise, 226, 236, 237
Tursiops truncatus, 235
Turtle, 231
Tuscaloosa, Alabama, 77
Tutwiler, Julia S., 147
Tyndale, Sharon, 32

Ua mau ke ea o ka aina i ka pono (motto), 18
Ulmus americana, 114–15, 118
"Under God the People Rule" (motto), 22
"The Union" (motto), 22
"Union, Justice and Confidence" (motto), 19
"United in Pride and Hope" (motto), 24
"United We Stand, Divided We Fall" (motto), 19
Upjohn, Richard M., 79, 87
Upson, Arthur E., 150
Ursus arctos horribilis, 235
Ursus californicus, 227
U.S. Virgin Islands: bird, 145; capitol, 92–93; fairs & festivals, 314; flag, 73–74; flower, 105; governors, 441; histories, 470; legal holidays, 189–90; license plates, 210; motto, 24; name, 14; nicknames, 14; observances, 190; postage stamp, 224; seal, 51; song, 153; tree, 122; university, 361–62
U.S.S. *Nautilus*, 228
U.S.S. *Texas*, 242
Utah: animal, 243; bird, 142–43; capitol, 89–90; cooking pot, 243; emblem, 12, 243; fairs & festivals, 304–5; fish, 243; flag, 70; flower, 104; fossil, 243; fruit, 243; gem, 243; governors, 432; histories of state, 466; insect, 243; legal holidays, 182–83; license plates, 207; motto, 22–23; name, 12; nicknames, 12; postage stamp, 222; railraod museum, 243; rock, 243; seal, 45; song, 152; sports teams, 451; tree, 120; universities, 357–58
"Utah We Love Thee" (song), 152
Utes, 12

Vallejo, California, 78
Valley quail, 128

Vandalia, Illinois, 81
Vandiver, Willard, 7
Vermont: amphibian, 243; animal, 243; beverage, 243; bird, 143; butterfly, 243; capitol, 90; coat of arms, 46; fairs & festivals, 305–6; flag, 70; flavor, 243; flower, 104; fossil, 243; fruit, 243; gem, 243; governors, 432–34; histories of state, 466–67; insect, 243; legal holidays, 183; license plates, 207–8; mineral, 243; motto, 23; name, 12; nickname, 12; observances, 183; pie, 243; postage stamp, 222; rocks, 243; seal, 46; soil, 243; song, 152; tree, 120; university, 358
Vermont poplar, 113–14
Viceroy butterfly, 231
Victorian architecture, 78
Victorian Gothic architecture, 79, 86
Vidalia sweet onion, 230
Viola palmata, 103
Viola papilionacea, 104
Viola sororia, 102
Violet, 99, 102, 103
Virgil, 18
"Virgin Islands March" (song), 153
Virgin Valley black fire opal, 236
Virginia: artisans center, 243; beverage, 243; bird, 143; boat, 243; capitol, 90; dog, 244; emergency medical services museum, 244; fairs & festivals, 306–7; fish, 244; flag, 70; flower, 104; folk dance, 244; folklore center, 244; fossil, 244; governors, 434–36; histories of state, 467; insect, 244; language, 244; legal holidays, 183; license plates, 208; motor sports museum, 244; motto, 23; name, 12; nicknames, 12; observances, 183–84; outdoor dramas, 244; postage stamp, 222–23; seal, 46–47; shell, 244; song, 152; sports hall of fame, 244; sports teams, 451; tree, 120; universities, 358–60; war memorial museum, 244
"Virtue, Liberty, and Independence" (motto), 22
Virtute et Armis (motto), 20
Volunteer State (Tennessee), 11

W. C. Kruger and Associates (architects), 86
Wabash River, 231
Waid, Willa Mae, 152
Wakefield, Nebraska, 231
Walleye, 234, 241
Walter, Henry, 87
Walter, Thomas U., 87

Ward, Dr. Joseph, 22
Washington: arboretum, 244; bird, 143–44; capitol, 90; dance, 244; fairs & festivals, 307–8; fish, 244; flag, 70–71; flower, 104; folk song, 152; fossil, 244; fruit, 244; gem, 244; governors, 436–37; grass, 244; histories of state, 467; insect, 244; legal holidays, 184; license plates, 208; motto, 23; name, 12; nicknames, 12; observances, 184; postage stamp, 223; seal, 47; ship, 244; song, 152; sports teams, 451; tartan, 244; tree, 120–21; universities, 360
Washington, George, 6, 12, 13
"Washington My Home" (song), 152
Water elm, 114–15
Water maple, 119
Weakfish, 228
Web-foot State (Oregon), 10
Webster, Daniel, 21, 220
Weiss, Dreyfous and Seiferth (architects), 82
Wells, George A., 150
Wesley, John, 112
West, Sir Thomas, 3
West, William R., 87
West coast hemlock, 120
West coast swing dance, 227
West Virginia: animal, 244; bird, 144; butterfly, 244; capitol, 90–91; coat of arms, 47–48; fairs & festivals, 308–10; fish, 245; flag, 71; flower, 104; fruit, 245; governors, 437–38; histories of state, 467–68; legal holidays, 184–85; license plates, 208–09; motto, 23; name, 12; nicknames, 12; observances, 185; postage stamp, 223; seal, 47–48; songs, 153; tree, 121; university, 360
"The West Virginia Hills" (song), 153
"West Virginia My Home Sweet Home" (song), 153
Western hemlock fir, 120
Western meadowlark, 134, 137, 140
Western soft pine, 116
Western spruce, 110
Western wheat grass, 238, 241
Western white pine, 113
Western yellow pine, 116
Weymouth pine, 114
Wetmore, James A., 78
Wheat State (Kansas), 5
Wheeling, West Virginia, 90–91
"When It's Iris Time in Tennessee" (song), 152

Where America's Day Begins (Guam), 14
"Where the Columbines Grow" (song), 148
White, 230, 239
White, Harry K., 90
White, Wilbert B., 151
White and lavender columbine, 98
White bass, 239
White birch, 116–17
White cornel, 104
White cypress, 114
White elm, 114–15
White holly, 111–12
White kukui blossom, 99
White maple, 119
White Mountain State (New Hampshire), 8
White oak, 111, 113, 114
White perch, 232
White pine, 6, 113–115
White poplar, 113
White pupu shell, 99
White spruce, 111, 119–20
White trillium, 103
White whale fossilized skeleton, 243
White-tailed deer, 231, 234–36, 239, 240, 245
Whitewood, 113, 114
"Who We Are" (poem), 241
Wild apricot, 104
Wild blueberry, 232
Wild crocus, 104
Wild haw, 101
Wild prairie rose, 100, 102
Wild rice, 234
Wild rose, 100, 204
Wild turkey, 126, 136, 141, 233
Wilder, Walter R., 90
Williams, Roger, 11, 221
Williamsburg, Virginia, 90
Willing, George M., 4
Willow goldfinch, 143–44
Willow ptarmigan, 127
Wilson, Charles C., 89
Wind flower, 103
Winter, Charles E., 153
Wisconsin: animal, 13, 245; beverage, 245; bird, 143; capitol, 91, 223; coat of arms, 48; dance, 245; dog, 245; domestic animal, 245; fairs & festivals, 310–11; fish, 245; flag, 71; flower, 104–5; fossil, 245; governors, 438–39; grain, 245; histories of state, 468; insect, 245; legal holidays, 185; license plates, 209; min-

eral, 245; motto, 23, 223; name, 11–12; nick-names, 12; observances, 185; postage stamp, 223; rock, 245; seal, 48; soil, 245; song, 153; sports teams, 451–52; symbol of peace, 245; tree, 121; university, 360; wild life animal, 245

Wisconsin River, 12

"Wisdom, Justice, Moderation" (motto), 18

"With God, All Things Are Possible" (motto), 21

Wolverine State (Michigan), 7

Wood duck, 136–37

Wood thrush, 144

Wood violet, 104

Woolly mammoth, 226

Wren, Carolina, 141

Wright, Allen, 10

Wright, Gladys Yoakum, 152

Wylie, Lottie Bell, 148

Wyoming: bird, 143; capitol, 91; dinosaur, 245; fairs & festivals, 311–12; fish, 245; flag, 71–72; flower, 105; fossil, 245; gem, 245; governors, 439–40; histories of state, 468; legal holidays, 185–86; license plates, 209; mammal, 245; motto, 23; name, 13; nicknames, 13; observances, 186; postage stamp, 223; reptile, 245; seal, 48–49; song, 210; tree, 121; university, 361

"Wyoming" (song), 153

Ximenex, Ortuno, 2

"Yankee Doodle" (song), 148

Yankee-land of the South (Georgia), 4

Yellow, 230

Yellow and orange air plant, 99

Yellow breast, 145

Yellow cedar, 105

Yellow cottonwood, 113–14

Yellow cypress, 114

Yellow daisy, 101

Yellow elder, 105

Yellow fir, 118

Yellow jessamine, 103

Yellow pine, 116

Yellow poplar, 113

Yellow spruce, 110

Yellowhammer, 126

Yellowhammer State (Alabama), 1

Yellow-shafted woodpecker, 126

Yellow-top, 100

"You Are My Sunshine" (song), 149

Young, Ammi B., 90

Youngest State (Hawaii), 4

Yucca flower, 102

Zanesville, Ohio, 87

Zebra longwing, 228

Zebra swallowtail, 241

Zerene eurydice, 227

Zia, 86, 203–4

Zinnia, 99

Zizania aquatica, 234

About the Authors

BENJAMIN F. SHEARER is Vice-President for Student Affairs at Neumann College in Aston, Pennsylvania. He and his wife Barbara are authors or compilers of several books published by Greenwood Press.

BARBARA S. SHEARER is Director of Public Services and External Relations at the Scott Memorial Library, Thomas Jefferson University, in Philadelphia. She and her husband Benjamin are authors or compilers of several books published by Greenwood Press.